HISTORY AND HISTORIANS
IN THE NINETEENTH CENTURY

DISCARD

George Peabody Gooch, eminent British historian, was born in 1873. He was educated at King's College, London and Trinity College, Cambridge and studied in both Berlin and Paris. A Member of Parliament from 1906 to 1910 and again in 1913, he was President of the Historical Association (1922-1925), National Peace Council (1933-1936), and editor of the *Contemporary Review*. He has received Hon. D. Litt. degrees from Oxford and Durham and is an Honorary Fellow of Trinity College. Since the war he has been living in Chalfont St. Peter, Buckinghamshire.

Among the author's other books are HISTORY OF OUR TIME, GERMANY AND THE FRENCH REVOLUTION, NATIONALISM, HISTORY OF MODERN EUROPE, 1878-1919, RECENT REVELATIONS OF EUROPEAN DIPLOMACY, and STUDIES IN GERMAN HISTORY. His latest book, UNDER SIX REIGNS, was published last fall.

HISTORY AND HISTORIANS
In The Nineteenth Century

By G. P. GOOCH

With a new introduction by the author

BEACON PRESS   BEACON HILL   BOSTON

New historical survey and Preface © 1959 by G. P. Gooch

First Published in 1913 by Longmans, Green and Company

First published as a Beacon Paperback in 1959 by
arrangement with Longmans, Green and Company

Printed in the United States of America

Library of Congress Catalog Card Number: 59-6390

Third printing, August 1965

PREFACE TO THE BEACON PRESS EDITION

I feel highly honoured to see my name added to the distinguished list of writers whose works are appearing at a price which enables them to find many new readers. I hope that some of those readers may derive something of the pleasure from reading my book which I experienced in writing it fifty years ago. *History and Historians in the Nineteenth Century* is my favourite among my writings, mainly because it deals with a subject of inexhaustible interest — the whole dramatic story of civilisation. As Pope said, 'The proper study of mankind is man.'

An octogenarian historian can look back with profound satisfaction at the progress achieved during his lifetime in every sphere of study and research. Today we survey the evolution of mankind and the totality of human experience with wider knowledge, clearer vision, and cooler heads than in the far off days of my apprenticeship. The general standard of scholarship is definitely higher. We are less cocksure, less dominated by prejudices, less prone to plausible generalisations. Our inspiring ideal and our paramount obligation is to deserve the unstinted confidence of our readers. As Ranke declared in a memorable phrase: 'the writing of history is a matter of conscience.' No strident advocate of his race, his country, his party or his church, has a claim to enter the temple of Clio. If I were asked to draw up Ten Commandments for historians I should put at the top: 'Remember your moral responsibility to your readers.' Historians, like other people, are creatures of flesh and blood, and the author's personality will always peep through the printed page; but we must do our utmost to play fair, to understand the life of distant times and ideas which we do not share. No student should base his conception of such controversial themes as the Reformation and the French Revolution on a single writer or a single book, for in some spheres where our deepest feelings are involved full agreement is too much to demand. All I ask is that scholars should regard themselves, not as gladiators struggling in the arena amid the plaudits of their respective supporters, but as a band of brothers dedicated to the single-minded pursuit of truth. Readers of this volume will judge for themselves how far each of the many historians described in these pages reaches or approaches this lofty goal.

People often speak of 'the verdict of history,' 'the philosophy of history,' 'the science of history.' There is no agreed verdict, only individual verdicts; no agreed philosophy, only a welter of conflicting ideologies; no agreed science, only the application of scientific methods. We continue our eager and never-ending search for truth, but the sphinx smiles at us and keeps her secrets. Are there or will there ever be final answers to the questions prompted by our study of the human adventure? If so, they have not yet been found.

September 1958.   G. P. G.

PREFACE TO THE SECOND EDITION

SINCE the destruction of the stock of the fifth impression in the Blitz of December 29, 1940, the book has been out of print in England. A reprint was issued by Peter Smith in New York in 1949. In the present edition the text has been revised and the bibliographical notes have been brought up to date. The task of continuing the survey through the first half of the twentieth century on the same scale must be left to younger hands. The new Introduction merely attempts to indicate the main achievements of the last four decades.

G. P. G.

January 1952.

PREFACE TO THE FIRST EDITION

THE object of this work is to summarise and assess the achievements of historical research and production during the last hundred years, to portray the masters of the craft, to trace the development of scientific method, to measure the political, religious and racial influences that have contributed to the making of celebrated books, and to analyse their effect on the life and thought of their time. No such survey has been attempted in any language. The development of modern historiography is only treated incidentally in the excellent handbooks of Bernheim and Gustav Wolf. Langlois offers little more than a skeleton. Flint and Molinier deal with France alone. Wegele confines himself to Germany and halts on the threshold of the nineteenth century. Fueter's admirable 'Geschichte der neueren Historiographie,' published in 1911, provides a comprehensive review from Petrarch to our own day; but the main portion of the book is devoted to the earlier centuries, and its methods and aims differ fundamentally from those of the present work, in which the curtain rises on Niebuhr. The evolution of German, French and Anglo-Saxon scholarship is related in detail, and is followed by a brief survey of the achievements of other States. The six international chapters which conclude the volume describe departments of study in which scholars of every nation have co-operated, namely, the recovery of the ancient world, the exploration of ecclesiastical history, and the reconstruction of the wider aspects of the life of humanity. For a bird's-eye view of the ground which is here examined in detail I may perhaps be permitted to refer to the closing chapter of the closing volume of the 'Cambridge Modern History.'

G. P. G.

January 1913.

CONTENTS

RECENT HISTORICAL STUDIES

THE dramatic events of the First World War focussed the attention of scholars and students on recent European history, more perhaps in Germany than anywhere else. On the collapse of the Hohenzollern Empire the fathers of the Weimar Republic courageously decided to reveal the diplomatic secrets of the Imperial régime. The main burden of *Die Grosse Politik der Europäischen Kabinette, 1871–1914*, was borne by Friedrich Thimme, who carried through his task with amazing energy and enriched his fifty volumes with controversial annotations; for his disapproval of the *Flottenpolitik* and his dislike of the slippery Bülow were unconcealed. The decision to place Germany's cards on the table was censured in some quarters on the ground that the victors would never follow suit; but the conviction of the editors that other Governments could hardly shirk the challenge was justified when Great Britain, France, Austria and Russia successively presented their evidence on the background of the First World War. Italy alone held back. Less formidable in scope was *Die auswärtige Politik Preussens, 1858–1871*. At last it became possible to compare the whole record of Bismarck's diplomacy with that of his spineless predecessors and his blundering successors.

A third major German enterprise during the inter-war years was the monumental edition of Bismarck's *Gesammelte Schriften*, planned as an expression of national gratitude in dark days to the founder of the Hohenzollern Empire. A large portion of the nineteen enormous quartos was new, and a mass of material scattered through various publications was analysed by a team of experts. Gerhard Ritter edited the incomparable autobiography, restoring the original title of *Memories and Reflections*; Andreas collected many hundred records of conversations with the superman over half a century; Petersdorff provided a selection of letters, Schüssler of the speeches. The heaviest burden was borne by the indefatigable Thimme, whose six volumes of *Politische Schriften* form the most valuable portion of the work. Beginning with most of the despatches from Frankfurt already published under the Chancellor's direction, and those from St. Petersburg and Paris published by Raschdau long after his death, the editor proceeded to the almost unexplored years between 1862 and 1870. The attitude towards Austria before 1866 emerged in an unexpected light. While the old man's memory exhibited the drama as the working out of a pre-arranged plan, the contemporary documents revealed a statesman feeling his way towards his goal and not at the outset convinced of the necessity of war. As a result of the new material we now read the most impressive of political apologias with more critical eyes. The detection of factual errors and misrepresentations, however, leaves its value as the expression of a unique personality unimpaired.

The loss of the First World War enhanced the admiration of most Germans for the realist who had proclaimed that 'politics are the art of the possible' and had averted hostile coalitions by limiting his risks. Erich Marcks, the oracle of Bismarckian studies, abandoned his project of a full-length biography when the narrative had reached 1851, on the reasonable ground that the full story of his hero could only be told in the form of a history of his time. His last and greatest work, *Der Aufstieg des deutschen Reichs*, published in 1936, summarised events and tendencies from the close of the Napoleonic era till the summons of the ruthless Junker to the helm and described the story of the *Reichsgründung* at full length. The work occupies a place in the select class of large-scale German historical classics which includes Ranke's *Reformation Era*, Treitschke's *Germany in the Nineteenth Century*, and Koser's *Frederick the Great*. Marcks had grown to manhood when the Iron Chancellor was in command, and the volumes of the septuagenarian scholar retain something of the patriotic exaltation of his youth. After prolonged reflection on the whole available evidence he concluded that the transformation of the anaemic Deutscher Bund into a viable nation-state, to which Germans had as much right as other peoples, could have been achieved by no less drastic means.

Similar melodies were heard in Brandenburg's documented *Die Reichsgründung* and in two works by Arnold Oskar Meyer. *Bismarck's Kampf mit Oesterreich am Bundestag zu Frankfurt, 1851–1859*, utilised the despatches of the Austrian representatives with whom the Prussian *virtuoso* engaged in unrelenting strife; and boundless admiration for his hero shines out even more brightly in his large biography published in 1943, enriched by new material supplied by the family. The three volumes entitled *Die Rheinpolitik Kaiser Napoleons III von 1863 bis 1870*, edited by Hermann Oncken, reveal the most secret thoughts of the Imperial schemer at Paris. The reports of Richard Metternich, the Austrian Ambassador, make an astonishing story of ambition and intrigue which is summarised in a lengthy Introduction. The conclusion drawn by Oncken is that the France of the Second Empire was a bad neighbour and that Bismarck took the right course. A more dispassionate narrative of the making of the Hohenzollern Empire was supplied in the eighth, ninth and tenth volumes of Alfred Stern's *Geschichte Europas 1815–1871*, a work based on decades of research in foreign archives and composed in the cooler atmosphere of Switzerland.

Two large-scale accounts of Bismarckian and post-Bismarckian Germany have been written from widely different standpoints. Adalbert Wahl's four massive volumes, *Deutsche Geschichte 1871–1914*, provide the most comprehensive account of the political and cultural life of the Reich and all its component parts ever written by a single scholar, but it is also something of a political tract. In many European countries, he complained, there had been a decline since the French Revolution, and it had not yet reached the end. Material progress had been achieved at the cost of spiritual retrogression, and organic elements such as the Estates had yielded to a levelling Parliamentary democracy. It was Bismarck's incomparable service not only to found the German Reich but to provide it with a suitable constitution, capable of defending it alike against predatory socialism and doctrinaire cosmopolitanism.

The Bismarckian Old Guard in Germany has not had things all its own way. Ziekursch's *Politische Geschichte des deutschen Kaiserreichs*, though inferior in scope and learning to the treatise of Wahl, is no less a political argument. While most German historians in the inter-war era, exasperated by humiliation and defeat, glorify the Iron Chancellor at the expense of his successors, he declines to burn incense on the altar. He regrets that he provided the Hohenzollerns with such enormous power that a Frederick the Great on the throne or a Bismarck beside it was required for its prudent use. The edifice was top-heavy, and the democratic *Zeitgeist*, which the Chancellor scorned, proved victorious. Ziekursch sheds no tears over his fall, but William II and his short-sighted advisers stumbled from one blunder to another. When the testing time came in 1914 Germany lacked the institutions and the solidarity needed to confront the ordeal. The same spirit of nineteenth-century—we may almost say Gladstonian—liberalism inspires the impressive three-volume life of Bismarck by Erich Eyck, who sharply castigates his ruthless methods at home and abroad. A subsequent volume on the reign of William II finds equally little to praise, and deplores the lack of national training in the art of self-government. For the foreign policy of the last of the Hohenzollerns we turn to Oncken's *Vorgeschichte des Weltkrieges* and Brandenburg's *From Bismarck to the World War*, the latter an acknowledged masterpiece. Among the crowd of biographies and autobiographies of the time Johannes Haller's life of Eulenburg and Bülow's Memoirs stand boldly out. The latter's apologia, one of the least convincing of its class, damaged the reputation of the writer more than that of the sovereign and other foes on whom he took his revenge.

Among German students of pre-Bismarckian times several names deserve honourable mention. No recent work on the Middle Ages found such enthusiastic readers as the scintillating portrait of the Emperor Frederick II, *stupor mundi*, by Ernst Kantorowicz, but Davidsohn's massive volumes on the early history of Florence rest on firmer foundations. Hintze greeted the quincentenary of the coming of the Hohenzollerns to Brandenburg with a masterly survey of the achievements of the dynasty. The fourth volume of Delbrück's *Geschichte der Kriegskunst*, bringing the narrative from the Renaissance to Napoleon, completed his most ambitious historical enterprise. Himself a combatant in 1870 and the biographer of Gneisenau, his authority is recognised by military students. The evolution of armies and armaments, the literary oracles from Machiavelli to Clausewitz, the commanders from Gustavus Adolphus to the Wars of Liberation, and the historic battles are his theme. The book, he explains, was written not merely for soldiers but for all lovers of history.

To readers reared on Ranke's *Reformation Era* and the opening volumes of Janssen's *History of the German People*, it is a delight to study Willy Andreas' massive monograph *Deutschland am Vorabend der Reformation*, which holds the balance between the traditional Protestant picture of pre-Lutheran darkness and the traditional Catholic rejoinder that demoralisation followed instead of preceding the Wittenberg revolt. Of equal importance was Karl Brandi's panorama of the reign of Charles V, based on the researches of a lifetime. Schnabel's *Deutschland im neunzehnten Jahrhundert* covers the same period as Treitschke's masterpiece in a quieter temper and from a widely different standpoint. While 'the Bismarck of the Chair' glorified Prussia and scourged her enemies at home and abroad, the treatise of the South German Catholic is less a narrative than an assessment of the political, economic and cultural life of the German people. Four stout volumes bring the story to the year of revolutions, and the author, now a professor at Munich after the stormy intermezzo of the Second World War, is at work on the sequel. He is read with most pleasure by those who prefer Stein to Bismarck and the gentler breezes of the South to the bleak climate of Berlin. As Max Lehmann's biography of Stein superseded the enormous compilation of Pertz and the admiring tribute of Seeley, so Gerhard Ritter, perhaps the most productive of living German historians, has in large measure superseded Max Lehmann.

Veit Valentin's stout volumes on the German revolution of 1848-9 breathe the liberalism of the loyal Frankfurter who watched the activities of Prussia with critical eyes. The later volumes of Sombart's immense treatise, *Der moderne Kapitalismus: Historisch-systematische Darstellung des gesamten Europäischen Wirtschaftslebens von seinen Anfängen*, described the eighteenth, nineteenth and twentieth centuries. His analysis of the material and psychological factors in the evolution of capitalism through the centuries, though sharply criticised by Below and Brentano, impresses by its range and originality. The stimulating *General Economic History* by Max Weber, the most fertile and encyclopaedic mind of his time in the German academic world with the exception of Tröltsch, was compiled from the lecture notes of the Heidelberg Professor and of some of his hearers after his death in 1920. Wolfgang Michael lived just long enough to complete his monumental work on England in the eighteenth century, the fifth volume reaching his target of 1760. Hartung's masterpiece, *Deutsche Verfassungsgeschichte*, has been revised and brought down to the emergence of the Weimar Republic and the Nazi dictatorship.

The most arresting figure in German historiography since the First World War is Friedrich Meinecke. Winning his spurs as the biographer of Boyen and the author of *Weltbürgertum und Nationalstaat*, he continued his studies of European thought since the Middle Ages. *Die Idee der Staatsräson*, which may be described as an expansion of Acton's pregnant Introduction to Burd's edition of the *Prince*, traced the conflict between politics and morals through the writings of publicists and statesmen from Machiavelli onwards, through Richelieu and Frederick the Great, Hegel and Treitschke. No German scholar since Dilthey, whose stature has been recognised by the collection in twelve volumes of his penetrating essays, has analysed ideologies with such insight and subtlety. Of equal significance was *Die Entstehung des Historismus*, a survey of the transition from the unimaginative and generalising rationalism of the *Aufklärung* to the genetic relativism of the Romantic Movement, culminating in Ranke's celebrated aphorism that all the centuries are equal in the sight of God. Dismissed by the Nazis from the editorial chair of the *Historische Zeitschrift* which he had adorned for forty years, Meinecke proceeded in his autobiography to describe his intellectual evolution and his contacts with scholars and statesmen of two generations. Another veteran, Walter Goetz, collected an able team of specialists for the *Propyläen-Weltgeschichte* in ten volumes.

Several Austrian historians increased their fame within and beyond the frontiers of their fatherland. Oswald Redlich, the *doyen* of mediæval studies, continued his learned monographs into extreme old age. No Austrian work of the inter-war years rivals in importance Dopsch's *Wirtschaftliche und Soziale Grundlagen der Europäischen Kulturentwicklung aus der Zeit von Cäsar bis auf Karl den Grossen*. Having made his name before the First World War by his volumes on the social history of the Carolingian era, he pushed his researches back to Caesar and Tacitus and reconstructed the factors of mediæval civilisation—political institutions, land systems, the classes, the Church, industry and trade. His interpretations aroused widespread criticism, for he proclaimed in ringing tones the abiding influence of Imperial Rome. The battle of the Roman and the Teuton was still raging in the lecture rooms, and Dopsch stood forth as the doughtiest Romanist since Savigny and Fustel de Coulanges. We are shown an unbroken cultural continuity, the Germans gradually assimilating the Roman heritage without much wanton destruction. Like Fustel he tends to underestimate the value of the 'barbarian' contributions to mediæval civilisation and to exaggerate the vitality of Roman institutions, and Vinogradoff declared that he was stronger in economics than in law.

Ritter von Srbik, the greatest of Austrian historians since Arneth in the field of modern history, produced two major works which no student of nineteenth-century Europe can neglect. The first full-length biography of Metternich brought him at a bound into the front rank. The most eminent of Austria's statesmen since Kaunitz would have welcomed this sympathetic presentation by a scholarly conservative of his lifelong efforts to combat the democratic and nationalist ideology of the French Revolution and to foster the steadying conception of a European community. Yet Srbik never suggests that Metternich was creative. While fully recognising the power and learning of the book, some critics complained that he credited the pillar of European conservatism with a more coherent system of political ideas than he possessed. In *Der Zerfall Österreichs* Viktor Bibl, his colleague at Vienna and his only rival in the field of early nineteenth-century Austrian history, painted a far less flattering picture of the man whom he regards as little more than an able opportunist with reactionary instincts. Srbik's second major work, *Deutsche Einheit*, traces in greater detail the story of Austro-Prussian rivalry in the middle decades of the nineteenth century which had been so eloquently described in Friedjung's *Kampf um die Vorherrschaft in Deutschland*. But whereas the Jewish scholar wrote without access to the State archives, Srbik was allowed to explore the *arcana imperii*, and added to his four volumes of narrative five volumes of documents on Austria's German policy, 1859–66. Though a patriotic Austrian he was wholly free from the traditional bitterness towards Prussia, and he preached the ideal of *Gesamtdeutschland* as it emerged from Bismarck's Dual Alliance in 1879. It was natural that so friendly an Austrian recorder of a long quarrel should be offered by the Nazis a chair at Berlin and equally natural that he should decline. His later years were devoted to a valuable large-scale record of German historiography since the Middle Ages.

Two other veteran Austrian scholars added to the laurels they had won before the First World War. Joseph Redlich commenced an elaborate survey of the political systems and constitutional changes in the Hapsburg dominions since 1848 with a sketch of the reforming era of Maria Theresa and Joseph II, but *Das Österreichische Reichs- und Staatsproblem* was planned on too generous a scale and remained a torso. Writing after the fall of the Hapsburgs he was the first historian to utilise the records of the Ministerial Councils and conferences by which the internal development of the Empire since the Metternich era was shaped. The first enormous volume brings the story to 1861, the second to the *Ausgleich* of 1867. The portraits of Bach, Schmerling, Beust, Deak and other leading actors are vividly conceived, and those who have thought of the elderly Francis Joseph as a machine rather than a human being will discover in these pages an impetuous young ruler who took his full share in discussions and decisions. The story is continued on a smaller scale in his biography of the Emperor, which was enriched by personal knowledge of many actors in the drama.

Friedjung devoted his later years to a survey of the Hapsburg Empire since 1848, but only lived long enough to cover the reactionary decade of Schwarzenberg and Bach. His *Zeitalter des Imperialismus*, which was also interrupted by death when the third volume was nearly completed, is of value mainly for the treatment of Balkan politics, in regard to which his acquaintance with Aehrenthal brought him inside knowledge. The least productive of a gifted circle of friends was Pribram, whose edition of the *Secret Treaties of Austria-Hungary*, from 1876 to the First

World War—with an elaborate Introduction on the making and evolution of the Triple Alliance—lit up many dark corners of Bismarckian and post-Bismarckian Europe. Among the achievements of a younger generation the most notable are Hugo Hantsch's two-volume *Geschichte´ Österreichs*, a much needed summary of a century's research, and Count Egon Corti's biographies of the Emperor Francis Joseph and his unhappy brother Maximilian.

During the inter-war period no French scholar laboured so zealously as the veteran ex-Foreign Minister Hanotaux to arouse interest in the history of his country, and his glowing patriotism found vent in three large cooperative works. To the *Histoire des colonies Françaises*, in six volumes, he contributed an Introduction, and to the *Histoire de la Nation Française*, in fifteen, the Introduction and the closing volume on the nineteenth century. A third enterprise, an illustrated record of the First World War in fifteen volumes, breathes the passionate Germanophobia of his friend Poincaré. After an interval of over thirty years he returned to the task in which he had won his spurs, collaborating with the Duc de La Force in his continuation—though not the completion—of his monumental work on Richelieu. All his writings, he declared with truth, had one object—France. In the field of mediæval studies no single work rivals in importance René Grousset's large-scale *Histoire des Croisades*. The brisk debate on early French political and social institutions initiated by Fustel de Coulanges and Flach has been continued on sounder lines by Ferdinand Lot, Marc Bloch, Petit-Dutaillis, Halphen and Fawtier.

The second half of the sixteenth century continues to attract more attention than the first, and the interest in Catherine de Medici never flags. The first adequate biography was written by Mariéjol, and Lucien Romier's volumes, *Le Royaume de Catherine de Medici*, filled in the background. Braudel's encyclopædic *La Méditerranée et le Monde Méditerranéen a l'époque de Philippe II* is as much a sociological survey as a political narrative. No recent work on the seventeenth century approaches in importance Abbé Brémond's large-scale history of the Church under the early Bourbons, which ranks with Sainte-Beuve's classic treatise on Port Royal. Henri Sée continued Tocqueville's task of exploring the social system and economic conditions of the provinces of North-Western France in the seventeenth and eighteenth centuries, and presented an equally unflattering picture of the Ancien Régime. His largest effort, *Histoire Économique de la France*, bringing the survey down to 1914 in two volumes, appeared after his death in 1936. The last work of the Comte de Ségur contains perhaps the most convincing portrait of Marie Antoinette ever painted. Lavisse crowned the editorial labours of a long life by the cooperative *Histoire de France contemporaine*, 1789–1919, to which the veteran Seignobos made the largest contribution.

No French historian of the inter-war years generated so much heat as Albert Mathiez. Breaking away from the bourgeois radicalism of his master Aulard, he emerged as the standard-bearer of the Fourth Estate, re-editing Jaurès' *Histoire Socialiste* and founding the *Annales de la Révolution Française*. In a long series of monographs based on indefatigable research he reviled Aulard's hero Danton as a bad Frenchman and a bad man, while Robespierre appears as the unselfish champion of the common man, Thermidor as a catastrophe, not a deliverance. Mathiez is strongest where Aulard is weakest, namely, in social and economic history. His popular history of the Revolution is the most authoritative Left Wing interpretation since Michelet. Though few of his readers are likely to share his Marxist approach or his glorification of a fanatical doctrinaire, none of his many books can be ignored. On his death in 1932 the primacy in the field of Revolution studies passed to Georges Lefebvre, who succeeded to the editorship of his journal and shared his interest in social and economic phenomena. Standing midway between the rival camps of Aulard and Mathiez, he inspires greater confidence than either. His most popular monograph, *La France en 1789*, summarises generations of research on the hectic months between the meeting of the States General and the Women's March to Versailles. A companion volume, *La Grande Peur*, attributes much of the excitement and excesses of the opening phase of the drama to the fear of famine, robbery with violence, and royalist revenge. A little book on the Directory paints a less contemptuous picture than that in Vandal's dazzling masterpiece. Lefebvre may be classified as Left Centre, more sympathetic to the Revolution than Madelin but free from the paradoxes of Mathiez. He never forgets Renan's priceless aphorism : *la vérité est dans les nuances*.

Since the death of Frédéric Masson Madelin has been the *doyen* of Napoleonic studies. While his masterly narrative of the Revolution in the series *Histoire de France racontée à tous* was notable for its dryness of tone, his admiration of Napoleon is unconcealed. The Revolution appears as an unfortunate but unavoidable intermezzo, interrupting the unfolding of the greatness and glories of France. In his volumes *Le Consulat et l'Empire*, in the same series, we are shown not only the inspired soldier but the restorer of order, the supreme administrator, the fearless author of reforms which held their place while dynasties and governments rose and fell. In the closing phase of his long life Madelin undertook the longest and most important biography of his hero since Thiers, the sixteen volumes of which are at the same time, to a much fuller extent than with his brilliant predecessor, a history of France during the years of revolution, glory and defeat.

No major work has appeared on post-Napoleonic France since the First World War. Pouthas has done justice to Guizot, and Baumont and Renouvin have surveyed the Third Republic in their admirable volumes in the series *Peuples et Civilisations*. The large-scale unfinished life of Briand by Georges Suarez, who was shot as a collaborator after the expulsion of the Germans, comes nearest to our English political biographies, and Poincaré recorded his services to his country as Premier and President from 1912 to 1918 in ten complacent volumes of narrative and diary. Daniel Halévy's narrative of the early years of the Third Republic supplements the classical treatise of Hanotaux on the decade of Thiers and Gambetta. No recent work on modern France, however, compares in significance with his brother Élie Halévy's *Histoire du Peuple Anglais au dix-neuvième siècle*, unfortunately planned on too large a scale and left a torso in six volumes. No foreigner has combined in the same degree a knowledge of every aspect of modern English life and thought with a sympathetic yet critical analysis of our character and outlook.

The two world wars and their aftermath slowed down production less in England than in Germany and France. The success of the *Cambridge Modern History* encouraged the Cambridge University Press to launch a series of ambitious enterprises—the *Ancient History*, the *Medieval History*, the *History of the British Empire*, the *History of India*, the *History of British Policy*, the *History of Poland*, the *History of English Literature*, and the *Economic History of Europe*. While such works, enriched by contributions from foreign experts and by invaluable bibliographies, are mainly for students, Herbert Fisher's *History of Europe* and Trevelyan's *History of England* and *English Social History* from the age of Chaucer have been eagerly welcomed by the general reader at home and abroad.

The Anglo-Saxon centuries have at last been mapped out by R. H. Hodgkin and Stenton, making full use of archæological research and of the fruitful labours of the English Place Names Society. In the post-Norman period no achievements compare in importance with Tout's six-volume *Chapters in Mediæval Administrative History*, which emphasises the vital significance of the King's Household as the real executive of the kingdom, and with Powicke's *Henry III and the Lord Edward*, an encyclopædic picture of politics and society in the thirteenth century. Holdsworth lived long enough to complete the first comprehensive survey of English law down to 1700. Though Coulton's picture of the mediæval Church and in particular of monasticism has been criticised as unduly dark, no one questions his unsurpassed knowledge of the sources, while his inspiration as a teacher is enshrined in an array of monographs by his pupils. Little and Rose Graham, David Knowles and Cheney, have studied the religious orders in England, Plucknett and Helen Cam English mediæval institutions. Eileen Power's early death removed a social historian with something of Maitland's imaginative flair. In the foreign field we may note Barraclough's studies of mediæval Germany, Sir George Hill's monumental *History of Cyprus* down to the Turkish conquest in the sixteenth century, and Steven Runciman's spirited *History of the Crusades*.

Recent study of the Reformation era in England owes much to the labours of Pickthorn, Canon Maynard Smith and Father Hughes. Allen's superb edition of the letters of Erasmus moved steadily forward. After adding a portrait of Wolsey to the list of his sixteenth-century monographs, Pollard devoted his later years above all to the foundation of the Institute of Historical Research. Neale's concise biography of Elizabeth, so much more understanding than the nagging indictment of Froude, earned the distinction of foreign translations. More important are his detailed analyses of the composition, methods and activities of the Elizabethan House of Commons and Rowse's colourful panorama of Elizabethan England. Tawney's *Religion and the Rise of Capitalism* developed a fruitful line of enquiry opened up in a celebrated essay of Max Weber. The most valuable of Firth's later writings was the judicial analysis of Macaulay's *History of England*. Lady Burghclere found more to excuse in Strafford than Hallam and Macaulay. Veronica Wedgwood has performed the difficult task of providing a readable narrative of the Thirty Years War and has painted a brilliant portrait of William the Silent. Keith Feiling's impressive volumes on the Tory party in the seventeenth and eighteenth centuries registered a wide departure from the Whig tradition. G. N. Clark's survey of the later Stuarts is one of the outstanding successes in the *Oxford History of England*. Arthur Bryant has done justice to Pepys' labours at the Admiralty, and Andrew Browning's unflattering portrait of Danby ranks in importance with the Shaftesbury of Christie and the Halifax of Miss Foxcroft.

Two major works have been devoted to the age of Anne. George Trevelyan stands above the battle in a way which his famous relative could scarcely have done had he reached his goal. *The Reign of Queen Anne* is likely to hold its place as long as Gardiner's story of the constitutional struggle of the seventeenth century. Equally brilliant but less judicial is the four-volume biography of Marlborough by the most distinguished of his descendants, who follows his hero's career in politics and war with unflagging enthusiasm. In describing the battles Winston Churchill is in his element, and his magical style makes the conflict of Whigs and Tories not only readable but fascinating. Unlike Trevelyan, who thinks the Tories were right in ending the War of the Spanish Succession by a compromise peace, the born fighter regrets the tame conclusion to so many years of glory and sacrifice.

No one has succeeded in making the parliamentary manœuvres of the first two Georges really interesting, but Basil Williams eulogised Chatham and Stanhope and did his best with the fussy Newcastle and the showy Carteret. Lord Ilchester told the story of Henry Fox and of Holland House from the family archives. More challenging were the volumes in which Namier discarded the traditional view that the young George III, under the influence of his mother and Bute, inaugurated a new era by attempting to revive some form of dynastic autocracy. His evidence and arguments have coloured all subsequent discussion, and his analysis of the political structure of England in the third quarter of the century broke fresh ground. Butterfield has issued instalments of a full-length study of Fox which no one had attempted since Lord John Russell. Norman Sykes has analysed the relations of Church and State in the eighteenth century. The story of the French Revolution, which no leading English scholar since Carlyle except Morse Stephens had tried to master, has been told with a detachment impossible to Frenchmen by J. M. Thompson in the best English survey of the years 1789–94, and in his full-scale biography of Robespierre, whom he explains from his speeches, articles and letters. The most important recent English contributions to the story of the Great French War are contained in Oman's vast *History of the Peninsula War* and in the later volumes of Fortescue's *History of the British Army*. At the other end of Europe we welcome Gibb and Bowen's *Islamic Society and the West*, a comprehensive sociological analysis of the impact of Western civilisation on Moslem culture in the Turkish Empire in the eighteenth century.

Most recent outstanding English works on the nineteenth

century have dealt with foreign affairs. Webster's volumes on Castlereagh and Palmerston and Temperley's study of Canning are based on such exhaustive research at home and abroad that the work will scarcely have to be done again. The latter's survey of Great Britain and the Near East was interrupted by death after the appearance of the first volume, which opened with a study of the Ottoman Empire in its decline and acquitted Stratford Canning of the charge that he hustled his country into the Crimean War. Of equal merit is Seton-Watson's analysis of the rival Near Eastern policies of Disraeli and Gladstone, in which the author's lifelong sympathy with the Balkan Christians is clearly revealed. His histories of Roumania and Czechoslovakia, the surveys of Russian history by Bernard Pares and Sumner, E. H. Carr's elaborate study of the Bolshevist régime, and Adolphus Ward's *History of Germany from 1815*, are all of the first rank. Gooch's volumes, *Before the War*, study the problems and performance of ten European statesmen who piloted the Great Powers through the opening years of the twentieth century as mirrored in the vast official publications. Recent German policy has been illuminated in Wheeler-Bennett's monographs on Brest-Litovsk, Hindenburg and Munich, all of them enriched by the author's contacts with leading actors in the drama. Lloyd George's eight volumes on the First World War and the settlement, Grey's dignified account of his stewardship, and Churchill's epics on the two desperate conflicts, are almost as valuable for the revelation of their authors' personalities as for the material they contain.

In the domestic field no work on recent times compares in importance with Clapham's *Economic History of Modern England*, to which his official *History of the Bank of England* may be regarded as a supplement, and his posthumous *Economic History of Britain to 1750* as an introduction. Lipson's three volume *Economic History of England* has superseded Cunningham in the Universities. Monographs on the sufferings and struggles of the working class in town and country by Dr. and Mrs. Hammond combine emotional fervour with diligent research. Among the many official political biographies, a *genre* in which England excels, Garvin's homage to Joseph Chamberlain (continued by Julian Amery), Lady Gwendolen Cecil's impressive portrait of her father, and Mrs. Dugdale's affectionate record of her uncle Lord Balfour, hold pride of place. Winstanley's studies of the University of Cambridge in the eighteenth and nineteenth century are based on the Newcastle papers and other little-explored manuscript sources, and Charles Mallet provided the first full account of the fortunes of Oxford. *The Victoria History of the Counties of England*, now issued under the auspices of the Institute of Historical Research, pursues its leisurely way.

The most challenging figure among recent American scholars was Charles Beard, who was less interested in the political struggles at Philadelphia and Washington than in the broad sociological approach. Though not a Marxist, his whole thought was coloured by the economic factor. He traced it in treatises on the making of the Constitution and in the shaping of Jeffersonian democracy, which championed the small farmer of the interior against the capitalist of the Atlantic seaboard. His most ambitious work, in which his wife collaborated, *The Rise of American Civilisation*, followed by *America in Mid-Passage* and *The American Spirit*, abandoned the political interpretation of Bancroft and Channing, and, carrying on the Turner tradition, unfolded his story as the exploration and exploitation of a continent. That he devoted his closing years to a violent attack on Franklin Roosevelt's character and foreign policy was a source of regret to his friends. In the last half-century an increasingly critical attitude towards the Colonial period was exemplified in the surveys of C. M. Andrews, George Beer and James Truslow Adams, while a more sympathetic understanding of the economic system and mentality of the South was illustrated in the writings of Ulrich Phillips and William Dodd, subsequently American Ambassador at Berlin. The 'New History' preached and practised by James Harvey Robinson and his school stressed the significance of cultural and economic factors. No American work on the ideology of the Middle Ages since the writings of Henry Charles Lea compares in importance with Lynn Thorndike's gigantic *History of Magic and Experimental Science*. Carl Becker's analysis of the Declaration of Independence is a masterpiece. Washington found a competent interpreter in D. S. Freeman, Lincoln in Randall and Allan Nevins, Woodrow Wilson an ardent admirer in Stannard Baker. A detailed survey of the United States after the Civil War was provided by Oberholtzer. No single work, however, compares in importance with the *Dictionary of American Biography*.

In the wider field of world history Haskins dedicated himself to the Normans, Dana Munro to the Crusades. Nef has studied the history of War since the end of the Middle Ages in connection with the rise of industrial civilisation. Merriman followed up Prescott's trail in his massive *Rise of the Spanish Empire*, Conyers Read produced a full-length study of Walsingham which ranks among the finest historical biographies of our time, and Cheyney filled the gap of the last fifteen years of Elizabeth left by Froude.

Gottschalk's four volumes on Lafayette's life up to 1789, full of new material, supersede all previous biographies, and Gulick has described the struggles of the Austrian Republic. The edition of Jefferson's writings, papers and correspondence in fifty volumes, begun in 1950, is both a worthy tribute to the idolised author of the Declaration of Independence and a contribution of unique significance to the story of the foundation of the United States. W. S. Lewis' monumental Yale edition of Horace Walpole's Correspondence, which includes the letters he received, is as welcome an edition to our knowledge of the eighteenth century as the integral publication of the Boswell papers recently discovered in Scotland and Ireland. In the sphere of contemporary history nothing equals in importance the vast cooperative *Economic and Social History of the World War*, edited by Shotwell and financed by the Carnegie Endowment for International Peace. Sidney Fay wrote the first and fairest treatise in any language on the origins of the conflict, emphasising the special responsibility of Austria and Russia for the catastrophe, while Bernadotte Schmitt's treatise on the actual outbreak of hostilities upheld the older view of the over-shadowing guilt of Berlin. For the diplomacy of the First World War as viewed through American spectacles we must turn to the four volumes of the papers of Colonel House, edited by Charles Seymour. Less controversial are the four scholarly volumes by William Langer on the relations of the Great Powers after the foundation of the Hohenzollern Empire. Among the throng of American books on the approach and course of the Second World War none rivals in importance Cordell Hull's voluminous Memoirs, the more appetising fare of the Harry Hopkins Papers, skilfully edited by Robert E. Sherwood, and Samuel Morison's large scale *History of the U.S. Naval Operations*. J. W. Thompson, one of America's leading mediævalists, supplied the most comprehensive survey of historical scholarship through the ages ever attempted.

The smaller or less academically productive States of Europe continue to provide some works of high quality. From Sweden came Heckscher's comprehensive study of Mercantilism. In Holland we welcome Geyl's *History of the Netherlands*, at once warmly patriotic and scrupulously critical, the third volume of which has reached the eighteenth century. Japikse, who had given history lessons to Queen Juliana, edited the correspondence of John de Witt and of William III with his bosom friend Bentinck. The outstanding achievement in *Kulturgeschichte* is the picture of the waning of the Middle Ages in France and the Netherlands by Huizinga, the Dutch Burckhardt, who shows how small a part in the transition to the modern world was played by classical influences. In Belgium Pirenne, the most brilliant of Belgian historians, completed his spirited narrative, though he was more at home in the Middle Ages than in modern times. In Denmark Aage Friis devoted his later years to elucidating the complicated problem of Schleswig-Holstein in the Bismarckian era with the aid of the Danish archives. In Italy two Prime Ministers, Giolitti and Salandra, explained their respective attitudes before and during the First World War in plausible apologias. The veteran Benedetto Croce, who had begun his illustrious career in the field of Neapolitan history, described the fortunes of United Italy down to her entry into the First World War in 1915. The Mussolini régime, which he hated and despised, was obliquely attacked by depicting the young constitutional state in relatively favourable colours. Senator Luigi Albertini, formerly editor of the *Corriere della Sera*, employed the leisure of his later years forced on him by the Fascist dictatorship in the compilation of his three gigantic volumes, *Le Origini della Guerra 1914*. Among recent Spanish scholars the veteran Pidal succeeded Altamira as the chief interpreter of early and mediæval Spanish civilisation, and edited the latest cooperative *Historia de Espana*. More familiar to Anglo-Saxon readers is Madariaga who, while unwilling to live in Franco's Spain, has revealed his undiminished attachment to his country by a life of Columbus and an eloquent vindication of the record of the Spanish Empire in the New World. In Czechoslovakia the Memoirs of Masaryk and Benes are indispensable to the student of the First World War. Halecki, Dyboski and other Polish scholars made valuable contributions to the *Cambridge History of Poland*. In Roumania the murder of Jorga by the Iron Guard deprived the Balkans of their most learned and productive scholar.

In Russia the Marxist blight has paralysed disinterested research. The High Priest of the new orthodoxy was Pokrovsky, a pupil of Kluchevsky and Vinogradoff, and an active member of the Communist party. After years of exile, the revolution of 1917 gave him his chance. Appointed to a high post in the Ministry of Education, he created institutions for the study of history on Marxist lines. As the head of the archives he published the secret treaties of the Tsarist era in the *Krasny Archiv* and inaugurated the Russian equivalent of *Die Grosse Politik*. The philosophy embodied in his *Brief History of Russia*, which received the blessing of Lenin, is simplicity itself. Since the basis of human activity is the satisfaction of our needs, the struggle for economic power between various social groups forms the main theme. The ruling class, whether feudal or bourgeois, has always employed historians to present the historical process in a manner conducive to its interests. All historical writings, indeed, reflect the class ideology of the author, and the old ideal of objectivity is not only impossible but undesirable. 'Every real historian is a politician.' Karamsin's rendering of Russian history was succeeded by the bourgeois interpretation of Soloviev, Kluchevsky and Platonoff. When the domination of the landowners and the bourgeoisie was over, it became necessary to rewrite history in terms of the unceasing struggle of the manual worker for justice, which could only be obtained and preserved if his champions secured a monopoly of power. The depressing tale of the last of the Romanoffs has been told from different angles in the apologias of his Ministers Witte and Kokovtseff, Iswolsky and Sazonoff. Trotsky's *History of the Russian Revolution* is a Marxist classic.

The study of the Ancient World is inevitably a.cooperative enterprise. Here the *Cambridge Ancient History*, with its superb plates and exhaustive bibliographies, holds pride of place. No other work conveys such an impression of the magnitude of the recent additions to our knowledge of a dozen civilisations, and no chapter in the annals of historical inquiry during the last half-century compares with the succession of thrills in the resurrection of the Ancient East. No one came so near to covering the whole field as Eduard Meyer, whose monumental *Geschichte des Altertums* was kept more or less up to date by himself till his death in 1928 and subsequently by other hands. Among scholars of a slightly later generation no one compares in range with Rostovtseff, whose two-volume *History of the Ancient World* is based on his lectures at Wisconsin and Yale.

Egyptology, the *doyen* of the archaeological sciences, has continued to verify the familiar tag : *ex Africa semper aliquid novi*. Even more sensational than the finds of Mariette, Maspero and Flinders Petrie was the discovery in 1922 by Howard Carter after years of search of the first unrifled tomb of an Egyptian ruler. The artistic splendours of the young Tutankhamun suggest the opulence of the Eighteenth Dynasty and the immensity of our loss in the spoliation of other royal shrines. The romantic story is recorded by an eye-witness in the biography of Breasted by his son. Only second in interest was the discovery shortly after by the American archæologist Reisner of the burial chamber of Queen Hetephras, the mother of Cheops, founder of the Fourth Dynasty and builder of the Great Pyramid at Giza ; but the significance of the only partially intact tomb of the Old Kingdom is diminished by the fact that the furnishings had been transferred from the original burial place higher up the river and that the mummy has disappeared. A second unrifled tomb, of the Twenty-second Dynasty, was discovered by Pierre Moret in 1939.

The later years of Flinders Petrie's long and laborious life, described in his *Seventy Years of Archaeology*, were mainly devoted to excavation on the Palestine side of the frontier. Near Gaza he explored the large fortified Hyksos city Tell-el-Aijul, abandoned, perhaps owing to malaria, about 2000 B.C. but not destroyed, with the walls of houses intact up to 6 or 8 feet, and the pottery suggesting a high standard of civilisation. To him and de Morgan we owe our first acquaintance with pre-dynastic times. Recent researches at Badari, Deir Tasa and elsewhere have rendered it possible to reconstruct and name the principal phases, which are described in Elise Baumgärtel's *Cultures of Prehistoric Egypt*. Despite the labours of Maspero in the eighties, Petrie in the nineties, and the German Orient-Gesellschaft on the eve of the First World War, Tell-el-Amarna has yielded new treasures to the zealous workers of the Egypt Exploration Society. In the last half-century the technique of Egyptological research has become an exact science. Useful summaries of the recent research are provided in *The Legacy of Egypt*, edited by Glanville, and *The Splendour that was Egypt* by Margaret Stuart. Less sensational than the recovery of monuments and objects of art by the spade, but of no less assistance to the historian, is the ever increasing mastery of the numberless inscriptions and written records in the valley of the Nile and the museums of many lands by the philologists with Erman and Sethe, Breasted and Alan Gardiner at their head. Idris Bell has devoted himself to the new science of papyrology. In the cooperative *Dictionary of Ancient Egyptian* the seed sown by Champollion over a century ago has grown into a mighty tree.

Southern Mesopotamia has claimed even more attention during the last four decades than the Valley of the Nile, for de Sarzec's revelation of Sumerian civilisation at Tello whetted the appetite of archæologists. As far back as 1854 Taylor, British Consul at Basra, identified the so-called 'Mound of Pitch,' a few miles from the Euphrates, as Ur of the Chaldees, the home of Abraham. Immediately after the First World War the soundings of Campbell Thompson and Hall revealed the magnitude of the task, and in 1922 the University Museum of Pennsylvania proposed to the British Museum a joint expedition to Mesopotamia. Ur and Tell-el-Obeid, four miles away, were selected for the first assault, and Leonard Woolley was placed in command. Seven years later the Director summarised the sensational results in his fascinating little book *Ur of the Chaldees*, and the exploration continued till 1934. Here was the best preserved Jiggurat, or tower-temple, in Mesopotamia, for the more celebrated Tower of Babel has vanished without trace. The story of three thousand years was mirrored in the art treasures of the royal graves, from 3500 B.C. onward, discovered in 1926. Current ideas of early civilisation were revolutionised when the proud claim to cultural seniority was transferred from Egypt to Sumerian Mesopotamia.

Robberies there had been in the cemetery at Ur, but about half was intact, including precious stones, marvellous mosaics, and the tomb of Queen Shub-ad with a gold cup near her head. No religious symbols were found, but the expectation of a future life was grimly suggested by the skeletons, male and female, neatly laid out in rows, not slaves but courtiers, gaily attired for the death ceremony, accompanying their king-god for service beyond the grave. After the great days of the First Dynasty, the glories of Ur were revived and surpassed nearly a thousand years later by Ur-Nammu, whose authority extended from the Persian Gulf to the Mediterranean. His dynasty was overthrown by the Elamites of South Persia, and after the subsequent sack of the city by the Babylonians about 1885 B.C. darkness descended for 500 years. About 1400 B.C. it was restored by a Babylonian king, and centuries later was rebuilt by Nebuchadnezzar, King of Babylonia. The last chapter of the chequered fortunes of Ur was its conquest by Cyrus, King of Persia. At Warka, close by, the Germans resumed their labours which had been interrupted by the war of 1914. Further north an Anglo-American expedition under Langdon explored Kish, near Babylon. At Susa, in South Persia, the work commenced by de Morgan and the Délégation Française en Perse was resumed by de Mecquenem, and marvellous painted pottery of the oldest Elamite civilisation was found. Meissner's comprehensive *Babylonien und Assyrien* summarised the labours of nearly a century in the vast spaces of Mesopotamia. In North-west Persia Aurel Stein and Herzfeld explored Tepe Sialk, Tall-i-Bakun and other promising sites, while Mortimer Wheeler unearthed the pre-Aryan cities of Harappa and Mohenjo-daro dating from the third millennium B.C.

The two capitals of the Hittite Empire, the earlier, Boghaz-keui in Cappadocia, the later, Carchemish, on the Euphrates, having been explored before the First World War, the most urgent task was the decipherment of the thousands of tablets and inscriptions found by Winckler in the northern capital in 1906. After years of study Hrozny published *Die Sprache der Hethiter* in 1917, followed by a selection of texts with tentative translations. Though his classification of Hittite as an Indo-European tongue is not universally accepted, his services are everywhere recognised. So great has been the progress of archæological and philological research that two series of the Schweich Lectures by Cowley and Hogarth (1920 and 1926) were devoted to the Hittites, and Garstang's *Land of the Hittites*, published in 1910, appeared as virtually a new work, *The Hittite Empire*, in 1929. It is now clear that for two centuries, from about 1400 B.C., the Hatti kings were the chiefs of a large confederacy and the leading power in Asia Minor, reaching as far West as the Aegean and pushing East and South to the Euphrates and Syria. A large-scale investigation of Hittite and pre-Hittite civilisation was undertaken by the Oriental Institute of the University of Chicago under the direction of von der Osten and Schmidt. Scores of new sites were found, the most important of which was Alishar. The epoch-making discoveries of Arthur Evans in Crete were described by himself in his old age in the sumptuous volumes of *The Palace of Minos*.

The lands lying between the Hittite sphere of influence on the North, the Mesopotamian Empires on the East, and Palestine and Phoenicia in the South, have been diligently explored, and the little-known people called Mitanni has been put on the map. A pearl of great price was discovered by Schaeffer in 1929 at Ras Shamra, a port on the North Syrian coast opposite Cyprus, and the labours of many years were described in the excavator's Schweich Lectures. When written records begin Ugarit, as it was called in the Tell-el-Amarna letters and other ancient records, was inhabited by a Semitic people trading with Egypt, Asia Minor and Mesopotamia. After the decline of the First Dynasty of Babylon the city enjoyed its greatest prosperity under Egypt in the fourteenth and fifteenth centuries B.C. The finds are of extraordinary interest as revealing conditions among the Canaanites at the time of the arrival of the Israelites in the South. The library founded by King Nigmed about 1500 B.C. contained hundreds of cuneiform tablets in several languages, including Sumerian-Babylonian dictionaries, treaties, laws, wills, letters and religious texts. Here, too, was the earliest known Semitic alphabet, related to Phoenician and Hebrew. Here was the first evidence of the religion of the Canaanites as described by themselves instead of being seen through the darkly tinted spectacles of the Israelites. Here are the deities, El the Supreme God, Baal, Dagon and the rest, so familiar from the fulminations of the Old Testament. The long life of Ugarit, dating back to Neolithic times, ended in defeat and destruction about 1200 B.C. Only less important was the excavation by Baron Max von Oppenheim of Tell Halaf, the sculptures and pottery of which go back to the fourth millennium. Here ruled Tushratta, King of Mitanni, whose letters to Amenhotep III were found at Tell-el-Amarna, one of them announcing the departure of his daughter to be Queen of Egypt. The city was engulfed by the Assyrian tide in the ninth century B.C.

Despite a generous flow of American dollars, excavations in Palestine continue to be disappointing as regards inscriptions and art treasures, but valuable work has been accomplished in half a dozen cities. The recovery of ancient Jerusalem is impeded by the fact that the built-over site can only be tested by tunnelling. In Samaria, the northern capital, the plan of the walls and palaces has been traced. In Jericho, Lachish and Bethlehan Egyptian objects facilitate the dating, and in the latter inscribed ostraka of the sixth century B.C. were a welcome surprise. At Megiddo the labours of the Oriental Institute of Chicago, financed by Rockefeller, were rewarded by the discovery of gold ornaments and ivories, treasures which are rare in an oft plundered land. Though several excavated sites reach back to the fourth millennium, we know far less of the life and thought of Palestine before the coming of the Israelites than of early Egypt and early Mesopotamia. The main interest of Palestinian archæology lies in the general confirmation of the Old Testament historical narratives. For instance, the exploration of Jericho harmonises with the Jewish narrative of the destruction and rebuilding, and facilitates the dating of the invasion of Palestine under Joshua. Such direct verification of the Bible story is exceptional, but the indirect result of a century of archæology in enabling us to reconstruct the setting of the drama is considerable. Moreover the discovery that writing was known to the Hebrews before the ninth century B.C. strengthens the probability that the historical narratives rested on a more solid foundation than oral tradition. Many aspects of the progress of scholarship are recorded in the forty volumes of Schweich Lectures on Biblical Archaeology.

In the sphere of Greek history the first outstanding event of the inter-war years was the second edition of Beloch's *Griechische Geschichte*, which grew from four volumes to eight. After a prolonged interruption caused by the entry of Italy into the First World War, he returned to his home in the Eternal City. It had been his youthful ambition to supersede Curtius, and the dream was fulfilled. It was the dearest wish of the veteran scholar, whose interest increased rather than flagged when he reached the Hellenistic era, that he might carry his narrative through the little-known period from the third century to Sulla ; but it was not to be. Scarcely less important is the richly illustrated *Social and Economic History of the Hellenistic World* by Rostovtzeff, who, like Vinogradoff before him, left the Russian prison-house for the free air of the Anglo-Saxon world. Kahrstedt's volumes on the institutions of Sparta and Athens are the nearest equivalent to Mommsen's *Römisches Staatsrecht*. New ground opened up by archæology was surveyed in Minns' richly illustrated *Scythians and Greeks in South Russia* and in Rostovtzeff's *Iranians and Greeks in South Russia*. Tarn's masterly volumes on Alexander the Great, the first reprinted from the *Cambridge Ancient History*, the second a collection of studies, provide the most satisfying interpretation of a world figure about whom our sources are lamentably incomplete. Wilcken's sumptuous *Urkunden der Ptolomaerzeit*, enriched by an Introduction and Commentary, continued his fruitful labours in the domain of papyrology. In addition to a delightful autobiography published in his eightieth year, the last decade of the strenuous life of Wilamowitz, the greatest German Hellenist since Böckh, yielded two massive treatises, each in two volumes, *Platon* and the posthumous *Der Glaube der Griechen*. The latter covered the whole field up to Plotinus, who has been sympathetically interpreted in the masterpiece of Inge. Of equal importance were A. B. Cook's majestic treatise *Zeus, A Study in Ancient Religion*, and Werner Jaeger's *Paideia: The Ideals of Greek Culture*, which received the honour of an English translation. In the field of archæology nothing rivals in importance the excavations of Carl Blegen on the site of Troy, where the activities of Schliemann and Dörpfeld had left much still to discover and explain.

In the field of Roman studies the two Italian veterans, Ettore Pais and Gaetano de Sanctis, continued their labours on the Republic. Eduard Meyer's elaborate vindication of Pompey against Caesar and his studies of the Punic war may be regarded as appendices to his unfinished *Geschichte des Altertums*. Beloch's *Römische Geschichte bis zum Beginn der Punischer Kriege* is lively and controversial. Comprehensive surveys of the social and economic history of the Roman Empire, largely based on the *Corpus Inscriptionum*, were made by Rostovtzeff and Tenney Frank, the latter the leading American classical scholar of the inter-war period, who captained a cooperative enterprise in five volumes. Only less important than the Inscriptions has been the collection and classification of the coins of the Empire by the numismatists with Mattingly at their head. In England the Republic has been surveyed by Heitland, and Rice Holmes paid tribute to Augustus. In France Léon Homo has devoted himself to the Empire. Otto Seeck completed his panoramic *Geschichte des Untergangs der antiken Welt* by a sixth volume bringing his story to the fall of the Western Empire. Marching on a broad front, he tells his readers as much about Augustine, the heresies and the Theodosian Code as of the invasions of Huns and Vandals. Dessau, another of Mommsen's pupils, came nearer to filling the gap left by the master with his *Geschichte der Römischen Kaiserzeit*. The whole of the first volume is claimed by the majestic figure of Augustus. The first half of the second reaches Vitellius, while the second half reviews the conditions and administration of the different parts of the Empire during the first century. Of no less importance is Ernst Stein's massive *Geschichte des Spätromischen Reiches*, the first volume of which spans the period from Diocletian to the fall of the Western Empire, the second, published after his early death, continuing the narrative till the death of Justinian. In the field of Roman archæology the decade of excavations at Dura Europos, a third-century fortified outpost on the Euphrates, by Rostovtzeff for Yale University is of primary importance.

The impetus given to Byzantine studies during the generation preceding the First World War has been fully maintained. No recent work exceeds in importance Bury's *History of the Later Roman Empire from the death of Theodosius II to the death of Justinian*, which superseded his early treatise on the same subject though it covered a shorter period. When the most erudite of British historians and the only scholar who contributed to the three Cambridge Histories, Ancient, Medieval and Modern, died in 1927, the lead in England was taken by Norman Baynes, whose volume on Byzantine civilisation in the Home University Library provided the first popular survey of the results of recent research, while the cooperative work entitled *Byzantium*, edited by himself and H. Moss in 1948, supplied more advanced students with much of what they need. Among younger British Byzantinists Steven Runciman, Joan Hussey and Jenkins have been hard at work. William Miller, who lived for many years in Athens, described mediæval Greece and the coming of the Turks. The leading Greek expert, Andréadès, explored the economic and financial history of the Eastern Empire. Authoritative surveys have been made by Uspensky, Director of the Russian Archæological Institute at Constantinople, Vasiliev, who in his new home in Wisconsin rewrote the volumes first published in Russian, Heisenberg, Krumbacher's successor as editor of the *Byzantische Zeitschrift*, Ostrogorski, and most recently in the three massive volumes of Louis Bréhier, Diehl's successor as the *doyen* of Byzantine studies in France. Dvornik's *The Photian Schism: History and Legend* defends the greatest of the Patriarchs of Constantinople against attacks by the Roman Church. In the sphere of archæology nothing compares in importance with the excavation of the Imperial palace at Constantinople in the thirties. For English readers the most convenient guide to the intricacies of Byzantine history from the eighth century till the final catastrophe of 1453 is the fourth volume of the *Cambridge Medieval History*. The reappearance in 1950 of the *Byzantinische Zeitschrift* under its distinguished editor Franz Dölger of Munich was a welcome sign that the quasi-paralysis of the Second World War was over. The invaluable *Encyclopædia of Islam*, of which the first instalment appeared in 1913, and of which Sir Thomas Arnold was the English editor, was completed in four stout volumes, with a supplement published in 1938.

The investigation of Christian origins never flags, but the experts continue to disagree on the dating and authority of the Gospels, above all of the Fourth. Only less important than the treasures of Oxyrhynchus, which have kept scholars busy for half a century, are the Chester Beatty papyri, ranging from the second to the fourth century A.D., containing portions of nine books of the Old Testament and of fifteen of the New, parts of the Book of Enoch, and a second century homily by Melito of Sardis. The chief result of the finds, which are summarised in Sir Frederic Kenyon's *The Bible and Archæology*, is to establish an earlier date for the text of the New Testament and for the formation of the canon than had been generally assumed. The heaviest task of Harnack's closing years, which are described in the full length biography by his daughter, was his treatise on Marcion, a theme on which he had won a prize half a century earlier. Eduard Meyer's *Ursprung und Anfänge des Christentums* carries us through the apostolic age. The excavations beneath the mighty fabric of St. Peter's have yielded the richest harvest in the field of Christian archæology since de Rossi's labours in the catacombs.

The Early Church and the early Middle Ages have inspired several works of importance, among them the cooperative *Histoire de l'Église*, edited by Fliche and Martin, and Hans von Schubert's *Geschichte der Christlichen Kirche im Frühmittelalter*, which begins with Clovis and ends with the fall of the Carolingians. Horace Mann brought his *History of the Popes* from Gregory the Great down to the fourteenth century in eighteen volumes. In the Preface to the nrst volume of his *Geschichte des*

Papsttums von den Anfängen bis zur Höhe der Weltherrschaft, published in 1930, which bore the title *Römische Kirche und Imperium Romanum,* Erich Caspar explained that a history of the Papacy must be more than a history of the Popes in chronological sequence. It must be first of all the history of an idea—the primacy of Rome. The imposing volume ends with Leo I in the middle of the fifth century, when the fall of the Western Empire left the stage free for the Papacy. The second volume brought the record to 752, when the work was interrupted by death.

While Caspar devoted his life to the Early Church, Johannes Haller divided his energies between the Papacy and modern Germany. His *Geschichte des Papsttums,* written for the general reader as well as for the expert, was begun too late in life and only reached the thirteenth century in three volumes. From the Catholic camp came Etienne Gilson's imposing analysis of Scholasticism, *La Philosophie du Moyen Age,* summarised in his Gifford Lectures, *The Spirit of Mediæval Philosophy,* and Martin Grabmann, the Munich oracle of Thomist scholarship. Dempf's *Sacrum Imperium,* with the sub-title *Geschichte und Staatsphilosophie des Mittelalters und der politischen Renaissance,* traces the development of political ideas and ideals from the New Testament, the Early Church and Augustine to Hildebrand and Aquinas, Dubois and Marsilio, Dante and Wycliff, concluding with the age of the Councils. Tröltsch's masterpiece, *Die Soziallehren der Christlichen Kirchen und Gruppen,* which has been translated into English, illuminates the whole field of Church History. If the story of the Papacy proved too large a theme for a single scholar's span of life, so was the Church in Germany. The publication of Hauck's monumental *Kirchengeschichte Deutschlands,* which he had hoped to bring down to the Peace of Augsburg in 1555, had only reached the fourteenth century at his death in 1918; but the second half of the fifth volume, continuing the narrative till the eve of the Council of Basle, was sufficiently advanced for publication. The great collection of Papal Regesta of the early Middle Ages, inaugurated by Paul Kehr before the First World War with materials from Italy and Germany, has been extended to other countries. The Bollandist *Acta Sanctorum,* after three centuries of cooperative endeavour, has reached the month of December.

Passing to the Reformation we note the Prussian Academy edition of Ranke's *Deutsche Geschichte im Zeitalter der Reformation* with an admirable Introduction by Joachimsen. The most striking item in the material from the historian's unpublished papers is a lengthy eulogy of Luther written for the tercentenary of 1517 in a mood of youthful exuberance which was quickly outgrown. On Kawerau's death in 1918 the presidency of the Luther Commission, which is responsible for the vast Weimar edition of his writings, passed to Karl Holl, the first volume of whose *Gesammelte Aufsätze zur Kirchengeschichte* is devoted to the reformer. Kalkoff's critical volumes on Hutten came as a surprise to the elder generation which had been reared on the eloquent eulogy by David Friederich Strauss. Pastor's gigantic *History of the Popes* since the end of the Middle Ages, based on the Vatican and other Italian archives, the first volume of which had appeared in 1886, reached its thirteenth volume in 1928, the year of his death, which brought the narrative to 1664; and posthumous volumes carried it down to the close of the eighteenth century, which had always been his goal. No work of our time—perhaps of any time—in the domain of Church History has made such an opulent and enduring contribution to knowledge. Hubert Jedin's *Geschichte des Konzils von Trient*, when completed, seems likely to supersede all previous narratives. The vast *Dictionnaire de Théologie Catholique*, begun in 1900 and completed in 1950, is the most important achievement of recent French Catholic scholarship, and is of use to members of all churches and of none.

Though philosophies of history are less in fashion than during the nineteenth century, the quest for its purpose and its laws—if such there be—continues. That every thinker has his own angle of vision is not surprising, and we need not be discouraged by the failure of our predecessors to agree. Some of the boldest attempts to guess the riddle of the sphinx have been analysed in Collingwood's posthumous volume *On History*. The problem of interpretation has been complicated since the days of Bossuet by the realisation of the relatively recent emergence of what we call civilisation. The background of time has been enlarged almost out of recognition by the pundits of anthropology, mostly English, among them Myres and Marett, Arthur Keith and Fleure, Gordon Childe and Mortimer Wheeler, J. G. D. Clark, editor of the *Proceedings of the Prehistoric Society*, and Osbert Crawford, founder and editor of *Antiquity*. The facile dogmatism, whether theological or pseudo-scientific, which was natural in the era of limited horizons is out of date in the middle of the twentieth century when new light from the distant past, excellently summarised by Glyn Daniel in *A Hundred Years of Archæology*, flashes into our field of vision from year to year. By far the larger part of the story of mankind tells, not of states and individuals, but of growing needs, changing values, useful inventions, widening perspectives. Every student requires a nodding acquaintance with pre-history in order to grasp that man, the raw material of his craft, has always been not only a fighting but an experimenting and a reflecting animal.

Tröltsch's *Der Historismus und seine Probleme*, published in 1922, surveyed the main attempts at a philosophy of history since the eighteenth century, and three recent attempts at interpretation have aroused discussion all over the world. Spengler's *Decline of the West: an Outline of a Morphology of History* sought the key in multiple periodicity, a succession not of transitional stages, as previous thinkers had believed, but of completed cycles. Civilisation, he argued, passes from childhood to old age not once alone but again and again. One civilisation after another moves forward to its appointed end. Western civilisation is the latest of these recurring cycles, which advance and recede like the tide on a shelving beach. For the familiar chronological sequence—ancient, mediæval, modern—which is only applicable to Europe, Western Asia and North-east Africa, he substitutes four cycles, Indian, Arabian, Antique and Western, the latter beginning about A.D. 900. Each is subdivided into Spring, Summer, Autumn, Winter. The civilisation of the West, now entering its winter months and replacing spiritual activities by practical aims, has only about a couple of centuries to run. Spengler discovers no enduring progress, no guiding spirit, no ultimate goal, merely an endless repetition of approximately similar experiences.

To this depressing quasi-biological determinism Arnold Toynbee's *Study of History*, perhaps the most significant achievement of English scholarship since Frazer's *Golden Bough*, offers a flat negation. Agreeing with Spengler in envisaging world history as the record, not of centuries or continents, but of civilisations, he rejects every kind of determinism. Reviewing the rise and fall of twenty-one civilisations, he concludes that their capacity or their failure to survive is due to concrete ascertainable causes, not to any inhibiting biological law. No known civilisation was or is fated to die : the deciding factor is its response to the challenge of nature and man. Spengler sees us caught up in a process so rigidly predetermined that no gift of prophecy is needed: in its broad outlines the future will be as the past. In Toynbee's eyes modern man, with an accumulating store of memories to steer him, has a fair chance of averting the doom which has overtaken so many experiments. Rejecting the oversimplified interpretation of history as primarily a struggle for economic control, he emphasises the significance of spiritual factors. We are out on the broad open road, not in a *cul-de-sac*.

While Spengler and Toynbee deal exclusively with the record of human experience, Croce disdains the customary chronological approach. The past, he declares in *History, its Theory and Practice*, exists for us solely as a subjective idea of what happened. All history is contemporary history in the sense that we can only think of the past with the mind of our own day. The notion of sequence, indispensable for the practical purposes of life, fails to provide us with objective reality. The sole reality is subjective—what we think about concrete things which we know have occurred. History is not a science: unlike the world of nature, it has no ascertainable laws. Nor can any philosophic system be extracted from it, for every mind and every age regards it from a different angle. While facts are historical, interpretations are purely subjective. To Croce the average historian is a mere chronicler, for facts only become history when they have passed through the crucible of an individual mind. We talk glibly of cause and effect, but no historian can forecast the future, since history never repeats itself. The annals of civilisation record the instinctive and unceasing struggle of man to escape from the limitations of barbarism, and the yardstick of progress is the increasing possibility of self-realisation. Here Croce changes from the critic to the prophet, and a warmer note comes into his voice. His whole system is at once far less mechanistic and depressing than that of Spengler. He rejects determinism as decisively as Toynbee, and salutes the conception of liberty as fervently as Acton himself. 'Give me liberty to know and to utter above all other liberties.' The ringing words of the *Areopagitica* should be inscribed in golden letters in every library and every lecture room in the land. For the historian needs light and air if he is to fulfil his duty of recovering and interpreting the past.

The British Foreign Office documents 1919-1939 continue to appear, and those of the German Foreign Office captured by the Allies in 1945 are being published in an English translation. Of special interest are the *dossier* relating to the Hohenzollern candidature in 1870, the papers of Holstein, the *Éminence Grise* of the Wilhelmstrasse, and the text of the Schlieffen Plan.

In the sphere of British medieval studies the three chief items are Runciman's majestic *History of the Crusades,* Knowles's studies of the Religious Orders in England, and Powicke's narrative of the thirteenth century in the *Oxford History of England.* The most notable works on the Tudor era are Father Hughes's account of the Reformation, Neale's elaborate studies of the Elizabethan Parliaments, and Rowse's colourful panorama of the Elizabethan age at home and abroad. Of the new *Cambridge Modern History,* which supplements but does not supersede the older work, two volumes (on the Renaissance and on the eighteenth century) have appeared. On the seventeenth century we may note Veronica Wedgwood's reconstruction of England on the eve of the Civil Wars, and Christopher Hill's Marxian interpretation of the social and religious background. It is instructive to compare Ogg's presentation of the reigns of James II and William III with that of Macaulay a century ago. De Beer's annotated edition of John Evelyn's diary includes the portions previously omitted. Valuable additions to our knowledge of the eighteenth century have been made by Norman Sykes's life of Wake, Archbishop of Canterbury, Plumb's life of Walpole, Sherrard's life of Chatham, and by a group of writers — among them Butterfield and Richard Pares — arguing vigorously about Namier's interpretation of the structure of politics in Georgian England. Churchill's *History of the English-Speaking Peoples* is chiefly of interest for its literary quality and its revelation of the author's ideology. Gooch has continued his portraits of the Enlightened Autocrats and contrasted them with the nerveless autocracy of Louis XV. Cobban has traced the decline and fall of the *ancien régime* in France. Harold Acton has described the rule of the Bourbon Kings in Naples and Sicily. Keith

Feiling has defended the record of Warren Hastings in India. Jane Norton's edition of Gibbon's Letters (3 volumes) supplements and supersedes the collection published sixty years ago.

In the nineteenth century we may mention Thompson's life of Napoleon III, Taylor's *Struggle for Mastery in Europe, 1848-1919,* and life of Bismarck, Hugh Seton-Watson's picture of Russia under the last three Tsars, Mack Smith's story of the antagonism between Cavour and Garibaldi in the Risorgimento, Hales's sympathetic biography of Pio Nono, and Brogan's suggestive sketch of French history since Napoleon. Medlicott's *Bismarck, Gladstone and the Concert of Europe* continues his treatise on the Congress of Berlin. The *Victoria County History* and the *Oxford History of English Art* move forward steadily; the large-scale biographical *History of Parliament* is in the hands of Namier, Neale and other scholars. Douglas, assisted by a group of specialists, is editing a selection of English Historical Documents covering the whole of English history in twelve volumes.

Among large works dealing with the twentieth century we must mention Carr's volumes on the early years of the Communist regime in Russia and Macartney's survey of Hungary since 1929. Harold Nicolson's authorized life of George V and Wheeler-Bennett's authorized life of George VI reveal the useful role of the sovereign who, in the familiar formula of Thiers, reigns but does not govern. The Duke of Windsor records his interrupted career in *A King's Story.* Alexander Werth has continued his eye-witness surveys of the French political scene in a study of Mendès-France, Bullock has written the best life of Hitler, Elizabeth Wiskemann has described the sufferings of Germany's eastern neighbours, Poland and Czechoslovakia, before, during, and after the Second World War. English political history before the Second World War is illustrated by Blake's biography of Bonar Law, Evelyn Wrench's life of Geoffrey Dawson, editor of the *Times,* and the reminiscences of Amery, Dalton, and Lord Templewood. On the coming and course of the war Churchill's six volumes, supplemented by Arthur Bryant's selections from Lord Alanbrooke's vivid journals, will always find readers. The Annual Survey of International Affairs, inaugurated by Toynbee under the auspices of the Royal Institute of International Affairs, was interrupted during the war; the vacuum is being filled by a series of cooperative volumes not all limited to the events of a single year.

A century ago Marx compelled students of history to devote

more attention to economic factors. In the atomic age we are becoming increasingly aware of the role of science in the evolution of mankind. Two major works, Needham's survey of *Science and Civilization in China,* and the *History of Science and Technology,* edited by Charles Singer, make steady progress. The archaeologists are widening our horizon by pushing ever further back the origins of civilisation. Kathleen Kenyon has revealed Jericho as the oldest of cities, and the Dead Sea Scrolls continue to be deciphered and debated. Gordon Childe and Mortimer Wheeler have kept us informed of the exciting discoveries in many lands.

Next to Churchill's narrative of the Second World War no recent English work has attracted such world-wide attention as Toynbee's *Study of History,* completed in 1954 by volumes 7 to. His knowledge of the rise and fall of civilisations is encyclopedic, but his theme is too vast for him to escape sharp criticism by specialists. No aspect of his study has aroused more discussion than his emphasis on the role of the World Religions and his denial of the uniqueness of any of them. The whole treatise reveals the author's deep interest in Asian peoples and his rejection of our complacent assumption of European superiority.

In the United States, interest in the Founding Fathers never wanes. The publication of the enormous mass of Jefferson's papers will require many years. Freeman's masterly biography of Washington has been completed after his death with a seventh volume written by other hands. Theodore Roosevelt's correspondence in 8 volumes supplements his autobiography and the official life by Bishop. Link's large biography of Woodrow Wilson is more critical in tone than Stannard Baker's official narrative. Hoover has described the whole of his career; Truman only his seven years in the White House. The chief item in the sphere of medieval studies is a vast cooperative History of the Crusades, edited by Setton. The first volume of a life of William Cecil by Conyers Read continues his Elizabethan researches which began with his life of Walsingham. The late Godfrey Davies continued to the Restoration the story of Stuart England which was begun nearly a century ago by Gardiner and carried on to the death of Cromwell in 1658 by Firth. May has begun a comprehensive survey of the closing phase of the Hapsburg Empire, and Hans Kohn has written a history of Panslavism. Langer and Gleeson's *World Crisis and American Policy 1937-40,* based on official sources but not an official enter-

prise, supplements Cordell Hull's impressive apologia. Schlesinger
has begun a large-scale record of the Roosevelt era. Among documented surveys of the war Samuel Morison's *History of American
Naval Operations* is outstanding.

No living French scholar is so widely known as the Abbé Breuil,
whose researches in South Eastern Europe and South West Africa
have enriched our knowledge of prehistoric man. Gilson has increased his fame by his *History of Christian Philosophy in the
Middle Ages.* The vast cooperative Catholic *Histoire de l'Église,*
edited by Fliche and Martin, is nearing completion. Another co-
operative enterprise, *Histoire des relations internationales,* is edited
by Renouvin who has himself contributed two volumes on the
nineteenth century. Crouzet's *L'Epoque Contemporaine: à la
recherche d'une civilisation nouvelle,* completes the *Histoire géné-
rale des Civilisations* of which he is Editor. Of recent works on
the Second World War none surpasses in dramatic interest the
two documented volumes of General de Gaulle's apologia. André
Maurois' biographies of Victor Hugo and George Sand, filled with
new material, contain a good deal of political and social history.
Saint Marc's *Emile Ollivier* vigorously defends the short-lived
experiment of the Liberal Empire.

In Germany, the *Historia Mundi,* planned by Fritz Kern,
directed since his death by Valjavec, and published in Bern, has
reached the eighteenth century. Containing contributions from
many lands, it provides the most comprehensive up-to-date survey
in any language of the evolution of man. Erich Eyck, the biographer
of Bismarck, has completed his survey of recent German history
with his two volumes on the Weimar Republic. It is enriched by
personal knowledge of many leading actors. Gerhard Ritter has
traced the close relations of the army and the state in Prussia, and
has described the internal resistance to Hitler in the life of
Goerdeler, one of his many victims. Srbik, greatest of Austrian
historians, crowned his life-work with a survey of the German
mind since the Renaissance, with special reference to the writing
of history. Friedrich Hertz, now a British citizen, has published
in English a study of the German public mind down to the
Treaty of Westphalia — not a history of political theory but a
record of what people thought about the state and society. In
Belgium, Ganshof, *doyen* of the medievalists, has contributed the
introductory volume to Renouvin's *Histoire des Relations Inter-*

nationales. In Holland, Geyl has turned from his *History of the Netherlands* to analyse French views of Napoleon and to criticize the methods and message of Toynbee's *Study of History.* In Italy, interest in recent history has been stimulated by the publication of the *Documenti diplomatici Italiani* and by Salvatorelli's and Salvemini's pictures of the Fascist era. In Spain, Madariaga, now a British citizen resident in England, has described the rise and fall of the Spanish Empire in South America in a series of biographies. Behind the Iron Curtain the insistence on Marxian interpretations continues to paralyse historical scholarship which cannot flourish except in unfettered freedom.

CHAPTER I

FROM THE RENAISSANCE TO THE FRENCH REVOLUTION

I

THE Middle Ages produced meritorious historical writers such as Otto of Freising and Matthew Paris, Joinville and Froissart, whose testimony to events of their own time was fairly trustworthy, but the essential conditions of study did not exist.[1] Printing was unknown and books were rare. The critical treatment of documents had not begun, nor was it realised that there was any need to treat them critically. Happy in the treasures of his monastic library, the pious chronicler did not stop to investigate their value, and copied the errors of earlier compilations into his pages. Though the forging of charters was a regular trade, the means of discovering deception had not been invented. Recorded events were accepted without challenge, and the sanction of tradition guaranteed the reality of the occurrence. Finally, the atmosphere of the Middle Ages was saturated with theology. The influence of Augustine weighed with almost physical pressure on the mind of Europe for a thousand years, diverting attention from secular history and its problems. In view of the constant interposition of Providence, the search for natural causation became needless if not impertinent. History was a sermon, not a science, an exercise in Christian evidences, not a disinterested attempt to trace and explain the course of civilisation.

The transformation in the outlook of mankind, which gathered force in Italy in the fifteenth century, favoured the conditions in

[1] The best surveys of historiography since the Renaissance are by Fueter, *Geschichte der neueren Historiographie*, 1911, third edition 1936; J. W. Thompson, *A History of Historical Writing*, vol. ii. 1942 (New York); Moriz Ritter, *Die Entwicklung der Geschichtswissenschaft*, 1919; and Fritz Wagner, *Geschichtswissenschaft*, 1951. Wegele, *Geschichte der Deutschen Historiographie*, 1883; Meinecke, *Die Entstehung des Historismus*, 1936, and Srbik, *Geist und Geschichte vom deutschen Humanismus bis zur Gegenwart*, 1950, are indispensable for Germany. Flint, *Historical Philosophy in France and Belgium*, 1893, and Monod, 'Du Progrès des Études historiques en France,' *Revue Historique*, vol. i., are useful for France. For the latest period the co-operative work *Histoire et Historiens depuis cinquante ans, 1876–1926*, 2 vols., 1928, is important, especially for the minor countries.

which objective methods and a genetic conception of history could
arise. The revelation that the classical world was not a shadowy
tradition but a brilliant reality stimulated curiosity and reflection.
The spirit of inquiry was further encouraged by the discovery of
the New World and the establishment of closer relations with the
East. Within a couple of generations the realm of space and the
horizon of learning were doubled. While the frontiers of knowledge
were being pushed back, a change scarcely less momentous was
beginning to appear in the intellectual atmosphere. The increasing
corruption of the Church, the development of town life, the expansion of commerce had already begun to act as solvents of the theological spirit; and the seduction of pagan culture, at once lofty
and frankly human, accelerated the process of emancipation. The
Italian Renaissance stands not so much for a conscious revolt
against authority as for the secularisation of thought. A joyous
pride in man, in the power of his mind and the beauty of his body,
succeeded to the brooding asceticism of mediæval ideals. For
speculations on the spiritual nature and posthumous prospects of
man were substituted inquiries into his earthly achievements. The
Middle Ages, which began with Augustine, ended with Machiavelli and Rabelais, Columbus and Copernicus.

The new spirit was reflected in the field of historical study.
The earliest masters of the new learning, Petrarch and Boccaccio,
were the fathers of modern historiography. They were, however,
only amateurs, and the finished model was provided by the
Florentine Bruni, the first historian who on principle employed
criticism. Aiming at the closest possible reproduction of the
classics, Bruni and his brother humanists condemned themselves
to sterile imitation, but they took the step without which progress
was impossible by substituting natural for supernatural causation. A further stage was reached when Machiavelli and
Guicciardini lifted historiography out of the realm of literature and
related it to the life of states. Tradition began to appear rather as
a challenge than a command. Lorenzo Valla exploded the Donation
of Constantine, and Æneas Sylvius, the humanist Pope, confronted marvels and legends in a spirit of healthy scepticism.
Humanistic historiography quickly spread over Europe.[1] The
pleiad of scholars whose rays illuminated the court of the Emperor
Maximilian, himself an historian, aroused interest in the heroes
and achievements of the Teutonic races. Celtis lectured on the *Germania* of Tacitus. Cuspinian edited Jordanes and Otto of Freising,
Peutinger and Beatus Rhenanus plunged into the study of

[1] See Joachimsen, *Geschichtsauffassung in Deutschland unter dem Einfluss
des Humanismus*, 1910.

German antiquities. They introduced into Central Europe the ideal and the methods of secular study and disinterested scholarship.

It was of such men that Goethe was thinking when he declared that the Reformation had thrown back European culture for a hundred years, for the brief career of humanism in Germany was rudely cut short by the appearance of Luther. Theology once more became dominant, and secular studies were engulfed in the whirlpool of confessional strife. Yet the fever contained within itself the germ of its cure. The controversialists of the Middle Ages appealed to principle, their successors to history. Protestantism sought to prove that the Church of the Medici Popes was not the Church of the early Christians and to show how degeneration had taken place. The Catholics, for their part, attempted to confound their enemies by revealing facts of which they were unaware. In the fierce struggle victory, not truth, was the aim, but precious documents were brought to light. When Flacius and his collaborators, under the auspices of the Lutheran princes, hurled the Magdeburg Centuries at the enemy, the Curia directed Baronius to prepare an exhaustive refutation and placed the Vatican archives at his disposal. Though, as Casaubon was to show, the mighty edifice was to some extent a house of cards, and though its author was ignorant of Greek and accepted forgeries and legends with childlike faith, the mass of new material and the apparent completeness of the reply rendered the appearance of the Annals one of the decisive events of the Counter-Reformation.[1]

Though the seventeenth century witnessed a gradual decline of confessional virulence, historical studies remained in large measure ecclesiastical. The great school of Anglican divines, from Ussher to Bingham, whose situation midway between Rome and Geneva was favourable to a balanced view of controversial questions, produced works of enduring importance on the early Church. The Belgian Jesuits, under the guidance of Bolland and Papebroch, began a collection of *Acta Sanctorum* on so vast a scale that it is still in progress.[2] Even greater were the services rendered by France. The Gallican theologians subjected Ultramontane claims to severe scrutiny, while the Jansenist Tillemont gathered materials for his priceless works on the Church and the Roman Empire, and Baluze explored the history of the Avignon Popes. Above all, the Benedictines of St. Maur[3] began to pour forth the great series

---

[1] See Mark Pattison, *Isaac Casaubon*, chap. 6, 1875.

[2] See Delehaye, *The Work of the Bollandists, 1615–1915*, 1922.

[3] The best account of the Benedictine scholars is to be found in the volumes of Emmanuel de Broglie on Mabillon and Montfaucon, 1888 and 1891.

of works which threw light on almost every province of ecclesiastical history. No page in the annals of learning is more glorious than that which records the labours of these mighty scholars in an age when an abstract Cartesianism was the dominant philosophy, when the State stood aloof, and when public interest was hardly born. The century which started from Baronius and culminated in Mabillon cannot be accused of stagnation.

Though the main theme of historians during the sixteenth and seventeenth centuries was the Christian Church, subjects of a secular character attracted the attention of isolated inquirers, for the most part laymen. Pithou and Pasquier explored the origin of French institutions, Du Cange mapped the little known territory of the Byzantine Empire, D'Herbelot summarised existing knowledge of the East, and Mézerai wrote the history of France in the critical spirit of a constitutionalist. Mariana presented his countrymen with a national history of Spain, and Zurita compiled the Annals of Aragon. In Italy the effort of Sigonius to reconstruct the institutions of Rome stands out as an isolated achievement. In England Bacon wrote the Life of Henry VII and Lord Herbert of Henry VIII, Camden laboured at British Antiquities, and Selden traced the history of law. In Germany Conring conducted profound investigations into the origins of German law. But it was in Holland that secular scholarship had the widest scope. Scaliger had made his home among the Dutch long before he published the monumental treatise which founded scientific chronology. Gruter's collection of inscriptions was prepared under his eye, and the long series of works by the Leyden Professors on classical antiquity continued his tradition.

Among the few attempts that were made to determine the principles and methods of historical study the treatise of Bodin stands out as a bold and brilliant achievement. At the height of the religious wars the French publicist envisages history as a secular subject and approaches it in a scientific spirit. In language which anticipates Montesquieu he indicates the influence of geographical situation, climate and soil on the character and fortunes of nations, while on the other hand he calls attention to the influence of personal position, patriotic and religious bias, and opportunities of knowledge on the views and the value of writers. No such insight into the operation of environment had been possessed by any previous thinker, and nothing was added to it for a couple of centuries. In the region of criticism a few results were obtained, though rather in the nature of anticipations than of definite conquests. Spinoza declared that the Old

Testament must be treated like any other historical work, and Père Simon incurred the wrath of Bossuet when he began to apply critical methods to the Jewish Scriptures. Launoi earned the name of the *dénicheur de Saints* by his ruthless handling of the records of the martyrs, and Perizonius suggested that the early history of Rome was legendary. Above all, Mabillon laid the foundations of the science of Latin diplomatic in *De Re Diplomatica* in 1681.

With the eighteenth century the scope of historical study rapidly widened. While the task of collecting material was steadily pursued, a more critical attitude towards authorities and tradition was adopted, the first literary narratives were composed, and the first serious attempts were made to interpret the phenomena of civilisation. We may glance at the output of the century under these four heads.

In the storage of erudition the French Benedictines maintained the supremacy they had established in the seventeenth century. Ruinart sifted the records of the early martyrs, Montfaucon laid the foundations of Greek palæography and classical archæology, Bouquet collected the historians of France, Clément compiled the first comprehensive chronology in his ' L'Art de vérifier les dates,' Sainte-Marthe wrote the history of the provinces of Christian Gaul, Vaissete and De Vic compiled the Annals of Languedoc, Rivet commenced the mighty 'Histoire littéraire de la France' which is still in progress. While all around them was changing, these scholars found happiness in their tranquil labours till their congregation was swept away by the Revolution. Muratori's stupendous labours in collecting the sources of Italian history, in compiling its annals and discussing its antiquities secure him a place by the side of Mabillon. Tiraboschi compiled a record of Italian literature which is still not only unrivalled but unapproached. In Germany Leibniz collected the early records of the House of Brunswick and commenced the *Origines Guelficae* which were completed long after his death. The Austrian Jesuit, Eckhel, devoted his life to the collection and classification of coins. In late seventeenth and early eighteenth century England, Wharton and Strype, Hearne and Madox, Hickes, Rymer and Wilkins continued the traditions of Tanner and Dugdale and rendered possible the intelligent study of the Middle Ages.[1] Their erudition has never been surpassed, and their works remain inexhaustible storehouses of learning to which serious students must have continual recourse.

[1] The admirable volume by D. C. Douglas, *English Scholars*, 1939, describes the great collectors between 1660 and 1730.

Though the great collectors rarely applied critical tests to their material, sources and traditions began to be scrutinised with greater freedom. On the eve of the eighteenth century Bentley exposed the Epistles of Phalaris; during its course Astruc discovered the composite nature of Genesis, Reimarus and Semler initiated the critical discussion of the Gospels, and Vico challenged the unity of the Homeric poems. Valuable results were obtained in the Memoirs contributed by the members of the French Academy of Inscriptions and the debates to which they gave rise.[1] The greatest interest was aroused by the prolonged discussion of the credibility of the records of early Rome initiated in 1722 by Pouilly, who boldly declared that nothing was certain before Pyrrhus. The Abbé Sallier, scenting danger to religion, denounced him as an atheist. Fréret intervened as a peacemaker, suggesting that truth and legend were often mixed. The subject was independently investigated by Beaufort, whose work on the Uncertainty of the Early Centuries of Roman history confirmed the conclusions of Pouilly and anticipated the arguments of Niebuhr. The contribution of the Academy towards the formation of critical methods was by no means exhausted by these debates. Fréret, its illustrious secretary, taking all antiquity for his province, carried chronology beyond Scaliger and Petavius and analysed the sources of Greek mythology, while his study of Oriental languages led him to suspect the affinity of the Indo-European races. 'If he had enjoyed the liberty which we possess,' declares Thierry, 'the science of our institutions and our social origins would have been born a century earlier.' In the later part of the century the attention of the Academy was largely directed towards archæology to which the partial excavation of Herculaneum gave a marked impetus; and De Brosses and Barthélemy brought back valuable results from Italy before Winckelmann had crossed the Alps.

The critical study of history was assisted by the great atmospheric change which has won for the eighteenth century the title of *Saeculum rationalisticum*. The seventeenth century had witnessed sporadic outbursts of scepticism, checked by a lively fear of temporal penalties. As its successor dawned a cool blast blew across Europe, and by the middle the sun of the *Aufklärung* was high in the heavens. Within the lifetime of Fontenelle France passed from the world of Bossuet to the age of Voltaire, from Port-Royal to the *Encyclopédie*. The criticism of existing practices and inherited beliefs reacted on one another. The fashion of

[1] See Maury, *L'Ancienne Académie des Inscriptions et Belles-Lettres,* 1864.

throwing doubt on testimony and tradition was set by Bayle, but it was to Voltaire more than any other man that the new attitude towards the past was due. While Bayle was a sceptic, Voltaire was a rationalist, and the crushing weight of authority could only be overthrown by a whole-hearted champion of the might and majesty of reason. With all his intellectual and moral failings Voltaire claims a high place among the influences which prepared the world for historical science. By allowing his razor-edged intelligence to play freely over vast ranges hitherto unchallenged by critical thought, he did much to destroy the blind credulity against which erudition alone was powerless.

The seventeenth century witnessed the appearance of works of high value relating either to events in which their authors had takon part or to the immediate past by Sarpi and Pallavicini, Davila, D'Aubigné and De Thou, Clarendon and Burnet, Hoofd and Puffendorf; but surveys of national life were scarcely attempted. In the eighteenth century a polished narrative of English history was produced by Hume, a less readable but far more scholarly history of Scotland by Robertson. Hénault compiled a chronological handbook on which Frenchmen were nourished till the coming of Sismondi. Mascov recorded the fortunes of Germany, Johannes Müller the epic of the Swiss cantons. Schlözer narrated the story of Slavonic Europe, and Pütter explained the institutions of the Holy Roman Empire. Cellarius abandoned the traditional framework of the Five Monarchies, which had prevented a rational conception of the development of civilisation; and a group of obscure English writers produced the first comprehensive Universal History, which, though destitute of literary qualities, brought together a mass of material not easily accessible, and which, in translations and abridgments, held its own till it was superseded by Rotteck and Schlosser almost a century later. Above all, Gibbon constructed a bridge from the old world to the new which is still the highway of nations, and stands erect long after every other structure of the time has fallen into ruins.[1]

Though the history of States naturally formed the main object of study, other aspects of the life of humanity began to claim attention. The first comprehensive Church History was written by Mosheim in the cool atmosphere of the University of Göttingen. Art as a product and mirror of civilisation received its first adequate treatment from Winckelmann, whom Goethe called a new Columbus. In his History of Osnabrück Justus Möser,

---

[1] For Gibbon, see Bury's Introduction to the *Decline and Fall*, 1896; G. M. Yo*n*g, *Gibbon*, 1948. *Gibbon's Autobiography and Letters*, 1896, are supplemented by *Gibbon's Journal*, ed. D. M. Low, 1929.

described by Herder as the author of the first German history with a German head and heart, made the first sociological approach. Above all Voltaire founded a new genre, later known as *Kulturgeschichte*; his 'Siècle de Louis XIV' was the first picture of the multiform life of a civilised State. A few years later his 'Essai sur les Moeurs' portrayed the moral, social, economic, artistic and literary life of Europe from Charles the Great to Louis XIII. His subject, he declared, was the history of the human mind. He desired to trace the steps by which society had passed from the barbarism of the Middle Ages to the civilisation of his own time, to indicate the growth of enlightenment and social refinement. The sparkling brilliance of the style and the novelty of treatment combined to secure an ever-widening influence for a book which more than any other work of the century enlarged the horizon of historical study. Despite its glaring faults the historiography of the *Aufklärung* marks a real advance. It put an end to the era of mere compilation. It widened the scope of history from a record of events to a survey of civilisation. It attempted to introduce critical standards and sociological methods.

Finally, the eighteenth century witnessed a bold advance towards the philosophic interpretation of the life of humanity.[1] The rudimentary conception of progress in Bacon's aphorism, *Antiquitas saeculi juventus mundi*, was developed by Pascal: 'The whole succession of human beings through the whole course of ages must be regarded as a single man, ever living and ever learning.' In the literary quarrel of the Ancients and Moderns, Perrault maintained that we should not only admire the achievements of the classical world but perfect them by the addition of all that we had subsequently learned. In a fine image he declared that the interruption in the Middle Ages was only apparent, like a river which flows for some distance underground. Fontenelle maintained that, though the life of a nation passed through stages like the individual, there was no decline. His scientific studies indeed suggested to him a certain relation between the movement of human history and 'the great and universal movement which has directed all nature.' The doctrine of perfectibility appealed to the new-born enthusiasm for man which meets us constantly throughout the eighteenth century, from the Abbé Saint-Pierre at the beginning to Godwin, Condorcet and the *Illuminati* at the end.

These utterances were rather the expression of generous hopes than the reasoned product of philosophic reflection. No rational

---

[1] See Delvaille's massive *Essai sur l'Histoire de l'Idée de Progrès*, 1910; Bury, *The Idea of Progress*, 1920; and Cassirer, *Die Philosophie der Aufklärung*. 1932.

interpretation of history was possible till the doctrine of evolution
was enunciated by Leibniz. 'Nothing happens all at once,' we
read in 'Nouveaux Essais,' 'and nature never makes jumps. I
call that the law of continuity. In starting from ourselves and
going down to the lowest, it is a descent by very small steps, a
continuous series of things which differ very little—fishes with
wings, animals very like vegetables, and again animals which
seem to have as much reason as some men.' As nature advanced
by small steps, so humanity moved slowly and painfully forward.
The lonely Neapolitan thinker, Vico, in discussing the laws of
change in his 'Scienza Nuova,' regarded the process of history
as a natural phenomenon.[1] 'First the forests, then the huts, then
the villages, then the cities, and finally the academies.' The
principle was further elaborated in Turgot's Discourse at the Sor
bonne on the Successive Advances of the Human Mind. History,
he declared in terms to which we can add little, was the life of
humanity, ever progressing through decay and revival, each age
linked equally to those which have gone before and those that are
to come. Anticipating Comte, he outlined the law of the three
states through which the human mind passes in its progressive
apprehension of reality. Progress was nothing narrower than the
gradual evolution and elevation of man's nature, a combined advance in material well-being, mental enlightenment and virtue.
Cousin has called Turgot the father of the philosophy of history,
and no one has a better right to the name. Further contributions
to a theory of progress were made towards the end of the century
in Germany. At the close of his life, as from a lofty watch-tower,
Lessing surveyed the panorama of history and recorded his impressions in the pregnant aphorisms of 'The Education of the
Human Race.' The human mind, he declared, was greater than
any of the influences that moulded it. Religion was a progressive
revelation, and religions were the school-books which man uses
in his progress, each helpful at a certain stage of development,
none of them final. It is the thought of Pascal without the framework of his theology. But the most detailed and exhaustive investigation into the conditions and nature of progress was contained
in Herder's 'Ideas on the History of Humanity.' Deeply impressed
by the influence of cosmic factors, he emphasised the existence of
similar laws in history and nature.[2] At the end of the century
Burke proclaimed the organic continuity of historic life and the
debt of every age to its predecessors in his Reflections on the
French Revolution.

[1] See H. P. Adams, *Vico*, 1935.
[2] See Haym's great biography, 2 vols. 1877–85.

In addition to these speculations on the nature of progress, serious endeavours were made to explain particular factors of civilisation. Montesquieu, himself a lawyer, investigated the origin and influence of laws and institutions, explaining that they must be judged not by abstract principles but by their suitability to the circumstances of time and place. Of no less importance was the study of the economic elements in historical development. Hume reached some illuminating sociological generalisations in his Essays, but it was the glory of Adam Smith to relate the rise and fall of nations to their economic resources and policy. A generation later Malthus built his law of population on a basis of elaborate historical induction.

Though work of high merit and enduring value was thus accomplished during the eighteenth century, several obstacles impeded the growth of genuine historical science. In the first place the spirit of the *Aufklärung* was unfavourable to the historical sense. The seventeenth century had witnessed a gradual fall of the theological temperature, and Bossuet's 'Histoire Universelle' may be taken as the last considerable work of the theological era. But with its secularisation history entered on a career attended by new and scarcely less formidable dangers. The abstract and absolute standard, the failure to realise the differences in atmosphere and outlook in different ages, and the zeal for political and philosophic propaganda were hostile to patient research and disinterested investigation.[1] The conception of continuity was the property of a few isolated thinkers. The more popular doctrines of the social contract, with its assumption of deliberate action, and of the law of Nature, with its idealisation of primitive society, were the negation of history. The French Revolution defiantly turned its back on the past, as the sleeper shakes off the nightmare which has oppressed him. Thus the tendency of the age encouraged writers to content themselves with superficial inquiry and facile generalisations. Bolingbroke urged the study of modern history as politically useful, but condemned erudite research as learned lumber. Robertson wrote the Life of Charles V without learning German. Some of the most popular books of the century, such as Schiller's narrative of the Thirty Years War, were the fruit of meagre learning and an untrained judgment.

The limitations of the *Aufklärung* were most apparent in its treatment of the religious sentiment and of the Middle Ages. A knowledge of Greece and Rome was fairly general, partly owing

[1] See Meinecke's masterly work, *Die Entstehung des Historismus*, 2 vols. 1936, and Dilthey, 'Das achtzehnte Jahrhundert und die geschichtliche Welt' in his *Gesammelte Schriften*, vol. iii.

to the familiarity of the cultured classes with classical literature, partly because the ideas and institutions of the ancient world formed the inspiration of reformers. But the Middle Ages were like a sealed book, not only to the deist and the rationalist but to the Trinitarian. 'Enthusiasm' was equally distasteful to the believer and the sceptic. Hume dismissed the Anglo-Saxon centuries, the time of the making of England, as a battle of kites and crows. Voltaire declared that the early Middle Ages deserved as little study as the doings of wolves and bears, and revealed his incapacity to understand mediæval Christendom in 'La Pucelle.' Robertson's famous Introduction to the Life of Charles V is tainted with ignorant disdain. Gibbon's contempt for religious feelings and belief blinded him to the significance of many of the principal objects on his long journey. It was his immortal service to show how the Roman Empire lived on, but of the new world into which it survived he understood as little as other men. It was only towards the end of the century that sympathy for the Middle Ages came in like a flood with the Romantic movement.

A second disability was the lack of the critical faculty in dealing with the value and testimony of authorities. Histories of France began with copious details of Pharamond, and Rollin paraphrased Livy. To Johannes Müller all chronicles and charters seemed of equal value so long as they were old, and his popularity was largely due to the brilliant rendering of the patriotic legends of Tschudi. Where scepticism existed, it was often as uncritical as credulity. La Mothe le Vayer, in his Discourse on the uncertainty of history, declared that a wise man would doubt all things except divinely revealed truths; and Bayle was equally the enemy of reason and faith. The learned Jesuit Hardouin maintained that the history of the ancient world was fabricated by monks of the thirteenth century, the real authors of Thucydides, Livy and Tacitus. Despite Mabillon, the technique of research was still in its infancy.

A third reason why historical study made no greater advance was the almost entire absence of teaching. It was indeed recognised that history was essential to the education of rulers. Bossuet declared that it was the counsellor of princes, and wrote his 'Histoire Universelle' for the instruction of the Dauphin. Fénelon composed a Life of Charlemagne for the Duke of Burgundy. Histories of the Powers were specially written for the youthful Joseph II. But in the statutes of Henri IV for the University of Paris history is not mentioned, and it found no place in the curriculum of the Jesuits, the educators of half Europe. Fénelon gave it no place in his 'Education des Filles.' The Cartesians disparaged it, and Malebranche declared that there was more truth in a single principle of metaphysics than in all historical books. The ignorance in which children were compelled to grow up provoked occasional remonstrance. Fleury expressed the wish that everyone should know the history of his town and province. Rollin lamented that no time was allowed in school for the teaching of the history of France, 'which it is a disgrace for every good Frenchman to ignore'; and he added that he felt himself a stranger in his own country. D'Alembert declared that it was scandalous for children to leave school without any notion of the history of their country. A few isolated attempts were made to impart instruction. George I founded a Chair of Modern History at both Universities, but the Professors, among whom was the poet Gray, rarely or never lectured. Not till the creation of a Chair of History and Morals at the Collège de France in 1769 did France recognise the claim of history to rank with the older sciences. The youth of Germany was better supplied. The foundation of Göttingen in 1757 inaugurated advanced teaching by scholars of acknowledged competence, whose influence will be traced in later chapters.

A fourth disability was the restriction placed on the access to documents and on the liberty to announce results. The expense and danger of travel rendered it difficult for a student to consult the authorities he needed for his task, and his troubles were increased by the miserliness with which the possessors of archives guarded their treasures. Manuscripts were regarded as useful for the determination of practical questions of law and precedent. When an archivist was appointed in East Friesland in 1729, he was informed by his employers that 'after learning the secrets of our house he must carry them to the grave and reveal them to nobody.' No one was allowed to use the archives at Stuttgart without the express permission of the Duke. The title of Court Historiographer possessed a real meaning when its holder was regarded as the defender of the glory and dignity of the dynasty. It was in this spirit that Puffendorf was commissioned to write the life of the Great Elector, and Leibniz to investigate the origins of the House of Brunswick. When Muratori was collecting for the *Scriptores*, several Italian princes refused him access to their archives on the ground that he might find arguments against their territorial pretensions. A single false step might ruin a career. Thus when the Jacobite Carte mentioned in a note the case of an Englishman who had been cured of the king's evil by the touch of the Pretender, the grant given by the Common Council of London was withdrawn and the work was boycotted. The trade of historian was scarcely less dangerous than that of a journalist. Mézerai, an old Frondeur, was deprived of his pension for some comments on the fiscal expedients of the predecessors of Louis XIV. Giannone was exiled for his history of the Kingdom of Naples, and died in prison. Fréret was sent to the Bastille for maintaining that the Franks were not of Gallic race. Père Daniel was fiercely attacked for eliminating Pharamond and other legendary heroes commonly called the first four Kings of France, and the Abbé Velly found it necessary to restore them to their thrones. In Austria the censorship was particularly oppressive during the long reign of Maria Theresa, the entrance of foreign books being almost entirely checked. A brief interval of enlightenment occurred when the Emperor Joseph succeeded his mother, but obscurantism returned with his death.

In addition to the dangers which historians incurred from the operations of the secular censorship, they were confronted in Catholic countries by the might of the Church. Though the paralysing influence of the Index and the Inquisition was felt most directly in the realm of speculation and science, it was hardly less fatal to disinterested historical research. Sincere Catholicism was no defence against accusation and condemnation, and even Muratori was only saved by the intervention of his friend Benedict XIV. To realise the sterilising effect of the censorship, lay and ecclesiastical, we must not forget that the fear of its penalties probably prevented the writing of as many books as it condemned. Thus the conditions which rendered it possible to set forth the truth without fear or favour were as rare as the will to learn it and the critical equipment required for its discovery. For the liberty of thought and expression, the insight into different ages, and the judicial temper on which historical science depends, the world had to wait for the great North German scholars at the opening of the nineteenth century, the age of the Second Renaissance.

CHAPTER II

NIEBUHR

THE first commanding figure in modern historiography, the scholar who raised history from a subordinate place to the dignity of an independent science, the noble personality in whom the greatest historians of the succeeding generation found their model or their inspiration, was Niebuhr.[1] Of the influences which combined to mould his mind and character the earliest and the deepest was that of his father. The great traveller was one of the most remarkable men of his time. With rare energy he had set himself to learn the languages and study the history of the ancient East on being chosen to accompany an expedition sent by the King of Denmark. Beginning with a year in Egypt, followed by a prolonged sojourn in Syria and Arabia, he visited India, returning through Persia, Baghdad, and Palestine. During the years immediately preceding and following the birth of his only son he was engaged in arranging and publishing the results of his journey. His wide and accurate scholarship and his knowledge of unknown and little known lands procured an instantaneous success for his massive volumes, which found their way into every country in Europe. When Barthold was in England, in the last year of the century, he was delighted to find the name of his father a household word, and he grew up with the determination to be worthy of him.

The brief life of Carsten Niebuhr by his son throws a welcome light on the youth and early studies of the historian of Rome. 'He taught us geography and history, French, English and mathematics, and helped me with Latin. When we read Cæsar, he would spread out D'Anville's map of ancient Gaul on the table, and I

---

[1] *The Life and Letters of Niebuhr*, Eng. edition, 1852, is among the most impressive of biographical memorials. The best brief survey is in Classen, *B. G. Niebuhr*, 1876. Eyssenhardt, *B. G. Niebuhr*, 1886; Lieber's *Reminiscences of Niebuhr*, 1835; Nissen's article in *Allg. Deutsche Biographie*, and Otto Mejer's lecture in his *Biographisches*, 1886, are also important. A new edition of his *Briefe*, edited by Gerhard and Norvin, appeared in 2 vols. 1926-9. The best surveys of modern German historiography are by Below, *Die deutsche Geschichtschreibung von den Befreiungskriegen*, 1924; Acton, 'German Schools of History,' in his *Historical Studies*, and Srbik, *Geist und Geschichte Vom Deutschen Humanismus bis zur Gegenwart*, 1950.

had to find every place.' He used to tell his son stories of the East, when sitting on his knee before bedtime, instead of fairy tales. Mohammed and the early Khalifs, the spread of Islam and the rise of the Turks, were soon familiar to the boy, who at the age of ten wrote on the historical geography of Africa. There is an obvious resemblance to the familiar picture in Mill's Autobiography. In both cases the fathers succeeded in cramming their sons' heads in tender years with a boundless mass of information and in launching them into intellectual manhood a decade earlier than other boys, but Niebuhr was spared a violent emotional crisis. Though the historian, like the philosopher, was never young, his youth was tranquil and happy. The nearest neighbour was Boie, a member of the Göttingen school of poets, and friend of most of the literary men of the day. Barthold looked back gratefully to the man 'who introduced me to much which would perhaps have long remained unknown to me.' Boie, on his side, draws a picture of the lad at fifteen busy with a manuscript of Varro from the library at Copenhagen, and reports that he dreamed of nothing but manuscripts and variants. At sixteen he was 'a small miracle of knowledge and intellectual maturity. He will infallibly become a scholar of the first rank.' At twenty 'there is the making of a great man in him.' A more powerful influence was that of Voss, the translator of Homer. The Odyssey appeared in 1781, and in 1782 he records that the Niebuhr children talked of nothing but Odysseus and Penelope. Homer was the only poetry which Carsten appreciated, and his son shared his enthusiasm. Voss, he wrote later, began a new era in the understanding of antiquity, because he felt and explained it as if its figures had been his contemporaries.

Carsten wished his son to continue the work of geographical exploration, but the opposition of the mother prevented the realisation of a plan which never appealed to him. The father then resolved that he should be a diplomatist. The lad, however, quickly recognised where his true work lay, and at nineteen he wrote the memorable words: 'If my name is to live, it will be as an historian and publicist, as a classic and philologist.' At Kiel he studied philosophy and law as well as history, and became interested in the system of Roman property. His leisure during the following years was devoted to problems of the ancient world. 'I know no one else of such talents and industry,' wrote Nicolovius, who met him in 1797; 'his soul is like a bee, for he collects all the good of our opulent time and never touches poison.' Before he conquered fame at a stroke he had already won the reputation of boundless learning. It was to a series of external events that the student of history owed his transformation into an historian. In the words of his friend Bunsen, 'Niebuhr's life is more intimately connected with the deepest movements and struggles of suffering humanity in his day than that of any other great writer of his age.' On leaving the University he became private secretary to the Danish Minister of Finance. His prolonged visit to Great Britain, at the age of twenty-three, was designed to widen still further his knowledge of administrative methods, and furnished him with that insight into English history and conditions which amazed his visitors in later life. Returning to Denmark he entered the service of the Government, and for six years helped to direct the financial and commercial policy of the country, with special reference to the banking and commerce of its colonies. His fame reached Berlin, and a few weeks before the Prussian kingdom collapsed at Jena he was pressed to transfer his services. The Niebuhr family was German on both sides, and the offer was accepted. For the next four years he laboured to reconstruct the finances of the country. His work was recognised to be of the highest value by Hardenberg, Stein, and the King. The impression which once prevailed that his tenure of office was a failure has been removed by the publication of the documents relating to his resignation.

Niebuhr had followed the French Revolution from its inception in the French press. His attitude throughout was one of distrust and dislike, though Voss and other friends greeted it with enthusiasm. 'Rousseau,' he declared a generation later, 'was the hero of most intellectual people in my youth, and in most parts of Germany the great mass of the nation at first approved the Revolution.' From his earliest years he manifested the horror of violent change which accompanied him through life and was to hasten his death. He was well aware of the abuses of the old régime, and his personal acquaintance with the Émigrés at Hamburg was to fill him with a lasting contempt for their class; his ideal was orderly development by process of law. When the forces aroused by the Revolution were harnessed to the chariot-wheels of Napoleon, his dislike of the Revolution hardened into a hatred of France as fierce as that of Stein and Fichte, while his love for Germany grew into a passionate desire for service. His detestation of revolutionary methods was deepened by his knowledge of England. In later life he referred Bunsen to Burke for political philosophy. In his conversation with Lieber at Rome he often remarked that without his study of England he could never have understood the history of Rome. 'The ever-growing perfection of the British constitution and freedom since 1688,' he wrote, 'affords the noblest picture of collective national wisdom and virtue that history can offer. Without a single form being altered or abolished, the possession of freedom has gradually spread through the whole nation. The greatest freedom existed in all things, the greatest freedom a people ever enjoyed. Never perhaps was a land in better circumstance than England at the time of the French Revolution. She was the pride and the envy of the world.' He had little belief in the merits of particular political forms, and was convinced, as he declared in his preface to Vincke's treatise on English institutions, that British liberty rested far more on administration than on the constitution. He was blind to the deep shadows in the realm of George III, but he learned the value of a strong central government resting on a broad basis of administrative decentralisation.

Armed with copious learning and a varied experience of affairs, Niebuhr entered on the great task of his life. During the scanty leisure of his official career in Denmark he had composed several dissertations on the ancient world, and on resigning his place he resolved to devote himself to the study of Roman history. The newly founded University of Berlin provided a rallying-point for all who desired to rebuild the shattered fabric of the Prussian state[1]; and no one more profoundly agreed with the famous declaration of the King, 'We must make up by intellectual strength what we have lost in material power.' He would write 'to regenerate the young men, to render them capable of great things, to put before them the noble examples of antiquity.' He was urged to deliver lectures, and in 1810 he began the course out of which grew the Roman History. Lacking experience of public speaking he read his lectures, which proved an immense success. His profound earnestness, the enthusiasm for learning which inspired the new University, and the exaltation which thrilled Prussia as the War of Liberation approached, combined to attract a large and distinguished audience.

Niebuhr enjoyed the lectures as heartily as his hearers and he looked back on the three years during which they were delivered as the happiest of his life. Savigny was not flattering his friend when he told him that he was opening a new era for Roman history. He believed, as no one before him had done, in the ethical significance and the patriotic stimulus of historical study. He felt himself speaking to his countrymen as directly as Fichte in his 'Addresses to the German Nation.' 'The evil time of Prussia's humiliation,' he declared later to Lieber, 'had some share in the production of my history. We could do little more than ardently

[1] See Lenz, *Geschichte der Königlichen Friedrich-Wilhelm Universität zu Berlin*, vol. i. 1910.

hope for better days and prepare for them. I went back to a great nation to strengthen my mind and that of my hearers. We felt like Tacitus.' Three sets of lectures had been delivered, two on Roman History, the third on Roman Antiquities, when the national uprising of 1813 summoned the larger part of his audience to the battle-field. Meanwhile, he had transformed the first two courses into a book which appeared in two volumes in 1811–12, with a dedication to the King. Though almost entirely rewritten many years after, it inaugurated the systematic study of Roman history.

The investigation of regal and republican Rome had been fitfully pursued ever since the revival of learning; but few had attempted to form a clear and coherent conception of the life of the state or of the stages of its growth. Machiavelli had used Livy as a peg on which to hang his own political reflections and maxims. Montesquieu had made a courageous attempt to discover the causes of the growth and decay, but his knowledge was scanty and he was at the mercy of his materials. Numberless writers had transcribed and abbreviated Livy; but no one before Niebuhr re- garded Rome as above all a great state, the institutions of which, political, legal and economic, must be traced to their origin and followed through their successive changes. His experience of government enabled him to approach the problem with an insight which no previous historian had possessed: no one but a states- man, he declared, could write the history of Rome. He had grasped the truth that the early history of every nation must be rather of institutions than of events, of classes than of individuals, of customs than of laws. The story of Roman development is built round the struggle of patricians and plebeians, which origin- ated in the racial differences of conquerors and conquered. He painted a clear picture of the political issues at stake, and enabled the world to form a vivid conception of the state from its origins to the Licinian Laws. The agrarian problem was for the first time fully investigated. What Grote was to do for the Athenian demo- cracy, Niebuhr achieved for the Roman republic by making it as real and intelligible as a state of the modern world.

His second great achievement was the critical examination of the sources and credibility of early Roman history. To his scepti- cal forerunners Niebuhr owed little or nothing. Beaufort he only read after completing his own work, and pronounced clever but too exclusively destructive. Of Vico's speculations he appears to have been ignorant. He was certain that the accepted narrative could be neither true nor wholly false. In the quest for a critical method he was entering upon an almost untrodden path, but a

new era had been opened by the publication of the 'Prolegomena
to Homer.' He had thoroughly assimilated Wolf's method and
results, and it was in large measure from him that he derived his
belief that the history of early Rome had been enshrined and
transmitted in poems. He approached his inquiry with a feeling
of deep responsibility. 'In laying down the pen,' he wrote, 'we
must be able to say in the sight of God, "I have not knowingly
nor without earnest investigation written anything which is not
true."' Yet he possessed an almost boundless self-confidence. He
declared that he had 'a correct and very rapid judgment, a faculty
scarcely capable of deception in discovery of the false and incorrect.' He was aware of the revolution he was effecting. 'One
could not have maintained these things in earlier times without
danger to life and liberty. Philologists would have cried treachery,
the theologians high treason, and public opinion would have
stoned one.' His power of divination was as real to him as the
illative sense to Newman. 'I am an historian,' he writes to a
friend, 'for I can make a complete picture from separate fragments, and I know where the parts are missing and how to fill
them up. No one believes how much of what seems to be lost can
be restored.' Using another image, he declared, 'I dissect words
as an anatomist dissects bodies.' On another occasion the historian
is compared to a man in a cell whose eyes gradually become so
accustomed to the darkness that he can perceive objects which
one newly entering not only does not see but declares to be invisible. Niebuhr's method resembles conjectural emendations of
Bentley, Cobet and Munro.

What were the channels through which the deeds and circumstances of early Rome reached the earliest chroniclers whom we
possess? Adopting a suggestion of Perizonius, he replies that
knowledge was conveyed by songs, funeral panegyrics and annals
kept by the Pontifex Maximus. Some of the songs were separate,
while others formed a cycle—'an epopee, which in depth and
brilliancy of imagination far surpassed all that later Rome was
to produce.' He proceeds to review the legal period, labelling
some events mythical and others historical. Romulus and Numa
are fabulous. From Tullus Hostilius to the first secession of the
plebeians is partially historical. 'Between the purely poetical and
the completely historical age there is in all nations a mythico-
historical era.' In a masterly review August Schlegel [1] rejected the
theory of ballads, and censured the historian for describing them
with a precision as if they were before him. If they had existed
we might surely have expected to find some quotation from them,

[1] *Werke*, xii. 444–512.

or some reference in a commentator or a grammarian, but he failed to adduce the slightest evidence that they ever existed. His practice of divination again brought no small danger with it. His faculty for remote inferences, for detecting implications in a statement or an allusion or an omission, led him to the discovery of useful clues, but from its very nature it was incurably subjective. Though dim objects are seen for the first time by the keen eye of the trained scholar, they must not remain invisible to lesser mortals. Macaulay complained that he did not always distinguish between a proved truth and a hypothesis. Cornewall·Lewis devoted his 'Inquiry into the Credibility of Early Roman History' to an unsparing denunciation of his 'occult faculty of historical divination,' declaring that all labour bestowed on the period before Pyrrhus resembled the search for the philosopher's stone or the elixir of life. The fairest criticism came from Schwegler, who essayed to stretch the bow of Ulysses a generation later. 'At first, disagreeing in many points, I gradually came more and more to agree. In the chief questions he almost invariably found the right path. Indeed many of his hypotheses in reference to constitutional questions admit of a much better defence than their author supplied.' This general judgment is confirmed in the course of his work, in which he discusses most of Niebuhr's contentions. While rejecting the hypothesis of ballads, dismissing many of his conclusions on ethnology, and declaring him somewhat unfair to the patricians, Schwegler pronounces his analogical method extraordinarily successful, above all in his reconstruction of Roman institutions, which he was the first to understand.

When the lectures were interrupted by the War of Liberation, Niebuhr sought permission to enter the army, but the King wisely replied that he could serve the state more effectively in other ways. He accordingly founded a newspaper in which he endeavoured to inspire his countrymen in the great struggle. When the war was over, he accepted the task of discussing with the Vatican the government and administration of the Catholic population which had been added to Prussia. He believed that the mission would not last long, but the Prussian Ministry were unable to determine the details of his instructions, for which he had to wait several years in Rome.[1] Though finding little satisfaction in the work of the Embassy, his exile brought compensations with it. The journey opened with the sensational discovery of a manuscript of Gaius at Verona, but his expectation of finding further treasures in the Vatican was disappointed. His search, which was not

[1] The whole question and Niebuhr's share in it are explained in O. Mejer, *Zur Geschichte der römisch-deutschen Frage,* 1871.

very deep, was only rewarded by a few fragments of Sallust and Cicero; but he witnessed the beginning of the long series of discoveries by Mai, notably the fragment of Cicero's 'Republic' which he helped him to edit. He steadily increased his knowledge of the ancient world, and sent an occasional paper to the Prussian Academy. He interested himself in the remains of Rome, and aided the large archæological enterprise planned by his friend and secretary Bunsen.

When the Concordat was signed Niebuhr resolved to return to Germany and continue his studies. Vigorous efforts were made by his old pupil, the Crown Prince, to win him for Berlin but he determined to make his home in Bonn. It is with the University of the Rhineland that the last and most productive period of his life is associated. It was there that the 'Roman History' assumed its final shape, there that his lectures on ancient and modern history left an ineffaceable stamp on their hearers, there that he became the acknowledged monarch of European scholarship. The Berlin lectures had been written out, but at Bonn he spoke freely from the abundant stores of his mind. 'He was as excited,' writes a pupil, 'as other men are when discussing the politics of our own age and country. His thoughts came so rapidly that he could not always finish his sentences. But his sincerity, and above all the vivid descriptions of men who were to him living realities, carried his hearers away.' When the great teacher was gone the notebooks of his hearers were produced, and the lectures were published in ten volumes. Imperfect as they are and lacking the author's revision, they are none the less of considerable interest. They reveal his immense knowledge of the ancient world, and contain his opinions on men and events with which his published writings do not deal. The lectures on Rome are particularly welcome, as they carry the story beyond the point reached by the 'Roman History.' The latter, which deals far more with the institutions and structure of the state than with the individuals who composed it, conveys no notion of the intensely personal attitude from which Niebuhr approached the past. His experiences, above all the central incident of his life, the struggle with France, coloured his whole thoughts and erected nationalism and the dread of revolution into the dominant principles of his political philosophy. No part of his lectures is more suffused with his own personality than that in which he relates the collapse of Greece before the might of Macedon. Demosthenes is Stein or Fichte, Philip is Napoleon, Chæronea is Jena. His most burning indignation is reserved for the regenades who welcomed the conqueror, and in his scathing denunciation of Phocion we sense what he thought of Dalberg and

Johannes Müller. The course on the French Revolution is hardly
more personal than many of the lectures which deal with the
world of two thousand years ago. Niebuhr's activity also extended
into many branches of philology. He undertook a collection of
Byzantine historians, and himself edited Agathias. In company
with Brandis he founded the *Rheinisches Museum* and contributed
largely to its pages. His vision ranged prophetically over the
future. In 1829 he foretold that Nineveh would be the Pompeii
of Middle Asia and that a Champollion would arise for Assyria.

The chief occupation of the years at Bonn and the crown of
his achievement was the new edition of the History. The relation
of the earlier to the later work was explained in the preface to
the first volume, but in declaring that it was entirely new and
incorporated only a few fragments of the former he exaggerates
the differences. It is true that every chapter was rewritten and
that the notes were multiplied; but the method is the same and
the results are rarely different. The existence of ballads is still
assumed, and the divinatory technique is applied with unabated
confidence. It is still a string of dissertations rather than a narrative. In the preface to the second volume he declares the constitution to be his main object, and its history could only be recovered
by a minute examination of the sources. 'The discussions may be
prolix, but I wished to assert nothing arbitrarily.' It is the most
unreadable of historical classics, because the text is loaded with
matter usually relegated to notes and appendices. 'One imagines
oneself,' remarks Taine, 'at the bottom of a mine, with the murky
light of a lamp, close to a miner scratching laboriously at the hard
rock.' Despite these disadvantages, the new edition gained an
immediate and resounding fame. 'No discovery of an ancient
historian,' he wrote proudly to Savigny in 1827, 'would have
taught the world so much as my work, and all that may come to
light from ancient sources will only confirm or develop my principles.' Goethe, who had expressed a wish after the first edition
that all history should be treated in the same manner, read the
new version and repeated his congratulations. Nowhere was it
so warmly welcomed as in England. Macaulay declared that it
created an epoch in the history of European intelligence, though
his admiration diminished in subsequent years. Excellently translated by Thirlwall and Hare, and defended by them against the
onslaught of the *Quarterly Review*, it became a text-book at the
Universities. Accepting Niebuhr's results, Thomas Arnold composed a History of Rome in which the rough stones were polished
and fitted into an harmonious structure. A few lesser men continued to transcribe Livy as if Niebuhr had never lived, but the

chariot of learning moved a stage forward. Scarcely was the second volume in print when the great historian died. Fragments of the third appeared in 1832, bringing the story down to the first Punic war.

Niebuhr was cut off at the age of fifty-five in the fullness of his powers and at the height of his influence, but he had begun to live ten years earlier than other men, and he had felt the troubles of his country as his own. He was afflicted with a growing irritability which alienated friends and disposed him to gloomy views. He lost faith even in England, which he described as dying of the cancer of egotism. He had never cast off the shadow of the French invasion, and when the Revolution of 1830 broke out his over-wrought imagination believed that a repetition of that terrible experience was at hand. He was filled with morbid apprehensions for the safety of his wife and children. His health, already shattered by the burning of his home and library and by the news from Paris, was too weak to resist a chill caught in the closing days of 1830. Goethe declared that Niebuhr's thoroughness and depth encouraged him to perform his own duties in the same conscientious spirit. He left an ineffaceable impression of greatness and goodness in men so different as Stein and Schleiermacher, Frederick William IV, Dahlmann and Jacobi, Arndt and Schön, Savigny and Cornelius, Lieber and Bunsen. Savigny declared that the 'Roman History' gave him courage to write the history of Roman law; Ranke that Thucydides, Fichte and Niebuhr were his masters; Grote that it was impossible to pronounce his name without veneration and gratitude; Waitz that he owed more to the Roman History than to any other book. In the words of Mommsen, all historians, so far as they are worthy of the name, are his pupils.

CHAPTER III

WOLF, BÖCKH AND OTFRIED MÜLLER

WHILE Niebuhr was interpreting the Roman state the study of Greek civilisation was also entering on a new career. After the disappearance of the great school of Renaissance scholars at the end of the sixteenth century, Greek studies rapidly declined.[1] A revival was inaugurated by Bentley, and continued by the Leyden triumvirate, Hemsterhuys, Valckenaer and Ruhnken. The Dutch scholars, however, confined themselves to philology. About the middle of the eighteenth century the excavation of Pompeii and Herculaneum aroused new interest in classical archæology, and in obedience to this impulse Winckelmann left Dresden for Rome in 1758.[2] Through him Greek art, which had been ignored since the Renaissance, was once again recognised as a revelation of the Greek spirit not less eloquent than literature. A new chapter began when Zoega[3] made his home in the Eternal City in 1783. Like many young students before and after him, the Danish scholar dreamed of mastering the whole of Greek literature and antiquity. He began by cataloguing collections of coins, proceeded to investigate the origin of obelisks, and devoted his later years to classical bas-reliefs. Though his last undertaking was interrupted by death it is one of the cardinal works of archæology, its plates surpassing all previous reproductions and its text revealing wide knowledge of Greek mythology and religion. Though he never wrote a popular work, his learning and critical power place him beside Winckelmann and Visconti among the founders of scientific archæology. His work and ideas became known through his pupil Welcker, who produced a German edition of the bas-reliefs, collected his letters, and published a volume of his Dissertations.

While Greek art was being studied and interpreted in Rome, a revival of Greek studies was taking place in the German Universities. Lectures on classical archæology were delivered by

---

[1] The best summary of classical studies since the Renaissance is in Sandys' *History of Classical Scholarship*, vols. ii. and iii., 1908. For Germany see Bursian's monumental *Geschichte der classischen Philologie in Deutschland*, 1883; for Holland, Lucian Müller's *Geschichte der klassischen Philologie in den Niederlanden*, 1869.

[2] See Justi's magnificent biography, 2 vols., 2nd ed., 1898.

[3] See Welcker, *Zoega's Leben*, 1819, and the excellent biography in *Allg. Deutsche Biog.*

Christ at Leipzig before the middle of the century, but it was above all at Göttingen that the horizon began to widen. Gesner surveyed the art and antiquities as well as the literature of the ancient world, and instituted the first philological *Seminar*. When Gesner died, the Hanoverian Government invited Ruhnken to succeed him. The great Leyden scholar refused, but recommended Heyne,[1] who had known Winckelmann at Dresden and sat at the feet of Christ and Ernesti. His advice was taken, and Heyne entered on half a century of fruitful teaching. For the first time the whole field of classical life was covered in lectures. His archæological course was based on Winckelmann, and that on classical antiquities contained a good deal of historical material. Though he produced no first-rate work, lacked exact scholarship and outlived himself, his achievement was immense. He first seized and revealed classical philology as a whole. He founded the historical conception of antiquities and institutions, mythology and religion. But his greatest work was his pupils, of whom it has been calculated that more than three hundred became teachers. Among them were Zoega, the Schlegels, Thiersch, Wilhelm von Humboldt, Bunsen, Brandis and Lachmann. We owe a charming biography of the master to his pupil, colleague and son-in-law, Heeren, who portrays him as the friend and counsellor of studious youth.

I

The greatest of Heyne's pupils was the one who owed him least. When Wolf[2] entered Göttingen in 1777 at eighteen, he was already master of several languages, ancient and modern, and demanded to be matriculated as a student of Philology. He was told that there were only four faculties—Theology, Law, Medicine, and Arts—and that he must enter one of them. He persisted, and was inscribed as he desired. But though his wish was thus gratified, he was sadly disappointed with Heyne. He went to the lectures on the Iliad, but soon ceased to attend them. Young as he was, he saw that the Professor was not a textual critic, and that his approach to classical literature was rather æsthetic than scientific. After two years he left Göttingen, and four years later obtained a Chair at Halle at the age of twenty-four.

[1] See Heeren's biography, 1813. The best appreciation is by Leo, in *Festschrift z. Feier d. Hundertfünfzigjährigen Bestehens d. Gesellschaft d. Wissenschaften zu Göttingen*, 1901.

[2] See Reiter, F. A. Wolf, *Ein Leben in Briefen*, 3 vols., 1935. Mark Pattison's well-known essay, *Essays*, vol. i., 1889, is the best brief sketch. Arnoldt, *Wolf in seinem Verhältnisse zum Schulwesen u. zur Pädagogik dargestellt*, 1861–2, deals with the teacher. Cp. Paulsen, *Gesch. d. Gelehrten Unterrichts*, ii. 208–227, 1897.

Wolf's teaching during his twenty-three years' residence at Halle breathed a new life into classical study throughout Germany. He first conceived classical philology as a science in itself. When Wilhelm von Humboldt defined it as 'the knowledge of human nature as exhibited in antiquity,' he summarised the interpretation which Wolf had made familiar. His lectures were in the highest degree stimulating, and his students repaid him by enthusiastic devotion. Goethe came over from Weimar to hear him. Lessing's bust stood in his lecture-room, typifying the spirit of critical inquiry. His courses covered every department of the classical world—literature, antiquities, geography, art, numismatics, and a general introduction to classical study. Several of them were published after his death from the notes of his hearers. Though imperfectly reproduced, they show his immense knowledge of every province of classical learning and modern scholarship, while the clear, pointed comments help us to imagine the effect they produced. We are not, however, solely dependent on the notes of his hearers for our knowledge of his conception of antiquity. When the French invasion of 1806 led to the closing of the University and the dispersal of the Professors, Goethe urged him to utilise his enforced leisure to write. He took the advice, and wrote his grand fragment on classical study.[1] He declares that he had felt the need of such an outline since he began to lecture in 1783. It was his desire to raise the knowledge of antiquity to the dignity of a philosophico-historical science. We must avoid the mere accumulation of particulars without an idea of the spirit which binds them into a whole. This noble essay, which breathes the same profound veneration for the study of classical antiquity as Niebuhr's 'Letter to a Young Philologist,' became an inspiration for teachers and the programme of a century's work.

Wolf's most celebrated work, the 'Prolegomena to Homer,' written in Latin, is one of the cardinal books of the modern world.[2] Being asked to revise the text of Homer for a new school edition, he intended to write a short preface, but the Introduction grew into a book of two hundred pages published in 1795. That the Homeric poems reached their final form generations if not centuries after their composition was widely believed by the scholars of Alexandria, and was reaffirmed by Perizonius, Vico and other modern writers. Robert Wood's striking work on the Genius of

[1] Reprinted in his *Kleine Schriften*, 1869.
[2] The best account is in Volkmann, *Geschichte u. Kritik d. Wolfschen Prolegomena*, 1874. Jebb, *Homer*, 1887, and Bury, in 'The Cambridge Ancient History,' ii., chap. 18, give brief sketches. There is a German translation in Reclam's *Universal-Bibliothek*.

Homer, published in 1769, was translated into German, and his thesis that writing was unknown till long after the creation of the poems became the corner-stone of Wolf's edifice. Villoison's edition of a Venetian manuscript of the Iliad, revealing wide differences from the commonly received text, confirmed him in the conviction that it was the work of several bards. The idea of oral transmission came readily to a generation which had welcomed Ossian as an echo of the primitive Celtic world. The presupposition of the Wolfian hypothesis is the absence of writing for literary purposes before Solon. Under such conditions the composition and transmission of long epics was impossible. The 'Homer' that we know is the blending of poems by various authors, probably in the time of Pisistratus. In the interval many changes were made by the rhapsodists, and further modifications in the taste of the time were introduced by the editors. That several of the original songs were by a poet named Homer is highly probable. It is Wolf's masterly handling of the subject rather than his originality that renders his work so memorable. He threw a flood of light not only on the origin of the Homeric poems but on the nature of epic poetry in general.

Voss's translation had made Homer familiar, and the 'Prolegomena' made a profound sensation throughout Europe. There had been nothing like it since Bentley's demolition of the Epistles of Phalaris. Ruhnken, to whom as 'the prince of critics' the book was dedicated, was shaken in his belief in the unity of the poems, though too old to surrender it. Voss rejected it. Schiller sarcastically remarked that each of the seven cities which claimed Homer could now have its piece. Goethe, who at first approved the idea, returned to the traditionalist camp. In certain quarters there was talk of 'impiety.' On the other hand, Wilhelm von Humboldt and the Schlegels, Ilgen and his greater pupil Gottfried Hermann, welcomed the work as at once convincing and original. Two influential voices supported its conclusions but denied its originality. Herder declared that he had always believed Homer to be a constellation and the Iliad and Odyssey by different hands, adding that he had long ago called attention to the distinction between natural and artificial poetry. Heyne went further and accused Wolf of borrowing ideas from his old teacher. Wolf was nettled by the denial of originality and stung to anger by the charge of plagiarism. In a series of Open Letters to Heyne he declared that his old master had never hinted the belief which he now avowed. It was a moral weakness that Wolf should have been more concerned to establish his originality, which was less than he claimed, than to emphasise the thoroughness and method in which he surpassed all his predecessors and critics. Though his central contention as to the late use of writing has been overthrown and the volume is now only read by Homeric specialists, it contributed more than any other work to launch the critical movement which was to raise nineteenth century scholarship above its predecessors. With the closing of Halle by the French invasion his career as a successful teacher came to an end. His work was continued by his disciples, among whom must be numbered men who were never his pupils in an academic sense.[1] Humboldt was directed to Greek studies by him, assimilated his view of antiquity, and interpreted it to the world; and it was through Humboldt that the spell of the Greek world was cast upon Schiller. Goethe's debt was repeatedly declared by the poet himself. It was chiefly through the poets that the classics passed into the consciousness of the German people.

II

Wolf's successor in the leadership of Greek studies was his pupil Böckh.[2] Leaving Halle in 1806, at the age of twenty-one, he became Professor of Greek Philology at Heidelberg. He was conscious of his powers, successful as a teacher, and surrounded by congenial companions. Heidelberg was at that moment the citadel of romanticism. The chief teacher of classical antiquity was Creuzer, whom he described fifty years later as 'my benefactor,' and among his close friends were Brentano, Arnim and Görres. During his residence he published studies on Plato and the tragedians, and began his work on Pindar's metres which rendered the poet intelligible to the modern world. He followed the precedent set by Wolf in delivering an encyclopædic course. His fame spread rapidly, and in 1810 he migrated to the new University at Berlin which he was to adorn for fifty-six years. While covering the whole field of classical philology in detailed surveys, his general course exerted the widest influence. His notes for the course, delivered twenty-six times, were in continual process of revision, and a full and reliable version of these celebrated lectures was published after his death.[3] After explaining that an encyclopædia must be a whole, not an aggregate, he proceeded to review chronology, life, trade, religion, science, literature and philosophy.

---

[1] Cp. Lothholz, *Das Verhältniss Wolfs u. W. v. Humboldts zu Goethe u. Schiller*, 1863.

[2] Max Hoffmann's *August Böckh*, 1901, contains an admirable biography and copious correspondence. The best brief sketch is in Stark, *Vorträge u. Aufsätze*, 1880.

[3] *Encycl. d. philologischen Wissenschaften*, 1877.

The early years at Berlin were chiefly devoted to the study of the economic life of Greece, which had been almost entirely neglected. He composed a dissertation on the Silver Mines of Laurium for the Prussian Academy, and in 1817 published his greatest work, 'The Public Economy of Athens.' Revised in 1851, and appearing in a third and enlarged edition in 1886, the centenary of the author's birth, it is the only German historical work written before Ranke which has not been superseded. Dedicated to Niebuhr, it achieved for Athens the resurrection which Niebuhr had accomplished for Rome. It was Böckh's supreme achievement to transform classical philology into an historical science. The preface declared that the science of Hellenic Antiquities was still in its infancy, and a survey of the whole field was the more necessary as most students were engaged in minute philological researches. The immense achievements of Athens were only rendered possible by physical force, which in its turn rested on the public and private economy of the state. By the end of the Persian war the financial system was fully developed, while the Macedonian conquest involved new arrangements. It is of the intervening period that the book gives a detailed description.

The money needed for the public service, and the relation of taxation to the means of the people, could not be ascertained without knowing the prices of articles and the wages of labour, for which the evidence is scanty. Investigation follows into the quantity of money in circulation and into the gradually increasing supply of the precious metals. The prices of land, mines, houses, slaves, cattle, clothes and food are examined, and the conclusion is reached that the necessaries of life were cheap and wages low owing to the presence of slave labour and resident aliens. A discussion follows of the public expenditure and its objects—defence, the civil service, the assemblies, police, the administration of justice, buildings, religion, the celebration of festivals, and the poor. In addition to these regular charges, frequent wars exercised a disturbing influence. The ordinary revenues were derived from state property, mines, customs, poll-taxes, legal fees, fines and confiscation, supplemented by tribute from allies. Extra revenues, necessitated by wars, were obtained from a special property tax, an arbitrary impost, or loans. Böckh begins and ends his work with a warning not to regard the Greeks as wiser or better than ourselves. Their pecuniary dealings were by no means free from stain. Statesmen were always trying to discover some method by which the mass of the people might be supported out of the public revenues rather than by individual industry. Far too much was spent on soldiers' pay; foreign possessions were maladministered; allies were oppressed. Depravity and moral corruption were rampant even in the most brilliant period of the leading State. 'The Greeks, with all the perfection of their art and the freedom of their government, were more unhappy than is commonly believed. Even in the times of their glory they bore within themselves the seeds of that destruction which was to befall them.'

'The Public Economy of Athens' first made known to the modern world the daily life of a state of antiquity. From a mass of isolated indications Böckh constructed a finished picture. His approach was historical, not æsthetic, his sole aim an objective reconstruction of a vanished world. The achievement, like that of Winckelmann, opened up new vistas. The whole economic organism of the Athenian state stood revealed, and a realistic view of Greek civilisation became for the first time possible. Though he was accused of confusing wealth with the precious metals and his estimate of population was challenged, no one has contested his right to rank as the author of the first work of a scientific character on the history of Greece. Twenty years later he published a volume, which may be regarded as a continuation, on the Weights and Measures of Antiquity. In studying the collection of coins in the Berlin Museum he had discovered an unexpected connection between different lands. The book discusses in detail a range of subjects only hinted at in the earlier work, and embraces the whole of the ancient world. Like all his writings it combines an infinite capacity for minute investigation with a wide vision. His survey of the weights, measures and coinage of Greece, Italy, Sicily, Egypt, Palestine, Phoenicia and Babylonia not only founded comparative metrology, but revealed the relations of the nations from the Tiber to the Euphrates and the unity of the civilisation of the Mediterranean states. His exact and careful scholarship may be judged by comparing the work with Heeren's treatise on the trade and commerce of antiquity. Two years later he utilised the discovery of some inscriptions to explain the nature and administration of the Athenian marine.

In writing 'The Public Economy of Athens' he had found one of his most valuable sources in inscriptions. The Prussian Academy had been reorganised by the Humboldts about the same time as the foundation of the University with which it has ever since worked in the closest relation. Böckh believed that its object was to carry out undertakings too large for individual scholars, and several joint enterprises were set on foot. Of these by far the most important was the plan of a collection of Greek Inscriptions. Inscriptions in the Near East had been copied by travellers from

Cyriac of Ancona in the fifteenth century onwards; but the number was small, and the collections of Gruter and his successors were chiefly Latin. Authentic records were often imperfectly copied, and forgeries were common. Fourmont, sent by the Académie des Inscriptions to Greece, falsified much that he found, destroying or burying the originals to prevent discovery. The emissaries of the Society of Dilettanti were more conscientious. But no Eckhel arose to sift the grain from the chaff, and to render the inscriptions scattered through innumerable publications available for the needs of scholarship. It was therefore a happy inspiration which led Böckh in 1815 to propose a Corpus of the inscriptions of antiquity, beginning with those in the Greek language. Funds were granted in the expectation that the enterprise would be finished in four years, and fill one large volume or two small ones. Neither Böckh nor the Academy realised the magnitude of their undertaking, for the work is still in progress, and has cost more than ten times the sum originally allotted. In undertaking the task the Academy rendered the greatest service to the study of Greece that it has ever received. In the legacy of the ancients the inscriptions are of scarcely less significance than their buildings, their sculpture and their writings. They shed new light on familiar subjects and illuminate tracts of territory on which rays shine from no other quarter.

The limit was fixed at the foundation of the Eastern Empire, and a Commission was appointed to carry out the enterprise under Böckh's direction. The main object was to collect, classify and explain the inscriptions already known. Though the dispatch of scholars to verify the originals and to discover new material was discussed, it was not in the forefront of the programme. The main burden of the vast enterprise fell on the editor, for his colleagues, except Bekker who was sent to Paris and London, rendered little assistance. In 1825 the first part appeared, and in 1828 the first volume was complete. Böckh arranged his inscriptions, as Eckhel his coins, geographically, and his choice was generally approved. But the scholarship of the volume was sharply attacked by Gottfried Hermann,[1] who carried on the English and Dutch tradition of pure philology. Like everybody else, he declared, he had looked forward to the edition, but his hopes were disappointed. He proceeded to accuse Böckh of misreading many inscriptions, and concluded that no part of the work could be accepted without verification.

[1] *Über Böckh's Behandlung d. Griechischen Inschriften*, 1826. For Hermann see Köchly, *Gottfried Hermann*, 1874, and Jahn's address in his *Biographische Aufsätze*, 1866.

Böckh vigorously defended himself.[1] There was nothing useful, he contended, in the criticism except suggestions as to readings, which, however, must always remain uncertain. 'I have studied inscriptions for many years,' he added, 'and he has not.' Hermann replied, and the pupils of the protagonists entered the field. The warfare was not only between two scholars but between rival schools. The Leipzig Professor believed linguistic studies to be the kernel of philology, since other problems could only be approached through linguistic interpretation. He knew and cared little for the politics and art, religion and philosophy of the ancient world. He had no conception of historical development. With such ideas it was natural that he should regard Böckh and his pupils as endangering philology by subordinating it to other studies, and that he should exaggerate the importance of mistakes. It was not till twenty years had elapsed that the veteran leaders of the rival schools renewed the friendly relations of their early days. The Corpus, being partially based on copies by untrained hands, was not a perfect work, and many of Hermann's criticisms were well founded. Some of the inscriptions Böckh failed to understand. The epoch-making work of his pupil Kirchoff on the Greek alphabet rendered it possible to date and locate many records which appeared to offer no clue. The cardinal importance of copying from the original has come to be recognised. Moreover, the opening up of Greece and the Near East and the labours of scholars of every country have enormously increased the number of items. Nevertheless much of Böckh's epigraphic work was of an enduring character, and none of his contemporaries could have done it so well. When the second volume appeared in 1843 he handed over the editorship to younger men, while continuing to render occasional assistance. The third and fourth volumes, which owed much to Curtius and Kirchoff, were completed by 1859, the entire work containing 10,000 entries. The main occupation of the great scholar's later life was chronology. The Moon Cycles, like the Metrology, showed that his vision swept over the whole of the ancient world. And while his profound dissertations widened the boundaries of knowledge, his addresses on ceremonial occasions held aloft the ideal of accurate and disinterested scholarship.[2] By his patriarchal age, his immense range, and the almost infinite number of his pupils, Böckh occupies a position in regard to classical studies similar to that of Ranke in the history of modern Europe.

[1] *Kleine Schriften*, vol. vii., 1872.
[2] They are collected in his *Kleine Schriften*.

III

Böckh's principles were carried far and wide by the generations who sat at his feet. The pupil who was dearest to his heart, who owed most to him and paid his debt most fully, was Otfried Müller.[1] The young Silesian attracted attention even in his school-days by the facility with which he learned the classical languages and wrote Latin and Greek verses. At Breslau he plunged into the study of philosophy and ancient history. The precocious youth came to Berlin and entered the lecture-room of Böckh in 1815 at the age of eighteen. The choice between the literary and the historical approach to antiquity had been made before he left Breslau, but he was confirmed in his decision by his new teacher. Mythology already interested him more than any other department of study. His knowledge was the amazement of his teachers and comrades, and the thought of a history of Greece took root in his mind.

At the age of nineteen Müller entered on his career of author-ship by his Doctor's thesis on Ægina. This wonderful monograph, which traced the history of the island to the Frankish conquest, was dedicated to Böckh, and the delighted master rewarded him by a glowing review in which he emphasised the insight and complete-ness of the work.[2] Curtius was later to compare the first production of his beloved master to Justus Möser's History of Osnabrück. The foundation was laid by an examination of the topography, followed by a study of race, religion, antiquities, sea-power, trade, art and government. Many passages revealed a knowledge that went far beyond his subject. 'If he goes on with similar con-tributions,' Böckh wrote, 'we shall have a history of the Greeks of which till now there has been no conception.' The master realised in a flash that the pupil had become a colleague. The correspond-ence which now began is of the highest value, not only for the life and studies of the friends but also because it enshrines the noblest ideals of German scholarship.[3] 'You gave me the idea of a true philology,' writes the pupil, 'and I still feel in the same relation to you as of old.' When Müller in the preface to 'The Dorians' de-clared that he could not say how much of Böckh had gone into the book, the master replied, 'If I have been anything to you, you

---

[1] The best accounts are by K. Dilthey, *Otfried Müller*, 1898, and Curtius in *Altertum u. Gegenwart*, vol. ii., 1882. R. Förster's *Rede*, 1897, is useful. Lücke's *Erinnerungen an Müller*, 1841, are the testimony of a friend and colleague. O. and E. Kern, *Carl Otfried Müller, Lebensbild in Briefen*, 1908, is of value for his personality.

[2] Reprinted in Boeckh, *Kleine Schriften*, vol. vii., 1872.

[3] *Böckh u. Müller im Briefwechsel*, 1883.

have more than repaid it, and I am in your debt. But we will leave this striking of balances. May the unquenchable striving for truth strengthen the bond by which we are united.' The two men completed each other, each possessing precious qualities that the other lacked. Böckh was a realist, suspicious of mountain paths where the foothold was hazardous. Müller was a creative and original mind, fascinated by speculative problems and revelling in daring generalisations. It was precisely the relationship of Stubbs and Green.

While every part of the history of Ægina was carefully studied, it was the twilight before the Persian wars that attracted him most. Müller looks down in spirit on the island from the Athenian mainland. This faculty of compelling nature to throw light on primitive history was new in Greek study, and was one of the elements which he added to the legacy of his master. Here, too, we find his notion of the origin of the Greek people, and here the beloved Dorians are favoured at the expense of the enemy at Athens. Here also by his use of coins and monuments he reaps the first-fruits of the archæological labours which were to fill so much of his life. He determined to carry on his investigations, and within a year a volume on Orchomenos and the Minyæ was ready. Like its predecessor it began with a full description of the country drawn from the records of travellers, proceeded to discuss the legends of origin and colonisation, and sketched the art and culture. It appeared as the first part of a 'History of Hellenic Races and Cities,' and was to prepare the way for a history of Greece. He had discovered the greatness of the Æolic Minyæ and traced their wanderings in the port of Iolkus, where the memories were preserved in the legend of the Argonauts, in Thessaly and Bœotia, in Laconia and the Islands and Cyrene. His guide is the local legend, and he believed, like Niebuhr, that the historical might be winnowed from the mythical. But his method carried him, as it had carried Niebuhr, further than subsequent scholars could approve. Böckh remarked that though he agreed with the chief results, the subject itself was too vague to be thoroughly cleared up. 'It is a slippery path,' he wrote, 'that of mythology, which you are following. A holy fear keeps me from springing over the wall, though I like sometimes to peep through a slit.' At the same moment Müller's friend Buttmann was endeavouring to show that the Minyæ were as mythical as the Centaurs. His criticism of the value of the legends of their colonisation and relationships was more accurate than Müller's, but half a century later Schliemann was to establish the reality of Orchomenos as a contemporary of Tiryns and Mycenæ.

Before the book was published Müller was appointed Professor at Göttingen. When Welcker left for Bonn in 1819, Heeren, who managed the University, asked Böckh if he would approve the appointment. Böckh replied that he was the model of a scholar, and that he had never seen such modesty in a young man nor such a fine moral sense. Though he was only just of age, he was fully competent to take the post. During his early years at Göttingen Müller laboured steadily at the Greek races and states. In 1824 appeared 'The Dorians,' the work which first made his name widely known. The volumes, for which Böckh sent him the relevant inscriptions, dealt for the first time with a people who played a leading part in Greek history. 'I try to seize the essence of the Dorian stock, as of a man, by its doings,' he wrote; but it is dangerous to personify a race. The Dorians, Ionians and Æolians were not so different as he believed. Such differences as existed arose far more from their fortunes and their homes than from innate qualities, and he underestimated the degree of unity achieved by centuries of intercourse. Again he errs in his excessive admiration for the Dorian stock, in which he saw the true Hellenism. He was fascinated by the 'noble simplicity' of Sparta, the reverence for tradition, the lofty ideal of womanhood. Yet despite its obvious faults, the influence of the book was healthy. It was the first example of a comprehensive summary of a race in its inner development as well as its outward fortunes, carried out with a wealth of knowledge and a breadth of vision never surpassed. While Böckh only laid the foundation for a history of Athens, Müller wrote the first important work of actual Greek history.

The 'Minyæ' and the 'Dorians' were both praised and censured for their bold handling of the problems of mythology, and it was in reply to the attacks on the latter work that he wrote his 'Prolegomena to the Study of Mythology.' He had already defined his general attitude in reviews of Creuzer and Voss.[1] In discussing the former's *Symbolik*, he had expressed his gratitude to the man who had raised the science to the height at which it stood, but the idea that priests clothed religious ideas in symbols of which the key was lost he dismisses as nonsense. In regard to Greece he declared that he could hardly read a page without disagreement, and he totally rejects the elaborate dogmatic system which Creuzer builds up out of the myths. On the other hand he refuses

---

[1] Reprinted in *Kleine Deutsche Schriften*, 1847–8. The best account of Creuzer is in Stark, *Vorträge u. Aufsätze*, 1880. Cp. his autobiography, *Aus dem Leben eines alten Professors*, 1848. For Voss we have Herbst's great biography, *J. H. Voss*, 1872–6. The best sketch of Lobeck is in Lehrs, *Populäre Aufsätze*, 1875.

to adopt the negative conclusions of Voss, who declared that the Mysteries possessed no secrets, and that they merely dealt with fables of the birth, loves and quarrels of the gods. He refused to admit that they had no symbolic or allegorical meaning, or that the universal testimony to their sacredness was groundless. The middle position assumed by Müller in the bitter controversy between Creuzer and Voss, and maintained when Lobeck restated the negative conclusions of the latter with immensely greater learning, afforded a steadying influence in the early years of the new science. The little volume, written with great clearness and power, was the first attempt at a systematic discussion of the methods and aims of mythological study, and pointed the direction in which research was to travel. Rejecting Creuzer's far-fetched habit of seeking for Oriental origins, he turns to the locality in which each myth originated or with which it was most closely associated. Neither Creuzer nor Voss, he declared, understood the essence of myth, which was, in fact, the oldest poetry of a people, the creation of the folk-soul, the original form of its reflection and observation. The conception had been advanced by Herder, and was soon to be applied by Jakob Grimm to the Teutonic races. Müller's chief interest lay in the study of local myths, legends of migrations, and the relations of local cults. But he was wrong in believing that there was no myth without its locality, and his race gods, such as the Dorian Apollo, sometimes lacked accuracy of attribution.

An important part of his duty at Göttingen was to teach archæology. Heyne's lectures had created a demand, which Welcker, with his intimate knowledge of Italy, had developed. Surrounded by engravings and plaster casts Müller seemed to bring the ancient world to life. With his love of beauty he seized the significance of the object before him, and restored its geographical and historical environment. He believed Greek art, like Greek religion, to have sprung up spontaneously. He lived long enough to learn from Böckh of the frequent intercourse of the nations, and excavations were to reveal foreign influences, but he went less astray than Creuzer, who transformed the Greeks into a debtor nation. His lectures and researches found permanent form in his 'Handbook of the Archæology of Art,' a work of scarcely less importance in the history of Greek studies than 'The Public Economy of Athens.' It was the creation of a new discipline, the first guide to a subject of enormous magnitude and uncertain frontiers. One of his conspicuous gifts was the power to reduce vast masses of material to order and symmetry. Rewritten a few years later by the author, revised in 1847 by Welcker and reprinted in 1878, the Handbook has been the guide and companion of generations of students. The work suffers from Müller's usual fault of overstating the independence of Greece, but, subject to this correction, it provided a no less trustworthy than brilliant survey of the whole artistic evolution. In 1832 he supplemented it by his 'Monuments of Ancient Art,' for which he chose the plates and wrote the text. His minor works on archæology fill five volumes. No German since Winckelmann had done so much to make Greek art a living element in classical study.

While Müller was believed to be wholly engrossed in mythology and archæology, he surprised the world by the publication of a work on the Etruscans, whose history Niebuhr pronounced the most obscure in all antiquity. With the synthetic power which distinguished him he reconstructed the civilisation of a people whom he believed to be immigrants from the East. Applying his usual method he examined the natural features of the country, surveying every aspect of the public and private life of the State —history and government, industry, religion and art, science and manners. Despite Niebuhr's contention that some of his ideas had been appropriated, the work is highly original. Half a century later the work was reprinted by Deecke, who declared its art so wonderful that it was a duty to revive the book. Despite the immense accession of knowledge from the excavation of the cities and cemeteries of Etruria, it is still of value, and is unlikely to be wholly superseded till the key to the Etruscan language is found.

During the later years of his short life Müller worked at a popular history of Greek literature which he brought down to the fifth century, and which, in German and Italian, French and English dress, enjoyed a wide and lasting popularity. But his youthful dream of a history of Greece had never ceased to haunt him, and with his fortieth year he felt it was time to begin. There was only one more indispensable preliminary. In the request for a year's leave he wrote: 'From the beginning of my publications I have always contemplated a systematic and detailed history of Greece. I have given twenty years to studies directed to this end. I am now as ripe for the task as I ever can be, and I must begin soon if I am not to be too late. I need a knowledge of the places in order to compare and revise the results of my own geographical and topographical studies with the reality. A few months in Greece would be of incomparable value for my whole life.' The country had been first systematically studied by Stuart and Revett in the middle of the eighteenth century, and their work was continued by Leake, the Pausanias of modern Greece, whose topographical writings appeared during the formative period of

Müller's life.[1] When it was suggested to Böckh that he ought to visit Greece, he replied with a smile that he knew what it looked like. Müller, on the other hand, though he boasted that he would need no guide in Athens, fully recognised the importance of a personal acquaintance with the country and its monuments. He contemplated not less than twelve volumes, half narrative, the other half notes, proofs and dissertations, depicting the complete historic life of the Greek people. What the 'Dorians' did for a single stock was to be essayed, with matured power and ampler knowledge, for the whole race. The request was granted, and after a prolonged stay in Rome he reached Athens in 1840, where he was met by his pupil Curtius, in whose letters [2] we follow the closing weeks of his life. After a vigorous onslaught on the capital and the Peloponnesus, Thebes and Orchomenus, fever struck him down at Delphi, and he was carried back to Athens to die. His death was the greatest loss that Greek studies sustained during the nineteenth century. In the eloquent words of Curtius, 'He fell a martyr in the land of his spirit, like a hero on his shield, in the fulfilment of his calling and in the preparation of greater, riper works.' Unlike his master Böckh and his pupil Curtius, he possessed a touch of genius. He is the Shelley of the academic renaissance, the young Apollo in the historical pantheon.

The labours of Böckh and Otfried Müller in reconstructing the history and civilisation of Greece were ably seconded by a band of zealous scholars. Welcker [3] devoted a long and fruitful life to the study and co-ordination of Greek art, literature and religion. Meier and Schömann explored the legal institutions of Athens. Ritter and Brandis wrote the first scholarly histories of Greek philosophy, Ideler, at once an astronomer and a philologist, reconstituted the chronology of the ancient world. In every direction the opening decades of the century witnessed a new and deeper insight into the life and thought of the mother of European culture.

[1] The best summary of Leake's life and work is in Curtius, *Altertum u. Gegenwart*, vol. ii., 1882.

[2] *Ernst Curtius, Ein Lebensbild in Briefen*, 1903.

[3] Kekule, *Das Leben Welcker's*, 1880, is one of the best biographies of a classical scholar.

CHAPTER IV

EICHHORN, SAVIGNY AND JAKOB GRIMM

THE treatment of law and institutions may be absolute or relative.[1] The former sets up a system in conformity with an ideal formed by reason; the latter studies legal principles and methods in relation to the social needs from which they spring. The eighteenth century was dominated by the philosophic conception, the nineteenth by the historical. The transition occurred during the same wonderful years which witnessed the renaissance of Greek and Roman studies. While the new era of classical research is connected with Berlin, the historical study of jurisprudence is identified with Göttingen.[2] Though Gesner and Heyne made the Hanoverian Alma Mater the centre of philological studies for half a century, the political and historical sciences had always been strongly represented. Pütter in German law, Martens in International law, Spittler, Schlözer, Gatterer in history, Achenwall in statistics, formed a galaxy of which no other European seat of learning could boast. Of Pütter, the teacher of Hardenberg and innumerable statesmen and officials, Göttingen was particularly proud. It was his method in his lectures and his writings to explain current law by German history. But though he saw, as Montesquieu had seen, that law could only be understood by reference to the past, it did not occur to him to regard it as itself an expression of the national life. The distinction of being the founder of the historical school of jurisprudence belongs not to him but to one of his pupils.

Hugo first realised that the law of a people could only be understood through the national life itself, since it was itself a part and expression of that life.[3] This fruitful conception dawned on him about the time that he became Professor at Göttingen in 1788, and is clearly expressed in the preface which he wrote in the

---

[1] See the later volumes of Landsberg's monumental *Geschichte der deutschen Rechtswissenschaft*, and Gierke's masterly address, *Die historische Rechtsschule u. die Germanisten*, 1903.

[2] See G. von Selle, *Die Georg-August Universität zu Göttingen, 1737–1937*, 1937; and Hunger, *Die Bedeutung der Universität Göttingen für die Geschichtsforschung am Ausgang des achtzehnten Jahrhunderts*, 1933.

[3] The most authoritative account of Hugo is in Savigny's *Vermischte Schriften*, vol. iv., written in 1838 on the jubilee of his doctorate. Cp. O. Mejer's essay in his *Biographisches*, 1886.

following year to a translation of Gibbon's chapter on Roman law. 'Roman law is splendid when we study it without any thought of our own customs, constitution and religion; when one simply learns to know the Romans themselves and to observe how their law developed, and then thinks of what is happening now among ourselves, and reflects why it was that men who were at bottom like ourselves were in many ways so different in their doings and arrangements.' He went on to say that though Gibbon came nearest this ideal, it had never been completely attained. Nor was it his good fortune to realise it himself. History, he declared, must be studied not to illustrate but to discover principles: natural law must give place to historical law. Yet he never embodied these fruitful ideas in a work of any magnitude. His text-books were dry and forbidding, and while still a middle-aged man he saw himself passed in the race.

While Hugo pointed out the road, it was the glory of his greatest pupil to be the first to travel along it. The early life of Karl Friedrich Eichhorn,[1] son of the Orientalist, was passed in an atmosphere of learning. Like most other *alumni* of Göttingen he studied law, political science and history. On finishing his University career he determined to see the machinery of the Empire at work, and with this object visited Wetzlar, Regensburg and Vienna. It had been his intention to become a practical jurist, but soon after his return he accepted a chair at Frankfort on the Oder. The first volume of his 'History of German Law and Institutions' appeared in 1808 when he was twenty-seven. 'If I had had guidance,' he wrote in 1828, 'I should have learned more in one year than I did in ten. If I had been told that all understanding of law rested on historical perception, I should have arranged my studies correctly ten years before I found the right way by my own groping.' This passage appears to contradict utterances in which the historian acknowledges a deep debt to his teachers. The explanation is that he only grasped the real tendency of Hugo's teaching when his student days were over. He had learned from him the necessity of the historical study of law, but he had heard nothing but Roman law from his lips. Pütter connected law with the history of the state, Eichhorn with the life of the nation.

Eichhorn brought to his task an intensity of national feeling which none of his teachers had possessed. His interest in public affairs had been aroused by the French Revolution, and the catastrophe of 1806 stirred him, as it stirred Niebuhr, to the

---

[1] The standard monograph is by the great canonist, Schulte, 1884. Frensdorff's article in *Allg. Deutsche Biog.* is excellent. Lörsch, *Briefe von Eichhorn*, 1881, gives a selection of letters.

depths. He resolved to dedicate himself to the redemption of Germany by teaching his students to love their country and its history; it was in this spirit of constructive patriotism that he wrote the first volume of his celebrated work. The preface declares that now, when the constitution of the Empire was in a state of violent transition, it was more important than ever to look back at the past and to seize its relation to the present. His task was to bring order into the mass of material which had been collected, to pass beyond the labyrinth of errors and hypotheses to the sources themselves. His ambition was not to discuss legal antiquities but to construct a foundation for existing institutions and ideas by means of a history of the state and of public law. The novelty of the plan was not more remarkable than the success with which it was carried out. In a letter from Savigny, when Eichhorn's broken health led him to take a gloomy view of things, that consummate scholar used these words: 'You call me happy in comparison with yourself as a master of Roman law. Then listen to the simple truth. If I have any merit it lies in my having followed the way already mapped out. But how is it with you? You have opened the way in German law without a forerunner and given this science a wholly new life by speech and pen.' Savigny's judgment is the testimony not only of an affectionate friend but of impartial posterity. Eichhorn inaugurated a new era not less decisively than Niebuhr. If he did not reveal such intellectual power, the foundations were more secure.

Eichhorn found on the one hand collections of laws and documents, on the other text-books for the use of practitioners. There was rich material for the Empire, for the separate states, for the Church, for the classes, but it had never been critically examined or wrought into a coherent whole. The history of German Public Law was chiefly a record of dynasties, wars, and territorial changes. Emphasis was laid neither on its development nor on its character as an expression of national life. Realising that certain elements of current German law grew from Roman or ecclesiastical soil, he included foreign systems in his survey. Law was presented as the product of all the factors that influence the life of a nation. Though it was impossible for a single man to tell the whole story from the sources, he performed his task with a power which ranks him among the founders of historical science. He traced the connection between the legal ideas and institutions of different ages, and revealed the continuity of evolution. No jurist and few historians contributed so powerfully to the awakening and fostering of the spirit of nationality. The value of the work was immediately recognised. Its sale was enormous, and from its appearance the

history of German law became an indispensable part of the training of students of jurisprudence. The highest compliment it
received was an invitation to the new University of. Berlin. No
sooner was he installed than the War of Liberation commenced.
He was one of the earliest volunteers, fighting at Leipzig, entering
Paris with the Allies, and winning the Iron Cross. In later life the
consciousness of having shared in the liberation of his country
was more precious to him than his immense reputation. When the
restriction of academic freedom in Prussia during the years of
reaction became irksome, he accepted an invitation to return to
his own University. It was during the twelve years at Göttingen
that he reached the highest point of his professorial fame.

In addition to his main achievement Eichhorn wrote a treatise
on Private Law, which may be regarded as a supplement to the
History; for in dealing with inheritance, serfdom and the family,
the principles of the historical school are fearlessly applied. In
1829 he was compelled by ill-health to resign his chair, but he
retained strength to write a third important work on ecclesiastical
law. Like the *Privatrecht* the new treatise was an elaboration of
the brief discussion in the author's main work. The discussion of
Protestant law, hitherto utterly neglected, occupies only a part
of the massive work. Half a volume is devoted to prolegomena,
describing the officers of the Church, the decretals, the relations
of Church and State and of Catholics and Protestants. This sketch
of Church history from the legal and institutional point of view
was of great value, being written with a deeper knowledge of law
than historians possessed and a wider knowledge of ecclesiastical
history than lawyers could claim. The objective spirit in which the
Roman Church was treated was a refreshing novelty. 'I am a
Protestant by inner conviction,' he wrote, 'but I am without any
hostile feeling to the Catholic Church and its adherents.' He respected it as a great historical phenomenon and a valuable conservative force. The treatise exerted a profound influence on the
teachers and students of ecclesiastical law, not least on the handbook of Richter by which it was superseded. The author declared
it to be his ripest work, and such a consummate judge as his pupil
and biographer Schulte has confirmed the opinion.

Eichhorn's later life produced no literary work except occasional essays and the revision of his earlier writings. The steady
demand for his History enabled him to keep it up to date. He
was conscious of the shortcomings of the first volume and, after
revising it twice, virtually rewrote it for the fourth edition in
1834. Even then he declared it to be the weakest part of the work,
though he profited by Jakob Grimm's study of legal antiquities.

He declared that the study of the codes, the capitularies and the formulæ must be pursued for a long time before anyone could flatter himself that he really understood the early Middle Ages. On returning thanks for his reception into the Prussian Academy in 1839 he modestly declared: 'I only venture to regard my work as useful in so far as it has perhaps contributed to win for these studies new friends.' For a time it seemed sufficient to fill up the gaps that the master had left and to follow the lines of research which he had opened up. Later it became clear that there were faults of construction as well as of detail. His view of the Roman origin of towns was unfounded. He had not realised the full measure of difference among the Teutonic peoples, nor did he afford adequate recognition to the law which was practised but not written. In some cases he generalised too boldly from local and temporary phenomena. Yet these faults scarcely diminish the enduring significance of his achievement. All Germany expressed its gratitude on the occasion of his jubilee in 1851. 'We jurists,' declared Wilda, 'whatever branches of jurisprudence we have especially studied, whether we have been your hearers or have otherwise benefited by the fruits of your labours, revere you as our great teacher and master. But your achievements do not belong to scholarship alone. The quickening of the study of German law is a national deed of far-reaching importance. Time will emphasise this more and more. Universal reverence will be paid to the name of the man who fought for the freedom of his fatherland and revealed its identity to the German people.' The prophecy has proved correct. 'His book,' wrote Schulte in 1884, 'is still unapproached, still less rivalled.'

Eichhorn bequeathed to scholarship a method and a model, but the world of ideas in which he lived has passed away. The reverence for the past which he shared with Niebuhr and Savigny grew into a rigid conservatism which provoked a revolt against the historical school. A strong monarchy, rooted in the respect and affection of the people, was his ideal, and it never occurred to him that a more advanced political education brought with it the need for different institutions. While the strength of the historical school consisted in its recognition of the continuity of history, its danger lay in the temptation to hamper the creative energies of the present.

II

If Eichhorn gave the first consummate example of the historical treatment of law, it is to his life-long friend that we owe the fullest explanation and the most brilliant defence of the method itself. Losing his parents while still a child, Savigny[1] became the ward of an assessor in the Imperial Court at Wetzlar, where he learned his first lessons in law. A term at Göttingen introduced him to Spittler and Hugo, and at the age of twenty-one he began to teach at Marburg. In 1803 he published a treatise on the Roman Law of Possession which won immediate success and which, revised at frequent intervals during the author's life and after his death, retains its place among the classics of legal literature. He now began to collect material for the work with which his name will ever be associated. While Eichhorn desired to find the roots of existing law in German history, Savigny determined to trace the influence of Roman law throughout the Middle Ages.

In 1804 he started on a prolonged tour through the libraries of Western Europe. In 1808 he accepted a professorship at Landshut, but two years later was summoned by Humboldt to teach Roman law at the newly founded University of Berlin. He was a consummate lecturer, and his class-room was always crowded. 'His lectures,' wrote Bluntschli,[2] 'were of a wonderful clearness and certainty of expression, so beautifully arranged that he could print them without revision, and yet so free that they gave the impression of the freshest thought. His appearance at the desk had something stately and noble. The confidence of a man who was master of his material was enthroned on his open brow. The great, clear eye shone when he explained and analysed juristic conceptions.' 'Even to-day,' wrote Sybel in 1888, 'I hold Savigny for the most perfect academic teacher of the century.'

Though sharing to the full the patriotic enthusiasm of the era of liberation, Savigny felt it his duty to oppose the demand for the codification of the law which grew out of the new consciousness of national unity. The plan, which was as old as Leibniz, was put forward by several jurists, of whom the most important was Thibaut, the famous Heidelberg Professor.[3] He had studied at Göttingen and was well acquainted with the standpoint of the new historical school, but he believed that a philosophical treatment of law was needed to achieve consistency and to remodel the products of the past in the light of the needs of the present. In his

---

[1] The best studies are by Rudorff, 1862; Landsberg (in *Allg. Deutsche Biog.*); Ennecerus, 1879. Ihering's striking appreciation is in his *Gesammelte Aufsätze*, vol. ii., 1882. Foreign views are represented by Mignet in *Nouveaux Éloges historiques*, 1877, and J. E. G. de Montmorency in *Great Jurists of the World*, 1913. For his correspondence, see Stoll, *Friedrich Carl von Savigny*, 3 vols., 1927–39.

[2] *Denkwürdiges*, i. 62–5, 1884.

[3] Thibaut left a deep impression on his pupils. See Walter, *Aus meinem Leben*, 91–4, 1865.

essay on the necessity of a code, 'written in fourteen days out of the warmth of my heart,' he raised the standard of legal reform. Germany had now rescued her honour and won the possibility of a happy future, but there were still many obstacles to its realisation. The Fatherland remained a mosaic of little states, and the existing law was a curious mixture. Roman law was foreign and the fruit of a period of decline. The old German law-books were full of anomalies. No human being could survey the whole of so vast and ill-arranged a territory. A simple code, constructed in a German spirit, would render it easy for judges and possible for ordinary citizens to master the subject. The task should be carried out by statesmen and scholars in combination. Such a code would bind together the inhabitants of different states, even if they were condemned to remain politically separated. If it was contended that the traditional system was known and reverenced, the answer was that a code drawn up after emerging from the fires of the Napoleonic wars would be holy in the eyes of their children.

Thibaut's pamphlet, glowing with patriotic feeling, voicing the new-born demand for a closer unity, and emphasising the practical disadvantages of an antiquated system of law, created a profound impression; but Savigny intervened with a reply so convincing that the project was abandoned for two generations. In the preface to the second edition of the 'Vocation of Our Time for Legislation,' he explains the genesis of the first. 'It appeared at a time which can never be forgotten by those who lived through it. For years the fetters which bound our country to the arbitrary rule of a foreigner had been drawn tighter and tighter, and it seemed that it must end in the annihilation of our nationality.' When the deliverance came, it was possible once more to discuss such matters of domestic interest. He begins by frankly admitting the reality of the demand for a code, both on practical and sentimental grounds. He recognised the feeling that Germany was called on to show herself not unworthy of the times, and admitted that certain changes must be made, as the French code had been eating into the German organism like a cancer. The popularity of codes dated from the eighteenth century. Men longed for a mechanically precise administration of justice and for laws which, divested of all historic association, should be equally adapted to all nations and times. But now that the historical spirit had been awakened, there was no room for this shallow self-sufficiency.

Savigny proceeded to explain his notion of the origin of positive law. 'For law, as for language, there is no moment of cessation. It is subject to the same movement and development as every other expression of the life of the people.' In its earliest shape it is simple. Later it enters on a double life, remaining, indeed, an expression of the community but becoming a science in the hands of the jurists. In by-laws and town laws we often find the survival of primitive practice. 'All law was originally formed by custom and popular feeling, not by jurisprudence—that is, by silently operating forces, not by the arbitrary will of a lawgiver.' He next turns to the practical difficulties of a code. Where were the materials? And how was it possible to anticipate every case and to frame a decision before it occurred? A body of precedents, often contradicting one another, would arise outside the acknowledged law. Roman law derived its greatness from its possession of leading principles. While the Roman state was alive and developing, no code was constructed or even proposed: the Codes were the products of decay and synchronise with its virtual disappearance. The Napoleonic Code was a thoroughly bad piece of work. Not every age had a vocation for law any more than for art. There were no jurists capable of making a great code. The task would be too great for a single brain, and the work of a committee would lack unity. Existing law should be improved by legislation, while disputed points might be cleared up and old customs might be recorded. Finally a code, even if practicable, would do nothing but harm. It would destroy the study of the past, paralyse juristic thinking, and inspire no reverence. 'History is a noble instructress, and only through her can living contact with the primitive life of the people be maintained. The loss of this connection would rob the nation of the best part of its spiritual life. When the Jews were tired of waiting for the laws of God, they made a golden calf, and the genuine tables of the law were broken to pieces upon it.'

Savigny's treatise, though successful in its immediate purpose, was a strange mixture of profound reasoning and of glaring fallacies. He gravely undervalued the merits of the philosophy of law, without which there could be no higher synthesis. Though he was right in saying that the time for codification had not come, he was wrong in declaring that it would never arrive. Historic law must be tested by and adapted to the needs and the rights of man. It is only a step from the 'Vocation' to a championship of inveterate abuses and to the shelter of hoary usurpations behind the ark of legitimacy. Yet, despite his exaggeration of the evils of codes and of the difficulties in making them, he gave weighty expression to the historical nature of law. He showed that law, like language, was an expression of the life of the people, growing by natural process out of their experiences and needs. The jurists were no more the authors of law than the grammarians of language: they only developed what the folk-life created. Part of this product remained customary, while other portions were turned into 'laws.' The legend of the 'wise lawgiver' disappeared for ever. Savigny, like Burke, voices the reaction against the eighteenth century.

The controversy excited immense interest. In collaboration with Eichhorn he founded a ' Journal of Historical Jurisprudence' to defend and illustrate his views. The opening article, which may be regarded as a popular summary of the 'Vocation,' dismissed his opponents as the unhistorical school. Thibaut did not reply to the 'Vocation,' but he refused to accept the new label, suggesting as a fairer description of himself and his friends 'the historico-philosophical school.' When certain of Savigny's pupils spoke of him without the courtesy that their master had shown, he retaliated in a brilliant pamphlet, 'The So-called Historical and Unhistorical School.' A good deal of the heat, he declared, was due to the unfortunate choice of terms. He in nc way despised the historical study of law, but he protested against the subjection of the present to the past. The controversy ended, so far as it concerned the two protagonists, with Savigny's explanation of his position in the preface to his ' System of Modern Roman Law.' He had used the title 'historical school' because this department of legal study had been unduly neglected, and he had no wish to depreciate other methods. It was untrue that he desired to subject the present to the government of the past, or German to Roman law. He had merely insisted on the living connection with the past, and had declared that only by its study could the true nature of the present be grasped. No part of law was immutable. This explanation of his position, he believed, should end the struggle and lead to the disuse of party names. His wish was fulfilled since the controversy entered on a new stage. His conception of law as an organic growth became the common possession of men of all schools, while the philosophic approach was brilliantly vindicated by Ihering.

In addition to being the principal champion of the genetic treatment of law, Savigny was the author of one of the most valuable investigations ever made into its history. The 'History of Roman Law in the Middle Ages' began to appear in 1815. The book falls into two periods, the first comprising the six centuries before Irnerius, in which the survival of Roman law can be proved in great detail, the second containing the four succeeding centuries, when it became the object of systematic study. The first two volumes form the backbone of the work. Their theme is the survival of Roman law after the fall of the Empire, despite the convulsions of the barbarian invasions. It was his object to trace its survival in every part of what had once been the Empire. This could only be accomplished by an inquiry into the fortunes of the peoples to whom it had been a living reality. If they had been annihilated, their law could not have survived. If they had lost personal freedom or the public life of the time had wholly ceased, Roman law could hardly have continued. 'For law is a piece of public life, bound to all its parts in many ways, and it must die if the life disappears.' Moreover the application of the old law could have been scarcely possible in the German states of the Empire without Roman judges and courts.

Savigny traces the survival of Roman law in the institutions of the towns, the local customs, canon law and academic study, and concludes that what had been regarded as a renaissance in the twelfth century was merely an increase of interest. He begins by sketching the legal institutions of the Empire in Italy and the provinces, passing to those of the Germanic peoples and finally to the countries conquered by the Teutons. In the greater part of the Frankish monarchy and in Lombardy the Roman Rectores gave place to German courts with civil and military authority. Did the destruction go deeper and affect the municipalities? The common opinion that in Italy they were destroyed he believed to be wrong. The Germans, he declared, never attempted to root out or even to Germanise the Romans. Indeed the position of the latter was freer and happier than in the days of Imperial decay. Their property as a rule was secure, and their vitality is proved by the survival of so much of the language. Moreover the constitution of the town could be easily amalgamated with German practice. A further reason for the survival of the Roman constitution of the towns was that the Germans cared little for urban life. Passing to the evidence for the continuity of legal instruction he declares that, though there were no special schools, teaching was given as a part of Roman literature in many grammar schools. Roman law continued to exist and to expand through the medium of written sources and by the practice of the courts. Of these the first was far the most important, and Savigny attempted to collect the traces, whether verbal reproductions or obvious derivations. Among these sources are the law-books compiled for the Romans in several states, those of the Germans containing scraps of Roman law, charters, contracts, wills and commentaries. Many scholars had seen that Roman law was in operation throughout the Middle Ages, but this was of little value unless it was known which parts were used and what degree of favour each of them enjoyed. The second volume marshals the evidence for survival among the Burgundians, the Visigoths, the Franks, the Ostrogoths, the Lombards, the Anglo-Saxons, in Byzantine Italy and in the writings of the Church. He often spoke of himself as a pioneer, and his main contention is universally accepted. It was an immense achievement to prove the continuity of Roman law during the dark centuries between the fall of the Western Empire and the rise of the Bologna jurists. It was not surprising that, having convinced himself of the central fact, he should at times admit evidence that failed to satisfy a more exacting age. His most serious error was to assert the continuance of the Roman town constitution in Lombardy, a mistake corrected by the masterly researches of Karl Hegel, son of the philosopher.

The second part of the work deals with the fortunes of Roman law from the twelfth century to the Renaissance. The main feature of this period was the systematic study of texts, and its history is therefore to be found in the lives of the jurists. After an analysis of the sources he discusses the conditions of the revival of jurisprudence. The Lombard towns were rich and populous, and their commercial life raised many problems for which the Teutonic laws were unsuitable. They were therefore driven to the study of Roman law. The great chapter on the Universities, above all that of Bologna, was a contribution to the history of mediæval learning of the highest value. The last three volumes contain notices of the life and writings of the glossators. The author realised that they could be nothing more than a work of reference, but he maintained that it was necessary for someone to undertake a complete survey. Throughout the book the beneficent influence of Roman law and its contribution to the education of the world is asserted with unwavering conviction. The whole work, with its emphasis on continuity, might be described as a gigantic appendix to Gibbon's 'Decline and Fall.' Savigny's later life was mainly devoted to a detailed investigation of the Roman elements in current German law. Dying in 1861 at the patriarchal age of eighty-two, he had lived long enough to witness the application of historical methods to every branch of law and to be hailed throughout Europe as the greatest jurist of the century.

III

In the same wonderful decade which witnessed the earliest works of Niebuhr, Böckh, Savigny and Eichhorn, Jakob Grimm founded the science of Teutonic origins.[1] Bodmer had published part of the

---

[1] The history of the science is best studied in Raumer's *Geschichte d. Germanischen Philologie*, 1870, and Paul's *Grundriss d. Germanischen Philologie*, vol. i., 1891.

Nibelungen, and some of the minor poets interested themselves in
the Minnesinger, but the study of antiquities was thoroughly
uncongenial to the *Aufklärung*. A new epoch opened with Herder,
who paved the way for the historical study of literature by his
conception of nature-poetry, of the folk-soul, of language as a
treasure-house to which the centuries brought their contributions.
He loved the childhood and youth of literature, the world of
Homer, the Eddas and the Volkslieder. 'I do not believe,' he
declared in 1793, 'that the Germans have less feeling than other
nations for the merits of their ancestors. I think I see a time
coming when we shall return more seriously to their achievements
and learn to value our old gold.' Herder's interest came to be
shared by a growing number of his countrymen as the romantic
movement increased in strength. Johannes Müller described the
Nibelungen as the German Homer, Bürger attempted to reproduce early models in his ballads, and Musäus utilised the sagas for
his tales. Tieck's emotional personality found nurture in the songs
and romances of the Middle Ages. August Schlegel's lectures in
Berlin declared war on the canons of the *Aufklärung*, and von der
Hagen was encouraged by them to publish old German poetry.
Fouqué began a series of mediæval romances. Arnim and Brentano published their great collection of folk-songs known as the
Wunderhorn, which brought back the Middle Ages in a flood and
inspired a generation of German lyrists. The romanticists rendered
a priceless service to historical studies. They enriched the imagination by their presentation of the many-coloured life of other ages
and countries. They doubled the intellectual capital and widened
the horizon of their time. But they were artists, poets, dreamers,
not scholars, philologists, historians. It was the glory of Jakob
Grimm [1] that, growing up in their circle, he added to their best
characteristics the critical scholarship which they lacked.

Born in Hesse in 1785, Grimm entered Marburg University
and, in obedience to the wish of his father, enrolled himself as
a student of law. His intellectual interests were awakened by
Savigny, who became his hero and model. 'What can I say of his
lectures,' he wrote half a century later in his Autobiography,
'except that they exercised a decisive influence in my whole life?'
It was to him that he dedicated the 'Grammatik,' declaring that
his heart had longed to do public homage when he was able to

---

[1] Scherer's *Jakob Grimm*, 2nd ed., 1885, is one of the best of German
monographs, and there is much of value relating to the brothers in Scherer,
Kleine Schriften, 1893. Weinhold, *Rede auf Grimm*, 1863, is authoritative.
Grimm's brief autobiography is printed in his *Kleine Schriften*, vol. i.,
1864. His correspondence fills many volumes.

offer something worthy of his old master. It was in his library that he made acquaintance with early German literature, and it was from him that he learned the historic piety which stamps the lifework of both teacher and pupil. If this friendship was the first important event in his life, the second was the appearance of Tieck's edition of the Minnelieder. Through Savigny he made the acquaintance of Arnim and Brentano, and the *Wunderhorn* was enriched from his stores. A fresh, almost uncultivated field, declared Grimm long afterwards, was before them. Goethe and Schiller had cared little for the Middle Ages. Bodmer had put the key in the lock, and the Romantics had turned it. When in 1805 Savigny took him to Paris to help in collecting material for the history of Roman law, he undertook researches on his own account. 'I have been thinking,' Wilhelm had written to his brother, 'that you might look for old German poems among the manuscripts. Perhaps you might find something unknown and important.' Soon after his return, Jakob determined on a collection of German sagas and fairy-tales. He quickly discovered that many were international and was forced to survey all Teutonic and Romance literatures, glancing also at those of the Slavonic world and the East. He drank deeply at the springs of Creuzer and Görres, and studied comparative grammar and early law. In these first few years of his intellectual awakening he mapped out the vast territories to the cultivation of which he was to devote his long and strenuous life.

Beginning with reviews and essays the brothers rapidly arrested the attention of scholars; and the 'Mährchen,'[1] the first volume of which was published in 1812, made the name of Grimm a household word throughout Germany. They accomplished for the fairy-tale what Arnim and Brentano had done for the Volkslied. Herder had remarked that a collection of children's stories would be a Christmas present for the young people of the future. His forecast was fulfilled, but the main object of the work was to reveal the national wealth. The brothers strongly disapproved of the liberties which Arnim and Brentano took with their precious material. 'They care nothing for a close, historical investigation,' wrote Jakob to Wilhelm in 1809; 'they are not content to leave the old as it is, but insist on transporting it to our own time, to which it does not belong.' With their childlike natures and delight in folk-poetry the Grimms were ideal interpreters of the fairy-tale to the modern world. More than any other part of the romantic

[1] See Hermann Grimm's article, *Die Brüder Grimm u. die Mährchen*, in his *Beiträge z. deutschen Culturgeschichte*, 1897. Hermann Grimm was the son of Wilhelm.

output the 'Mährchen' became part of the life of the German nation. The collection of German sagas which followed'was less successful. Most were already in print, though a few were added from oral tradition. A strange mixture of Christian and heathen elements, of magic and history, they were of the utmost value as a revelation of the popular mind. Grimm declared that the earliest history of every people was the Folk-Saga, which was always epic. He agreed with Arnim's dictum that epics composed themselves, and with the paradox of Novalis that there was more truth in the tales of the poets than in the chronicles. The Romanticists grasped the cardinal truth that the historian had to reconstruct the life and achievements of the peoples. History had neglected sagas and ballads because they contained no 'facts.' These views were powerfully expressed in the essay, 'Thoughts on Myth, Epic and History,' but his teaching was not without grave flaws. He attributed to the sagas more historical substance than they possessed. In his devotion to folk poetry he was unjust to other and later types. The conscious he reckoned inferior to the unconscious, individual effort to the spontaneous creations of the community. He loved to regard mediæval literature, like mediæval cathedrals, as the anonymous expression of the soul of a people.

The repetition and development of the romanticist views of early literature led to a sharp criticism by August Schlegel, who ridiculed the contention that epics and folk-songs write themselves.[1] That we do not know the authors is no proof that they grew alone. The saga and the heroic lay were the common property, not the common product, of their age. 'When we see a lofty tower rising above the habitations of men, we know that many hands brought stones for its construction; but the stones are not the tower. That is the work of the architect.' Without nature there is no life, but without art there is no form. All poetry is the combination of nature and art. Schlegel laughed at their reverence for the unimportant, their enthusiasm for old wives' fables and nursery rhymes. In the latter criticism there lurks something of the arrogance of the *Aufklärung*, but the essay as a whole came like a keen, cool breeze. The indictment extended to Grimm's etymology. The study of old German literature, declared Schlegel, could only succeed if based on exact grammatical knowledge. Grimm felt the justice of the criticism and began to turn to grammatical studies. Rask, whose Icelandic grammar he had praised on its appearance in 1811, had said that philology should not so much decree how words should be formed as describe how they had been formed and altered. This principle found a ready

[1] August Schlegel's *Werke*, xii. 383-426.

response in Grimm, who entertained the same reverence for language as for folk-poetry. The grammarian must be the student, not the teacher of language. Writing in the noonday of the *Aufklärung*, Adelung despised dialects, and constrained the language with bit and bridle. Others urged the expulsion of certain words and the alteration of many more. The attack on ancient forms was as repugnant to Grimm as an outrage on morals. The production of a bald uniformity was like the method of the Terrorists in the French Revolution, and the fabrication of new words was a sin. It was the wrinkles and warts that gave the incommunicable stamp of home, as on a familiar face. In place of learned pedantry and levelling reform he offered historical grammar, which taught respect for every living element.

The laws of language had been outlined by Wilhelm von Humboldt in 1812 in his masterly essay on the Basques. He urged the combination of the study of language and history, and the investigation of the characteristics of nations as the necessary accompaniment of grammar. The structure of language was organic, but its formation was disturbed by borrowings and imperfect assimilations. Every language consisted of organic parts and inorganic accretions. These ideas were adopted by Grimm in his German Grammar, the first volume of which appeared in 1819. The purpose of the book was to reveal the operation of law in language as in history, and the key could only be recovered by careful comparison of all Teutonic languages and dialects. His chief thesis was that all the families of German speech were closely related, and that the present forms were unintelligible without a reference to the oldest. He made full use of the work of his predecessors, above all of Hickes and Rask, and, in another field, of Bopp, but he introduced the comparative method into Teutonic philology. In the purely German territory he had to lay the foundations himself, and an architectural whole appeared where there had been nothing but isolated details. The book gave far more than its title suggested, for it was in truth a history of the Teutonic languages. Grimm's masterpiece formed one of the instruments by which historical science has ever since made its advance. The most competent of judges, Benecke, declared that he did not know whether most to admire the author's insight or knowledge. His old critic, Schlegel, hastened to express his congratulations. Following his guide the reader rejoices in the ever-increasing light, till an ordered world meets his gaze.

The work was out of print in a year, and in 1820 its author began to rewrite it. He made new and important discoveries as he worked, and the printed sheets were revised by Lachmann.

The arrangement of material was improved, and the second edition was in many respects a new work. The most important
addition was the statement of 'Grimm's Law,' or the explanation
of the change of letters. There were laws of sound. No words
could be traced to a common origin unless the differences in their
sounds could be explained by a law of variation. In this way the
relations of peoples could be recovered, and some knowledge of
the early life of humanity be obtained. Three further volumes of
the 'Grammatik' were published, the latest attacking the problem
of syntax. When the publisher inquired whether Grimm preferred
to complete or revise his work, he chose the latter. Though incomplete, it is beyond comparison the most important work ever
devoted to German philology. No one had ever penetrated so
deep into the innermost recesses of language and seized its intimate relation to life. In becoming a philologist Grimm did not
cease to be a poet. His creative insight is continually flashing light
on dark places. Adelung had asked what sense there could be in
giving a sex to lifeless things and abstract conceptions. Grimm
answers by trying to retrace the paths along which primitive
fancy moved. In its early forms language is concrete and pictorial;
in its later, abstract and intellectual. This view of the transition
from the sensible to the rational was a weighty contribution to
the history of mankind.

Between the first two and the last two volumes of the 'Grammatik' Grimm published his work on Legal Antiquities, a picture
of early German life from a particular angle.[1] The differences he
had shown to exist between the early and later stages of literature
and language existed equally in the realm of law and religion. He
had warmly adopted Savigny's view of the nature of law and had
hailed the 'Vocation' with delight. He was especially interested
in symbolic actions, the forms in which conceptions expressed
themselves. In an early essay on Poetry in Law he had declared
that they had grown in one bed. The poet and the judge alike
uttered the common thoughts. He was unjustly accused of failing
to treat the subject historically or to trace the gradual transformation of institutions, but his task was wholly different from that of
Eichhorn. He confined himself to the sensible, the visible, the
pictorial element, the customs and uses, the actions and forms
which an unlettered age demanded. His chief authorities were the
so-called Weistümer, or dooms, and early literature and legend.
No jurist could have written the book, for no jurist possessed
the requisite knowledge of the languages and literatures of the

---

[1] On Grimm as a jurist, see Hübner's admirable monograph, *Jakob
Grimm u. das deutsche Recht*, 1895.

early Teutonic world. While Eichhorn desired to discuss the foundations of modern law and practice, Grimm never troubled himself about later developments. Every usage possessed its importance as an expression of the folk-spirit.

The book was hailed with delight by the jurists of Germany. Savigny rejoiced in the brilliant development given to his own teaching. Eichhorn was warm in his praise, without fully realising its creative character, Michelet gave intense satisfaction to the modest author by building his own 'Symbolic Origins of French Law' on its foundations. Grimm truly declared that his book was a work of suggestion. Its suggestiveness is still unexhausted a century after its appearance, and its influence may be traced in every subsequent writer on early Teutonic law. Closely allied to the Legal Antiquities was the edition of Weistümer, or dooms, of which four volumes appeared during his life and three others after his death. 'Unless I am blinded by enthusiasm,' he wrote, 'this collection will enormously enrich and almost revolutionise our legal antiquities, make important contributions to a knowledge of law, mythology and customs, and give warmth and colour to our early history.' They played the same part in law as folk-songs and fairy-tales in mythology and poetry. In both cases he used popular tradition to illustrate and explain written memorials. But the earliest date from the thirteenth century, and he erred in employing them as illustrations of far earlier times.

A further aspect of early Teutonic life was explored in the 'German Mythology.' Görres and Mone had studied the survival of heathen practice and belief without employing critical methods. 'In my books,' declared Grimm in the preface, 'I have tried to show that the language of our ancestors was not rough and wild but fine and harmonious; that they did not live in hordes but were free, moral and law-abiding. I now desire to exhibit their hearts full of belief, to recall their magnificent if imperfect conceptions of higher beings.' Literature, sagas, fairy-tales, customs, language were made to yield their contribution, and a mass of oral matter was collected. The old world revived with its brilliant colouring and fantastic shapes. The stage swarmed with gods, swan-maidens, nixies, cobolds, elfs, dwarfs and giants. Mythology being a creation of the poetical spirit, his talent was peculiarly fitted to deal with it. The Introduction unfolds a great picture of Christianity spreading over Europe while heathenism retreats step by step. Beginning with the gods, we pass to the lesser mythological beings, to the elements and the seasons in relation to human life, to the personality of animals and plants. The world of light is paralleled by the world of darkness, by demons, witches and magicians. The 'German Mythology' took its place among the classics of European scholarship. But though it is often regarded as his most perfect work, and though its vitality and insight are marvellous, it is not without serious faults. The picture of Teutonic civilisation is too rosy, and he credits early times with customs and beliefs of subsequent growth. A few years later considerable portions were superseded by Adalbert Kuhn's researches in Indo-Germanic mythology and Mannhardt's investigations into popular cults. Yet it was none the less the foundation on which the science of Teutonic heathenism has been reared, and it holds an honoured place beside the 'Grammar' and the 'Legal Antiquities' among the works which recreated ancient Germany.

Grimm's later life was chiefly occupied by linguistic studies. His 'History of the German Language,' published in 1848, was rather a series of dissertations than a connected narrative, and may almost be described as an appendix to the Grammar. A good many of the results of the earlier work were modified in consequence of the works of Bopp and Pott. The researches of Zeuss had interested him in ethnography; and though parts of the work are fantastic and some of its identifications of early tribes incorrect, the attempt to throw the light of philology on ethnology and culture was not without importance. The 'German Dictionary,' the last great task of his life, was suggested to the brothers by a publisher, and accepted by them in return for a living wage. It was to include all words from the age of Luther to the age of Goethe. The first part appeared in 1852, and the letter 'F' had been almost completed when Jakob Grimm died in 1863, full of years and honours. 'All my works,' he wrote in one of his last essays, 'relate to the Fatherland, from whose soil they derive their strength.' These simple words may serve as an epitaph for one who was at once a great patriot and a great scholar, and who carried through life the heart of a little child.

Jakob's earliest and most effective helper was his brother Wilhelm.[1] Their studies began together at Marburg, and their publications were joint till the elder brother turned his attention seriously to grammar. During the middle decades of their lives their paths led in different directions, but their closing years witnessed a renewal of co-operation. The Dictionary is no less a memorial to their joint labours than the 'Mährchen.' In addition to the works in which he assisted his greater brother, Wilhelm's

---

[1] Jakob's address on his brother is in his *Kleine Schriften*, vol. i. Their *Briefwechsel aus der Jugendzeit* was published in 1881. Tonnelat, *Les Frères Grimm*, 1912, gives a good account of their early collaboration. Cp. Scherer's article in *Allg. Deutsche Biog.*

independent production was of the highest value. His greatest achievement was his study of the German heroic saga. His scope was far narrower than that of his brother. It was his instinct rather to select a limited territory and to examine every corner of it with loving care than to roam over immense tracts of country. He lacked the creative genius of Jakob, but he was the more exact and careful worker. The relations of the brothers form one of the idylls in the history of scholarship, and they remain associated in the memory as they appear in the frontispiece of the Dictionary. They loved the German people, and their love has been richly repaid. They rank next to Goethe and Schiller among the spiritual influences which have made Germans all over the world conscious of their unity.

The Grimms grew out of the romantic circle, but they owed less to any of its members than to Benecke,[1] librarian and Professor at Göttingen, who was the first to make lectures on early German literature and language part of the ordinary curriculum. He assisted the brothers in their early researches, lending them books from the library, and encouraging them by favourable reviews. His first important publication was an edition of the fables of Bonerius, which marks the beginning of scientific lexicography. His talent was philological rather than literary, but in this sphere he was unrivalled. Each word was examined in its historical development and the finest shades of meaning extracted. Each monument of early poetry was studied in the light of its time and place. Benecke was not only, in the words of Jakob Grimm, the inaugurator of grammatical knowledge of early German literature at the Universities, but also the founder of the strictly historical method of studying this branch of literature, which had hitherto been judged by æsthetic standards.

While many philologists rendered valuable assistance, Lachmann[2] shares with Jakob Grimm the honour of ranking as the joint founder of the scientific study of early German literature and language. Born eight years later he learned exact philology under Hermann at Leipzig and owed his initiation into Teutonic studies to Benecke. At the same time he continued his classical studies, and the aged Heyne foresaw his pupil's eminence. His edition of Propertius contained the germ of all his future achievements in different departments of philology. His aim was the

[1] Their correspondence with Benecke, published in 1889, reveals a charming intimacy. Cp. Scherer's article in *Allg. Deutsche Biog.*

[2] See Hertz, *Lachmann*, 1851; Jakob Grimm's *Kleine Schriften*, vol. i.; Leo, *Rede zur Säcularfeier Lachmanns*, 1893; and *Briefwechsel der Brüder Grimm mit K. Lachmann*, 1925.

reconstruction of the text as the author wrote it, on the authority
of the best manuscripts. The emendations in which philologists
rejoiced were not to be thought of till the manuscripts had been
examined. In 1816 he turned to the Nibelungen, the present form
of which he attributed to the thirteenth century. He gradually
obtained an unequalled insight into the metric and philological
characteristics of mediæval poetry, reconstructing texts from an
exhaustive study of all available manuscripts. The 'Grammatik'
was warmly welcomed, Lachmann declaring that it put them all
to shame for their ignorance. The two men now entered into close
relations, and in his preface to the second edition Grimm declared
that it was impossible to describe the help of Benecke and Lachmann. 'Such full and open communications as Lachmann has
vouchsafed me must have been experienced for their value to be
understood.'

When Lachmann was appointed to a Chair in Berlin in 1824,
he had acquired an incomparable knowledge of the printed and
manuscript sources of early German literature, which enabled him
to pour forth critical masterpieces in rapid succession. His first
work was Hartmann's 'Iwein,' for which Benecke gave him his
collections, and which he declared to be the first critical edition
of an old German poem. The 'Iwein' was followed by an edition
of Walther von der Vogelweide, which first made the poet intelligible, and by the works of Wolfram. 'My aim,' he declared, 'was
to make visible one of the greatest poets in his full splendour.'
Returning to the Nibelungen he published the text in 1826 and his
critical investigations ten years later. It was possible, he contended, to trace twenty separate songs, but his reconstruction of
the poem was widely assailed. Into the field of German literature,
as into Homeric studies and New Testament criticism, Lachmann
brought fruitful ideas which, even when not accepted in their
entirety, worked like a leaven long after his premature death. In
his obituary notice Grimm declared that philologists were of two
classes—those who studied words for the sake of things and those
who studied things for the sake of words. He himself belonged to
the former, Lachmann to the latter. 'Born to be an editor,' he
added, 'Germany has never seen his equal.' He made a history of
mediæval German literature possible. His true master was Bentley,
whom he pronounced 'the greatest critic of modern times.' But
while Bentley sometimes reached his most brilliant results by
a flash of genius, Lachmann won his triumphs by industry and
insight into the variations of language and metre. While Grimm
failed as a Professor and founded no school, Lachmann's lectures
were the starting-point of many a career. Otto Jahn dedicated his

first important work to his 'incomparable teacher.' Simrock's versions of the mediæval classics were built on his foundations. Moritz Haupt, his successor and literary executor, saluted him as the supreme master. Müllenhoff's encyclopædic *Deutsche Altertumskunde* could hardly have been written had he not paved the way. Zeuss, the founder of Celtic philology, stood on his shoulders. Though not a professional historian, he supplied historians with a key to large tracts of the life and thought of the early Germanic peoples.

CHAPTER V

THE MONUMENTA

WHILE the romantic movement aroused interest in early German literature and legend, the systematic study of German history was the result of the fiery ordeal of the Napoleonic wars. The religious and political disunion of Germany rendered it difficult for her inhabitants to realise their unity. Lessing and Herder, Klopstock and Wieland, Goethe and Schiller felt themselves citizens of the world. It required the overwhelming disaster of Jena, the execution of Palm, and the humiliations of the French occupation to teach the sacredness of the Fatherland. 'Shake your chains as you will,' said Goethe, 'he is too strong for you; you will never break them.' 'Prussia is done for,' declared Napoleon; 'she has disappeared from the map of Europe.' The two greatest minds of the age were equally blind. The regeneration of Prussia was a national achievement. Stein came from Nassau, Hardenberg and Scharnhorst from Hanover, Gneisenau and Fichte from Saxony, Niebuhr from Schleswig-Holstein. The political independence and the spiritual unity of the country were won by the same terrible struggle. Though Germany had to wait half a century for unification the flame of patriotism continued to glow, and the noblest architect of liberation turned to a new task of national service.

I

The need of a collection of the sources of mediæval history had been keenly felt during the eighteenth century, but all plans were wrecked on the impossibility of securing the co-operation of scholars and on the lack of financial support. Historiography was particularist or cosmopolitan, not yet national. On the downfall of Napoleon, Germans began to realise more fully the value of their possessions. In 1814 Savigny informed Jakob Grimm of the plan of a society for the study of German history and an edition of its sources.[1] 'You and your brother,' he added, 'would make ideal secretaries; think about it and win others for the project.' The scheme, for which he hoped to receive official assistance, included the foundation of historical societies in each state co-

---

[1] See Steig, *Goethe u. die Brüder Grimm*, chap. 10, 1892.

operating in common tasks. The plan embraced Austria, Switzerland and the Netherlands, and included not only the sources of history but of literature, language and art before the Reformation. The magnificent ideal quickly broke down by its own weight. Its successor was to be more modest and more successful.

When the war was over Stein withdrew almost completely from public life.[1] He had always been interested in history, and he now employed his leisure in its systematic study. He realised the need of a critical edition of the sources, and he felt that such a work would serve the purpose of patriotism no less than of scholarship. 'Since my retirement,' he wrote in 1816, 'I have wished to quicken the taste for German history and facilitate its study, and thereby to contribute to the preservation of the love of the common fatherland and of our great ancestors.' Eichhorn, whom he asked to interest the scholars of Berlin, entered warmly into the scheme, and a plan was drawn up and forwarded to Hardenberg; but neither the King nor the minister gave the project any encouragement. In 1818 Stein brought his project before the representatives of the Confederation at Frankfurt, but here again he met with disappointment. There was still but little interest in German history, while Metternich and his disciples suspected liberalism and revolution to be lurking behind any undertaking of a 'national' character. Determined to wait no longer, he provided a large sum of money and persuaded several of his Westphalian friends to do the same. Early in 1819 the Society for the Study of Early German History was founded at Frankfurt, and a journal began to appear, containing preliminary discussions and communications. One scheme after another was put forward, and the vast extent of the undertaking and the necessity of consulting the archives of many countries became ever more apparent. The title, *Monumenta Germaniæ Historica*, was selected by Stein; and the famous motto *Sanctus amor patriæ dat animum*, was adopted as expressing the spirit in which the work was conceived.

The first volume of the 'Archiv' contained a long list of volunteers and patrons, including such eminent names as Eichhorn, Schlosser, Wilken, Dahlmann, Raumer, Heeren, Niebuhr, Humboldt, Jakob Grimm and Goethe. But the competent scholars to whom Stein could look for assistance were few. The

---

[1] The full story of Stein's relations with the *Monumenta* must be read in Pertz's vast biography, vols. v. and vi. Neither Seeley, Max Lehmann nor Gerhard Ritter devotes much attention to it. The introduction to Wattenbach's *Geschichtsquellen im Mittelalter*, Dümmler's article, 'Über die Entstehung der Monumenta Germaniae,' *Im Neuen Reich*, 1876, and Bresslau, *Geschichte der Monumenta Germaniae*, 1921, are useful.

romanticists had paid little attention to history, and of the historians in active service some declared they were too busy, while the assistance of others was not worth having. Stein gave attention to the minutest particulars both of the business and the literary sides of the enterprise, but he was only an amateur. It was while he was almost overwhelmed with the difficulties of his gigantic enterprise that timely aid arrived. Pertz [1] at this time was archivist at Hanover. He had written a book on the Merovingian Mayors of the Palace, to which his old master Heeren had contributed a flattering preface. Stein was greatly impressed by it, and was delighted when he expressed his willingness to edit the Carolingian sources. In 1820 he invited the young author to go to Vienna to search for manuscripts. Pertz accepted the commission with alacrity, and on his way he visited his patron at Nassau. The veteran statesman and the young scholar were strongly attracted to each other, and the partnership to which history owes such an incalculable debt was formed. When Dümge, the first editor, was induced to retire in 1822, Pertz was at once appointed. 'He is an excellent young man,' wrote Stein to Niebuhr; 'the whole work must be entrusted to his hands, and the selection of colleagues must be left to him.'

Before the enterprise was out of danger many difficulties had still to be overcome. Dahlmann withdrew on account of the Carlsbad decrees, declaring that such a work could not be carried on in an atmosphere of suspicion and repression. Stein was greatly annoyed, and spoke bitterly of 'those irritable and unreasonable beings, the scholars.' His chief wrath, however, was reserved for the rulers who stubbornly refused their help. 'Governments,' he wrote, 'send costly expeditions to Egypt and Brazil. The history of the Pharaohs, the life of gazelles and monkeys is studied, but nothing is done for the history of our people.' The Emperor of Austria, Gentz told Pertz, disapproved of all societies, even historical societies, as he did not know to what use German history might be put. These difficulties, however, were surmounted, and in 1824 the definitive plan of the work was published. It was to consist of five parts—Writers, Laws, Imperial Acts, Letters and Antiquities, of which only the first two were taken in hand. The work would properly have begun with the Goths, the Franks and the Lombards, but for this period it was essential to consult manuscripts in many libraries. To wait till the earliest sources were ready for publication would be to defer the commencement of the

[1] See Pertz's *Autobiography and Letters*, 1895; Waitz's articles, ' Die Zukunft der Monumenta Germaniae,' *Historische Zeitschrift*, vol. xxx., and 'Pertz u. die Monumenta Germaniae,' in *Neues Archiv*, vol. ii.

undertaking for years. Pertz, therefore, determined to start with the Carolingians. Stein had often told his friends that he would not live to see the appearance of any part of his great undertaking, and when the editor was at last able to send him the first volume in 1826, his delight was unbounded. He who was usually so reserved in the expression of his feelings declared his 'unspeakable joy.' He chivalrously added, 'Yours is the greatest part of the merit; my part was only to have helped.'

Pertz brought to his task unquenchable enthusiasm, a wide knowledge of the printed sources of mediæval history, and a thorough competence in the handling of manuscripts. His colleague and successor Waitz declared that his transcripts and collations were among the best ever made, better than of most who later set themselves up as censors. The volume marks an epoch in historical study. It was the first time that German texts had been edited on the same critical principles as the works of classical writers. Of course it was not perfect. Some manuscripts were credited with too much, others with too little authority. The criticism was rather textual than historical, but it was a not unworthy beginning of the greatest co-operative historical work of the century. The second volume appeared in 1829, and in 1835 the first volume of the Laws was issued. When Pertz resigned the editorship after half a century, he could look round on twenty-five stately folios, containing the Scriptores from the Carolingians to the Interregnum and an almost complete collection of the Leges, in nearly every one of which his own work was to be found. Only those who know the miserable condition in which the national annals then stood, imperfectly and incompletely printed in different books, can realise the immense advance made when all the sources were collected and critically arranged. Though his edition of the laws and capitularies was radically imperfect, his life-work rendered the critical study of mediæval history possible. The greatest compliment to Pertz was when Ranke remarked, 'Without your great work I could never have attracted a circle of young men to these studies.'

The great statesman to whose initiative the work was due, and without whose energetic support it would never have been accomplished, passed away in 1831. He followed the revival of historical study with lively satisfaction, greeted Raumer's 'Hohenstaufen' and Stenzel's 'Franconian Emperors' as works of scholarly patriotism, and foretold Ranke's supremacy. Böhmer was not indulging in flattery when he declared that Stein knew history better than most of the professors. Many years later Pertz was to discharge his debt of gratitude to his beloved patron in the portentous biography which it is equally difficult to read and to neglect. After his death the whole burden rested on the shoulders of the editor. The progress of the work was only rendered possible by the generosity of Böhmer and other individuals. Some contributors worked badly, others failed to fulfil their promises. But Lappenberg was a tower of strength, while such brilliant recruits from Ranke's *Seminar* as Waitz and Köpke lent their aid. As the years passed Pertz became increasingly dictatorial, and conflicts with his colleagues were not uncommon. One of the most brilliant of them, Jaffè, quarrelled violently with his chief. Stenzel found the rein too tight and withdrew his co-operation. But the fault was not wholly on one side. Waitz testified after his death that they had worked harmoniously, and in a memorial address Ranke declared that he had always refrained from joining in the general cry which forgot his virtues in his failings.

The most helpful among Pertz's friends in the critical days was Böhmer,[1] who in his early life had drunk in the enchantments of Frankfurt. The instinctive love of his city and the traditions to which it bore witness was intensified by seeing the French invader in the streets. 'Old Frankfurt,' he wrote later, 'was my first love. In my school days I used to wander about and look at the ancient buildings. In Napoleon and his followers I saw incarnate devilry.' Studying jurisprudence at Göttingen he came to entertain a profound dislike for Roman law, and maintained that the German people had been spoiled by the Roman jurists. His reverence for the Middle Ages was increased by the writings of Johannes Müller, whom he described as the greatest German historian. Like Goethe he was among the earliest admirers of the Boisserée collection. In 1818, at the age of twenty-three, he set out for Italy, visiting Freiburg and Strassburg on the way. 'No one,' he wrote, 'will ever convince me that the Middle Ages, which created such works, were a time of barbarism.' In later life he used to say that none could realise how hard it had been to convince people of the beauty of early German architecture and painting. He became the friend of Grimm, Hagen, Uhland and other Germanists, and through Brentano entered the circle of Catholics who were working for the revival of religious life. Though nominally a Protestant, his historical and æsthetic sympathies were wholly Catholic.

[1] Janssen wrote his life and collected his correspondence in 1868. The biography fills the first volume. Ranke's address is in his *Abhandlungen u. Versuche, Neue Sammlung*, 535–44, 1888, Döllinger's in *Akademische Vorträge*, vol. ii., 1889.

Böhmer declared that he was not driven to history by curiosity, ambition or dilettantism. 'It was love of the Fatherland, the conviction that the knowledge of the past could be instructive for the present, the hope that the true might lead to the good.' In his memorial address Döllinger pronounced him the purest patriot, the most German soul he ever knew. 'His whole being was in the thought of the German fatherland, in work for its honour and prosperity.' He had begun to study mediæval sources when his course was determined by a meeting with Stein in 1823. 'To him it is wholly due that I have assisted patriotic studies.' He aided Pertz with his plans, became secretary and treasurer of the Society, and undertook numerous journeys in search of material. His ideal was Mabillon, a man equally learned and pious, the author not of pretentious narratives but of collections from which a true knowledge of the Middle Ages could be constructed. 'For people and fatherland,' he wrote in 1829, 'that is the motto of my life.' In this spirit of national piety he undertook the Imperial Acts. 'Written by those who knew the truth, their credibility is scarcely ever in doubt.' They reflect every variety of political and legal relationship, and their rays illumine periods where the chronicles fail. He published the first volume of the 'Regesta' in 1831, and it was a keen regret that Stein, 'my fatherly friend, perhaps the last great German of the old time,' had not lived to see it. It received a warm welcome, Grimm hailing it as one of the most important works of German historical literature. The Emperors came to life when their movements could be followed and the documents issued from the Imperial Chancery could be studied in connection with the place and circumstances of their composition.

Arnim had compared the early world to a city sunk below the waves, its foundations remaining, its old streets and squares still visible, from which many a valuable treasure could be rescued. Intent on salvage, Böhmer determined to produce cheap and handy collections of important, rare or new material, with a characterisation of each piece. A far more living picture, he declared, could be formed from these originals than from all modern works put together. The first volume of the 'Fontes Rerum Germanicarum,' appearing in 1843, was mainly devoted to Ludwig of Bavaria, the second to the thirteenth century, a third to the twelfth. They were sent forth in the hope that they might be used by teachers in schools and stimulate the historical consciousness of Germany. 'To know what has been and is no more, to see how much of what is rooted in the past still stands—that seems to me the beginning and condition of all higher culture. It is of special importance for a people which wants to raise itself, not by continuing the last few centuries of decadence, but by linking itself on to the earlier times of power and greatness.' He urged that each state and province should form an historical society and was delighted when the Lower Rhine led the way. In 1844 he published the first volume of a revised edition of the 'Regesta,' which was in fact a new work. The documents were far more numerous and the extracts much fuller, while short essays on each ruler were added. Giesebrecht declared that it was his eternal merit to have unlocked the inner heart of the Empire's history, and that his works were as epoch-making as the *Monumenta* itself. Huillard-Bréholles declared that his own vast work on the Emperor Frederick II could not have been compiled had not Böhmer led the way.

Though Böhmer never wrote narrative history, his views were in no way concealed. He was equally convinced that lack of religion was the greatest evil of his time and that Protestantism was unable to reconstruct society on a Christian basis. He yearned for a reunited, visible Church. Brentano said of his friend, 'He is more Catholic than I.' The Reformation, he declared, was the greatest misfortune of the German nation, and he never forgave it for subjecting the Church to the State. The Church was the noblest and most magnificent product of history. In the conflict of Empire and Papacy he was on the side of the latter. 'I cannot bear the contemptuous judgments of venerable institutions, the belittling of the Church and its blessed activity.' He left money for historical work to be carried on 'in a Roman Catholic sense.' In his last illness, he declared, 'I have always regarded the Church as the Mother to whom we owe the best that we possess. May it regain its lost power over men's minds.' He was a child of the Middle Ages born out of due time, an orphan in a strange world. 'What an error,' declared Ranke, speaking both as a Christian and an historian, 'what an error to think that one period has been especially favoured by God!' Böhmer was one of the most original personalities among nineteenth century historians. His judgments of men and institutions were biassed, his technique was radically imperfect, and the 'Regesta' had to be edited afresh by a team of specialists; but he ranks with Stein and Pertz among the heroes of the *Monumenta*. He was not exaggerating the significance of his work when he wrote, 'The furrows I have ploughed and the seed I have sown will not be blown away by the first wind.'

II

If the *Monumenta* was the chief product of the new spirit of nationalism,[1] its effect was also seen in the narratives of the centuries when the German Empire was the leading power in Europe. The most learned work of this class was Wilken's 'History of the Crusades.' A pupil of the elder Eichhorn, Wilken[2] developed a keen appetite for Oriental history and literature, and became Professor at Heidelberg in 1805. A friend of Johannes Müller, Arnim, Brentano and other members of the Romantic circle, he approached his subject with genuine sympathy. Though the first volume sometimes failed to distinguish saga from history and was superseded by Sybel, the later volumes were far more critical and retained their value for two generations. The work rested on a thorough knowledge of Oriental sources, and presented the first full and authoritative picture of an eventful chapter in European history. Warmly welcomed by his contemporaries, it was praised by such competent judges of a later generation as Giesebrecht and Kugler. A still higher compliment was paid it in 1880 when Röhricht declared that there was only one opinion of the work in the learned world and that a third of the book was still unsurpassed.

No writer took a more active part in fostering the new-born interest in national history than Luden,[3] whom Johannes Müller called his adoptive son. In 1808, a year after Fichte had delivered his 'Addresses to the German Nation,' he lectured at Jena on the study of German history. 'Not only was the auditorium filled,' he declared, 'but the anteroom, the staircase and the court. I wish that we Germans would study like children the life of our beloved parents, dominated by the holy thought of the Fatherland. In these days what could quicken and comfort us more than the return to the happier times of old, when the tree that is now broken stood proudly erect? What could strengthen us to virtue and action more than the example of our fathers?' The very spirit of nascent German nationalism breathes in these glowing words. If the present was dark, the past shone with a steady radiance. 'It is the happiness of German history that the Germans never sank to the level which is the shame of other peoples, but always strove with powerful determination for what

[1] The Heeren and Ukert series of histories was undertaken by Perthes, the publisher, in a similar spirit. *Perthes' Leben*, vol. iii., 25–41.

[2] See Stoll, *Friedrich Wilken*, 1896.

[3] See his *Rückblicke in mein Leben*, 1847, and Herrmann, *Die Geschichtsauffassung Ludens*, 1904.

they held to be the true worth of mankind. Their character has never changed.'

Luden's 'History of the German People' was published in twelve volumes between 1825 and 1837. 'The time of indifference to German history,' declares the preface, 'is past. A generation ago the Middle Ages seemed to be a starless night, faintly lit by a pale northern light. The few who dared to enter this gloomy world and tell others what they saw got thanks only from a few friends. Their books were often named but seldom read. But then the awful time of misfortune broke the bonds of indifference and prejudice. The need of self-respect sent us back to our fathers. We learned hope from our own earlier triumphs. Now the first enthusiasm is gone, the magic is past, the first need is satisfied. But the delight in what we found has strengthened the desire for further search. Anyone who feels a taste for history should study above all the history of his fatherland. It is not a duty but an instinct of the human heart.' His admiration for German character is as ardent as ever. A history of the Middle Ages should start from the Germans and return to them. 'Of the new peoples they stood highest both in power and in culture.' The main purpose of the book was political and ethical. 'I hope my book will strengthen the patriotic sense.' His ambition was realised, but no works are more quickly superseded than patriotic histories. After visiting him Dahlmann wrote to a friend, 'He will never go any further.' He was right. Luden remained throughout life the ardent patriot of the era of Liberation.

Among Luden's pupils was Voigt,[1] who declared that his admiration for the Middle Ages was aroused by the Jena Professor. His work on Hildebrand was suggested by his master, 'to whom I owe everything that I am.' The Pope was portrayed as a great reformer, worthy of the reverence of all good men. The book, which was bitterly attacked in certain Protestant circles, contributed to the growing tendency to regard the Middle Ages with insight and sympathy. Voigt's future studies were determined by his removal to Königsberg, where he found the archives of early Prussia and the Teutonic Order. His History of Prussia to 1527 appeared in nine volumes, dedicated 'To the Fatherland.' It was an elevating task, he declared, to watch the heroism and sacrifices of their fathers in defence of their land. The hero of the book is Hermann von Salza. 'The supreme prize in research is when the spirit is raised to reverence and the heart is filled with enthusiasm at the sight of great and good men.' Voigt first narrated the early

[1] See Lohmeyer's article in *Allg. Deutsche Biog.*, and Döllinger's *Akademische Vorträge*, vol. ii.

history of Prussia from the documents, but he confined himself to the archives of the Order. He glorified the knights and despised their foes. He resented the charge of partisanship, but the whole performance is a typical product of the romantic age. Superior in learning to his master, he belongs equally to the pre-critical era.

Of the historians in whose pages the heroic figures of Germany became familiar by far the most popular was Raumer.[1] The dominant influence in his early studies, as in those of most of his generation, was Johannes Müller, of whom he speaks with warm gratitude in his Memoirs. As a young man he chose the Hohenstaufen for his theme, and undertook a prolonged visit to the libraries of Italy in pursuit of material. When asked at the Vatican whether he was 'of our religion,' he adroitly replied that he was studying the Hohenstaufen and was of the religion of that time. He obtained permission to examine manuscripts, and used a number of Papal letters of the highest value. The book appeared in 1823–5, and was eagerly read. It was the first luminous and comprehensive treatment of a great epoch in German history. Sismondi had recently described the struggle of the Lombard cities and Barbarossa from the standpoint of the former, and in his pages the Hohenstaufen were tyrants. Raumer, on the other hand, recognised that both parties were fighting for a great principle. Of the two great rulers who dominate the drama the picture of Barbarossa was the least successful, but the brilliant personality of Frederick II, *Stupor Mundi*, was revealed to the world in his pages. The stage is European and more than European. Several dramas are in progress at the same time—the struggle of East and West, of Empire and Papacy, of Imperialism and the Italian cities, of orthodoxy and heresy. Raumer fully understood that events are only the skeleton of history. Sketches of life and thought, of the Albigenses and the Mendicant Orders, are scattered through the narrative, while the two concluding volumes are entirely devoted to culture. This was the most novel part of the whole work, dealing with the classes and the towns, law and economics, science and art. His survey of the organisation of the state, crown ⁕rights, personal and legal relations, was warmly praised by Ranke. The sixth volume, almost wholly devoted to the Church, was a notable achievement for a Protestant historian.

[1] See his *Lebenserinnerungen*, 1861; Ranke, *Abhandlungen u. Versuche, Neue Sammlung*, 578–81, 1888; and Reumont, *Friedrich Wilhelm IV.* chap. 3, 1885. Schack declared that his name was as immortal as Barbarossa and Manfred, *Ein halbes Jahrhundert*, vol. i. 208, 1888.

A grave fault prevented the 'Hohenstaufen,' despite its shining merits, from entering the class of histories which survive their authors: it was written before the science of criticism was created. Raumer had conscientiously explored the printed and some of the manuscript sources of his period, but he lacked the equipment necessary for their valuation. Stenzel rather unkindly spoke of it as 'a remarkable success for a man without any proper training.' He was never attracted by the methods of Wolf and Niebuhr, and the Middle Ages were still refracted through the lens of the romantic movement. Though new editions succeeded one another during the author's life and one appeared after his death, the authority of the work steadily diminished. Yet it did more than any other book of the time to arouse interest in the Middle Ages, and was the parent of dramas and novels through which a knowledge of the heroic period of German history filtered down among the people.

The highest level of merit among those who devoted themselves to national history before the appearance of Ranke was reached by Stenzel.[1] The dominant influence of his early life was that of Johannes Müller.[2] He was severely wounded in the War of Liberation, and was among the first to promise support to Stein's project of the *Monumenta*. 'In 1810, when I began to teach, the idea seized me of writing the history of Germany from Charles the Great to Rudolf of Hapsburg. I wanted to tell my fellow-countrymen how bold and free their fathers were and how they maintained their independence.' He started in the middle, choosing a period in which the sources were numerous and stopping where Raumer had begun. His 'Franconian Emperors,' 1024–1125, was based on the first really critical examination of mediæval sources. Giesebrecht later declared that no one had studied the period more profoundly or more impartially, adding that his book inaugurated the critical study of the Middle Ages. 'In many of the most famous works of the day,' wrote Stenzel, 'all sources are accepted which make history attractive. I defy anyone to show me a statement in my book which I cannot substantiate from the best authorities.' He emancipated himself from the romantic idealisation of the Middle Ages. The core of the work is the reign of Henry IV, whom he depicts as one of the greatest and best of German rulers. Unlike his friend Voigt, he contends that Hildebrand's desire to reform the Church was increasingly overlaid by the mad ambition to rule the world. The detailed narrative of the struggle ranks with Raumer's picture of Frederick II

---

[1] See the excellent life by his son, K. G. Stenzel, 1897.
[2] See Henking, *Johannes Müller*, 2 vols., 1909, 1928.

in interest and surpasses it in critical value. 'I have worked at my book for seventeen years—the last eight of which were exclusively devoted to the sources of a hundred years. How much time a critical edition would have saved me, and how much have I missed for lack of it!' Though the work as a whole was superseded a generation later by the masterpiece of Giesebrecht, it takes its place among the books to which historical science owed its origin.

CHAPTER VI

RANKE

I

WHILE the school of romantic nationalism was still in the ascendant, a new spirit was introduced into the theory and practice of history.[1] Born in 1795, Ranke may have heard the thunder of the guns at Auerstädt and he saw the flying Germans, closely followed by the victorious French, pass through his native village. At school the boys copied Napoleon's bulletins on their slates. But the future historian was more interested in the past than the present. A native of Thuringian Saxony he was surrounded by historical memories. Memleben spoke of Henry the Fowler and Otto the Great, the Kyffhäuser of Barbarossa. At Schulpforta he laid the foundation of the exact knowledge of classical literature from which he derived unceasing satisfaction throughout life. He already possessed the serenity which was to be an element in his fame. 'Our father,' wrote Heinrich, 'at first feared Leopold would

---

[1] For the vast literature on Ranke see Helmolt, *Ranke-Bibliographie*, 1910. Correspondence and memoranda were published by Dove in 1890 as *Zur eigenen Lebensgeschichte*. *Das Briefwerk* and *Neue Briefe* appeared in 1919. Much of biographical interest is to be found in Heinrich Ranke's *Jugenderinnerungen*, 1877; Hitzig's *Ernst Ranke*, 1906; his son's recollections in *Deutsche Revue*, January–February, 1903; and forty letters in *Deutsche Revue*, 1904–6. The best of the larger monographs is Guglia, *Ranke's Leben u. Werke*, 1893. Lorenz, *L. v. Ranke*, 1891, is too theoretical. The biography and essays in Dove's *Ausgewählte Schriftchen*, 1898, are of the highest value. Nalbandian, *Ranke's Bildungsjahre u. Geschichtsauffassung*, 1902, and T. H. Von Laue, *Leopold Ranke, The Formative Years*, 1950, are useful. The appreciations by Sybel, *Vorträge u. Abhandlungen*, 1897, Giesebrecht, 1887, and Moriz Ritter, 1896, are important. Reumont's article, *Historisches Jahrbuch der Görres-Gesellschaft*, 1886, contains their correspondence. Among foreign estimates may be mentioned those of Reuss, in *Revue Historique*, vol. xxxi., Guilland, in *L'Allemagne Nouvelle et ses Historiens*, 1899, and Gooch, 'Ranke's Interpretation of German History' in *Studies in German History*, 1948. Winckler's *L. v. Ranke, Lichtstrahlen aus seinen Werken*, 1885, classifies his more notable utterances. The German Academy's edition of his writings was interrupted by the Second World War after the publication of *Germany in the Reformation Era* and the *History of Prussia*. The latest appreciation, and one of the best, is by Srbik, *Geist und Geschichte vom deutschen Humanismus bis zur Gegenwart*, vol. i., 1950.

be affected by the Greek tragedies; but he regarded them purely as works of art, which he appreciated without allowing them to excite his feelings.' At Leipsic he studied theology and classical philology, the few historical lectures that he attended repelling him by their lack of grasp and reflection. He learned to read the Old Testament in Hebrew, but cared little for dogmatic studies. He enjoyed Gottfried Hermann on the Greek poets, but devoted most of his attention to the ancient historians, above all Thucydides. Niebuhr, he afterwards declared, convinced him that historians could exist in the modern world. He read Kant with interest and Fichte with admiration. When Stenzel asked the young student if he intended to devote himself to history, he replied in the negative. The seven years spent as teacher in the Gymnasium at Frankfurt on the Oder were more decisive than school or university, for it was there that he turned from philology to history. He never regretted his long apprenticeship, and maintained that it was impossible to familiarise young men too much with classical antiquity.

Ranke was turned to history not by current events, like Niebuhr and the patriotic school, but by his professional duties. He loved to lecture on Livy and Herodotus, read Niebuhr again with increased admiration, and welcomed Böckh's realistic picture of the Athenian State. He gradually extended his vision beyond the ancient world to the *Völkerwanderung* and the Middle Ages, composing fragments on the Carolingian era from the Chronicles. The first indication of a book dates from 1820, when he wrote that he wished to learn something of the life of the nations in the fifteenth century, of the new sprouting of the seeds sown by antiquity. In reading Guicciardini and Paolo Giovio he found their differences too great to be reconciled, and resolved to clear up the difficulty by studying the other main authorities of the period. This done he determined to write his own account of the time. Thus the 'Histories of the Romance and Teutonic Peoples' was written rather for the author's satisfaction than for the public. In rebutting the charge of slender philosophic and religious interest he declared that it was precisely that which had drawn him to history. His letters to his brother Heinrich repeatedly expressed the hope to reach nearer to God. 'Every action testifies to Him, every moment, above all the connection of history.' The service of history was a holy work, purifying the soul. 'We remove the shell of things and reach the essence.' This kernel was human personality, revealed in action, suffering, effort. He was particularly attracted by the human side of history. 'It is so sweet to revel in the wealth of all the centuries, to meet all the heroes face to face, to live through everything again.' His début revealed both his interest in personality and the religious complexion of his mind. He had often declared the deciding factor in history to be men of action, and the titles of his chapters emphasise his sense of their importance. We hear less of the peoples than of their princes, less of conditions than of actions. The Introductory Essay endeavoured to establish the unity of the Romance and Germanic peoples dating from the *Völkerwanderung*, expressing itself in the Crusades and in the common institutions and ideals of Latin Christianity. Thus a single process of development might be traced. Regarding history as an object lesson in ethics and religion, he depicts the shameless moral corruption of Italy as sealing her doom.

Though a thin film of theology floated on the surface, the main body of the work was unaffected. In one of the precious fragments dictated in old age Ranke declared that his discovery of the difference in the portraits of Louis XI and Charles the Bold in 'Quentin Durward' and in Commines constituted an epoch in his life. 'I found by comparison that the truth was more interesting and beautiful than the romance. I turned away from it and resolved to avoid all invention and imagination in my works and to stick to facts.' The preface announced, in words which have become classical, the spirit in which the book was written. 'History has had assigned to it the task of judging the past, of instructing the present for the benefit of the ages to come. To such lofty functions this work does not aspire. Its aim is merely to show how things actually were.'[1] The great figures of an age rich in commanding personalities are soberly portrayed, the peoples surveyed without bias. His passionless tone is not the result of indifference. When judgment is pronounced, it is the more weighty from its rarity. Of the death of Alexander VI he writes: 'A limit is set to human crime. He died and became the abomination of the centuries.' He accepts every manifestation of life—the gay court of Charles VIII, the fanaticism of Spain, the majesty of the Venetian aristocracy. The book constituted a distinct advance in the objective treatment of European history, and will always retain its interest as the earliest work of the greatest of modern historians, but its merits are a little below its reputation. As its title indicates, it is a collection of histories rather than a history. His intention had been to extend his survey to 1545, but he became increasingly conscious of the limitations of his only book resting exclusively on printed authorities, and never continued it. It thus remains a fragment—a convenient summary of the main

[1] 'Er will bloss zeigen wie es eigentlich gewesen.'

external facts of twenty years of European history, which adds nothing to the knowledge and little to the interpretation of the age. Half a century later he was only persuaded with difficulty to include it in his collected works.

If the beginning of the critical era of historiography is commonly held to date from the publication of Ranke's first work in 1824, it is owing rather to the elaborate appendix than to the narrative. In this famous discussion of his authorities he first applied to modern history the principles of Niebuhr. There was nothing new in his maxims that the nearest witness to the event was the best, and that the letters of the actors were of more value than the anecdotes of the chronicler. The novelty of his method lay in his determination to seize the personality of the writer and to inquire whence he derived his information. 'Some will copy the ancients, some will seek instruction for the future, some will attack or defend, some will only wish to record facts. Each must be separately studied.' Applying this method he reached some startling results. Guicciardini he pronounced wholly unworthy of his fame. Much of his material was copied from other books, much was false, much was doubtful, speeches were invented, treaties altered, important facts misrepresented. Ranke admires his fine political instinct, his universal outlook, his freedom from ecclesiastical bias, but he goes too far in denying him nearly all the virtues of an historian. Next in interest was the discussion of Machiavelli, whose 'Prince' was a tract for the times, prescribing poison only because they were out of joint. The analysis of the life and the temper of the two great Florentines inaugurated the serious study of their historical writings, and the dissection of the lesser authorities enabled future historians for the first time to use them intelligently. He never wearied of expressing his debt to Niebuhr, whose bust occupied the place of honour in his study, but he declared in old age that in his critical disquisitions he had not thought of Niebuhr or of anybody else. 'My practice arose by a sort of necessity, in its own way.'

The reception of the work of the unknown Frankfurt teacher was highly favourable. The only hostile criticism came from Leo, who disparaged its learning, its philosophy and its style. Ranke was fully conscious of its imperfections, and the Preface hinted that it might seem hard, disjointed and colourless. Yet its merits were obvious, and were rewarded by a call to Berlin.[1] 'It is as if the door to my true life at last opens, as if I can at last spread my wings,' he wrote. But though the University was at its zenith,

[1] See the correspondence in Lenz, *Geschichte der Universität zu Berlin*, vol. iv., 457–76, 1910.

there was no great scholar to vindicate the claims of modern history. Hegel, then at the summit of his fame, had as little use for Ranke as Ranke for Hegel.[1] He was only Professor Extraordinarius, and his lectures were delivered to small audiences. Yet the friendship of Savigny and the salon of Rahel and Varnhagen opened a new world. The mystic Schubert[2] has drawn a charming picture of the young Professor, merry, alert, sunny, a delightful companion. The historian later attributed the increased polish of his writings in part to his acquaintance with the intellectual women of Berlin, but his greatest joy was in the archives. Among their treasures were forty-seven volumes of the relations of Venetian ambassadors in the sixteenth and seventeenth centuries, which pointed the way to more serious studies than had gone to the making of his first book. His acquaintance with the Venetian reports constituted an epoch in his life, for they revealed in a flash that the history of modern Europe must be rewritten in the light of fresh and contemporary material. They opened a spring of inexhaustible fertility with which he could resuscitate the scenes and actors of three centuries. Finally they confirmed his habit of writing history with the detachment of an onlooker, and he caught from the experienced diplomatists of the Republic something of their reserve and their fine shades of judgment.

With the aid of the Venetian reports he quickly constructed his 'Ottomans and the Spanish Monarchy of the Sixteenth and Seventeenth Centuries,' designed as the first of a series of works bearing the general title of 'Princes and Peoples of Southern Europe.' Like its predecessor the new work contained a picture gallery of rulers and statesmen, but he now undertook a study of conditions as the background of events. Though less than one hundred pages are devoted to Turkey, the Ottoman system, military and civil, stands out in bold relief. The constitution, trade, finance and administration of the Spanish Empire in the Old and New World are described in greater detail. Yet the recognition of conditions does not diminish his sense of the importance of personality. In Turkey he shows how everything depended on the Sultans, and carefully portrays their characters. In Spain he pronounces the princes the mainspring of the vast machine, and traces the decay of the seventeenth century in large measure to the degeneracy of the dynasty. It is one of the merits of the book to have offered the first intelligible picture of Philip II. The study of Don John of Austria revealed a new lightness of touch. Bettina, Goethe's 'Kind,' described the work as *wunderschön*. If that was

---

[1] See E. Simon, *Ranke und Hegel*, 1928.
[2] *Selbstbiographie*, vol. iii., 603–5, 1856.

only the language of friendship, the book was none the less an advance on his own earlier achievement and on that of contemporary historians of modern Europe.

As the 'Romance and Teutonic Peoples' brought the call to Berlin, the 'Princes and Peoples' procured the inestimable privilege of subsidised travel. Starting in 1827 Ranke did not return for nearly four years. 'The object of my scientific journey,' he wrote, 'is to discover and use unknown sources for the history of modern States, especially those of Southern Europe.' His immediate object was to obtain material for an Italian volume of the 'Princes and Peoples.' But before reaching Italy he was to be drawn aside for a time into a new and almost unknown world. During his year's residence at Vienna he made the acquaintance of the scholars who were endeavouring to further Slavonic culture, among them Kopitar, the archivist, and his friend Wuk Stephanowich, who, after taking part in the revolution, had left Servia when the Turkish power was restored. Wuk's collection of Serb folk-songs had attracted the notice of Jakob Grimm, who translated a selection, and of Goethe, who devoted an essay to them. Ranke entered eagerly into the problems and aspirations of the Slavonic world, and the 'History of the Revolutions in Servia' was written in Vienna. In the preface to the third edition, published in 1879, he declared that the work was based on an outline by Wuk, which was confirmed by personal examination of the witnesses whom Wuk had consulted. A detailed study of their customs, religion and poetry explained how the Serbs had survived centuries of subjection. The narrative ended with the revolt of Milosh Obrenovich and the beginnings of an ordered polity. In later editions the story was brought down to date and enriched by wider study. Ranke was deeply convinced of the incapacity of the Turk to govern Christian peoples, and watched with sympathy their efforts to overthrow his rule. The book broke virgin soil. No Teutonic scholar was in a position to pronounce a critical judgment on the work, but its power was unmistakable. 'This little book,' wrote Niebuhr to Perthes, its publisher, 'is the best contemporary history we possess. Ranke has shed everything which offended in his earlier manner.' Goethe, to whom the author sent a copy, was not less pleased, and expressed a wish to know more of him. Though not one of his most celebrated works, and perhaps a little too rosy in tone, it was a genuine contribution to knowledge and, in its enlarged form, remains an indispensable guide through one of the less known chapters of modern history. It was his only excursion into the field of East European studies.

Ranke's sojourn in Vienna introduced him to another set of

influences which proved of permanent importance in the development of his mind and thought. He had given little attention to
politics before he came to Berlin, and in Rahel's salon he met
Börne and other men and women of radical tendencies. He began
to seek in the French Revolution the key to French politics and
to the conflicting schools of thought throughout Europe. It was
with his interest thoroughly aroused and his views only partially
formed that he made the acquaintance of Gentz, to whom he
brought an introduction from Rahel. That brilliant man, once
the ornament of her salon and the interpreter of Burke, was now
sixty-four. Though not in office he stood at Metternich's right
hand. In repeated conversations with him Ranke learned much
of the secret history of the last generation, but his greatest service
to the historian was to introduce him to Metternich. While rejecting the absolutism favoured by the all-powerful Minister and
his henchman, he left Vienna with an immensely enlarged knowledge of European politics.

Despite the attractions of Servian history and political discussion, the greater part of Ranke's time in Vienna was spent in
the archives. He was delighted at the wealth of treasures from
Venice which had not been restored. An unknown history of
Europe seemed to open out before him. Among the jewels was
Sanuto's diary, which no one had yet seen. He found that the
statutes of the Inquisition copied by Daru from manuscripts in
Paris were forged in the seventeenth century. As the spurious
statutes had left a deep stain on the fame of the Republic, he was
glad to reveal their true character. His researches were continued
in Venice itself, where he began and where he was to end his
Italian journey. His main object in obtaining permission to visit
the Venetian archives was not so much to study the history of the
Republic as to procure material for the series of works on European history which had begun to shape themselves in his mind.
The researches begun at the Frari were continued in the libraries
of Rome and Florence, whence he took home materials which were
to be of use throughout his life. His plan of an Italian volume of
the 'Princes and Peoples' was soon abandoned, as he found that
the Popes were enough for a separate work. The treasures of the
Vatican were closed to him, but he found some compensation in
the liberality of the great families. 'Unless I am misinformed,' he
wrote, 'the value of the Vatican sinks into insignificance compared with the wealth of private collections, above all the Bar-
berini.' He found all and more than all that he had hoped from
his Italian journey. 'I am satisfied and know for what I live; my
breast fills with joyful emotion when I think of the happiness of

constructing an important work. I swear daily to carry it out, without swerving a finger's breadth from the truth as I see it.'

During his residence of over two years in Italy the historian published nothing except a lengthy study of Don Carlos, exploding the scandal which had lain heavy on the memory of Philip II. His 'Venice at the End of the Sixteenth Century,' though it did not appear till 1878, was doubtless written in Italy. He showed that her historical life never corresponded to the conception of the theorists who presented the constitution as a perfect and logical whole, a philosopher's dream. A second essay, published in 1831, proved that the conspiracy of 1616 was the work of mercenaries who planned to seize and plunder the city, not a far-reaching design of Spain as it had appeared in the pages of Daru. A third, on the Venetians in Morea, sketched the administration of part of the oversea Empire. Among other articles conceived or partly written in Italy were those on Savonarola, Filippo Strozzi and Consalvi. The Italian journey holds as prominent a place in the life of Ranke as in that of Goethe. He remarked later that he had never learned or thought more than during those crowded years. He recrossed the Alps with a deeper insight into the political development of modern Europe than any historian had ever possessed.

The first few years after his return were largely claimed by a task which he had not foreseen. The French Revolution of 1830 had given such a powerful impetus to democratic ideas that the Prussian Government became alarmed, and Perthes, a keen poli. ticiaṅ as well as a successful publisher, suggested to the Foreign Minister the foundation of a journal to combat French influences. Count Bernstorff approved. The proposal that Ranke should undertake the work probably emanated from Savigny, who favoured a middle course between rationalism and traditionalism. In this spirit the *Historico-political Review* was launched in 1832.[1] The editor was the chief contributor, but Savigny and other eminent men assisted. It quickly became clear that the ideal of a conservative rival to the activity of Rotteck and to Heine's scintillating letters from Paris to the *Allgemeine Zeitung* would not be fulfilled. But the *Review*, though it exerted but little influence in Prussia and none at all beyond its frontiers, played an important

---

[1] The best accounts of Ranke as a publicist are in Diethe's massive monograph, *Ranke als Politiker*, 1911; Meinecke, *Weltbürgertum u. Nationalstaat*, chap. 12, 1908; and T. H. von Laue, *Leopold Ranke, The Formative Years*, 1950. Varrentrapp's article, ' Ranke's Historisch-politische Zeitschrift,' *Hist. Zeitschrift*, vol. xcix., is a useful summary. Oncken, '*Aus Rankes Frühzeit*, contains correspondence about the Review.

part in the life of the historian. His gospel was that of Savigny and the Restoration. Government was only in very small degree a matter of outward form. Constitutions were no panacea and did not suit every country. The Republican idea had been wafted across the Atlantic during the American War of Independence and had been trumpeted abroad by France. Even worse was the doctrine of the sovereignty of the people, which threatened the stability of every government. Like Niebuhr he believed in maintaining local privileges and institutions, and he preferred estates to parliaments. He was well content with the honest and efficient government of Prussia. His historical contributions to the *Review* were more numerous and more important than those which bore a directly political character, but some of the former were intended to teach political lessons. The famous dissertation on the Great Powers emphasised the individuality of states and the danger from the levelling rationalism of the French Revolution. He proceeded to express his fundamental notions of the development of humanity. History, he declared, was not such chaos as it appeared at first sight. There were creative forces, moral energies at work which gave it value and meaning. States were intellectual entities, creations of the human spirit, thoughts of God. No people could live for itself, and the character of each only developed in contact with the whole. The core of his message was the duty of states to safeguard their individuality by developing along the lines of their historic growth.

The *Review* came to an end in 1836, for its circulation was too small to cover expenses and its influence was nugatory. Ranke was no journalist and had no taste for polemics. His conservatism and unflinching opposition to French ideas lost him his liberal friends. Varnhagen began to copy unfriendly gossip into his diary, and Alexander von Humboldt remarked that he had gone over to the reaction. 'Poor Ranke,' sneered Heine, 'a pretty talent to paint little historical figures and paste them together, a good soul, as good-natured as mutton.' Yet the *Review* was hardly more to the taste of the Gerlachs, Radowitz and other reactionaries who surrounded the Crown Prince. A disciple of Burke, not of Haller, he never ignored the importance of associating the people in some form with the work of government. Though he wrote important memoranda for the guidance of Frederick William IV and was consulted by the scholarly Maximilian of Bavaria, he never again took an active part in political controversy. A last echo of the *Review* may be heard in the Inaugural lecture delivered in 1836, on his appointment as Ordinary Professor, on the relations of History and Politics. Every state possessed its individuality.

The statesman must know his state and its history as a pilot must know not only the course but the vessel. Universal doctrines of government, dear to the eighteenth century, were worthless and dangerous. Armed with this gospel of the individuality of states and the historic unity of the European family, he now resumed his study of the leading Powers in their internal development and in their relation to one another.

II

While occupied with the *Review*, Ranke found time to write a book which won him his place among the great historians of the world. The first volume of the 'History of the Popes' appeared in 1834, the second and third in 1836. His object was to exhibit the Papacy as a factor in the development of Europe, transforming itself like other members of the European system. An objective study, he declared, was no longer difficult. 'What is there in the present day which can render the history of the papal power of importance to us? Not its relation to ourselves, for it no longer exercises any essential influence nor creates in us any apprehension. It can now inspire us with no other interest than what results from the process of its history and its former influence.' This tranquillity of spirit is consistently maintained throughout the work. Profoundly convinced of the inner unity of all the Christian Churches, he looked with tolerance on external differences. He writes with sympathy and admiration of the great figures and movements of the mother Church. His irenic nature reveals itself in his account of the fleeting moments when reconciliation seemed within sight, and he writes with admiration of Contarini and other peacemakers. The Popes of the Counter-Reformation become human and intelligible, and he gladly recognises genuine religious feeling, as in Loyola and the Jesuits. He was not the first Protestant to write sympathetically of the Roman Church. Johannes Müller had eulogised the Church of the Middle Ages as the representative of intellectual liberty against temporal despotism, and the romanticists had expressed enthusiasm for Popes and saints. Ranke treated the Papacy as a great historical phenomenon without regard to the controversies of the day and without romantic enthusiasm. This approach rendered possible the fruitful investigation of some of the most important tracts of European history, and constitutes the first title of the book to immortality.

The 'History of the Popes' is notable not less for its wealth of information than for its objective treatment. That he seized the main outlines of three centuries so clearly that subsequent research has done little more than fill them in was owing not only to the new material which he collected but to the critical treatment of his sources, printed and unprinted. The analyses of Sarpi and Pallavicini are classical examples of his art. In approaching the vast compilation of the great Venetian he declares himself to have been seized with a sort of terror. Difficult enough to master in any case, the reader must be on his guard at every step; for Sarpi's chief authorities were reports which have since disappeared and he saw the Papacy in the light of the quarrel with the Republic. Pallavicini's reply contained many documents from the Vatican, but was rather a polemic than a history.

Armed with a tranquil judgment and a critical knowledge of the sources Ranke entered on his course. The Introduction briefly traces the Papacy through the Middle Ages, emphasising its work as the great unifier of European civilisation. The narrative broadens in the fifteenth century and deals in detail with the foundation of the Papal States as one of the Powers of Italy. The kernel of the book is the Counter-Reformation, of which Ranke was the first authoritative interpreter. The revival of spiritual life, the Catholic re-conquest of Southern Germany, the foundation of the Orders make a brilliant picture. There is something epic in the great struggle when new crusaders, succeeding the sinners and triflers of the Renaissance, rolled back the tide of Protestantism. The title of the work, 'History of the Popes,' not History of the Papacy, emphasises the historian's interest in the concrete realities of human character, but he never forgot to show how the individual is determined by the atmosphere and traditions of his office. 'Of what little importance,' he exclaims, 'is even the strongest mortal in the face of world-history!' Less dramatic but of greater novelty was the analysis of the internal pattern of the Papal States, their administration and finance, the growth and influence of the princely families, their buildings and their patronage of art. No part of the work is more brilliant than that which describes the achievements, at home and abroad, of Sixtus V. In the seventeenth century the Papacy became more and more an Italian State and its influence waned. This part of the work contains the celebrated digression on Christina of Sweden, one of the most highly wrought portraits in his gallery. The survey of the eighteenth century is a mere sketch. In its original form the work ended with the Restoration, but in revising it for the collected works forty years later the author briefly continued his narrative till the fall of the Temporal Power.

The 'History of the Popes' was not only a great achievement

of historical research but a work of art. Ranke had reached the maturity of his powers. Without ever attempting flights of eloquence, his luminous and measured style produces its effect. From time to time he interrupts the narrative to utter a grave reflection on the significance of the scenes he describes. It was while engaged on the 'Popes' that he wrote, 'No history can be written but universal history. I am enchanted by the loftiness and logic of the development and, if I may say so, by the ways of God.' The work for the first time revealed his resources of research and judgment, narrative and portraiture. It combined spaciousness with a mastery of detail, a faculty of generalisation with minute accuracy. It was quickly translated and became one of the indispensable books of historical literature. Höfler and Theiner took up arms for the Roman Church, but Döllinger and other Catholics expressed their admiration of its tone and learning. In the Protestant world criticism was to come later from the school which desired to use history as a bludgeon. Gustav Freytag, lamenting the dispassionate treatment of the foes of Protestantism, pronounced it to lack the last touch of historic truth.

The charge of indifference to Protestantism was to be victoriously rebutted in the work which followed. In the preface to his 'German History in the Reformation Era' he declared that public life in the fifteenth and sixteenth centuries rested on the Imperial Diet, which had never been properly investigated.[1] 'I desired to study the development of the constitution, and in 1836 I found what I sought.' Ninety-six volumes, extending from 1414 to 1613 and containing the reports of the Frankfurt deputies, provided the key. He told Savigny that he felt an obligation to place the history of the origins of Protestantism beside his picture of Catholicism. He supplemented his researches at Frankfurt by discoveries at Weimar, Dresden and Dessau, while at Brussels he found a mass of correspondence of Charles V. At Paris he consulted part of the Simancas archives which had not been returned. He also utilised a good deal of the material which he had brought from Italy. 'Anyone,' he wrote, 'who has a natural tendency to impartiality must feel himself assisted by this juxtaposition of opposites to give each his rights.' To a far greater degree than his previous works the 'Reformation Era' was based on manuscript materials. 'I see a time coming when we shall build modern

---

[1] The book should be read in the Academy edition which contains a valuable Introduction and a lengthy unpublished early sketch of Luther. See also Gustav Wolf, *Quellenkunde der Deutschen Reformationsgeschichte*, and Schnabel, *Deutschlands Geschichtliche Quellen und Darstellungen in der Neuzeit*, vol. i., 1931.

history no longer on the accounts even of contemporary historians, except where they possessed original knowledge, much less on derivative writers, but on the relations of eye-witnesses and the original documents.'

Five volumes appeared in rapid succession between 1839 and 1843, a volume of extracts from authorities following in 1847. A foundation was laid by a detailed investigation of the Imperial Constitution and the attempts to reform it. If on reaching the Reformation he devotes far more attention to political than to theological problems, it was in no sense because he underestimates its religious aspect. 'History is religion,' he wrote, 'or at any rate there is the closest connection between them. As there is no human activity of intellectual importance which does not originate in some relation to God and divine things, so there is no nation whose political life is not continually raised and guided by religious ideas.' From the thirteenth century the Church had been decaying; the yoke of dogma was becoming too heavy to bear, worship was growing paganised. 'I do not know if any reasonable man can seriously wish this system to have lasted unchanged.' The kernel of the Reformation was the return to the Christian revelation, and the personality of Luther was the deciding factor. Seldom does Ranke speak so warmly of any human being. His deed, he declares, was the result of a purely spiritual struggle. Far from being a reckless innovator, he was one of the greatest conservatives that ever lived; but he had the strength to hold on to the ground he had won, unlike Melanchthon, who was too ready to compromise. Though he once more writes with sympathy of the Ratisbon discussions, he does not really regret the failure of reunion. To those who lamented the breach in the spiritual unity of Western Europe he rejoined that fundamentally it was the same Christian stream flowing through two channels instead of one. 'The parallel progress of European culture has taken the place of ecclesiastical unity.' His leniency to the reformers appears when he reaches the double marriage of Philip of Hesse and its quasi-approval by Luther and Melanchthon. Yet the portrait of Charles V is also drawn with sympathy. He had sketched his beginnings in the 'Princes and Peoples,' and he now followed him to his abdication. He admired his fidelity to the impossible ideal of the unity of Christendom. The book is a contribution to the history of European politics as well as to that of Germany in the era of the Reformation. We read of the Turks before Vienna, the sack of Rome, the Reformation in Switzerland, the conspiracy of Wullenweber. No work on the German Reformation has ever had such a wide scope.

Though it never obtained the same European popularity as the 'Popes,' its success in Germany itself was far greater, and in 1841 he was appointed Historiographer of the Prussian State. The one belonged to the world, the other to the Fatherland. Dove has compared its position as a national classic to that of Macaulay's History. Protestant critics who had detected a lack of warmth in the 'Popes' were delighted at the vigorous convictions of its successor. 'In reading the earlier works,' declared Sybel, 'my enjoyment is exactly the same as in visiting a gallery of excellent pictures and statuary. Utterly different is my feeling when I open the "Reformation," which is impregnated with the enthusiasm of a German patriot for the greatest act of the German spirit.' Treitschke pronounces it his masterpiece, its style warmed by the love of country. Moriz Ritter asserts that he never reached the same level again. Roscher saluted him as the greatest living historian. The author did not wholly agree with these verdicts. At the age of ninety he remarked that he had been told that it was far inferior to the 'Popes.' 'I felt that too. It seemed to me impossible to make a readable book out of the Acts of the Reichstag and theology. I did not try for readers in the great world but strove to satisfy German erudition.' The historian's instinct was not much at fault, and the progress of research has treated it less kindly. From Döllinger and Janssen Germany was to learn that his view of the eve of the Reformation was too dark and of the Reformation itself too rosy. Luther's fame does not stand where it did. We learn little about the mass of the people, their conditions and their aspirations, and the chapter on the Peasants' Revolt is one of the weakest. Though the book is mainly a political history, more care should have been taken to indicate the doctrinal points at issue. Except for a discussion of Justification by Faith on the occasion of the meeting of the Council of Trent and of the controversies of Flacius and Major, there is little theology in its pages.

The 'Reformation,' the reception of which was 'beyond all expectation,' was followed by the least popular of Ranke's major works. His first intention was to study the French Revolution; but on reaching Paris in 1843 he failed to obtain access to the archives he needed, and stumbled on the despatches of Valori, French ambassador at Berlin during the early years of Frederick the Great. Returning home he plunged into the Prussian archives, but he soon found that to understand the work of the Great King it was necessary to explore the activities of his father. An introductory survey of the growth of Prussia was added, and the 'Nine Books of Prussian History' appeared in 1847–8.[1] The work

[1] It should be studied in the Academy edition.

was a study of the rise of a Great Power, with special reference to the reign of Frederick William I and the early years of his son. Ranke was born in Saxony, and lacked enthusiasm for his adopted country. He always remained a German, with a friendly feeling for Austria unknown among Prussian historians. Indeed he was a dualist till Bismarck converted him. The coolness of the tone struck every reader. The King of Prussia was dissatisfied with the first two volumes, but approved the third. Though never a popular favourite, it possessed solid merits. As Prussian historiographer he was the first to be allowed the use of the State papers which had been closed to Preuss. In the words of Koser,[1] the final arbiter, it extended and deepened the knowledge of the first half of the eighteenth century as no work before it. Its greatest achievement was to reveal the personality, system and significance of Frederick William.[2] Brushing aside the gossip of Wilhelmina, he depicted the King as the founder of the efficient Prussian administrative machine. In his study of Frederick the Great, which ended on the eve of the Seven Years War, he reveals no hostility to Austria. He refuses to discuss the legal question of the claim to Silesia, adding the curious words, 'Happily this is not the task of the historian.' He recognises the particularism of Prussia, and finds no trace of the long term national policy with which Droysen was to credit her. It is an almost purely political narrative. The sketch of the *Aufklärung* is curiously meagre. The fascinating 'digressions' in the 'Popes' are absent. 'I am not surprised at Ranke's failure,' wrote Carlyle to Varnhagen. 'If I were a Prussian or even a German I should protest against his Frederick the Great.' He was grieved by the cold reception of a work to which he had devoted patient research, but the disappointment of the public was largely due to the expectations which his two previous masterpieces had taught it to cherish. Many years later he revised and enlarged the book the solid merits of which were no longer contested.

During his sojourn in Italy Ranke had resolved to write the history of France and England in their universal aspects, and to this double task he devoted the greater part of the next twenty years. In 1850 he revisited Paris and was delighted at the wealth of the material that he found. 'I am astonished,' he wrote, 'that the French leave it to me to discover part of their history.' The

---

[1] In *Forschungen zur Brandenburgischen u. Preussischen Geschichte*, vol. i.

[2] His reading of the King was attacked by Häusser (Ranke's 'Preussische Geschichte,' *Ges. Schriften*, vol. i, 1869), and Zimmermann, *Die neueste Preussiche Geschichtschreibung*, 1848.

'French History' began to appear in 1853. Great States and peoples, declared the preface, possessed a double character, one national, the other belonging to the destinies of the world. The universal side of France was particularly prominent, for political ferments had often originated there. 'Ambitious, warlike, incited by national pride, the French have kept their neighbours in constant excitement, sometimes liberating the oppressed, more often oppressing the free.' This reading of French psychology is repeated at intervals throughout the work. 'It is peculiar to France,' he comments on the adventures of Francis I, 'from century to century to break through the circle of legality.' Yet though the tone of the book is not altogether friendly, it is free from the disparagement which disfigures the pages of Sybel and Treitschke. Ranke wrote less as a German than as a European.

The detailed narrative begins with the sixteenth century, the connecting link between mediæval and modern France being found in the elaboration of a monarchial system from Philip Augustus onwards. In the religious wars of the sixteenth century his sympathies are with the *Politiques*. He speaks severely of the native duplicity of Catholicism, and declares that there had been nothing like the massacre of St. Bartholomew since Sulla's proscriptions. Yet he does not blame the apostasy of Henri IV. With the accession of the Bourbons the stream reaches its greatest breadth. The character and policy of the King and Sully's economic reforms are minutely studied. The greatness and ruthlessness of Richelieu are impressively suggested and he has hard words for Mazarin's vanity and greed. The picture of the reign of Louis XIV, the culmination of the absolute monarchy which is the main theme of the work, was the first adequate presentation of the Augustan age. While condemning his foreign policy, he emphasises the services of the King to literature, science and art. He was one of the first to do justice to the fine qualities of Madame de Maintenon. With the death of Louis XIV the end is in sight, and the narrative closes with a brief sketch of his successor.

Learned Frenchmen, declared Ranke, had long remarked how insecure was the foundation of their traditional history, but he was the first to demonstrate it in detail. His researches in the archives not only of France but of Italy, Germany, Belgium, England and Spain enabled him to look all round his subject. The most abiding result was to emancipate French history from the memoir-writers. No part is more admirable than the analysis of its most famous authorities. Davila's 'History of the Civil Wars' came largely from De Thou. Richelieu's Memoirs were almost wholly spurious, those of De Retz genuine but grossly

misleading. On reaching Saint-Simon he emphasises the late date
of composition and the violence of his prejudices, and confronts
him with the contemporary authority of Dangeau and the correspondence of Charlotte of Orleans with her German relatives. The
'French History,' with its mass of new material and its gallery of
portraits, was welcomed nowhere more heartily than in France.
Saint René Taillandier, who knew and admired all his books, sung
his praises in the *Revue des Deux Mondes*, and Thiers hailed him
as the greatest historian in Germany and perhaps in Europe.[1]

Ranke passed from France to England, to which he devoted
his longest work of research. His wife was English, and Macaulay's
essay on the 'Popes' had made his name a household word. Presenting an introduction from the King of Prussia to the Prince
Consort the historian remarked, 'I come to study.' The Prince
gallantly replied, 'And you are studied here.' He explored the
archives not only of London but of Dublin, and made valuable
discoveries in the priceless collection of Sir Thomas Philipps. To
master the foreign relations of the country he paid special visits
to Paris and the Hague. The 'English History' was constructed
on the same plan as the French, the common object being to study
the epochs in which its influence on the development of mankind
was most marked. 'In the last two centuries the glory of their
arms abroad lay nearest to the heart of the French nation, the
legal settlement of their home affairs to that of England.' He hints
that, though it would be folly to challenge Macaulay in his own
peculiar sphere, it might be useful to have an independent representation of events. He approached his new task with unusual
sympathy. France was the country of absolutism, innovation and
aggression. England was orderly and conservative. 'Nowhere
have more of the institutions of the Middle Ages been retained.'

---

[1] The following criticism of the 'French History,' despite its exaggeration, is of interest. 'Ten years have passed,' wrote Gindely to Helfert from
Simancas in 1861, 'since I became acquainted with Ranke's writings; and
I accepted the general opinion that he had made magnificent discoveries
in foreign archives. But I found myself obliged to go critically through
the "Popes" and the "French History." The shallowness of his studies
in the latter is astonishing. Not only is he lacking in a complete knowledge
of the printed literature, but he even resorts to deception, wishing to make
his readers believe that he has worked through the archives. The chief
of these, the archives of the Foreign Office, he does not indeed cite, for he
was never there till the present year; but he repeatedly cites the splendid
Simancas collection in the Archives of State, of which he never saw a dozen
volumes. His citations are mere crumbs stuck together in a chance fashion
to produce the appearance of being the results of systematic study.'
Quoted from A. W. Ward's article on Gindely, *Eng. Hist. Review*, July,
1893.

Following his usual practice, he opens with a brief sketch of early English history. The narrative broadens with Henry VIII, of whom he paints a portrait scarcely affected by Froude's recent volumes. 'He had no real sympathy with any living man. Men are to him only instruments which he uses and breaks to pieces. But he has an incomparable practical intelligence. We follow the course of his government with a mingled sense of aversion and admiration.' Once again he showed that he was fully alive to the place of personality in history. After concluding his survey of Elizabeth, he remarks that under no dynasty had great national changes been so dependent on the personal aims of princes. The kernel of the book is the foundation of Parliamentary Monarchy and the two revolutions of the seventeenth century. He refused to accept the partial defence of James I then being commenced by Gardiner, and rates Charles I, both as man and ruler, above his father. Realising that Anglicanism was not Catholicism, he commends the sincerity and depth of his religious convictions. 'There was something of the martyr in him, if the man can be so called who values his own life less than the cause for which he is fighting and, in perishing himself, saves it for the future.' His capital fault was his inability to understand other minds. His attempt to rule without Parliament rendered failure inevitable, and the future of Great Britain was involved in victory over Stuart principles. Pym appears not as a defender of law and tradition but as one of the greatest of revolutionary leaders. The picture of Cromwell is painted without much sympathy, but he seizes the capital fact that the conservative elements in him were as numerous as the destructive. Ranke was also the first to establish with a wealth of new material the European character of the Revolution of 1688. With the death of William III the path narrows and it ends with the accession of George III. The main value of the work lies in the new light thrown on the relations of England to the Continent, and the reaction of those relations on her internal life.[1] Of scarcely less importance was the presentation of the domestic struggle from the point of view of a foreigner far better equipped than Guizot. If it has less life and colour than some of its predecessors, it possesses a weight and dignity that he never surpassed. The analyses of Clarendon and Burnet are of first-rate importance. Without ever becoming widely popular, its place as an historical classic is secure.

[1] Even Bergenroth, who attacked the first volume in the *Grenzboten*, admitted the excellence of this feature.

III

The 'English History' completed the cycle of works embracing the Great Powers of Europe which Ranke had planned during his sojourn in Italy, and the execution of which had filled forty laborious years. They were followed by a number of writings which belong rather to the class of historical monographs. His 'Contributions to German History, 1555–1618,' took up the story at the point where the 'Reformation' had dropped it. The admiring study of the tolerant Ferdinand I and Maximilian II had appeared in the *Review*; but the portrait of Rudolf II was new, and there is no more interesting canvas in the historian's gallery than this mysterious ruler, with his stricken brain and his love of the occult world. A more important venture was the 'History of Wallenstein.' Ranke had often touched the Thirty Years War, but his new work was based on fresh research at Brussels, Dresden and Vienna. The great soldier was of peculiar interest, since tradition and scholarship alike were uncertain whether to regard him as a traitor or a man of honour. Hurter, the historiographer of the Hapsburgs, naturally denounced him. Ranke's Wallenstein is a gigantic egoist, greedy to obtain territory and to found a dynasty; but, though he toyed with treason, the final act of treachery was not committed. While everyone trusted Gustavus Adolphus, no man had confidence in his rival. Completely indifferent to religion he found it easy and militarily profitable to be tolerant. The subsequent discovery of his relations with Sweden renders the later chapters antiquated; and for once Ranke accepted documents—the reports of Sezyma Raschin—which proved to be spurious. But the book retains its interest, and a corrected edition was issued by Hallwich, the greatest of Wallenstein scholars.

The works of the seventies reflect the *annus mirabilis*. Ranke welcomed the result of the war as a triumph of conservative over revolutionary Europe, but he was free from national rancour. 'Who of us all,' he asked, 'is uninfluenced by the French spirit?' 'Against whom are you fighting?' inquired his old friend Thiers when they met in Vienna after the fall of Napoleon III. 'Against Louis XIV' was the reply. He had already begun study on the Origin of the Seven Years' War, and in the summer and autumn of 1870 he completed it. The preface described it as his tribute to the events of the day, but the work was no less objective than its predecessors. On the capital question, still undecided, as to the responsibility for the war he declares that Frederick desired peace at that particular moment, but that he always intended further acquisitions in order to safeguard what he had. If the 'Seven

Years' War' was in the nature of an appendix to the 'Prussia, a larger work was in part devoted to a still later chapter of Frederick's reign. 'The German Powers and the Fürstenbund, 1780–90,' rested on a mass of material drawn from German, Austrian and Dutch archives. The portrait of Joseph, the hero of the book, is painted with genuine sympathy. That of Frederick William II emphasises, perhaps a little too generously, the better side of a ruler who has few friends. Having thus dealt with Prussia in the later part of the eighteenth century he returned to the origins of the state. In 1867 he had begun to publish a complete edition of his works, revising and sometimes adding to them. In no case was the alteration so great as in the 'History of Prussia,' the first Book of which was transformed into four. The appearance of Droysen's colossal work had rendered the chapters on early Prussia obsolete; but the new Books, while freely employing his material, quietly rejected the national rôle which his ardent colleague assigned to the early Hohenzollerns.

The next work returned to the beginnings of contemporary history. 'The Origin of the Wars of the Revolution,' though one of his least important works, is interesting for the author's view of the French Revolution. He underestimates the autocracy of the last two French monarchs and their colossal mistakes, and the responsibility for the outbreak is attributed almost entirely to the opposition of the clergy and *noblesse* to reform. His hostility to the ideas of the Revolution is undiminished, but the judicial habit never forsakes him. By their foolish interference the Powers excited the national pride of France. The conflict was rendered inevitable by the sharp contradiction of two hostile worlds, the clash of the revolutionary with the conservative idea. In maintaining his ground Sybel declared that Ranke only knew part of the material, and added, 'I do not see ideas outside men, which lead them like demonic forces against their will. I see rather men form their intellectual system and act in accordance with it.' While Sybel, the National Liberal, held it to be reasonable for the sovereigns to dictate to France, his conservative master does justice to the French point of view.

At the age of eighty-one the veteran scholar issued a large work on Hardenberg, which serves as a continuation of the 'Fürstenbund' and the 'Wars of the Revolution.' Hardenberg had ordered that his papers should not be touched for half a century after his death. When the time arrived the seals were broken by Bismarck himself and the documents were entrusted to the Nestor of German historians. The authentic papers covered only part of the minister's life, but they contained a highly important Memorandum on Prussian policy in 1807, and other pieces of considerable value. Of the five stout volumes entitled *Denkwürdigkeiten des Fürsten Hardenberg* published in 1877 two contain the. editor's narrative. His contribution, without the documentary material but utilising the Haugwitz papers and other sources, fills three volumes in the Collected Works entitled 'Hardenberg and the Genesis of the Prussian State, 1793–1815.' The work opens with a brief sketch of his career before entering the Prussian service at the age of forty, but this is the only piece of genuine biography in the whole work. He justifies the Treaty of Basel as not only politically wise but as ushering in eleven years of neutrality 'which were almost the most fruitful in German literature.' Yet, unlike Sybel, he is never unfair to Austria, and recognises that in 1809 she stood for the freedom of Europe. The chapter on Jena is written without emotion. The work ends in 1813, the later years of the statesman's life finding no elucidation in his papers. Treitschke has pronounced the 'Hardenberg' far inferior to Ranke's earlier works in artistic beauty and historical judgment, but it is none the less a solid contribution to the history of the Napoleonic era and reveals the historian's poise when dealing with the crisis of his country's fate. A minor editorial duty was the publication of the correspondence of Frederick William IV with Bunsen, and the historian gladly undertook the task of elucidating and defending the policy of his old master. The personal devotion commanded respect; but the portrait was generally judged too flattering, and it was in reference to this volume that Treitschke harshly pronounced him too much of a courtier to tell the whole truth about great people. Other aspects of the reign were dealt with in the biography contributed to the German Biographical Dictionary in 1878.[1] The mass of work that had followed the 'English History' was immense. There was not a chapter without value, but he seemed to have lost the power of appeal to the general reader. The bright colours and realistic portraits had disappeared. Only an occasional and perfunctory chapter on literature recalls the breadth and fullness of the earlier works. The charge that he neglected personality at last began to have some substance.

In the spring of 1880 Ranke informed his publisher of a new work on Universal History, the first two volumes of which appeared at the end of the same year. The world was astounded at the audacity of an octogenarian sitting down to such a task. Would he live to finish it? Would his brain bear the prolonged

[1] See Kaufmann, 'Ranke u. die Beurteilung F. W. IV,' *Hist. Zeitschrift*, 1902.

strain? The historian himself knew the risks, but his resolution
had been taken after long and serious thought. For several years
he had been unable to read and write, and had to work through
two secretaries.[1] Original research had become impossible. 'He
told me,' records Giesebrecht, 'that one reason was his incapacity
any longer to work in the archives, and it was impossible to
live without work.' He had at first thought of writing his autobiography, weaving round it the movement of the century; but he
finally determined on a book like Humboldt's 'Kosmos' which
would be at once the natural conclusion of his achievement and
an emphatic assertion of the unity of history.[2] His whole life had
been a preparation for the task. 'The return to the classics,' he
wrote to Reumont, 'gives me special pleasure. I use my school-
books and the little sketches I made in Frankfurt, so that age and
youth are joined.' Though he had published little on the Middle
Ages, he had repeatedly covered the ground in his lectures, for
which he possessed full notes. He had minutely studied many of
the more important sources in his *Seminar*. He was, moreover, in
touch with the results of mediæval scholarship through an army
of pupils. His mind was synthetic, and he stood above the rivalries
of race and creed. It was impossible, he declared, to rest in the
history of single peoples. The race had won in the course of ages
an heirloom in material and social advance, religion and the creations of genius, memories of great events and great men which
unified mankind. There was a general historical life, which moved
progressively from one nation or group of nations to another.
Starting from this conception of a single process he excludes the
origins of society as unknown and the peoples of the East as
standing aloof from the main stream.

A brief survey of Egypt and the civilisations of Hither Asia
leads to the Greece of the Persian wars with which the detailed
narrative opens. He closely follows Herodotus and Thucydides.
He is fair both to Demosthenes and Philip, and is strongly attracted by the typically universal figure of Alexander. 'With all
our sympathy for the freedom of Greece we are tempted to find
some compensation for its destruction in the fuller influence of the
Greek genius on the world.' The volume ends with the Diadochi
and a glance at Sicily and Carthage. With Pyrrhus we reach Rome,
whose early history is only sketched in outline. While employing
Mommsen throughout, he retains his independent judgment,

[1] Vivid pictures of his methods are drawn by Wiedemann, 'Sechzehn
Jahre in der Werkstätte Ranke's,' *Deutsche Revue*, 1891–3; and Georg
Winter, 'Erinnerungen an Ranke,' *Nord u. Süd*, Aug. 1888.
[2] See Masur, *Rankes Begriff der Weltgeschichte*, 1926.

shunning exaggeration and invective. He respects Pompey without claiming greatness for him, and denies that Cicero was the
Varnhagen of antiquity. His task is to winnow the important from
the trivial, to mark the position of Rome in the chain of universal
history. The first two volumes of the 'Weltgeschichte,' though the
edition was exhausted in a week, form by far its least important
part, and are the least authoritative of Ranke's writings. The vast
collections of Greek and Roman inscriptions and the testimony of
archæology, to name only two new sources, were unknown to him.
Nor had he assimilated the results of critical study in regard to
origins, whether of early Israel or early Greece. The judgment of
Eduard Meyer is severe. 'He lacked real preparation for his task.
He had only occupied himself with antiquity in his youth, yet felt
himself justified in virtually ignoring the scientific work of half
a century. Under such circumstances the attempt could only issue
in total failure.' [1]

In the third volume, devoted to the Roman Empire, the chapter that attracted most attention was on the origin of Christianity.
'In pronouncing the name of Jesus Christ,' he wrote, 'though I am
a good evangelical Christian, I must decline to discuss the religious secret which, being incomprehensible, is beyond the grasp
of history. Of God the Son I can speak as little as of God the
Father. The historian can only show the combination of world-
historic influences in which Christianity appeared and by which its
operation was conditioned.' Whereas Judaism could never become
universal, the message of Christ provided the foundation on which
the conception of a higher community could arise. His interest
in the Christian Church is further revealed in the fourth volume
which deals at length with Athanasius and Arius, Julian and Neo-
platonism. With the Völkerwanderung he reached a period on
which he could speak with greater authority. The sixth volume,
extending to the death of Otto I, was the last he saw in print.
While engaged on this he made use above all of Giesebrecht. 'The
beginnings of our historical association,' he wrote to the author of
the Kaiserzeit, 'floated before me. I often feel as if I was in the
midst of these friends. I thank you and my other pupils for your
writings on the ninth and tenth centuries.' He reached his ninetieth birthday at the end of 1885 in perfect possession of his
powers, like an aged ruler gazing out over his kingdom. [2] He
hurried forward with feverish haste, despite almost continual
sufferings. 'Inter tormenta scripsi,' he wrote to a friend. When he
died in May 1886 he had reached the death of the Emperor
Henry IV. The seventh volume was dictated in four months. His

[1] Geschichte des Altertums, vol. i., pt. 1, 250, 1910.   [2] Acton.

gigantic plan was almost accomplished, for he had determined to give merely a sketch of modern history. As a substitute for the unwritten volumes of the later Middle Ages Dove published the manuscript of his lectures, completed by notes of his hearers, bringing the story to 1453.

The 'Weltgeschichte' was a wonderful production, considered merely as the intellectual achievement of a man between eighty and ninety who could no longer read or write. It was written for and best appreciated by those who already knew a good deal. Though it deals above all with broad tendencies, the importance of the individual actor is more fully recognised than in some other works of his old age. 'On the summit of deep, universal, tumultous movements,' ran his last dictated words, 'appear natures cast in a gigantic mould, which rivet the attention of the centuries. General tendencies do not alone decide; great personalities are always necessary to make them effective.' In speaking of Alexander he remarks that the spectator can hardly tear himself away from the Paris bust when he thinks of the deeds and qualities of the man it represents. His portraits of Alexander and Demosthenes, David and Constantine, Charles the Great and Otto I, Nicholas I and Hildebrand are alive.

The only attack came from the Catholic camp. The Jesuit Michael[1] hotly denounced his treatment of the Roman Church, and pronounced his attitude to Christianity the fundamental error of the book. Ranke, he declared, was a rationalist without wishing to show it. He failed to understand the Church and the Papacy, and praised Julian and Mohammed. There can be few readers of the 'Weltgeschichte' who would accept the verdict that it is anti-Catholic and anti-Christian. The work breathes a deeply religious spirit, and the author's intense interest in religious life and thought is manifested in the prominence he devotes to ecclesiastical history. But his faith was not of a kind that supplied him with an easy key to the problems of history. In the private lectures to King Maximilian[2] he declared it impossible to prove a directing will leading mankind from point to point or an immanent force driving towards a goal. All generations were equally justified before God and stood in equally direct relation to Him. Moral ideas could expand only in area, not in quality. Beyond Christianity it was impossible to go. Humanity contained within itself endless developments appearing in obedience to unknown laws. History was the record of divine manifestations imperfectly understood.

[1] Michael, *Ranke's Weltgeschichte*, 1890.
[2] *Über die Epochen der neueren Geschichte*, published in 1888 with an excellent introduction by Dove.

Lamprecht's criticism,[1] in some ways so perverse, rightly emphasises the essentially mystical character of his outlook.

Ranke's faults were negative rather than positive. His contemporaries complained less of what they found than of what they missed. The ardent nationalist lamented his cosmopolitan tranquillity, the moralist his ethical neutrality, the materialist his cloudy transcendentalism. Droysen scoffed at the objectivity of the eunuch. Treitschke wrote scathingly of the soft sunlight, scarcely veiled by occasional clouds, which illumined an elegant circle of high-born and refined men. On reading the 'Prussian History' Strauss sighed for the brush of Rembrandt. Menzel complained of his kid gloves. Acton pronounces that the world was much better and very much worse than he chose to say. On his ninetieth birthday Mommsen, with an undercurrent of protest, remarked, 'You are the most indulgent of us all.' The verdict of Gregorovius was that he went through history as he would go through a picture-gallery, writing acute notes. Sybel regretted that while Niebuhr's innermost feeling was ethical, Ranke's was æsthetic, and that he surveyed the past with the eyes not of a statesman but an artist. Reuss contrasts him with Michelet and Mommsen, where we feel the passion rise in the soul of the narrator and quicken his style.

Such judgments indicate that the critic belongs to a rival school, yet the most loyal disciples admit that there were spots on the sun. His harmonious nature made him to some extent blind to great tides of emotion and outbursts of passion, to the sublimities and degradations of life. It was well that he did not carry out his plan of a history of the French Revolution. In dealing with individuals and nations alike he was most at home in the middle regions of human experience. In another direction his work was incomplete. When the history of states has been written and the development of the European system has been made clear, the life of the people and the ideas that govern and explain action have to be described. There is a tendency to survey events too much from the windows of the council-chamber, to neglect the masses, to overlook the pressure of economic forces. The Venetian Relations, which helped to make his fortune and to which he attributed a somewhat excessive value, exerted a permanent influence on his mind. It is, above all, in the greater attention to the evolution of society that a later generation has advanced beyond his theory and practice.

Ranke's services to history can be rapidly summarised. The first was to divorce the study of the past as much as humanly

[1] *Alte u. neue Richtungen in der Geschichtswissenschaft*, 1896.

possible from the passions of the present, and to describe how things were—*wie es eigentlich gewesen*. His attitude is nowhere more concisely defined than in his obituary of Gervinus. 'He often declares that science must establish relations with life. Very true, but it must be real science. If we first choose a standpoint and transport it into science, then life operates on science, not science on life.' His own strong opinions usually remain locked in his bosom. In his dramas there are few heroes or villains. The second service was to establish the necessity of founding historical construction on strictly contemporary sources. He was not the first to use the archives but the first to use them well. When he began to write, historians of high repute believed memoirs and chronicles to be primary authorities. When he laid down his pen, every scholar with a reputation to make or to lose had learned to content himself with nothing less than the papers and correspondence of the actors themselves and those in immediate contact with the events they describe. Thirdly, he founded the science of evidence by the analysis of authorities, contemporary or otherwise, in the light of the author's temperament, affiliations and opportunity of knowledge and by comparison with the testimony of other writers. Henceforth every historian had to inquire where his informant obtained his facts. It is Ranke's glory to have rendered the history of modern Europe more fully intelligible, to have established its unity and portrayed the leading actors in the drama. He was congratulated by Arneth on having given a masterpiece to every country. He was the greatest historical writer of modern times, not only because he founded the scientific study of materials and possessed in an unrivalled degree the judicial temper, but because his powers of work and length of life enabled him to produce a larger number of first-rate works than any other member of the craft. It was the Goethe of history who made German scholarship supreme in Europe, and he remains the master of us all.

CHAPTER VII

RANKE'S CRITICS AND PUPILS

I

RANKE lived long enough to be recognised as the greatest historian of his time and to see his pupils in command of almost every historical chair in Germany. But the position of supremacy was only achieved after a prolonged struggle with captious critics and rival schools of thought. The first attack, and the only one to which he ever paid the compliment of a reply, came from Leo.[1] Like many other young men he was inspired by the fiery nationalism of Vater Jahn, and among the hot-headed youths who denounced the enemies of liberty on the Wartburg in 1817 few seemed less likely to become a pillar of the reaction. But with the murder of Kotzebue a drift towards conservatism set in, which was strengthened by the influence of Haller and Hegel. A visit to Italy bore fruit in a work on the Constitution of the Lombard Towns. No historian seemed more likely to win for himself a high place in scholarship, or better qualified to criticise the first work of the young Frankfurt teacher. The style, he complained, was a pale copy of Johannes Müller, the philosophy was superstition, the judgments unhistorical. Ranke was deeply hurt by this onslaught, which he characterised as the outburst of an angry schoolmaster confronted by a new method. A violent retort from Leo ended the controversy, and in the same year he left Berlin for Halle; but he continued to censure Ranke's 'timid avoidance of personal views' as unmanly, and dismissed his writings as porcelain painting, the delight of ladies and amateurs.

A more serious obstacle to the acceptance of Ranke's methods and the recognition of his authority was the didactic school of which the chief figures were Rotteck, Schlosser and Gervinus. For more than a generation Rotteck was the chief historical and political oracle of South Germany.[2] A native of Baden and the son of a French mother, he early assimilated French ideas and

[1] See Krägelin, *H. Leo*, 1908. His memoirs, *Aus meiner Jugendzeit*, 1880, only reach to the age of 23.
[2] See Röpell, *Rotteck*, 1883, and Ganter, *Rotteck als Geschichtschreiber*, 1908. The fourth volume of his *Gesammelte u. nachgelassene Schriften*, 1841–3, contains a life by his son, the fifth his correspondence.

adopted Rousseau as his master. Appointed Professor at Freiburg in 1798, he used his chair as a tribune and a pulpit. 'I revere history,' he declared, 'as a wise counsellor and judge.' His lectures formed the basis of his 'Universal History,' which began to appear in 1812. In the frank words of the preface, it was launched as a work of propaganda. Its aim was not only to enrich the mind but to strengthen the will and train the character of youth. 'My noble young friends, I desire to show you the great teachings, the elevated pictures of the past, to awaken love and admiration for the splendid characters of old, to kindle a passion for righteousness, freedom and fatherland.' His attack on Alexander, his invective against Rome for suppressing the freedom of the world, his onslaughts on every sort of despotism, were aimed—and were well understood to be aimed—at the Emperor on the Seine. In the preface to the second edition, written in 1821, he reminded his readers that the first volume was published before the retreat from Moscow revived the hope of liberty. 'History was then the only instrument by which wisdom could be taught.' After Waterloo the work was not less needed to encourage the fight for constitutional liberty. Though placed on the Index and forbidden in Austria, it was allowed to circulate freely throughout Germany, and translations into English and French, Italian, Danish and Polish made it in some degree the bible of Liberal Europe. The author witnessed the appearance of the thirteenth edition before his death in 1840. A twenty-fifth edition appeared in 1866, while an abridgment enjoyed a popularity scarcely less than that of the larger work. Lacking both learning and style, its spell was due to the fact that an age hungry for liberty found in it encouragement to persevere in the demand.

More of a moralist and less of a politician than Rotteck, Schlosser[1] was the most influential writer and teacher of history in Germany during the years in which Ranke was climbing the ladder of fame. In a short autobiography he records the disappointments of his student life at Göttingen. 'I was soon healed of the delusion of the German Professors that they were the lights of the world.' For a time he shared the prevailing cult of Johannes Müller, naming him the German Thucydides, but he quickly outgrew his admiration. He served no master, his censorious spirit invariably finding more to blame than to praise. He roamed at

---

[1] Weber, *F. C. Schlosser*, 1876, contains an autobiography, a biography, letters and fragments. Gervinus' striking tribute is in Gervinus, *Leben von ihm selbst*, 150–215, 1893. The best later appreciations are by Lorenz, *Die Geschichtswissenschaft*, 1–89, 1886, and Dilthey, *Gesammelte Schriften*, xi. 104–64.

large over the field of history, and after reaching the age of thirty produced monographs on Abelard and Beza. In the preface to the latter he strikes a didactic note which was to sound throughout his life. His object, he declared, was to wean his contemporaries from evil tendencies by the teachings of history. A year or two later he published a substantial volume on the Iconoclasts, one of the first adventures of a modern historian into the Byzantine world. In 1811 he began to write his 'Weltgeschichte,' the first of the two large works to which he owed his fame. His intention was to cover the whole field of history in three small volumes. The first, extending to the fall of the Western Empire, rested on the conscientious study of the original authorities. A second edition, largely expanded, appeared under the title of 'A View of the History and Culture of the Ancient World.' Since Rotteck was a mere compiler, it was largely through Schlosser that classical antiquity swam into the ken of the cultured middle classes of Germany. The final title of the work was 'Universal History for the German People,' edited by a pupil in nineteen volumes from the master's writings, to which he contributed a survey of the modern centuries.

Parallel with the 'Weltgeschichte,' Schlosser was engaged for several decades on a work of much greater importance. A visit to the libraries of Paris in 1822 was followed by two little volumes on the eighteenth century, which in turn were expanded after a second visit in 1834. The eighth and last volume only appeared in 1860, the year of his death. The most valuable and interesting pages are those which are devoted to the intellectual life of France, Germany and England. He warmly admires such bold spirits as Reimarus and the Deists, Thomasius and Lessing, Campomanes and Febronius. The political survey, extending from the war of the Spanish Succession to the fall of Napoleon, is of inferior merit and embodies little original material. He commends the aims if not the methods of the Philosophic Despots, but his attitude towards princes is one of almost monotonous depreciation. He speaks with loathing of the coarse brutalities of the petty German Courts, Versailles and St. Petersburg, and of the marketing of Hessian soldiers. He condemns the harsh selfishness of the British aristocracy, and recalls the starving Irish, the children in the factories, the poor rotting in the workhouses. His ambition was to tear off the mask with which lies, ambition and greed had tried to cover the misdeeds of the mighty. His contempt for the servile swarm of flatterers is not less than for courts and titles. Gentz is denounced as a sophist who lies in order to revel at the tables of the great. Yet Schlosser was no flatterer of the people. He had little belief in the power of constitutions to improve the world, and he had no political system to advocate. He denounces the excesses of the Revolution, as he had chastised the feuds of Athens and Rome. He refused to join in the glorification of the Wars of Liberation, and, without defending Napoleon, placed some of his actions in a more favourable light. Though respecting real piety in all its forms, in Sailer as in Spener, he regarded priests as accomplices in tyranny with princes. He condemned clericalism and obscurantism wherever he found it. He scourges the Jesuits in the days of their prosperity but condemns their ruthless expulsion. He was often called the modern Cato, and there was much of the early Roman in him. His favourite author was Dante, and his works reflect the sombre atmosphere of the Inferno. He was a cosmopolitan of the eighteenth century, a child of the *Aufklärung* who had learned the categorical imperative from Kant.

Schlosser's gospel was proclaimed not only in his writings but in his lectures at Heidelberg, and all witnesses agree in their description of the size and enthusiam of his audiences. His greatest pupil, Gervinus, has left a striking picture. 'At last I found what I had so long sought in vain. He spoke to heart and head with equal power. His lectures were filled with magnificent *aperçus* before which the gates of history sprang open.' But such an original personality was rather an inspiration than a reliable guide. He convinced his hearers of the lofty mission of history without teaching them how to become historians. He denied the possibility of objective history, maintaining that no man could ever obtain perfect knowledge of the inner connection of events, but he made no very strenuous efforts to procure such information as was available. He despised the researches of Ranke and spoke with contempt of the dust of archives. Like Leo he outlived his fame and his influence. In the preface to the concluding volume of the 'Eighteenth Century,' written a few months before his death, he confessed himself no longer strong enough for the task of warning and improving his generation. There was something pathetic in the consistency with which he clung to the doctrines and methods of his early manhood while historical studies were advancing by the light of other stars. 'Schlosser lamented to me,' wrote Strauss in 1858,[1] 'that the younger historians, including Gervinus, lay so little stress on morality in history, though Gervinus is a highly moral man.' His lecture-room emptied and his ideals were ignored. His greatest, indeed his only disciple, in the eloquent *apologia* written on his master's death, recognised the change. Opinions on Schlosser, he wrote, were no longer unanimous; he was accused of formlessness, self-righteousness, censoriousness. The first charge

[1] *Briefe*, 397.

was true, but the graver counts in the indictment rested on a misapprehension of his aims. The object of his books was less to convey instruction than to teach men to live. 'I have a feeling,' he concludes, 'that if a man had done nothing more than be to another what he was to me, that alone would be enough to give his life the highest value.' Schlosser himself would have been more gratified by this personal confession than by any tribute to his erudition. He was indeed rather a moralist and a publicist than an historian. Yet this man of scanty research and narrow philosophy was one of the main intellectual and moral forces for nearly half a century, and was long held to be the rival, if not indeed the superior, of Ranke.

The name of Gervinus[1] is inseparably connected with that of Schlosser. Both were men of rare intellectual vigour, both sought in history a guide to life. But though the disciple was not less austere, he was more of a politician than a moralist. While Schlosser called the age to repentance, Gervinus summoned it to action. The master's appeal was to the individual conscience; the pupil spoke to the nation. In his Autobiography he records his omnivorous reading at school of history and literature and his composition of poetry and dramas. A year in Italy was chiefly devoted to Florentine history, above all to Machiavelli. Of his 'Florentine Historiography' more than half was devoted to the author of the 'Prince.' A true patriot in a vicious age, he dared all for the good of his country: far from representing his time at its lowest, he could afford to despise his contemporaries. He was, moreover, the father of the scientific handling of history. 'As I sought rather enlightenment than the accumulation of material,' wrote Gervinus long after in his Autobiography, 'I could not have fallen in with anybody more suitable. Machiavelli combines history and politics.' The little book won golden opinions from Schlosser and Dahlmann, and the French Revolution of 1830 strengthened his interest in politics. 'The annihilation of fifteen years of reaction in a few July days awoke the belief that the day of political development for Germany too was dawning, but I felt she must avoid hasty and premature change.' His cautious attitude was expressed in a vigorous attack on Börne's pretensions to be a political Luther and in a warm eulogy of Dahlmann's 'Politik.' Each essay as it came from his pen was a call to action.

[1] See Gervinus, *Leben von ihm selbst*, 1893; Ranke, *Abh. u. Versuche, Neue Sammlung*, 567–76, 1888; Döllinger, *Akademische Vorträge*, vol. ii., 1889; Zeller, *Vorträge u. Abhandlungen*, vol. ii.; Dörfel, *Gervinus als historischer Denker*, 1904. His correspondence with the Grimms and Dahlmann fills the second volume of *Briefwechsel zwischen J. u. W. Grimm, Dahlmann u. Gervinus*, 1886.

In 1837 he was to show that his interest in public affairs was not merely academic. He had been appointed to a chair at Göttingen a few months before the separation of the English and Hanoverian crowns brought to the throne Ernest Augustus, whose first act was to tear up the constitution. Nowhere was the indignation more intense than in the University which formed the glory of the Kingdom. Seven of the leading Professors, among them Gervinus and Dahlmann, Ewald and the Grimms, united in a resounding protest, and were immediately deprived of their posts. The action of 'the Göttingen Seven' is a landmark in German history, signalising at once the growing strength of constitutional principles and the emergence of the Professors as an influence in politics. The courageous declaration made the name of Gervinus for the first time familiar throughout Germany, and the plaudits encouraged him in his resolve to awaken his countrymen to political self-consciousness. 'The active life,' he declared in his 'Historik,' written at this moment, 'is the focus of all history. All the forces of mankind concentrate on action.'

Among the methods he employed was the composition of a history of German poetry. 'The age which seemed to me called to undertake a reconstruction of civic life continued to write poetry. I soon became convinced that the epoch of real greatness in German poetry was past.' Literature, moreover, was mere dilettantism while great and serious work was waiting to be done. A nation must concentrate its powers. 'You must decide,' he wrote in the dedication of the fourth volume to Dahlmann, 'whether I have succeeded in a subject which is as a rule discussed æsthetically. Our belles-lettres have become a stagnant bog, filled with such poisonous substances that men are sighing for a storm from without. If the life of Germany is not to stand still, we must attract the talents which have now no goal to the practical work of the State.' The book was a pantheon in which there was no more room, for the last of the immortals was Goethe. Though the motive was practical, the 'History of German Poetry' possesses a value of its own. Rejecting the æsthetic criticism that had been dominant, he endeavoured to seize the connection of writings and their authors with their time. It was this attempt to place literature in its historical setting that renders the work a landmark. It was, moreover, in its earlier portions, almost wholly new. For the first time Germany possessed a detailed narrative of her literary growth. Jakob Grimm hailed it with enthusiasm, expressing special admiration for its patriotic spirit.

On the completion of the 'History of German Poetry,' Gervinus was called to Heidelberg, where his lectures drew large audiences.

His aim, as ever, was to fire his hearers with worthy political ambitions. In 1847 he founded the *Deutsche Zeitung*, with the aid of Dahlmann, Droysen, Häusser and other Professors, to demand constitutional government and to work for German unity. The refusal of the Imperial crown by Frederick William IV transformed him into a bitter critic of Prussia. He now devoted himself to the chief historical undertaking of his life, but before approaching his main task he wrote a volume of prolegomena. The 'Introduction to the History of the Nineteenth Century' may be read by itself without regard to the bulky work of which it forms the vestibule.[1] For the last three or four centuries, he declared, history has been moving in a single direction, in spite of hindrances and curves, from the freedom of the individual to that of the masses. Modern history is the struggle of the democratic ideas thrown up by the Reformation with the aristocratic structures of the Middle Ages and the absolutism of the crown. Since Napoleon individuals have been of little importance, and the movements of the time are carried forward by the instinct of the masses. Will the Fourth Estate now triumph? Germany already possesses intellectual and religious freedom, and she awaits political emancipation.

This eloquent tribute to the strength of democracy was followed by a prosecution for treason in Baden. The author was comdemned to imprisonment and his book to destruction; and though the sentence was reversed, it revealed the dangers of democratic propaganda. The first volume of the History appeared in 1855 with a flattering dedication to Schlosser. 'It will follow up your work on the eighteenth century, and if you find it in part worthy to be considered a continuation my ambition will be more than satisfied. I have learned from you such deep-rooted reverence for the majesty and greatness of history that it alone would make me free from passion, favour or fear. I hope I may exhibit something of that splendid sanity with which your writings are penetrated.' There is a good deal of Schlosser in the book, but the tone is more serene. Parts of the work, above all the volumes relating to the revolutions in South America and the Greek war of independence, provided a detailed narrative of little-known events. In dealing with Central Europe he claimed that the history of the Congresses was related for the first time from authentic documents, but the most interesting sections to-day are the surveys of literature and intellectual movements. His strength lay in his width of vision, in his interpretation of the ideas fermenting beneath the crust of things. His book was described by Treitschke, an unfriendly witness, as one of the most thoughtful histories in existence. He is

[1] It was translated into English in 1853.

everywhere on the side of the opposition—in Greece, Italy, Spain, America, Central Europe. Metternich is the evil genius of the time, his statesmanship an utter failure. Gentz, his tool, was bought by Austria, and prostituted his great powers to the cause of absolutism. Frederick William III only escapes equal condemnation because his despotism was feeble and ineffective. The brightest spot of Central Europe was South Germany. The chief benefactors of their age were not rulers but writers.

Gervinus keenly sympathised with the democratic movement of the nineteenth century, but he was insensitive to the equally strong nationalist current that was beginning to flow. He had always maintained that Italy could never become a single state, and even when unification was in sight he demanded a federation. The man who had exhorted his countrymen to political activity witnessed the unification of Germany without enthusiasm. He declared that the Middle States of Germany could boast a far more glorious history than the two Great Powers' by which they were overshadowed. In his eighth and closing volume, which ends with 1866, he explains the war of 1864 by Bismarck's desire to distract attention from domestic problems, and pronounces him destitute of moral ideas. The events of 1866 moved him to indignation, and he was only partially consoled by the victories of 1870. In the preface to the fifth edition of the 'History of German Poetry,' written after Sedan, he declares that Dahlmann and the Grimms, to whom he had dedicated his book, would not have given way to this intoxicated enthusiasm. 'I am a neutral, belonging to no party, neither aristocrat nor democrat, possessing no ties of interest with any state or princely house. I have always urged a federation, not a Prussian hegemony based on force.' Political freedom had at all times seemed to him a far greater prize than national unity and national strength. In Acton's words he personified the middle-class German from the smaller towns of the smaller states. It is not surprising that to a fiery nationalist like Treitschke he 'hardly belonged to any nation.'

The 'History of the Nineteenth Century' is now almost forgotten. While narrating the progress of constitutional movements he carried his readers with him, but his indifference to the spirit of nationality with which Germany was throbbing created an estrangement. Moreover there were other obstacles to success. His style had never been attractive, and he became increasingly prolix. His inability to appreciate men of whose policy he disapproved gives the book a one-sided character. The life-long enemy of doctrinaires was himself one of the greatest doctrinaires of the century. He had scoffed at Ranke's mild judgments, remarking that

he tried to wash without getting wet, but the censorious fashions of
Gervinus and his master are out of date. We may, however, echo
Ranke's generous words on the death of his old critic: 'It is best
that not all should attain to historical science by the same path.'

II

Unlike his friend Savigny, Ranke owed little of his influence
to his lectures. We possess several accounts of his method, which
closely agree in the main points. 'The first impression when he
appeared at the table,' writes Sybel,[1] 'was one of astonishment.
The great head framed with dark curly hair set on a little figure,
the incessant movement that followed the play of thought with
hasty gesture, the lecture itself, now stopping to search for the
right expression, now rushing forward in headlong rapidity, all
this seemed strange and almost repellent. But when one grew
accustomed to these habits one was carried away by the rich profusion of the content, the colourful and plastic grace of the form,
while the independent research and the originality of conception
appeared throughout.' 'The unusual liveliness,' records Giesebrecht,[2] 'was at first disconcerting. The lecture was thoroughly
prepared. The notes lay before the teacher, but his words came
forth as a creation of the moment and at times his material seemed
to overwhelm him. The stream rarely flowed evenly. First it would
issue slowly and then so rapidly that it was difficult to follow; or
again there would be a long pause, because the speaker seemed
unable to find the word which conveyed the picture of his fancy.'
'Ranke's lectures,' testifies Hermann Grimm,[3] 'chained me from
the first word to the last. He filled beginners with the feeling that
they were witnessing affairs with the experience of veteran statesmen. He spoke as if he had been present at all the incidents which
he described.' Two sketches of the later years may complete the
picture. 'He spoke without great animation,' writes Reuss,[4] who
attended his lectures in 1862, 'and was only audible on the front
benches. But sometimes he arrived with a more rapid step, produced some new book from his pocket, and discussed in animated
improvisation questions of method and criticism arising out of it.
Then his wrinkled face lit up with a singular flame, he gesticulated
like a young man, and those who were attentive and advanced
enough to profit by the oracles were amply compensated for many
dull sittings.' 'To understand his lectures,' declares Cherbuliez,

[1] *Vorträge u. Abhandlungen*, 1897.   [2] *Rede*, 1887.
[3] *Beiträge z. deutschen Culturgeschichte*, 38, 1897.
[4] *Revue Historique*, vol. xxxi.

'incredible application was needed. His voice was low and indistinct, at once monotonous and languishing. But the animation of his face and the vivacity of his gestures bore witness to his interest. It was with his eyes that he recounted.' His courses were continued till 1871, when ill-health compelled him to desist.

It was not in the lecture-room that Ranke's influence as a teacher was most effective. The famous 'school' by which historical method was revolutionised was founded in his own study. His *Seminar* began in 1833, and was attended by a group of students, every one of whom was to win fame in the boundless fields of research. 'We, his most intimate disciples,' wrote Giesebrecht after the master's death, 'whom he collected round him in his home, found opportunity to gaze at close range into the workshop of this untiringly creative mind. Our admiration was aroused by his wide knowledge, his many-sided culture, the rapidity with which he seized points and his genius in criticism. He would break into joyous laughter when he succeeded in destroying a false tradition or in reconstructing events as they occurred. At this time, when his name was becoming known in every wider circles, I made his intimate acquaintance and felt myself powerfully attracted by him. He was in the full strength of early manhood, and everything in him was movement and zeal.' Other traits are added by Sybel in his memorial address. 'The *Seminar* was founded for those who chose history as their profession. He allowed free choice of theme, but was always ready with suggestions. Sins against the canons of criticism met with a merciless judgment couched in friendly terms. The master encouraged each talent to develop along its own lines.'

The *Seminar* would have in any case influenced the world by leaving an ineffaceable stamp on its members, but it was to make a more direct appeal. In 1834 Ranke persuaded the University to offer a prize for an essay on Henry I. Waitz and Giesebrecht, Köpke and Hirsch competed. The prize was won by Waitz, but the unsuccessful candidates had also learned to love mediæval history. The merit of the essays and the enthusiasm aroused in their authors suggested to Ranke that his pupils should undertake some co-operative task. Though his own studies lay chiefly in modern history, he directed them to the more difficult paths of the Middle Ages. As Stenzel had chosen the Franconians and Raumer the Hohenstaufen, the Saxon Emperors were selected. 'Unforgettable were the hours we spent on the Annals,' wrote Giesebrecht in his memorial notice of Köpke.[1] 'The charm of the first attack on a large literary undertaking was heightened by the co-operation of a number of young men at work on a common task with which

[1] *Historisches Taschenbuch,* 1872.

they were to appear before the world, desiring to honour both their incomparable teacher and themselves. We were led by Waitz, and a close friendship arose between us. The circle soon broke up, some leaving Berlin, but each of us had found his life-work.' Ranke wrote the preface to the Annals, which began to appear in 1837. The first volume was Waitz's prize essay on Henry I, revised and enlarged. Köpke and Dönniges shared Otto the Great. The two later Ottos were undertaken by Giesebrecht and Wilmans. The authors built up an unvarnished narrative of events on the basis of the whole available material. These little volumes, following on Stenzel's narrative, inaugurated the critical study of the Middle Ages.

Before approaching the three great scholars whose names are imperishably associated with their master, we may glance at one or two other members of that famous circle. Köpke, who had won the second prize in the competition on Henry I, became a colleague of Ranke at Berlin and collaborated in the *Monumenta*. At his death his old master declared in touching words that it was God's grace to have been connected with so pure a soul for more than a generation. Hirsch likewise became Professor at Berlin, and devoted the greater part of a short life to his monumental study of the Emperor Henry II. Wilmans rendered valuable service to the *Monumenta*. Dönniges, after a brief professorial career at Berlin, entered the service of Maximilian of Bavaria and exchanged history for diplomacy. Adolf Schmidt edited the first serious historical review, the pages of which were largely filled with the contributions of his fellow-pupils. Among others who passed through the *Seminar* in its early years were Nitzsch and Duncker, Burckhardt and Gneist, Roscher and Pauli.[1]

The master always declared that he had never seen such burning zeal in any pupil as in Jaffé,[2] a Polish Jew, who early resolved to attempt for the Popes what Böhmer had achieved for the Emperors. In 1851 appeared the 'Regesta Pontificum' to the accession of Innocent III, containing 11,000 documents, letters and bulls, many copied direct from manuscripts discovered by himself. The work left Böhmer far behind in critical method, and was of scarcely less value for the Empire than for the Church. He next threw himself into the work of the *Monumenta*; but on the ground of its slow progress he devoted his later years to the inde-

[1] Ranke's *Zur eigenen Lebensgeschichte*, 1890, and *Neue Briefe*, 1949, contain much of his correspondence with his pupils. There is interesting material in ' Briefe an Ranke von einigen seinen Schüler,' *Hist. Zeitschrift*, vol. cvii.

[2] See Dove's article in *Allg. deutsche Biog.*, reprinted in *Ausgewählte Schriftchen*, 1898.

pendent publication of materials for German history in handy form, modelled on Böhmer's 'Fontes.' Each of the six volumes of his 'Bibliotheca Rerum Germanicarum' was grouped round a man or a place—Boniface and Hildebrand, Charles the Great and Alcuin, Corvey and Bamberg. Furnished with introductions and summaries and containing a good deal of new material, they facilitated the study of the Middle Ages at first hand. His suicide at the age of fifty-one deprived German scholarship of one of its most brilliant brains.

Among Ranke's pupils was Maximilian of Bavaria.[1] After attending the classes of Heeren and Dahlmann at Göttingen, the prince passed to Berlin, and a life-long intimacy commenced which was to bear golden fruit for historical studies. Looking back on his royal friend in his ninetieth year Ranke declared that, though inferior to Frederick William IV in personality and breadth of culture, he was peculiarly thoughtful. On his death he wrote of him as 'my best friend, my truest pupil, my most eager reader, my kindest patron. Though we disagreed in many things, there was never a shadow between us.' Their letters breathe affection and intellectual sympathy. 'I have not only read but studied your book on the Reformation,' wrote the Catholic prince in 1845. The correspondence ranged over national and international politics as well as scholarship. When the abdication of Ludwig I in 1848 brought Maximilian to the throne, he determined to utilise his friendship with the greatest of German historians: what his father had done for art he would do for historical science. 'It is my earnest desire,' he wrote in 1853, 'to bring you to Munich. My object is the planting of the new historical method and the foundation of an historical school in Bavaria like that of North Germany.' The letter was signed 'Your old pupil.' Ranke refused to desert Berlin, but in the following year he visited the King at Berchtesgaden, and delivered the lectures on 'The Epochs of Modern History' which were published after his death.

The King realised that for the fulfilment of his aim scholars must be imported. As Ranke was not to be had, he accepted his advice to call Sybel, who was shortly followed by Cornelius and Giesebrecht. The next step was to found the Historical Commission of the Bavarian Academy,[2] with Ranke as President and Sybel as Secretary. Though bearing a Bavarian title and supported

[1] See Dove, 'Ranke u. Sybel in ihrem Verhältniss zu König Max,' in *Ausgewählte Schriftchen*, 1898; and Ranke's memorial address, *Abh. u. Versuche, neue Sammlung*, 507–16, 1888. Part of their correspondence was published in the *Deutsche Revue*, 1904.

[2] See Sybel u. Giesebrecht, *Die Historische Commission*, 1858–83, 1883; and Moriz Ritter's article in *Hist. Zeitschrift*, vol. ciii.

by Bavarian funds, the Historical Commission formed a common ground for all German-speaking historical scholars, and has done more to further historical studies in Germany than any other institution. Ranke virtually chose the first members, and the annual meetings brought together the leading historians of Germany, Austria and Switzerland. Among its publications are the 'Dictionary of German Biography,' the 'Histories of the Sciences,' the 'Chronicles of the German Towns' (with which the name of Karl Hegel is inseparably connected), the 'Annals of the Mediæval Empire,' and the 'Acts of the Imperial Diet' (in which Julius Weizsäcker won enduring fame). Of more local interest was the correspondence of the Wittelsbachs during the sixteenth and seventeenth centuries. A large part of this immense burden was borne by Ranke's pupils, who also took a leading share in the *Historische Zeitschrift* founded in 1859 under the editorship of Sybel. Before the death of the King in 1866 he had the satisfaction of knowing that his ideal had been fully realised. The credit of the idea belongs to the ruler. That it was carried out is the merit of his beloved teacher.

When Ranke was surrounded by his children and grandchildren he used to say, 'I have another and older family, my pupils and their pupils.' His son relates that he was prouder of Sybel's 'French Revolution' than of any of his own books. 'With Waitz and Sybel,' he wrote to Giesebrecht in 1877, 'you make my glory as teacher complete.' The oldest and the greatest was Waitz.[1] While at school he devoured Niebuhr's revised volumes as they appeared. 'From him I learned to love constitutional history, and to emulate him became my highest goal.' He studied law at Kiel and, like Mommsen, passed from law to history. On entering Berlin in 1833 at the age of twenty he attended the lectures of Savigny, but soon found his true vocation in Ranke's *Seminar*. 'I met him in Ranke's circle;' wrote Sybel half a century later, 'and still remember how his superior knowledge and incisive criticism impressed me, while his friendliness made his acquaintance a delight. Conscientiousness was ever his leading characteristic.' He won the hotly contested prize on Henry I, and, next to Ranke himself, was the leading spirit in the Saxon Annals. It was intended to add a series of critical studies of the sources, but only one volume appeared. Ranke had pointed out in the *Seminar* that

---

[1] See E. Waitz, *Georg Waitz*, 1913. The best appreciations are by Kluckhohn, *Vorträge u. Aufsätze*, 1894; Wattenbach in *Abhandlungen der Berliner Akademie*, 1886; Sybel, *Vorträge u. Abhandlungen*, 1897; Frensdorff in *Allg. deutsche Biog.* A brief autobiography is prefixed to his little volume, *Deutsche Kaiser*, 1862.

the Chronicle of Corvey was of little value, and Waitz and Hirsch proved it a forgery. It was his first important discovery. When help was needed for the *Monumenta*, Ranke recommended Waitz. By copying and collating manuscripts in many archives he produced editions which surpassed in value those of Pertz his chief. The record of his fruitful activity may be read in his contributions to the journal of the Society. His life was to end, as it began, in devotion to the work with which his name is more closely associated than any other scholar except Pertz himself. His old master watched his rapid advance with rapture. 'Your bold progress,' he wrote in 1838, 'evokes my greatest sympathy and joy. You are treading the path of Baluze and Mabillon.' Later he wrote, 'It will be counted merit to me in my biography to have contributed to direct such a force as yours to the study of history.'

The next chapter opens in 1842 with his appointment to Kiel, where he began the chief task of his life. The first volume of the 'German Constitutional History' appeared in 1844, and was naturally dedicated to Ranke. 'It is a sign of my grateful memory of the time when you were both teacher and friend, a proof of my affection and love.' The second edition, issued in 1865, renewed the dedication. 'It is a gift from one of the many who think of you with gratitude and love, you who taught us the methods of strict historical research and deep penetration into the life of all times and peoples.' The third edition, published in 1879, once more gave expression to the undying gratitude of the author to his octogenarian master. The first volume dealt with the origins, customs and institutions of the early races of Germany till the Frankish conquest of Gaul, and was in large measure a commentary on Tacitus, whose testimony is accepted as thoroughly trustworthy. He expresses a high opinion of the Germans and their civilisation, examines the family, inheritance, wergeld, the classes, political institutions and the army, making full use of Grimm's 'Legal Antiquities' and of Scandinavian scholarship. He declares popular assemblies to have been the central point of the life of the State. Monarchy, apart from mere military leadership, existed, though it was not universal. When charged with drawing a dim picture, he replied that he could not say more than he found in the sources. 'We cannot recreate the life in its entirety, as we know it chiefly from foreigners and from later developments, but its general character is certain.' The work was at once recognised as authoritative. Waitz was the first to master the whole mass of material and to interpret it in the light of other Teutonic experience. It did not, however, escape criticism. Sybel challenged his view of kingship, declaring that early German society knew nothing of royalty, which was derived later from Roman sources. Waitz issued a lengthy reply and lived long enough to see his view of kingship as German not Roman generally accepted. A comprehensive attack was to come a generation later from Fustel de Coulanges, who rejected his picture of a high civilisation among the German tribes.

The second volume dealt with Merovingian institutions, which he pronounced to be of pure German origin. The third and fourth volumes covered the Carolingian era, the fifth to the eighth being devoted to the Saxon and Franconian dynasties and bringing the survey down to the twelfth century. If the latter half of the work is inferior in interest and value to the former, the historian can scarcely be blamed. From the Carolingians to the Hohenstaufen the history of German law was almost a blank, and it is Waitz's merit to have been the first to map the country. The value of the attempt was recognised, even though Sohm and other admirers hinted that it was rather a collection of materials than a constitutional history. While the first four volumes were thoroughly revised by the author, the last four had to wait for revision by his pupils after his death. The 'Constitutional History' rendered possible the reconstruction of the political life of mediæval Germany, but it naturally failed to appeal to the amateur. Waitz lacked the literary skill which makes Stubbs readable and sometimes delightful. Nor did he weave his material into a broad narrative of national development like the Oxford Professor. Moreover his work, though twice the length of its English counterpart, covers a far shorter period. It is rather a series of massive dissertations than a history. Yet while lacking popular appeal it amply fulfils the demands of science. It superseded Eichhorn for the early Middle Ages, and even after the emergence of Brunner it remains a work to which the student of Teutonic institutions must have frequent recourse.

Waitz was keenly interested in the fortunes of his native Schleswig-Holstein, and was drawn into active politics by Danish encroachments. He was a deputy of the University in the Holstein estates, aided Droysen with materials for his defence of the historic rights of the Duchies, and was driven from Kiel in 1848. At Frankfurt he worked with Dahlmann and Droysen, sharing their hopes and disappointments. His interest in the Duchies survived his departure, and he set to work to compose their history. Two volumes brought the story to 1660. 'When I left Kiel,' he wrote in the 'Letter to Jacob Grimm,' which served as preface, 'I thought that this would bind me to the country. Schleswig-Holstein must never despair of the future of the German fatherland.' It was left incomplete, because he had not time to study all the archives. It was while thus engaged that he discovered materials which he worked into his great monograph on Wullenweber. His studies in many archives enabled him to recreate the manifold activities of the Hansa League in the sixteenth century, to revive the impressive figure of the Lubeck burgomaster, and to unravel a curious chapter in the history of European diplomacy. The 'Wullenweber' is the most lively of his books, and is the only one in which the foreground is occupied by a personality.

On his expulsion from Kiel Waitz accepted a call to Göttingen. His courses covered a wide range, and were frequented by jurists as well as historians. 'He had full notes,' records Kluckhohn, 'and attended more to them than to his hearers, but the lectures lacked neither life nor movement. He spoke so slowly and clearly that it was possible to write almost everything down, and we were anxious not to miss a word. His audiences were not large, but were composed of the best material.' During a quarter of a century numberless mediævalists went to Göttingen for their scientific baptism. His method was that which he had learned at Berlin, and Ranke was justified in saying 'Your pupils are my pupils.' The most vivid picture of the famous *Seminar* has been painted by Gabriel Monod,[1] who was a member in 1868. When the eager young Frenchman expressed his gratitude for his writings, Waitz replied that his best and most successful works were his pupils. 'My books will be superseded and forgotten, but they will have helped to make scholars who will write better ones.' His immense influence seemed to Monod to spring largely from his moral qualities; it was obvious that he desired to form men as well as savants. Critics used to complain that he never encouraged his pupils to rise above the technical study of sources, but he knew that artistic sense and philosophic grasp could not be taught. His influence undoubtedly led to the cult of detail, and Monod admits that some came to think that only the infinitely little could be effectively studied. If his bent was thus rather towards intensive than extensive culture, the benefit to mediæval studies of an army of exact workers cannot be exaggerated.

In addition to his professorial duties, the unending labour of the Constitutional History, and unceasing co-operation in the *Monumenta*, Waitz carried out a vast quantity of miscellaneous work.[2] The *Forschungen zur deutschen Geschichte*, which he persuaded the Historical Commission to establish, was carried on under his direction for a quarter of a century, and almost every

---

[1] In *Portraits et Souvenirs*, 1897.
[2] See Steindorff's *Bibliographische Übersicht*, 1886.

number contains a contribution from his pen. He published a
volume, based on his lectures, on political science, another on the
Emperors from Charles the Great to Maximilian. He revised and
enlarged his youthful work on Henry I. He enlarged Dahlmann's
bibliography of German history. He shared in the direction of the
Historical Commission, and rendered valuable assistance to the
Hansa Historical Society. As Ranke gradually withdrew from
active work, Göttingen took the place of Berlin. The famous
scholar loved the University of his adoption, and it was with
reluctance that in 1875 he accepted the call to assume the supreme
direction of the *Monumenta*, for which he had worked for forty
years. The great national enterprise, now amply subsidised,
entered on a new life. Reverting to the activities of his youth, he
visited foreign archives in search of manuscripts, and again re-
recorded his experiences in the journal. Mommsen, Sickel and other
leading scholars lent their services, and the Director was aided by
many of his old pupils. After his death his editorial policy was
sharply attacked by Ottokar Lorenz,[1] who complained that he
published worthless sources and too many selections from foreign
writers, while the work as a whole lacked chronological or geographical sequence. It is arguable that one or two works should
have been omitted, but Waitz's ten years' stewardship stands out
as a period of wisely directed activity.

Among those who welcomed his return to Berlin was his old
master. Ranke was never tired of expressing his admiration and
affection for his greatest pupil. 'My chief joy,' he wrote in 1865,
'is the friendship with which a man like you repays the stimulus
he perhaps received from me in youth.' 'That which we began
quietly,' he wrote in 1884, 'has grown to be a great tree, in which
the birds of the air make their nests. I told Waitz at that time that
he seemed to me to be destined to become the German Muratori.'
Master and pupil died on the same day, the former aged ninety, the
latter seventy-three. The one transformed the study of modern,
the other of mediæval history. While Ranke's books were read all
over the world, Waitz wrote for scholars, and it is only scholars
who can measure the magnitude of his services.

The second of Ranke's pupils to obtain world-wide fame was
Giesebrecht,[2] whose early monograph on Otto II was one of the

---

[1] Preface to vol. ii. of *Deutschlands Geschichtsquellen*, third ed., 1887.
Waitz was defended by Weiland, *Hist. Zeitschrift*, vol. lviii.

[2] See Riezler, *Gedächtnissrede*, 1891; Heigel, *Essays aus neuerer
Geschichte*, 1892; Sybel, *Vorträge u. Abhandlungen*, 1897. Acton's brief
appreciation, reprinted from the *English Historical Review* in *Historical
Essays and Studies*, 1907, is a masterpiece.

best of the Saxon Annals. The Emperor had been neglected both by contemporary and modern historians, overshadowed by his great father and his brilliant son. A year later he performed a task which ranks high among critical achievements. A chronicle of the time of Henry III was partially known through fifteenth and sixteenth century writers. From these indications he set to work to reconstruct the lost annals, and a generation later the discovery of Aventin's copy of the 'Annales Altahenses' established the accuracy of his workmanship. A grant enabled the young scholar to spend three years in Austria and Italy, which he used in amassing material for the work on the mediæval Empire which he had already resolved to undertake. He had learned from Ranke the secrets of the critical art, but he possessed other qualifications for the task of his life. He had grown up amid memories of the French occupation and the Wars of Liberation. Like his master he was never affected by the liberal ideas and constitutional movements of his youth, and he disliked France as the source of revolutionary contamination. The Berlin riots of 1848, of which he was an eye-witness, strengthened his conservative leanings. To prepare for a better future it was necessary to return to the noble ideas of the past—a powerful Empire, a vigorous Church, a God-fearing people. 'From my youth up,' he wrote, 'I have been filled with the conviction that the German nation can only regain its lost place in the world by closer unity. For decades I have given this conviction unflinching utterance and have championed it in every sphere open to me, and from this my book has grown.'

After twenty years of study the first volume of the 'History of the German Imperial Era' appeared in 1855. The term *Kaiserzeit*, he explained, was invented to denote the time when the Emperors controlled the fortunes of the West, when the German races became one people, when Germany reached the highest point in her history. The country had suffered and still suffered so grievously from disunion that all Germans ardently desired to revive a single, mighty state, though they disagreed as to the means of its realisation. Perhaps the study of this distant time might contribute to agreement—the time which speaks to us in the lofty minsters, the walls of ancient cities, the mossy castles, the sagas and the ballads. Modern ideas were so different that it was hardly realised that the men of old were of the same flesh and blood. 'I desire to bridge the gulf between science and the people, and I wish to be judged in the light of that endeavour.' His first plan was to offer a simple narrative, without notes or references; but as the book contained much that was new he felt it his duty to satisfy the legitimate demands of students. None the less he hoped that it would be read by

teachers in schools and even by their best pupils. Let them learn
how greatness once came from the Christian and heroic virtues of
their forefathers. 'History teaches that the soul is more than the
body. The science of German history is a torch which lights our
path and throws its beams forward as well as backward.' The
work was dedicated to Frederick William IV, the Christian King,
who loved the Middle Ages as much as he himself did.

It was the historian's intention to bring his narrative to the
end of the Hohenstaufen, and to complete it in three volumes;
but the plan was modified owing to its phenomenal success, and
when he died thirty-four years later he was still in the reign of
Barbarossa. The work, though incomplete,[1] embraced three centuries crowded with incident and romance. Beginning with a slight
sketch of the Carolingian Empire the narrative broadens with the
Saxon Emperors. The middle portion describes the epic struggle of
Henry IV and Hildebrand, and the closing volumes are dominated
by the majestic figure of Barbarossa. The whole era is depicted
as one of heroism and piety. He speaks of the great Emperors
with a sort of mystical fervour. The picture is aglow with colour
and aflame with national pride. 'The Empire,' he declares, 'made
the Germans one people. In the tenth century the name of
German was rare, in the eleventh it was common; it betokened
the people of might, the people by whom things were decided, the
people of peoples.' In his memorial notice of Ranke, Giesebrecht
declares that his lack of moral warmth diminished his popularity.
'Most readers of historical books seek not only instruction but
moral stimulus.' This tonic the *Kaiserzeit* offered in abundant
measure to a dispirited generation. It is an epic, related with epic
breadth. He said of his master that he was a great painter of
situations but not a great narrator. The verdict on his own
achievement is just the reverse. He was greatest as a narrator. In
his fragment of 1884, 'The Old Pupils,' Ranke declared that
Giesebrecht had a poetical vein and knew how to write in the far-
off days half a century before. Of the three great pupils he is the
only master of style. Waitz lacked literary faculty. Sybel's prose,
though clear and vigorous, was destitute of grace and charm.

If the public was captured by the moral fervour and the decorative style, the book won the applause of a smaller and more
critical audience by its scholarship. His reputation as a critic was
confirmed and extended. Böhmer hailed him as the soundest of
mediæval scholars. 'His notes,' declared Acton, 'contain the most
penetrating and instructive discussion of authorities to be found

---

[1] A sixth volume, in which B. von Simson continued the narrative to
the death of Barbarossa, appeared in 1895.

anywhere in modern literature.' To specialists, indeed, they were a richer prize than the text. With Giesebrecht criticism was a constructive, not a destructive science. Even Scheffer-Boichorst was impressed, and remarked to Simonsfeld, who undertook Barbarossa for the *Jahrbücher*, that his work was needless, since Giesebrecht was enough. Though a champion of the Empire, he has a genuine admiration for the Papacy. He describes events, but is sparing in judgments on the ideas which underlie them. His volumes were read with equal delight by Protestants and Catholics in North and in South Germany.

The only discordant note was struck by Sybel. In an address to the Bavarian Academy in 1859, on Narratives of the Imperial Era,[1] Sybel praised its technique, its literary talent, its warm religious sense, and its sincere patriotism, but he challenged its dominating thesis. While Giesebrecht believed that the Empire was both national and beneficial, to Sybel this conception appeared fundamentally unsound. The reverence for the old Empire, he declared, was quite recent. Raumer had painted in the æsthetic, not the historic spirit. 'Each stately and brilliant figure finds its place and receives its colour, but he never inquires what the country lost or gained by them.' Giesebrecht was far ahead of his predecessors in knowledge and technique, but he failed to bring his subject to the test of principles. Had he done so, he would have found that the Emperors gravely damaged the German nation by their universalism, and that their true policy was to build up a compact and vigorous national life. He contrasts Henry the Fowler, 'the first King of the German nation, the founder of the German Kingdom, the finest star in the broad firmament of our history,' with Henry VI, poised at a giddy height and reaching out a conquering arm in every direction.

This spirited attack provoked a reply, not from Giesebrecht himself who always avoided controversy, but from Ficker,[2] who accused Sybel of importing contemporary conceptions and controversies into a far distant age. Nationalism was then unknown, and the tendencies of the age were to universalism. Otto's Empire was neither a world monarchy nor a national state but grew naturally out of the time. Italy suffered most after the fall of the Empire, and Dante longed for its restoration. The Empire fell, not because it was founded on false principles but because Sicily destroyed the German kingship. Without the Empire Germany would have gone to pieces sooner. Ficker's little volume, resting

[1] Published 1859 and never reprinted.
[2] See ch. 13; 'Der Streit mit Sybel,' in Jung's admirable life of Ficker, 1907.

on profound knowledge, was an effective defence of the main
lines of Giesebrecht's conception. Sybel returned to the charge
in a booklet 'The German Nation and the Empire,' claiming that
he tested policies by their compatibility with German interests.
The centralised empire of Charles the Great was detrimental to
youthful races, which needed free play. Henry I was a national
King without Imperial pretences. Otto the Great, the second
founder of the Empire, reverted to the claim, half Roman, half
Christian, to rule over Christendom. The fall of the Empire in
the thirteenth century was a blessing for German nationality.
The book ends by repudiating Ficker's contention that nineteenth century Austria represented the mediæval Empire. She
had been purely dynastic and clerical, and had never given a
thought to the well-being of Germany of which Prussia was the
true leader. In this academic tournament Waitz took up a middle
position.

The polemic against Austria removed the question from the
tranquil sphere of historical discussion, but a different and more
justifiable charge came from another quarter. In a forcible
pamphlet a Slavonic scholar protested against the idealisation
of the German race.[1] In a national work admiration for the race
and its history was natural, but here it passed all bounds. The
historian's pages were filled with references to German love of
freedom, German loyalty, German thoroughness. 'Our race had
to fulfil its destiny for its own honour and for the good of mankind.' It was a Power 'ordered by God,' with a world-historic
mission. The author had two moral standards, one for Germans,
another for the rest of mankind. He declared German rule to
have raised the moral standard of Italy, though his own pages
recorded the terrible devastations of German armies. The book,
declared the critic, was full of contradictions. While the Germans
were the embodiment of every virtue, the centuries were dark
and bloody.

Giesebrecht's cult of the Empire and pride in his race helped
to make his book the political and moral influence that he had
desired. He declared that historiography always followed the
great impulses of public life. 'Ours is more national now because
we are all more conscious of nationality. It will first show its full
strength when a German state renders us master of our own
destinies.' In 1871, when the happy consummation had been
reached, the historian confessed that the old Empire had neither
saved the nation from splitting up nor kept German territory
inviolate. That the new Empire had taken a better form than

[1] Lepar, *Über die Tendenz von Giesebrecht's Geschichte*, Prague, 1868.

that which he had glorified was a crowning mercy. 'Your great work,' wrote Ranke to his old pupil in 1878, 'fills me with joy and satisfaction. You combine criticism with a loving, poetic patriotism, and your presentation is at once virile and childlike. It is a work that has grown into the time and its movements.' But just because it formed such an intimate part of its time, a new time has left it behind. We have outlived the romanticism which possessed Giesebrecht hardly less strongly than Raumer. The goldén glow has faded into the light of common day. It is a record of action rather than a study of problems. Constitutional, economic and intellectual elements are almost wholly neglected. Yet its sterling scholarship preserves it from the total oblivion which has overtaken nearly every monument of the romantic and patriotic oohoolo.

Giesebrecht, like Macaulay, succeeded in his ambition of writing a book which people would read; but, unlike Macaulay, he commanded the general confidence of scholars. When Sybel's pugnacity made him impossible in Munich, King Max wrote to Giesebrecht: 'My whole hope of furthering historical studies lies in you.' He arrived in 1862 and succeeded where his predecessor had failed. He proved himself to be, as Ranke described him in 1863, 'a pure, well-meaning, deeply cultured and trustworthy man, gentle but not without a kernel.' He was an original member of the Historical Commission, and on his arrival in Munich became its secretary. As the President became too infirm to attend the annual meetings, he represented him and carried out his double task with unflagging energy. On Ranke's death he modestly refused the reversion, which passed to Sybel. In 1874 he revived the series of histories begun by Heeren and Ukert, and when Waitz took over the *Monumenta* he joined the board of control. His academic tasks and the repeated revisions of his earlier volumes impeded the progress of the *Kaiserzeit*; but the quality of the work showed no deterioration, and the reign of Barbarossa is one of its most perfect parts. His position among historians has been defined by Acton. 'He never became a European classic, like Ranke and Mommsen. He was neither the head of a school like Waitz, nor the chief of a party like Sybel. Disciples of Baur knew more than he of the growth of doctrines, and disciples of Richter about ecclesiastical institutions. Sohm and Gierke were superior to him in politics and law, Ficker and Denifle were more powerful originators. He did not speak with authority of things that came before Clovis or after Manfred. Nobody turned to him for explanation of the civil code, the rise of universities, the philosophy of Abelard, or the significance of Citeaux.

His limitations were distinctly marked and they were part of his strength. He spent a long life in mastering a single epoch and writing a single book. But among all his countrymen employed on the Middle Ages no one was more widely known and read and trusted; and the *Kaiserzeit* was the nearest mediæval equivalent of the *Römische Geschichte* and the *Zeitalter der Reformation.*'

The youngest and most brilliant of Ranke's three great pupils was destined to a career widely different from the tranquil fortunes of Waitz and Giesebrecht. Sybel[1] devoted his strength to renewing the connection of history with politics which his master had done his utmost to break, and it is only in his early years that he can be counted a member of the Ranke school. A child of the Rhineland, he grew up in an atmosphere more liberal than was to be found elsewhere in North Germany; but the Protestants, who were almost lost in the Catholic mass, looked to Prussia as their champion. Thus the future spokesman of the National Liberals learned at home the two dominating principles of his later career—constitutionalism and Prussian hegemony. Like Waitz, he pored over Niebuhr's Roman History while still at school, and learned to love Burke, 'who was a permanent influence in my political orientation.' Reaching Berlin in 1834, at the early age of seventeen, he was at once admitted into Ranke's *Seminar*, and he was never weary of expressing his gratitude to his incomparable master. 'You have shown me the way to science,' he testified in 1867, 'you have always been my model. I have no dearer hope than that my name will be worthy of a place in the long list of your pupils.'

Sybel took no part in the Saxon Annals, but his Doctor's dissertation on Jordanes, suggested by his master, won the praises of Waitz and, in a later generation, of Mommsen. Among the theses that he defended in the examination was that the fortunes of peoples depended on individuals, not on institutions, and that the writing of history *sine ira et studio* was a false ideal. Thus he already began to show the independence which was later to lead him far from his youthful moorings. 'Ranke opened for Sybel the portals of the temple of science,' declares Bailleu with truth, 'but he made his own way inside.' His first important work was likewise the outcome of the suggestion of his master, who had pointed out that William of Tyre and Albert of Aachen were dangerous guides. Acting on this hint he examined the whole range of sources and wrote his 'History of the First Crusade.' Ranke hailed the book as a wholly admirable achievement, and

[1] See Varrentrapp's biography prefixed to Sybel's *Vorträge u. Abhandlungen*, 1897.

declared himself proud to possess such a pupil. He destroyed many legends, robbed Peter the Hermit and Godfrey of Bouillon of their aureole, and constructed a plain tale from the best authorities. The pious Höfler complained that he put the chroniclers under the anatomical knife. The book remained the standard account of a great European event till Kugler and Röhricht— a long life for the work of a young man of twenty-four.

Sybel, now Docent at Bonn, lectured on the *Völkerwanderung*, and was soon immersed in the study of early German institutions. 'The Origin of German Kingship,' published in 1844, covered part of the same ground as the first volume of Waitz, which appeared in the same year, but reached widely different conclusions. The *Völkerwanderung*, he declared, was only intelligible if the Germans were semi-nomadic. Tribal organisation was incapable of producing a true state life, which arose from the fructifying influence of Roman culture. Among the greatest debts of German civilisation to Rome was monarchy. Leo, who had emphasised Roman influences in the political development of the Germans, was loud in his praises; but Waitz maintained that his view degraded the Germans, and rejected his theories of Roman influence and the tribal constitution.

The Middle Ages cast no glamour over Sybel, and the year of the 'German Kingship' witnessed the first of his many bouts with the Roman Church. A vast number of pilgrims, calculated at a million, came to Trier to view the Holy Coat. The young Docent was disgusted, and with the aid of a colleague rapidly collected material for a booklet in which he declared that he had found traces of twenty other Holy Coats. Thousands of copies were sold and a second part was added in reply to Catholic criticisms. Though the authors declared that their attack was not on the Roman Church but on a false relic, the Catholics never forgave him, and Sybel was confirmed in his conviction that Catholicism was the stronghold of obscurantism. The champion of Protestantism was rewarded by a call to his first professorial chair at Marburg. The lectures which it was his duty to deliver on the modern world and on German history since 1815 increased his interest in the problems of his own time, while the misrule of the Elector of Hesse provoked his indignation. His conversion from a mediævalist was completed by the events of 1848, which led him to the French Revolution. Henceforth the academic allegiance to Ranke is at an end, and the life of Sybel becomes merged in the fortunes of the Prussian School.

CHAPTER VIII

THE PRUSSIAN SCHOOL

RANKE began his career and founded his school in the era of political stagnation between the Wars of Liberation and the revolution of 1848, but in the middle of the century the attitude of detachment from the burning problems of the day became impossible. In the making of the German Empire no small part fell to the group of Professors who by tongue and pen preached the gospel of nationality and glorified the Hohenzollerns.

I

The spiritual father of the Prussian School was Dahlmann.[1] The French invasion filled him with indignation, and, in company with Kleist, with whom hatred of Napoleon amounted to monomania, he walked across Germany to Aspern after the battle to join the Austrian forces. Though he had never attended a lecture on history, he was appointed to a chair at Kiel in 1812. His first publication was a study of Saxo Grammaticus, applying the critical methods which he had learned from Wolf at Halle. Scandinavian circles were scandalised by the overthrow of their idol, but Stein was so delighted that he invited him to aid the *Monumenta*. He agreed to help, but after some minor contributions withdrew on the ground that certain members of the reactionary Bundestag had become connected with the enterprise. The middle years of his life were devoted to a history of Denmark. He loved Teutonic antiquities and, like Freeman, sought traces of the freedom which was the pole-star of his life. Written with sympathy, learning and power, the work, which carried the story to the Reformation, won him honourable fame among the scholars of Europe. It is not, however, as an historian but as a political teacher that he claims a place in a chapter on the Prussian School. He had early reached the conviction that

[1] Springer's *F. C. Dahlmann*, 1870–2, is a full and masterly biography. The best appreciations are by Waitz, *Rede auf Dahlmann*, 1885; Treitschke, *Aufsätze*, vol. i., 1865; Lorenz, *Die Geschichtswissenschaft*, chap. 2, 1886; Sybel, *Drei Bonner Historiker*, in *Vorträge u. Aufsätze*, 1874; Marcks, *Männer u. Zeiten*, vol. i., 1911; and Dilthey, *Gesammelte Schriften*, xi., 164–85. Janssen's study in *Zeit- u. Lebensbilder*, 1889, gives the Catholic view.

constitutional monarchy was the best form of government, and his treatise on Political Science, published in 1835, embodied his demand. His sincerity was tested in 1837, when he joined in the resounding protest against the action of the King of Hanover. Ejected from Göttingen he found refuge at Bonn, where he reached the highest point of his influence. His histories of the English and French Revolutions were frankly political, warning rulers of the consequence of attacking or refusing constitutions. Emerging again in 1848, he battled manfully for a liberal Empire under Prussian hegemony. After his bitter disappointment he gave up writing, but he continued to teach the doctrines of nationality and constitutionalism. The testimonies of colleagues and pupils to his massive personality are unanimous. Waitz spoke of him as granite and bronze, and declared that no one did more to spread the idea of a single Reich. Sybel describes his impressive oratory and restrained passion. Treitschke devoted one of his finest essays to the master to whom he owed more than to any other man.

The Prussian School owed part of its strength to the fact that its members were not all Prussian by birth or residence. Häusser[1] was won for history by the lectures of Schlosser at Heidelberg. His talent developed rapidly, and at twenty-seven he issued a detailed history of the Palatinate. The treatment of the Middle Ages was superficial, but with the Reformation the stream broadens and deepens. The Thirty Years War is narrated at length, and the life and culture of Court and people in the seventeenth and eighteenth centuries are illustrated by new material. The full-length portrait of Karl Ludwig, the kernel of the book, is painted with remarkable power. In relating the fortunes of the Palatinate he never forgets the wider problems which confronted the German people. In addition to his great monograph he wrote detailed criticisms of historical works in the *Allgemeine Zeitung*.[2] He never appreciated Ranke's greatness, and found him artificial and anæmic. His hero was Dahlmann. Historians of the study, he declared, were common, historians of life were rare. As the Year of Revolution approached he joined in the demand for national unity and a constitution for every State. He wrote on the Schleswig-Holstein question, assisted Gervinus with the *Deutsche Zeitung*, and entered the Baden Parliament, where his eloquence made him a prominent

---

[1] The best accounts are by Marcks in *Heidelberger Professoren*, vol. i., 1903; Kluckhohn, *Vorträge u. Aufsätze*, 1894, and Wattenbach, *L. Häusser, Ein Vortrag*, 1867.

[2] Republished as *Gesammelte Schriften*, 2 vols., 1869.

figure. At Erfurt he declared that Prussia was the nucleus on which the crystal of the German State must grow. In a biography of his friend List he emphasised his endeavours for a fuller and more virile national life.

Häusser's main occupation from 1850 to his early death in 1867 was the history of Germany during the revolutionary and Napoleonic wars. No detailed German narrative of that moment-ous generation existed, and in the South the French version of the time, recently confirmed by Thiers, was still dominant. That a Baden Professor should come forward with a warm tribute to Prussia's services to the fatherland in the hour of trial was an event in the political as well as in the academic world. The work appeared between 1854 and 1857, and was eagerly welcomed throughout the country. The author lived to issue a second and third edition, enriching his pages with a mass of new material. He begins with a rapid sketch of the Empire from the peace of Westphalia, with special reference to Prussia. He expressed a warm admiration for the Great Elector and Frederick William I, and hails Frederick the Great as a new model of kinship. The narrative proper begins with the accession of Frederick William II who is treated with marked severity. He defends the peace of Basel and draws Thugut in the darkest colours. The period of revival is described in a spirit of militant patriotism. The apostasy of Johannes Müller is castigated, Fichte and Arndt are exalted, and the heroic story of Hofer is related in full. The fourth volume deals with the Liberation, from Leipzic to Waterloo. Napoleon is the incarnation of foreign domination, Stein the deliverer. Little attention is devoted to internal reforms, and the references to literature and opinion are meagre. It is a pæan to the statesmen and soldiers of Prussia, an emphatic warning against the seductions of French ideas.

Häusser, declared Treitschke in his preface to the fourth edition, made no attempt to write for specialists. 'His aim was higher. After French scholarship had long dominated our his-torical vision, he first taught us to look at the Wars of Liberation with German eyes.' No work did more to awaken the political consciousness of the German people, but it possessed no qualities capable of prolonging its authority. Treitschke's first volume was to provide a briefer but far more brilliant study of the period, and more recently the Bavarian Heigel traversed the ground, paying special recognition to the movement of ideas, which Häusser almost entirely neglected. His influence was exerted not only by his books but by his lectures. His course on German history was attended by the townspeople of Heidelberg, officials and princes; among his hearers were many who were to take an active part in founding the Empire. His chief task, declares Wattenbach, was to make good citizens and good Germans. He was penetrated with a sense of the commanding rôle which a strong and united Germany would play in the world, and was convinced that such unity could only be achieved through Prussia. Everywhere we feel the man of action behind the scholar. In presenting the treaty of Versailles to the Baden Chamber Jolly declared with truth that, more than any other man, Häusser had taught the youth of South Germany the larger patriotism.

Another member of the Prussian School at whom we must glance before reaching its three greatest figures was Duncker.[1] Co-operating with Dahlmann, Droysen and other Professors at Frankfurt, he declared that the German question was not one of freedom but of force. He succeeded Dahlmann at Bonn, and acted as political adviser to Crown Prince Frederick. He entered the Prussian Chamber and supported Bismarck in his conflict with Parliament. Appointed Director of the Archives at Berlin in 1867, he co-operated in publishing the Acts of the Great Elector and the political correspondence of Frederick the Great. He wrote a number of valuable essays, chief among them a massive dissertation on Prussia during the French occupation. His writings breathe an almost mystical devotion to the dynasty, and on the death of his bosom friend Droysen he was appointed Historiographer of Brandenburg. Though his main achievement was the 'History of Antiquity,' we learn from Treitschke that he considered his share in the struggles for German unity the best work of his life.

II

The eldest of the three great figures who made the Prussian School celebrated all over the world and profoundly influenced German politics was Droysen.[2] Born two years after Jena, the son of a military chaplain of Blücher's corps, his first recollection was the sound of the guns which announced the entry of the Allies into Paris. At Berlin he plunged into Greek history and literature, and his first important achievement was a brilliant

[1] See Haym's biography, 1891, and Treitschke's tribute in his *Aufsätze*, vol. iv., 1897.

[2] Gustav Droysen's full-length biography of his father, 1910, only reaches 1848. The best surveys are by Meinecke, *Schaffender Spiegel*, 146–210, 1948; Hintze, *Historische u. politische Aufsätze*, vol. iv. (reprinted from *Allg. Deutsche Biog.*); Max Duncker, *Abhandlungen zur neueren Geschichte*, 1887; and Dove, *Ausgewählte Schriftchen*, 1898.

translation of Æschylus, followed by a rendering of Aristophanes which ranks with Voss' Homer and Schlegel's Shakespeare. While still at the University he determined to write a life of Alexander the Great, and the volumes on Hellenism which followed won him a solid reputation. Unlike most historians of Greece, he belived that she deserved her fate because she could not secure unity or power. When appointed Extraordinary Professor of Ancient History and Classical Philology at Berlin in 1836, it appeared as if he would dedicate himself wholly to antiquity, but a call to Kiel in 1840 altered the current of his life.

The lectures on the Era of the Wars of Liberation, delivered in 1842–3, were revised and published in 1846, and mark the beginning of the change. 'Our youth,' declared the preface, 'no longer believes in the deeds of prowess and the enthusiasm of that age. My object is to express and justify the love of and belief in the fatherland.' His pages pulse with fire and emotion. He shows that the characteristic of the era, expressing itself equally in the New and the Old World, was the revolt against absolute monarchy and aristocracy. 'Our faith gives us the assurance that God's hand guides events, both great and small, and the science of history has no higher task than to justify this faith.' The divine plan was the association of the people in the life of the state. Napoleon was defeated by the Prussian people. Thus the American revolt, the French Revolution, and the uprising of Prussia were three connected steps towards liberty and nationality. They had been followed by reaction and stagnation, and the fourth step was still to take. After this preliminary survey he turns to a detailed investigation of the period. He shows that the modern state began with the Reformation and reached its model in Louis XIV. Frederick the Great introduced a new conception of monarchy, but the state was still only a machine. Old Europe was rotten, and Rousseau was right to attack the evils of government and society. The revolt of the American colonies was the dawn of a brighter day. Droysen sympathises with the French Revolution, and praises the character and work of the French. The war of 1792, he declares, was defensive, and he pronounces the murder of Poland a far greater crime than the death of Louis XVI. The Revolution conquered the distinction between the people and the state, and Mirabeau rightly foretold that it would make its way round the world. A detailed account of the reforms of Stein and the growth of German patriotism leads up to the Wars of Liberation. The lines are large and bold, and he was never again to achieve such richness of colouring. The text of the book is rather liberty than nationality.

Frederick William IV accepted a copy of the first volume, but returned the second on account of the pages on the Holy Alliance and the disrespect to his father. Yet if the specific message of the Prussian School—German unity under the Hohenzollerns—is not yet delivered, the call to action, the identification of history with politics, and the glorification of Prussian statesmen and soldiers, indicate the road along which the author had begun to travel.

When Denmark attempted to tighten her hold on the duchies Droysen issued a pamphlet urging them not to sever their fortunes from Germany. He was sent to Frankfurt by the Provisional Government to secure recognition, and among the many Professors who gathered in the *Paulskirche* none delivered his message in more ringing tones. Germany, he declared, must rally round Prussia. To the Hohenzollerns belonged the place vacant since the fall of the Hohenstaufen. In his greatest pamphlet, 'Memorial of a Schleswig-Holsteiner,' he declared that Prussia must not content herself any longer with being the second power in Germany. This vigorous declaration, which ranks with Treitschke's most eloquent utterances, was admired by Bismarck, and, though coldly received by the King, it was believed to have won the approval of the Prince of Prussia. He devoted the remainder of his life to the problem which the Frankfurt Parliament had tried to solve. The 'Life of Yorck' was designed to remind the German people of the sacrifices and triumphs of their fathers. The three volumes of this biography are primarily a study of the Wars of Liberation grouped round the personality of one of its leading figures. He was allowed to use the archives of the General Staff, and he obtained precious information from Schön, the sole survivor of the heroic age. Their correspondence[1] reveals his lively interest in the work, but the historian soon found himself forming a different opinion of Yorck. While his verdict is on the whole favourable, Schön declared that there was no trace of the hero in him and that he was merely lucky. He hailed the first volume as excellent, but as the work advanced the differences became acute, and he finally dismissed it as a bad novel. The publication of Schön's papers in 1875 was to show how passionate was his temper and how treacherous his memory, and the reputation of the book survived the displeasure of the critic. It mattered little to its readers if the old soldier received rather more than his due, for the work was above all a military narrative, an arresting picture of an heroic chapter in the life of the German people. It breathes an atmosphere of moral exhilaration which came like a refreshing breeze

[1] See Schön, *Briefwechsel mit Pertz u. Droysen*, 1896.

in the dark days of Olmütz, and its lively style and narrative power secured it readers outside professional circles.

When Droysen's politics made his position in Kiel impossible, he found refuge at Jena where he began the principal task of his life. Though the first attempt to create a German Empire had failed, he never doubted that it would come as soon as Prussia woke up to her duty. For the moment she appeared to have forgotten her mission, and it was the aim of the 'History of Prussian Policy' to remind her of it. History was to bear witness that the Hohenzollerns alone, from their unswerving fidelity to German interests as a whole, were fitted to restore the Empire. The story opens with the granting of the Mark to Frederick of Hohenzollern by the Emperor Sigismund, and the first volume ranges over a wide field, embracing the Councils of Constance and Basel and the Hussite wars. The second depicts the chaos of the Empire under the Emperor Frederick, the settlement of the Mark, and the personality of Albert Achilles. With the Reformation, of which Droysen is an ardent champion, the pace quickens, as the rôle of Brandenburg was secondary, but room is found for a full-length picture of the Elector Joachim II. In these early volumes some attention is paid to internal conditions; but with the Great Elector, who is reached in the fourth volume, the material becomes so abundant that the historian virtually limits himself to foreign policy. Promotion to Berlin in 1859 rendered it easier to consult the archives. The investigation of the reign was facilitated by the official publication of the secrets of many archives, a vast enterprise in which Droysen himself took part. Penetrated with the mission of Prussia, he had attempted with scanty success to trace it back to the entry of the Hohenzollerns into the Mark; but with the Great Elector the German Idea becomes visible, even if it was not the lodestar of Prussian policy. The 'territorial time' ended and the Prussian state began.

After such a full-blooded personality Frederick I is an anæmic figure. As literature and art are outside the scope of the book, the reign presents comparatively little material, and its main achievement, the securing of the crown, provokes disgust at the obsequiousness to Austria. Very different is the estimate of Frederick William I, to whom three volumes are devoted. With scant courtesy to Ranke, Droysen declares that only his relations with his son had been thoroughly studied, and that he had been so caricatured that it was necessary to investigate his domestic as well as his foreign policy. He would reveal him as the champion of the peasants, the founder of the incomparable Prussian bureaucracy, the creator of a disciplined army. Droysen's detailed study confirmed in essentials the portrait which Ranke had drawn. The closing volumes were devoted to Frederick the Great, in the publication of whose correspondence and State Papers he co-operated. A full discussion of the claim to Silesia leads to a verdict in his favour, and the royal sceptic would have read the apologia of his champion with a smile. The fourteenth volume, which appeared after his death in 1886, covered the years of peace.

The 'History of Prussian Policy,' representing the heroic labours of over thirty years, ranks among the outstanding achievements of German scholarship. Few works rest so largely on the study of manuscripts, and few contain so much new material. Except for the Great Elector, however, where the harvest was gathered by other hands, he only used Prussian archives. He defended himself on the ground that, as they were too vast for a single life to cover, it was impossible to consult others. He added that it was his task to explain Prussian policy from the standpoint of its authors. But history seen exclusively through Prussian spectacles was bound to be one-sided, and Droysen read into his sources what was not there. The main fault of the book is that it predates modern political conceptions. 'The four hundred years revealed a regularity of growth and a definiteness of tendency which find their expression rather than their cause in the rulers. What has founded and maintains and directs this state is, if I may say so, an historical necessity. In this national calling it finds its justification and strength.' He paints the early Hohenzollerns as loyal to Germany, nationalist, working for the reform of the Empire till they saw that the first need was for the reformation of the Church. With the Reformation Protestantism became part of the national idea, and Austria ceased to share the growing intellectual life of the German people. Since 1555 the centre of gravity was to be found in the territories, not in the Empire. The Thirty Years War revealed the bankruptcy of the old system. With Austria Catholic and cosmopolitan, Prussia became the only possible head of a German nation. He did not exaggerate the powerlessness of Austria to regenerate Germany, but his interpretation of Prussian policy in terms of nationalism was a fundamental error.

The sharpest criticism came from the Guelf historian Klopp.[1] The conception of dualism, he declared, was radically false, as till 1740 the Hohenzollerns were loyal to the Empire—indeed more loyal than any other dynasty. Frederick the Great broke with the Hapsburgs in the interests of Prussia, not of Germany. The Austrophil Catholic was a political enemy, but Droysen's

[1] *Kleindeutsche Geschichtsbaumeister*, chap. 3, 1861.

contention was equally rejected by members of his own school. No competent historian accepted his interpretation of the early Electors, and his distinguished pupil Erdmannsdörffer 'denied the originality of the Great Elector, maintaining that he was influenced by his counsellors, above all by Waldeck, who was the first to recognise the national vocation of the Prussian State. The picture of Frederick the Great carried little more conviction, even Sybel declaring that his attacks on Austria were in no way determined by national preoccupations. His greatest pupil, Koser, though admiring the great King as much as his master, knows nothing of a German mission. In revising his 'Prussian History' in 1874 Ranke ignored the new gospel, remaining fair and almost indulgent to Austria, and cool to the Hohenzollern heroes. The 'History of Prussian Policy' was not intended to be a work of art but a storehouse of material and a patriotic act. It is curious that he should have made so little effort to give literary form to his results, and even Ranke groaned at the prospect of having to read it. Though students dare not neglect the most exhaustive survey of the foreign policy of a state ever written, most readers will be content to assimilate his established results in the lighter pages of his successors.

After the struggle of 1848-9 Droysen never again engaged in active politics, but he watched the realisation of his lifelong ideals with rapture. His time was fully occupied by his writings and professional duties. We owe a singularly vivid picture of his teaching to Frédéricq, the distinguished Belgian Professor. 'He began low, like a great preacher, to obtain complete silence, and you could hear a pin drop. He revealed a profound sadness at the falsities that passed under the name of history, often sighing with anger and contempt. Every moment there came a biting jest. There was great originality and much *verve*. The lecture ended with Homeric laughter at some anecdote told with irresistible humour. I never attended such an entertaining course, and rarely heard such serious and solid stuff.' The lectures to which he devoted most thought were those on methodology, notes for which he published in 1858, and which passed through many editions. He had sat at Hegel's feet, and the leading conception of the 'History of Prussian Policy'—the national idea working itself out through the centuries over the heads of men—was thoroughly Hegelian. There is still more of Hegel in the *Historik*,[1]

---

[1] There is an American translation, with a sketch by his pupil Krüger, Droysen's *Principles of History*, 1893. A greatly enlarged version of the *Historik*, based on the lecture notes and edited by Hubner, appeared in 1927.

which is so condensed that some of its aphorisms are scarcely intelligible. Though recognising the immense power of ideas, he emphasises free will and the responsibility of the individual. 'History is not the light and the truth, but a search therefor, a sermon thereon, a consecration thereto. It is the moral world regarded in its evolution and growth. Beginning and end are hidden from us, but we can detect the direction of the stream. From history we learn to understand God, and we can only understand history in God.' Passing to the world of reality, he emphasises the power and majesty of the state. 'The state is not the sum of the individuals whom it comprehends, nor does it arise from their will. Authority is the essence of its life, as love in the family, faith in the Church, and gravity in the world of matter.' The work ends on a practical note. 'Historical study is the basis for political improvement and culture. The statesman is the historian in practice.'

III

The Year of Revolutions which decided the destiny of Droysen was also of decisive importance in the career of Sybel,[1] who had been for some time drifting steadily away from Ranke's moorings. In his famous preface of 1824 the master had disclaimed any desire to instruct the present from the past, but that was precisely what the pupil was becoming ever more determined to do. In an address in 1847 on Universities in relation to political life he urged them to revive the spirit of the Wars of Liberation. 'The true academic policy is to penetrate every study with interest in public affairs and to keep in view its value for national concerns.' In 1848 he entered the Hessian Chamber and took part in the Vor-Parlament at Frankfurt, and his experiences strengthened his resolve to extract and apply the lessons of the past. The final renunciation of allegiance took place in 1856 in his celebrated address on the position of historiography. Ranke's all-round receptivity, he declared, sometimes ran the risk of weakening the ethical severity which the perfect historian needed. The beginnings of a better way had been shown by Mommsen. Despite this outspoken attack, the affectionate relations of the two men were in no way disturbed. In dedicating the third

[1] In addition to the biography by Varrentrapp in Sybel's *Vorträge und Abhandlungen,* 1897, see Schmoller, *Rede auf Sybel u. Treitschke,* 1896; Bailleu's articles, *Deutsche Rundschau,* Oct. 1895, and *Allg. Deutsche Biog.;* and Marcks, *Männer u. Zeiten,* vol. i., 1911. Guilland's chapter in *L'Allemagne nouvelle et ses historiens,* 1899, is very critical.

volume of his 'History of the French Revolution' to 'my revered teacher and fatherly friend,' he said, 'I desire to take the opportunity of again confessing myself as your pupil.'

No feature of the upheaval of 1848 impressed Sybel more than the number and zeal of the Socialists, and he determined to write a brochure on Communism in the French Revolution. Once transported into that land of marvels, he could not so easily escape. The pamphlet grew into five volumes and claimed the greater part of thirty years. The Revolution was known in Germany chiefly through the sketch of Dahlmann and the translation of Mignet, neither of which rested on original study. The pupil of Ranke at once saw the necessity of reaching the sources. At Berlin, though not allowed to see the despatches of the Prussian minister at Paris, he was permitted to use the archives of the War Office. On a visit to Paris in 1851 he found rich treasures in the War Office and the National Archives, where he noticed the acts of the Committee of Public Safety. 'What dust!' remarked the historian. 'Respect it,' answered the librarian; 'it is the dust of 1795.'[1] He also found useful material at the Hague. The Prussian, British, and Austrian archives were freely opened to him in time for subsequent editions. Finally, in 1866, Madame Cornu persuaded Napoleon to allow him to explore the Foreign Office. Sybel's pages thus presented to the world the first authentic picture of important aspects of the Revolution.

As a young man he had learned to love Burke, and had written an essay on his view of the Revolution before becoming its historian. Though a convinced champion of constitutional government and sympathising with the emergence of the Third Estate, he shared Burke's horror of Jacobinism. Unfettered liberty of the individual led to anarchy, mechanical equality to the destruction of freedom, the sovereignty of the people to mob-rule or a military dictator. His ideal was a strong government resting on the middle class, and his ambition was to convince German Liberals that French liberty was poison. While Dahlmann had depicted the Revolution as a constitutional struggle, Sybel pronounced it above all a social upheaval. He boldly challenged the popular distinction between 1789 and 1793, and directed attention to the tyranny and anarchy of the opening months. The sole authors of the war were the Girondins, led by Brissot; for the Powers of central and eastern Europe were more interested in Poland than in the domestic controversies of France.

The work was hailed with enthusiasm in Germany. Häusser classed it with Mommsen and Droysen, and declared that its

[1] See his 'Pariser Studien' in *Vorträge u. Abhandlungen*, 1897.

wealth of material and novelty of view would mark an epoch. Gustav Freytag proclaimed its importance for the political education of the nation. Moriz Ritter found in it a happy combination of the methods of Ranke and Niebuhr, the former in the connection of foreign and domestic events, the latter in the emphasis on economic and social conditions. Its merits were indeed considerable. Making no attempt to describe the familiar dramatic scenes, he investigated the development of parties and policy. His research in foreign archives revealed the diplomacy of the European rulers with whom the Revolution came in collision. The most brilliant achievement of the book was to establish the connection of east and west, and to exhibit the Revolution as part of the process of the destruction of the old Europe. In the words of Acton, he stands aloof from the meridian of Paris. Its continuation to the year 1801 enabled him to throw light on the little-known period between the Terror and the Consulate. Revised up to 1880, it incorporated the scholarship of a generation. Yet the work was disfigured by grave faults. It was in fact, if not in intention, a polemic. 'It is an attack,' declares Guilland, 'not only on the Revolution but on the mind and history of France.' The lesson of the book is the political incapacity of the French: in his desire to disperse the halo of heroism attaching to the Revolution, he turns giants into pygmies. The gospel of liberty and equality appears to him an appeal to greed and passion, not a demand for justice. Like Taine he accumulates the evidences of excess and overlooks the durable work of the Convention. He has no word of appreciation for the heroism of the Volunteers. He fails to recognise the generous emotions of a people, to allow for the staggering difficulties of their task, to admit the ceaseless intrigues of the Court. He rashly declares that Marie Antoinette was ready to work constitutional monarchy, and that, if restored, the fall of feudalism would have been recognised. His exclusive attribution of the war to the Girondins was rejected by Ranke. He was almost equally hostile to Austria, and Thugut is made the scapegoat of the Coalition. Leopold, he declared, was guiltless of the outbreak of the war, but Austria was mainly responsible for its unhappy course, and the treaty of Campo Formio was a betrayal. Vivenot sharply attacked the traducer of the Hapsburgs; and Hüffer, a Westphalian Catholic and for a time Sybel's colleague at Bonn, based a very different story on a more exhaustive study of the archives. Beside the madness of France, the greed of Russia and the selfishness of Austria, Sybel's Prussia stands out as the model state.

The book is not only disfigured by national and dynastic

bias; it is a purely external narrative. 'You will have a notion of things,' remarks Sorel, 'but you will not see the men. You know what the Prussian Ministry and the Viennese Cabinet have done or tried to do, but the peoples, their passions, their characters remain in shadow.' We witness rather a conflict of diplomatists than the birth of a new world. It dwarfs the Revolution itself not less than the actors in the drama, for it was only one of the three expressions of the end of the old era, ranking with the destruction of Poland and the fall of the Holy Roman Empire. 'These three events are connected, for their foundation is the same. In each it is the Middle Ages which are crumbling away. Everywhere a new policy triumphs, the modern military monarchy, levelling and centralising.' He scarcely noticed that the Revolution was by far the most important event in European history since the Reformation. Frederic Harrison's verdict, 'little more than a German Alison, the laborious tirade of a wrong-headed partisan,' does injustice to its learning and power; but though it is a book which no student of the revolutionary epoch dare neglect, few of its foreign readers are likely to share its standpoint or to adopt its interpretation.

Sybel's dislike of France and Austria was equalled by his distaste for Catholicism, which he regarded both as anti-national influence and an enemy of free research. To be an Ultramontane and a German patriot, he declared in an early essay, was impossible. 'One cannot serve two masters at the same time, the Pope and the King; a choice must be made.' To invite such a man to Munich was a bold experiment, but Maximilian was determined to create an historical school, and Ranke urged his old pupil to accept. Sybel entered eagerly into the King's plans, became one of the favourites of his Round Table, aided Ranke in the foundation of the Historical Commission, and became its first secretary. But his most important achievement at Munich was the creation of the *Historische Zeitschrift*. 'We want an organ,' he wrote to Waitz in 1857, 'to represent a definite scientific tendency and method. Every year history takes more and more the place of philosophy.' In his Introduction to the first number he described it as independent and scientific; but it took its character from the Editor, who rules out feudalism, which wished to revive dead elements, radicalism, which replaced organic revolution by caprice, and Ultramontanism, which subjected national development to foreign control. Oldenbourg, the publisher, writing after the historian's death in 1895, described him as an ideal editor, quick, tranquil and firm.[1] In later years he handed over

[1] See his article in *Historische Zeitschrift*, 1895.

most of the detail to younger men, retaining only the general control.[1]

As Sybel lost no opportunity at Munich of giving expression to his views by pen and tongue, the prejudice against the northerner naturally increased. 'I am four-sevenths politician and three-sevenths professor,' he confessed to Bluntschli. The King told him that he did not wish him to go but could not defend him if an agitation arose. He therefore seized the opportunity of a vacancy at Bonn caused by the death of Dahlmann to withdraw from a difficult position. He celebrated his arrival by the publication of his reply to Ficker, 'The German Nation and the Empire,' in which he declared that, as Prussia had shown herself the true leader of Germany, Austria must go. 'As sure as the stream flows forward, Germany will form a close union under the lead of its strongest member.' He was, however, one of the most determined of Bismarck's opponents in the years of conflict. He entered the Prussian Landtag and with Gneist and Virchow led the opposition to the Government, desiring to refuse supplies for the war of 1864. Sadowa effected a sudden and permanent conversion. While Mommsen and Virchow remained in the old camp, Sybel became one of the founders and leaders of the National Liberals. Bismarck, who had lately scoffed at the Professors for believing that they could unite Germany by talk about liberty, quickly recognised the value of their support, and on the jubilee of Sybel's doctorate publicly expressed his gratitude for his 'long co-operation in common work for the fatherland.' No German greeted the stupendous events of 1870 with greater thankfulness. 'What have we done,' he cried, 'that God's grace should allow us to witness such mighty things?' Like Ranke, however, he was soon dismayed by the growth of socialism and materialism, and was so alarmed by the growth of the Centrum that he re-entered the Landtag in order to support the Government in the *Kulturkampf*.

In 1875 Sybel was appointed Director of the Prussian Archives. He inaugurated the great series of 'Publications from the Archives,' advised the Berlin Academy to publish the Political Correspondence of Frederick the Great, and persuaded the Government to found an Historical Institute in Rome when Leo XIII threw open the Vatican archives. But the main task of his closing years was to describe the founding of the German Empire. The suggestion came from Bismarck, who promised him the use of the archives. After relating the fall of the Holy Roman Empire, he remarked, no plan could appeal to him more than the resurrection of the German Empire. His second great work was

[1] See Meinecke, *Erlebtes*, i., 182–4, 1946.

written far more rapidly than the first. He had taken an active part in many of the events, and the only archives that he was able to consult lay ready to his hand. He aimed at a plain narrative of the diplomatic and military efforts of Prussia. The first five volumes appeared in 1889; the sixth and seventh, bringing the story to the declaration of war by Napoleon III, in 1894. A year later he was dead.

'I have nowhere sought to hide my Prussian and National Liberal opinions,' he wrote in the preface. Yet the work is less polemical than the 'History of the French Revolution.' Beginning with a rapid sketch of modern German history, the narrative becomes detailed with Bismarck's accession to power in 1862. William I is reverently painted. 'His faith was the bread of life, the consolation of his grief, the unique rule of his actions.' Rössler, however, wittily remarked that in the title, 'The Founding of the German Empire by William I,' there was a misprint, and that it should run 'in spite of' instead of 'by.' (*Trotz* for *durch*.) Yet, though Bismarck is the hero of his drama, he fails to convey a realistic impression of the Iron Chancellor. He is too correct, too colourless, too tame: a critic complained that he had transformed the tiger into a tame cat. He devotes many hundred pages to the diplomatic crises which preceded the wars of 1864, 1866 and 1870, and in each case attributes the responsibility to the enemy. He softens the double-dealing in the Schleswig-Holstein problem, omits to state how Bismarck goaded his master to war in 1866, and conceals the mission of Lothar Bucher to Madrid. The Ems telegram, we are told, was shortened, not altered. Prussian policy is throughout irreproachably loyal and correct, and Bismarck is always in Sunday clothes. The work was an apologia, anticipating the *Reflections* which were to appear after the statesman's death. The Memoirs of the King of Roumania revealed the whole story of his brother's candidature for the Spanish throne, and the best antidote to this voluminous eulogy is Busch's diary. Yet, though he maintains that Bismarck had no wish for war, he cannot regret the outbreak of the conflict which realised the dream of his life. 'He who has had the happiness to live through these first days of the national resurrection will retain their memory as a holy possession for ever.' He entertains no unfriendly feelings towards Napoleon, whom he describes as by nature a man of peace who loved to think and dream. In some addenda[1] written shortly before his death he also exculpated the Empress Eugénie. The real culprit was Gramont.

The book met with a mixed reception. The clearness of

---

[1] Published in *Historische Zeitschrift*, vol. lxxv.

arrangement and skill in unravelling the threads of complicated diplomatic situations were unreservedly praised. Meinecke spoke of the wonderfully beautiful consummation of his lifework. 'All his ideas are able to combine in tranquil harmony—the strong, national state with its roots in history, the free constitutional life resting on the real force of the nation, the conquering personality of the statesman, the dominance of ethical laws in history.' Such enthusiasm was misplaced. It is inferior in learning, power, and originality to the 'History of the French Revolution.' Some complained that it was too official, omitting the conflicts of Bismarck with the Court, others that it was too exclusively diplomatic. Internal politics were neglected before 1866. Those who expected sensational revelations from the archives were disappointed. Though he had known all the leading actors in the drama, he failed to make the scenes live. The picture lacks atmosphere and background. Among his critics was the young Emperor, who was angered by the subordinate rôle attributed to his grandfather. When the Verdun prize was assigned to Sybel he vetoed the award, and on the fall of Bismarck excluded the historian from the archives of the Foreign Office. The aid of Bismarck and the diaries of other leading actors enabled him to complete his journey, but the later volumes are of less value. Though Ottokar Lorenz devoted a large volume to magnifying the rôle of William I, his estimate of Bismarck's share in the great transformation has never been overthrown. His work remains of value as the official statement of the Prussian case, but it has to be checked at every point by the testimony of other witnesses. Friedjung and Srbik have given the Austrian side of the story, and La Gorce has stated the case of France.

Sybel's two chief works are still consulted, but they never became widely popular. Though full of information they are disfigured by strong prejudices. He went through life waving the Prussian banner and waging war against France, Austria and the Roman Church. History was a vast arsenal which furnished him with weapons of attack and defence. Moreover, he lacked the magic of style. We miss the serenity of Ranke and the colouring of Treitschke. He possessed a powerful mind, but lacked imagination and subtlety. Some of his friends considered that he was fashioned rather for the forum than the library. In truth he belongs as much to the history of Germany as to the annals of scholarship. He was the leader of the brilliant group of historians who harnessed their studies to their politics, and played a considerable part in preparing their countrymen for the momentous changes which culminated in 1870.

IV

The youngest, greatest and last of the Prussian School was among the most striking personalities of the century. As Hutten's name stands for the revolt against the Pope and Körner's for the uprising against Napoleon, so Treitschke[1] represents the ascent of Germany from the paralysis of the Bund to the glories of 1870. The most eloquent of preachers, the most fervid of apostles, the most passionate of partisans, he most completely embodies the blending of history and politics which it was the aim of the School to achieve. Curiously enough the most fiery champion of Prussian claims was a Saxon of Czech descent. But for a grave illness in childhood, resulting in almost total deafness, he would have followed his father's profession and entered the army, and his sympathies were always with action. At sixteen the precocious schoolboy gave expression to the ideal of German union under Prussia in the presence of Beust. His convictions were strengthened at Bonn, where he attended the lectures of Arndt, now aged eighty-three, 'not to learn anything, but to see the hale old man.' But the main influence was Dahlmann, who took a keen interest in the brilliant lad. 'He told me I must serve my fatherland; as he gave me his hand with a piercing look, I gained courage and became conscious of how much I had to do.' It was at this time that he deeply pondered Pertz' massive biography of Stein. 'I cannot express how the study of this mighty man delights and elevates me. He only thought of his duty, like the humblest official.' He finished his University career at Heidelberg, where he heard Häusser proclaim the same doctrine that he had learned from Dahlmann.

He read widely in history and literature as well as in political science, but his first publication was a little volume of Patriotic Poems. He had written verse since the age of nine, and some of the pieces show poetical talent. The veteran Arndt spoke warmly of the verses, but they were not widely noticed and were never

---

[1] The fullest biography is by Petersdorff in *Allg. Deutsche Biog.* Schiemann, *Treitschke's Lehr- u. Wanderjahre*, 1896, only extends to 1867. Leipprand, *Treitschke im deutschen Geistesleben des neunzehnten Jahrhunderts*, 1935, is useful. Gooch, 'Treitschke in his Correspondence,' in *Studies in German History*, discusses the three volumes of his letters edited by Cornicelius, 1908–20. The best appreciation is by Marcks, *Treitschke, Ein Gedenkblatt*, 1905. For his personality see Hausrath's vivid volume, *Zur Erinnerung an Treitschke*, 1901. Among shorter appreciations the best are Schmoller, *Rede auf Sybel u. Treitschke*, 1896; Bailleu, *Deutsche Rundschau*, Oct.–Nov. 1896; Headlam, in *English Historical Review*, 1897. Guilland's chapter in *L'Allemagne nouvelle et ses historiens*, 1899, is hostile.

reprinted. A second volume, published in 1857, attracted no more attention. His first appearance as a publicist was in his dissertation on the Science of Society, which, in opposition to Riehl and other thinkers, he asserted to have no existence. The only science was that of the state, which was society organised as a unity. The state, he added, was necessary and primeval, and no contract was needed to create or maintain it. One day, he concluded, the German state would fulfil its destiny, and Prussia was the nucleus round which the broken fragments must unite. The same doctrines were more openly expressed in the writings which now began to become known to wider circles. The appreciation of Kleist virtually discovered the poet patriot whose fame steadily advanced from that moment. The 'Prince of Homburg' supplied him with the strong meat that he craved, and the essay closes with its famous line, 'In Staub mit allen Feinden Brandenburges.' The studies of Otto Ludwig and Hebbel reveal his devotion to drama; those on Milton, Byron, Lessing and Dahlmann give eloquent utterance to his enthusiasm for liberty.

At the age of twenty-five the young scholar delivered lectures at Leipzic on German history, to which crowded audiences listened as they had listened to Fichte half a century earlier. He taught that Prussia could only become a rallying point for all Germans as a constitutional state. All that was new and fruitful in the nineteenth century, he declared in his essay on Liberty, was the work of liberalism, but liberty rested more on a wisely-ordered national life and a good administration than on the power of Parliaments. England possessed a state, but valued it little. Germany lacked it, and therefore was more conscious of its worth. He now determined to write a sketch of the Bund from 1815 to 1848 in order to exhibit the sinful waste of national strength. His plan widened into a history of Germany, and the work which was expected to be completed in three years filled the remainder of his life. 'We need an Emperor,' he cried in his address on Fichte; 'Austria cannot give us what we want, for she is neither free nor German.' A still greater effect was produced by his oration on the jubilee of the battle of Leipzic, which echoed through Germany. 'One thing we still lack—the state. Ours is the only people which possesses no general legislation, which can send no representatives to the meetings of the Powers. No salvo salutes the German flag in a foreign port. Our country sails the sea without colours, like a pirate.' He was profoundly impressed by the example of Italy. What Piedmont had done Prussia could do.

Treitschke demanded a Germany that should be not only one empire but one state. Prussia was to annex the smaller states, and the princely houses were to disappear. 'Believe me,' he wrote to Freytag, 'only the good sword of the conqueror can unite these lands with the North.' Such doctrine was little short of treason in Saxony, and the outcry became even louder. Thus when Mathy, a native of Baden, procured the offer of a Chair at Freiburg in 1863, it was accepted.[1] Baden was at once the most national and the most liberal of the smaller States, and its ruler was closely connected with Prussia by marriage. On the other hand, the students were mainly Catholic. 'It is a parson's town,' he wrote to Freytag. 'The difference between Catholicism and Protestantism is much deeper than good people think. It is not a difference between certain dogmas, but between slavery and intellectual freedom.' The Bishop forbade Catholic students to attend his lectures, but his Protestant hearers enjoyed a rare treat. His colleague and lifelong friend Hausrath describes the effect of his eloquence, and remarks that he reminded him of a Hussite warrior. The year following his arrival he composed his greatest essay, 'Federation and Centralisation,' demanding that Prussia should attack the small States. 'My father will grieve over it,' he wrote, 'but in these things the duties of a son are not the only ones.' Prussia, he declared, had done all that was really great in Germany since 1648, and was herself the supreme political achievement of the German people. Only the Courts desired the existing system to continue, under which Germany was a mere geographical expression. The essay was an act, and revealed the first political writer of the day. Like Sybel, he at first mistrusted Bismarck, but he soon convinced himself that the Chancellor was determined to strengthen Prussia. The two men met in 1866 on the eve of the war, and Bismarck pressed him to accompany the army and write manifestoes, to be rewarded by a Chair at Berlin. The historian refused on the ground that he wished to be independent, and that he could not become a Prussian official till the Constitution was respected. None the less, when Baden joined Austria, he resigned his Chair at Freiburg. 'I long for the North,' he wrote; 'I belong to it with my whole being.' In the moment of victory he launched a flaming pamphlet on 'The Future of the North-German Middle States,' demanding the annexation by Prussia of Hanover, Hesse and Saxony, 'ripe and over-ripe for annihilation.' It was not surprising that his sorely tried father at this point publicly repudiated his son's attacks on the King.

Treitschke succeeded Häusser at Heidelberg in 1867. He was

[1] See *Briefe Heinrich von Treitschkes an Historiker und Politiker vom Oberrhein*, ed. by W. Andreas, 1934.

now a national figure, but he was regarded as more of a publicist than an historian. In sending the first volume of his Essays to his father in 1865 he wrote, 'That bloodless objectivity which does not say on which side is the narrator's heart is the exact opposite of the true historical sense. Judgment is free, even to the author.' Almost every essay carried its political message. In the attack on Bonapartism and French Policy, which soon followed, the faults of his method outweigh the brilliance of his style. Rulers were of two sorts—servants of the state and egoists. Napoleon was a monster, not a statesman—a grandiose Attila, a monstrous Genghis Khan, who loved war for its own sake. But in truth France was little better than her tyrant.[1] Like Sybel, but more offensively, he denounces the French as vain and turbulent, brave but lacking solidity, unable to perform the commonplace duties of life. France was a bad neighbour, oscillating between anarchy and despotism. The celebrated essay on Cavour is of higher quality. He wrote best when he wrote with sympathy, and next to Bismarck Cavour was his chosen hero. The detailed survey of the history of the United Netherlands taught the same lesson of unification. He watched the gathering of the storm-clouds in 1870 with feverish anxiety. On the outbreak of war he wrote, 'What a humiliation we have escaped! Had not Bismarck so cleverly edited the telegram, the King would have given way again.' His 'Ode of the Black Eagle' was the best war-song of the year.[2] After the decisive battles he published a pamphlet, 'What do we ask from France?' contending that Alsace was German. Like Freytag he did not desire the Imperial title, which he held to smack of Bonapartism. Victory, he declared, opened up infinite perspectives for Germany, who, with her rich moral culture, would become instructress of the nations. He was surprised by the ready patriotism of the South which destroyed his pet scheme of annexation. He feared that a federation could never be so strong as a unitary State, but what was good enough for Bismarck he was willing to accept. He entered the Reichstag in 1871 as a National Liberal, and took an active part in the debates on the *Kulturkampf*, but he was disappointed with Parliamentary life. 'Of all the institutions of our young Empire,' he wrote in 1883, 'none has proved so bad as the Reichstag.'

After the realisation of his dreams Treitschke settled down to write the 'History of Germany in the Nineteenth Century' which he had planned ten years before. He accepted a call to Berlin in 1874, remarking that as he had to spend half the year

[1] See Irmgard Ludwig, *Treitschke und Frankreich*, 1934.
[2] Reprinted in *Zehn Jahre Deutscher Kämpfe*, 269–71.

in the Prussian archives he might as well live there. Ranke had not favoured the appointment, regarding him as a publicist, not an historian. Other scholars shared his misgivings, and the new Professor was only admitted to the Berlin Academy shortly before his death. Yet he was to produce one of the greatest historical works of the century. 'I desire to write a history of the Bund,' he had announced in 1861, 'to show the idle masses that the foundations of political existence, power and liberty, are lacking, and that no salvation is possible but by the annihilation of the small states.' But with the disappearance of the Bund he resolved to attempt a panoramic view of the men and policy, institutions and ideas, which had prepared the way for the new Germany. The first volume, published in 1879, surveying the revolutionary and Napoleonic period, formed an introduction to the detailed narrative. While Häusser had dealt with governments, Treitschke presented the national life as a whole. The author of the 'Patriotic Poems' found in poetry the true mirror of the national spirit. The backbone of the volume was the story of Prussia, but the emphasis on her providential rôle was not incompatible with considerable severity towards Frederick William II. The volume closes with the War of Liberation and the Congress of Vienna. Despite its great bulk it was received with enthusiasm and sold by thousands.

The second volume, extending to the Carlsbad decrees, deals with a far less exciting story but rests more largely on original research. Its opening chapter, filling over a hundred pages, surveys the art, literature and scholarship of the Restoration, and ranks among the greatest of his achievements. A chapter dealing with the reorganisation of Prussia after the war is followed by a sketch of the South German States. The latter part of the volume describes the struggle between the liberal spirit which spoke through the Universities and the heavy hand of Metternich which forced the German princes to do his bidding. A critic declared that he should have written a Prussian, not a German History, since the Prussian chapters were as good as the others were bad. The aggressively Prussian standpoint provoked angry criticism. The most formidable attack came from the Strassburg Professor, Baumgarten,[1] the distinguished historian of Spain and Charles V, who was angered at Treitschke excusing in Prussia what he censured in Austria and abusing the more liberal ideas of the minor States. His indignation found utterance in a pamphlet, 'Treitschke's German History,' which created a

[1] See Erich Marcks' admirable biography prefixed to Baumgarten's *Aufsätze u. Reden*, 1894.

sensation. His standpoint, he declared, was defensible before 1870, but not after, and his attacks were more calculated to revive than to bury particularism. What Rome was to Janssen Prussia was to Treitschke. He could stimulate and inspire, but no one dare look to him for instruction. He revealed an almost incredible failure to understand non-Prussian Germany. Admirable in its delineation of intellectual life, the book was ruined by its political prejudices. A controversy between the historian and his old friend ensued, and Treitschke declared that his critics would have a different tale to tell when he reached Frederick William IV. Erdmannsdörffer pointed out some details in which the critic himself had gone astray, and Sybel explained that the 'Deutsche Geschichte' had attacked not liberalism but doctrinaire radicalism. Yet the damaging impression left by Baumgarten's attack was never effaced, for, though the tone was too shrill, he fastened on the fundamental flaw of the work.

These defects were less noticeable in the third volume, which extended to 1830. The long story of the Zollverein is commenced, and the importance of Motz was for the first time established. The gem of the volume is the celebrated chapter on the smaller States of North Germany, their rulers, their politics and their culture, a marvellous series of skilfully-etched vignettes. The fourth volume covers the closing decade of the long reign of Frederick William III, and deals mainly with the growth of constitutional ideas. The Zollverein story is completed, the Austrian influence becomes less oppressive, and Prussia begins to assert her place in the national life. The fifth, published in 1894, related the golden dawn of Frederick William IV and his brilliant circle. It was the most perfect part of the work, and possessed a certain mellow tranquillity. No one could accuse him of painting a courtier's portrait of the King; but though he lamented his political infirmities he seized the nobility of the man, and when he chastises it is more in sorrow than in anger. He was now sixty, and his eyesight was becoming weak. He had reached 1847, and was eager to embark on the year of revolution. 'God cannot take me away,' he said to Bailleu, 'till I have written my sixth volume.' But it was not to be. His health rapidly declined, and in 1896 he died.

The 'Deutsche Geschichte' is the nearest continental equivalent to Macaulay's History. Before he wrote little was known of Prussian history and still less of the minor states between the downfall of Napoleon and the Year of Revolutions. But his work was far more than a political narrative. It presented an encyclopædic picture of national development. He made a dull period live. He depicted the epoch, not as an era of decay, but as a gathering of the forces which were to lead to unity and a time of incomparable intellectual activity. Alone of the Prussian School he embraces culture in his vision, and he devotes infinite care to the movement of opinion and the course of literature and scholarship. His style is of incomparable richness and power, and he is a master of humour and pathos. The slight excess of rhetoric in the early essays and addresses has disappeared. He is the only literary artist of the Prussian School. In the magic of style and in throbbing vitality he equals Mommsen and leaves all other German historians behind.

The vivid personality which constitutes one of the main charms of the book is also responsible for its main defects. 'I get too easily excited,' he wrote to Sybel in 1864, 'but in time I hope to become an historian.' In 1882 he recognised that he would never change, confessing that his blood was too hot for an historian. His pen was a sword. His colleague Schmoller testifies that he loved and hated with elemental, almost volcanic force. To Freytag he confessed that the patriot in him was a thousand times stronger than the Professor. Friends compared him to Hotspur, to the Cid, to Young Siegfried. While Ranke was the most objective, Treitschke was the most subjective of leading German historians. No one would class him among 'good Europeans,' and indeed such a compliment would have been rejected with scorn. 'Only a stout heart,' he wrote, 'which feels the joys and sorrows of the fatherland as its own, can give veracity to an historical narrative.' He wrote history less to record than to teach. Only the Jesuits excelled him, said Bamberger bitterly, in the attempt to make instruction serve a special purpose. He hurls missiles at Austria, France, Russia and the Jews. He roundly condemns England as utilitarian and hypocritical, advancing to the conquest of an Empire with the Bible in one hand and an opium pipe in the other: by the side of the grasping Englishman the German was an idealist. He despises Louis Philippe and Leopold of Belgium as bourgeois and commercial Kings. But though the Germans are the best of the peoples, they are not all of equal merit. Prussia is the chosen nation. By the time he wrote his history Treitschke had conquered his dislike of the Junkers. The Zollverein and the Prussian army were the instruments of unity. The nobility, he declares, were more far-sighted and self-sacrificing than the bourgeoisie. His sharpest arrows are aimed at Young Germany, which he detests as Jewish, radical and Francophil. He writes of Heine and Börne as the corrupters of youth, the enemies of the Fatherland.

Treitschke was too much of a politician not to take part in

the controversies which arose during the last twenty years of his life. Two elements of the new Germany aroused his special indignation. He regarded socialism as anarchy, declaring that it should be met with force, not argument. In a fiery article, 'Socialism and its Patrons,' he denounced the Professors who went halfway to meet it. Schmoller, the most distinguished representative of the 'Socialists of the Chair,' issued a dignified reply, convicting the historian of misunderstanding their position. He was even more alarmed by the growing influence of the Jews. He was dismayed to witness the power in finance and journalism of men to whom patriotism and Christianity were nothing. He had no wish to reimpose disabilities, but the utterances of the famous historian synchronised with the foundation of anti-semitism by Stöcker. Among his academic colleagues were Jewish scholars, and Mommsen took the lead in organising a reply which accused him of destroying Lessing's great heritage of tolerance.

Treitschke fought his battles over again in his lectures. The crowded audiences listened to unmeasured attacks on France and England, socialism and the Jews, pacifism and Parliamentary Government. The course on Political Science, delivered many times throughout his life and published from notes after his death, provided the opportunity.[1] His main themes were the necessity of a strong State, an executive independent of party majorities, and the training of virile citizens. In an early essay he had sung the praises of war. 'The hope of banishing war is not only meaningless but immoral; its disappearance would turn the earth into a great temple of selfishness.' 'Our age is an age of iron,' he wrote later; 'if the strong vanquishes the weak it is the law of life.' The duel was a no less indispensable moral tonic than war. It was a lamentable end for a man who had rendered eminent services to his country that he should become the champion of absolutism and heat the fires of chauvinism by wild and whirling words. Like the Junkers he hailed the accession of William II with rapture, but the fall of Bismarck broke the spell. He attacked Caprivi and his master with so little reserve that he was threatened with Sybel's fate of exclusion from the archives. In his rich and full-blooded personality noble and repulsive elements were intermingled. There was a distinct strain of genius in 'the Bismarck of the Chair.'

With the death of Treitschke in 1896 the Prussian School disappeared. Its members were the political schoolmasters of Germany at a time of discouragement, and braced their countrymen

[1] An English translation in two volumes, with an Introduction by Lord Balfour, appeared in 1918.

to the efforts which culminated in a mighty Empire. It had grown out of a national need, and its *raison d'être* ceased when the need was satisfied. If the main purpose of history is to stir a nation to action, Droysen, Sybel and Treitschke were among the greatest of historians. If its primary aim is to discover truth and to interpret the movement of humanity, they have small claim to a place in the first class. The stream of historical studies, temporarily deflected by their powerful influence, began to return to the channel which Ranke had marked out for it. Moriz Ritter dedicated his life to the Counter-Reformation and the Thirty Years War. Erdmannsdörffer painted the first objective portrait of the Great Elector. Koser's biography of Frederick the Great is the most impressive work since Treitschke in the field of German history. Delbrück devoted himself to Gneisenau, Max Lehmann to Scharnhorst and Stein. Riezler worked at Bavarian history, Schiemann at Russia under the Tsar Nicholas I, Dietrich Schäfer at the Hanse towns. Erich Marcks, who made his name with monographs on the later sixteenth century, has written with unfailing judgment of Bismarck and his master, and Meinecke has traced the development of political opinion from the eighteenth century to 1848. Lenz and Hintze have devoted themselves to Prussian history. The voluminous 'Acta Borussica,' published by the Berlin Academy under the guidance of Schmoller and other experts, revealed the structure and methods of Prussian administration and industry during the eighteenth century. We live in an age of smaller achievements but more assured results.

V

In Austria historical production of a high quality is of recent date. When Pertz sought collaborators for the *Monumenta* at Vienna, Gentz replied that the formation of a society for the study of German history could not be agreeable to the Emperor. The censorship was active and vigilant, and the archives were only opened to men whose dynastic and religious orthodoxy was guaranteed. It was not till Arneth[1] became Director that the Metternich system was finally discarded. On visiting London he was struck by the liberality with which the archives were opened to every student, while his own country forbade the inspection even of its minor treasures. In Vienna the records were the *arcana imperii*, belonging to the dynasty as exclusively as the Crown Jewels. He gradually broke down the barrier, and his life of Prince Eugene contributed both to his own fame and to the

[1] See his autobiography, *Aus meinem Leben*, 2 vols., 1893.

glory of the House of Hapsburg. For the first time the eventful career of the brilliant soldier and statesman, 'the greatest man who ever worked for the benefit of Austria,' was traced with the aid of his own letters. It was, indeed, the first historical work produced in Austria to be widely read.

Arneth was now trusted in official circles, and the archives were placed at his disposal for the main task of his life. The 'History of Maria Theresa,' based throughout on the archives, presents a full-length portrait of the two most attractive figures in the long line of Hapsburg rulers. He approached his task with the enthusiasm inspired in every Austrian by Maria Theresa, 'the most brilliant personality in Austrian history.' Her courage during the years of struggle made her the idolised ruler of her peoples, and her fame shone the more brightly by contrast with her great antagonist. Arneth admits the ability of the King whom she always described as 'the wicked man,' and her son denounced as a rogue of genius; but while the Empress kept her word at whatever cost, Frederick was fundamentally dishonourable. When the peace of 1748 brought a breathing-space she turned to the work of reconstruction. She abolished the exemption of the nobles from taxation, reorganised the administration and judicature, codified the law, reformed the army. Despite his admiration for her noble character and high ability, Arneth is by no means blind to her weaknesses. Her greatest fault was bigotry. She hated the Jews and was anxious to expel them from her dominions. She detested Protestants and was a convinced supporter of the censorship. A second failing was her autocratic temper. Though tenderly attached to her consort, the Emperor, she never allowed him to take part in affairs. She disliked contradiction and was extremely jealous of her prerogatives. The most important event of the years of peace was the appointment of Kaunitz to the Chancellorship. The relations between the Empress and her adviser, here traced for the first time in detail, do credit to both. Though he was a sceptic and a libertine, she never wavered in her confidence. After the Seven Years War Joseph entered the Government, and during the latter half of her reign she was no longer the undisputed ruler. She had given him a careful education, and she rejoiced in his high qualities; but his urge to alter whatever appeared capable of improvement led him to condemn many of the arrangements with which the Empress was satisfied. Though an orthodox Catholic he detested clerical influences. When supported by Kaunitz he usually carried his point, but the constant friction darkened his mother's closing years.

Few books have contributed more to a comprehension of modern history than Arneth's ten volumes on Maria Theresa. They gave the Austrian side of two great European wars, related the fortunes of the outlying parts of the Empire—Belgium, Bohemia, Hungary, Lombardy—as well as of the hereditary possessions of the Hapsburgs, and described every aspect of the life of the realm—finance and law, education and religion. Above all, it allowed Maria Theresa, Joseph and Kaunitz, to reveal themselves in their own letters. The historian's later years were mainly devoted to the publication of the immense correspondence of Maria Theresa and her children. The volumes which excited most interest were those containing the letters from and to Marie Antoinette. In 1864 Hunolstein and Feuillet de Conches published collections of the Queen's letters which aroused doubts as to their authenticity, and the controversy was set at rest by the publication of the originals in Vienna. While the historian was engaged on the life of Maria Theresa he was appointed head of the archives in 1868. In 1863 even Ranke had been refused permission to see the despatches of the Austrian ambassador in Paris in 1756. Arneth now welcomed historians from every country. When attacked for admitting Sybel, the inveterate enemy of the House of Hapsburg, he rejoined that Prussians could only be converted from their false views of Austrian policy by examining the records.

Where Arneth led, a band of eager students followed.[1] Oswald Redlich's massive life of Rudolph of Habsburg and Ludo Hartmann's volumes on Italy in the Middle Ages found readers outside academic circles. Krones wrote the first comprehensive survey of the growth of the Austrian State. Klopp,[2] a north German friend of the King of Hanover who followed his patron into exile, devoted his life to the defence of the Hapsburgs and *gross-deutsch* principles. Beginning with a violent attack on Frederick the Great as the author of the dualism which had ruined Germany, he passed to a rehabilitation of Tilly and a study of the early years of the Thirty Years War, in which Gustavus Adolphus and the Protestant princes appear as the enemies of the German nation. The main occupation of his later life was a gigantic 'History of the Fall of the House of Stuart.' The work, which deals far more with Continental than with English history, is useful for its new material, but it is disfigured by its author's predilection for Austria and hostility to France. The period of

[1] The activities of the Academy, founded in 1847, are described by R. Meister, *Geschichte der Akademie der Wissenschaften, 1847–1947*, 1947.
[2] See W. Klopp, *Onno Klopp*, 1907.

the Revolutionary and Napoleonic wars has been explored by Vivenot and Zeissberg, Beer and Schlitter, Wertheimer and Fournier. The Restoration era was described by Anton Springer. The revolution of 1848 was studied by Helfert, the last representative of the age and spirit of Metternich, while Friedjung presented the Austrian side of the struggle which ended at Sadowa.

The foundation of the Historical Institute at Vienna in 1854 by Count Thun, Minister of Education, inaugurated the systematic study in Austria of the Middle Ages.[1] It was to a German scholar that it owed its reputation as one of the finest schools of mediæval study. Sickel,[2] the son of a Saxon pastor, was won for philology by Lachmann. Expelled from Berlin in 1849 for his politics, he learned his trade in Paris in the École des Chartes. Arriving in Vienna he was invited to lecture on palæography and became Director in 1867. Needing material for his teaching he edited the 'Monumenta Graphica Medii Aevi,'[2] containing two hundred facsimile documents from Austrian and Italian archives. A prolonged study of Carolingian manuscripts led to an unrivalled acquaintance with the forms of the time. The 'Acta Carolingorum' marks the culmination of the science founded by Mabillon, which had been recently carried forward by Delisle's work on the 'Regesta' of Philip Augustus and Huillard-Bréholles' vast collection of the Acts of the Emperor Frederick II. In 1874 he joined the Directorate of the *Monumenta* and undertook the Diplomata, himself producing two volumes covering the Saxon Emperors. Now recognised as the greatest living master of Diplomatic, Sybel persuaded him to co-operate in a collection of Imperial documents of the Carolingian and Saxon dynasties in facsimile. His appointment as first President of the Austrian Institute at Rome in 1881 was a fitting reward of his labours. Devoting his life to the editing of documents his fame is confined to the world of scholars, but there it is secure.

The mediæval studies of Vienna were rivalled by the labours of Innsbruck. Ficker, a native of Catholic Westphalia,[3] early made the acquaintance of Böhmer, by whom he was recommended to Count Thun. Appointed to the capital of Tyrol in 1852, he laboured without intermission for half a century. Like Sickel, he was a master of Diplomatic, but he was also a productive author. His defence of the mediæval Empire against Sybel made him

---

[1] See Santifaller, *Das Institut für österreichische Geschichtsforschung*, 1950.
[2] See Erben's excellent article, *Hist. Vierteljahrschrift*, vol. ix., and Sickel, *Römische Erinnerungen*, 1947.
[3] See Jung's massive biography, *Julius Ficker*, 1907.

widely known as a vigorous controversialist not less than an erudite historian. His first important book was a study of the constitutional position of the Princes of the Holy Roman Empire which was hailed by Waitz as epoch-making. A journey to Italy in 1861 was devoted to profound researches in the archives, which laid the foundation of his 'Studies in the History of Italian Administration and Law,' a vast encyclopædia of learning, equally valuable for law and government, the Empire and the Church, Germany and Italy. In knowledge of mediæval law and institutions he has never been surpassed, and he ranks with Waitz and Stubbs, Brunner and Maitland among their most authoritative interpreters. He also devoted many years to the editing of documents. Böhmer's 'Regesta' were creditable as a first attempt but even his friends could not conceal from themselves their technical inadequacy. The revised edition, undertaken by Ficker and his pupils, doubled the value of the work. The great treatise on Diplomatic grew out of the work on the 'Regesta,' and offered the first trustworthy guide through the maze of the chancelleries. His influence as a teacher was immense, and German scholars crossed the frontier to learn his critical methods.[1]

[1] The labours of a more recent generation are described in *Österreichische Geschichtswissenschaft in Selbst-darstellungen. Her. von N. Gross*, 1950.

CHAPTER IX

THE ROMANTIC SCHOOL IN FRANCE

I

THE French Revolution constituted as decisive a breach with tradition in historical scholarship as in Church and State.[1] The Jacobin looked on the past as a foul dungeon from which the human spirit had only just escaped into the light of day. The National Assembly ordered a holocaust of papers relating to the noble families of France in the Place Vendôme, and Condorcet delivered a discourse suitable to the occasion. 'To-day Reason burns the innumerable volumes which attest the vanity of a caste. Other vestiges remain in public and private libraries. They must be enveloped in a common destruction.' Throughout the country deeds were burnt to the accompaniment of pealing bells, while the people danced to the cry of *Vive la République*.[2]

The two groups of workers which had made France the centre of historical research for a century were swept away. The Benedictines had ceased to produce scholars of the calibre of Mabillon and Montfaucon, but much solid and loyal work was accomplished. In 1790 Dom Brial[3] wrote to a friend that, despite the confusion, Dom Clément was finishing the last sheets of 'L'Art de vérifier les dates,' but that all the other works in which the Congregations were engaged were suspended. 'Dom Clément,' he adds, 'is fairly well for his age, but he shares our chagrin at events.' Three years later Dom Clément was dead, and the curtain falls. The fate of the Congregations was shared by the Academies, but, as there was nothing except their royal origin to connect them with the old régime, they were quickly revived in a modified form. When the Terror was over, a new body called the Institute was created, with departments of science, literature and art and a new

[1] For summaries of French scholarship in the nineteenth century see Thienot, *Rapport sur les Études historiques*, 1867; C. Jullian's Introduction to *Extraits des Historiens français*, 1897; Halphen, *L'histoire en France depuis cent ans*, 1914; Moreau, *L'Histoire en France au XIXe Siècle*, 1935; Larat, *Les Historiens du dix-neuvième Siècle*, 1947.

[2] See Despois, *Le Vandalisme révolutionnaire*, 1868, and Laborde, *Les Archives de France pendant la Révolution et l'Empire*, 1867.

[3] Dom Brial, 'Deux Lettres,' in *Société de l'Histoire de France, Notices et Documents*, 1884.

Academy of Moral and Political Science. The Institute invited
Dom Brial to continue Bouquet's collection of chronicles, to
which he had already devoted many years. 'Almost alone,' writes
the editor in 1801, 'I accomplished the thirteenth volume; and
on receiving it from me they saw the importance of making use
of the Benedictines, and are now planning to continue the collection of the historians of the Crusades, the "Gallia Christiana," and
other works. These undertakings are still nothing but projects,
but they prove that we have emerged a little from the state of
barbarism in which we were plunged.'

The promise of the early days of the Consulate was deceptive,
and France entered on a period of rigid despotism no less unfavourable to historical study than the chaos of the Revolution.
The Collège de France remained,[1] but the Professor of History
found it advisable to select his subjects from the ancient world.
The most important event during the Revolution was the creation
of the National Museum by Lenoir.[2] The fall of the Ancien Régime
was followed by a wholesale destruction of artistic treasures as
the symbols of a despotic and superstitious age; but at the height
of revolutionary vandalism Lenoir intervened at the risk of his
life, and shepherded many of the threatened monuments into the
Convent des Petits-Augustins. The Museum, arranged with loving
care by its curator, exerted an even greater influence on historical
study than on art. Scattered in many churches, the monuments
had produced little impression; collected under one roof and
arranged in chronological order, they compelled attention.

In the last year of the Consulate Napoleon abolished the
Academy of Moral and Political Science and created a department
of Ancient History and Literature: no place was found in the
Institute for modern and mediæval history. When he became
Emperor his conception of the utility of historical study appeared
to undergo a change. In 1806 he utilised the weeks of leisure after
the Jena campaign to dictate two long memoranda.[3] He suggested
a sort of University or enlarged Collège de France, in which there
would be Chairs of Roman, Greek, Byzantine, French, English,
and American history. There would also be instruction in special
subjects, among them the history of legislation from Rome to
the Consulate, and the evolution of the art of war in France.

---

[1] See Monod, 'La Chaire de l'Histoire au Collège de France, *Revue
Historique*, vol. xo.
[2] See Courajod, *Alexandre Lenoir*, 2 vols., 1878–86, and article in
Revue Historique, vol. xxx.
[3] See *Correspondance de Napoléon*, vol. xv., 102–110, and Lefranc,
Histoire du Collège de France, 1893.

'There is one part of history which cannot be learned from books, that of the time nearest our own. There is always a gap of fifty years before one's birth.' The Professors would have to know everything up to the moment when they were speaking. 'It is often said that history can only be written long after the events. I do not agree. One can say what occurred one year after an event as well as a hundred years. It is more likely to be true because the reader can judge by his own knowledge.' The University was to possess a strictly practical character. 'I do not want philosophy nor ecclesiastical history but the history of facts.' The magnificent plan conceived at the Castle of Finkenstein remained a dream and was indeed impossible of realisation. France did not possess the men, and even if scholars had been available the Emperor would have treated them as state functionaries. Any savant innocently accepting an appointment would have found himself in a gilded cage.

The spirit which would have reigned was revealed with brutal frankness only a year later. In 1808 the Abbé Halma, librarian to the Empress, applied to the Emperor for permission to continue Velly and Hénault. The Minister of the Interior replied that the Government must reserve its encouragement for objects of more serious interest. The Emperor, when informed of the response, dictated the following memorandum[1]: 'I do not approve of the principles enunciated by the Minister of the Interior. It would be most useful to continue both Velly and Hénault. It is of the highest importance to make sure of the spirit in which the continuation will be written. I have directed the Minister of Police to see to the continuation of Millot, and it is my desire that the two Ministers should arrange for the continuation of Velly and Hénault. The work must be entrusted not only to authors of real talent but to trustworthy men who will present the facts in their true light and offer healthy instruction by leading the reader up to the year 8. It will be necessary in every line to make apparent the influence of the Court of Rome and the feebleness of the Valois and the Bourbons, to paint the massacres of September and the horrors of the Revolution with the same brush as the Inquisition and the massacres of the *Seize*. The perpetual disorder of the finances, the pretensions of the Parliament, the absence of regularity in the administration, must be brought out, so that the reader breathes a sigh of relief on arriving at our time. When this work, skilfully performed and written with the proper tendency, has appeared, no one will have the wish or the patience

---

[1] See *Correspondance de Napoléon*, vol. xvi., 489–91, and Merlet, *Tableau de la Littérature Française*, 1800–1815, vol. ii., 1883.

to do it again, especially when, so far from being encouraged by the police, he would receive discouragement.' This cynical memorandum explains the stagnation of historiography under the Empire: history was subject to the Minister of Police. A volume of the Abbé Millot's 'Histoire de France' was suppressed on the ground that it contained things contrary .o the glory of the armies of France. A play on Belisarius was forbidden lest it might suggest the fate of Moreau, another on Henri IV because it was undesirable to recall the most popular monarch who ever sat on the French throne.

Napoleon's sole merit in the sphere of historical studies was to appoint Daunou[1] to the control of the national archives. The wholesale destruction of documents had produced a reaction, and in 1794 a Commission was founded with Camus, a scholarly Jansenist, at its head. Before 1789 it was estimated that not less than 10,000 depôts existed, of which 400 were in Paris alone. Instructions were now issued, and to a large extent obeyed, that documents should be brought together and preserved in the capital of each Department. In 1804 Camus was succeeded by Daunou, who possessed a wide knowledge of historical literature and commanded universal respect. Though he had entered the priesthood in early life he had welcomed the Revolution and accepted the Constitution Civile, but he had always been a moderate. During the Directory he devoted himself chiefly to education and took a leading part in the foundation of the Institute. On the establishment of the Consulate he retired from political life, and it was to the scholar not the politician that the Emperor entrusted the archives. Though he had never been numbered among the avowed partisans of the Empire, Napoleon more than once turned to him for assistance. When the conflict with the Papacy approached, he was commissioned to write a book on the Temporal Power of the Popes, and accepted the task without hesitation. He had thrown off his orders and his theology at the outset of the Revolution, and entertained a wholehearted contempt for the Roman Church. His thesis was that since the ninth century the Papacy had been the chief cause of the misfortunes of Europe. He sympathised with religious belief, but declared emphatically that the temporal power must disappear.

---

[1] The best study of Daunou is by Guérard, *Notice sur D.*, 1855. Cp. Taillandier, *Documents biographiques sur D.*, 1841. There are excellent appreciations by Mignet, *Notices et Mémoires*, vol. i., 1843; Sainte-Beuve, in *Portraits contemporains*, vol. iv.; Le Clerc, in *Histoire Littéraire de la France*, vol. xx.; and S. de Sacy, *Variétés Littéraires*, vol. ii., 1858. All these writers knew him personally.

The book belonged to the class of histories which the Emperor appreciated, its purpose being to provide the Government with a weapon in the prosecution of its policy. Daunou was more profitably employed in continuing for the Institute the unfinished works of the Benedictines. Towards the end of the Empire, assisted by Dom Brial and Ginguené, he resumed the 'Histoire Littéraire' where it had been interrupted at the twelfth century, and remained the soul of the enterprise during the rest of his life.

The most important of the few historical books of the time was Flassan's 'History of French Diplomacy.' 'While Napoleon was First Consul,' writes the author in the preface to the second edition, 'he informed a deputation of the historical class of the Institute that he desired a work on the diplomacy of France.' The commission was accepted, and the first history of a nation's diplomacy ever written appeared. Many documents and treaties were published for the first time, but its value lay exclusively in the materials. It closed, as the Emperor desired that all histories should close, with a flattering reference to himself. Laying down his pen at the opening of the Great War, Flassan reminds his readers that France then entered on a period of confusion which lasted 'till the appearance of power directed by genius.' Fulsome though the tribute was, the Emperor declared that he had made indiscreet use of his opportunities, and condemned the attempt to reveal to the world the secret springs of the political machine. Such a ruler could appoint historiographers but he could not produce historians.

The only work of importance by a member of the Emperor's circle was the 'Venetian History' of Daru,[1] who organised supplies for the Imperial armies, accompanied his master on campaigns, and·after the Moscow disaster became Minister of War. The plan was formed in 1797, and at the plundering of the Queen of the Adriatic he secured a number of valuable documents. The volumes appeared in rapid succession between 1815 and 1819, and gained immense popularity throughout Europe. The narrative is grave and tranquil, but the picture is drawn in sombre colours. The secrecy and severity of the Government and the moral corruption of the people are emphasised, and the whole work marches towards the conclusion that when Napoleon intervened the victim richly deserved her fate. Daru's volumes were the work rather of a publicist than of a scholar, and patriotic Venetians charged him with a design to decry the Republic. He rejoined that he had written with warm praise of the valour, the

[1] See Sainte-Beuve, *Causeries du Lundi*, vol. ix.

art and the industry of Venetian citizens. But Count Tiepolo,[1] his most formidable critic, declared that the worst charges were based on worthless sources, and published two volumes of rectifications. Stimulated by these and other criticisms, Daru undertook new researches and incorporated his results in successive editions. Among his readers was Napoleon at St. Helena, to whom Lord Holland forwarded the volumes, and whose comments on the death-struggle of the Republic were incorporated in the second edition. The work retained its place as the standard history of Venice till it was superseded a generation later by the more scholarly narrative of Romanin.

During the years of Napoleonic rule, a period of coercion and sterility, Chateaubriand's writings were setting free the springs of emotion, enlarging the imaginative horizon and stimulating the historical sense.[2] Though his knowledge was fragmentary and his temperament averse from systematic study, to him more than any other man is due the flowering of historical studies in France under the Restoration. In literature he was but carrying on the traditions of Rousseau and Bernardin de Saint Pierre; in history it was his supreme achievement to unlock the Middle Ages. His first work is of interest not as a preparation for but as a contrast to his riper productions. Written in England in 1797, the 'Essay on Revolutions' is remarkable for its detachment from the shibboleths of contending parties. Though a noble and an *émigré*, he declares that the French Revolution was inevitable, but he rejects the illusions of its champions. His task is to discover its causes and to forecast its consequences by a survey of similar upheavals. His study of Greek history reveals that most modern battle-cries were familiar to the classical world, and he concludes that humanity moves in a circle. The French Revolution would probably collapse like the others, and progress would once more prove a delusion. Indeed Europe appeared to be nearing a dissolution, for societies perished without a religion. Christianity was discredited, and there was nothing to replace it.

The 'Essay on Revolutions' was quickly followed by the author's religious conversion. The new Chateaubriand appeared in the *Génie du Christianisme*, the publication of which in 1802 was an event in politics, religion, historiography and literature. Synchronising with the Concordat, it gave an incalculable impetus to the current that was bearing France away from the

---

[1] *Rettificazioni della Storia del Daru*, 1828.

[2] The most important books on Chateaubriand are by Sainte-Beuve, *C. et son groupe littéraire sous l'Empire*, 2 vols., 1849, and Cassagne, *La Vie politique de C.*, 1911. Cp. Bertrand, *La Fin du Classicisme*, 1897.

traditions of the eighteenth century. Its religious impressiveness has long since disappeared, its scholarship is superficial, and it is now read purely as literature, but a century ago it was hailed as a masterpiece of apologetics. In a series of pictures the beauties of Christianity were displayed in dazzling colours—its dogmas and its legends, its mysteries, its ritual and its art. But he does more than vindicate its claim to be the dominant factor in modern civilisation: he connects it with the glories of ancient France. He argues from its beauty to its truth. His appeal is to the emotions and the imagination. Few books possess less of the historical spirit, but few have had a more far-reaching influence on historical studies. Its influence was confirmed and extended by the appearance of 'Les Martyrs' in 1809. The Romans and the Franks live again, and the virtues of the Christians throw a soft halo over the picture. There is but little exaggeration in the eulogy passed on Chateaubriand in 1840 by Augustin Thierry. 'All who in different ways pursue the paths of this century have met him at the source of their studies as their first inspiration. There is not one who cannot say, as Dante said of Virgil, "Tu duca, tu signore et tu maestro."'

The first effect of the forces which Chateaubriand had set in motion was seen in Michaud's 'History of the Crusades.'[1] The Emperor granted him permission to consult the archives, and the first volume of his work appeared in 1811. While the eighteenth century saw in the Crusades nothing but an orgy of superstition, Michaud explained the sentiments out of which they grew and recalled the heroism they evoked. His own convictions made him sympathise with events inspired by religious motives, while in rendering justice to the Middle Ages he found another opportunity of dissociating himself from the Revolution. He endeavoured to show that the Crusades were not only defensible as an expression of faith but of real utility in the development of European civilisation. It was more than a purely religious interest to thrust back the Eastern invaders, while the confrontation of Europe and Asia diminished ignorance, established commercial relations, and led to the growth of towns. Though lacking brilliance and distinction, the book found a ready welcome from a public which had been schooled by Chateaubriand. Like Daru, Michaud spent the rest of his life in improving his work and enlarging his knowledge. He published a *Bibliothèque des Croisades*, in which he incorporated material translated for him by an Orientalist, and towards the end of his life set out to visit the

[1] See Mignet, *Notices et Mémoires historiques*, vol. i., *Réponse à M. Flourens*; and Sainte-Beuve, *Causeries du Lundi*, vol. vii.

scenes of his drama. There was nothing of the passionate pilgrim about the careful student, who said that he had gone to Jerusalem not to reform the errors of his life but to correct the mistakes in his history.

While Michaud was studying the Crusades, Raynouard[1] began to explore the language and literature of the Troubadours. He won renown as a dramatist by his tragedy on the Templars, whom he surrounded with the aureole of martyrdom, and whose vindication he pursued by a volume of documents relating to their trial. The Troubadour poems were collected and published in six volumes, but he was more interested in the form than the matter. He advanced the contention that Romance was the only child of Latin, and in consequence the mother of French, Italian, Portuguese, Spanish and Catalan. Further research was to show that romance was the elder sister, not the mother of the languages of Latin Europe; but though the keystone of the edifice was loose, he inspired interest in the brilliant civilisation of the Midi.

A more powerful and original mind had dedicated itself to the same province before the appearance of the selections from the Troubadours. No French scholar of his age was so international in his interests as Fauriel.[2] The friend of Bopp, the elder Schlegel and Corais, the translator of Baggesen, the interpreter of Manzoni, the student of Homer, Arabic and Sanskrit, he possessed a mind like a reservoir fed by innumerable channels. His collection of Greek folk-songs, with a masterly Introduction, introduced Europe to a new literature. Towards the end of the Empire he began that profound study of the civilisation of the Midi to which he devoted the rest of his life. Before Raynouard and every other scholar he realised the beauty of the culture which was destroyed by the Albigensian crusade. In tracing its origin his studies led him back to the era of Greek colonisation, and he determined to survey the civilisation of the Midi in a series of works, the first connecting ancient Gaul with the general history of antiquity, the second recording the invasions and domination of the Franks, the third reaching from the fall of the Carolingians to the conclusion of the Albigensian wars. Only the second of the three parts was completed; but the 'History of Southern Gaul under the Franks' is itself a substantial work in four volumes. Anticipating the contention of Fustel de Coulanges, he maintains that the invaders brought nothing but ruin and chaos. The South resisted

---

[1] See Mignet, *Portraits et Notices historiques*, vol. i., and Sainte-Beuve, *Causeries du Lundi*, vol. v.
[2] See Galley, *Claude Fauriel*, 1909.

better than the North, because it was more strongly Latin and was attacked with less energy. That the invasion rejuvenated the corrupt frame of the Roman province he emphatically denies. The work opens with a broad survey of the civilisation of the fifth century in Roman Gaul and among the invaders respectively. The fortunes of the Merovingians and Carolingians are only followed in so far as they affect the South, and the main thread is the survival of Latin culture throughout the centuries of barbarism. In his enthusiasm for the beautiful South he fails to recognise the value of the work that was being accomplished in the North, and the importance of Charles the Great escapes him. The third part, dealing with the brilliant civilisation of the centuries that followed the break-up of the Carolingian Empire, was to have been the crown of the whole work. Portions of the immense material which he had collected were utilised in the courses which he delivered at the Sorbonne on Provençal poetry and Dante, published after his death by his friend Julius Mohl. These admirable lectures treat literature as a mirror of civilisation, and throw light on the language and literature, society and morals of the world of the Troubadours. His vast learning made him the guide, philosopher and friend of the generation of historians who grew up under the Restoration. Guizot and Cousin, Thiers and Mignet owed much to his encouragement, and Augustin Thierry never wearied of acknowledging the debt to his friend and master.

Of less brilliance and originality than Fauriel but far more productive was Sismondi,[1] who was descended from a family of Ghibellins which had been expelled from Italy in the sixteenth century and had fled from France to Geneva at the revocation of the Edict of Nantes. When the Revolution broke upon Switzerland he lost his home and sought refuge in Tuscany. His first celebrated work, the 'History of the Italian Republics,' began to appear in 1807. He had intended at the outset to study the constitution of the cities, but he soon perceived that to understand their organisation he must survey not merely the legislation but the entire life of the people. Thus imperceptibly his task widened into the story of Italy from the fall of the Western Empire to his own time. The heart of his subject was the history of the Republics from the twelfth to the sixteenth century. To

[1] See *Sismondi, Fragments de son Journal et Correspondance*, with biographical introduction, 1857. The best appreciations are by Mignet, *Portraits et Notices historiques*, vol. ii., 1852; Sainte-Beuve, Lundis, vol. vi.; Scherer, *Nouvelles Études sur la Littérature contemporaine*, 1876; and Loménie, *Galerie des Contemporains*, vol. vii.

enter the labyrinth, he declared, a clue was needed. History taught that government and laws were the most essential factor in the character of peoples, not climate or race. Nowhere was this more clearly seen than in Italy, whose greatness varied directly with the volume of liberty she enjoyed. When she lost it under Charles V her influence disappeared, her energy of character, activity in commerce and distinction in art vanished. The lesson emerges that no State can become or remain great without liberty. 'It can exist in monarchies as well as in republics, in federations no less than in a single city. The duty of every ruler and every citizen before God and man is to introduce the guarantee of liberty into the constitution, whatsoever it be. Through it and it alone will men be truly men. Tyranny is a continuous revolution, and a people would be mad if they did not deliver themselves from it.' History was only of use for its lessons, and it was the duty of the historian to see that they were properly taught.

The introductory volume carries the reader rapidly through the dark centuries that followed the fall of the Western Empire in 476, and the detailed narrative begins with the struggle of Barbarossa and the Lombard cities. Though an enthusiastic supporter of the League he none the less senses the greatness of the Emperor. Indeed his passionate love of liberty makes him strict rather than indulgent to its guardians. Scattered through the volumes are chapters which reveal how far short of the ideal every state has fallen. The movement towards despotism at last becomes irresistible. 'The peoples had not remained faithful to the love of liberty and country, and personal passions had arisen,' he laments. As vigilance relaxes despotism creeps in. The tragic story of enslavement since 1530 is dispatched in half a dozen chapters, and the history lesson is at an end. In an early essay Freeman declared Sismondi's work to be immortal, and praised its eloquence, depth and didactic force. This enthusiastic eulogy was modified in later years, and the arrangement of material was declared to be faulty. The pious Manzoni, while warmly praising the book as a whole, protested against his treatment of the Church,[1] but no one could fail to be impressed by the power of the book. What Grote was to do for Greece, Sismondi accomplished for the Italian Republics.

The historian had reached middle age before he visited Paris. 'If we must love a nation,' he wrote to the Countess of Albany, 'I know none to be preferred to the French.' Like

---

[1] *Vindication of Catholic Morality against the Charges of Sismondi,* 1836, Eng. Trans.

Benjamin Constant he welcomed Napoleon on his return from Elba as the defender of national independence and the opponent of European reaction. After completing the 'Italian Republics' he braced himself to a still larger task. The first volume of the 'History of the French' appeared in 1821, the twenty-ninth, bringing the story to the death of Louis XV, after his death in 1842. He maintained that the history of France, like the history of Italy, had never been properly written. 'No modern history has been absolutely free from those necessary lies, those respectful reticences which destroy our confidence and our comprehension of events. Frenchmen have always employed history to establish the rights of kings or nobles, parliaments or people, instead of seeking for the causes of errors with a view to avoiding their repetition. I shall write without subterfuge, or indulgence. The absolute power of one or many is a poison.'

Sismondi's survey is based on original study, unlike those 'compilations from other compilations' which he aspired to supersede. It provided the first intelligible account of the fall of the Roman administration in Gaul, the character of the Germanic invasions, the structure of feudalism, the rise of the communes, the influence of commerce and industry on political development. 'I know I lack some qualities of an historian which others possess,' he wrote; 'but I can render one testimony to myself, and I am confident posterity will confirm it—I have always sought the truth and spared no labour to find it.' That he was not a Frenchman made it easier for him to apply the critical eye. It suffers nevertheless from grave faults. Like Schlosser and Rotteck he judges men and events of past times by the standards of his own, and for lack of imagination fails to understand the atmosphere and outlook of other ages. 'There is for an historian a holier mission,' he wrote a month before his death, 'than that of working to extend the renown of a people, and that is to judge every event by the great touchstone of the laws of morality, to castigate cruelty, greed and perfidy wherever they appear.' But his justice is not tempered with mercy or even with understanding. The austere republican weighs the monarchs in the balance and finds them wanting. The Protestant rationalist, whose family had been driven out by Louis XIV, denounces the intolerance, the luxury, the worldliness of the Catholic clergy. St. Louis was 'the only French King who constantly guided his actions by a feeling of duty,' but he was the founder of absolute monarchy. The Crusades provoke him to lamentations over the cruelty of the contending parties, while the Albigensian wars and the sufferings of the Jews are described with burning indignation. The vices of the Valois are related with loathing disgust. He dwells with most pleasure on pioneers like Etienne Marcel and l'Hôpital. His first book was a hymn to liberty, his second a philippic against the blighting despotism of kings and priests.

This lack of relativity did not escape his more discerning readers. 'In his virtuous indignation,' remarked Barante,[1] 'Sismondi becomes the personal enemy of all the kings, nobles and bishops of the past.' 'I am sure that he is truthful and therefore that he thinks he is just,' wrote that acute and charming critic, the Duchesse de Broglie; 'but as he does not possess the necessary imagination to transport himself to another time, he sees actions independently of motives and sentiments. His hatred of priests is wearisome, and he judges Hugh Capet as he would judge a Genevese syndic of the nineteenth century.' In striking contrast to the shrill depreciation of the ruling powers is his enthusiasm for the towns. Wherever large towns existed, in France or elsewhere, a republican spirit was manifest. That the Communes gained their liberty from the crown is a legend. 'The French people conquered for themselves what they possessed at the point of the sword, as liberty should always be acquired.' His rigid Puritanism would alone have sufficed to make it impossible for his book to obtain popularity in France, but its chances were further limited by defects of style. There is but little art in his composition and little movement in his narrative. Themes which stir the pulse of other writers evoke no response in him. He coldly remarks that Joan of Arc was only possible in an age of superstition. Even those who admired his sterling qualities lamented that the kernel was hidden in such a prickly husk. 'Sismondi interests me,' wrote Sainte-Aulaire to Barante, his brother historian, 'as much as it is possible to be interested when one is bored. I am sure you will not make us pay this price for the instruction that you give us.' While he was at work Guizot was subjecting mediæval France to a profound analysis and Michelet was irradiating it with the gorgeous hues of his fancy. In the last weeks of his life Sismondi wrote, 'I have given the French nation what it did not possess, a complete picture of its existence.' It is the fate of the pioneer that he aids his successors to place him on the shelf.

A more vivid method was inaugurated by Augustin Thierry,[2]

[1] These quotations are from Barante, *Souvenirs*, vol. iii., 1893.

[2] See Renan's affectionate tribute in *Essais de Morale et de Critique*, 1857; Brunetière's centenary address, *Revue des Deux Mondes*, Nov. 15, 1895; *Revue de Synthèse historique*, vol. xiii; Georges Valentin, *Augustin Thierry*, 1895, and K. J. Carroll, *Some Aspects of the Historical Thought of Augustin Thierry*, 1951. Arbois de Jubainville, *Deux Manières d'écrire*

who convinced his countrymen that the past was not dead and that its actors were men of like passions with ourselves. Few passages in French literature are more familiar than that in which he has related the origin of his historical vocation as a lad of fifteen. 'In 1810 I was finishing my classes at the college of Blois when a copy of ''Les Martyrs'' fell into my hands. We fought for the book, and it was agreed that each should have it in turn. When it came to me I remained at home all day. As the dramatic contrast of the savage warrior and the civilised soldier unfolded itself, I was more and more impressed. The effect of the war-song of the Franks was electric. I rose from my seat and, marching up and down the room, I shouted, ''Pharamond, Pharamond, nous avons combattu avec l'épée.'' This moment of enthusiasm was perhaps decisive for my vocation. I had no consciousness of what had occurred. I even forgot it for some years. But when, after the inevitable uncertainties as to the choice of a career, I devoted myself entirely to history, I recalled this incident in its smallest details. Such is my debt to the writer of genius who opened and dominates the century.'

The glowing picture painted in 1840 is perhaps a little over-coloured, but it correctly traces Thierry's earliest interest in history to the inspiration of the greatest of the romantics. 'As I advanced in my studies, the lively pleasure arising from the contemporary pictures of men and things was blended with a dull anger at our modern writers who have travestied the facts, misrepresented the characters, and clothed everything in false or uncertain colours. I seemed to have found my true vocation—not only to light up some corners of the Middle Ages, but to plant the flag of historic reform for France.' The Benedictines had collected facts but not understood them, had furnished materials for history but not written it. The stupendous events of the last fifty years had taught everyone a lesson. With this added experience it was possible to understand much in the Middle Ages that had been hidden, to read between the lines of the chronicles, to clothe skeletons with flesh and blood. The historian needed erudition, knowledge of life, imagination; if one or more were lacking he could not do his work.

It was in this spirit that the famous book on the Norman Conquest was composed. If Chateaubriand had fired his imagination as a lad, it was Scott who most deeply influenced his mind.[1]

l'Histoire, Critique de Bossuet, Thierry et Fustel de Coulanges, 1896, contains a severe criticism.

[1] See Maigron, *Le Roman historique à l'époque romantique; Essai sur l'influence de Walter Scott*, 1896.

'My admiration for this great writer was profound; it grew as I contrasted his wonderful comprehension of the past with the petty erudition of the most celebrated historians. I saluted the appearance of "Ivanhoe" with transports of enthusiasm.' He learned from Hume that English institutions contained more of aristocracy than of liberty. 'The idea struck me, that dates from a conquest.' As his researches continued he found that states now homogeneous revealed signs of early racial differences which became stronger as they were traced backwards. In some countries the classes faithfully represented the races, the conquerors surviving as a privileged caste. This key appeared to him to unlock English history till the accession of Henry VII. England was then one nation, but there were still more Norman names among the country squires than among artisans and traders. The book is thus the elaboration of a theory in the guise of a narrative. Its success was unprecedented. For the first time since Voltaire an historical work had been produced in France of supreme literary distinction. Thierry saw everything in colour and relief. He had learned from Scott, 'that great master of historic divination,' that the scenes of the past could be brought to life by the power of imagination. The Middle Ages seemed dull because no one understood how to interpret their monuments. In his hands the texts not only recorded facts but revealed a world. When he was old and blind he sometimes asked Renan, then a young man, to aid him in research. 'I never witnessed without astonishment,' testifies Renan, 'the promptness with which he seized a document and adopted it for his narrative. The least fragment revealed to him an organic whole which, by a sort of regenerative power, rose complete before his imagination.' Where others discovered Providence or the action of general causes, he saw the struggles of living men and women. History ceased to be a procession of shadows across a darkened stage. He ends a chapter with the emphatic words, 'These men have been dead for seven hundred years, but what of that? For the imagination there is no past.'

The 'Conquête d'Angleterre' was the revelation of a new art. Its ardent sympathy with the people secured it a warm welcome at a moment when the best minds of France were at war with the last of the Bourbons. Moreover, the explanation of centuries of English history by a simple formula made a profound impression on a generation that was beginning to feel the need of new interpretations not less than of wider knowledge. Yet the thesis was false. The political results of the Conquest, on which he lays little stress, were profound; the social and moral consequences, on which he insists, were temporary. That racial antagonism is the master-key to the centuries following the battle of Hastings is not an exaggeration but a delusion. Becket is exalted into the champion of the down-trodden Anglo-Saxons, but his theory of racial cleavage blinds him to the fact that the career of the Archbishop was simply an episode in the European struggle between Church and State. In his preface he naïvely remarks 'I have a sort of partiality for the conquered.' His sympathies are with the crowd. Brunetière called him the most democratic and the most socialistic of historians. A child of the romanticists, he was stronger in imagination than in criticism. He took the chroniclers as he found them. He employs the 'Roman de Rou' for the landing of the Conqueror, and even quotes his speech before the battle of Hastings—an exercise as rhetorical as the orations in Thucydides and Livy.

No sooner had Thierry achieved his resounding triumph than he lost his eyesight. Chateaubriand remarked in his gallant manner, 'History will have its Homer, and I am the first of his admirers.' Despite this terrible affliction he continued his labours, and his later works are in some respects superior to that which gained him fame. The 'Récits des temps Mérovingiens' were scarcely less popular than the 'Conquête.' It was a mistake, he declared, to dismiss the Merovingian epoch as the most confused and arid period in French history: such a narrator as Gregory of Tours did not appear again till Froissart. The life of the nation emerged as if by magic from the dust of the chronicles. His favourite theory of the conflict of races finds ample scope. He pictures Gallo-Roman civilisation struggling against Frank barbarism. The Merovingians were seen to be as interesting as other rulers. His limpid style and ardent sympathies were never more decisively displayed, but his artistic instinct sometimes carries him away. He is not wholly guiltless of adding touches to his narrative for which his sources give no authority. He unlocked the shadowy Merovingian age, but its systematic exploration neeedd more exact scholarship. When he published his 'Récits' in a collected form in 1840, he added to them 'Considerations on the History of France.' The core of the nation, he declares emphatically, by blood and laws, by language and ideas, was Gallo-Roman. The Franks substituted vassalage for the Roman social order which they found, and in the North Teutonic influence almost obliterated the earlier culture. But in the South an emancipating movement, starting from Italy, made itself felt in the towns where the débris of Roman municipalities still existed. In the towns were born self-government and equality before the law.

They made the *tiers état*, and the *tiers état* made the nation. As civilisation grows, the racial factor declines in importance.

The later years of the historian's life were influenced by the school which owed its foundation to Guizot. When invited in 1836 to edit documents relating to the growth of the communes, he accepted without hesitation. His long introduction, later published as a separate volume, is his ripest work. The student of chronicles became the student of charters. We hear little of the conqueror and the conquered, and he recognises that the obvious traces of the Frankish conquest had vanished by the tenth century. He sketches the rise of the bourgeoisie, reconstructs old municipal France, and brings the story of the States General down to the triumph of absolutism. The book is not without mistakes. He shares the error that the Roman municipalities lingered on. Luchaire censured his use of modern terms such as liberty and equality, and maintained that he made the towns more democratic than they were. Giry criticised his theory of the relation of the gild to the town. But the book is more than a sketch of municipal institutions; it is also his final reading of French history. His theme is the gradual elevation of all classes and the fall of aristocratic barriers. His main achievement was to introduce a new figure, the people, and to set it, where it ought to be, in the foreground of the picture.

The fame of Amédée Thierry[1] is overshadowed by that of his elder brother, but his books enjoyed scarcely less popularity at the time of their appearance. The 'History of the Gauls before the Roman Conquest' attempted to build up a connected story from the fragmentary sources. Mainly relying on the aid of philology, he traced their wanderings and settlements in Italy and Spain, Greece, Asia Minor and Syria. They were brave and generous, he declares, but lacked the instinct of union. With its virtues and weaknesses the Gallic blood was still dominant in the veins of France. His 'Gaul under Roman Administration' possessed less novelty. The book is a pæan on Roman rule. The Romans, he contends, found Gaul barbarous and left it civilised. His writings, though neither profound nor critical, did much to arouse interest in history.

A third member of the romantic school was Barante,[2] who, like Thierry, was profoundly influenced by Scott. Believing that the old chroniclers had only to be known to be loved, he selected

---

[1] See Mignet, *Nouveaux Éloges historiques*.

[2] See Guizot, *M. de Barante*, 1867, and Sainte-Beuve, *Portraits contemporains*, vol. iv. Barante's *Souvenirs*, vol. iii., 1893, contains much correspondence relating to his principal work.

the age which was illustrated by Froissart, Monstrelet and Commines. The first two volumes of the 'History of the Dukes of
Burgundy' appeared in 1824. Of all Scott's novels none had
aroused so much interest in France as 'Quentin Durward,' and
Barante chose the century which it had illuminated. Its success
exceeded all anticipations. The Duchesse de Dino told the author
that she had devoured rather than read the book, and that there
was nothing to criticise and nothing to desire. Beginning with the
battle of Poitiers, in which the first Duke of Burgundy took part,
and ending with the battle of Nancy, in which Charles the Bold
fell fighting, the theme possesses artistic and dramatic unity. But
it is far more than a history of Burgundy. It is also a stage on
which appear Du Guesclin and the Black Prince, Joan of Arc and
Louis XI. A second cause of its success was the author's good
fortune in his sources. His object was to reveal to his countrymen
the wealth they possessed in their chronicles, and he determined
not to intervene between them and his readers. He quotes long
passages in full; at other times he summarises his sources with a
slight touch of archaism. 'There is no more historian or author,'
he wrote; 'it is the truth itself which the eye of the reader beholds.'
The preface may be described as a dissertation on the words of
Quintilian which adorn the title-page, *Historia scribitur ad nar-
randum, non ad probandum*. Most historians, he asserts, fail to
convey the interest of their sources because they insist on looking
at the past with the standards of their own time. People must be
brought to life, and then the reader can draw any conclusion that
he likes. 'I have tried to restore to history the interest that the
historical novel has borrowed from it. Before all it must be exact,
but I think it can also be true and living.' He had removed every
trace of his own work and added neither judgments nor reflections. What he thought of the occurrences of four centuries ago
mattered little. The manifesto provoked a good deal of criticism,
even among those who acclaimed the book. Guizot, after con-
gratulating him on his success, went on to say, 'If you had presented the system in a somewhat less absolute manner, if you had
said that the *genre* should vary with the subject and that your
method was especially suited to the epoch you were treating,
there would be practically nothing to contest.' To another
friendly critic Barante replied that his preface had a particular,
not a general reference. 'I had no desire to lay down absolute
rules: other times and other subjects would not admit of this
method. But one must not mix up things which are mutually
exclusive. A philosophical purpose cannot be combined with the
delights of narration and the dramatic painting of events. I

wanted people to see the fifteenth century instead of hearing it described.' The work now seems lifeless and artificial, and the modern student demands something more than a paraphrase of the chronicles.

II

Though Michelet[1] was too individual to be styled a member of any group, he approached most closely to the school of Augustin Thierry. Combining his passionate love for the people with a grandeur and poetry of his own, he stands out as the greatest literary artist who has ever devoted himself to history in France. Owing to his intense interest in himself, his outer and inner life is known in detail. The only child of a small Paris printer, his earliest recollections were of grinding poverty. He grew up a nervous, excitable, under-nourished lad, ignorant of the common joys of children. When his mother died he resolved never to separate from his father. The latter had an unswerving faith in his son, and made sacrifices to send him to a *lycée*. He lived to witness his fame, and the historian expressed his gratitude by providing a comfortable home for the old age of the parent who had made his career possible. His mind developed rapidly, and his strongest impression came from Lenoir's Museum. 'It is there and nowhere else that I experienced the vivid realisation of history. I remember the emotion, always the same and always lively, which made my heart beat when, as a small child, I passed under those solemn arches and gazed at those pale faces. I was not quite certain that all these marble sleepers might not be alive; and when I approached the hall of the Merovingians I was not sure that I might not see Chilperic and Fredegonde arise.'

While still uncertain as to his vocation, Cousin persuaded him to learn German and to translate Vico. He needed some philosophic interpretation of civilisation, and in the great Neapolitan he found the harmony of science and faith. 'He is the prophet of the new world. He first showed the rôle of Providence exercising itself, not in the narrow limits of a religion like Bossuet, but in man humanising himself through society.' His emphasis on the contribution of the masses to civilisation, his conviction that the social condition of a people was mirrowed in its law and poetry,

---

[1] The best appreciations are by Monod, *Renan, Taine, Michelet*, 1894; Jules Simon, *Mignet, Michelet, Henri Martin*, 1899; and Faguet, *Le dix-neuvième Siècle*. Much biographical material is to be found in Monod, *Jules Michelet*, 1905; Mme. Quinet, *Cinquante Ans d'Amitié, Michelet-Quinet*, 1899; and Noel, *Michelet et ses Enfants*, 1878. Two posthumous volumes, *Ma Jeunesse*, 1884, and *Mon Journal*, 1888, bring the story to 1823. There is a good article in the *Quarterly Review*, Jan. 1901.

and his use of etymology as a key to human origins, struck notes of delighted response. The translation of the *Scienza Nuova*, which conveyed the spirit rather than the letter, made it known not only to France but to Europe. Michelet achieved for Vico what Dumont accomplished for Bentham.

In 1827, the same year in which the translation appeared, he was appointed to teach history and philosophy at the École Normale and published his first narrative work. The 'Précis d'Histoire Moderne' superseded the chronological tables and bald summaries which were in universal use, and offered a survey of the development of civilisation from the fifteenth century to the French Revolution which brought the chief events and the leading actors into strong relief. Its freshness is partly due to the fact that it was largely based on original sources. For the first and last time Michelet wrote simply and concisely. The book is a well-kept garden, not a tropical forest. Never before had a writer of genius and learning set himself to compose a book for schools. A year later he visited Germany. Before starting he met Quinet, who had recently translated Herder's 'Ideen,' and commenced an historic friendship of half a century. He brought back an undying veneration for German philosophy and scholarship, and he loved to recall his debt. 'Germany is the bread of life for strong minds. She made me greater by Luther and Beethoven, Kant, Herder and Grimm.'

When Michelet crossed the Rhine the learned world was ringing with the praises of Niebuhr, whom his youthful enthusiasm for Virgil and his studies of Vico had prepared him to appreciate at his full worth. The plan of a history of Rome rose before his mind. In 1830 he visited Italy for the purpose of his book, and in the following year appeared his volumes on the Roman Republic. Like Arnold, he removes the mass of scaffolding and allows the grandeur of the design to emerge in bold relief. But his book is far more than a reproduction of Niebuhr. The factor of race is minimised, and the nation is represented as the moral image of its dwelling-place. The passion for symbolism, which adorns and disfigures his later work, now makes its appearance. The Samnite wars were not the strife of two races, but the conflict of the plain and the mountain. Cato the Elder is 'the old Italian genius,' Cæsar 'the man of humanity.' The book ends with the death of Cæsar. His assertions about early Rome are much too positive, and he makes no serious attempt at a critical analysis of his sources, though rejecting Niebuhr's theory of lays. But the work rests on wide foundations. Topography, language, law, literature, inscriptions, medals are used to supplement the chronicle and the legend. Though only a sketch of a vast subject, it is full of ideas and throbs with life. 'An incomparable work,' declared Monod half a century later, 'full of original and profound views, and in some respects not yet surpassed.'

The 'Introduction to Universal History,' published in 1831, ranks among the most brilliant productions of its author. Briefly and eloquently he marks out the position which the chief nations have occupied. 'With the world began a war which will only finish with the end of the world, that of man against nature, mind against matter, liberty against fatality. History is nothing but the record of this ceaseless struggle.' Following the course of the sun, which is the course of civilisation, we see the dominion of nature diminishing at every stage. India is at her mercy, like a child at its mother's breast. Persia introduces the principle of light, which will one day confound the principle of darkness. Egypt accepts the immortality of the soul. The Jews worship Jehovah above and apart from nature. Greece and Rome develop the arts and sciences, but they fall because they are not rooted in liberty. Christianity glorifies the spirit. Modern Europe is an organism, one part of which is unintelligible without the rest. Germany is the land of renunciation, of sympathy, of mysticism. Italy is individual and independent, the heir of Rome, the land of politics and law. England is proud, heroic, aristocratic, the first of modern nations to struggle for liberty while caring nothing for equality. France, on the other hand, is constructive, free, democratic. The Revolution of 1830 is the consummation of French history; it is her proud destiny, having won liberty for herself, to inaugurate the era of democracy, which is liberty incarnate. The governing idea of the survey had been stated in Quinet's introduction to his translation of Herder. 'History is the drama of liberty, the protest of the human race against the world which enchains it, the freedom of the spirit, the reign of the soul.' In one particular this analysis is utterly arbitrary and unscientific. He begins with India, but China is older and at the same time less despotic and superstitious. The parallelism of history and the sun breaks down at the start. Again Egypt is reached before Judæa, though the latter is east of the former. He traces the progress of freedom, but fails to prove that history is nothing more than its realisation.

The 'Introduction to Universal History' was a hymn to the glories of France as the principal actor in the drama of liberty. Michelet's next task was to treat her history in detail, and at his creative touch she became a person. The first six volumes of the 'History of France' are his most perfect and enduring work.

They were written when his genius had reached its fullest development and before his imagination had become diseased. His object is 'the resurrection of the life of the past as a whole,' the land and the people, events, institutions and beliefs. Though his work is based on original sources, he makes large use of his brother historians. 'I owe much to the conscientious history of our venerable Sismondi, and the beautiful narratives of the Thierrys have never left me. I owe even more to the writings of Guizot and to his kindly interest.' The first volume sketches the centuries before Hugh Capet, and characterises the races out of which a united nation was to arise. The Celts are credited with sociability, love of action and rhetoric. The Germans are impersonal and dreamy, and a vague indecision rests on their features. The second volume examines the stage on which the drama is played. The 'Tableau de France' is not only one of the most signal achievements of the historian's genius, but the application of a new instrument of interpretation. Michelet was the first to realise the full importance of the geographical factor in the development of his country. He maintained that political divisions corresponded to physical divisions, and that each province had its peculiar rôle as each organ its function in the human body. He sketches the provinces in turn, their features, their climate, their inhabitants, their character, their contribution to the national life. Resting on a generous recognition of the manifold elements of which France was composed, the book is of all the large scale French histories the most truly national.

Michelet provides tableaux rather than a record of events. He hurries across large tracts of territory, and lingers over individuals and occurrences that strike his imagination. Of these gorgeous scenes the earliest is the fall of the Templars, the documents relating to which he edited for Guizot's collection of State Papers. The most famous depicts Joan of Arc, the summit of his achievement and one of the glories of French literature. His moving narrative reproduces the atmosphere of the Middle Ages, its burning life, its blending of patriotism and religion, its exaltation and degradation. The radiant figure of the Maid stands out against the dark background of France under Charles VI. Scarcely less exquisite are the pages devoted to mediæval art and to the 'Imitation,' 'the most beautiful of Christian books after the Gospels.' The sixth volume, containing a powerful full-length portrait of Louis XI, embodied more new material than any of its predecessors. As a result of his researches, declared the author with pride, the conventional figures of Scott and Barante had entirely disappeared. His judgments are on the whole very fair.

He pays little attention to kings, but he is not their enemy, and St. Louis has never had a more devoted admirer. The Church is treated with sympathy, and parts of the book seem an echo of the 'Génie du Christianisme.' He never forgets that he is writing a history of the whole nation. The soul of France had grown by the complex influences which transform individuals. 'Who has modified, smelted, transmuted these elements, made them a body? France herself, by internal labour, by mysterious parturition, blended of necessity and liberty.' He scornfully repudiates the doctrines of race, the influence of conquest, the providential rôle of great men. Organic life cannot be explained, for it is a mystery.

The greatest of Michelet's gifts was his sympathetic imagination. No writer has ever approached the history of France with such passionate and filial love. 'If I surpass other historians it is because I have loved more.' The supreme actor merges his own personality in the parts that he plays, and his power of expression equals his power of imagination. What he sees he can make others see. The most casual entry in his note-books is as personal as the most highly wrought passage in his published writings. The grain of sand is transformed by the microscope into a vision of glory. His pages blaze with colour. Taine has compared him to Doré and Delacroix, Monod to a great musician. He is the Victor Hugo of history. But these unique gifts involve the lack of certain qualities which the historian should possess. His heart was too full, his emotions too intense, to see life steadily and see it whole. Like Carlyle he leaps onto the stage, rebukes and encourages the performers, interjects asides to the audience. His glance lacks precision, and we dare not trust ourselves to his guidance. His passion for symbolism aids his readers to visualise the past, but the symbol often swallows up the reality. The imagination creates as well as reveals. There is something of the atmosphere of the gorgeous East about his work. 'He recalls to me,' wrote Heine, 'the large flowers and powerful perfumes of the Mahabharata.' We are still in the romantic movement, the world of colour, passion and poetry.

The work was received with mingled feelings.[1] Its novelty and power, its learning and beauty, were recognised on all hands, but its mysticism came as something of a shock to the sceptical liberalism of the Bourgeois Monarchy. Nisard, for half a century the oracle of classical criticism, pointed out the lack of order and

---

[1] The criticisms are summarised in Monod's article, 'Les Débuts d'Alphonse Peyrat dans la Critique historique,' *Revue Historique*, vol. xcvii.

method, and blamed its lyrical exaltation. Sainte-Beuve, who had shed his romantic skin, refused to review it on the ground that he was too much out of sympathy. Sismondi, on receiving a copy from the author, replied that he was filled with astonishment and admiration. 'You give me new discoveries at every page on the ground at which I myself have worked so long, but I cannot accept a personality in the peoples which makes the personality of individuals disappear. Your interpretation is wholly novel. Whether it will convert me is another matter.' In Catholic circles it found warmer praise. Chateaubriand commented that he had always felt that French history needed to be rewritten, and Michelet had done it. Montalembert, an old pupil, declared that he was stupefied by its colossal erudition and incomparable *nerve*, and praised the impartiality of his treatment of Catholicism.

When Michelet reached the dawn of modern history he interrupted his survey. When a determined attack on University teaching was launched by Louis Veuillot and his ultramontane associates, Michelet and Quinet, the most popular Professors in France, flung themselves into the fray, delivering simultaneously a course of lectures on the Jesuits. Every address was a battle-cry, and Paris rang with the sound of conflict. Believing that intellectual and political freedom was at stake, the Professors hit out vigorously. The course on 'Priests, Women and Families' held up the confessor to reprobation as the destroyer of the home. The crusade against the Jesuits developed into an attack on Christianity, and Guizot cannot be blamed for bringing the courses to an end. Michelet's emergence as the leader of the anti-clericals so soon after his glorification of the mediæval Church led to embittered charges of apostasy. He replied that he had sought baptism at the age of eighteen as a means of entering into communion with an august historic institution but had never accepted its dogmas. Jules Simon testifies that he was already a rebel in his lectures at the École Normale in 1834. But though there is no ground for a charge of apostasy, his attitude towards the Church underwent a permanent change. He confessed that his picture of mediæval Christianity was an ideal, not a reality, and he now began to feel his way towards new political principles. The July Monarchy came in on the flood of liberal enthusiasm, but from 1840, when Guizot was called to the helm, it set itself to combat democratic aspirations.

As Thiers and Mignet had used the French Revolution to overturn Charles X, so Michelet and Lamartine employed it to undermine his successor. The former dreamed of a regenerated

France, free alike from Church and Monarchy, based on the principles of justice, a France in which the poor and the humble would come by their rights. This vision was embodied in the 'History of the French Revolution,' his second great work, which differs widely in spirit and aim from his first. His task is no longer merely to resuscitate the past: he is less the painter than the preacher, and into none other of his works did he pour so much of his own spirit. 'The Revolution is in us, in our souls. In principle it was the triumph of law, the resurrection of justice, the reaction of ideas against brute force. It began by loving everything. In its benevolent period the whole people were the actors; in the period of cruelty only a few individuals.' Its early days were sacred: never since Joan of Arc had there been such a ray from on high. After centuries of oppression the people emerged, reorganised society, set an example to the world. Through the smoke and flames he perceives the growth of a new France, a new Europe. He begins by discussing the new conception of justice from which the Revolution arose. Voltaire had answered the question, Can there be religion without justice and humanity? Rousseau had founded social right on an impregnable basis. 'Let them stand for ever on the same pedestal, twin apostles of humanity. When they have passed, the Revolution is already accomplished in the mind of France.' The outbreak is painted in the warm hues of admiring sympathy, and he renders intelligible the days of credulous enthusiasm and infinite hopes. His 'Fête of the Federation' stands with his 'Joan of Arc' as one of the shining achievements of French literature. In 1789, he declares, France became conscious of her liberty, in 1790 of her unity. Her heart was full of magnanimity, clemency and pardon. The artificial barriers between classes, parties and nations fell away, and the soul of the people was revealed in unsullied radiance. Never did a great revolution cost less blood or tears. She appeared to the world in the guise of the angel of liberty. 'From the Rhine, the Netherlands, the Alps the voice of suppliants reached her. She had only to step beyond her frontiers for them to kneel before her. She came not as a nation but as Justice, Eternal Reason, demanding nothing of men but that they should realise their own highest aspirations. Happy days of our innocence! France had not entered on the path of violence, nor Europe on that of hatred and envy.' Mirabeau and the early leaders made the mistake of believing in the monarchy, and their work needed supplementing, but their successors proved unequal to the task. France was saved in spite of the Terror, which delayed the success of the Revolution for half a century. Marat was the ape of Rousseau,

Robespierre a pedant,[1] the September Massacres an indelible stain on the national honour. But the enemies of the Revolution no more escape than its false friends. The Queen was guilty, for she called in the foreigner. The King played fast and loose with his promises, and his death, though a blunder, was not a crime. The revolt of the Vendéans was incredible ingratitude. But there is little bitterness in the book. 'All find their reconciliation in the heart of France.'

With the exception of Carlyle, Michelet's book is the most brilliant picture ever painted of the greatest event in modern history, and Aulard described it as the truest, though not the most exact, history of the Revolution. 'From the first page to the last,' wrote the author at the end of his task, 'there is only one hero— the people.' He loves Danton because he sees in him the truest incarnation of the soul of the people. The work thus gains artistic and historic unity. Destruction and reconstruction are seen to be parts of the same process. The book was a contribution to knowledge as well as to interpretation. He used the registers of the Commune of Paris, which perished with the destruction of the Hôtel de Ville in 1871. During his residence at Nantes after the *coup d'état* he explored the archives for the history of the Vendée risings. Above all, he had learned innumerable details from his father and other eye-witnesses of every episode of the Revolution. But though the book possesses conspicuous merits, his judgment of the Revolution is unacceptable. The voice of the people is the voice of God. Whatever was good in the Revolution was the work of 'the people'; whatever was bad was the work of somebody else. The ferocious passions of the mob, the hatred and envy which accompanied the vast upheaval, are hardly suggested. If he is too tender to the masses, he is too harsh to the Church. He regards the Revolution as a struggle between two conceptions of life, rationalist democracy versus Christian monarchy. The men were won for the Revolution, but the women remained in the hands of the priest, to whom above all was due the halting of the advance. The execution of the work is not less faulty than its general conception. Some events are described with infinite detail, others no less important are scarcely noticed. The book swarms with errors and suffers from exaggeration and effervescence. It is the epic of radical democracy, the most eloquent defence of the ideals of the Revolution ever written.[2]

---

[1] It was above all his view of Robespierre that was attacked by Robespierre's devoted biographer, Hamel, in *Michelet Historien*, 1869.

[2] For the gratitude of anti-clerical republicans see Spuller, *Figures disparues*, vol. i., 1886.

After an interruption of ten years Michelet returned to the task which had been interrupted by the struggle with clericalism. Louis Napoleon was now on the throne, the Church was powerful, democracy was discredited. His personal position was precarious. His refusal to take the oath lost him the Professorship to which he had been reappointed on the fall of Louis Philippe, and his post in the Archives followed it. He found comfort in the society of his devoted second wife,[1] and in observing and recording the wonders of bird and insect, sea and mountain. But his spirit was soured. While the Middle Ages had been described by a happy man, the later volumes breathe hatred and disenchantment. There is less research, less care, less reflection. He generalises from isolated facts, his prejudices become more strident, he refers great events to trivial causes. In too many pages we listen to a scurrilous pamphleteer.

Each of the eleven volumes of the new series bears a title. That on the Renaissance yields to none of its predecessors in power and brilliancy, though its preface strikes a frankly anti-Christian note. The Reformation, like the Renaissance, is glorified as a revolt against the Middle Ages and a forerunner of 1789.[2] As the work advanced its faults increased. The gossip of memoir writers is greedily swallowed, and no Court scandal is too disgusting or improbable to find credence. He speculates on the legitimacy of Louis XIII and Louis XIV, and with the Regency and Louis XV hints at incest. Manuscript journals of the physicians of Louis XIV are called in to solve problems of high politics. The King's life divides into a period of success and of failure—before and after the operation for fistula. Foreign policy is increasingly neglected. From a history of the nation the book often degenerates into a series of *causeries* on the Court. One critic described it as 'a bad book and a bad act,' and Montalembert wrote mournfully of his old teacher as a fallen idol. On the other hand, it abounds in striking ideas and in brilliant pictures. Many of its pages are beautiful and precious, and the sympathy for the poor and suffering is deep and real. The chapters on the revocation of the Edict of Nantes ring with noble indignation. He is incomparable on the corruption of the Valois, the pride of the Grand Monarque, the madness of Law. Nor is he without his moments of generosity. He feels something of the greatness of

---

[1] See the *Lettres à Mlle. Malairet*, 1847–9, a volume in the *Œuvres Complètes*.

[2] These two volumes are the text of Taine's brilliant appreciation in his *Essais de Critique et d'Histoire*.

Henri IV and Sully, and weeps over the grave of the Duc de Bourgogne.[1]

The 'Bible of Humanity' reveals the extent to which the mystical and romantic elements lived on beneath the acrid rationalism. Each civilisation is a verse written in the eternal, ever-growing book. India, Persia, Egypt, Judæa, Greece, Rome, Christianity are stages in this revelation of reason and justice. The power of magical evocation remains, but the faculty of criticism, never strong, almost disappears. The war of 1870 and the Commune broke his heart, and the three volumes on Napoleon which followed reveal incurable decline. His genius and method were too individual to found a school, but his writings and lectures exerted a profound influence. Many a young student could echo the words of Monod. 'I owe my vocation for history to him; I am not a disciple, but I am inspired by a deeper feeling, that of filial gratitude.' No historian has loved France more tenderly. To him that loved, much may be forgiven.

[1] One of the sanest criticisms of the later volumes is by Sainte-Beuve, *Nouveaux Lundis*, vol. ii. The indignation of Catholic royalists may be seen in de Broglie, *Questions de Religion et d'Histoire*, vol. i., 1860, and d'Haussonville, *Études biographiques et littéraires*, 1879.

CHAPTER X

THE POLITICAL SCHOOL.—GUIZOT, MIGNET, THIERS

THE school which was founded by Thierry and reached its summit in Michelet grew out of the romantic movement and perished with it. By its side arose a group of writers whose object was rather to explain than to narrate, for whom the individual was of less interest than the state, the anatomy and physiology of history of greater importance than its outward form and colour. Among its main interests were the structure of society, the evolution of forms of government, the relation of states to one another.

I

Guizot was the child of Protestant parents and always retained the grave austerity of French Protestantism.[1] His father had revolted against the excess of the Revolution and paid the penalty with his life. The son remained through life a moderate liberal of 1789. He quickly became known as a young man of wide erudition and marked ability, and in 1812, at the age of twenty-four, Fontanes appointed him *suppléant* to Lacretelle in the Chair of History at the Sorbonne. On the fall of the Empire he entered public life. He had already won a prominent place among the small but distinguished group of the Doctrinaires or Whigs who followed Royer-Collard. As their representative he journeyed to Ghent to persuade Louis XVIII to grant a Constitution, and during the early years of the Restoration he occupied a series of high administrative posts. In two remarkable pamphlets he urged the claims of the middle classes to be the deciding influence in politics, and preached the ideals of the *Juste Milieu*. The predominance of the educated bourgeoisie was the true mean between the rival absurdities of divine right and the sovereignty of the mob. The foes of society were absolutism and Jacobinism. At that moment the counter-revolution was the enemy. The ground that had been won in the Revolution must never be surrendered,

---

[1] See Guizot's voluminous Memoirs and the correspondence published after his death. The best biography is by Bardoux, 1894. The best appreciations are by Jules Simon, *Thiers, Guizot, Rémusat*, 1885; Faguet, *Politiques et Moralistes*, vol. i.; and Woodward, *Three Studies of European Conservatism*, 1929. The volumes of Pouthas are almost entirely political.

but it could only be permanently maintained by the equilibrium of a genuinely constitutional monarchy.

The fall of the Doctrinaires in 1820 restored Guizot to his Chair, and the first course, on the origins of representative government, gave expression to his enthusiasm for English institutions. Of greater importance were the lectures on the institutions of France, which, like their predecessors, were the vehicle of political propaganda. Indeed so closely did they approach to the burning problems of the hour that the Professor was silenced in 1822. Part of the course appeared in 1823 in his 'Essays on the History of France.' His object was to inquire how free, aristocratic and monarchical institutions struggled and combined until the tenth century. The first and most important essay treats of municipal government in the Roman Empire. Why did that Empire fall? Slavery, luxury and despotism had all existed throughout the Imperial era. Guizot came nearer an explanation when he recalled that it was largely an agglomeration of towns, and explained how the curiales, who controlled municipal affairs and were responsible for the revenue, sank under the burden. When the middle classes were ruined by taxation it had no other resources. The following essays, dealing with the establishment of the Franks in Gaul, the causes of the fall of the Merovingians and Carolingians, the institutions of the Franks and the feudal régime, reveal a convinced Germanist. The closing essay on the causes of the establishment of the representative system in England explains how the competing interests of King, nobles and commons resulted in an equilibrium which allowed of the growth of a free and orderly government.

After describing mediæval England in his lectures and essays and modern England in his pamphlets, Guizot plunged into the constitutional struggle of the seventeenth century. He begins his 'History of the English Revolution' with the accession of Charles I. No attempt was made to discover new materials or to dramatise the conflict. It is an engraving, not a picture. We are in the hands of a statesman engaged in the search for practical lessons who is in no doubt as to which side was right. The contrast with the French Revolution is continually before his eyes. England wisely made no attempt to break the natural course of events. The leaders of the popular party appealed to precedent and merely resisted the abuse of the royal prerogative. There were several causes of this fundamental difference. The English Revolution was political, not social. It sought liberty, not equality. It was religious, not rationalistic. It was carried through by men of property and high intelligence like Hampden and Pym, the pioneers of the movement towards rational liberty which has changed the face of the world.

The work was interrupted by a return to his Chair in 1828, and it is on the lectures delivered in the next three years that his world-wide fame as an historian rests. He left an ineffaceable impression on his hearers. Jules Simon declared that he was eloquence incarnate, but unlike most eloquent men he expressed himself with great conciseness. Political allusions were now rigorously excluded. He appeared to his audience to treat of human affairs as if he stood above the petty struggles of humanity. The 'History of Civilisation in Europe,' with which he began, was a triumph of condensation. The modern world, he declared, was superior to the ancient because it combined valuable elements which previously existed in isolation. The Roman Empire bequeathed the municipal system, a written law, and the idea of Imperial rule. The Christian Church contributed lofty doctrines and a world-wide organisation. The barbarians brought with them personal liberty and the habit of voluntary association. These elements needed a prolonged period for their amalgamation, and the Middle Ages were the battle-ground of their claims. Feudalism and ecclesiastical pretensions must be treated with respect as incorporating venerable traditions or responding to widely felt needs. But the main organ and symbol of progress during the later Middle Ages was to be found in the growth of a middle class between the aristocracy and the peasantry, for its existence involved in the long run representative government. The Reformation encouraged the critical spirit, and the Puritan Revolution marked the triumph of self-government in England and the beginning of its conquest of the civilised world. The course ends on the eve of the French Revolution, which the growth of the *tiers état* in numbers, intelligence and wealth rendered inevitable. The lectures constituted an enormous advance in the interpretation of history. He sweeps the field as from a lofty watch-tower. His eyes are on the distant horizon and the collective achievement. His philosophy of history is an unshakable belief in Providence, but the transformations of society are explained on purely secular grounds. The influence of individuals, however, and the chapter of accidents are underestimated, and the epochs dovetail too neatly into one another. There is peril in mingling with the crowd, but there is also danger in surveying the changes and chances of mortal life from the summit of Olympus.

Guizot followed his first course by a detailed examination of the development of civilisation in France, which he chose as a mirror of the destinies of Europe. He begins by describing the social and intellectual, civil and religious condition of Gaul before the German invasion, the character and institutions of the Germans beyond the Rhine, and finally the invasion itself and the interaction of the barbarian and Romanised societies. In the civil order he sketches the origin and character of the barbarian codes. In the religious world he describes the internal organisation of the Church and its relation to civil society. Intellectual life is illustrated by a survey of the scanty literature. The character and policy of Charles the Great, his administrative reforms, his influence on legislation and education, are minutely studied. A sketch of the Church and the development of theology and philosophy brings the survey to a close. In thirty lectures the life of five conturies is analysed with extraordinary skill and ample learning. In 1830 he began a similar investigation of the feudal period, which he defined as extending from Hugh Capet to Philippe le Bel. When he had completed his survey of feudalism and the monarchy, the course was ended by the revolution of 1830, which launched the historian on the troubled sea of politics. The abrupt termination of the 'History of Civilisation in France' is one of the heaviest losses which historical science ever sustained, for even in its fragmentary form it stands out as one of the great achievements of the first half of the century. Guizot was the first to dissect a society as the anatomist dissects a body, the first to study the functions of the social organism as the physiologist those of the animal. It is a model of arrangement, doing justice to the vast variety of phenomena which make up civilisation while keeping steadily in view the unity of national life. The lectures demonstrated the possibility of a scientific treatment of history. No one has surpassed him in his capacity to seize the ideas which underlie events, to discern the innner changes which govern outward transformations, to recover the intellectual tendencies of an epoch.

The criticisms suggested by the course of 1828 were equally relevant to its successors. Guizot himself declared that the historian has a threefold task. He must collect his facts and know how they are connected—that may be called historical anatomy. He must discover the organisation and life of societies, the laws which preside over the course of events—that is the physiology of history. 'But do you know also their external physiognomy? Have you before your eyes their individual features? The facts now dead once lived; unless they have become alive to you you know them not. The investigation of facts, the study of their relation, the reproduction of their form and motion, these constitute history, and every great historical work must be judged by these tests.' This passage is at once a testimony to Guizot's lofty conception of the duties of the historian and a sentence on his own limitations. The recreation of the past is beyond him. He admired Scott and Fenimore Cooper and recommended their novels, but he shows no trace of their influence. He lacks narrative and descriptive power, pictorial and dramatic imagination, interest for the individual and the particular. His record is too symmetrical. The most penetrating criticism came from Sainte-Beuve.[1] 'Guizot's writings form a chain from which you cannot remove a link. His aim is to rule and to organise the past as well as the present. I doubt if it is given to man to embrace the causes of his history with this completeness and certitude: he finds it almost beyond his strength to understand the present. History seen from a distance undergoes a singular metamorphosis; it produces the illusion—the most dangerous of all—that it is rational. The follies, the ambitions, the thousand strange accidents which compose it, all these disappear. Every accident becomes a necessity. Guizot's history is far too logical to be true.' To remind himself how history is fashioned Sainte-Beuve took down from his shelves the Memoirs of de Retz.

Guizot employed his position as a Minister to further the interests of history in many ways. The organisation of historical studies in France dates from the reign of Louis Philippe. In the words of Thierry, history became a national institution. The first of his undertakings was the formation of a Société de l'histoire de France,[2] with the aid of Thiers, Mignet, Barante, Fauriel, Raynouard, Guérard and other well-known scholars. Its activities included new editions of the chroniclers and the publication of manuscript material, such as the letters of Mazarin and the records of the trial of Joan of Arc. On the death of Barante in 1866 Guizot, who had watched over its fortunes throughout, became President, to be succeeded on his death by Léopold Delisle. Of far greater importance was the project for the publication of the manuscript sources of French history at the expense of the State. The idea was not new.[3] Moreau, who became the historiographer of France at the close of the reign of Louis XV, conceived the idea of obtaining copies of charters and documents. A Cabinet des Chartes was founded in 1762, and the main burden

---

[1] *Causeries*, vol. i.

[2] See Jourdain, *Notices et Documents à l'occasion du 50ième Anniversaire*, 1884.

[3] See the exhaustive work of Xavier Charmes, *Le Comité des Travaux historiques*, 3 vols., 1886.

of transcription was undertaken by the Benedictines. The suppression of the Order ruined the enterprise, but the labour of copying innumerable charters just before the storm in which so many of the originals disappeared was not thrown away. In 1833 Guizot proposed to the King that the State should undertake the publication of manuscripts. The utmost efforts of isolated individuals, he declared, could only produce partial and limited results. Untold riches lay buried in the archives of France. Louis Philippe was sympathetic, and a committee was formed at the Ministry of Public Instruction to act as a centre and guide for local endeavours. Among the earliest volumes of the *Documents Inédits* were the works of Mignet on the Spanish Succession, Thierry on the *Tiers État*, and Guérard's editions of Abbey Cartularies. Differing from the *Monumenta* and the Rolls series in confining itself to unpublished material, the magnificent enterprise proved of priceless aid in the development of historical studies in France. A final service was the revival of the Academy of Moral and Political Sciences.

When the ministry and the monarchy fell together in 1848 Guizot returned not to the unfinished history of his own country, but to that of the land in which he sought refuge from the storm. During the reign of Louis Philippe his only literary effort was a French edition of the writings and correspondence of Washington. The grave and eloquent panegyric which served as an Introduction repeated his well-known convictions. The Anglo-Saxon race, he declared, had known how to conduct its revolutions in both hemispheres, and it was with a heightened admiration for England that he resumed his studies of the Puritan revolution after an interval of a quarter of a century. Though much light had been thrown upon the period, the later volumes differ little from the earlier. His chequered career made the storms of the seventeenth century more real to him, and he excels in analysing the debates and recording the movement of ideas. But there is no more colour than of old. There are no flowery paths nor sunlit landscapes. His main task is still to teach and to warn. He is as convinced as ever of the beneficence of the revolution, but experience has made him a little more critical. He virtually accepts Carlyle's demonstration of Cromwell's sincerity but rejects the estimate of his statesmanship. Of the three great Anglo-Saxon revolutions led by Cromwell, William III and Washington, the first was the least successful. Cromwell founded nothing, because he pursued, however unwillingly, a revolutionary policy. He speaks with the greatest severity of Vane, Ludlow and the doctrinaire republicans of a type only too familiar to the minister of Louis Philippe. Though his lofty austerity and aloofness is not to everybody's taste, it produces the same feeling of confidence as a volume of Ranke. He had intended to bring his history down to 1688, but the desire to write his Apologia led him to end with the Restoration. While the early volumes on Charles I contained no fresh material, new light was shed on the foreign policy of the Commonwealth, and the volumes on Richard Cromwell were a real contribution to knowledge. The series ended with a volume on Monk. Though the 'English Revolution' is inferior in importance to the 'Civilisation in France,' it was a notable contribution to the interpretation of a momentous crisis and may still be read with interest.[1]

II

In the early years of the Restoration two young Provençals set out for Paris, linked in intimate friendship and inspired by similar ideas and ambitions. Mignet,[2] the elder, who occupies the higher place in the hierarchy of French historians, was born at Aix in 1796. The overwhelming events connected with the fall of the Empire intensified his interest in politics, and his home became a centre of political discussion. Among the visitors was Thiers, who left Marseilles to study law at Aix. The friendship thus begun lasted without a cloud for sixty years. The young advocates watched the excesses of the Restoration with growing anger; but while Thiers was already dreaming of office, Mignet combined historical study with his practice, and won a prize offered by the Academy of Inscriptions for a study of the Institutions of St. Louis. His essay impressed men so different as Daunou and Dom Brial, and deserved its welcome, not merely for its picture of the Christian King and his code but for its luminous survey of feudal and monarchical France. It contains, moreover, the first indication of the author's historical ideas which resemble those of Guizot. 'How consistently things act, how they accomplish themselves necessarily and make use of men as means and events as occasions! From the beginning of the French monarchy it is less men who have guided things than things which have directed men. Under the first two dynasties France reveals a tendency to independence, culminating in feudal anarchy; in the third, a tendency to order, culminating in absolutism, followed by a tendency to liberty, culminating in the Revolution.' Here is

---

[1] Cp. Taine's brilliant essay in *Essais de Critique et d'Histoire*.

[2] The fullest account is by Petit, *François Mignet*, 1889, the best appreciation by Jules Simon, *Mignet, Michelet, Henri Martin*, 1890.

the full-grown Mignet—his subordination of individuals, his power of condensing thought, his first avowal of that determinism for which he was to be so often attacked.

The young historian came to Paris in 1821 to receive his prize and to pursue his fortunes. Thiers followed him, and the friends found employment on the press. Their articles attracted the notice of Talleyrand, and in a few months they were familiar figures in the salons of the Opposition. Mignet had no intention of allowing journalism to monopolise his energies, and began a course at the Athénée which Sainte-Beuve described when both had become famous.[1] 'I well remember the first lectures in which he approached the sixteenth century and the Reformation. The young historian of twenty-six spoke of the St. Bartholomew and the causes which led up to it. Everyone felt himself dominated by the grave accent and the telling phrase. The slightly Puritan pronunciation and the weighty delivery redoubled their effect, coming from a young man so full of brilliance and smiling with grace. He possessed both austerity and culture, both reflection and candour.' At a moment when Guizot had been silenced and Daunou's conscientious discourses were followed by a mere handful of students, Mignet's lectures were an event. A second course on the English Revolution, seasoned with attacks on the government, was no less successful.

The growing reaction of the later years of Louis XVIII strengthened the Liberal Opposition, and France was divided into the friends and foes of the Revolution. Mme. de Stael's 'Considerations,' published in 1818, had aroused keen interest. 'The book entirely changed current opinion,' records Mme. de Boigne,[2] 'by boldly speaking in honourable terms of the Revolution. Where she set the example, panegyrics poured forth and few minds had the balance to extract the good grain from the bloodstained tares.' It was, however, rather a discussion of principles than a narrative of events. The bare summaries of Lacretelle satisfied no one, and France was eager for further enlightenment. The friends now resolved to attack the dynasty through a glorification of 1789. In his lectures Mignet had shown how the work of 1640 required for its completion the work of 1688, and drew the inference that constitutional government could never be safe except under a dynasty honestly prepared to accept it. He now applied the lesson to his own country. His 'Précis of the French Revolution,' written during four months' absence from Paris, appeared in 1824. Its success was immediate and enduring. It was quickly translated into many languages, six separate versions

[1] *Portraits contemporains*, vol. v.   [2] *Memoirs*, vol. ii., 277–8.

appearing in Germany. The highest tribute to the book is that, though based on scanty research and never rewritten, it still maintains its utility.

Though Mignet had no access to new material, he had learned a good deal from Talleyrand, Daunou and other surviving actors. He utilised the experience of his witnesses without sharing their passions, and rescued the cause of the Revolution from those who had served it badly. His greatest gift was to seize and reproduce the connection of events. He revealed it as an organic whole to a generation which knew it as a legend and a tradition. He showed that it was not an accidental convulsion but the logical result of history and the mother of a new society. Cool though the temperature be, he leaves no doubt as to his convictions. The introduction establishes the necessity of a far-reaching change and this necessity dominates the book. Even if a legitimate revolution falls into excesses, that is no ground for rejecting its principle. Yet he never pleads that the end justifies the means. He sternly condemns the Terror, whose only method of government was death. Louis XVI combined the two qualities which make good kings, the fear of God and the love of the people. The Revolution goes its way, with many good men on the wrong side and many bad men on the right.

The 'Précis' has often been criticised for its lack of warmth. Croker pronounced it a post-mortem anatomical lecture.[1] 'It has a compactness,' declared Carlyle,[2] 'a rigour as of riveted rods of iron, the symmetry, if not of a living tree, yet of a well-manufactured gridiron; it is without life, colour, or verdure.' Taine grumbled that there was not enough devil in him. Mignet's admirers reply that it was precisely his self-possession which enabled him to estimate the actual results of the Revolution. A more serious indictment came from Sainte-Beuve,[3] who challenged the implication that it had to follow a certain course, and declared that he forgot the vast difference which would have been made by the survival of Mirabeau or the early death of Robespierre and Napoleon. The indictment was repeated by Chateaubriand,[4] who, while eulogising the book as 'eloquence applied to reason,' accused the author of a belief in inflexible destiny and described him and Thiers as the founders of 'the fatalist school.' These charges are exaggerated. Mignet recognised the power of great movements to override individual interest or volition, but he had no belief in iron laws. Jules Simon, the apostle of idealism and

[1] *Essays on the French Revolution*, 1857.
[2] *Critical Essays*, vol. vi.   [3] *Premiers Lundis*, vol. i.
[4] Preface to *Études historiques*.

free will, roundly declared that his friend was accused of fatalism because he believed in logic. At the most it was but a rationalistic version of Bossuet's principle, *L'homme s'agite, Dieu le mène.*

The book was an incident in the campaign against the Bourbon dynasty, and Mignet returned to his journalism. With the accession of Charles X, of whom Royer-Collard acidly observed that he always remained the Comte d'Artois, reaction became the settled policy of the government. It was largely against the *National*, a paper founded and edited by Mignet, Thiers and Armand Carrel, that the Ordonnances of Polignac were aimed in July 1830. The order to suspend publication was disobeyed, and next day it printed the protest of the journalists of Paris, drawn up by Thiers and Mignet, with the name of the latter at the head of the list. The three editors took their lives in their hands, and to them more than any other men was due the expulsion of the Bourbons. Mignet could have had high office, but he wisely refused to embark on the tumult of political life. He contented himself with the directorship of the Archives of the Foreign Office, a post for which he was better fitted than any of his countrymen.

On receiving a pressing invitation to aid Guizot in the publication of the sources of French history, Mignet undertook to collect and edit the documents relating to the Spanish Succession. Four volumes brought the story to the Peace of Nymwegen; but though the documentary part was not completed, the Introduction, which traces the story to its close, ranks with the masterpieces of historical literature. It is unsurpassed for insight, judgment and learning, for clearness and firmness in thought and style. In addition to exhibiting the relations of France and Spain, and indeed the grouping of the European Powers, for over half a century, it provides a gallery of portraits of the leading statesmen of the age. In these pages Mazarin first received justice as a diplomat, and the figure of Lionne, his successor, is revived. The Grand Monarque himself appears in a new light, for no one can study Mignet's volumes without the conviction that he was more than a man of pleasure and ceremony. The work, with which diplomatic history was born, was hailed with applause in the world of scholarship, and has never been superseded.[1] The 'Spanish Succession,' though for obvious reasons the least popular of his works, was his most precious contribution to history.

The work of Mignet's later life dealt almost exclusively with the sixteenth century. The first of his masterly monographs was devoted to Antonio Perez, whose romantic story possesses the

[1] There is a fine eulogy in Legrelle, *La Diplomatie française et la Succession d'Espagne*, 1895, which continued his work.

interest of a novel. But it is much more than a study of a brilliant adventurer; it is a contribution to our knowledge of the reign of Philip II. The relations of Perez to Princess Eboli, the real causes of the murder of Escovedo, the loss of its privileges by Aragon are for the first time elucidated. From Philip to Mary Stuart was but a step. Mignet's volumes grew out of Labanoff's great collection of the Queen's correspondence, supplemented by the despatches of the Spanish ambassadors at Simancas. While accepting the Casket letters, he believes that Mary was passionate rather than vicious, and that her later life was purified and chastened by her sufferings and courage. The theme was chosen, not for the personality of the Queen, but for her rôle in the religious struggle. We witness a war between principles rather than between persons. His book has been superseded by the mass of material discovered since its publication, but it was the first balanced portrait, and it is still a useful corrective to the competing extravagances of her biographers. From Mary Stuart he returned to the great Emperor whose figure had attracted him when he began to study the Reformation. The mystery of his retirement had been solved by Stirling-Maxwell and Gachard; but he adduced new proofs that it was the result of diplomatic not less than physical or religious reasons, and that some of the main currents of European diplomacy flowed through the portals of the remote Spanish monastery. From the closing scene of the eventful reign he worked back to its opening. A series of articles on the rivalry of Francis and Charles was reprinted from the *Revue des Deux Mondes*, with little change, in two volumes. The survey, which was not continued beyond 1529, contained more new material than any of his narratives. It presented a picture of European politics based on the archives of France, Spain and Austria, and checked by the reports of the Venetian ambassadors. Mignet's legacy is relatively small in volume but of the finest quality. Every phrase is studied, every judgment has been weighed. He is the Ranke of France, and he disputes with Guizot the title of the greatest French historian of the first half of the nineteenth century. 'The elevated, august and even sacred character of history,' declares Sainte-Beuve, 'is engraved on everything he writes.' Like Guizot, he was interested in men mainly as they influenced institutions and movements, and considered them rather as workers than as personalities. No historian has done more to apply the methods and spirit of scientific research to the life of states.

In another department his fame is equally secure. When Guizot revived the Académie des Sciences morales et politiques in 1833, Mignet was among the earliest of the new members, and in 1837 he was appointed Perpetual Secretary. For decades his immense knowledge, his capacity for business and his sound judgment made him the ruler and guide of that illustrious body. So great was the respect for him, records his successor Jules Simon, that no proposals were made unless they possessed his approval. The addresses delivered by the Perpetual Secretary gave the *éloge* a new life and a classic form. The same qualities of style and thought which distinguish his historical works adorn the appreciations of his colleagues. These solid and scholarly studies reveal an intimate acquaintance with philosophy, economics and law, no less than history, and some are gems of analysis and criticism. To read the four volumes of *éloges* is to walk down a gallery of Greek statuary. What Michelet achieved by colour Mignet accomplished by purity of line. Heine scoffed at him as a 'coiffeur de vieilles perruques,' adding that if there was no hair on the head he always managed to hide the skull under a wig of phrases. This was merely Heine's way of saying that he was an indulgent critic. When the gulf was too wide, as in the case of Michelet, he left the task of appreciation to his successor. In the portraits of the statesmen and thinkers of the Revolution he returns to the field where he won his spurs. The *éloge* of Droz sharply attacks Rousseau's doctrines as 'false, mischievous and unintelligent.' He censures as fatalism the contention that in its later stages the Revolution could not be stopped, but for its constructive work his admiration remains undimmed. 'It is the immortal glory of the Constituent Assembly to have registered in laws the principles which the reason of sages has scattered in books. These principles have become the patrimony, henceforth inalienable, of the human race. When men have once seen the truth in its splendour they can never forget it. Sooner or later it triumphs, for it is the thought of God and the need of the world.'

III

In the same year that Mignet began to write his 'Précis,' his *alter ego* undertook a detailed narrative of the French Revolution. The moment when the actors in the drama were about to expire, declared Thiers,[1] was the proper time for writing its history, since their testimony could be collected by men who did not share their passions. The opening volumes were sketchy and careless, but their success determined him to devote more attention to his task.

[1] The best lives are by Mazade, 1884, and Rémusat, 1889. Jules Simon's study of his friend and leader, in *Thiers, Guizot, Rémusat*, 1885, is masterly. Allison, *Monsieur Thiers*, 1932, is a useful American sketch.

His object was frankly political. The full results of the Revolution, he taught, could only be attained by the expulsion of the old dynasty. A convinced monarchist, he used to say, 'We must cross the Channel, not the Atlantic'; but it was constitutional monarchy alone to which he owed allegiance. He combines an unshakable conviction of the justice and necessity of the Revolution with a detached view of its agents. 'We have to uphold the same cause, but we are not bound to defend their conduct. We can separate liberty from those who have rendered it disservice.' Like Mignet, he disengages the essence of the movement from its horrors. The charge of fatalism was warmly repelled in one of the first of the many articles which Sainte-Beuve was to devote to his writings.[1] 'To reproach him for presenting things in so perfect a connection, in an order apparently so inevitable, is to reproach him for having cleared up what was obscure.' The accusation might have been avoided if he had manifested as much indignation against the executioners as he displayed sympathy for the sufferers. He is an outspoken opponent of the Terror, warmly admires the private virtues and courage of the royal family, and blames many actions of the Revolutionists; but he felt too grateful to Carnot and the Jacobins for repelling the invader to inflict heavy sentences. Jules Simon remark that his adversaries mistook an explanation for an absolution, and Thiers himself boasted that no one could point to a word which excused crime. He wrote at a time when the principles of the Revolution were being hotly challenged, and he had no wish to put weapons into the hands of its foes.

Thiers' book is a narrative of events, not a study of causation or conditions. While Mignet's pages are weighted with judgments and reflections, Thiers hurries on to the next incident and leaves the reader to do his own thinking. It is typical of his methods and of his temperament that the curtain rises on the storming of the Bastille. He keeps on the surface of events, paraphrasing the *Moniteur* and Lacretelle. On the other hand, the handling of such financial problems as the currency and the maximum is excellent. The Italian campaigns are vividly described, and the study of military organisation and strategy is illuminating. The chief characteristic of the book is its freshness of treatment. It was said of Guizot that he had the air of having known from all eternity what he had only learned that morning. Thiers had the air of only having learned that morning what he communicated to his readers. Few books leave such an impression of youthful buoyancy. Every detail interests him, and he is assured that it will interest his readers. 'He marshals a hundred thousand facts as a skilful

[1] *Premiers Lundis*, vol. i.

general marshals a hundred thousand men,' said Sainte-Beuve.[1] For the first time a detailed narrative of the greatest event in modern history was available, and two hundred thousand copies were quickly sold.

The 'History of the French Revolution' scarcely deserved its popularity, but some of the charges against it are greatly exaggerated. 'Thiers has one reference,' wrote Carlyle,[2] 'and that is only to a book, not to a page or a chapter. A superficial air of order, clearness and calm candour is spread over the work; but inwardly it is waste, inorganic. No human head that honestly tries can conceive the French Revolution so. A critic undertook to find four errors per hour by way of bet, and won. Yet readers may peruse Thiers with comfort in certain circumstances, and even profit; for he is a brisk man of his sort, and does tell you much if you know nothing.' The complaint that Thiers only once quotes an authority is answered by turning to the work itself. Moreover, there were few books to which readers could be referred. The ten volumes were produced during four years of incessant political fighting, but, though many errors were due to carelessness, many arose from lack of information. Nor is the charge of wholesale misconception better founded. Like Mignet he misread the Girondins and overpraised the Directory, but his general approval of the aims and results of the Revolution, combined with repudiation of the Terror, represents the broad verdict of history. The faults of the book are that its author never realised the importance of obtaining new material, and that it was conceived and executed as an incident in a political campaign.[3] Throughout life he was more of a politician than an historian.

Thiers entered the service of the King whom he had called to the throne, but when Guizot became supreme in 1840 he partially withdrew from political strife. He had brought his narrative down to the end of the Directory, and he now took up the thread where he had dropped it. The political motive which had prompted the earlier work was absent from the later. Though Louis Philippe had dispensed with his services, Thiers had no desire to overthrow constitutional monarchy. The revival of the Napoleonic cult was the result, not the object of the book. The Emperor had charged Bignon[4] in his will to write his history, and his old servant

---

[1] See the admirable article in *Portraits contemporains*, vol. iv.

[2] *Critical Essays*, vol. vi.

[3] Cp. the severe analysis in Croker's *Essays on the French Revolution*, 1857.

[4] See Mignet's *éloge* in *Portraits et Notices historiques*, vol. ii.; Häusser's detailed review in *Gesammelte Schriften*, vol. i., 1869; and Geyl, *Napoleon: For and Against*, 37–44, 1949.

devoted the remainder of his life to the task, in large measure relating what he had himself seen and heard. His narrative, a dignified
handling of a great theme, is the work of a whole-hearted admirer.
There are no shadows in the picture, no hint of censure in the
hour of defeat. The Emperor was baffled in 1812 by the burning
of Moscow, which was an act of barbarians, and by the exceptional winter, which no one could foresee. At Leipzic Germany,
like Spain before her, was spurred to revolt by English gold and
the unsleeping hate of the Coalition. He believes that his master
was beaten by the Cabinets, not by the peoples of Europe. We
breathe the atmosphere of the Imperial bulletins, and the bias
is so naïve that it ceases to be dangerous. A shorter but more
critical work was written a few years later by Armand Lefebvre,[1]
whose father had been commissioned by the Restoration Government to relate the diplomatic history of the Interregnum. He collected a good deal of material, but died before he was able to
make use of it, and his son continued his labours. He respects
Pitt and Nelson, and realises the folly of the Emperor's attacks
on the nationalities. He knew little of foreign sources, but his
researches in the French Foreign Office constituted a real advance
in Napoleonic study.

While Bignon and Lefebvre only investigated certain aspects
of the Emperor's work, Thiers determined to survey his achievements as a whole. He had had practical experience of administration and diplomacy. He had visited the battlefields of Germany,
Italy and Spain. He had discussed Napoleonic finance with Baron
Louis, and Napoleonic strategy with Jomini and Foy. He was
familiar with the correspondence of the Emperor, his ministers
and his police agents. The 'History of the Consulate and Empire'
is a work of a far higher order than the 'French Revolution,' and
provided the first adequate account of the greatest of historic men.[2]
The first seven volumes, bringing the story to Tilsit, appeared in
the closing years of Louis Philippe. The First Consul emerges as
the saviour of France alike on the battlefield and in the cabinet.
'His only motive at that time was to do good.' The conclusion of
the Concordat, 'an admirable work, the finest of his achievements,'
appears as a political idyll, the Pope and the First Consul as
friends and colleagues. In his former work Thiers' sympathies had
been on the side of popular government; now, though despotism
is never overtly applauded, the Bonapartist overshadows the
Liberal. The explanation is to be found in a speech delivered in

---

[1] See Häusser, *Gesammelte Schriften*, vol. i., and Geyl, *Napoleon*,
45–52.
[2] See Geyl, *Napoleon*, 53–67.

1841. 'I love the Revolution because it is the regeneration of my country, but had not Napoleon saved it it would have been ruined.' Brumaire was necessary and therefore legitimate. The execution of Enghien was a deplorable accident, for only the sleep of Réal prevented a reprieve. He is the ideal despot, fertile in resource, matchless in action, yet no stranger to humanity and pity. Royer-Collard caustically remarked that Thiers had written the history of the Consulate as a man who would have liked to make it himself. In foreign policy the colours are no less brightly tinted. There was not a country, he declares, through which the French armies passed which did not become better and more enlightened. He has no condemnation for the treatment of the Queen of Prussia. A fleeting reference is made to the execution of Palm without naming him, and Eylau is described as a brilliant victory. Even the Continental System finds a champion.

The more sober volumes written during the Second Republic are largely devoted to the perfidious seizure of Spain, of which he provided the first clear and connected account. There is no justification for Lanfrey's remark that he only censured the war because it failed. His sympathies are wholly with the Spaniards. 'The people were led by truer feelings than the educated classes. They acted nobly in rejecting benefits offered by a strange hand.' He makes no attempt to screen their terrible excesses, but the defence of Saragossa covers many sins. When the scene shifts to Central Europe we find further evidence of a more independent attitude. He realises that the Germany of 1809 is different from that of 1806, and he admits that the conduct of the conquerors made all Germans hate them. The Austrians were right to fight in 1809, and they fought in a new spirit. Thiers was one of the earliest victims of the new Brumaire in 1851, and the subjection of France made him more critical of the uncle and model of his enemy. 'Napoleon allowed himself to be led in all things beyond the bounds of reason.' He is no longer the sword of the Revolution but a despot like other despots. With a glance at the Second Empire the historian laments the growing servility. He maintains that the Russian enterprise was equally indefensible from a political and military point of view. He is loud in his admiration of Alexander's noble pride and of the sublime patriotism of Moscow, and concludes his narrative with words of crushing severity. 'These tragic events resulted not from this or that mistake but from the one great error in going to Russia at all. And in this error lay a greater—the desire to attempt everything against right, against the wishes of the peoples, without a thought for the blood with which he conquered.' The narrative of the uprising of Germany is less powerful. Thiers could not read German, and he had only the vaguest notion of the personalities and forces of the Wars of Liberation. While he dimly feels the greatness of Stein, his warmest admiration is reserved for Metternich, whom he met after the aged statesman had fallen from power. But when France is invaded his sympathy revives. After the return from Elba he presents the Emperor as a man of peace and a constitutionalist. In the Waterloo campaign he adopts the legends of St. Helena. Yet the work closes with a list of capital errors and an emphatic warning. 'Who could have foreseen that the sage of 1800 would be the madman of 1812? Yes, one could have foreseen it, remembering that omnipotence carries within itself an incurable malady. In this great career, where there is so much to teach soldiers, administrators and politicians, citizens must learn never to deliver their country to a single man.'[1]

In the preface to the twelfth volume, written in 1855, Thiers explains the spirit in which he approached his task. 'I feel shame at the mere idea of doing an injustice, the more as I have myself been misjudged. To judge men fairly we must extinguish all passion in our souls and remember our own weakness.' The supreme need of the historian is intelligence. 'Whoever has clear insight into men and things possesses the true genius of history.' Can we accept the testimonial which the historian presents to himself? Has he extinguished passion in his soul? Have outward events left no mark on his work? These questions are rarely answered as he would wish. 'Thiers,' said Lamartine, 'is the accomplice of fortune; he only recognises the wrong when it is punished by failure.' The judgment of Lanfrey is similar.[2] 'His work is the epic of matter. He has no appreciation of moral forces. *Tu ne réussis pas, donc tu as tort*—that is his whole philosophy.' If this be the verdict of a rival, we may admit that at times the glory of France was more to him than liberty or morality. The rise of Napoleon the Little was to teach him that if despotism is to be resisted it must be at the outset.

Little as Thiers knew of Germany, his knowledge of England was still less, and one of the blots on his work is his failure to do justice to the policy of Pitt and the genius of Wellington. He

---

[1] Nisard declared Thiers' verdict too severe. *Considérations sur la Révolution et Napoléon*, 1887.

[2] 'L'Histoire du Consulat et de l'Empire,' in *Études et Portraits politiques*, 1880. Cp. the able articles in the *Edinburgh Review*, April and July, 1858.

knew little of foreign archives or of the researches of foreign scholars. He accepted without question Metternich's version of Austrian policy. His claims to technical knowledge of military affairs have not passed without challenge; yet, though he is no professional like Ségur or Napier, his interest in war did much to win for his book its enduring popularity. Thiers, remarked Lamartine, was as much predestined to relate the campaigns as Napoleon to undertake them. His treatment of finance has received more unqualified praise. On the other hand, we learn little of administration, still less of public opinion, religion or literature.[1] That a work in twenty volumes carries its readers to the end without fatigue and without impatience is a tribute as much to the style as to the subject. Thiers achieves his effects by lucidity and mastery of detail. He will not praise the passage of the St. Bernard till he has measured the distances and calculated the depth of snow on the passes, the height of the mountains and the number of ammunition carts. On another page he declares that he has not hesitated to give the price of bread, soap and candles. 'The art of narrating in the degree he possesses it,' remarks Émile Ollivier, 'is more than talent—it is genius.' Sainte-Beuve never wearied in his admiration. 'It is a rare satisfaction to read a series of volumes so easy and so full, where we are never met by a difficulty of thought or expression, and where we watch in comfort the spectacle of the greatest events.' The style is remarkably level but there are no purple patches.

The 'Consulate and Empire' must always occupy a prominent place in historiography. It was written by one of the foremost political figures of the century. It was among the main factors in the growth of the Napoleonic legend. Lamartine christened it the book of the century. Flint declared it perhaps the most interesting history ever written on the same scale, Rémusat the most magnificent monument of contemporary literature. It was precisely because the book was a political event as well as a literary achievement that contemporaries found it difficult to criticise impartially. Lanfrey denied Thiers every quality of an historian. Charras and Quinet, who waged war against the Empire from beyond the frontier, attacked the volume on Waterloo. Jules Barni,[2] another exile, hurled his thunderbolts from the safe distance of Lausanne. The Comte de Martel[3]

---

[1] The fullest and most authoritative criticism of his book is by Häusser, *Ges. Schriften*, vol. i., 352–586.

[2] *Napoléon et son historien, M. Thiers*, 1869.

[3] *Thiers, un historien fantaisiste*, 1883–7. For a sketch of this strange person see Masson, 'Un Explorateur d'Archives,' in *Jadis*, vol. ii.

devoted three volumes to proving that the historian was a charlatan and a liar. Count d'Haussonville pointed out the mistakes in the narrative of the Emperor's relations with the Church. Tocqueville curtly remarked that the history of the Empire was still to write, Taine that Thiers did not love truth. But critics and admirers agree that no work has ever given such an impetus to the study of the Napoleonic era.

CHAPTER XI

THE MIDDLE AGES AND THE ANCIEN RÉGIME

I

INTEREST in the mediaeval history of France was aroused by Augustin Thierry and Barante, Guizot and Michelet, but its systematic study owes most to the École des Chartes.[1] The idea of a school where savants could train young students emanated from De Gérando in 1820, and in 1821 a royal decree was signed approving the proposal 'to assist the Academy of Inscriptions in its labours.' A dozen students joined, but the institution soon flickered out. Revived in 1829, its fortunes steadily improved, and a journal was established. It was largely from among its *alumni* that editors were found for the 'Documents Inédits' and contributors to the 'Histoire littéraire de la France.' The work of Dom Rivet had reached the twelfth volume in 1763, bringing the narrative to 1167, but was then discontinued for lack of interest and only resumed under Napoleon. The scholarship improved when Victor Le Clerc[2] succeeded Daunou as chief director. On reaching the fourteenth century, he undertook a preliminary survey of its literature and science, its political and social conditions, following the example of Dom Rivet for the twelfth and Daunou for the thirteenth. Le Clerc not only wrote largely himself but trained younger scholars of the calibre of Renan and Hauréau to aid him in his formidable task.

No one produced more enduring work on the Middle Ages in the second quarter of the century than Guérard,[3] one of the earliest pupils and later a teacher and Director of the École des Chartes. His life-work was to edit the Chartularies of the great Abbeys, and the Polyptique of the Abbot Irminon won him European fame. It contained full details of the vast estates of the monastery of St. Germain-des-Prés in the time of Charles the Great, and revealed the relations of classes and the methods of land-holding. The comprehensive Introduction is one of the glories of French scholarship. Guérard traces the growth of political and

[1] See *Livret de l'École des Chartes*, 1821–91, 1891.
[2] See Renan's charming sketch of his master in *Mélanges d'Histoire et de Voyage*, 1878.
[3] See N. de Wailly's *Notice sur Guérard*, 1855.

social institutions, the conditions of persons and lands, from the German invasions. He rejects the contention that Gaul was civilised and regenerated by the Frank invaders, against whom he draws a severe indictment. He traces the manor to Roman legislation, and maintains that the framework of Roman society and administration remained erect till the collapse of the Carolingian Empire. Reprinted in an abridged form in 1896, it shares with Guizot's lectures the merit of being the most important contribution to the study of early France produced in the first half of the century.

Among the most brilliant mediævalists of a younger generation was Quicherat,[1] who, after passing through Michelet's lecture-room, learned stricter methods at the École des Chartes. It was mainly at his suggestion that it undertook the foundation of a journal, of which he was the first editor. Deeply impressed by Michelet's picture of Joan of Arc he collected the sources of her trial. The five volumes of material, with copious notes and explanations, were followed by a short but masterly study of the heroine, and the complete work provided a model for the critical handling of mediæval sources. He was also the founder of mediæval archæology. A Chair of French Archæology was founded for him at the École des Chartes in 1847, and his lectures created an extraordinary impression. His knowledge of the monuments and antiquities of France was unrivalled. The world of scholarship impatiently waited for a comprehensive work, and Michelet, to whom literary production was no effort, vainly urged his old pupil forward. Yet his authority was none the less uncontested because he could point to no imposing treatise.

With the death of Quicherat in 1882 the primacy among French mediævalists passed to Léopold Delisle,[2] an *alumnus* of the École des Chartes and a pupil and friend of Guérard. Appointed to the manuscript department of the Imperial Library in 1852 he became its head in 1874. For sixty years he poured forth a never-ending stream of publications. Supreme in palæography, diplomatic and criticism, he threw light on every part of the French Middle Ages. Though his chief task was the cataloguing and editing of the treasures in his keeping, he contributed to the 'Histoire littéraire' and occasionally produced monographs, among them his well-known study of the Norman peasantry in the thirteenth century. Though only a name to the

[1] See the notice prefixed to his *Mélanges d'Archéologie et d'Histoire*, vol. i., 1885, and Giry's appreciation in *Revue Historique*, vol. xvii.

[2] See *Quarterly Review*, April, 1911, and Poole's tribute in the *Transactions of the British Academy*, 1911.

great public, he was reverenced by scholars all over the world. His editions of the Acts of Philip Augustus and of the Gascon rolls were recognised as models by younger men. His eightieth birthday evoked international homage, and a bibliography of his writings was compiled. In 1905 he was harshly dismissed from his post, but found refuge among the treasures of Chantilly. At the age of eighty-three, the year before his death, he published a massive Introduction to a collection of charters of Henry II relating to France.

Of scholars whose output roughly begins with the foundation of the Third Republic a few may be mentioned. Trained by Waitz and himself a specialist in Merovingian sources, Gabriel Monod[1] laid every student of history under an abiding obligation by the foundation of the *Revue Historique* in 1876. Among the chief contributors was Auguste Molinier,[2] whose first great achievement was the revision of the massive Benedictine history of Languedoc. An immense number of new documents were added, and the long excursuses of the editor form the most valuable part of the work which, in its new as in its original form, is an indispensable instrument of the mediævalist. His lectures at the École des Chartes, where he had been a student, formed the basis of his volumes on French mediæval sources, the accuracy and completeness of which render them a priceless possession. The Introduction, which fills a large part of the fifth volume and was the author's last work, presents a concise but masterly survey of the evolution of historical composition, criticism and instruction in France. Of scarcely less significance was the achievement of Giry.[3] Educated at the École des Chartes he turned his attention to the Communes, correcting the views of Thierry on the origin and development of municipal institutions. Recognising the endless diversity of circumstance, he cautiously avoids making kings or lords the systematic protectors or enemies of town liberties, and his monographs on St. Omer and Rouen are models of research. By his lectures at the École des Hautes Études, founded by Duruy in 1868, and at the École des Chartes, Giry exerted a wide influence. An irreparable loss to mediæval studies was the early death of Julian Havet,[4] who discovered that a number of documents on which historians of the Merovingian era had relied were forgeries.

[1] See the obituary in *Revue Historique*, vol. cx.
[2] *Ibid.*, vol. lxxxv.
[3] *Ibid.*, vol. lxxii.
[4] See the sketch by his brother Louis prefixed to his *Œuvres*, vol. i., 1896.

The most conspicuous though not the soundest of French mediævalists of the latter half of the century was Fustel de Coulanges.[1] He was one of the first students of the French School at Athens, and after the phenomenal success of 'La Cité Antique' he was eager to trace the connection between the classical and the Teutonic world. His articles on Justice in Antiquity and the Middle Ages, which appeared in 1871 in the *Revue des Deux Mondes*, indicated the direction of his thought. In 1872, at the age of forty-two, he launched a thunderbolt in the pages of the same review. The German invasions of the fifth century, he declared, had no direct influence on the history, religion, customs, government or structure of society. The barbarians brought nothing but confusion, and their arrival simply favoured the development of the feudalism already existing in germ. Modern aristocracy was based on territorial feudalism, which only arose after the distinction of races had disappeared. In 1875 he published the first instalment of a 'History of the Institutions of Ancient France,' hoping to follow it with a volume on feudalism, another on royalty and the States-General, and a fourth on absolute monarchy. But the storm of criticism that greeted it convinced him that he must make sure of his foundations before building his house. Thus began the monumental work which occupied his every thought for the rest of his life. Hitherto he had stated conclusions rather than proved them. He would now make each chapter a dissertation, setting forth his proofs in full. The enlarged work dealt with Roman Gaul, the German invasions, Merovingian institutions, and the lands. The fifth and sixth volumes, left unfinished at his death and edited by his most eminent pupil, Camille Jullian, were dedicated to vassalage and Carolingian institutions.

Fustel's views were set forth with crystal clearness and extraordinary power. Gaul fell an easy prey to Rome and never revolted, for Rome was the higher civilisation. But the fourth century witnessed the growth of a powerful aristocracy, while the middle classes fell into poverty and the central authority began to crumble. Power passed to the great landowners who could neither fight nor govern. At this moment began the Frank invasions, due to the break up of old German institutions and in general to the absence of fixed habits and ideas. The Franks

---

[1] See Guiraud, *Fustel de Coulanges*, 1896; Tourneur-Aumont, *Fustel de Coulanges*, 1931; Sorel, *Notes et Portraits*, 1909; Herbert Fisher, *Eng. Hist. Review*, January 1890; Monod, *Revue Historique*, vol. xli. Arbois de Jubainville hotly attacks him in his *Deux Manières d'écrire l'Histoire*, 1896. Kehr's article in *Historische Zeitschrift*, vol. lxxi., is typical of German depreciation.

brought nothing of their own, for they had nothing to bring. Their institutions, as Sybel had contended, were derived from Rome. The invasion was not a conquest but a pacific settlement of Romanised Germans. The Gallo-Romans were neither reduced to serfdom nor treated as inferiors. The Kings were the heirs of the Emperors and aped their ways, absolute over Franks and Gauls alike, but little real change occurred. The cities were un- molested and the taxes but slightly modified. The Merovingian régime was in the main a continuation of the Lower Empire. Germanists, he declared, had overlooked the witness of Rome and read Teutonic evidence with national prepossessions. All the agricultural characteristics of the manor existed under the Empire and were plainly apparent in Merovingian times. But though the invasion itself changed but little, it was followed by momentous transformations. Feudalism arose in the organisation of property and individual relations. A new method of holding property appeared in the *beneficium*, a relation not established by law but arising privately, and society was modified by the dependence of free men on one another, often for the sake of protection. Thus aristocracy grew, and with the decay of the Carolingian power it became supreme. The Franks were not the authors of the change, but they aided it and gave it some new traits: for instance the judicial system of Frankish Gaul was German, and the *comitatus* favoured the growth of feudal rela- tions. 'I am both German and Roman,' he declared, 'or rather I am neither.'

The critics caused Fustel to elaborate his method. It required years of analysis for a day of synthesis, he declared. All his works derived from the *Discours sur la Méthode*. All opinions about history, even those most generally held, must be regarded with suspicion; the historian must approach his task not only without presuppositions but without working hypotheses. The second step is to go straight to the texts. The researches of other scholars may be of use but are more likely to lead the student astray. Historical science is the interpretation of documents, for which an unbiassed mind and a mastery of the language of the originals are sufficient. In the next place, the historian must look at things as contemporaries saw them, not as they appear to the modern mind; his readers should never know if he is republican or monar- chist, liberal or reactionary. He must explain things but not attempt to judge their value or discover their ultimate causes. Race, climate, Providence, are mere counters, not coin of the realm. He rejects the notion that a nation's destinies are fixed in advance. We see the concrete changes and explain how one state of society is transformed into another: beyond lies the frontier between history and speculation.

This rigorous limitation of aim is at once his strength and his weakness. His concentration on the original authorities of a period in which they are so scanty that they can be mastered by a single mind gave him an easy mastery within the confines of his subject, and his acquaintance with Roman history was an initial advantage. He boasted of being the only man who had studied every Latin text from the sixth century B.C. to the tenth century of the Christian era. Most of his critics avoided coming to close quarters with him, for he was always ready with a battery of texts. He possessed an almost unique power of grouping facts round a central contention. He was, moreover, a great literary artist, though he regarded praise of his style as something like a reflection on his science. 'His words possessed a geometrical rigour,' declares his pupil and biographer Guiraud of his lectures; 'it was the eloquence of the savant, indeed of the mathematician, abstract without being arid, sparing in images and rich in formulæ. The heart was not touched, the mind was not charmed, but the intelligence was utterly satisfied.' His books are of lapidary precision. He opened up fresh veins of inquiry and touched nothing that he did not illumine.

The faults of his method are as obvious as its merits. His Cartesian doubt often led him to start with a bias against current conceptions. 'He delights in a sort of aristocratic isolation,' complained Monod, 'and feels that he has only grasped a thing when he sees it differently from his predecessors.' He used to say, 'I am Guérard's pupil,' and Guérard was the only scholar for whom he felt real respect. In the second place he underestimated the difficulty of arriving at the truth. He believed history to be an objective science, the secrets of which could be extracted by the same methods as in the physical sciences. To collect, interpret and compare the whole of the original texts must, he believed, lead to conclusions on which there could be no controversy. 'Do not applaud me,' he said one day to an enthusiastic audience, 'it is not I that I speak to you but history that speaks by my mouth.' He regarded his results as independent of himself and felt criticism as something like blasphemy. The dissent of competent scholars never led him to modify his conviction, not only that he had reached the truth, but that truth was easy to reach. Yet before the interpretation of texts is commenced we must establish their authenticity. 'Fustel,' wrote Arbois de Jubainville, 'had not the most elementary notion of diplomatic. A large number of Merovingian charters were forged by Jerome Vignier in the seventeenth

century, and when Julien Havet showed that some of those he
had used were forgeries, he replied that false charters were almost
as useful as real, since the forger copied the rules.' Even his
treatment of authentic sources was challenged, and Monod
pointed out that he once gave a text three different meanings.
Again he forgot that the interpretation of texts and technical
terms demanded knowledge of juristic conceptions. He failed to
realise that the light from the texts leaves great spaces of time
and whole groups of problems in shadow. As he only studied a
limited period and area, complains Brunner, he often misunderstood the sources; and Kehr declares that he never appreciated
Germanic law.

Was Fustel so entirely without personal prepossessions as
he supposed? Critics have hinted at a connection between the
date when he reached his conclusions and the conclusions themselves. His post at Strassburg, an outpost of France, gave him a
special interest in the problem of Franco-German relations, and
when war came in 1870 he compiled a pamphlet on French claims
to Alsace. When the struggle was over he wrote a stinging article
on the methods of German historians, whom he roundly accused
of sacrificing truth to racial and dynastic passions. For half a
century, he complained, French historians had praised Germany,
contrasted the chastity of the Germans of Tacitus with the corruption of the Gauls, and hailed the Frankish invasion as a blast
of pure, bracing air. They blamed the invasion of Italy by
Charles VIII and the ambition of Louis XIV. The royalist historian depreciated the nineteenth century and the republican
disparaged the Ancien Régime. German historians, on the other
hand, were an organised army of patriots: science was a means
to an end, and that end the glorification of the fatherland. 'We
shall continue to profess that erudition has no fatherland. But
we live to-day in an epoch of war, and it is almost impossible
for scholarship to retain its former serenity. Can we be blamed
for defending ourselves?' The historian who wrote such words
on the morrow of the invasion may well have had a subconscious
bias in discussing the early relations of Gauls and Germans; but
the manuscript of his courses before 1870 reveals that his main
positions had already been reached. A further criticism is suggested by the complete exclusion of individuals from his field of
vision. Almost the only recognition of personality in his chief
work is a passing reference to the feebleness of the later Merovingian rulers. His interest is in institutions, not in life. His fame
as a teacher is secure, but his results are nowhere accepted in
their entirety. His structure does not compare in solidity with

the edifice in which Brunner has traced the development of early German society and law.

The study of French mediæval institutions has been eagerly pursued, but most of the investigations have related to a period subsequent to that which Fustel described. In *Les Origines de l'ancienne France*, Flach traced the growth of feudalism, or, as he prefers to call it, the seigneurial régime, which resulted from the anarchy following the fall of the Carolingians. Before that time, he declares, there were lords but not vassals. Like Fustel he argued that France owed little to Teutonic influences but much to the Celts and, like Fustel, he is not a very trustworthy guide. While Flach's chief object was to depict the growth and relation of classes, Luchaire explored the institutions of the early Capetian monarchy down to the death of Philip Augustus, which he proved from the charters to be essentially absolute. Ferdinand Lot and Halphen explored the Carolingian era, Chalandon the Norman Kingdom in Sicily, Picot the early history of the States-General. A masterly survey of the evolution of French institutions was undertaken by Paul Viollet. Welcome light has been thrown on the Middle Ages by scholars who are not political historians. Hauréau traced the evolution of scholasticism, Jourdain investigated the influence of Aristotle, Renan analysed the publicists of the time of Philippe le Bel. The history of literature was summarised in the co-operative work of Petit de Julleville. The epics and romances of chivalry were explored and popularised by Léon Gautier and Paul Meyer. The greatest name in French mediæval scholarship outside the bounds of political history is that of Gaston Paris,[1] who succeeded his father at the Collège de France in 1872. His doctor's thesis on the legend of Charlemagne became a classic, and by his editions of romances, his contributions to the 'Histoire Littéraire,' and his literary surveys he became the guide of generations of students. Romance philology, created by Diez, was enlarged and vivified by Gaston Paris, the Lachmann of France. He learned the chronological development of the language so exactly that when he knew the date of a work he could restore the primitive forms where they had been altered by copyists. All previous narratives have been superseded by Lavisse's co-operative *Histoire de France*.

II

The Ancien Régime presents difficulties to the French historian owing to its connection with the battles of his own time.

[1] See Ker, *Essays on Mediæval Literature*, 1905, and Monod's notice in *Revue Historique*, vol. lxxxii.

The republican freethinker cannot always do justice to an epoch of political and ecclesiastical autocracy, while the Catholic royalist tends to gloss over the failings of the Absolute Monarchy. But these temptations are losing their power day by day.[1] The first half of the sixteenth century has been far less studied than the second. Poirson's well-known volumes still provide the fullest summary of the reign of Henri IV. He contented himself with the printed material on the ground that if he were to dive into the archives his book would never be finished. The King appears as the greatest of the *Politiques*, the restorer of France to her position among the Powers, the skilful administrator, the fosterer of agriculture and industry, the patron of art, literature and science. No room is found in the four stout volumes to deal with the peccadilloes of the man, and there is a tendency to depict the King as too liberal, too constitutional, too modern. A masterly survey of part of the ground has appeared in Fagniez's study of agriculture and industry under the fostering hand of Sully and his master. A valuable contribution to the religious life of the century has come from the Society for the History of French Protestantism founded in 1851. In its Bulletin, in the collection of the correspondence of the French reformers, and in 'La France Protestante,' the biographical dictionary of the brothers Haag, are to be found treasures beyond price.

The Grand Siècle has been well worked. Batiffol presented a new Louis XIII—a man of some resolution and resource, tenaciously attached to his royal prerogatives. Richelieu has formed the theme of two works of outstanding importance. After devoting many years to editing his Letters and Papers, Avenel wrote the best detailed study of the Iron Cardinal; but his volumes made no pretence to a complete picture of the most illustrious of French statesmen. He omits the foreign policy, which he considers admirable, and confines himself to the internal administration, which he judges with severity. When Richelieu was called to the helm there were at least some traces of liberty in France, some traditions of independence; when he died he had founded a choking absolutism on the ruins of the *noblesse*.

A few years later Hanotaux commenced a more ambitious work. The first volume of the 'History of Richelieu' appeared in 1893, the preface announcing that he had already laboured fifteen years at his task. The drama opens with a detailed account of the first thirty years of the life of the hero, his family, his theological studies, his relations with Cardinal Du Perron, with the saintly

[1] Caron et Sagnac, *L'État actuel des Études d'Histoire moderne en France*, 1902, contains useful material.

Bérulle and with Père Joseph, his energetic administration of his diocese, culminating in a brilliant picture of the young Bishop at the meeting of the States-General in 1614. Arrived at his entry on the public stage the historian paints an elaborate survey of the state of France in 1614—Paris and the provinces, the monarchy and the administration, the finances, justice, the army, the States-General, the provincial assemblies, municipal life and liberties, the Protestants, the *noblesse*, the lawyers, the bourgeoisie, the peasantry. It is a grandly conceived vestibule, ranking with Michelet's survey of mediæval France and Macaulay's third chapter among the masterpieces of historical sociology. The second volume brings the narrative down to 1624, when Richelieu became the uncrowned King of France. At this moment the historian became Foreign Minister, and when he regained his leisure he turned his attention to the Third Republic. He had advanced far enough for his general conception of the Cardinal's character to emerge. He depicts him not only as practical, positive and cool, but as accessible and straightforward. Michelet's Cardinal is a sphinx; the hero of Hanotaux is a man of simple psychology, as direct in thought as decisive in action. Every historian of the French monarchy must pronounce on its governing principle of centralisation. Avenel, following Tocqueville, found in it the germ of decay. Hanotaux envisages it as the matrix in which the unity of the nation was achieved.

Light was thrown on almost every aspect of Richelieu's personality and career by Fagniez's monumental life of Père Joseph. Hitherto known only as the Cardinal's shadow, the base intriguer of De Vigny's 'Cinq Mars,' he appeared not only as a skilful diplomatist but as a man of high character and lofty imagination. While never dominating Richelieu's policy he was almost as much a colleague as an agent, though he preferred to work behind the scenes. While the Cardinal's mind was essentially secular and his first thought was the greatness of France, the monk's governing principle was the greatness of the Church. Eager to eject the Turks from Europe, to convert the Protestants, to suppress Jansenism, he saw in a powerful monarchy the instrument by which his religious projects might be realised. Before his best friend the Cardinal wears no mask, and we catch glimpses of human weakness and weariness that his contemporaries never suspected.

While Richelieu's greatness was a living tradition it is only recently that the figure of Mazarin has been revealed in its true proportions. The disgust of Saint-Simon was typical of French feeling towards the statesman who was at once a foreigner, the enemy of the *noblesse*, and one of the most rapacious ministers of modern times. That a juster view now prevails of the man whom Richelieu thought worthy to succeed him is mainly due to Chéruel,[1] who edited his correspondence and wrote the history of his administration. Though there is no hero-worship in his volumes, he shows how largely the Italian Cardinal prepared the power and splendour of France under Louis XIV. He pronounces his external policy successful and glorious, his internal policy memorable for his defeat of a turbulent aristocracy. No attempt is made to render his personality attractive or to deny his shameless greed. A more colourful picture of the stormy years when Mazarin ruled France is presented in the Duc d'Aumale's[2] full-length history of the Condé princes in the sixteenth and seventeenth centuries. When the fall of Louis Philippe and the *coup d'état* of 1851 barred the way to further public service for his sons, the scholarly Duke resolved to explore the family archives. On the first two volumes being printed the whole edition was seized at the binder's. The embargo was removed in 1867, and when the offending work appeared the world learned that it was only the author's name that was dangerous. The remaining volumes appeared at intervals, the seventh and last in 1895. The latter half of the vast enterprise was devoted to the life of the great Condé. The author's experience of war gives value to the judgments on his campaigns, and the battle pictures of Rocroy, Lens and the Faubourg St. Antoine are masterpieces of description. The work was completed at Chantilly after the return from his second exile, surrounded by memories of the Prince, but the Duke's admiration for his hero does not blind him to the indefensible character of the Second Fronde.

The later years of Louis XIII and the troubled times of the Fronde occupied the last two decades of Cousin's[3] long and laborious life. His discovery of the text of Pascal's *Pensées* in 1843 led him to the exquisite personality of his sister, and suggested a series of studies of famous women of the generation that preceded the personal rule of Louis XIV. The most attractive of his portraits after Jacqueline Pascal is Madame de Hautefort. At once the object of the platonic affection of the King, the friend of the Queen and the enemy of Richelieu, she had a difficult part to play, but she never thought of her own interests. A very different type is Madame de Chevreuse, who loved intrigue not

---

[1] See Rocquain's *éloge* in his *Notes et Fragments d'Histoire*, 1906.

[2] See Picot's *éloge*, 1897, E. Daudet's biography, 1898, and the *Correspondance du Duc d'Aumale et de Cuvillier-Fleury*, 1910–1912.

[3] See Barthélemy Saint-Hilaire's biography, vol. ii., 178–256, 1895.

less than Madame de Hautefort hated it, and who with the energy and determination of a man matched her wits against Richelieu. The most notable of Cousin's portraits was Madame de Longueville, the sister of Condé. The elderly philosopher was twitted with playing the part of *cavaliere servente* to the fair sinner; but though he admires her beauty and her brains, he never applauds her conduct. He intended to devote no less than four volumes to her life; but only two were written, the first dealing with her youth, the second with her life during the Fronde. The edifying story of her retreat and penitence in Port Royal was never told. La Rochefoucauld cynically confessed that he seduced her in order to gain the influence of Condé, and it was her lover who tempted her into the Fronde. Once engaged, her hatred of Mazarin was implacable. Throughout his works Cousin scolds the factious nobility, and, though no lover of absolutism, sides with the monarchy and its loyal servants against their enemies.

Cousin's heroines touch Mazarin at so many points that he dallied with the idea of writing the life of the great minister. He published a series of articles in the *Journal des Savants* on his Carnets or note-books, which he was the first to analyse, and devoted a volume to the little known period of his youth. The picture of the soldier who lived by gambling and of the ecclesiastic who never became a priest was not attractive, but it revealed the man who impressed Richelieu in 1630. In addition to Cousin's political studies, he threw light on the literary society. Madame de Scudéry's once famous romance, 'Le Grand Cyrus,' published in ten volumes between 1649 and 1654, had become a mere name when he disinterred a key to its characters. Cyrus himself was Condé, while Madame de Longueville and the other leading figures of the Court played their part in the drama. Armed with his discovery the historian summarises the information supplied by this forgotten witness. A final vignette was Madame de Sablé, the author of maxims which inspired La Rochefoucauld and of portraits which anticipate La Bruyère. Turning to history late in life his works were imperfect, but the sharp attack of Taine[1] was overdone. Cousin, declared his young critic, offered rhetorical commonplaces in stilted language. He worshipped the seventeenth century but failed to convey its spirit. He had no eye for character, and, compared with Sainte-Beuve's 'Port Royal,' his volumes were only a collection of material.

The first and still the most satisfactory picture of the reign of Louis XIV was painted by Lavisse in his co-operative history

[1] In *Les Philosophes Classiques*.

of France.[1] 'Le Roi Soleil' fails to dazzle his latest biographer. Rejecting Saint-Simon's systematic depreciation he pronounces the King a man of ordinary intelligence. His Spanish blood revealed itself in his love of etiquette, his devotion to the forms of religion, his dream of world-empire. It was his misfortune that he received no instruction in administration. His best quality was his love of work. He understood the army and foreign affairs, and knew more about Europe than any of his advisers. He was not a bad man, but he overstrained France, and the supreme condemnation of his work is the fall of the monarchy in 1789. Colbert is depicted as ambitious, unscrupulous, often base, though the grandeur of his aims is recognised. 'If the monarchy could have been saved, Colbert would have saved it.' He alone saw the need of fundamental changes and protested against the King's extravagance. Lavisse's volumes, written more in sorrow than in anger, form melancholy reading. Crediting Louvois with administrative capacity, he sharply condemns his harshness and selfishness. The full treatment of religious life and thought—Jansenism, Gallicanism and Protestantism—of culture, of administration and finance, of trade and industry enhances the value of one of the most masterly works in French historical literature.

For detailed knowledge of the reign we must turn to the biographies and monographs. Chéruel's elaborate study of Fouquet displays his usual judgment and research. Camille Rousset's voluminous biography of Louvois, based on the War Office papers, defends the fame of the War Minister whom Saint-Simon detested as the evil genius of the King. Ségur's volumes on Luxemburg, *le tapissier de Notre-Dame*, have revived one of the most brilliant figures of a brilliant age. Legrelle accomplished the arduous task, which Mignet left unfinished, of tracing the history of the long negotiations relative to the Spanish Succession. The Duc de Noailles and Lavallée made it possible to appreciate Madame de Maintenon. Count d'Haussonville, in a work equally distinguished by scholarship and literary charm, explored the relations between France and Savoy and painted an exquisite portrait of the Duchess of Burgundy, 'the Rose of Savoy,' who illuminated the dull Court of the aged monarch with the radiance of a sunbeam.

Historians of Louis XIV possess a special advantage and face a peculiar difficulty in Saint-Simon. Already known by short extracts the most celebrated of Memoirs appeared in 1829, and for a generation exerted an almost hypnotic influence. The

[1] For Lavisse see Doumic, *Écrivains d'aujourdhui*, 1894, and *Some Historians of Modern Europe*, ed. B. E. Schmitt, ch. xi.. 1941.

position of the author at Court, his intimate acquaintance with its leading figures, the unparalleled fullness of detail, the extraordinary power of observation, the wonderful gallery of portraits and the unflagging vivacity of style, render it difficult to envisage the Grand Monarque except through his spectacles. Yet he was a passionate partisan, and his pages breathe his undying resentment against 'the bastards,' their royal father, Madame de Maintenon and all who espoused their cause. We owe it chiefly to three scholars that his authority has been overthrown. In a brief but masterly analysis Ranke measured his prejudices and emphasised the superior value of strictly contemporary information. A far more exhaustive analysis was made by Chéruel, the editor of the first critical text, who showed how many of his anecdotes were contradicted by contemporary records and how many of his portraits needed correction. Finally de Boislisle devoted his life to a monumental edition which, though interrupted by death before the Regency is reached, is one of the glories of French scholarship. Utilising the voluminous papers of Saint-Simon published in 1880, he not only supplied a commentary but added a mass of material illustrating every aspect of the time.

The rise and fall of Jansenism has been described in one of the most celebrated works on seventeenth century France. Sainte-Beuve[1] chose the saints and scholars of Port-Royal for his theme when invited to deliver lectures at Lausanne in 1837. The austere piety of the Jansenists had a good deal in common with the spiritual Protestantism of Vinet, of whom the great critic said that he helped him to understand the inner meaning of the movement. Eighty-one lectures were written in six months and read from manuscript, but the publication lasted nearly twenty years. The first two volumes were little more than a revision of the lectures, but the last three were almost a new work. He had been led very close to the portals of the Catholic Church by Lamennais, but when the master broke with Rome and lost his faith, the pupil lapsed into life-long scepticism. None the less he approached Jansenism in a friendly and almost a reverent spirit, describing it as an attempt to return to the primitive Church. He quotes with approval Royer-Collard's dictum, 'He who knows not Port-Royal knows not humanity.' He shows how it put a stamp upon its inmates, how it became itself a collective

[1] The fullest account of his work on Port Royal is in Michaud's important volume, *Sainte-Beuve avant les Lundis*, 1903; cp. Séché, *Sainte-Beuve*, 2 vols., 1904. Sorel's essay, 'Sainte-Beuve et les historiens,' in *Études de Littérature et d'Histoire*, 1901 and the longer study in *Notes et Portraits*, 1909, are authoritative. The publication of his voluminous correspondence is in progress.

individuality. Saint-Cyran and Arnauld are followed by Mère Angélique, De Sacy, Pascal, Tillemont, De Rancé, Nicole, Racine, each with his own clearly marked personality yet stamped with the cachet of the group.

The short but brilliant episode of the Regency has received far less attention. Though Saint-Simon's wonderful portrait of his friend and patron gives on the whole a discriminating picture of the man, his volumes have to be used with extreme caution. In particular the sketch of Dubois, whom he can never forgive for corrupting the youth of the Duke, conveys no adequate notion of his real ability and aims, and it was the achievement of Émile Bourgeois to explore his foreign policy and to follow his dazzling fortunes. While condemning his subservience to the dynastic ambitions of his master and his attempt to play the part of the arbiter of Europe, he recognises the value of his work for the army, finance and commerce, and rebuts the charge that he was personally corrupt.

The publication of his secret correspondence by Boutaric in 1866 revealed a new Louis XV, no longer a mere *fainéant*, but keenly interested in foreign affairs, above all in the fate of Poland, the country of his wife. But while the royal diplomat sometimes recognised what ought to be done, he lacked the energy to carry it through. The chief of the secret cabinet was the Comte de Broglie, and the most important result of Boutaric's book was to determine the Duc de Broglie[1] to learn more of his ancestor's career. The appearance of ' Le Secret du Roi' in 1878 was a literary event. Boutaric had given only the instructions of the King to his agents and his replies to their questions; the correspondence of the agents themselves he had not found. The Duke discovered that of his grand-uncle at the Foreign Office, and added material from the family archives. ' What Louis concealed from the world was what was best in himself. There was often good sense, morality and patriotism behind the scenes, while on the stage strutted licentious frivolity.' But though there were gleams of sense, there was never a sustained effort of will. The skill with which a sterile diplomacy is made readable is beyond praise, and the imbroglio of a double policy, the secret always in danger of being discovered by the King's own ministers, introduces a touch of comedy.

When the story of the secret negotiations had been told the Duke turned to the official diplomacy of the reign. The first volumes, entitled ' Frederick the Great and Maria Theresa,' cover the first two years of the War of the Austrian Succession. France had opposed Austria since the time of Henri IV, and it was

[1] See Fagniez, *Le Duc de Broglie*, 1902.

Belle-Isle's plan to re-establish the Empire free from Austrian preponderance; but the flaw of the scheme was that it involved co-operation with Frederick, who abandoned his ally directly he had got what he sought. Prussia went to war for Silesia, France for an idea, and success was rendered impossible by her incoherence and weakness in diplomacy and in arms. A still more terrible mistake was committed than that of merely undertaking a needless and unprofitable war: by supporting Frederick France helped to foster the growth of a remorseless enemy. In painting his darkly shadowed portrait of the great King the historian is thinking of Bismarck and Moltke. The works which follow bring the pitiful story to the conclusion of the war in 1748. He admires the high character of D'Argenson, but deplores his blindness and his blunders. If the honour of France was saved it was by her soldiers, by Belle-Isle's winter retreat from Prague and by the campaigns in which Marshal Saxe shed a last ray of glory on the declining monarchy. Maria Theresa is drawn with a loving hand. Only Louis XV is below his task.

After devoting nine volumes to the War of the Austrian Succession, the appearance of 'The Austrian Alliance' in 1897 seemed to suggest that the Duke was about to embark on the Seven Years War; but he was now an old man, and the work was an epilogue. He concludes that the new grouping arose not from the resentment of the Pompadour at a jest of Frederick II or her delight at a supposed compliment from Maria Theresa, but from mutual interest. Austria had desired it since 1748 and Louis was not averse. Yet even here, though French policy was back on the right road, the historian contrasts its vacillations with the skill of Kaunitz and the Empress. Moreover the change came too late. By this time Austria was weak and Prussia was strong. The foreign policy of Louis XV has been further explored by Vandal, who traced his relations with Russia, and by Waddington, who wrote the history of the Seven Years War in a spirit fairer to Frederick the Great and with a wider knowledge of foreign archives than the Duke possessed. For the life of the Court and the frail beauties who presided over it, the society, art and morals of the period, the sparkling anecdotage of the brothers De Goncourt is still of value. Among the studies of the salons of Paris a high place is held by the Marquis de Ségur's exquisite volumes on Madame Geoffrin and Julie de Lespinasse.

The later years of Louis XVI fall within the orbit of the Revolution, but the earlier part of the reign has been somewhat neglected. The publication of forged letters of Marie Antoinette[1]

¹ See Farrer's *Literary Forgeries*, 1907.

by Hunolstein and Feuillet de Conches in 1864 led Arneth to publish the correspondence of Maria Theresa with her daughter and the Austrian Minister in Paris Mercy d'Argenteau from the archives of Vienna, and thus to render possible a critical study of the Queen's character. The first adequate biography was furnished by La Rocheterie. The first volume of Ségur's *La Chute de la Monarchie* is devoted to the ministry of Turgot, whose noble aims are recognised but whose hasty methods are censured. In his desire for an enlightened despotism rather than for the co-operation of classes he was behind the best thought of the time. The King is portrayed as a reformer, eager to economise but overruled by the Queen and the vested interests of the Court. The second volume on Necker's first tenure of the Ministry of Finance carries the melancholy story to 1781 when intervention in the American War of Independence had increased the economic embarrassments of France.

Several works of importance throw light on the Ancien Régime without confining themselves to any single reign. The instructions given to French Ambassadors between the Peace of Westphalia and the Revolution, edited by Sorel, Rambaud, Hanotaux and other scholars of the first rank, throw light on diplomatic relations with almost every country in Europe. Émile Bourgeois traced French diplomacy from the days of Richelieu in his indispensable *Manuel de Politique Étrangère*. Funck-Brentano proved how seldom the Bastille was the living tomb of political offenders. Babeau and Henri Sée reconstructed the life of the provinces, and Avenel explored the system of prices and wages. Sainte-Beuve's incomparable gallery of portraits illustrates almost every aspect and incident in the life of France since the Renaissance. Henri Martin's volumes on the Ancien Régime were the best part of an undistinguished work which held its own as the national history for many years and was only superseded by Lavisse's co-operative *Histoire de France*.[1]

[1] See Hanotaux, *Henri Martin*, 1885; Jules Simon, *Mignet, Michelet, Henri Martin*, 1890. H. de l'Épinois, *Henri Martin et son Histoire de France*, 1872, voices Catholic and monarchist criticism.

CHAPTER XII

THE FRENCH REVOLUTION

I

THE study of the French Revolution,[1] inaugurated by Thiers and Mignet in the twenties, was carried further in the following decade by two works of widely different character and tendency. The first was the vast 'Histoire Parlementaire' of Buchez[2] and his disciple Roux. Buchez was a convinced republican, who, like many clever young men of his generation, had joined and abandoned the Saint-Simonians. He had developed a curious system in which Catholicism and socialism were blended, and in the Revolution he saw the highest result of civilisation. Since equality is Christian, all hindrances to its attainment must be removed, an assumption which led straight to a glorification of the Jacobins and Terrorists. The purest character of the Revolution was Robespierre, whose beneficent work was cut short by Thermidor. The book contains not only the debates in the Assembly but extracts from the proceedings of the Jacobin Club and the Commune, from trials, newspapers and pamphlets, and immediately took its place beside the *Moniteur* as an indispensable authority.

A more serious attempt to explain and judge the Revolution was made by Droz,[3] who as a young man had fought in the army of the Rhine, and who in 1811 devoted himself to the main task of his life. The 'History of the Reign of Louis XVI during the years when it was possible to avoid or to guide the Revolution' announced its standpoint in the title. His pages are a pæan to Lally-Tollendal, Malouet and other constitutional royalists of the English school, the rejection of whose proposals in September 1789 is held to mark the fatal lapse from reason to passion. 'The moment one can direct a revolution is short. That moment is now

[1] See appendix to Acton, *Lectures on the French Revolution*, 1910; Paul Janet, *Philosophie de la Révolution française*, 4th ed., 1892; Thompson, *Life of Robespierre*, vol. i., Introduction, 1935; Clare Brinton, *A Decade of Revolution*; Gooch, 'The Study of the French Revolution,' in *Maria Theresa and other Essays*, 1951; Cobban, *The Causes of the French Revolution* (Historical Association, 1946); and Paul Farmer, *France reviews its revolutionary Origins*, 1944.
[2] See Flint's *Philosophy of History*, ch. 7.
[3] See Mignet, *Portraits et Notices historiques*, vol. 2.

past. Providence grew weary.' A third volume, disguised as an appendix, follows the attempts of Mirabeau to reconcile the Monarchy with the Revolution. 'Till the end of the Constituent there was a chance, however small, of guiding the movement.' In his admirable *éloge* Mignet rightly rejected the contention that the mistakes of 1789 or even the death of Mirabeau made a peaceful transition impossible, but the value and interest of a thoughtful work are not destroyed if its theory of a fatal moment is rejected.

Three histories which began to appear in 1847 differed equally from Buchez and from Thiers, Mignet and Droz. While the three latter were constitutional royalists, Lamartine, Michelet and Louis Blanc were ardent republicans. All alike desired to overturn the throne. 'La France s'ennuie,' declared the poet in ominous words. Louis Philippe owed his accession and his fall in almost equal degree to the labours of historians. The most nakedly political of the three works was that of Lamartine.[1] His verses had flowed from him without effort, and he made no serious attempt to prepare himself for his new task. It was enough for him to know the outlines of the plot: his imagination could supply the rest. Though it bears the title of a history of the Girondins, it is virtually a history of the Revolution and carries the narrative down to Thermidor. No man ever sat down to write with a more slender equipment of the qualities of an historian. He transposes dates, omits subjects which do not interest him, invents incidents. He attempts a resurrection, like Michelet, but without Michelet's careful preparation. He was naturally a humane man, and he never directly glorifies crime, but his governing purpose was to exalt the Revolution. Discovering himself in the Girondins, above all in Vergniaud, he glories in their idealism and paints in dazzling colours the imaginary Last Supper. When they are gone he transfers his devotion to Robespierre, a disciple of Rousseau and almost a new Christ. But the individual on whom he lavishes the whole resources of his pathos and eloquence is Charlotte Corday. Her history, of which we know little and of which Lamartine knew less, fills half a volume, the scanty facts being eked out with a wealth of imaginary incidents. The story of 'the angel of assassination' ranks with Michelet's picture of Joan of Arc among the supreme achievements of French prose; but the one is history, the other romance.

On the day of the publication of the first two volumes Lamartine wrote to a friend, 'I have staked my fortune, my literary

[1] See Deschanel, *Lamartine*, vol. ii., ch. 21, 1893, and Jules Simon, *Quatre Portraits*, 1895.

renown and my political future, to-day on a card. I have won. The publishers tell me there has never been such a success. While the critics shook their heads, the printers could hardly keep pace with the demand. 'J'ai pour moi les femmes et les jeunes gens,' wrote the joyful author; 'je peux me passer du reste.' He asked Dumas what he considered to be the reason of such a triumph. 'Because you have raised history to the level of the novel,' replied the novelist. The compliment is the severest condemnation ever passed on the book. It was drama, romance, politics—anything but history. Tocqueville, after working with him, declared in his 'Memoirs' that he had never known a mind less sincere nor one which had a more complete contempt for the truth. 'When I say he despised it, I am wrong. He did not honour it enough to occupy himself with it at all.'[1] When the Second Republic had come and gone and his brief glory as a statesman was over, the fame of his book quickly paled. Nettement[2] published a reply in which 113 pages were filled with errors of fact. Looking back from the cool obscurity of old age, the author expressed his regret for certain passages and recognised the danger of his teaching. It was too late. The most worthless and the most eloquent of books had done its work. The Constitutional Monarchy had been succeeded by the Second Empire.

The narrative of Louis Blanc[3] is a far more serious affair. The author had made his name in the early days of the July Monarchy as a republican journalist, and on the completion of the first decade of the rule of Louis Philippe published his 'Ten Years of French History.' The eloquent socialist pamphlet in five volumes was read all over Europe, and contributed more than any other work except the 'Girondins' to prepare the Revolution of 1848. Kings were depicted as the representatives of a dead past, the bourgeoisie as a hybrid monster corrupted by the love of lucre. The people, on the other hand, though the source of all right, were excluded from power. 'Soon every theory will have been tried except the simplest and noblest, that of fraternity. Till this is applied let us not despair.' His second work was not less an instrument of propaganda. 'I was brought up by royalist parents, and horror of the Revolution was the first strong sentiment that agitated me. But by study I learned to render homage to its great events and its great men.' No man could date its

---

[1] *Souvenirs*, 164–5, 1893.

[2] *Études critiques sur les Girondins*, 1848; cp. Biré, *La Légende des Girondins*, 1882.

[3] An adequate biography is much needed. There is a brief sketch in Spuller's *Figures disparues*, vol. i., 1886.

beginning. 'All nations have contributed to produce it. It is the glory of France to have performed the work of the human race at the price of her own blood. All the revolts of the past unite and lose themselves in it, like rivers in the sea.' History is the record and the result of the operation of the principles of authority, individualism and fraternity. The reign of authority lasted unchecked till the Reformation, which inaugurated individualism. The former led to oppression, the latter to anarchy. Fraternity, foreshadowed by Hus and the Anabaptists and first clearly announced by the Mountain, alone leads to liberty. The Revolution is a name for two distinct movements. The one, starting from Voltaire and represented by the Constituent Assembly, was a movement of the bourgeoisie for the profit of individualism; the other, deriving from Rousseau and interrupted by Thermidor, was based on fraternity. To realise that great ideal another revolution would be necessary.

Louis Blanc paints the close of the Ancien Régime in dark colours, but he is no great admirer of the early leaders of the Revolution. Mirabeau was a mixture of greatness and baseness, bought by the Court though lacking in nobility. The Girondins were pure individualists, the sons of Voltaire, ineffective and vain. Marat, representative of a new power, journalism, was a monster of cruelty. The Jacobins, on the other hand, were only stern by necessity. 'If the Revolution became irritated let us deplore it, but let us remember the thousand needless provocations.' The September massacres were not premeditated. There had been rumours of conspiracy in the prisons, and foreign armies were a few days' march from the capital. 'It is easy to understand how Paris fell into this satanic intoxication.' Hideous as was the cruelty, it was disinterested. The execution of the King was a gigantic blunder though not unjust. The task of the Revolutionists was to kill the monarchical idea, but the scaffold exalted and ennobled it. The later volumes are at once a mild condemnation of the Terror and a pæan to Robespierre. 'The Terror was not a system. It sprang, ready armed, from the entrails of the situation. Enveloped by intrigue and treason, it often struck down the innocent, but it always believed them to be guilty.' Attention had been too much concentrated on the horrors. 'After the battle the dead have been counted one by one and laid out bleeding before posterity. The lofty exertions of mind and the victories of thought have only been sketched. Yet there is the living history of the Revolution.' The Jacobins slew sadly and of necessity, to save themselves and the Revolution. Robespierre, who wished it to retain its energy while abating its fury, possessed little power. Thermidor was not a deliverance but a martyrdom, its victim a gentle and inspired enthusiast, a Puritan and a Stoic, the defender of the poor and the clear-sighted apostle of humanity.

In closing the twelfth volume in 1862 Louis Blanc declared that the book had been the delight and the torment of his life for eighteen years. Its value lies not in its philosophy, which is superficial, nor in its judgments, which are often grotesque, but in its patient unravelling of events.[1] 'His method is truly scientific,' declares Aulard,[2] 'as he alleges no fact without its authority. Some of his appendices are masterpieces of historical criticism. It is still the best general work for making the Revolution known.' His study of Croker's vast collection of pamphlets during his exile in England under the Second Empire opened up a rich quarry. The story of the Vendée revolt, a dark world into which Michelet had darted a few rays, was for the first time told in full. While most historians laid down their pens at Thermidor, he brought his narrative to the close of the Convention. He devotes more attention than any of his predecessors to finance and economic conditions. On the other hand, it is impossible to accept Aulard's verdict that he is the most impartial historian of the Revolution. Acton spoke of his frigid passion. 'I pity the reader,' wrote Louis Blanc at the close of his work, 'who does not recognise the accent of sincerity and the palpitations of a heart hungry for justice.' We recognise the accent of sincerity, but the palpitating heart interferes with the operations of the brain. He is the relentless enemy of the bourgeoisie, the uncompromising champion of 'the people.' He judges men according as they belong to the rival schools of 'individualism' and 'fraternity,' taking the former at their worst and the latter at their best.

While Michelet and Louis Blanc were busy with their pæans to the Revolution, a man of widely different temperament and training was investigating the soil out of which it grew. Tocqueville's 'L'Ancien Régime et la Révolution,' which appeared in 1855, was described by its author as a study, not a history; but it threw more light on its character than most histories and inaugurated its scientific exploration. Tocqueville[3] belonged to the *noblesse* of Normandy. His father was a peer, his mother a

[1] Lanfrey severely criticised it in an appendix to his *Essai sur la Révolution Française*, 1857. For a German view see Häusser's *Ges. Schriften*, vol. i., 1869.

[2] Letter in Jullian's Introduction to the *Extraits*, 1897.

[3] See *Memoir, Letters and Remains of de Tocqueville*, Eng. trans., 2 vols., 1861; *Correspondence and Conversations of Tocqueville with Nassau Senior*, 2 vols., 1872; G. de Beaumont, *Notice sur T.*, 1897. The best appreciations are by Mignet, *Nouveaux Éloges historiques*, 1877; Faguet,

granddaughter of Malesherbes. Finding little satisfaction in his career as a judge, he obtained leave to report on the penal methods of the United States. His real object was to study the problems of the New World. While the report on the penitentiary system is forgotten, 'Democracy in America' is one of the classics of political science. Though he does not present the United States as a model, he admires them. The federal constitution and the Supreme Court contributed to secure the separation of powers on which liberty rested. In most of the countries of the Old World centralisation had gone too far. Democracy began as the enemy of despotism, but it was as likely to become despotic as any other form of government. The author woke up to find himself famous, and Royer-Collard told him that there had been nothing like his book since Montesquieu.

Tocqueville entered Parliament, but failed to impress the Chamber or the country. On the fall of the Monarchy he became Foreign Secretary, but the *coup d'état* of 1851 brought his public life to a close, and after a short imprisonment he returned to his ancestral home to continue his studies of democracy. He wrote to a friend that he was resolved to discover and explain the causes, character and influence of the great events of the Revolution, the Empire and the Restoration. The Revolution itself was so colourful that it had occurred to no one to study its relation to the régime which it superseded. Realising the necessity of exploring provincial archives he made a prolonged stay at Tours, where he found a complete collection of the records and correspondence of the Intendants. He pursued his researches in Normandy and Languedoc, studying the decrees of the Parlements and the registers of the parishes, and gradually visualising the structure of society, the nature of feudal rights, the central and local administration in the eighteenth century.

His results were startling. 'As I advanced I was surprised to find at every moment traits which meet us in France to-day. I discovered a mass of sentiments which I had thought were the offspring of the Revolution, a thousand habits which the Revolution is believed to have produced.' Above all, the centralised administration was an inheritance from the Ancien Régime. France was subject to three governments: the King and his ministers, aided by the Intendants; the feudal powers and jurisdictions; and finally the provincial institutions. Of these the first

Politiques et Moralistes, vol. iii.; Sainte-Beuve, *Causeries*, vol. xv., and Scherer, *Études critiques*, 1863. The *Souvenirs* deal only with his political career. Marcel's *Essai politique sur T.*, 1910, deals fully with the publicist. The latest study is by J. P. Mayer, 1939.

was by far the strongest. The feudal powers, though annoying, were weak, the provincial institutions ghosts of their former selves except in Brittany and Languedoc. Behind the façade of a dissolving aristocracy he detected a powerful central machine gradually extinguishing local life, corporations and seigneurial jurisdiction. The second conclusion was that the Ancien Régime was less terrible than had been thought. There was much that was arbitrary but little real oppression. Feudalism as a political system, aristocracy as a political force, had disappeared, and the privileges that remained appeared all the more odious because the system of which they had formed a part was dead. 'Some good people have endeavoured to rehabilitate the Ancien Régime. I judge it by the sentiments it inspired in those who lived under it and destroyed it. I see that all through the Revolution, cruel as it was, the hatred of the old régime outweighed all other hates, and that during the perilous vicissitudes of the last sixty years the fear of its return has outweighed all other fears. That is enough for me.' A revolution was inevitable, not because the burden was intolerable, but because Frenchmen were growing less patient of abuses.

The book introduced a new perspective. Where others had seen a radical contradiction between the Monarchy and the Revolution, Tocqueville saw a logical continuation. The Ancien Régime was largely centralised; the Revolution centralised administration still further. The Ancien Régime had destroyed the greater part of feudalism; the Revolution destroyed the rest. Neither cared for liberty. The driving principle of the Revolution was equality, and it was equality before the law which the Monarchy had been striving to establish in its long struggle with feudalism. 'The Revolution was the sudden and violent termination of a task at which ten generations had laboured.' The second volume was interrupted by death. The commencement of the reforming movement extorts his admiration. 'A time of inexperience, no doubt, but of generosity, enthusiasm, virility and grandeur, a time of immortal memory, to which men will look back with admiration and respect.' Its weakness was that liberty was sacrificed to equality. The hatred of inequality was deep and inextinguishable, while the love of liberty was more recent and less profound. They met in the Revolution, and for a moment inflamed the hearts of Frenchmen with the noble ideal of becoming equal in liberty. It was but for a moment, and the anarchy which succeeded it led straight to despotism. It was a tragic result but not unnatural, for nowhere had men so completely lost the sense and practice of affairs. Thus the work was left half accomplished. It secured equal laws, regularity, uniformity, at the cost of increasing centralisation. It failed to achieve liberty.

Tocqueville's second book was received with the same enthusiasm as the first. It was indeed a second chapter of his treatise on democracy, a fresh warning, a renewed exhortation to his countrymen and to the world. 'To show men how to escape tyranny,' he wrote to a friend, 'that is the idea of both my books. To work in this sense is a holy mission, for which one should spare neither money, time nor life.' He was free from party ties and party passions. He shared the conviction of the Doctrinaires that liberty demanded a strong government which did not abuse its strength, and that the separation of powers was the secret of ordered freedom. 'No political writer of the century can compare with him,' pronounces Scherer; 'posterity will set up his bust at the feet of Montesquieu.' If his place as a publicist is secure, what of his fame as an historian? Can we accept his reading of the Ancien Régime and its relation of the Revolution? Sainte-Beuve charged him with injustice to Richelieu and Louis XIV. The Intendants, asserted the great critic, were better for the people than some royal governor, and centralisation begot equality before the law. A somewhat similar judgment was passed by the venerable Pasquier, the last survivor of the generation which knew the France that had vanished. The historian, he declared, exaggerated the absence of good elements of government and the consequent need of the Revolution. None the less, the conclusion that it changed less than had been supposed, that in many directions it only accelerated the tendencies of the Ancien Régime, has become the starting-point of subsequent scholarship. In the words of Scherer, he accomplished for the Revolution what the geologists had done for the history of the globe. He destroyed the cataclysmic theory and substituted the slow action of secular causes.

No one had expected Tocqueville, a Catholic and a royalist, to eulogise the Revolution, but the world was astonished at the attack upon Jacobinism by a republican freethinker, the friend and ally of Michelet. From his earliest years Quinet[1] devoted his pen to the defence of liberty. Chief among its enemies he reckoned

---

[1] See Mme. Quinet, *Edgar Quinet*, 2 vols., 1888–9, and *Cinquante Ans d'Amitié, Michelet et Quinet*, 1903; Heath, *Quinet, his Early Life and Writings*, 1881. For appreciations see Faguet, *Politiques et Moralistes*, vol. ii., Spuller, *Figures disparues*, vol. i., and Monod, 'Le Centenaire de Quinet,' in *Revue Historique*, vol. lxxxii. Quinet's *Histoire de mes Idées* only reaches his seventeenth year.

the Roman Church. Primitive Christianity rested on equality, but the Church had been unfaithful to the principle. Moreover, it proscribed thought, the organ of progress, and paralysed the countries where it was dominant. His lectures on the Jesuits at the Collège de France were a declaration of war. In a further course on 'Christianity and the French Revolution' he commends the Reformation as an attempt to return to primitive ideals, and bitterly laments its defeat in France. 'Alone of modern nations, France has made a political and social revolution before achieving a religious revolution.' The foundation must be laid before the house can be built. England and America, starting from Protestantism, achieved their purpose: France, starting from Catholicism, had failed. The criticism of current ideas was continued in his 'Philosophy of French History.' Nations, he declared, were destroyed by false notions as well as by enemies, and one of the most dangerous was that everything has been for the best. The Gauls were incapable of civilisation, and the Roman and Frankish conquests were therefore desirable. An earlier triumph of the Third Estate would have prevented the necessary unification of France. The Revolution was needed to assert the principle of freedom after the long reign of authority. This facile optimism overlooked the debit side of the account, and it was to this aspect that he called attention. Guizot thankfully recognised how good was the result of the historic process; Quinet reflected how much better it might have been.

Quinet's greatest and most enduring work, 'La Révolution,' which appeared in 1865, is an attempt to understand its aim, to separate its good and evil elements, to show where and why it failed. It was written in exile, without access to a good library, and was in no respect a work of research. Its interest lies in the personality of its author and the novelty of his attitude. He calmly declares that the Revolution as a movement needs no apologia: the task was to discover why such immense efforts achieved such disproportionate results. 'A whole people cried ''Freedom or Death,'' and meant what it said. Why did not men who knew so well how to die know also how to become free?' Two main reasons, suggested in his 'Christianity and the French Revolution' twenty years before, were that it grew out of a Catholic soil and neglected to substitute Protestantism for Catholicism. The first was its misfortune, the second its own fateful error. It could not build on the Ancien Régime nor on the religion which was one of its essential parts. It could not rest on the shadowy theism of Rousseau's Savoyard Vicar. The Civil Constitution antagonised the Church without destroying it.

Catholicism in any form was irreconcilable with the new liberty A further mistake was the adoption of violent methods. The death of the King was a gigantic blunder as well as a crime. The Terrorists committed a double sin. They continued the despotism of the past and fostered the despotism of the future. With the name of the Revolution on their lips they laboured unceasingly for its destruction. Within eight years of the execution of Louis XVI Napoleon was supreme, the Concordat was signed, and the 'Génie du Christianisme' was on every table. Despotism and Catholicism were again enthroned, and the work of emancipation remained to be done over again.

Quinet's book is powerful and eloquent, but its most original thesis is untenable. He attacks the Revolution for its violence, and in the same breath scolds it for not destroying Catholicism root and branch. Political convictions must be treated with respect, but religious convictions must be trampled down. His animosity against the Church diminishes the impressiveness of his attack on the Terror, and his regret that Protestantism was not forcibly established in a land of Catholics, deists and atheists reveals his limitations as a practical statesman. Yet his onslaught on Jacobinism was vigorous and effective. 'The key and novelty of my book is the criticism of the Revolution in the name of the Revolution.' It led straight to the Empire, to Waterloo, to 1851. Two generations of despotism were the price of its mistakes. The Terror destroyed the Revolution instead of destroying its foes. The book aroused intense excitement. It was the first outspoken attack by a man whose devotion to democracy was beyond suspicion. When the Second Empire crushed liberty, democrats found comfort and inspiration in the Revolution, but now the veil of the temple had been rent. The challenge was taken up with spirit by Alphonse Peyrat.[1] 'Quinet has outraged the purest and most devoted men, and in declaring that it was not worth its price has passed an insensate judgment.' In comparing its leaders to Caligula, Nero and Torquemada he was calumniating the Jacobins and the Committee of Public Safety. 'The spirit of liberty spread by the Revolution throughout the world renders any lasting tyranny impossible.' 'Everything in your book,' wrote Michelet, 'is great, strong, magnanimous. It is a triumph for me too, as you and I are the same person.' This was the voice of friendship, for the difference of view was profound. Michelet had condemned the Terror while assigning the major responsibility to the Émigrés and the counter-revolution; Quinet scourged it for conscious and deliberate crimes. Michelet rejoices that the

[1] *La Révolution et le Livre de M. Quinet*, 1866.

Revolution boldly substituted Justice for historical Christianity; Quinet laments that a purer form of Christianity was not established. The book must be in part interpreted as a shaft aimed at Louis Napoleon. 'It is an act of accusation against the Empire,' wrote the *Moniteur* with perfect truth. His quarrel with the Revolution for opening the door to Napoleon scarcely allowed him to realise how immense was the work that it achieved, and how great an impetus it gave to many of his own most cherished ideas.

While Quinet's volumes added nothing to the knowledge of events, Mortimer-Ternaux' 'History of the Terror' inaugurated the systematic study of the archives. His standpoint was one of moderate liberalism. The principles of 1789 are frankly accepted. 'We are the children of the French Revolution, and we will not blaspheme our mother.' The action of the Court was unwise, the achievements of the Constituent Assembly immense. But the same reasons which lead to the support of 1789 involve condemnation of 1792-3. 'Two principles dispute the world, liberty and despotism. Demagogy is one of the incarnations of despotism. To oppose demagogy is to oppose despotism.' The Terror was not the work of the nation, and France was saved in spite of it. It began, he declared, on June 20, 1792, with the invasion of the Tuileries. So abundant was his material that the work only covered a single year, and was terminated by death before he reached the establishment of the Revolutionary Tribunal. His eight volumes, filled with extracts from the registers of the Paris sections and reports to the Commune, are still indispensable.

Where Mortimer-Ternaux left off Wallon began. He had won fame among scholars by his 'History of Ancient Slavery' and among pious Catholics by his biographies of St. Louis and Joan of Arc, and it was not till the later decades of his long life that he turned to the Revolution. Campardon had published two weighty volumes on the Revolutionary Tribunal in 1866, based on the official reports of its proceedings, but Wallon's 'Histoire du Tribunal Révolutionnaire' published still larger quantities of new material and connected its activity with the general movement of the Revolution. We receive full details of the great trials, Charlotte Corday, Custine, the Queen, the Girondins, Égalité, Roland, Danton, Robespierre, ending with those of the members of the Tribunal itself; but its most hideous feature was the punishment of the young and the obscure. Wallon's last work touched another side of the problem of the administration of justice under the Terror. The 'Revolutionary Tribunal' dealt with Paris, the 'Representatives on Mission' with the provinces.

Though they repressed many local abuses they were terrible instruments of tyranny, and some of them were as remarkable for their incapacity as for their savage cruelty. The subsequent publication of the complete correspondence makes it clear that, though Wallon rightly emphasised the criminal side of their activity, he failed to do full justice to their labours in the organisation of national defence.

While the political side of the Revolution was being investigated, the first attempt at social history was made by the brothers de Goncourt, whose volumes on the Revolution and the Directory reconstructed the life and thought, the morals and amusements, the atmosphere and colour of the time. Their sources included newspapers, brochures, fly-sheets, caricatures, and reveal the profound dislocation of society and the rapid deterioration of morals. More serious were the researches of Adolf Schmidt, who, though a German, presented part of his results in a French dress. Based on the police reports addressed to the Minister of the Interior, his 'Tableaux de la Révolution française' bring us close to the life of the populace. We overhear the conversation of the crowd and learn what the women of Paris were thinking. He shows the influence of economic conditions, the antagonism of rich and poor, the effect of the *assignats* on prices, the famine, the increase of crime, the beginnings of socialism.

II

The most resounding attack on the Revolution since Burke came from an unexpected quarter. While Quinet wrote more in sorrow than in anger, it was reserved for Taine[1] to outlaw the Revolution as a whole. 'Of books that are strong enough to work a change and form an epoch in a reader's life,' declared Acton, 'there are two, perhaps, on our revolutionary shelf. One is Taine, the other Michelet. No man feels the grandeur of the Revolution till he reads Michelet, or the horror of it without reading Taine.'

The main interest of his early life was in philosophy, and after playing a sonata of Beethoven he pronounced it as beautiful as a syllogism. His teachers were struck by his extraordinary power.

[1] Taine's *Life and Letters* appeared in English, 1902–8. The best general surveys are by A. de Margerie, *Hippolyte Taine*, 1894; Giraud, *Essai sur Taine*, 1902; Chevrillon, *Taine*, 1932; and Lacombe, *Taine, Historien et Sociologue*, 1909. The best brief appreciations are by Boutmy, in *Taine*, *Scherer, Laboulaye*, 1901; Monod, in *Taine, Renan, Michelet*, 1896; Bourget, in *Essais de Psychologie contemporaine*, 1883; Sorel, in *Nouveaux Essais d'Histoire et de Critique*, 1898.

'He is easily first in everything,' wrote Vacherot, 'and the most industrious and distinguished pupil I have ever known at the École Normale. His erudition is prodigious for his age, and such passion for learning I have never witnessed. His mind is remarkable for rapidity of conception, subtlety, strength. But he judges and formulates too rapidly. He has a weakness for formulas and definitions, to which he too often sacrifices reality. His moral nature, however, is a stranger to any passion but truth, and is above all temptation.' More than forty years later the obituaries had merely to repeat this searching analysis of the young Normalien. He early reached the conviction that the methods of science must be applied to the record of civilisation, and his passion for exact observation was fostered by his studies in medicine and anatomy. He expounded his philosophy of history in the introduction to his famous work on English Literature. The three forces which in combination produce civilisation and determine its transformations are the race, the *milieu* and the moment. 'History is a mechanical problem. The only difference is that it cannot be measured by the same means or defined so exactly.' 'It is a science,' he wrote to a friend, 'analogous to physiology and zoology, not to geometry. My idea has lain on the ground since Montesquieu; I have only picked it up.' But Montesquieu never imprisoned history in an iron cage. Race, *milieu* and moment are factors which themselves require further analysis. Race is a product of history, not an ultimate element. The *milieu*, except in its physical aspect, is itself a result. Taine explains everything in a great man except his greatness, for the springs of genius are beyond plummet's sounding. The same oversimplification is apparent in the doctrine of the *faculté maîtresse*. Every man, he declared, was distinguished by a dominating characteristic; and he illustrated his contention in monographs on Livy and La Fontaine, in the studies of which the 'English Literature' is composed, and in his lectures on the Philosophy of Art. Yet many individuals are distinguished, not by one dominant characteristic, but by a harmonious balance of qualities. Again, the master faculty is in many cases a result. Livy is explained by his oratorical instinct—itself the outcome of a combination of intellectual and political influences. The fullness of life and the riddle of personality cry aloud for more subtle and discriminating treatment.

When the 'History of English Literature' was finished Taine composed the philosophic work planned while he was at college, and in 1870 his treatise on Intelligence appeared. The preface once more stated his theory of history in unmistakable terms.

'History is applied psychology. The historian notes and traces the transformations presented by a human molecule or group of human molecules, and explains them by their psychology— Carlyle of Cromwell, Sainte-Beuve of Port-Royal, Stendhal of the Italians, Renan of the Semitic race. For fifteen years I have contributed to these special and concrete psychologies; I now attempt a general and abstract psychology.' His famous sentence, 'Virtue and vice are products like sugar and vitriol,' became the symbol of French materialism, and Bishop Dupanloup issued a solemn warning to the parents and youth of France against the teaching of Taine, Renan and Littré.

A few months later the German invasion gave a wholly new orientation to his life. In December 1870 he wrote to Sorel, 'Our duty will be publicly to confess our faults, to discover in those faults the causes of our reverses, to spread knowledge of languages and history.' The Commune left a still more poignant memory. He became convinced that French civilisation was a veneer beneath which seethed the primeval passions of savagery. He had taken no great interest in politics before the war, but now they absorbed him. The first decisive result of his meditations was that England was on the right track and France on the wrong. His 'Notes sur l'Angleterre,' written during the war, express his admiration for the conservatism of the people. The island kingdom appeared to him the home of ordered liberty. His own country-men inspired him with terror, almost with despair. 'Your Memoirs,' he wrote to Guizot, 'prove that in the conflict between the nation and your government the nation was wrong. In general the French have acted and thought since 1789 partly like mad-men, partly like children.' In another image he compared France to a vicious horse mounted by bad riders. 'History shows that states, governments, religions, churches, are the only means by which the animal and savage man acquires his little portion of reason and justice.' While Rousseau taught that man was naturally good and was made bad by society, Taine believed that man was naturally bad and might be made a little less vicious by institutions. In this spirit he set to work to study the causes of the present discontents. His book was to be a sociological inter-pretation, not an historical narrative. His models were Guizot and Tocqueville on one side, Stendhal, Balzac and Sainte-Beuve on the other.

The first volume of the 'Origins of Contemporary France'[1]

[1] The fullest analysis is by Aulard, *Taine, Historien de la Révolution française*, 1907. For criticisms of the first volume see Sorel's review in *Revue Historique*, vol. ii., and Morley's *Miscellanies*, vol. iii.

appeared in 1875. The preface sharply challenges the whole
theory of democracy. Ten million ignorances do not make knowledge. The people can tell what sort of government they desire
but not what they need. To prescribe for the present one must
know the past. The Ancien Régime must therefore be studied as
a whole. The Court and the salons, art and literature, are known
to all, but they were not France. We must reconstruct the life
of the provinces, the bourgeoisie, the peasantry and the artisan.
Taine's picture is unfavourable without being hostile. He gives
full credit to the monarchy, the *noblesse* and the clergy for building up the nation; but the utility of the Crown had been forgotten
in its abuses, and the nobles had ceased to render the services
which had once justified their privileges. The Church is censured
for its intolerance, the unequal distribution of its vast wealth,
and its non-resident clergy; the merits of its humbler members
are fully recognised. The condition of the peasant, crushed by
taxation, is painted in dark colours. The grievances of the *tiers
état*, on the other hand, were rather sentimental than practical.
' Already, before the final crash, France is in dissolution, because
the privileged classes have forgotten their duties and responsibilities.' The determination to substitute a picture for a narrative
is legitimate, but in attempting to portray a century he draws
traits from different generations, and presents a description which
is not wholly true of any period. Compared with Tocqueville he
is merely a brilliant amateur.

The novelty of the volume lies in its derivation of the revolutionary spirit. The thesis is that the philosophy of the eighteenth
century was the product of the 'classic spirit,' which was invented
by Descartes and the essence of which was to pursue the absolute
and to worship uniformity. When the French mind turned to
politics it proceeded to prescribe according to the dictates of
pure reason. This neglect of the individual, the concrete, the real,
was the mark alike of literature, of the *Philosophes* and of the
Revolution, and its predominance was the main cause of the
tragedies of modern France. But the tendency which he condemns
should rather be called the deductive spirit. The classic tradition
was boldly challenged by Rousseau, the chief inspiration in
Taine's view, of the revolutionary leaders, and Montesquieu was
its open enemy. In the next place he forgets that the French
political theories of the eighteenth century were borrowed from
the thinkers of other lands. Thirdly, the deductive spirit was a
reforming and fertilising as well as a destructive influence. The
free play of the strongest minds of France led to a notable advance in tolerance and justice. Large parts of their programme

were suggested, not by deductive reasoning from abstract notions, but by observation of the society in which they lived. 'This vast and admirable effort of intelligence and speculation,' remarks Sorel with justice, 'was not fated to end in Utopias and Revolution.' It pointed to reform, not to anarchy. The comparison of France to a man, rather weak in constitution, who drinks greedily of a new liquor and falls to the ground foaming at the mouth, is utterly delusive. To attribute the Revolution to Rousseau is as childish as to attribute it to Plutarch. The book was greeted with general admiration, though it completely satisfied no one. Royalists noted with satisfaction that the Revolution was attributed in large measure to the *Philosophes*; Catholics welcomed the testimonial to the lower clergy; Republicans quoted his views as to the sufferings of the peasantry.

When Taine reaches the Revolution itself the relatively balanced attitude disappears.[1] In his 'English Literature' he had sharply criticised Carlyle's disparaging verdict. 'These madmen, these hungry sans-culottes, fought on the frontier for humanitarian interests and abstract principles. Generosity and enthusiasm abounded here as with you. They pursued philosophy as your Puritans religion. Their goal was the salvation of all, as your Puritans sought the salvation of self. They combated evil in society as your Puritans in the soul. Like them, they possessed heroism, but of a propagandist kind which has reformed Europe, while yours only helped yourselves.' The Commune and further study completely altered his favourable opinion. In a letter of 1878 he wrotes, 'Till I studied the documents I took the same view of the Revolution as other Frenchmen. Since Thiers we have chosen to live in a world of illusion. Drama, poetry, a vague humanitarian philosophy have magnified all these people.' A work was needed, he declared, based solely on contemporary testimony and official acts, without reference to the controversies of a later generation. 'I have written as if my subject was the revolutions of Florence or Athens.'

When the Duc de la Rochefoucauld-Liancourt brought the news of the rising in Paris, Louis XVI remarked, 'It is a revolt.' The duke replied, 'Sire, it is a revolution.' As the duke corrected the King, the historian corrects the duke. 'It is not a revolution,

---

[1] See the powerful essay, 'Taine et la Révolution,' in Scherer's *Études sur la Littérature contemporaine*, vol. vii. The work was also severely condemned by Martin Philippson, in *Hist. Zeitschrift*, vol. xli., Fagniez and Gazier in *Revue Historique*, vols. vii.–viii., Brunetière in *Histoire et Littérature*, vol. iii., 1885. Cochin's *La Crise de l'Histoire révolutionnaire*, 1910, defends Taine against Aulard.

but a dissolution.' With the fall of the central government disappeared the security of life and property. The distinction between the principles of '89 and '93 is contemptuously rejected. On being asked when the Terror began, Malouet had replied, 'On the fourteenth of July, 1789.' Taine shared his opinion. The golden dawn' never existed. Moderate men were never at the helm. Sound principles never prevailed. Bloodshed and rapine began at once, and the human tiger bounded forth from his lair. He gathered a good deal of valuable material in reference to the burning of châteaux, the maltreatment of nobles, and the influence of famine in the provinces. The Revolution, he declared, was in essence a transfer of property. 'That is its permanent force, its primary motive, its historical meaning.' No historian can now assert that the opening months were a period of peaceful reform, interrupted only by an occasional explosion like the march to Versailles. On the other hand, the label of 'spontaneous anarchy' is a gross exaggeration. There were thousands of villages in which the Ancien Régime fell without bloodshed or disturbance. The reader is told of no act of virtue or wisdom. He hears only of evil men and the crimes and follies they commit. The attack on the Bastille is attributed to popular frenzy, and no reference is made to the belief that the troops summoned by the Court were to be employed for a *coup*. The Constituent Assembly is allowed to have planted some useful germs in the domain of private law, but in the sphere of political and social reorganisation it acted like an academy of Utopias. Like a blind operator it destroyed not only the tumours but the living organs. 'It had only one fault left to commit, and this it committed by resolving that none of its members should find a place in its successor.' The King was retained as an impotent mockery. The 'spontaneous anarchy' of 1789 had become the 'legal anarchy' of 1791. 'Such was France—exhausted by fasting under the Monarchy, intoxicated by the bad brandy of the ''Contrat Social'' and a score of other heady beverages. The period of joyous delirium is over, and the period of sombre delirium is about to begin.'

The work was received with plaudits by Royalists and Catholics, and with indignation by Republicans of every school. Shortly before it appeared Taine wrote to his mother: 'The Revolution seen at close quarters is quite different from what is generally believed. It is a religion, and people will rush at me as if I was a blasphemer.' The attribution of the violence of the leaders to their philosophy is a gigantic delusion. Many of the actions of the Constituent were unwise, and the Civil Constitution was a colossal blunder, yet a definite reason can be assigned for every one of them independently of any philosophy. The Rights of Man were not only a declaration of abstract principle but a protest against concrete abuses. The dominant personality of the Constituent was Mirabeau, a Constitutional Royalist, one of the greatest of political realists, but Mirabeau is scarcely mentioned. Its mistakes were caused, not by the teaching of Rousseau, but by the inherent difficulty of regenerating France, and by its own inexperience.

The second and third volumes on the Revolution deal with the conquest of power by the Jacobins and with the use they made of it. Taine thought little of the Constituent, but he looks back to it with something like regret when he reaches the mediocrities of the Legislative and the pygmies of the National Assembly. In the Constituent there had been a handful of wise and sober men like Malouet and Mounier; the later Assemblies were filled with theorists, whose dominating principle was the sovereignty of the people, by which they understood, not the majority of French citizens, but the mob of Paris. The Jacobins installed a power at once terrible and imbecile, 'a fierce and suspicious Sultan, who, having appointed his viziers, holds his sabre ready at any moment to cut their throats.' On the foundation of maxims of universal liberty they erected a despotism worthy of Dahomey, a tribunal like that of the Inquisition, and human hecatombs like those of ancient Mexico. Visitors to the sanctuaries of ancient Egypt, on asking to see the statue of the god, were shown a crocodile lying on a purple carpet behind a richly embroidered veil. France possessed a similar theology, the tenets of which were formulated by Rousseau. 'In three years they conducted the crocodile into the sanctuary and installed him behind the golden veil on the purple carpet. The god naturally chose fat victims, but his voracity was so great that he also devoured the thin. Once or twice a year he devoured a fellow crocodile, or was himself devoured.'

Such is Taine's celebrated picture of Jacobin psychology. It is the kernel of his work, the part to which he gave most attention and by which his reputation as an historian must stand or fall. But was the Jacobin so unlike other men before him? Are his actions to be explained by his adoption of the theories of Rousseau? No serious student can answer these questions affirmatively. The heated feeling and violence of language recall the fevered accents of the 'Reflections on the French Revolution' and the 'Regicide Peace.' He professed to be a naturalist, but naturalists do not scream at the objects which they investigate. 'The Revolution,' declared Scherer in astonishment, 'has transformed the most abstract of our thinkers into an excited polemist.' In his anger he throws his determinism to the winds. We are dealing with a pessimist in a passion. He charges the Jacobins—the term is used generically—with regarding men as automata; but his own Jacobins are pure automata, strange monsters which never existed. He convicts them of blindness to the facts around them, but he is himself blind to the most important influences which guided their conduct. He depicts them springing fully armed from the brain of Rousseau, learning nothing, forgetting nothing, functioning in the void; whereas the real Jacobins, the members of the Jacobin Club, were monarchists during the opening phase of the Revolution. He warns his readers that he is not going to relate the history of diplomacy and war, yet he omits not only their history but their influence. He portrays the Representatives on Mission as wild beasts, of whom Carrier is the type, their actions governed by blood-mania. The Émigrés on the Rhine, the intrigues of the Court with foreign Powers, the flight to Varennes, the hostile armies massed on the frontier a few days' march from the capital, the Brunswick manifesto, the rebellion in the West— these menacing facts, without which the domestic history is un- intelligible, are left virtually unnoticed. The leaders were driven to madness, not by Rousseau, but by fear of losing the fruits of the Revolution. Taine confesses that he has only reached one conclusion in politics, namely that society is very complicated. He forgot that it is the duty of an historian in judging individuals to understand the nature of the problems by which they are confronted.

His letters show that he had formed his judgment of the Revolution before he began the detailed study of its sources. Having formed it, he sought for confirmation. Like so many amateurs he trusts too much to memoirs, and surrenders himself unreservedly to the guidance of Gouverneur Morris and Mallet du Pan. He swallows every scrap of hostile evidence. He con- densed and translated a volume purporting to contain the ex- periences of an English lady in France during the Terror, but more probably the work of John Gifford, an extreme anti-Jacobin of low character. By following his footsteps in the archives Aulard discovered how superficial was his research and how unscientific his method. He dipped into the bundles to find confirmation for his views and tears passages from their context. He only makes use of two newspapers, the *Moniteur*, the authority of which has been overthrown, and the *Mercure*, because Mallet du Pan wrote in it. Scherer remarked that he had plunged into the ocean of documents and been drowned. He collected a mass of details, many of them insignificant, while omitting matters of vital importance. It is his method, not his verdict, which leads Aulard to declare that the work is virtually useless for the purposes of history.

'For forty years,' wrote Taine in 1891, 'my work has been nothing but pure or applied psychology.' He wrote his 'Origines' in the same practical spirit in which he aided the École libre des Sciences Politiques. 'We want to fill with facts, figures, and documents, the heads which, if empty, would harbour Utopias.' He did his best to supply such instruction; but no teacher can help his countrymen by proclaiming a gospel of discouragement and despair, and no prophet can regenerate the State without faith in God or man. He held that where organised Christianity disappears public and private morals decay, but though he came to regard it as socially indispensable it remained for him intellectually incredible. He rejects alike the Church, the Ancien Régime, the Revolution, Napoleon, modern democracy. 'If the future wishes to understand the soul of France on the morrow of the Franco-German war, it will open this book, which in its despairing pages prolongs and renews the cry of the vanquished.'[1]

While Taine was thus engaged, his friend Albert Sorel[2] was at work on 'Europe and the French Revolution.' He possessed a far deeper knowledge of history and a more judicial mind, and his place as an historian is incomparably higher. After studying law in Paris the young Norman, on Guizot's advice, entered the Foreign Office, and when the conflict of 1870 broke out he displayed skill and judgment in drafting diplomatic documents. After the war, though Gambetta wished him to become Political Director of the Foreign Office, he withdrew from active diplomatic work. He threw himself into the life of the École libre des Sciences Politiques at the invitation of Boutmy, and, next to the founder, was the soul of the school for thirty years. His first important book, 'The Diplomatic History of the War,' contained despatches of some of which he was himself the author. But the main occupation of his life was the diplomatic history of the revolutionary period. The first-fruits of his studies appeared in the *Revue Historique* in detailed articles on the Treaty of Basel, the mission of Custine to Brunswick, and other aspects of

---

[1] Hanotaux.

[2] See Picot, 'Notice sur Sorel,' in *Séances de l'Académie des Sciences morales et politiques*, 1907; Boutmy, *Études politiques*, 1907; Monod in *Revue Historique*, vol. xcii.; *Discours à la fête en honneur de Sorel*, 1905, on completing his great work. There is a good article on the book in *Quarterly Review*, Oct. 1907.

international relations. The plan gradually arose in his mind of a comprehensive study of the struggle between Europe and the Revolution. His object was to exhibit the Revolution, which appeared to some the subversion and to others the regeneration of the old world, as the natural result of the history of France and Europe. Tocqueville had found the model of the internal policy of the Revolution in the reigns of Louis XIV and Louis XV. Sorel announced that in their foreign policy the revolutionists were the direct heirs of the Monarchy.

The first volume, the most novel and striking of the whole work, analyses the political methods and ideas of the eighteenth century. Europe was morally bankrupt. In his book on the Eastern Question Sorel had already brought a severe indictment against the Philosophic Despots. 'It has often been said abroad, and even repeated in France, that the Revolution and Napoleon upset the law of nations, and substituted for a kind of golden age of diplomacy, where right ruled without a rival, an age of iron in which might prevailed against all rights. To judge fairly we must know what was the conception of right and the practice of the representatives of the Ancien Régime.' The book revealed that in the partition of Poland Frederick the Great, Catherine II and Joseph II recognised no law but their selfish interests. These were the three Courts which were later to attack the Revolution, and France merely adopted the principles on which they had acted. A second reason for the decrepitude of old Europe lay in the reform movement which invaded every country during the eighteenth century. The ruin of ancient institutions left the throne isolated, the spread of rationalism encouraged men to challenge tradition, and the sweeping changes inaugurated by the Philosophic Despots led to further unsettlement. A revolution appeared inevitable in almost every country, and it broke out in Belgium earlier than in France. A third solvent was the pervading influence of French ideas and manners. For the first time since the Middle Ages there was a distinct community of ideas, but the fountainhead was no longer Rome but Paris. After analysing the weakness of Europe, he proceeds to show how the old régime in France prepared the way for the Revolution. Autocracy anticipated the omnipotence of the Chamber; Gallicanism pointed to the Constitution Civile; the persecution of the Protestants provided a working model for the attack on the Émigrés; the *journées* anticipated the *coups* of the Revolution; Richelieu and Louis XIV gave France a taste for dictatorship and founded the tradition of conquest. Thus both at home and abroad the weapons were ready for use.

Having thus set the Revolution in the main stream of European development, he proceeds to sketch its early stages and its effect on foreign opinion. He recognises the nobility of the ideas with which the leaders set out, but they soon began to play the rôle of conquerors and to demand the 'natural frontiers.' He never forgets the importance of individuals, but he believed in the compulsion of collective and hereditary tendencies. While the nation craved a strong government, the timid ministers of a timid King led it to anarchy. Thus power naturally passed to those who had a policy and were not afraid to act. Sorel is one of the fairest of historians. He is equally free from the bitterness of Sybel and Taine and from the lyrical transports of Michelet and Louis Blanc. He does full justice to the better side of the revolutionists, and never forgets the staggering difficulties by which they were confronted. He does not scoff at the Declaration of the Rights of Man, but he contests its practical value. He is fair to the Émigrés, distinguishing the earlier *intransigeants*, who endeavoured to arm Europe against their country, from the later, who were the victims of persecution. He is just to the Court, censuring its policy but comprehending its instincts. He emphasises the guarded character of the Declaration of Pillnitz and the essential moderation of the Emperor Leopold.

The third and fourth volumes deal with the war, defensive and offensive, and its relation to domestic policy. He agrees with Sybel that the Powers were too busy planning the destruction of Poland to desire a life-and-death struggle with France. But Marie Antoinette laboured to stir up war, Austria threatened to interfere in Avignon, and the King of Prussia prepared a plan of invasion before the French declaration of hostilities. He ascribes the direct responsibility to the Girondins, though the explosive forces of the Revolution and the old instinct of aggrandisement prepared the way. But his sympathies are none the less with his country in the conflict, for the integrity of national territory and the maintenance of the priceless conquests of the Revolution were at stake. Even when the French armies assume the offensive his blessing at first goes with them. In demanding the Rhine as a frontier they were only renewing the traditional policy of the Monarchy. To defend this frontier they needed to create a ring of tributary States. Thus the conquest of Belgium was justified, but that of Holland was not. He exhibits the intimate connection between the danger on the frontier and the worst excesses in Paris. Thus the advance of the armies and the Brunswick manifesto led to the September massacres; the execution of the King, as Danton said, was a reply to foreign dictation; the immolation of the Girondins followed the treason of Dumouriez. He acquits the leaders of Taine's ridiculous charge of being the slaves of certain abstract principles, and shows how their conduct is explained by their determination to resist the restoration of the old régime and to defend the frontiers; but he none the less sharply censures their excesses. He returns to the sound national tradition in supporting the principles of 1789 and condemning the Terror. Taine declared that while working at the Revolution he felt himself to be in a madhouse. Sorel's figures are human beings, oscillating between motives, built of the same stuff as other men. 'Taine,' comments Hanotaux in an eloquent passage, 'only sees the blood dropping from the scaffold; Sorel sees it spread over the battlefield to save the country and fertilise Europe. The Revolution made the national and democratic Europe in which we live.'

Sorel's judgment of the Revolution is not more admirable than his literary art. Dr. Trevelyan[1] salutes him as the modern Thucydides. The canvas is vast, but there is no confusion or prolixity. He excels equally in the analysis of ideas, the refinements of diplomacy, the portraits of men and women. The book breathes a deep though restrained patriotism, a chastened optimism, a wide tolerance. His researches, continuing and in part superseding Sybel, threw a flood of light on foreign policy and indirectly on the internal situation. Tocqueville connected the Revolution with the history of France, Sorel with the history of Europe. His book is at once the first adequate study of the Revolution as an international event and one of the fairest judgments of it as an episode in French history.

III

Though generations of students had laboured at the Revolution, its documentary exploration was pursued on a more comprehensive scale during the last quarter of the nineteenth century. After attracting attention by a work on the revolutionary orators, Aulard was promoted from Poitiers to a Chair of the History of the French Revolution founded for him at the Sorbonne in 1885 by the Municipal Council of Paris.[2] The Revolution, he declared in his inaugural lecture in 1886, did not begin in 1789 nor did it end in 1815. All the past prepared and announced it,

---

[1] An Autobiography and other Essays, 76, 1949.
[2] See La Révolution Française, No. 81, 1928 (Memorial Number); Georges Belloni, Aulard Historien de la Révolution Française, 1949, which warmly praises the man and the patriot no less than the historian; and Some Historians of Modern Europe, ed. Bernadotte E. Schmitt, ch. 3, 1941.

and its life continued both in the world of facts and in the souls of Frenchmen. 'Without sympathy one only sees the surface. To understand it one must love it. I am a respectful and grateful son of the Revolution which has emancipated humanity and science.' Hardly a third or a quarter of the documents had been even catalogued, much less studied. Its diplomacy was only beginning to be known. The economic history had still to be written, and the life of the assemblies and clubs to be reconstructed from the official records. This programme was carried out with extraordinary energy by the Professor and his pupils, who founded the Société de l'Histoire de la Révolution and took over the monthly review *La Révolution Française*. Of Aulard's own editorial enterprises the most important relate to the Jacobin Club and the Committee of Public Safety. Though the official record of the discussions of the club had disappeared, he reconstructed its history in six volumes from the newspapers and pamphlets of the time. He shows how it grew out of the Breton Club at Versailles, and how its members, far from being mere automata mouthing the formulæ of Jean Jacques, were in turn monarchists, Girondins and Montagnards. The work on the Committee of Public Safety was facilitated by the preservation of the register of discussions and resolutions. Greater difficulties arose in connection with the correspondence of the Representatives on Mission; but he collected a vast mass of material. These twenty-six volumes show the Committee at work, and reveal the full extent of the internal and external difficulties by which it was confronted. Among his other notable documentary enterprises are 'Paris after Thermidor,' 'Paris under the Consulate,' and 'Paris under the First Empire,' in which the reports of the police are largely employed.

Aulard's work as an editor is recognised on all hands to be critical and conscientious, and the writings in which he conveys the results of the researches of himself and his pupils have profoundly modified current views of the Revolution. The volumes entitled 'Lectures and Studies on the Revolution' illustrate many aspects of political, ecclesiastical and diplomatic history. It was not till 1902, after more than twenty years' study of the original authorities, that he ventured on a large narrative work in his 'Political History of the French Revolution.' The sub-title is 'Origins and Development of Democracy and the Republic.' He merely glances at the momentous events of the first three years. He has little to say of the Court, finance, economic conditions, diplomacy and war. His theme is the evolution and application of the two governing principles of the Revolution, the sovereignty of the people and equality. He shows how small a part was played by abstract ideas, though perhaps he allows too little place to the elements of passion and to the velocity of unchained instincts. The most striking novelty is the demonstration of the late origin of the republican idea. Champion's summary of the Cahiers had revealed the surprising moderation of the demands of 1789. No one except Brissot and Condorcet asked for a republic till the autumn of 1790, and the Legislative was as monarchical as the Constituent. The monarchy was overthrown, not by republicans, but by its own intrigues. The second contention is that the horrors of 1792–4 were due, not to 'Jacobin psychology,' but to the necessity of repelling the invader and of safeguarding the reforms already achieved. His thesis is that men who believed in the principles of 1789 and were grimly determined to uphold them acted exactly as might have been expected. Without defending the September massacres, he explains the state of mind from which they grew—the whole achievement of the Revolution at stake, the allied armies advancing towards Paris, the boasts of Royalist prisoners that their triumph was at hand. They were not the work of the Government nor of any responsible authority, but the instinctive action of a section of the Paris populace in face of a sudden and overwhelming danger. The interpretation of the Terror is of a similar character. The men of 1793 were the custodians of the Revolution and of the national territory. Against their excesses and cruelties must be set the supreme achievement that they saved France both from the return of the Ancien Régime and from invasion. No wonder he was the friend of Clemenceau, Jaurès and Anatole France. While Napoleon, he declared, had done more harm than good and his legend had been a curse, the Revolution had done far more good than harm.

Gratitude for the preservation of the Revolution in no way involves enthusiasm for all its champions. Marat with his dream of dictatorship and Robespierre with his State religion were reactionaries, and the latter treacherously murdered his magnanimous comrade, 'the great and good Danton.' Danton towers above his rivals, and many pages in the 'Études et Leçons' are devoted to his career. In an early sketch he rashly pronounced him irreproachable in public and private life, and declared that no figure of the Revolution was more moral, more human, more pure in regard to money or more free from hate. The real hero, however, is the people, and the credit for guiding the Revolution does not belong to Paris alone. The provinces chose the Constituent Assembly, organised the federation of

1790, and created the republican party in 1792. After the decisive victories of 1789 a rift began between the bourgeoisie and the masses, and Aulard's sympathies are with the latter. It was owing to them that the Revolution did not stop with the political changes of 1789 and that it came to mean a charter of emancipation for the toilers of the world. The Directory was a mere bourgeois republic and commenced the reaction, while the forward movement was completely checked by Napoleon. Self-government came to an end, and the separation of Church and State, which had worked well, was terminated by the Concordat. A great lassitude settled down on all classes, for liberty was dead. The merits of the work are conspicuous.[1] It is written with a mastery of the sources that no historian had ever approached, and ho makes the whole drama intelligible. But he is a partisan. His dislike of monarchy, feudalism and the State Church is only equalled by his gratitude to their destroyers. Jules Simon acidly described him as 'Professor of Revolution.' No other first class historian has come so near justifying the Terror as a patriotic necessity. The militant rationalist could not judge the Catholic opposition fairly. While Taine proclaimed that men are naturally bad and that the best are in the higher classes, Aulard, like Michelet and Jaurès, teaches that they are naturally good and that the most worthy are to be found at the bottom of the ladder.

Though Aulard was the greatest living authority on the Revolution at the turn of the century, valuable work was accomplished by many other scholars. Chuquet's[2] 'Guerres de la Révolution,' in eleven small volumes, is based on the archives of the War Office and the depots of the districts which formed the arena of the war, on newspapers and memoirs, and on a careful study of the ground. 'I have tried to make myself the contemporary of the combatants and to live with them in their camps. I have not written a party work.' He agrees with Sybel and Sorel that the Declaration of Pillnitz did not involve hostilities, but it was taken by France as a threat. 'The Prussian invasion unchained the Revolution and precipitated it on Europe.' The struggle was bound to come, and France and Europe were jointly responsible. 'How can we have declared war?' exclaimed Lafayette; 'we are ready in nothing.' Confusion, jealousies and distrust abounded; yet the soldiers were devoted to the Revolution, which opened military rank to the humblest privates. The

---

[1] A penetrating analysis is to be found in Faguet's *Discussions politiques*, 1909. Powerful criticisms came from Wahl, *Hist. Vierteljahrschrift*, 1902, and Glagau, *Hist. Zeitschrift*, 1903.

[2] There is a sketch of Chuquet in Bamberger's *Charakteristiken*, 1894.

Prussian army was in no better condition, and Brunswick disliked the invasion and expected it to fail. The succeeding volumes review the battles and campaigns from Valmy to Hondschoote. A serene impartiality marks the work. He fully appreciates the better qualities of Brunswick. He is more indulgent than Sorel to Dumouriez and Custine. The volume on Hoche traces the gradual refining of a rough and uneducated man. He recalls how Saint-Just restored discipline and confidence in the army. While honouring the heroism of the soldiers, he does not hesitate to condemn their excesses. Though war is his main theme, the author is equally at home in politics. The volume on Jemappes is accompanied by a survey of the revolution in Belgium, that on Mayence by a picture of the German Jacobins.

The social and economic history of the Revolution has been the object of increasing study during recent years.[1] A Commission de l'histoire de la Révolution, founded in 1903 at the instance of Jaurès, who remained its President till his death in 1914, undertook the publication of the Cahiers, which, when completed, will form a small library. The six volumes, published in the 'Archives Parlementaires' at the end of the Second Empire, neglected the documents of the villages, which are more valuable than the ambitious efforts of the three estates, often drawn up by lawyers and in many cases copied from models with a few local additions. A second task is the collection of data relating to the property of the Church and the Émigrés and to the royal domain. A third is to trace the stages of the abolition of feudal rights. The condition of the peasantry attracted the attention of Kovalevsky and other Russian scholars, and received detailed treatment in the socialist presentations of the Revolution by Jaurès and Kropotkin. Finance, from Turgot and Necker to the end of the Convention, was explored by Gomel, while Sagnac summarised civil legislation. Aulard and Mathiez have thrown light on the revolutionary sects, and La Gorce has described in detail the grievous trials of the Church from the standpoint of a Catholic Royalist. Chassin collected a mass of material relating to the risings in the Vendée, and Ernest Daudet followed the footsteps of the Émigrés. The immense success of the scholarly anecdotage of Lenotre shows that the attraction of the personal side of the Revolution is undiminished. But the main feature of recent research is the displacement of the picturesque by the study of conditions and ideas, not in the capital alone but throughout France.

[1] See Boissonade, *Les Études relatives à l'histoire économique de la Révolution Française*, 1906.

CHAPTER XIII

NAPOLEON

I

THE unbribed intellect of France opposed the author of the *coup d'état* of 1851, and its hostility is reflected in the historical literature of the period. The character and achievements of the first Napoleon[1] became a battle-cry, and strenuous efforts were made by friends and foes of the new régime to advance their principles under cover of historical research. The method favoured by the Bonapartists was the publication of new material. Baron du Casse, aide-de-camp to King Jerome, published the 'Memoirs and Correspondence of King Joseph,' followed by similar works on Eugène Beauharnais, Jerome and other members of the Imperial family. The Correspondence of Joseph suggested to Napoleon the Little an important resolution. Why should not the entire correspondence of the founder of the dynasty be collected and printed? As the work was too vast for a single editor, a Commission was appointed, on which the Imperial family was represented by Prince Napoleon and Walewski and scholarship by Sainte-Beuve. The work was completed in thirty-two volumes shortly before the downfall of its patron, and a magnificent *édition de luxe* was printed for presentations. Over a million francs had been spent on the rehabilitation of Napoleon. This immense work,[2] revealing his life almost day by day from Toulon to St. Helena, at once took its place as the foundation of serious study. For the first time it was possible to survey the whole activity of the diplomat, the soldier and the administrator, the principles of his government, the relations with his family, the lights and shadows of his character. To no ruler except Frederick the Great has such a monument been raised. But it was undertaken in the interest of the dynasty, not of historical science, and many letters of the highest importance were omitted. It purported to include everything which had not already appeared and

[1] There is a brief summary of Napoleonic studies by Driault in *Revue des Études Napoléoniennes*, vol. i., 1912. Geyl, *Napoleon: For or Against?* (translated from the Dutch, 1949) analyses the chief works of French historians.

[2] See the chapter, 'La Correspondance de Napoléon,' in Prince Napoleon, *Napoléon et ses détracteurs*, 1887.

which was not too trivial to print, and it was not till the appearance of supplementary volumes under the Third Republic that the dishonest character of the editing was realised.

The later volumes of Thiers went far to discount the hero-worship of the earlier, and no writer of standing came forth to acclaim the uncle of the reigning sovereign. The enemies of the dynasty, on the other hand, were active. Count d'Haussonville showed that, though the Concordat was useful to the Church, it was not indispensable, as Catholicism had already revived and the Churches were open. While the Church acquired little that it did not already possess, the civil power gained much, and the Organic Articles were fetters on the Pope and clergy. Thus the much-lauded Concordat was rather the subordination of the Church to the Imperial power than a concession to the religious feelings of the nation. When it was discovered that the author was hostile he was forbidden access to the archives, which were opened to Theiner in order to re-establish the claim of Napoleon to be the restorer of religion.

The most powerful blow was struck by one of the ablest of the journalists to whom the Second Empire was anathema. The *coup d'état* filled Lanfrey[1] with indignation and determined his life. He hated the régime with the undying hatred of Victor Hugo and Quinet; but he recognised that the responsibility did not rest on the reigning Emperor alone. If the 'History of Napoleon' did not produce the explosive effect of Lamartine's 'Girondins,' it none the less contributed to the downfall of the Second Empire. The austere Liberal allows no extenuating circumstances. The idol is swept contemptuously from its pedestal and trampled into a thousand fragments. Brumaire was the brutal overthrow of such liberty as had been left by the Jacobins. The Concordat was concluded solely in order to strengthen his own power. Pichegru was strangled by his orders. The Emperor married Marie Louise from vanity and because he wished to exchange an old for a young wife. The debt of the Code to the First Consul is a legend. The Legion of Honour was an instrument of self-aggrandisement. The crossing of the St. Bernard was no great achievement. Marengo was a defeat for the First Consul, a victory for Desaix. His foes, Madame de Stael, Hofer, Schill, Wellington, the Spaniards, are exalted. Their desertion of the tyrant softens the verdict on Fouché and Talleyrand.

[1] See the biography prefixed to the *Correspondance de Lanfrey*, 2 vols., 1883. For appreciations see Charmes, *Études historiques et diplomatiques*, 1893; J. Reinach, *Études de Littérature et d'Histoire*, 1889; Lot, in *Revue Historique*, vol. i.; and La Gorce, *Histoire du Second Empire*, v., 451-2.

A work such as this, half history, half pamphlet, could not aspire to a permanent place in literature. Napoleon is made to carry the burden of his nephew's sins as well as his own. Lanfrey's Napoleon is an ogre, not a human being. Such a portrait fails to explain the enthusiasm which greeted his accession to power and the immense hold he possessed on the admiration and loyalty of France for many years. The book is scarcely stronger in research than in judgment. His principal source was the newly published correspondence of the Emperor, and he was too ready to use such untrustworthy material as the Memoirs of Bourrienne and Fouché. On the other hand his narrative of the Spanish adventure was a real contribution to history, and his discovery that a letter to Murat, published in the Correspondence, was forged by Napoleon himself at a later date cleared up a difficult problem. The book has been compared to a searching north wind; both the manner and the matter suggest a bleak day in autumn when the leaves are falling. A fifth volume appeared in 1874, but its popularity in France ceased with its utility as a party weapon. Thiers' work was a panoramic survey of a period, Lanfrey's a splenetic attack on an individual. The work of the statesman, with all its faults, has outlived that of the journalist.

The indignation excited by Lanfrey's book among the admirers of the First Empire was partly modified by the knowledge that the primary object of attack was Louis Napoleon. Thiers forgave his critic and sent him to Berne as Minister of the Third Republic. Taine's[1] missile, on the other hand, discharged many years after the death of the exile at Chislehurst, was aimed at the first Napoleon alone. His book is not a biography but a psychological study. Unlike Lanfrey, he recognises to the full the transcendant genius of the man. He adopts Madame de Stael's verdict that he was more and less than a man. With his hatred of confusion, bloodshed and despotism it was natural that Taine should detest the heir of the Revolution and the greatest autocrat of modern times, but his readers were surprised at the unrelieved shadows of the portrait. Like Lanfrey he finds no mark of humanity. Tradition, he declares, was nothing to him. He was neither royalist nor Jacobin. He lived in utter moral isolation. The only signs of feeling were prompted by the death of his marshals, and they were soon forgotten. From beginning to end he was dominated by an overmastering egoism. He regarded human beings as objects, not fellow-creatures. He was like a hunter in pursuit of his prey. Principles, affection, gratitude, patriotism, had no meaning for him, and he believed that they

[1] See references at page 225.

had no meaning for others. He trembled with terror at Brumaire. He was mean, petty, vulgar, utterly lacking in self-control and self-respect, with the worst faults of the parvenu. He was restless, loquacious, explosive, almost epileptic. Ordinary social intercourse with him was impossible, and men who feared nothing else in the world trembled when he approached. He told Josephine of his amours, and we cannot be certain that he did not seduce his sisters. Under other circumstances he would have been a convict and the princesses prostitutes. Beneath the Imperial robes we see the naked animal.

It is a revolting picture, and Taine is aware that at first sight it may be difficult to accept. The difficulty, however, is removed by the application of a master-key: he belonged neither to his age nor country. He was an Italian of the Renaissance, a *condottiere* born out of due time, a contemporary of the Malatestas and the Borgias. That he caused the death of two or three million men and left France shorn of the fifteen departments acquired by the Republic seemed to the Bonapartists less damaging than the assertion that he was not a Frenchman. The portrait suffers from the same incurable disability as the study of the Jacobins. Taine allows nothing for the evolution of character and ideas under the pressure of events. The lieutenant of artillery is the same man as the exile of St. Helena. If there were no other fault the portrait would be worthless. But it is equally opposed to the sources. 'Ce qui manque,' commented Jules Lemaître[1] when the volume appeared, 'c'est la silhouette du petit caporal.' His pages are filled with quotations from Madame de Rémusat and Miot de Mélito, while friendly witnesses like Méneval and Mollien are rarely called. He accepts anecdotes of doubtful authenticity, attributes incidents to writers by whom they are not recorded, and combines passages from letters to different people.

The volume fell like a bomb in the Bonapartist camp. Princess Mathilde, in whose salon Taine had been for many years an honoured guest, shut her doors upon him. Her brother, Prince Napoleon,[2] came forward to defend the memory of his uncle and the outraged dignity of the dynasty in 'Napoleon and his Detractors.' Taine's book, he declared, was a libel from beginning to end. He was an entomologist, intended by nature to classify and describe collections of insects with pins through their heads. He greedily accepted the tittle-tattle which gathers round a conspicuous figure, and had nothing to say of Napoleon as the

---

[1] 'Taine et Bonaparte,' in *Les Contemporains*, vol. iv.
[2] A biography is urgently needed. There is a good sketch of this able but unattractive person in Spuller's *Figures disparues*, vol. ii.

greatest general who ever lived or of the heroic struggle of France against the armed might of Europe. The Prince proceeds to discredit his chief informants. Bourrienne was a venal wretch, treated by his master with culpable indulgence, and his Memoirs contain additions by another hand. Madame de Rémusat's real view of the Emperor is enshrined in her contemporary letters, filled with admiration and gratitude. Her original memoirs were burned, and those we possess were written under the Restoration. Miot de Mélito knew the Emperor but little, and it is doubtful if the memoirs bearing his name were his work. The Prince closes with an impassioned rhapsody on his uncle as the heir of the Revolution, free alike from selfishness and ambition, the incarnation of the glory of France, the knight without fear and without reproach. The volume spoke with the voice of dynastic loyalty, not of historical scholarship. That such conflicting portraits could be painted showed that the study of the Emperor was still in its infancy. The superman, indeed, had never passed out of politics. Under the July Monarchy the tide of feeling ran strongly in his favour, under the Second Empire strongly against him. Thiers was a politician, Lanfrey a journalist, Taine a philosopher. Historians had devoted far less attention to the Empire than to the Revolution, and it was not till the last decade of the century that it became possible to know Napoleon as he was.

II

No writer has done more to reveal Napoleon's personality or worshipped him with more passionate devotion than Frédéric Masson.[1] As a child he had heard stories from the veterans of the Grand Army and had felt their scars with his fingers. When France turned her back on the dynasty, he came forward with his services. He became the friend of the Prince Imperial, the literary counsellor of Prince Napoleon and Princess Mathilde. 'I have sung the same song for thirty years,' he wrote in 1906. 'The idea of Napoleon is not one of those one takes up and drops at will and with which one amuses leisure hours. It is dominating, absorbing, tyrannical. Haunted by what will doubtless appear a form of delirium, I finger with delight the papers on which his name is inscribed, I shiver before his writing, I intoxicate myself with his glory. I feel the same satisfaction in unmasking a man who betrayed him as a detective in arresting an assassin.' After assisting Prince Napoleon with his reply to Taine, he began to

[1] See Sorel, *Notes et Portraits* 1909, and Geyl, *Napoleon: For or Against?* 177–209.

pour forth the endless sequence of volumes for which he had long been collecting material. He commenced with a study of Napoleon and the Fair Sex, which was hardly calculated to raise the moral reputation of the hero. Some Bonapartists having attacked him for his revelation of the Emperor's weaknesses, he pointed out that this was only the first volume of a long series. 'I shall dedicate my life to him, for everything has shown me more and more that his history has still to be written. To get to the root of the matter I have endeavoured to envisage the man, the son, the husband, the lover, the father, the brother. The more deeply one studies his history, the greater does one's admiration for him become. One can do his memory no greater service than by making known the facts of his life. He was a being in whom his fellow-men can recognise a brother, for he shared the emotions common to mankind.'

The volume to which this rhapsody serves as preface is typical of all Masson's work. His devotion never leads him to suppress disagreeable facts. His position resembles that of the Catholic who admits blemishes in his Church, but never doubts its divine character. He marshals a formidable array of frail beauties on the stage, and suggests that behind them stands a crowd of the unknown and the unnamed. The most attractive chapter is devoted to Madame Walewska, the most disinterested woman who ever crossed Napoleon's path and the only one whom he really loved after Josephine's disloyalty had cooled his passion. Masson does not consider that any defence of the hero is required. He assures us that he confined himself for the most part to women to whom virtue meant nothing, that he paid them handsomely, and that he never allowed love to conflict with business. Indeed by a bold stroke he almost claims Napoleon's amorous adventures as a further proof of his superiority to other men. 'There was not a note in the gamut of human passion that he did not sound. He had as great a faculty for love as for thought or action, and was no less extraordinary as lover and husband than as warrior and statesman.' The success of the book was immense. The theme was of universal interest, the style was easy and flowing, the mastery of fact obvious on every page. Yet critics called attention to the complete lack of references, a complaint repeated on the publication of each successive volume. The author's defence has always been that many documents had been given him under the pledge of secrecy, that large numbers were in his own possession, and that his readers could trust his good faith. Though his good faith is not in doubt, it is his own fault that his fame is less secure in the study than in the salon.

The second volume of the elaborate portrait to which Masson had dedicated his life was entitled 'Napoléon chez lui.' The chief need of the time, he declared, was for minute details and an exact foundation. 'I, being suspected of having hypnotised myself with Napoleon, must beyond all others abstain from polemic and expressions of personal convictions.' This self-denying ordinance does not apply to prefaces, for he proceeds to denounce the tendencies of the day. 'The nation has now reached such a pass that only the religion of the Emperor can console it and rehabilitate it in its own eyes. He was the Revolution in its sublimity, the Fatherland in its sacredness. France has slept for eighty years, a prey to rhetoricians and placemen.' Happily there were signs of better times. Prince Napoleon's reply to Taine awoke the dormant passion for the mighty dead, and Marbot's Memoirs had awakened in all hearts a generous love for him (Celui) who for twenty years strove for France. When we reach the volume itself the historian keeps his word and gives us an objective picture of the daily life of the hero. We learn who were his valets, his secretaries, his doctors, and how he treated them; how he made his toilette, ate his meals and dictated his letters; how he talked at receptions and attended mass on Sundays; how the Austrian marriage brought a stiffening of etiquette and separated the Emperor still further from ordinary mortals. It is a picture of the ordered and methodical activity of one of the greatest workers who ever lived.

The next stage in the journey, though of less universal interest, was of greater importance to Napoleonic students. The young Napoleon was revealed to the world in 'Napoléon Inconnu' in 1895. On the eve of the second abdication the Emperor had taken out a bundle of papers and written on it 'To Cardinal Fesch.' The *dossier* found its way to Florence, where it rested till it was discovered by Biagi and published by him and Masson. The packet was found to contain Napoleon's early writings, letters, extracts from books, reflections and observations. The two volumes are filled with documents, accompanied by a biographical commentary. Masson exaggerates the interest of the early compositions; but though they offer no foundation for a picture of precocious intelligence, they show that he read widely and with care.

On the completion of 'Napoléon Inconnu' Masson entered on two large tasks, the execution of which ran parallel for many years. The first was to portray as husband and father, the second to trace his relations to the Bonaparte family. The former consists of five volumes, the first three of which are devoted to Josephine, the fourth to Marie Louise, and the fifth to the King of Rome. A Beauharnais legend had grown up, he declared, and it was therefore necessary to tell the truth and reveal her failings. The first volume relates her early fortunes, and exhibits the levity of 'the poor little Creole.' She was badly educated, her husband was a man of lax character, and the uncertainty of the future made her live for pleasure. The second volume, 'Joséphine Impératrice,' shows the same woman, frivolous, sensual and idle. While Napoleon was filled with a deep and passionate devotion for her, she laughed at his transports and lived in open adultery. He was unfaithful to her only after she had been unfaithful to him. Her extravagance was incurable and was the subject of constant friction with her economical master. She filled her place as wife of the First Consul with fair success, but she was never the Empress, and though she made herself agreeable she was never respected. The busy idleness of her life suggests the cruel phrase that she was something of the harem wife. All witnesses agree as to her affability and voluptuous grace, but she had no culture, no moral rule. The third volume, 'Joséphine répudiée,' deals fully with the divorce. Neither husband nor wife, declares Masson, ever thought their marriage really binding; and when he returned from Egypt, enraged by her infidelities, he had firmly resolved to divorce her. The pleadings of her children postponed the project; but his desire for an assured succession and the birth of a son to Countess Walewska finally determined him to take the step he had so long contemplated. The parting was affectionate, visits and correspondence continued, Eugène and Hortense remained attached to their step-father, and Josephine took a friendly interest in the King of Rome. It was the nemesis of such a butterfly existence that in the lifelong pursuit of pleasure she never found happiness.

Napoleon's second wife was a mere passive agent of other men's wills. While some Bonapartists have denounced her for treachery to her husband and to France, Masson rightly refuses to judge her as if she were French. Only a few of the hundreds of letters exchanged between the Imperial pair have survived, but despite this irreparable loss he draws a vivid and not unsympathetic picture. She was devoted to her father and soon became genuinely attached to her husband, who treated her with marked kindness. A change took place in the atmosphere of the Court. Etiquette was stiffened. The superman gave more time to meals, played games with her in the evening, saw fewer people, opened fewer letters, and worked less strenuously. When the days of trial came it was arranged that she should go to Vienna to regain her

health and join her husband in Elba. Correspondence continued
for a time, then suddenly ceased. The fallen despot attributed her
conduct to the Austrian Court, and continued to speak affec-
tionately of her till death. Masson believes that he never knew of
Neipperg. Marie Louise played her part as well as anyone had a
right to expect from a commonplace woman confronted with a
destiny to which she was unequal. The closing volume of the series
is devoted to the King of Rome. Napoleon, supreme as a lover,
was no less unique as a father. 'Paternal love such as his has never
been seen so powerful in any human being.' From the birth of
his son his whole thought was directed to his successor, and when
his own fall was assured he struggled to save the dynasty. The
mixture of love and dynastic ambition was fatal to the Empire.
Napoleon's *raison d'être* was the Revolution. 'The day when,
forgetting his point of departure and his mission, he thought
himself legitimate, the day he denied the Revolution, legitimism
devoured him and his Empire, his dynasty and his heir.'

Masson's largest and most important work, 'Napoléon et sa
Famille,' contains the most damning indictment of his brothers
and sisters ever penned. No one had ever attempted to trace in
detail the influence of his affections on his policy and fortunes.
The weakest as well as the most attractive feature of his character
was his tenderness for his family, his perpetual indulgence for
their faults, his illusions as to their merits. The contrast between
Joseph, idle but dignified, and Lucien, ambitious but undisci-
plined, is finely drawn, while the escapades of Caroline and
Pauline prepare us for their gallantries on a larger stage. Except
Louise, they were all greedy of money, their mother among
them. As prosperity increased, their utter mediocrity became
manifest to every one except the architect of their fortunes. But
though Napoleon only learned when it was too late that he was
leaning on broken reeds, he soon became aware of their moral
failings. 'You talk,' he remarked with biting irony, 'as if I had
dissipated the patrimony of the late King, our father.' By the
side of these grasping intriguers the children of Josephine shine
with a bright and steady effulgence, Hortense affectionate and
womanly, Eugène loyal and disinterested.

Joseph, Louis and Jerome became Kings, and Caroline a
Queen. The Empire became a family institution. Lucien, who
possessed genuine ability, was in disgrace, and the indolent
Pauline was too occupied with her gallantries and her jewels to
care for power. Elisa, handicapped by her ridiculous husband,
never became a star of the first magnitude. Joseph played his
part in Naples and Spain with statuesque inefficiency, while

Louis, morbid, obstinate and suspicious, stoutly resisted dictation in Holland. Jerome, the spoilt child of the family, without mind or morals, played the lord of misrule at Cassel. Caroline, dominated by restless ambition, kept her eyes steadily fixed on the succession for her husband or her son. But despite his perpetual disappointments the Emperor continued to believe that no political alliance was likely to be stable unless cemented by a family tie. The family system might have served in fair weather but when storms arose it was doomed to shipwreck. While anti-Bonapartist historians applaud the courage with which Louis defended his Dutch subjects against exploitation, Masson charges him with ingratitude to the author of his fortunes. The Empire, he contends, could only be maintained if the orders of its founder were loyally executed, and Napoleon had no choice but to depose his recalcitrant satrap and to incorporate Holland in French territory.

When a legitimate heir was born, the family system appeared less essential; but with the chance of succession gone, the main reason for the fidelity of the King and Queen of Naples disappeared. Masson believes that they began to intrigue with Napoleon's enemies as early as 1811, and suggests that they were also influenced by the nationalist secret societies of Italy. When the Emperor learned their treachery, his surprise and indignation knew no bounds. The defection of Bernadotte, Jomini and Moreau was a scandal, but the treason of Murat and Caroline appears to the historian an unspeakable crime. When the Empire begins to crumble, Masson's admiration for the hero is in no way diminished. Fatal errors of tactics were committed, but his faith in military autocracy remains unshaken. The volume on St. Helena is as much an indictment of England as a glorification of the demigod. 'If I hand on the torch of passion that I have received, I shall be satisfied; and if my picture of Napoleon gives wings to a salutary ambition, how proud shall I be. Let the Liberator come! Let him sweep away the parliamentary orgy where Circe presides, where the pigs, rolling in mud and blood, pursue their quarrels.' France lost the hegemony of Europe which she had possessed for two centuries, and England took it. For its recovery another Napoleon is needed. 'He is the incarnation of national policy, as old as France herself. He understands all her interests, knows all her needs, shares all her aspirations, defends all her rights.' Few readers will adopt his view of the hero, and indeed the bias is so obvious that it loses its dangers.[1] But, to do

[1] His views are conveniently summarised in his volume, *Sur Napoléon, Huit Conférences*, 1909.

him justice, there is little special pleading in his works. He does not attempt, like Arthur Lévy, to prove that in the conventional sense he was a good man. He admits that the seizure of Enghien was a violation of the law of nations, and that the family system, on which he built his Empire, was a mistake. It may be doubted if his principal work has served the Bonapartist cause, for readers may ask themselves whether the detestable family was not too high a price to pay for the hero.

Vandal,[1] the second of the triumvirate who engineered the revival of Napoleonic studies in France, was less productive than Masson, but his work is of higher quality. The policy of France in Eastern Europe, the subject of his first efforts, was also the theme of the volumes by which he won world-wide renown. As early as 1882 he had expressed his regret that she did not make the Russian alliance the basis of her policy in the eighteenth century; and he had the satisfaction of publishing the first instalment of 'Napoléon et Alexandre I'[2] in 1891, the year which witnessed the rapprochement between the Third Republic and the Empire of the Tsars. Its grace and power would under any circumstances have secured it a triumph, but its sensational success was due to its appearance during the years when enthusiasm for the Muscovite was at its height. Bignon and Lefevbre, Thiers and Lanfrey had explored portions of the French archives, but the Russian archives were not fully known till Tatistscheff and Vandal published their results simultaneously. While the Russian begins in 1801, the French scholar opens with Austerlitz and dispenses with detail before Tilsit. They agree that the alliance was bound to fail and that the responsibility for the breach rests on both sovereigns, but the Russian's admiration for Alexander is greater than that of the Frenchman. While Tatistscheff's volume is rather a collection of materials, Vandal's work is addressed to the cultured reader not less than to the specialist.

A single pregnant sentence announces the author's standpoint. 'Throughout his reign Napoleon pursued an unalterable goal—to assure by a serious peace with England the fixity of his work, the greatness of France, and the repose of the world.' To accomplish this it was necessary to conclude an alliance with Russia which would guarantee the Continent and leave him free to compel Great Britain to recognise his conquests. His reign was a battle of a dozen years waged against England, and his most crazy projects grew out of the need for defeating the island

[1] See Ségur, *Parmi les Cyprès et les Lauriers*, 1912.
[2] There is a good review in Sorel's *Lectures historiques*, 1894.

kingdom. Struck by her feebleness he conceived the iniquitous plan of stealing Spain from her dynasty, but the main object was to secure another weapon against the British foe. Thus the Russian alliance is but an episode in a titanic duel. 'At the end France falls at the feet of Europe after penetrating and transforming it. France has succumbed, but the French idea has triumphed.' After thus sketching the background of world politics he introduces the two protagonists. Napoleon is the impersonation of the Latin genius in his radiant clearness, his alert vigour, his imagination controlled by logic; Alexander derives from the northern races his lofty and indeterminate aspirations. No French historical writing is more brilliant than that which describes the meeting of the monarchs at Tilsit and the assembly of kings at Erfurt. 'The world is big enough for us both,' said Napoleon, and he proposed to partition it. Russia was to have Northern Asia and Constantinople, France to take Egypt and India.

Vandal shows clearly that the alliance was no sooner concluded than it began to decay. He demolishes the legend that Alexander was a loyal ally. Of the two the Tsar was the least true to his bond. The fascination of Tilsit soon lost its spell. Both sides soon began to play a double game, each negotiating secretly for alliances with other Powers, while Talleyrand busily sowed suspicion between them. Alexander stood aside in the Austrian war, and his refusal of a Russian princess as Josephine's successor indicated waning cordiality. With Marie Louise as Empress of France there was less need for the friendship of the Tsar. Though Vandal attributes the largest direct share in the breach of the alliance to Russia, he confesses that the ultimate responsibility rests on Napoleon. Spain haunts Napoleon as Poland haunts Alexander, and the misfortunes of both were the indirect consequence of the abuse of power. 'Let us recognise this providential justice which emerges sooner or later from events and strikes the guilty.' Napoleon had learned nothing from the opposition of the Spanish people, and when the quarrel came to a head 'he foresaw everything except the power of resistance which the soul of a great people finds in itself.' The narrative ends on the eve of the invasion. The alliance carried the seeds of death within itself, for it was based on war and conquest. The historian concludes by contrasting the new Franco-Russian pact, defensive in its character and respectful of the rights of other lands.

Vandal's volumes are as remarkable for their delineations of character as for their grasp of the tangled skein of diplomatic intrigue. His famous antithesis, *Napoléon c'est l'action, Alexandre c'est le rêve*, is scarcely consistent with his own pages, which reveal how much of the dreamer lurked in Napoleon and how much more than a dreamer was the Tsar, whom his rival in wrath described as a Greek of the Lower Empire. The picture of Alexander, beginning as Don Carlos with Czartoryski as Posa and learning under the stress of repeated defeats something of the wisdom of the serpent, is a triumph of psychological interpretation. Equally convincing is the portrait of Napoleon, dragging the ever lengthening chain of his own mistakes. His magic power reconciled France with herself and raised the French for a time above the level of humanity, but no one could wish for another such period. Of the minor actors Talleyrand and Metternich are sketched with special care. Vandal possesses the solidity and breadth of Sorel with an elegance and lightness of touch that are his own.

Vandal had hitherto busied himself with the external relations of his country. He was now to show that he could narrate her domestic history with not less power and brilliance. The main novelty of 'Napoléon et Alexandre' was the proof of the disloyalty of the Tsar. The main contention of 'L'Avènement de Bonaparte'[1] was that Brumaire was not the destruction of liberty but the restoration of order and prosperity. It was the thesis of Thiers revived and buttressed with new arguments. The work opens with a picture of the Directory drawn in the darkest colours. Violence continued, energy and enthusiasm had disappeared. After the exclusion of Carnot France found herself at the mercy of a worthless oligarchy, guided by Barras, who was distinguished by moral depravity in an age when base men were not rare. The roads were infested by robbers, corruption was universal, the finances were in disorder, political and religious liberty were unknown, the press was in fetters. Everywhere there was lassitude and inertia. The picture of tyranny and disorder, degeneration and discouragement, is the more striking because Vandal's habit is to avoid invective. Such a situation could not last in a country which knew by experience how easy it was to change the government; and Sieyès, who took the initiative, looked round for a successful general who would make the *coup* and become the ornamental figure-head of the new régime. His first thought was Joubert, and when Joubert was killed his mind turned to Moreau; but at this moment Bonaparte landed in France, and the ovations of the people gave Sieyès his cue.

If Vandal's first task was to show that Brumaire merely

[1] A cheap edition appeared in Nelson's series in 1912, with an introduction by Lord Rosebery.

executed the judgment of the people on the disreputable Directory, his second was to sketch the magical transformation which
followed the establishment of the Consulate. His view of the later
years of Napoleon is as severe as need be, but he refuses to allow
his knowledge of the end to colour his verdict on the beginning.
Far from destroying liberty—that had been destroyed already—
he rescued his countrymen from Jacobin tyranny. Though the
First Consul knew little of French politics he learned with extraordinary rapidity, and after Marengo he felt confident of his
destiny. One of the most striking features of the book is the proof
that his uncontested supremacy only dates from his first victory
as the representative of France. At first he was called Citoyen,
the tradition of republican simplicity was preserved, and Cam-
bacérès and Lebrun took their places beside their colleague in the
work of government. We see the First Consul attending com-
mittees and learning his trade, but his main principles were
already fixed. He declined to associate his assumption of power
with any form of reaction. Brumaire was the work of the moderates
of 1789, men who stood between the extreme parties as the
Politiques had stood between the Ligue and the Huguenots.

From a political point of view Marengo was the most important of Napoleon's battles with the exception of Waterloo. Had
he been defeated Fouché and other intriguers were ready to overthrow him: victory led straight to the Consulate for life and the
Empire. On his return he was greeted with greater enthusiasm
than had been witnessed since the Fête of Federation, and he
now began to speak as a master. The doors of the Churches were
open already; but the Concordat was a striking homage to tradition and sentiment, and its author hoped that it might be a
treaty of peace with the Catholic West. A second bold step was
to allow the majority of the Émigrés to return. What would have
been madness before Marengo was prudence after it. After years
of stress and confusion there was at last a sensation of convales-
cence. Robbery was put down with a high hand, economy was
introduced, the speculators whom the Directory tolerated were
suppressed, and justice was made pure and prompt. The closing
chapter is entitled 'Towards the Empire.' The people realised
how much depended on his life, and were anxious to avert the
return of anarchy or a Bourbon restoration. Thus, though a
despot, he was no usurper. He gave France the order which she
so urgently needed, but neither liberty nor peace. Vandal sympathises with the disappointment of the best minds in France, but he
asks what man of his time would have acted more generously.
'He is the pacificator of the French, the restorer of national

cohesion—that is his incontestable glory. If he had granted liberty too he would have shown himself superior to his century.' It is impossible to say if it was beyond his genius. It was certainly beyond his character.

Vandal's second great achievement enjoyed the same resounding success as the first. The style was easy and elegant, and the leading ideas stood out in bold relief. No one had seriously studied the Consulate since Thiers, and a mass of new material, illustrating public opinion as well as the acts of government, had accumulated. Some critics complained that he overestimated the services and statesmanship of Napoleon. His father was Postmaster-General under the Second Empire, and he himself was a friend of Princess Mathilde and Prince Victor Napoleon, but his acquaintance with the Imperial family left no trace in his writings. He wisely refuses to judge Napoleon *en bloc*. He maintains his right, while condemning the 'frenzies' of the Emperor, to applaud the work of the First Consul. His views as to the late emergence of Cæsarian ambitions and the originality of the policy of reconciliation are more controversial. Napoleon is entitled to the credit, if credit it be, of the Concordat; but Madelin has shown that part at least of the initiative in facilitating the return of the royalists must be attributed to Fouché, and that had it not been for the remonstrances of his advisers the Jacobins would have had more to suffer.

The third member of the famous triumvirate of admirers, Henri Houssaye[1] had served with distinction in 1870, and his experiences in defensive warfare in eastern France led him to study the campaign in which the first Napoleon had fought a losing battle in the same territory. As he proceeded he was filled with a great pity and a great enthusiasm. The result of his researches was published in 1888 under the simple title '1814.' Historians had hurried over the interval that separated Leipsic from the abdication. It is Houssaye's merit to have recovered the history of these months and to have revealed their treasures of heroism and devotion. Though the task was hopeless, the intrepidity of the troops equalled the genius of the captain. The desperate struggle is described with the pen of a soldier and a patriot. 'I have tried to be impartial,' he declares, 'but impartiality is not indifference. Where I see behind everything wounded France I have not been able to prevent myself trembling with pity and anger. Without taking the part of the Empire I have rejoiced at the victories of the Emperor and sorrowed with his

[1] See Madelin's biographical introduction to the posthumous volume on Jena, 1912.

defeats. In 1814 Napoleon is no longer the sovereign but the general, the first of the soldiers of France.'

Though the volume is almost wholly military, the historian does not forget the background. Since the beginning of the Spanish campaign and still more since the Russian débâcle France had been tired of war, and after Leipsic she longed for peace. Yet, bleeding and bankrupt as she was, four-fifths of the nation neither desired the fall of Napoleon nor even thought of it. The opposition came from the liberals, whose irritation was legitimate but inopportune. Two years earlier they might have stopped the aggression; now they merely paralysed the defence. He contrasts the ardour of the soldiers and the masses with the coldness and finally the desertion of the bourgeoisie and the upper classes. Though it was impossible to drive back the invader, there was no necessity for the restoration of the Bourbons. The Tsar, believing that France had no desire for them, was prepared to recognise Napoleon II, and only yielded on the assurance of Talleyrand and other malcontents that he was misinformed. Napoleon had 60,000 men and was prepared to defend the capital, but the defection of Marmont was the final blow. The abdication was the work of Frenchmen rather than of the invaders.

The volume, full of life and colour, of heroism and adventure, was welcomed with delight. The author's enthusiasm for the leaders of a forlorn hope struck a responsive note in the heart of a generation which had known the horrors of defeat and invasion. The military narrative deserved the praise it received, but the political judgments are open to grave criticism. Houssaye sympathises so profoundly with the soldiers and their great captain that he fails to comprehend those who opposed them. His fundamental error is to make Napoleon, even for a brief campaign, merely the defender of the French flag. He sees only the *Petit Caporal*, the good patriot, the friend of the peasant, the victim of treason. He was also the ruthless conqueror of Europe, and the campaign of 1814, in recording which the historian 'shakes with pity and anger,' was the reply of the injured peoples to the megalomaniac whose yoke they had borne too long. Many good Frenchmen believed, as Europe believed, that there could be no peace while Napoleon was on the throne; and Talleyrand, the chief villain of Houssaye's drama, has at least as good a claim to the title of patriot as the old master whom he had deserted before the crash.

The success of '1814' determined the historian to continue his narrative to the fall of the Empire. '1815,' dealing with the first Restoration and the Hundred Days, was almost wholly political. An exhaustive analysis of public opinion reveals the hostility of the army and of the masses to the Bourbons. The return from Elba is described in the most eloquent chapters that Houssaye ever wrote. On reaching the Hundred Days, he sketches the curious outburst of Jacobin feeling which the short experience of the Bourbons had provoked. The passions of 1793 revived, the hatred of priests and nobles returned, and the masses looked to Napoleon as the vindicator of the Revolution. He returned less as Emperor than as First Consul, the man of the people. 'Je suis issu de la Révolution,' he declared, and he set Benjamin Constant to draft a Constitution. But the Liberal Empire came too late. Though Houssaye disliked the Restoration, he is not able to show that it was really violent or arbitrary. The government of Louis XVIII was exceptionally mild, and there was but little change in the personnel of the administration. The unpopularity of the Bourbons was owing to little things, to mistakes of tact, to the pretensions of the Émigrés. There was no real popular movement during the Hundred Days. The Emperor himself had no illusions. 'They have let me come,' he observed to Mollien, 'as they let the others go.' Houssaye has no word of blame for the return from Elba. Those who welcomed the Emperor are 'patriots,' those who distrusted and opposed him are 'ultra-royalist.'

The third volume of the series is devoted to the Waterloo campaign. The sketch of the spirit and character of the army is of rare interest. The old troops were gone, but the new were even more eager for the fray. They lacked discipline and were therefore liable to panic, but their hatred of the foreigner amounted to frenzy, and they idolised their leader. 'Napoleon had never handled an instrument of war so formidable and so fragile.' And the Emperor was worthy of his soldiers. Houssaye rejects the contention that his hand had lost its cunning and that he was wrapped in lethargy at the crisis of his fate. 'His plan was one of his finest strategical conceptions. Everything failed owing to defects of execution, some by the Emperor himself, far more by his lieutenants.' It was Ney's fault that Ligny was not decisive, and it was Napoleon's fault that he did not destroy the English at Quatre-Bras. At Waterloo he performed all that was humanly possible. It was his intention to have begun the battle early in the morning, but the ground was too wet for the heavy artillery. Had it been dry Wellington would have been routed before the Prussians arrived. Though Napoleon lacked neither physical nor mental vigour, he confessed at St. Helena that he did not possess his old self-confidence. Even with the handicap of bungling

officers and untrained troops the disaster would have been a
crowning victory had the battle begun at the time he had planned.
Thus Houssaye once more plucks consolation from defeat.

The concluding volume deals with the second abdication and
the White Terror. The closing book bears the title 'France cruci-
fied,' and is written at white heat. Burning tears drop on the
tomb of the gallant Ney. 'Three-quarters of the population suffered with horror the insolent yoke of the victorious party, the
bâton of the Prussians, and the knife of the royalist cut-throats.'
Yet in a few years France recovered and once more took her place
among the great nations. 'With such vitality we must never
despair. How can we doubt of the destinies of a people which has
gone from resurrection to resurrection for a thousand years?' The
second restoration was a very different affair from the first, but
in scourging the authors of the reaction Houssaye appears to
forget that Waterloo and the White Terror were the result of the
return from Elba. He has no right to heap the whole blame on
the Powers and the royalists and to let the real author of these
calamities go free. His eloquent volumes are a precious contribution to our knowledge of the fall of the Empire, but they find no
place among that small class of works which satisfy the judgment
and the conscience of mankind.

The writings of Masson, Vandal and Houssaye, synchronising
in their appearance, exerted a profound effect on French opinion.
Lanfrey was forgotten, and little more was heard of Taine's
audacious contention that the Emperor was an Italian of the
Renaissance. Masson revealed the man, and, though the picture
was far from pleasing, it was at any rate human. Vandal recalled
the beneficent work of the First Consul. Houssaye depicted the
Emperor fighting the battle of France against the invader and
the hated Bourbons. The publication of Marbot's Memoirs in 1891,
breathing the very spirit of heroism and romance, made the
Grand Army live again. It seemed as if France had only just
awakened to the real greatness of her adopted son, and writers
vied with each other in proclaiming his virtues.

The most fervent of his worshippers was Arthur Lévy.
'Napoléon Intime' portrays a man whose leading qualities were
goodness, gratitude and cordiality. The work opens with
evidence of the hero's loyalty to his family and early friends.
There were no traces of ambition in early life, and after his first
sensational successes he forgot neither his family duties nor his
humble origin. His affectionate nature appears again in the
romance of his marriage. Had Josephine been faithful to him
he would have remained faithful to her. It required years to

persuade him to sacrifice his personal feelings to the national interest, and the divorce was as painful for him as for her. Marie Louise in turn quickly learned how indulgent and affectionate was the Corsican ogre at whose name she had trembled in Vienna. His love of children was intense, and they returned his love. His relations to his brothers and sisters exhibit him in an equally favourable light. The stories of incest were invented to amuse Louis XVIII. In his dealings with his officials we find innumerable traits of kindness and consideration. He never changed his servants if they behaved honestly. He only had three private secretaries, Bourrienne, who was dismissed for flagrant dishonesty, Méneval, whose Memoirs are a long pæan to his master, and Baron Fain. His valet Constant remained with him throughout. He was devoted to Desaix, Lannes and Duroc, and deeply mourned their loss. He paid Junot's debts, forgave Bernadotte his early treasons, and dealt gently with Moreau. He was never dazzled by his victories nor by the magnificent fêtes which were demanded by the people. His nature inclined to mercy and moderation. Lévy finds nothing to blame except the death of the Duc d'Enghien, which, nevertheless, was a proof not of cruelty but of determination to assure the safety of the State. There are ugly incidents in the hero's life to which no reference is made, and his rejection of the testimony of such witnesses as Madame de Rémusat and Madame de Stael on the ground that their advances had been repulsed is unconvincing.

A second work, 'Napoléon et la Paix,' essayed the still more formidable task of proving the greatest of conquerors a lover of peace. The words of the exile at St. Helena were literally true. 'I only conquered in my own defence. Europe never ceased to war against France, against her principles, against myself. The Coalition never ceased to exist, either secretly or openly.' He fought throughout for the frontiers gained by the Republic, and he would have been guilty of cowardice had he surrendered what he found. 'Not without misgiving,' writes Lévy, 'did I discover confirmation of a theory so opposed to the usual notions, and of course it is difficult to believe that the great captain hated the wars in which he gained so much glory.' If appearances are against him, it is only because we fail to realise the policy of his foes. 'The immutable rivalry of England, the fear of an improvised dynasty, the hope of putting a barrier to the expansion of the ideas of liberty, and the secret ambitions of all the Powers —these were the elements of the Coalitions on which his efforts for peace were shipwrecked.' His diplomacy was handicapped by his trustful nature. 'Nearly all his life he felt a sort of respectful confidence in Kings. He almost believed that hereditary monarchs belonged to a superior humanity.' He needed many painful experiences to remove the scales from his eyes. His deference for legitimate monarchs and his sincere desire to avoid war is exhibited most clearly in his relations with Prussia. His eagerness for a Prussian alliance was flouted by the beautiful Queen, who deliberately chose war.[1] In like manner he was the victim of England's undying hostility to France, and he declared at St. Helena that he had always desired peace with England by any means compatible with the dignity of the French nation. That he aimed at universal monarchy is a pure legend. Surrounded by enemies he was like a harassed bull, and his only safety lay in rapid strokes. *Cet animal est très méchant. Quand on l'attaque, il se défend.*

Lévy's work ends with the campaign of Jena, and he is therefore dispensed from illustrating the hero's pacific instincts from the incessant warfare of the later Empire. The closing pages, however, show how he would confront the problem. The dynasties of Naples and Spain were evicted because they violated treaties and plotted against France, while Vandal is assumed to have proved Alexander the author of the rupture of 1812. 'If he had been less devoted to peace and less inclined to respect the sovereignty of his enemies, Paris would not have seen Alexander, Frederick William and Francis within her gates, all of whom he could have deposed.' 'Though I have been called the modern Attila and Robespierre on horseback,' said the fallen ruler, 'they know better in their heart of hearts. If I were what they say I should perhaps still be reigning and they would not.' Lévy's work is learned and sincere, but even paradox has its limits. Like his hero he fails to detect the nations behind the governments. His portrait of Queen Louisa is a caricature, and he forgets that Fox and other Whigs who had stoutly opposed the war against the Revolution recognised that enduring peace with Napoleon was impossible. It is true that he had to deal with a situation he had not created, but there was not a country in Europe which would not have been glad to live at peace with him had he sheathed his sword.

A modified version of the theory of a pacific Napoleon is to be found in the pages of Sorel. The historian had originally intended to conclude his work by a rapid summary till 1815, but he devoted a volume to the Directory and three to Napoleon. The latter half of his work is markedly inferior in power, learning and above all in judgment, and his ignorance of the British archives often leads him astray.[2] 'The problem of the natural frontiers is the pivot of the war, and forms till 1815 the link

---

[1] This view of the war of 1806 is shared by Lenz, *Life of Napoleon.*
[2] See the severe criticism in Geyl, *Napoleon: For or Against?* 254–307.

which connects all the governments issuing from the Revolution. France cannot be blamed for trying to realise her traditional ambition; her error was in thinking that her new frontier could be held without European recognition or conquering beyond it. Thus the truces of Napoleon never possessed any security.' Europe fought to restore the old frontiers, France to defend them: he was merely his country's sword, the instrument of his countrymen's will. '1799 is the first operation of a siege, the siege of France, which lasts sixteen years, filled with attacks and sorties and the construction of distant bastions. In 1812 the greatest sortie was made, and the defenders of the beleaguered city were driven back from post to post. The war between Europe and the Revolution began with Valmy and ended at Waterloo.' In its later stages the conflict was degraded by the element of personal ambition, but Sorel ranged himself with Vandal and Lévy in emphasising the patriotism of the hero and the perfidy of the Powers. A less pacific and more convincing picture of Napoleonic diplomacy emerges from the scholarly monographs of Driault.

In addition to the works of his professed admirers,[1] Napoleon has recently been the theme of several books of outstanding importance. Starting with the documents published in Masson's 'Napoléon Inconnu,' Chuquet collected a mass of material relating to his life at Brienne and at Paris, his school-fellows and military comrades. Written with serene impartiality the 'Jeunesse de Napoléon' has taken its place as the standard authority up to and including Toulon. Madelin's superb biography of Fouché throws light on almost every stage of Napoleon's career from Brumaire to the second abdication. To the cool and sceptical Jacobin it was above all due that Brumaire was not followed by reprisals, that neither the royalists nor Jacobins were harassed, that the rebellion in the West was suppressed, that conspiracies were nipped in the bud, that the hostility of the Faubourg St. Germain was disarmed. Lady Blennerhassett's full length portrait of Mme de Stael is a work of the same calibre, though less friendly to-the Emperor. In a different field Lanzac de Laborie's comprehensive work, 'Paris sous Napoléon,' presents the first adequate picture of the internal life, society and administration of the Empire. Original material of great value has recently come to light. Marbot's Memoirs and Gourgaud's journal at St. Helena are important, the first for its atmosphere, the second for its facts. The Memoirs of Talleyrand, published by the Duc de Broglie,

[1] For an almost hysterical rhapsody see Georges Duruy's preface to Barras' *Memoirs*.

proved so lacking in interest that not a few suspected a forgery; they are certainly of less importance than the volumes of his diplomatic correspondence published by Pallain. A 'Revue des Études Napoléoniennes,' under the direction of Driault, began to appear in 1912. Victor Hugo's 'Toujours Lui, Lui Partout,' is as true as ever.

III

Of the four detailed histories of the Restoration that of Nettement[1] alone is favourable to the Bourbons. The author, a friend of the Comte de Chambord and one of the most powerful journalists of the middle decades of the century, obtained a good deal of information from Berryer and other leading actors. Vaulabelle reflects the moderate liberalism of the era of Louis Philippe, and Viel-Castel traces the Parliamentary discussions with extraordinary fullness from the same standpoint. The ablest of the four narratives is that of Duvergier de Hauranne, who played a prominent part in the events he describes. Beginning political life as a *Doctrinaire*, he welcomed the Revolution of 1830 and supported the new régime from his place in Parliament; but he joined the opposition when Guizot inaugurated a policy of hard-shelled conservatism, and helped to organise the banquets that warned the government of the wrath to come. Exiled in 1851 he devoted himself to the composition of his history, and lived long enough to welcome the Third Republic. His intention was to bring his narrative to 1848, but when he had reached 1830 he was an old man. His ten stout volumes possess enduring value as a record of the golden age of Parliamentary eloquence.

For nearly a generation the reign of Louis Philippe was mainly known through the diatribe of Louis Blanc. Guizot employed his old age in composing the voluminous Memoirs which not only offered a detailed defence of his conduct but enshrine the cautious spirit of the bourgeois monarchy. Not until forty years after the expulsion of the last King of France was a serious attempt made to narrate in detail the history of the reign. Thureau-Dangin, a right-wing Royalist, places in the foreground what Louis Blanc left in shadow—the Chambers and the Chancelleries. Free government, he declares, was rendered more difficult by the revolution of 1830, but not impossible. The reign forms part of the Restoration, which, despite its faults, gave France prosperity and honour, peace and ordered liberty. He detests republicans, radicals, socialists, free-thinkers, Saint-Simonians. Laffiitte is savagely attacked, Lafayette is dismissed as a senile

[1] See Biré, *Alfred Nettement*, 1901.

demagogue, Thiers as the evil genius of the reign. Even in literature he finds traces of 'the sunstroke of 1830.' Victor Hugo deteriorates, Lamartine turns politician, Balzac is impure, Eugène Sue vile. He despises the people, 'our drunken and ragged masters,' and censures all approaches of the bourgeois ruler to his humbler subjects. He has little respect for the King, though he warmly recognises his love of peace. The popular origin of the July Monarchy is an ineffaceable stain. The historian's favourite statesmen are Casimir-Périer and Guizot, who set their faces so sternly against democracy, but he is more conservative than Guizot, for he scoffs at 'the illusions of 1789,' and speaks of the impotent and destructive anarchy of the Third Republic. 'Everything indicates that God reserves for France the inestimable privilege of recommencing the experiment which was jeopardised in 1830 and violently interrupted in 1848.' The work of Thureau-Dangin on the Monarchy of July breathes the stuffy atmosphere of the Faubourg St. Germain, but his surveys of foreign policy, resting on a mass of unpublished material, are masterly.

The second Empire has been treated in two works of surpassing interest. The prolix apologia, of Émile Ollivier in fourteen volumes, designated 'L'Empire Libéral,' is a brilliant survey of its later years by one of its leading statesmen whose career was ended by the débâcle of 1870. The history of La Gorce, on the other hand, derives part of its value from its detachment. 'I have no relation by origin or memory,' he declares, 'either to the courtiers of the Emperor or to his adversaries.' Napoleon III had suffered first from adulation, then from calumny: there was no longer need for either. His reign was brilliant and deadly, superficial and tragic. He was a mixture of Machiavelli and Don Quixote, whom it was impossible to hate. However severe the judgment both on the ruler and the man, the impression left by the seven volumes is rather of melancholy than of anger. The 'History of the Second Republic,' which served as an introduction to the larger work, reveals La Gorce as a royalist and a Catholic. The overthrow of the Monarchy in 1848 produced a situation which could not last, but he condemns the *coup d'état* of 1851. The bourgeoisie, however, quickly rallied to the government, while the rapid development of the material resources of the country and the rebuilding of Paris kept labour employed. The discredited royalists, divided between Legitimists and Orleanists, made no trouble, and the Church responded with enthusiasm to the Imperial advances. 'The clergy,' he writes with gentle malice, 'love incense, for the sake of the religion they represent, and perhaps unconsciously also for themselves.' The Emperor made servitude more popular than liberty. But the vestal flame had not been wholly extinguished in 1851, and in the early sixties it began to burn with a stronger light. Thiers returned to public life, brilliant publicists like Paradol and Lanfrey began to voice the discontent, and Sainte-Beuve uttered a resounding demand for intellectual liberty. Rationalism and radicalism grew rapidly, and even during the glitter of the Exhibition of 1867 a feeling of instability was universal. With the appearance of Gambetta and Rochefort began a period of open war. In a masterly chapter on 'The Decline of the Empire' the historian traces the descent. Sedan merely gave the *coup de grâce* to the dying gladiator.

The work of La Gorce provided the first detailed survey of the foreign policy of the Second Empire. He censures the Emperor's Italian policy as leading straight to the destruction of the Temporal Power of the Pope. In the study of the relations of the Emperor with Prussia he is at his best. While Sybel never censures German dealings with France, La Gorce criticises the performers on both sides of the Rhine. He makes no attempt to hide the confusion, the weakness, the hesitation, the divided counsels of France. He recognises the genius of Bismarck, but denies him nobility of character. France deserved to be beaten, but Prussia did not deserve to win. The demand for guarantees against a renewal of the Hohenzollern candidature was a fatal error. When war broke out the bravery of the troops was neutralised by the inadequacy of the preparations and the incompetence of their leaders. While rendering justice to the generous ideas, the personal charm and the humanity of the Emperor, he draws a dark picture of his work. One critic declared that the book ought to kill Bonapartism. When all allowances were made, the Second Empire stood for autocracy and war. The reforms of Ollivier, to whom he pays eloquent tribute, came too late. 'Splendours and misery—in these two words lies the history of the Second Empire.' With the events of 1870 we reach a period so recent that definitive narratives are impossible. A few valuable monographs based on personal knowledge, such as Jules Simon's volumes on Thiers, Joseph Reinach's eulogy of Gambetta's brief Ministry, Rambaud's biography of Jules Ferry, Léon Say's volumes on finance, the lively Memoirs of Freycinet and Juliette Adam, throw welcome light on the early years of the Republic. Hanotaux' detailed narrative, written in a spirit of moderate republicanism, provides the most authoritative guide through the critical years of the Third Republic including the making of the Constitution and the abortive *coup* of 1877. The hero of the drama is the veteran patriot Thiers.

CHAPTER XIV

HALLAM AND MACAULAY

I

THE serious study of early England and the presentation of the results of archival research begins with Sharon Turner, whose 'History of the Anglo-Saxons' appeared between 1799 and 1805.[1] Though inferior in narrative power to Hume, his volumes constitute an enormous advance in scholarship. Writing in 1820, in the preface to the third edition, he declares that his ardent desire had been fulfilled. 'The taste for the history and remains of our great ancestors has revived and is visibly increasing.'

While Turner was at work a far greater man was preparing a treatise of wider scope and deeper significance. After some years at the bar Hallam[2] turned to literature, but he was forty-one before the 'Sketch of Europe in the Middle Ages,' published in 1818, the first important historical work produced in England since Gibbon, made him famous. Though he added a volume of notes and dissertations thirty years later, the treatise was never seriously revised, and it represents the immature scholarship of the early nineteenth century. Beginning with Clovis and ending with the Italian expedition of Charles VIII, it covers a thousand years. The preface explains that its chief object is to survey the modes of government and the laws of different countries. A further limitation is indicated in a passage which shows that the author was born in the century of Hume and Voltaire. He desires to present what can interest a philosophical inquirer. 'Many considerable portions of time, especially before the twelfth century, may justly be deemed so barren of events worthy of remembrance that a single sentence or paragraph is often enough to give the

---

[1] The best bird's-eye view of English historiography is by Sir Adolphus Ward, *Cambridge History of English Literature*, vol. xii., ch. 14, and vol. xiv., ch. 2. Peardon, *The Transition in English Historical Writing, 1760–1830*, 1933, is a scholarly monograph. There are useful sketches in A. J. Grant, *English Historians*, 1906, and Hugh Walker, *The Literature of the Victorian Era*, 1921.

[2] It is curious that there is no biography of Hallam. Mignet's obituary in *Éloges Historiques* is not one of his best. Herbert Fisher, 'The Whig Historians,' in *Pages from the Past*, 1939, contrasts his conservatism with Macaulay's radicalism.

character of entire generations and of long dynasties of obscure kings.'

Hallam's plan is to deal with the leading countries seriatim, reserving for later treatment the problems common to them all. The chapters on France, Italy and Spain offered a fairly detailed record, while the sketches of Germany and Eastern Europe were meagre. Of greater originality were the comprehensive dissertations on feudalism and the ecclesiastical power. He loves clerical domination as little as other Whigs, and speaks with scorn of the pretensions of Hildebrand and Innocent III. Fanaticism, superstition and intolerance he abhors. The work concludes with a comprehensive survey of the state of society and literature, education and commerce, which forms one of the earliest models of *Kulturgeschichte*. The picture is dark, and the historian confessed in later life that he had been perhaps a little too severe. As an attempt to recover the ideology and character of the Middle Ages it is scarcely more successful than the endeavour of Robertson, for both were utterly lacking in the sympathetic imagination which brings distant ages near and renders the unfamiliar intelligible. He cultivates a calm, judicial attitude, equally sparing of eulogy and invective. He is a lawyer, not an artist. 'He has rather the intelligence than the sentiment of the past,' declared Mignet in his sketch of a man whose temperament and methods had much in common with his own. He does not exhibit a drama; he draws lessons. His style suits his thought. Powerful and clear, though lacking subtlety and charm, it occasionally rises to a grave eloquence. On the other hand, it suffers from the sententiousness which afflicted so many historians of the time and reached a climax in Palgrave and Alison.

A third writer contributed to popularise the knowledge of the English Middle Ages, and produced a narrative which partially superseded Hume and remained the most popular sketch of our history till the appearance of Green. Lingard[1] won reputation as a serious historian by his 'Antiquities of the Anglo-Saxon Church.' Though the object of the book was to glorify the Catholic centuries, he wrote with a reticence that rendered it palatable to Protestant readers. The grounds of his reserve at a time when Catholicism was a despised sect were obvious, yet his work was hotly attacked by Bishop Milner as calculated to do as much harm as good to the Church. His success encouraged him to the more ambitious task which filled the remainder of his long life.

---

[1] See the excellent biography by Haile and Bonney, 1912. The *History* was abridged and continued in 1904.

In the preface to the 'History of England,' the first three volumes of which extended till the accession of Henry VIII, he declared that he had written without consulting modern historians, thus preserving himself from imbibing the prejudices and reproducing the mistakes of other writers. It gave no indication that the author was a Catholic priest, and few of his readers would have guessed it. His old foe, Bishop Milner, indignantly denounced it as calculated to confirm Protestants in their errors, but the majority of his communion, both in England and at Rome, approved his adroitness. His object, he wrote to a friend, was to make the Catholic cause appear respectable in the eyes of the British public. He is studiously reserved in his judgments of people and events, and the balanced portrait of Becket shows how different was his Catholicism from the Ultramontane rigour that came in with Pius IX. He has no sympathy with enthusiasm, and believes that Joan of Arc was deluded. The book is a purely political narrative, and little or nothing is heard of literature or society. It was the result of prolonged study, and was enriched by researches in the Vatican and other Italian libraries.

No real progress could be made without a fuller knowledge of unprinted sources. The Record Commission was appointed in 1800 to provide for the better arrangement, preservation and use of the national treasures. The manuscripts were scattered about in the Tower, the Rolls Chapel, the Chapter-house of Westminster Abbey and other places, unclassified and neglected. Rats and mice ruled supreme, and the approach of man was discouraged by high fees and galling restrictions. In these circumstances the Commission might have been expected to make good use of its powers, but it was doomed to comparative sterility by its composition. The Bishops, Cabinet Ministers and Privy Councillors who formed a large proportion of its members lacked the knowledge and the leisure to discharge their duties with success. It was said that no one who possessed any acquaintance with history was appointed till Mackintosh joined the Commission twenty-five years after its foundation. Documents of little importance, disgracefully edited, were published at enormous cost, and Rymer and other works, of which editions already existed were reprinted. In the words of Maitland, 'the scandalously bad elbowed the admirably good.'

It was chiefly owing to Harris Nicolas,[1] best known as the editor of Nelson's Letters, that public attention was aroused to the necessity of drastic changes. In a series of pamphlets he described the mortifying conditions under which he had had to

[1] See *Dict. Nat. Biog.*

conduct his studies. In his 'Observations on the State of Historical Literature,' written in 1830 and dedicated to Melbourne as Home Secretary, he expresses a hope that the new reign and the new ministry may inaugurate an improvement. 'The history of England is not merely imperfect and erroneous but a discredit to the country, for almost every new document proves the current histories false. Scarcely a statement will bear the test of truth. The Government prefers that the Records should perish rather than that they should be allowed to illustrate British history.' The Society of Antiquaries, founded in 1751, had not advanced historical knowledge so much as a single scholar like Hearne. The Record Commission, with greater resources, had accomplished little more. New Commissioners must be appointed, and their income should be devoted exclusively to the publication of manuscripts of importance. Largely as the result of his efforts a Select Committee was appointed in 1836, with Charles Buller as Chairman. The evidence given by Nicolas and other witnesses convinced the Committee of the urgent need of collecting, cleaning and classifying the records and facilitating their use. A new Commission was appointed, and from 1836 dates the more careful stewardship of our incomparable heritage.

The best work of the Record Commission had been accomplished by Palgrave,[1] whose practice of the law was accompanied by a passion for antiquarian research. His edition of the 'Parliamentary Writs' received discriminating praise from Nicolas, but the critic complained of the needless expense incurred in the publication, and a split ensued between the two scholars. Appointed Deputy-Keeper in 1838, he collected the treasures hitherto dispersed in many places into a single repository. In addition to publishing a mass of original matter, Palgrave wrote works of a more general character. 'The Rise and Progress of the English Commonwealth,' published in the year of the Reform Bill, was the first comprehensive study of our early constitutional history. It was the author's intention to bring his story down to the Stuarts, but the two massive volumes devoted to the period before the Conquest had no successors. Savigny's epoch-making treatise on the survival of Roman law had been finished some years earlier; but the English historian declared that he had reached his results before he read the German jurist, and independently of the remarkable work of John Allen, the friend and secretary of Lord Holland, on the growth of the Royal Preroga-

[1] See the Memoir by his son in Palgrave, *Collected Historical Works*, vol. i., 1919. His theory of English institutions is summarised in the Introduction to Vinogradoff's *Villainage in England*, 1892.

tive. Allen showed that the theory of royal power was the same
in all the nations which grew out of the Empire. This absolutism
derived from Rome, not from the Teutonic tribes. Yet the prerogative in England was never monarchical in the Continental
sense, and there was a wide gulf between Teutonic practice and
Roman theory. Though Palgrave defends his originality, he pays
his predecessors a handsome tribute in the preface. 'Two learned
men have thrown new light on the origin of laws and government
in Europe. Savigny clearly demonstrates the existence of Roman
communities far on in the Middle Ages, and Allen has shown how
much of our monarchical theory is derived from the government
of the Empire.' Thus the note is struck on the very threshold
which revealed him as one of the most uncompromising
'Romanists' of the century.

Palgrave gave an entirely new construction to Anglo-Saxon
history. He boldly challenges the current view that it is necessary to begin with political events and to proceed to institutions
and law. 'The history of the law is the most satisfactory clue
to the political history of England. The character of the people
mainly depends on their laws.' He speaks of law with deep
reverence. 'The function of the lawgiver is the highest exercised
by man. Legislation is a duty involving the most fearful responsibility which can devolve on any human being.' The English
Monarchy derives from the monarchical power of Rome and the
limitations of Teutonic practice. It was the Roman element which
saved us from becoming a nation of loose aggregates, the Teutonic
element which delivered us from absolutism. Of limiting influences
the most important were the free judicial institutions. The shires,
hundreds and townships were not mere administrative divisions
but political bodies. Such was the framework of society, and such
it remained despite invasions and changes of dynasty. The barbarian invaders of the Roman Empire changed only the forms of
villainage. The disappearance of the language of the Britons no
more proves the destruction of the British than the disappearance
of the Celtic language in Gaul argues the destruction of the Gauls
by the Franks. The invasion of the Danes and Normans left even
fewer traces. Mediæval England was built on Roman foundations.
Palgrave's volumes were bold and ingenious. His belief in continuity rested on his conviction of the *vis inertiae* of social conditions; but, though powerful and erudite, he is arbitrary and
fanciful. He sees Rome everywhere and shuts his eyes to traces of
the Teuton. The arrangement of his material could not be worse.
The first volume begins with chapters on the Roman Emperors,
and the second, described as 'proofs and illustrations,' should

have been called, as the *Edinburgh Review* suggested, 'supplementary thoughts.'

Palgrave's later and larger work, 'The History of Normandy and England,' was in some respects a continuation. No history of the duchy had yet appeared, and no one, he asserted, could write it unless he possessed the key. 'A dead set has been made against the Middle Ages as immersed in darkness and barbarity, and most of all against mediæval Christianity.' But, while they had been unjustly depreciated by Protestants and rationalists, they were now suffering scarcely less from injudicious defenders. If a balanced attitude was the first condition of success, the second was a clear appreciation of the influence of Rome. 'The doctrine on which all real understanding of mediæval and modern history depends is the deduction of authority from Rome and the continuity of the European States.' Thus the historian's second work, no less than the first, is a variation on the theme of Rome. He begins with a detailed history of the Carolingian Empire, and passes to the fortunes of the Norsemen before Rollo's settlement in Normandy. The second volume is devoted to the early dukes, and the third brings the story to the Norman Conquest. The fourth deals with Rufus and discusses the results of the Conquest. The work was interrupted by death in 1861, and the history of the Conquest itself was never written, but the author's view of its character was fully explained. In direct opposition to Thierry, he regards it as scarcely more than a change of dynasty. The Englishman champions the Normans as warmly as the Frenchman had championed the Saxons. He shows that the transfer of land was less complete and the fusion of races far more rapid than Thierry allowed. Such changes in law as were introduced were the work, not of the Conqueror, but of Henry II. Palgrave's volumes were of service in revealing the Norman dukes and in correcting Thierry's perverse conception of the Conquest, but they possessed a further merit. In discovering that the Roman Empire did not terminate in 476, he seized the key to mediæval history. 'Rome's cruelties, baffling conception by their infinity, her vices, her absolute hatred against God, received their chastisement,' he writes in his opening chapter; yet no one admired more than he her political genius. No part of his work is better than that which treats of the Carolingian Empire and its successors. 'When drawn within the magic circle of Imperial Rome,' declares Freeman[1] with truth, 'he rises to his full power.'

The faults of the work are even more conspicuous than its merits. Palgrave is garrulous, sententious, verbose. His nemesis

[1] *Edinburgh Review*, April 1859.

is that his books are unread and that his services to historical study are almost forgotten. A second fault is the uncritical use of authorities. It is true that he dethroned the False Ingulf, who had led Thierry astray, but he pays equal attention to authorities of very different value. Again, he concerns himself too exclusively with the history of institutions and rulers, too little with the national life. Even more than Hallam he surveys the scene through a lawyer's spectacles. Yet, despite his many faults, he occupies an honourable place among the pioneers. 'He would have been a great commander,' writes Maitland in his picturesque way, 'if an army had been forthcoming. We had our swallows, and beautiful birds they were; but there was spring in Germany.'

If Anglo-Saxon England owed something to Palgrave it owed far more to Kemble,[1] the first of British 'Germanists' as Palgrave was the first of British 'Romanists.' At Cambridge he was the friend of Arthur Hallam, the Tennysons, Maurice, Sterling and Milnes, but he left without taking a degree. His main interest at that time lay in action, not in learning. 'He is engrossed by a passion,' wrote his sister Fanny, 'which occupies his mind and time to the detriment, if not the exclusion, of all other studies.' He adored Bentham, and advocated the ballot, disestablishment and other advanced proposals. In a word, he was in 'a sort of frenzy about politics.' In 1830 he and a few friends went to Spain to help Torrijos in his ill-fated rising. On the conclusion of the tragic adventure he threw himself into Teutonic philology, and studied under Grimm. The main task of his life was to collect Anglo-Saxon charters and with their aid to reconstruct the social and political life of early England. His 'Codex Diplomaticus' contained about fifteen hundred documents in chronological order from the conversion of Ethelbert to the Norman Conquest, collected from collegiate, cathedral and other libraries. A good many had already been printed by Rymer, Hearne and other scholars, but whenever possible they were transcribed afresh. 'The stores of knowledge here laid open to the philologist, the jurist and the antiquarian,' he proudly declared, 'will produce results far beyond the limits of this country or age.' The Charters supply information concerning the law of real property, the nature of tenure, the authority of the King, the nobility and the Church, while household arrangements and the disposition of real and personal estate are known by the Wills. The chief merit of the work lies rather in the vast collection of material than in his

---

[1] See *Dict. Nat. Biog.* He often appears in Fanny Kemble's *Records of a Girlhood*, 1878. See also Vinogradoff's masterly introduction to *Villainage in England.*

treatment of it. 'Kemble was a great man,' pronounces Maitland, 'but, even according to the standard of his own time, not a very good editor of legal documents.'

'The Englishman has inherited the noblest portion of his being from the Anglo-Saxons. In spite of every influence, we bear a marvellous resemblance to our forefathers.' It is in this spirit of whole-hearted Germanism that Kemble wrote his greatest work. 'The Saxons in England' appeared in 1849, with a dedication to the Queen. The picture was mainly based on his own Codex and on Thorpe's collection of Laws. The work is not a narrative but a series of essays, each complete in itself, on institutions, classes and problems. Almost every aspect of society is presented, and a chapter on Heathendom sketches the intellectual background of the invaders. The dust of the workshop is often visible, but the volumes are full of new material and new views. Partly by an inquiry into local names, he shows that the Teutonic conquest began long before the recorded settlements. He agrees with Palgrave that the invaders easily conquered the Celts and did not destroy them, but the root of the social system was the mark which the invaders brought with them. As they were relatively few, they divided only a part of the land they had conquered, the rest remaining in the hands of the people under the title of Folkland for future use. Feudalism was born when this reserve fell to a few magnates. Free men could then no longer obtain fresh holdings, and had to seek subsistence from a lord. Land was the basis of political and social relations, both during the reign of free communities and when they were replaced by the manor. Neither Britons nor Romans left a trace in the life or institutions of their successors. The demonstration that Anglo-Saxon England was essentially Teutonic was sound, but the picture of the social structure was marred by grave errors. The mark, so far from being the type of settlement, was the exception. The conception of folkland as unoccupied territory held in trust was an illusion. On the other hand, his acquaintance with the charters enabled him to throw light on almost every province of law. Though his book is rather an encyclopædia than a history, it dominated English scholarship for a generation. Introduced into Germany by Konrad Maurer, it exerted an enduring influence on Teutonic students of mediæval institutions.

II

The success of Lingard's volumes on mediæval England was surpassed by their successors, which brought the narrative to the

Revolution of 1688. He excuses himself from personal judgments on the ground of 'my occasional ignorance of motives and causes, my inexperience in what is called the philosophy of history, but which has often appeared to me the philosophy of romance. Where the authorities are silent, I prefer to leave the reader to exercise his own judgment.' In describing the origin of the Reformation in Germany he admits the existence of grave abuses, and condemns the Papal bull against Henry VIII as vindictive; but the addition of the headship of the Church to the headship of the State debased the spirit of the people and led to passive obedience. He impartially condemns tyranny and cruelty whenever he finds it. 'The foulest blot on Mary's reign is her cruel persecutions of the reformers. The mind is struck with horror, and blesses the legislation of a more tolerant age.' In dealing with Mary Stuart he refuses to take sides, and in regard to Elizabeth he is hardly more pronounced. Protestants say her reign was happy, Catholics that it was a time of national misery. But though he refuses to judge the reign as a whole, he pronounces the Queen irresolute, mean and irritable, and suggests that her personal morality was bad.

The volumes on the Stuarts reveal the same cautious spirit. 'A suspicion has existed that I may occasionally be swayed by religious prepossessions. Nothing can be more easy than to throw out such insinuations, but I am not aware that any important error has been discovered.' He declares Laud and his enemies 'equally obstinate, equally infallible, equally intolerant.' The death of Charles I was 'an awful lesson to royalty to watch the growth of public opinion and to moderate its pretensions in conformity with the reasonable desires of its subjects.' Yet the victorious Puritans move him to stronger language than he usually permits himself. The conquerors of Wexford and Drogheda are 'ruthless barbarians.' Cromwell himself was overbearing, selfish, ambitious, and regarded dissimulation as the perfection of human wisdom. The eighth volume, appearing in 1830, completed the narrative with a guarded vindication of James II. Lingard's volumes presented the first modern narrative of the two critical centuries of English history. His religious attitude was that of a Gallican, his political standpoint that of a Whig. John Allen, in repeated attacks in the *Edinburgh Review*, charged him with suppression and perversion of facts. Hallam praised his acuteness and industry, but deplored his inveterate partiality. He was a partisan, declared Alison, but nobody concealed his partialities more skilfully, his bias appearing not in what he told but in what he concealed. Southey's criticism on the Reformation volumes swelled into his 'Book of the Church.' His tone gradually became more outspoken. He confessed that as he had to acquire credit among Protestants he was extremely cautious in the first edition of his work, and that when he had won it he introduced matter respecting the penal laws and other topics which he at first withheld. He attributed to his book 'the revolution in the Protestant mind as to the doctrines of Popery.' He improved it as new editions were demanded, and enjoyed the satisfaction of seeing it both abridged and translated into several languages before his death in 1851 at the age of eighty.

The first work on modern England of national and international importance was Hallam's 'Constitutional History from the accession of Henry VII to the death of George II.' Written while the Tory domination was still unbroken, it constituted a political manifesto. In a vitriolic article in the *Quarterly Review* Southey denounced 'its acrimony and its arrogance, its injustice and its ill-temper.'[1] Yet Hallam belonged to the extreme right of the Whig party. He detested political and ecclesiastical tyranny, but he had no confidence in the wisdom of the people, and the Reform Bill, though the work of his friends, went too far for his taste. His work is a sustained attack on the Tudor and Stuart despotism and a glorification of the principles of 1688. Hume was dethroned, and Tory views of the seventeenth century were generally abandoned. At the moment when the Reform Bill inaugurated a generation of Whig politics, he inaugurated a generation of Whig history. His influence was increased by the moderation of his tone and the austerity of his style, which has been compared to that of a State paper or the judgment of a great magistrate.

Hallam applauds the work of 'the majestic lord who broke the bonds of Rome.' Yet Henry figures in his pages as an able and ferocious despot, 'one of the many tyrants and oppressors of innocence whom the wrath of Heaven has raised up and the servility of man has endured.' Cranmer finds but little favour in his eyes. The Marian persecutions are condemned scarcely more severely than the cruel punishments of the Catholics by her sister. The Tudors were all arbitrary despots, and it was not till the conflict on monopolies at the close of the reign of Elizabeth that popular opinion began to assert itself. The Reformation was a beneficent movement carried through by worldly and selfish men. To a lover of law the Tudors were almost as offensive as the Stuarts, but to their subjects the yoke of the latter was far less

[1] Hallam angrily resented the attack. See Smiles, *John Murray*, vol. ii., 263–4.

tolerable. Hallam had no sympathy with Puritanism as a religious movement, but he was a wholehearted supporter of the resistance of the lawyers and the country gentlemen to the encroachments of the monarchy. Never had such a staggering literary blow been delivered at Personal Government. Lingard had mildly condemned the obstinacy of the first two Stuarts, and Godwin had inveighed fiercely against their despotism. But the grave denunciation of the apostasy of Strafford, the intolerance of Laud and the incorrigible insincerity of their master, exerted a far more profound effect. The attempt of Isaac Disraeli to rescue the character of James and Charles left public opinion unmoved. Speaking with a weight and an authority which no English historian had approached, Hallam delivered judgments from which there appeared to be no appeal. Yet he is by no means an unqualified admirer of the conduct of the popular party. He would have preferred the perpetual banishment of Strafford. He considers that Charles' power for mischief was broken in 1641 and that there was no need to resort to arms. He condemns the execution of Laud and the King.

In the light of subsequent research it is precisely this part of Hallam's celebrated treatise which is the most imperfect. He believed that there was a definite Constitution to break, and that the first two Stuarts broke it. Here he was inferior to Hume, who realised that they had an arguable case, since precedents pointed in different directions. Parliament possessed the power of legislation and the virtual control of supplies, but the continuous direction of foreign and domestic policy had always been the function of the Crown. Prerogative was not the enemy of law but a supplementary power covering matters for which the law did not specifically provide; in the test battles between Crown and Parliament the legal right was not always on the side of the latter. The Whig historian loves the Commonwealth and Protectorate little more than the Stuart despotism. 'He is a hanging judge,' declared Macaulay. 'His black cap is in constant requisition. In the long calendar there is hardly one who has not, in spite of evidence to character and recommendations to mercy, been sentenced and left for execution.' He recognises Cromwell's achievement in making England once again a Great Power, but he depicts him as a selfish despot of the Napoleonic type, and laments that he 'sucked the dregs of a besotted fanaticism.' On the other hand, he blesses the conservative revolution of 1688, and his discussion of that event forms a classical exposition of the Whig doctrine of government. A detailed account of the working of the newly defined constitution under William was followed by a brief survey of the reigns of his three successors. The 'Constitutional History' is one of the most impressive works in English historical literature. It became a text-book in the Universities, was quoted in Parliament, and was diligently studied as a guide by the youthful Victoria and her Consort. It was translated into French under the auspices of Guizot, and was inwardly digested by the friends of constitutional liberty all over the world.

If Hallam was the first authoritative exponent of Whig historical philosophy, Macaulay[1] was its most popular and most eloquent interpreter. It needed some effort to master the three volumes of the 'Constitutional History,' in which comment clogs the narrative, and laws and theories of government overshadow men and women; but everyone could read Macaulay, and those who shirked the stout volumes of the History could distil his views from a dozen sparkling essays. Together they shaped the opinion of the world till Ranke and Gardiner lifted the seventeenth century above the strife of Whig and Tory.

Like Thirlwall and the younger Mill, Macaulay showed extraordinary precocity. He wrote a 'Universal History,' essays and poems while other children are in the nursery. It was as difficult for him to forget as for other people to remember. On one occasion he wrote out a list of the Senior Wranglers, with their dates and colleges, for a hundred years. He declared that any fool could say his Archbishops of Canterbury backwards. He once remarked that if every copy of 'Paradise Lost,' 'The Pilgrim's Progress' or 'Sir Charles Grandison' were destroyed, he could reproduce them from recollection. His interest in politics came later, but was not less keen. The Evangelicals who frequented his father's house at Clapham were mostly Tories, but at Cambridge he learned to detest the Tory Government, and he left the University a convinced Whig. His first publications dealt with classical as well as modern themes. The Roman and Athenian sketches and the exquisite 'Conversation of Cowley and Milton on the Civil War' already revealed the power and ease of his style. With the appearance of the essay on Milton in the *Edinburgh Review* in 1825 the world became aware that a star of the first magnitude had arisen. The lightly borne knowledge, the wealth of allusion, the dazzling brilliance of the language were a revelation. 'The more

[1] See Trevelyan's classical biography, 1876; Cotter Morison's volume in the *English Men of Letters*, 1882; R. C. Beatty, *Lord Macaulay, Victorian Liberal*, 1938. Among appreciations may be mentioned Morley, *Miscellanies*, vol. ii., 1877; Leslie Stephen, *Hours in a Library*, vol. ii., 1892; Bagehot, *Literary Studies*, vol. ii, 1878; Herbert Paul, *Men and Books*. Macvey Napier's *Correspondence*, 1879, contains much material.

I think,' said Jeffrey, 'the less I can conceive where you picked up that style.' The great Whig organ had secured not only an accomplished essayist but a powerful recruit. Milton the politician is championed with not less enthusiasm than the author of 'Paradise Lost.' The first blow was struck at the Stuarts by the writer whose life was to be devoted to attacking their fame, and Cromwell was assigned a place beside Washington and Bolivar. If the article was too cocksure on grave questions of politics and taste, the defect was scarcely noticed by a generation which was accustomed to invective.

Four years later Macaulay explained his conception of the task of the historian in an essay entitled 'History.' To be a really great historian, he declared, was perhaps the rarest of intellectual distinctions. There were many perfect works of science, poems and speeches; there was no perfect history. Herodotus was a delightful romancer. Thucydides was the greatest master of perspective but not a deep thinker. Plutarch was childish, Polybius dull. No historian ever showed such complete indifference to truth as Livy. Tacitus was the greatest portrait-painter and the greatest dramatist of antiquity, but he could not be trusted. Modern historians were stricter in their notions of truth and superior in generalisation, but their bias led them to distort facts. Hume was a vast mass of sophistry. Southey wrote for the Anglican Church, Lingard for Rome. Gibbon hated the Church, Mitford the Athenians. While they were busy with controversy, they neglected the arts of narration. Facts were the mere dross of history. The ideal historian must know how to paint as well as to draw, and must embrace the culture as well as the actions of mankind.

This programme was carried out in the 'Essays,' of which some are of permanent value while others are only redeemed from oblivion by their style. The best are concerned with English history in the seventeenth and eighteenth centuries. Of these the essay on Hallam was among the earliest and most important. Under cover of a review, Macaulay takes occasion to deliver a violent attack on the Tory version of English history. The denunciation of Cranmer is almost as vigorous as that of Strafford, the 'insolent apostate.' He pronounces the whole life of Charles I a lie, and declares hatred of the liberties of his subjects to have been the ruling principle of his conduct. He brushes aside Hallam's weighty criticisms of the action of the Long Parliament. He confesses to a more unmitigated contempt for Laud, 'a ridiculous old bigot,' than for any other character in our history. He condemns the half-hearted prosecution of the war in its early stages, and it is only when we reach the last scene in 1649 that he utters a protest. Though no lover of Puritanism, his eloquent eulogy of the character and policy of Cromwell prepared the way for Carlyle. A dark picture of the Restoration leads up to the Revolution of 1688, 'glorious' for William alone. The essay on Hampden covers part of the same ground, but is written with greater restraint. The portrait of James I is in the historian's worst style; that of the stainless hero reveals his admiration for the man who shares with William the chief place in his affections. The essay on Mackintosh offered a reasoned defence of the Revolution. The studies of Horace Walpole and Chatham showed that his knowledge of the eighteenth century was not inferior to that of the seventeenth. The essays written after his return from India are weightier and less polemical. That on Temple is the ripest, and the second essay on Chatham is a masterpiece of portraiture. Of still greater merit is the biography of Pitt, written many years later for the 'Encyclopædia Britannica.' Not all the English essays reach these lofty altitudes. Macaulay's knowledge of the times before the Stuarts was scanty. That on Burleigh is mediocre, and the 'Bacon' was the most brilliant failure of his life. If the discussion of the Baconian philosophy, with its caricature of idealism and its philistine utilitarianism, is fatal to his fame as a thinker, the political narrative is scarcely better. The philosopher is exalted beyond all reason, the statesman debased beyond all justice. Though Spedding[1] swung the pendulum too far in the other direction a few years later, he at least exposed the glaring injustice of the essayist.

The two celebrated Indian essays, written shortly after his return from Calcutta, are among the most imposing of Macaulay's achievements. While every schoolboy, he complained, could date the leading battles of European history, few Englishmen knew even the names of the victories by which their race had won a foothold in Asia. Of the two 'Clive' is the more accurate but the less popular. The career of the lad who left an office stool to command armies in the field, won the battle of Plassey, rose to a dizzy height of fortune, was prosecuted by his countrymen for embezzlement and died by his own hand, was full of the colour and romance which he loved. 'Warren Hastings' put the great proconsul on the map. The conflict of the Governor-General with his Council on the one hand and the Indian potentates on the other provided a wealth of interest. The ruses by which British power was built up, the struggle with the Begums of Oude,

---

[1] His *Evenings with a Reviewer*, two vols., 1848, contained a sustained attack on the *Essay*.

the tricking of Nuncomar, follow each other in rapid succession. Over the scene broods the glamour of the opulent East, with its strange customs and glowing hues. The diabolical cleverness of the superman paves the way for the trial scene in Westminster Hall and the avenging thunderbolts of Burke. Though the picture is the most dazzling work of art in the author's gallery, it is one of the most inaccurate of his portraits. While Hastings owes his celebrity to Macaulay, his fame had to wait for vindication at other hands.

His knowledge of Continental history was limited, and he loses his sureness of touch when he embarks upon it. The essay on Machiavelli is almost as much a political dissertation as an historical study. The story of the War of the Spanish Succession is enriched by glimpses into the council chamber of Anne. The essay on Ranke's 'History of the Popes' hardly deserves its fame. In contrasting the skill with which the Papacy appropriated new movements with the blundering pedantry which drove forth Wesley, he overlooks the far greater failure of Rome to avert the Reformation. The essay on Frederick the Great is among the worst of his writings.[1] The caricature of Frederick William I is based on the memoirs of Wilhelmina, which are employed without a suspicion of their untrustworthy character. The King, he declares, could be best described as a cross between Moloch and Puck. Writing before the appearance of Ranke's 'Prussian History,' he cannot be blamed for failing to realise the significance of the founder of Prussian administration, but he might have caught at least a glance of the virtues hidden below a rugged exterior. The portrait of Frederick is scarcely more true to life. He is presented as a man of bad heart, a tyrant without fear, without faith and without mercy. To dub him a tyrant was to misconceive the 'enlightened despotism' which was one of the characteristic features of the century and effected many salutary reforms.

If Macaulay did not invent the historical essay, he found it of brick and left it of marble. His articles glitter like diamonds in the dusty pages of the *Edinburgh Review*. To compare his contributions with those of Sydney Smith, Jeffrey or Brougham is to measure the gulf which separated the old style from the new. What Shakespeare's plays achieved for the fifteenth century, Macaulay's essays accomplished for the seventeenth and eighteenth. He was the first English writer to make history universally interesting. A traveller in Australia recorded that the

[1] For German wrath see Häusser's *Ges. Schriften*, vol. i., and Du Bois-Reymond, ' Friedrich II in Englischen Urteilen,' *Reden*, vol. i.

three works he found on every squatter's shelf were the Bible, Shakespeare and the 'Essays.' The inscription on his monument in the chapel of his old college, *Ita scripsit ut vera fictis libentius legerentur*, is the simple truth. A work which appeals to men of all races must possess extraordinary merits. The secret of his power is that he is the most fascinating story-teller who ever wrote history. He has been called the Rubens of historiography. His tableaux linger in the memory as if one had seen them on the stage. In vividness of presentation he equals Carlyle, Motley and Michelet. Entering Parliament in 1830 and reaching at a bound the front rank of orators, he understood the spirit of Parliamentary government as no great historian before or after him. His dramatic power was accompanied by inexhaustible stores of knowledge which enabled him to enrich his narrative by a thousand vivid touches.

Though the dramatic instinct, experience of political life, and boundless knowledge went to the making of his best essays, the decisive factor in their success was style. To a generation accustomed to ponderous solemnity his prose, rapid, sparkling, transparent, came like a draught of water to a thirsty man. Yet it is sometimes better suited to an oration than an essay, and the coruscating eloquence becomes turgid and oppressive. Ossa is heaped upon Pelion till we groan beneath the load. The panegyric on Athenian culture in the early essay on Mitford would have been a wonderful piece of declamation, but in cold print it is almost nauseating. To read Macaulay is to take a rapid walk in a bracing air—immensely stimulating but not a form of exercise that suits every constitution or every time of life. In their high spirits, their assurance, their sumptuous pageantry, the 'Essays' are the work of a brain essentially young, and they appeal with the greatest force to the budding mind.

The omniscience of Macaulay is a legend. Though his store of knowledge was amazing, there were gigantic gaps in it. His mastery of classical literature was superb; but he knew practically nothing of the Middle Ages, except Dante and Petrarch, and even in English history before Elizabeth his equipment was that of the average cultivated man. His familiarity with the growth of Continental States was small. A master of the literature of modern England and the Latin South, he knew little of that of Germany. His acquaintance with religious and philosophic thought was extraordinarily limited. He was strangely ignorant of the patient scholarship which created historical science while he was writing his books. A second limitation is his political bias. Most of his essays appeared in a review the main object of which was the propagation of certain opinions. To apply the same standards to his essays as to those of professional scholars is to do him injustice. A political manifesto must not be judged by the same canons as a scientific treatise. There is no affectation of neutrality or indifference. He honestly believed that Whig principles were the alpha and omega of political wisdom. To the end of his days he was the man of 1832. Thus the most brilliant and popular of English historians is one of those who possess the least weight.

A third failure of the 'Essays' is their sledge-hammer brutality. Like a giant rejoicing in his strength, he deals out staggering blows. His admiring friend Mackintosh declared that he failed in little but the respect due to the abilities and character of his opponents. Melbourne wished that he was as cocksure about anything as Macaulay was about everything. Some offensive phrases were omitted or softened when the 'Essays' were republished in 1843, but the winnowing process was not very severe. 'I have beaten Croker black and blue,' he wrote, delighted at the opportunity of turning his review of an edition of Boswell into a furious attack on a political opponent. He lived to do public penance for his onslaught on the elder Mill, but he was rarely troubled by such qualms of conscience. The essays on Southey and Sadler, Barère and Robert Montgomery, are full of boisterous invective. He loves exaggerated phraseology. The verses of Frederick the Great were 'hateful to God and men.' 'We are tempted to forget the vices of Laud's heart in the imbecility of his intellect.' In comparison with the labour of reading Nares' 'Life of Burleigh' the treadmill is an agreeable recreation. With such a temperament there is little place for light and shade. 'La verité est dans les nuances,' declared Renan; but with Macaulay truth is sometimes bartered for a telling phrase or a resounding epithet. A final disability is the lack of insight into certain types of thought and character. His downright temper and straightforward nature made it difficult for him to understand complex personalities. He was too convinced of the finality of the outlook of his time— 'the most enlightened generation of the most enlightened people that ever existed'—to penetrate the mind of other ages. Carlyle tersely described him as 'an emphatic, really forcible person, but unhappily without divine idea.' The notes on his keyboard were few, the range of his emotional experience curiously limited. He had no sympathy with the passionate discontent of the disinherited or the yearnings of the mystic, and he frankly despised the speculations of philosophers from Plato downwards. He was neither a thinker nor a prophet, but a humane and cultured Philistine.

The college essay on William III showed that the personality of the Deliverer had made a deep impression on the young Whig, and the essays on Hallam and Mackintosh gave fervid expression to his admiration. In 1838 he planned a history of England from the Restoration to the death of George IV, and in 1839 he began to write. When the Melbourne Government fell in 1841 he expressed a hope that he might remain long enough in opposition to bring his narrative down to the death of Anne. But the labour proved far greater than he had anticipated. He gave up writing for the *Edinburgh Review*, refused the Chair of Modern History at Cambridge, and devoted himself wholly to his task. When death came suddenly in 1859 he had not even reached the end of William's reign. The republication of the 'Essays' in 1843 revealed the size of his public, and the 'inexhaustible demand' encouraged him in his heavier labours. On launching the first two volumes of the 'History of England' in 1848 he wrote with manly pride, 'I have had the year 2000, and even the year 3000, often in my mind.' 'I shall not be satisfied,' he wrote to Macvey Napier, 'unless I produce something which shall for a few days supersede the last fashionable novel on the tables of young ladies.' The ambition was realised. There had been nothing like it since 'Waverley.' The book was translated into the language of every civilised country, and honours poured in from foreign academies. Except for a bitter attack by his old enemy Croker in the *Quarterly*, critics of all schools joined in a chorus of congratulation. Even Alison, though pronouncing it one-sided, hailed it as a noble book.

The success was fully deserved. Though on the whole less dazzling than the 'Essays,' it was a far greater achievement.[1] It is the work of a riper mind, the vigour of youth combining with a new and welcome maturity. England, he declared, had need of both the historic parties. There is much more learning and thoroughness. He wrote slowly and took infinite pains both in collecting and shaping his material. 'He could not rest,' records his nephew and biographer, 'until every paragraph concluded with a telling sentence, and every sentence flowed like running water.' He found his reward in the enjoyment of his readers, among them men who read little else. A vote of thanks to him was carried at a meeting 'for having written a history which working-men can understand.' He was particularly gratified to learn from a reader in the printer's office that there was only one expression in the two volumes of which he did not catch the meaning at a glance. Twenty years of study went to compose the narrative of about

---

[1] It should be read in Firth's edition, 1913. Firth's posthumous volume, *Macaulay's History of England*, 1937, is a masterpiece.

the same length of time. Though only a fragment of the complete design, it is none the less the greatest historical work in the English language since Gibbon. 'It will be my endeavour to relate the history of the people as well as the history of the government, to trace the progress of useful and ornamental arts, to describe the rise of religious sects and the change of literary taste, to portray the manners of successive generations.' The famous third chapter on the condition of England in 1685 supplied a background to the drama. While the 'Essays' revealed a rare power of concentration, the success of the History depended on having plenty of elbow-room. It is the limitation of his method that it can only be applied to a short period, and one in regard to which information is plentiful.

After a rapid survey of English history before the Restoration, a brilliant chapter on the reign of Charles II and a panoramic view of the country, the detailed narrative starts with the accession of James II. Opening with the expedition of Monmouth and the Bloody Assizes, and culminating in the attack on the Universities, the trial of the seven Bishops, the coming of William and the flight of James, the story is a continual succession of arresting scenes. The volumes on James II end with an eloquent pæan to the Revolution of 1688, written under the shadow of 1848. 'It was a revolution strictly defensive. In almost every word and act may be discerned a profound reverence for the past. Of all revolutions the least violent, it has been of all revolutions the most beneficent. Its highest eulogy is that it was our last revolution. For the authority of law, for the security of property, for the peace of our streets, for the happiness of our homes, our gratitude is due, under Him Who raises and pulls down nations, to the Long Parliament, to the Convention and to William of Orange.' Seven years later two volumes on William III made their appearance. The heroic soul tried by a thousand vicissitudes, the cold exterior concealing a heart full of tenderness for his wife, for Bentinck and for Keppel, the complete subordination of self to the interests of Protestant Europe, combine into the most wonderful portrait Macaulay ever painted. Beside his towering figure even the best of the politicians, Whigs and Tories alike, appear puny and selfish. The preparation for these volumes was even more arduous than for their predecessors. 'I will first set myself to get, by reading and travelling, a full acquaintance with William's reign. I must visit Holland, Belgium, Scotland, France. The Dutch and French archives must be ransacked. I must see Londonderry, the Boyne, Aughrim, Limerick, Kinsale, Namur again, Landen, Steinkirk. I must turn over hundreds, thousands of pamphlets.' The programme thus noted in his journal was faithfully carried out. To this direct knowledge of the localities the History owes much of its vitality. Where all is brilliant, the siege of Londonderry and the massacre of Glencoe shine with peculiar lustre. The origin of the National Debt, the foundation of the Bank of England, and the expedition to Darien, form little monographs of skilful workmanship.

The 'History' is a pæan to the Revolution and to its principal author. A more critical generation adopts Macaulay's view of the blessings of 1688, but it regards the actors in the drama in a somewhat different manner. A few years after he laid down his pen the greatest of modern historians traversed part of the same ground. Ranke[1] contended that the Whigs to whom Macaulay attributed the merits of the Long Parliament of Charles II were hardly a separate body, and contested the picture of the Tories as ultra-clerical and ultra-monarchical. They urged war with France and arranged the marriage of Mary and William, both opposed by the Whigs, and they were as ready to fetter James as their opponents. They talked less of the right of resistance, but when the danger came to Church and Constitution they were as eager to defend them. Nor can Macaulay's portrait of James, of whom he speaks throughout with contemptuous loathing, be fully accepted. The picture of William suffers from excess of light, and the attempt to wash off the stain of Glencoe is a failure.

The exaggeration of virtues and defects and the inability to understand certain types of character reappear in the History. Marlborough is 'a prodigy of turpitude'—a miser, a profligate, a traitor, a murderer. In the words of John Paget,[2] who submitted the portrait to a searching analysis, 'documents are suppressed, dates transposed, witnesses of the most infamous character paraded as pure and unimpeachable, forgotten and anonymous slanders of the foulest description revived.' The plan of the descent on Brest, the betrayal of which is described as 'the basest of all his hundred villainies,' was already well known to Louis XIV. The Duchess appears as a shrew without talent or character. George Fox is pelted with abuse in the worst style of the early essays. The treatment of Penn aroused justifiable resentment in the Society of Friends. Aytoun sprang to the rescue of Dundee. Babington published a detailed reply to the picture of the character and social status of the clergy. Macaulay was too ready

---

[1] The approach of the two historians is discussed in Noorden's article, 'Ranke u. Macaulay,' *Hist. Zeitschrift*, vol. xvii.

[2] *The New Examen*, 1861, a powerful and interesting work.

to accept as evidence whatever he found in the pamphlets and broadsheets of the day. Speaking of the volumes on William III Mill declared them pleasant reading, but not exactly history.[1] 'He aims at stronger effects than truth warrants, and so carica- tures many of his personages as to leave it unaccountable how they can have done what they did. What a difference between him and Grote, who is less brilliant but far more interesting in his simple veracity, and because, instead of striving to astonish, he seeks to comprehend and explain.' 'Four hundred editions could not lend it any permanent value,' wrote Carlyle in his journal, 'there being no depth of sense in it, and a very great quantity of rhetorical wind.' These strictures are overdone, but Macaulay's grasp of one important aspect of his subject was limited. His picture of the revolution of 1688 is too insular. Where he supplies new material, as in the Triple Alliance, the treaty of Dover, Barillon's negotiations with the Opposition and the peace of Ryswick, he never grasps all the threads. Here again Ranke's European vision supplements the work of his predecessor. A final criticism must be hazarded. He is better at description than at explanation. No historian of the front rank has shown himself more blind to the invisible world of thought and emotion, or made less effort to fathom the depths on which the pageantry of events floats like shining foam.

The combined efforts of Hallam and Macaulay rescued the critical century of English history from the dominion of Hume, but Toryism found a new champion in Alison.[2] 'I was induced to adventure on a history of Europe during the Revolution,' he wrote, 'by the clear perception that affairs were hurrying on to some great social and political convulsion in this country. The passion for innovation which had for many years overspread the nation, the vague ideas afloat in the public mind, the facility with which Government entered into these views—all these had awakened gloomy presentiments in my mind.' The first volume appeared in 1833, the tenth in 1842. The preface is a singularly frank statement of his political and religious philosophy. 'If there is one opinion more than another impressed on the mind by an examination of the French Revolution, it is the perilous nature of the current into which men are drawn who commit themselves to the stream of political innovation.' Happily the follies of men are checked by a stronger hand. 'The actors were overruled by an unseen power, which rendered their vices and ambitions the means of vindicating the justice of the divine

[1] Mill's *Letters*, vol. i., 188–9, 1910.
[2] *Autobiography*, 2 vols., 1883.

administration, asserting the final triumph of virtue over vice, and ultimately effecting the deliverance of mankind.' The narrative breathes the same spirit of uncompromising Toryism. The Revolution was an outburst of anarchy, purely destructive in its principles and results; like other violent outbreaks, it tended to effect its own cure. 'From the death of Louis XVI a reaction in favour of order and religion began throughout the globe.' Among its champions was George III, 'who never lost power with the thinking few.' The work closes with a hundred pages of moral reflections. 'Democracy cannot exist and never has existed for long in an old society. It must either destroy the community or be destroyed itself.'

The 'History of Europe,' naïvely described by the author as a great effort in favour of the Conservative cause, became the bible of the Tory party, which found in it the tonic it needed during the early years of the reformed Parliament. It was not, however, its Toryism which procured it world-wide popularity for more than a generation. Alison himself rightly attributed his success to the surpassing interest of his subject and his priority in the field. Readers could afford to overlook his platitudes in return for the first comprehensive survey of the most eventful years in modern history. No gentleman's library in England or America was deemed complete without the massive volumes of the Scottish magistrate, and translations carried his message all over Europe. But the rising tide of democracy and the growth of disinterested historical scholarship gradually sapped his fame. A continuation of the History to the *coup d'état* of Louis Napoleon lacked the dramatic interest of its predecessor. Soon after the author's death in 1867 the 'History of Europe' began to be banished to the dusty recesses of the second-hand bookshop.

One scene of Alison's colossal drama was described in greater detail and with very different authority by Napier.[1] The 'History of the Peninsular War,' in which he received assistance both from Wellington and Soult, is the finest military history in English, but it reveals a bias as pronounced as that of Alison or Macaulay. 'The Spaniards have boldly asserted, and the world has believed, that the deliverance of the Peninsula was the work of their hands. This assertion I combat.' The primary cause of the downfall of Spain, he declares, was the union of a superstitious Court with a sanguinary priesthood. They were cruel and bigoted, ignorant and boastful, and the unmitigated ferocity they displayed in the war was a disgrace to human nature. The French, on the other

---

[1] For the extensive literature provoked by his book see *Dict. Nat. Biog.*

hand, excite his admiration, for they were so brave that only British soldiers could defeat them. Though he charges Napoleon with guile and tyranny, he pronounces him the greatest man in history, the most wonderful commander, the most profound politician. He expresses frank admiration for Soult and other French generals. The hero of the book is Sir John Moore. Even the Portuguese receive a tribute. The strong feelings of the author, however, rarely affect the value of the military narrative. The pictures of Albuera and the other battles and sieges in which he took part are more vivid than those which Kinglake, his only serious rival, was to paint of the Crimea. It is the work of a soldier who teaches that war is the rule of the world, and that from man to the smallest insect all living things are at strife.

In addition to the writings of Hallam and Macaulay, Alison and Napier, which were read all over the world, useful works were produced which appealed rather to students than to the great public. James Mill's[1] 'History of British India,' described by Macaulay during the debates of 1833 as 'on the whole the greatest historical work which has appeared in our language since that of Gibbon,' required an effort to read. The subject was remote, the treatment detailed, the tone of the work censorious. The Utilitarian philosopher described with scant sympathy a society resting on caste and tradition. At a time when Sir William Jones had encouraged an excessive admiration for Hindu civilisation, Mill's survey of the laws and institutions, manners and arts, religion and literature of the Indian peoples came as a bitter draught; but his judgment on the Company and its agents was no less severe. He spoke modestly of his 'heavy volumes.' The want of personal knowledge of India, which he maintained was an aid to impartiality, deprives it of touches which might have softened its rigid outlines. Sympathy and imagination are lacking. The value of the work lay in its mass of information and its analytical power. It took rank among the classics of its time, and won him a place in the India House. Revised and continued a generation later by Horace Wilson, it remained canonical for two generations and was adopted as a text-book for candidates for the Indian Civil Service. On the other hand, Max Müller[2] declared it responsible for some of the greatest misfortunes that had happened to India, even with the antidote against its poison supplied by Wilson's notes.

No writer of the age of Hallam and Mill was so unwearied in

[1] See Bain, *James Mill*, 1882, and Leslie Stephen, *The English Utilitarians*, vol. ii.
[2] *India: What can it teach us?* Lecture ii., 1882.

the publication of new material as William Coxe. His lives of the Walpoles, Marlborough and Pelham are still indispensable to the student of the eighteenth century, while his massive histories of the House of Austria and the Spanish Bourbons opened a new field of study. Though utterly lacking in narrative power and literary instinct. he was a conscientious editor, and his works formed a quarry from which abler men were to draw. More popular in treatment, though based on considerable study of manuscript sources, were Agnes Strickland's 'Lives of the Queens of England' and Tytler's 'History of Scotland,' the latter under- taken at the instigation of Walter Scott. A thoughtful and com- prehensive 'History of England during the Thirty Years' Peace' was compiled by Harriet Martineau, which is still worth consult- ing as the work of a well-informed contemporary.

CHAPTER XV

THIRLWALL, GROTE AND ARNOLD

I

THE classics had been more generally studied in England since the Renaissance than in any other country, and the first history of classical times with any pretensions to scholarship was written by an Englishman. On discovering that his friend Mitford[1] was a lover of Greek literature, Gibbon suggested that he should write a history of Greece. The work was begun without reference to the problems of the day, and the first volume appeared in 1784, but when the French Revolution broke out the historian used his work to strike at the Whigs and Jacobins. To those who admired the freedom of the Greek republics and asserted that their institutions were best calculated to produce happiness, he replied that it was a complete mistake to suppose that they secured well-being in the country of their origin. Security of person and property was unknown, the rulers were dominated by jealousy and greed, and society rested on a slave basis. Sparta, the best of them, made no pretence to democracy. For Mitford democracy is despotism; the British Constitution under George III the best the world had ever seen. He preferred Persians, Carthaginians and Macedonians to Greeks. He eulogised the Tyrants, while eagerly swallowing every scandal about democrats and demagogues. He naturally sides with Macedon, and denounces Demosthenes as a coward and a rogue. 'Mitford,' writes Freeman, 'was a bad scholar, a bad historian, and a bad writer of English. Yet we feel a lingering weakness for him. He was the first writer of any note who found out that Greek history was a living thing with a practical bearing.' Nearly all modern historians of Greece, declared Macaulay,[2] divested men of individuality and made them mere types; from this grave fault Mitford was free. But this was his only merit, and it was itself in part the result of his unbridled partisanship. The book owed its success mainly to its

[1] See the memoir by his brother Lord Redesdale in vol. i. of the edition of 1837. There are some interesting judgments on Mitford and his successors in Mahaffy's Introduction to the English translation of Duruy's *History of Greece*, 1892.
[2] 'Mitford's *History of Greece*,' in *Miscellaneous Essays*.

political bias. The Tories quoted it as a generation later they quoted Alison. 'Mitford,' wrote Macaulay in 1824, 'enjoys a great and increasing popularity. He has reached a high place among historians without being challenged. He should have been attacked on the appearance of his first volume. To oppose the progress of his fame is now almost a hopeless enterprise.' The slashing article delighted the Whigs, but it availed little against an established reputation, and a second edition, revised by the author, appeared in 1829. Yet the day of emancipation was not far off. The Reform Bill marked the birth of a generation completely out of sympathy with the historian's standpoint, while the appearance of two new histories of Greece, at once more scholarly and more liberal, provided effective substitutes.

In his attack on Mitford Macaulay expressed his longing for a real history of Greece, embracing not only its politics but its society, art and literature, in order that the modern world might become conscious of its debt. A few years later the first scholarly survey in any language was published by Thirlwall, who, after winning a fellowship at Trinity College, Cambridge, spent some years at the Chancery Bar.[1] In 1827 he was ordained and returned to Trinity, where he joined Julius Hare in translating Niebuhr. He accepted a crown living in Yorkshire, and in 1840 was appointed Bishop of St. Davids. When invited to write a history of Greece for Lardner's Cyclopædia, he gladly undertook the task. The first volume was published in 1835, the eighth in 1844. A revised and expanded edition appeared between 1845 and 1852. The author declared himself abundantly satisfied with its reception. His modest ambition was 'to leave the history of Greece in some respects in better condition than he found it.' Reserved in the expression of opinion and lacking colour and enthusiasm, he possessed none of the arts of popularity, but his faultless scholarship and balanced judgment made him the companion of students willing to take some trouble to reach their goal.

The work opens with a sketch of the geography of the Greek world, a discussion of the early races, and a picture of the culture of the heroic age. Unlike Mitford, who believed in the reality of the Homeric personages, the disciple of Niebuhr carefully distinguishes legend from history. His survey of the golden period

---

[1] See his *Letters*, 1881, and J. C. Thirlwall, *Connop Thirlwall*, 1936. For appreciations see *Edinburgh Review*, April, 1876 (by Plumptre), and J. W. Clark, *Old Friends at Cambridge and Elsewhere*, 1900. He often appears in Wemyss Reid, *Life of Lord Houghton*, 1890. For German influences on English classical scholars see Dockhorn, *Der deutsche Historismus in England*, 1950.

of Athens is cool, clear and business-like, but lacks colour and atmosphere. He never visited and never desired to visit Greece. There is no thrill in the narrative of Marathon, and the art and literature of the age of Pericles occupy but little space. The struggle at Syracuse loses something of its tragedy and Alcibiades much of his glitter. Thirlwall has no hero except Socrates. His chapter on the internal condition of Athens during and after the Peloponnesian war is a balanced summary. 'Fickle, passionate, often unjust, they were also capable of mercy and pity.' The struggle between Philip and Demosthenes was fully and fairly described. The latter appears to him 'good and great'—far greater than Phocion, who, though personally of high character, became the slave of the conqueror. Philip, though unscrupulous and intriguing, was not without generous instincts. Few historians have taken such a favourable view of Alexander's aims and achievements. 'His ambition almost grew, in the collateral aims which ennobled and purified it, into one with the highest of which man is capable.' His conquests were highly beneficial to the vanquished. But the blessings of his work which were experienced in Asia were barely felt in Greece. 'In many important respects her condition changed for the worse.' The book closes with a brief survey of events till the destruction of Corinth made Greece a Roman province. Thirlwall's merits are conspicuous. He incorporated the results of Böckh and Otfried Müller, Welcker and Droysen, Creuzer and Lobeck, who were recovering Greek antiquity for the modern world. His judgment was equal to his scholarship. Lord Houghton, who knew everybody, when asked to name the most remarkable man he had ever known, replied without hesitation, 'Thirlwall.' The faults of the book are negative, not positive. The actors are a little shadowy, and the drama has the air of having been acted long ago. It was left to a greater contemporary to bring the Athenian democracy back to life and to rivet the gaze of the world on its achievements.

At the age of twenty-eight Grote[1] began the systematic study of Greek history, and in 1826 he announced the views he had formed in an article on Mitford. While admitting the faults of the Greek democracies, he submits that they must be fairly judged. 'Compare them with any other form of government in ancient times and we have no hesitation in pronouncing them unquestion-

---

[1] See Mrs. Grote, *The Personal Life of George Grote*, 1873, and Bain's Introduction to Grote's *Minor Works*, 1873. For expert appreciations see Pöhlmann, *Aus Alterthum u. Gegenwart*, 1895; Lehrs, *Populäre Aufsätze*, 1875; Gomperz, *Essays u. Erinnerungen*, 1905; Freeman, *Historical Essays*, Second Series, 1873.

ably superior. That the securities they provided for good government were lamentably deficient we fully admit, but the oligarchies and the monarchies afforded no security at all.' He grapples with Mitford's contentions that the assemblies were fickle, the democracies unstable, the rich overtaxed, and castigates his gross blunders in scholarship. 'It is obvious,' he concludes, 'that an historian who can thus deviate from his authorities in recounting specific facts is still less to be relied on for accuracy in any general views. Should Greek history ever be written with care and fidelity, we venture to predict that his reputation will be prodigiously lowered.' The young banker had already made the acquaintance of Bentham and the elder Mill, and was regarded as a promising recruit of the small but influential group of Philosophic Radicals. When the Whigs returned to power in 1830 after their long eclipse he determined to enter Parliament, and from 1833 to 1841 he represented the City of London. With Roebuck and Molesworth he endeavoured to lead Grey and Melbourne further along the road of democracy than they cared to go. It was an experience of extraordinary interest and value, but he had no wish to prolong it; when the Whigs fell in 1841 he withdrew from the political arena. Two years later he retired from the bank, and devoted himself to his 'History of Greece,' of which the first volume appeared in 1846 and the twelfth in 1856. His scholarship was sound and he profited by 'the inestimable aid of German erudition.' He had carefully studied the early history of other civilisations. He was a trained metaphysician, to whom the subtleties of Greek speculation presented no difficulties. He was a convinced believer in democracy and ardently sympathised with the attempts made by the Greek States to realise it. Finally his experience of political life helped him to feel and make his readers feel the reality of the problems which the statesmen and thinkers of Greece attempted to solve.

The work begins with a survey of the traditions of early Greece, his view of which he had explained in an article on Greek Legends and Early History. No attempt to rationalise them could winnow the wheat from the chaff: they were simply the creation of the fancy of an imaginative people. This attitude governs the first two volumes of the History. 'I know nothing so disheartening and unrequited as the elaborate balancing of what is called evidence concerning these shadowy times and persons. If the reader blame me for not assisting him, if he ask me why I do not withdraw the curtain and disclose the picture, I reply, in the words of the painter Zeuxis, that the curtain is the picture.' He would not have devoted so much space to the legends had he not found them of interest as a revelation of the budding mind of man. As scientific views of the universe developed, myths came to be treated as allegories. He shows wide knowledge of sagas and legends and utilises the latest German scholarship. The discussion of prehistoric Greece concludes with an analysis of the Homeric poems. Steering a middle course between the Homeric authorship and the ballad theory of Wolf and Lachmann, he pronounces the Odyssey as in all probability the work of a single brain. The Iliad, on the other hand, was originally an epic on Achilles, on which other and minor episodes were grafted. Composed in the ninth century they were handed down by memory for about 200 years, and assumed the form in which we know them under Pisistratus.

'Historical Greece' opens with a brief geographical sketch. The narrative begins with the Spartan polity, and we reach firm ground with Solon, the first of the historian's heroes. At this point, when Greece begins to play a part in history, he surveys the world in chapters on Asia Minor, the Phœnicians, the Assyrians and the Egyptians. Having thus drawn a political map, he sketches the foundation of Greek colonies in the Mediterranean. The kernel of the book is the story of the Athenian democracy, which begins with the reforms of Cleisthenes. A rapid improvement, he declares, was wrought in the people. 'The active cause was the grand and new idea of the sovereign people, composed of free and equal citizens. It was this which acted with electric effect, creating a host of sentiments, motives, capacities to which they had before been strangers.' This exaltation lasted till about fifty years before the battle of Chæronea, when the Athenians fell to the level of other Greeks. 'Because democracy happens to be unpalatable to most modern readers, they have been accustomed to look on the sentiment only in its least honourable manifestations, such as the caricatures of Aristophanes. We must listen to it as it comes from the lips of Pericles.' The Persian wars showed that the Athenians could act as well as talk, but they were on their guard against victorious generals. Grote laments the fall of Miltiades after Marathon, but argues that he deserved his disgrace. Fickleness was not an attribute of the Athenians, for they were constant to Nicias and Phocion. They were faithful to their leaders so long as the leaders were faithful to Athens. After the Persian wars the Constitution reached its final form. Cleisthenes had swept away the distinctions founded on birth and diminished those founded on property. The remaining disabilities now disappeared. Athens was governed by a sovereign assembly of which every citizen was a member and from which all the officers of state were chosen. This government first substituted law for force, and was one of the best the world has ever seen. Its ideal character, if not its actual working, is enshrined in the immortal oration of Pericles. It was the golden age of rational liberty. 'No modern state presents anything like the generous tolerance we read of here.' Unfortunately it depended largely on Pericles himself, and when he was gone the decline began. 'His incorruptible public morality, his caution and firmness in a country where all these qualities were rare and their union still rarer, were without a parallel in Greek history.'

Grote is by no means blind to the faults of the Athenians. He censures the cruelties which disgraced their wars, and condemns the execution of the generals after Arginusæ as a breach of the law, though he believes them guilty. In praising Nicias for his incorruptibility, he adds that it was a quality rare in Greek public men. He sharply condemns the Sicilian expedition. On the other hand he contends that they have been unjustly condemned on more than one ground. He explains and defends ostracism as a mild substitute for impeachment and executions. He champions Cleon against the satire of Aristophanes and the malice of Thucydides. The chapters on the Sophists and Socrates are among the most original in the book. Like the Scribes and Pharisees, the Sophists are known from the descriptions of their enemies. 'I know few characters in history who have been so hardly dealt with. They bear the penalty of their name.' Their task was to teach young men to think, speak and act, to prepare them for the duties and responsibilities of citizenship. They were moralists, not philosophers, a profession, not a sect. There is no shred of evidence that their influence was bad or that the time of their popularity was an era of degeneration. He stigmatises as a legend the decline of Athenian character. 'It is my belief that the people had become both morally and politically better, and that their democracy had worked to their improvement.' Socrates was himself a Sophist, or public teacher, differing from the rest in the publicity of his teaching, his refusal of fees, and his missionary enthusiasm. That he was a good man does not prove that they were bad men or that his teaching was more useful than theirs. His contemporaries did not see him, as we do, through the golden haze of Plato's eloquence. Religious innovators have never been tenderly treated either in pagan or Christian times, and only Athens would have tolerated Socrates so long.

In the fourth century Athens is no longer the chief actor in the drama, but the lamp of Greek civilisation still burned as brightly as ever. Grote's admiration for Epaminondas is boundless. A greater soldier though a lesser statesman than Pericles, the famous

Theban alone reaches his stature. Agesilaus receives his due, and the historian lingers over the career of Timoleon, the Washington of antiquity. Athens herself had no lack of noble citizens, but they were powerless to avert her doom. That she was vanquished by brute force is no reason why we should bow the knee to her conqueror. He admits that her fall was in some measure due to herself. 'The Athenian of B.C. 360 had, as it were, grown old. He had become a quiet, home-keeping, refined citizen.' At such a time the influence of Phocion proved fatal. But for him Athens might have repulsed Philip before he became irresistible. Though he deplores his policy, Grote recognises his personal excellence, but in Demosthenes he salutes the union of virtue and wisdom. As Pericles incarnates the spirit of Athens in her glory, Demosthenes is the principal ornament of the declining Hellenic world. The neglect of his advice brought Greek democracy to a violent end on the battlefield of Chæronea.

The picture of Philip is hostile without being radically unjust. He was a good general, though he was lucky in having no competent Greek commander against him. He was not without culture; but he lacked moderation, held the oriental view of woman, and disgraced himself by drunkenness. His son Alexander was far worse. The prince whom Droysen had glorified and Thirlwall had praised appears to Grote, as to Niebuhr, a barbarian of genius, powerful only to destroy. He inherited his ungovernable impulses from his savage Epirot mother. The razing of Thebes was a cruelty unprecedented even in a cruel age. The murders of Philotas and Parmenio displayed his ruthlessness, that of Cleitus his unbridled passions. Fighting and conquering were both the business and the luxury of his life. His raid into Asia was like Attila's attack on Europe. On the death of Darius he assumed the pomp and adopted the habits of a Persian King. 'Instead of hellenising Asia he was tending to asiatise Macedonia and Hellas.' His 'cities' were only fortified posts to hold the country in subjection. Of all his foundations Alexandria alone flourished. While Greece had stood for liberty, Hellenistic Asia was incurably despotic. The only definite advantages of the Macedonian conquests were the improvement of communications, the growth of commerce, and the increased knowledge of geography. If the conqueror had lived he would probably have subjugated the habitable world, including Rome. But he and his father had done enough mischief. 'After Alexander the political action of Greece becomes cramped and degraded, no longer interesting to the reader or operative on the destinies of the world.' Demosthenes took poison to escape death at the hands of the Macedonians.

The Achæan League, 'a sprout from the ruined tree of Greek liberty,' never attained more than a puny life. Of all that had made Greece great only the schools of philosophy survived.

The work was received with a chorus of admiration. His old schoolfellow Thirlwall had once remarked, 'Grote is the man to write a history of Greece.' After reading the first volume he wrote that, high as were his expectations, they were very much surpassed. 'It affords an earnest of something which has never been done for the subject in our own or any other literature. It has afforded me some gratification that his views do not seem greatly to diverge from mine on more than a few important points.' After the first four volumes he confessed 'the great inferiority' of his own performance. 'I may well be satisfied with that measure of temporary success and usefulness which has attended it, and can unfeignedly rejoice that it will, for all the highest purposes, be superseded.' The admiration was mutual, for Grote declared that if Thirlwall's book had appeared a few years sooner, he would probably never have written. The 'History of Greece' is one of the great historical books of the world. The style lacks colour and grace, but few works make such an impression of sustained intellectual power. He confesses that it was planned when Greece became known through Mitford, and that its object was to provide a juster view. For him the Greeks were 'the people by whom the first spark was set to the dormant intellectual capacities of our nature,' and his volumes are a glowing tribute of gratitude and admiration. No writer before or since has done so much to make the world realise the importance of Greece for the statesman and the citizen. Well might Freeman declare that the reading of Grote was an epoch in a man's life. While others had celebrated the mother of philosophy and science, literature and art, he regretted that her literary glory had overshadowed her political greatness. Her highest achievement, her most precious contribution to humanity, was political liberty. Thus Greek history, and above all Athenian history, appeared in a new light. 'He is the first statesman,' wrote Lehrs, 'who has given us a picture of Greece.' There was hardly a fact of importance, declared Mill, which was perfectly understood before he re-examined it.

A century of research and discussion, the revelation of Mycenæan civilisation, the discovery of the 'Politeia,' have overthrown or modified many of his conclusions, but whatever else is read, parts of Grote must be read also. His preface shows that he was aware of one of the pitfalls of the historian. 'We have to judge of the whole Hellenic world, eminently multiform as it was, from a few compositions, bearing too exclusively the stamp of

Athens.' Despite this caution his book is rather Athenian than Hellenic. The earlier and later history suffers in consequence, and some of the minor states receive less than their due. His hatred of usurpers blinded him to the fact that the rule of the Tyrants was not the result of mere personal ambition but met a certain need. He overlooked some of the weaknesses of the Athenian State. 'Grote,' wrote Schömann,[1] 'has refuted not a few charges which have been brought against the Athenian Demos, reduced others to smaller proportions, and explained and extenuated what could not be praised. But though we gladly agree in all the good he says of the Athenians, it cannot modify our judgment of their democracy. Even the Athenian people soon experienced its mischievous effects.' Yet his partisanship is of the least harmful type. 'His work,' pronounces Freeman, 'is even more honourable to his moral than to his intellectual qualities, for he gives facts which tell against his own conclusions. We read what he says, not as the sentence of a judge but as the pleading of an advocate; yet it is a great thing to have the pleading of such an advocate.' Another obvious weakness is the neglect of economic influences. He does not see the gradual development of a gulf between the bourgeoisie and the proletariat. By terminating his narrative in the fourth century he evades consideration of the results of the system which he eulogised and which were already becoming obvious. Finally the conception of the work of Alexander is radically false. It was a grave error to regard him as a barbarian, as alien to Greece as Xerxes or Darius. The Macedonian dynasty was closely allied to Greek stock, the Macedonian Court was saturated with Greek influences, and Alexander, the pupil of Aristotle, was an enthusiastic student of Greek literature. Greek civilisation reached the modern world through his conquests not less than through Rome. Merivale remarked satirically that he had interrupted his story just where it began to be interesting, and Freeman wrote a history of the federations which showed how the political instinct of the Greeks adapted itself to the changed surroundings.

II

The critical study of Roman history in England was inaugurated by the translation of Niebuhr, but his fame owes most to Thomas Arnold.[2] No English scholar hailed the revised volumes with greater delight, and no one entertained a deeper veneration

[1] *Athenian Constitutional History as represented in Grote*, Eng. trans., by B. Bosanquet, 1878.

[2] See Stanley, *Life and Correspondence of Thomas Arnold*, 1844.

for the author, whom he visited at Bonn. ' It is a work,' he wrote, ' of such extraordinary ability and learning that it opened wide before my eyes the extent of my own ignorance.' He planned a history of Rome, not to rival the production of so great a man but because it was not likely to become popular in England. When Niebuhr died, he was more desirous than ever to restate his conclusions and continue his work. His ambition was to imitate his method of inquiry, ' to practise his master art of doubting rightly and believing rightly.' He approached his task with becoming modesty. 'As to any man being a fit continuator of Niebuhr,' he wrote to Hare, ' that is absurd; but I have at least the qualification of an unbounded veneration for what he has done, and I should like to try to embody the thoughts and notions I have learnt from him.' The first volume of the ' History of Rome ' appeared in 1838, and covered the period before the invasion of the Gauls. The legends are related in archaic style to suggest that they are only romances. In the story of the Kings he finds a little, but only a little, that is historical. In this part of his work it is the pen of Arnold and the voice of Niebuhr: even the bold hypothesis of the ballads is accepted. The second volume reaches the end of the First Punic War. The third, bringing the narrative within sight of the end of the Second Punic War, was almost completed when the author died in 1841. Thus Arnold's book, like that of his master, remained a fragment.

His early death decreed that his History should be remembered mainly as an adaptation of Niebuhr: had he lived longer he would have shown he could walk alone. He was far better fitted to portray the life of a state than to reconstruct the faint outlines of an early civilisation. His strength grows as he advances, and his third volume is as superior to the second as the second to the first. 'The most remarkable of his talents,' wrote his friend Hare, ' was his singular geographical eye, which enabled him to find as much pleasure in looking at a map as lovers of painting in a Raphael.' This gift, added to his interest in military affairs, enabled him to interpret Hannibal. His admirable style, easy and flowing yet full of colour, found in the Second Punic War a theme worthy of itself. It was a loss to literature that the hand which traced the portrait of the great Carthaginian was not spared to recount the fortunes of the Gracchi and the closing years of the Republic. The later part of an early sketch of Roman history was reprinted as a continuation, but it is a poor substitute for the unwritten volumes, and is chiefly of interest for the outspoken condemnation of Cæsar. 'In moral character the whole range of history can hardly furnish a picture of greater deformity.

Never did any man occasion so large an amount of human misery with so little provocation.' The portrait of Augustus is scarcely less severe, and the work forms a passionate indictment of Cæsarism. The fundamental principle of Arnold's conception of history was that it was a divine process, and that man was a moral being accountable for his actions. He scornfully rejects the plea that the laws of morality which govern private relations are inapplicable to the action of rulers. The greater the sinner, the greater the sin. The end never justifies the means. The moral test is never absent in the volumes on Rome, and it appears with added emphasis in the course delivered as Regius Professor of History at Oxford in 1841. In these once famous lectures we meet rather the theologian than the historian. History is the setting forth of God's glory by doing His appointed work. 'We are living in the latest period of the world's history. We are the last reserve of the world—its fate is in our hands. God's work on earth will be left undone unless we do it.' The Niebuhr era lasted for a generation and Arnold was the last of its prophets. In 1855 there appeared a work which denounced the method of divination and rejected the reconstruction of early Roman history. The scepticism of Cornewall Lewis exceeded all bounds, but it none the less revealed the unsubstantial character of Niebuhr's foundations. A year or two later his reign was brought to an end and Mommsen ruled in his stead.

While the Republic was eagerly studied in the pages of Niebuhr and Arnold, Imperial Rome was almost totally neglected till the middle of the century. In 1840 Merivale[1] undertook a short book on the Empire for the Society for the Diffusion of Useful Knowledge, but the Society failed before his task was accomplished. A visit to the Eternal City in 1845 increased his interest, and in 1850 the 'History of the Romans under the Empire' began to appear. The preface calls attention to 'the remarkable deficiency of our recent literature in any complete narrative of the most interesting period of Roman annals.' He wrote, he added, because Arnold had not written. But though he describes himself as Arnold's 'admirer and friend,' his political standpoint is fundamentally different. The first two volumes extend from the first triumvirate to the death of Cæsar, whose career is described as the prelude to the history of four centuries. 'The Imperium of his successors rose majestic and secure from the lines drawn by the most sagacious statesman of the Commonwealth.' In the preface to a later edition, he declares that he should have begun with the Gracchi. 'This would have shown the necessity for an

[1] See *Autobiography and Letters*, 1898.

entire reconstruction of society on a monarchical basis. The Roman oligarchy was the most wasting tyranny the civilised world has ever witnessed. Mankind groaned in misery and degradation that a hundred families might have the privilege of slandering and slaying one another. It deserved to perish, and its destroyers were benefactors to their species.' Merivale admired strong governments, and when Louis Napoleon made his *coup d'état* in 1851 he remarked that he would have done the same. He admits Cæsar's vicious private life, but his public work was beneficent. The two following volumes are devoted to Augustus, 'a man of genius.' He refuses to regard the early Empire as a despotism. There were bad Emperors, but as a whole they were kept within bounds by the Senate, and their joint rule brought peace and happiness to the Roman world. 'There has been no government in human history in which law and usage have been so carefully observed by the ruling power as that of the Empire from Augustus to Pertinax.' Though he deals leniently with the Emperors, he does not attempt to whitewash Tiberius, nor does he idealise Roman society. He admits a growing tendency to despotism, though he suggests that the Romans bore it easily because they were themselves despots. After the fall of the Julian dynasty the narrative moves more swiftly. The work ends with Marcus Aurelius, partly to avoid competition with Gibbon, partly because the constitutional period of the Roman monarchy then terminated.

Merivale's work was written at a time when it had no competitors. The scholarship was sound, the narrative clear and vigorous. He was a convinced and enthusiastic advocate of the Empire. He exposed the unfairness of Tacitus, Suetonius and Dion, and reminded his readers that they wrote long after the events they described. He rescued Claudius from undeserved contempt, and claimed for the Flavian period the admiration which Gibbon reserved for the Antonines. Domitian himself began as a reformer. If Arnold was tempted to judge rulers by too high a standard, Merivale asked too little of human nature. He was so much impressed by the outward success of the Empire that he paid little heed to its inner rottenness. He made Cæsar and Augustus the chiefs of a popular party who erected their rule on the ruins of a corrupt oligarchy, instead of a pseudo-democratic despotism like that of the Bonapartes. The book lost its authority, not because it was superseded by a later work on the same subject, but because it was based on literary sources alone. While it was being written Mommsen and his pupils were already laying the foundation of a deeper knowledge of the Empire in the 'Corpus Inscriptionum Latinarum.'

CHAPTER XVI

CARLYLE AND FROUDE

I

DURING the first half of the nineteenth century no British writer except Macaulay gave such an impetus to historical study as Carlyle.[1] While the English Whig employed history to justify his political convictions, the Scottish Calvinist used it to illustrate his ethical teaching. He devoted his early years to German literature, and it was not till he reached the threshold of middle age that he began to prepare for wider flights. His essay 'On History,' published in 1830, reveals his first thoughts. Pronouncing it to be the essence of innumerable biographies, he emphasises the contribution of the humble to the making of civilisation. 'Which was the greatest benefactor, he who gained the battles of Cannæ and Trasimene or the nameless poor who first hammered out for himself an iron spade? Battles and war-tumults pass away like tavern brawls. Laws themselves, political constitutions, are not our life, but only the house in which our life is led. Nay, they are but the bare walls of the house. all whose essential furniture is the work of a long-forgotten train of artists and artisans who from the first have been jointly teaching us how to think and how to act.' New and higher things are beginning to be expected of the historian. 'From of old it was too often observed that he dwelt with disproportionate fondness in senate-houses, in battle-fields, nay, even in kings' antechambers, forgetting that far away from such scenes the mighty tide of thought and action was still rolling on its course, that in its thousand remote valleys a whole world of existence was blooming and fading whether the famous victory was won or lost.' A criticism of Scott's 'History' in his journal about the same time reveals similar convictions. 'Strange that a man should think he was writing the history of a nation while he is chronicling the amours of a wanton young woman and a sulky

[1] The four volume biography by Froude, the six volume biography by David Alec Wilson, Carlyle's *Reminiscences* and correspondence, and Mrs. Carlyle's *Correspondence* provide abundant matter. Brief biographies have been written by Richard Garnett, 1887, and Nichol, 1892. Among the best appreciations are Morley, *Miscellanies*, vol. i.; Moncure Conway, *Carlyle*, 1881; Masson, *Carlyle*, 1885; Leslie Stephen, *Hours in a Library*, vol. iii. The essay in J. M. Robertson's *Modern Humanists*, 1895, is a powerful polemic.

booby blown up with gunpowder.' Two years later, in an essay entitled 'Biography,' he inquired whether the whole purpose of history was not biographic; and in a second pronouncement, 'On History Again,' he lays increased stress on its moral value. 'History is not only the fittest study but the only study, and includes all others. It is the true epic poem, the universal divine Scripture.' But when he began to practise his trade it became the biography of great men rather than the record of the unnumbered and the unnamed; and the narratives to which he devoted his middle and later life assumed precisely the character against which he had raised a warning finger in 1830.

By the time that Carlyle had reached the affirmations of 'Sartor' he was out of touch with the rationalism of the eighteenth century, but it was to that epoch that his interest unceasingly turned. His studies of Voltaire and Diderot convey his estimate of the *Philosophes*, his essays on Cagliostro and the Diamond Necklace flash light into the dark corners of the Ancien Régime, while the portrait of Mirabeau crosses the threshold of the new age. This striking group of articles was his first contribution to history, and forms an introduction to his masterpiece. The 'History of the French Revolution,'[1] published in 1837, won him a national reputation, and it is the only English historical work of the earlier half of the century, except Macaulay's 'Essays,' which is still widely read. Its merits are unique. In the first place, it is a piece of great literature. In a generation accustomed to the dissertations of Hallam, the pomposity of Alison, and the metallic brilliance of Macaulay, a book brimful of passion and poetry came as a revelation. By a supreme effort of creative imagination he succeeded in rendering the vision as real to his readers as to himself. ' It stands pretty fair in my head,' he had written, ' nor do I mean to investigate much more about it, but to splash down what I know in large masses of colour that it may look like a smoke and flame conflagration in the distance.' It is the most dramatic work in English historical literature, the most epic of historical narratives. To the author it was far more than a mere history of events, for it embodied his deepest moral and religious convictions. We hear the impassioned accents of a prophet calling sinners to repentance. On finishing his task he said to his wife, 'I know not whether this book is worth anything, nor what the world will do with it; but there has been nothing for a hundred years that comes more direct and flamingly from the heart of a living man.' To John Sterling he wrote that it

---

[1] See the editions of Fletcher and Rose, with introduction and notes, 1902. Cp. the appendix on Carlyle's errors in Alger's *Paris, 1789–94*, 1902.

was a wild, savage book. 'It has come hot out of my own soul, born in blackness, whirlwind and sorrow.' The reader has its great scenes stamped ineffaceably on his mind. The storming of the Bastille, the raid on Versailles, the fête of the federation, the flight to Varennes, the trial and death of the King, the Girondins and Danton, the brief tragedy of Charlotte Corday, the fall of Robespierre—these pageants we carry with us through life. No writer but Michelet has approached Carlyle in the power of rendering the atmosphere of horror and hope, of tense passion and animal fury. No less remarkable is the insight into the character of the leading actors. Lowell remarked that while the figures of most historians were like dolls stuffed with bran, Carlyle's were so real that if you pricked them they bled. Though misconceiving the Girondins like other historians of his age, he drew portraits of the King and Queen, Mirabeau and Lafayette, Danton, Robespierre and Marat, which require little alteration. 'Insufficiently informed but singularly impartial' is the verdict of Dr. Trevelyan.[1] He had not yet capitulated to the hero-worship which disfigures his later books. Sympathising little either with the old order or the new, he looks beyond the war-cries of party to the convulsive struggles of human souls.

Carlyle discovered the French Revolution for the English-speaking world, and painted a picture the colours of which are still undimmed; but the book suffers from grave faults, some arising from the circumstances of the time, others from lack of insight. His knowledge was extremely limited. He gave up the attempt to explore Croker's magnificent collection of pamphlets on learning that he could not consult them on their shelves. The study of the archives had not begun, and it never occurred to him that he ought to begin it. His main authorities were the *Moniteur*, the 'Histoire Parlementaire' of Buchez and Roux, the narratives of Lacretelle and Thiers, and a few volumes of memoirs. Building upon such slender foundations it was not surprising that a large number of errors crept into his pages. In an essay on 'Histories of the Revolution' he had sharply attacked the accuracy of Thiers, but his own accuracy was not beyond reproach. He accepted such legends as the drinking of a glass of blood by Mlle. Sombreuil, which dates from 1800; the sinking of the *Vengeur*, an invention of Barère; the prophecy of Cazotte, which was written after the events; and the last supper of the Girondins, the creation of Nodier. Barbaroux appears as the platonic lover of Mme. Roland in place of Buzot. The gravest of his mistakes occur in the narrative of the flight to Varennes. By making the distance 65 instead

[1] 'Bias in History,' in *An Autobiography and other Essays*, 74.

of 150 miles, and supplying the fugitives with a huge, clumsy vehicle, he changes a well-planned enterprise into a childish scheme which deserved to fail. In the next place, his book is less a history than a series of tableaux. The introductory chapters scarcely attempt to explain the catastrophe that follows, and the narrative ends abruptly with the whiff of grape-shot in 1795. The relations of France with Europe are overlooked, and the provinces are forgotten. Scenes of minor importance, such as the mutiny at Nancy, are treated at length, while constitutional and economic problems are omitted. He wearied of his task before the end, and the later part is very scrappy. No reader would learn how the Revolution developed and why one stage passed into another. To exalt the pageant is to condemn the history.

A third fault is more fundamental. Carlyle misunderstood the character of the event with which he had to deal. He pictured the whole nation as driven wild by misery and oppression, and prepared from the beginning for a complete upheaval. He thus conceived the Revolution as purely destructive, 'a transcendant revolt against the devil and his works,' a huge bonfire of the rotten feudalism of old France. 'I should not have known what to make of this world at all,' he said to Froude, 'if it had not been for the French Revolution.' This misconception arose not only from the error of isolating it from the European movements of the eighteenth century. As his friend Mazzini pointed out in a penetrating review, he lacked the conception of Humanity.[1] 'He does not recognise in a people any collective life or collective aim. He recognises only individuals. For him, therefore, there is not and cannot be any intelligible chain of connection between cause and effect.' That the Revolution was the parent of the nineteenth century, that beneath its horrors lay the seeds of a more generous life, that constructive work of a permanent character was accomplished, that it incorporated many ideas and tendencies of the Ancien Régime—all this was unknown to him. While Carlyle bids us witness the dusk of the gods, Michelet salutes the birth-pangs of democracy. No one can begin to understand the Revolution till he realises its dual character. He is the greatest of showmen and the least of interpreters. He described his work as 'one of the savagest written for several centuries, a book written by a wild man,' and it enjoyed a mixed reception. Wordsworth exclaimed that no Scotsman could write English. Hallam declared that he could not read it owing to its detestable style. The whole thing, wrote Prescott, both as to form and *fonds*, was perfectly contemptible; it was wrong to colour so highly

[1] *Life and Writings of Joseph Mazzini*, iv., 110–144, 1891.

what nature had already over-coloured. Yet the chorus of praise was far louder. Mill hailed it as one of those works of genius which are a law to themselves. Kingsley christened it the single epic of modern days. Critics of such different schools as Jeffrey and Arnold, Sterling and Thackeray, recognised its genius. Southey read it through six times. As a prose epic its position is unassailable, but its authority has long disappeared.

As the 'French Revolution' made its way but slowly, Harriet Martineau and other friends aided Carlyle to increase his resources by public lectures. Four courses were delivered, of which only the last and the best, on 'Heroes and Hero-Worship,' was published. The character studies of Mahomet, Dante, Shakespeare, Luther, Cromwell and Knox excited the enthusiasm of the audience. Every lecture was a sermon. 'I had bishops and all kinds of people among my hearers,' he wrote to his mother. 'I gave them to know that the poor Arab had points about him which it were good for them all to imitate. and that probably they were more quacks than he.' He had learned to think meanly of the capacity and virtue of the average man. 'The immense mass of men,' testifies Froude, 'he believed to be poor creatures, poor in heart and poor in intellect.' Like the Calvinistic theologians he thought that the elect were few. Without the sheep-dog the flock would go astray. It is no longer the unnamed benefactors of the race to whom he offers homage, but the men of elemental energy who overthrow crumbling institutions and carve out paths for their successors. The hero steers his course by facts, and to recognise the eternal verities is to serve God. From the thesis that the right cause wins it is only a step to the contention that the winning cause is the right one. Moncure Conway charitably maintained that what Carlyle worshipped was not force but work, the turning of chaos into order. That is true enough, but he cared little about the methods by which it was performed. In 1832 he declared himself 'a radical and an absolutist,' but the absolutist soon swallowed the radical. The crude doctrine of values which emerges in 'Heroes' dominates and disfigures much of his later work. In 'Past and Present' the conception of leadership wears its most engaging form in Abbot Samson, but in the essay on Dr. Francia, the Dictator of Paraguay, it assumes its most repulsive aspect. The 'veracious' man is he who entertains no scruples and tramples down the obstacles which bar the way to power. It never occurred to him to investigate the effects of autocracy either on the ruler or the ruled. The forerunner of Nietzsche forgot the golden truth expressed in Mill's dictum that where the schoolmaster does all the pupils' lessons they never advance.

In 'Heroes' Cromwell was described as 'a great and true man. While reading Clarendon in 1822 Carlyle had planned a study of the Civil Wars, and wrote a number of character sketches, which appeared after his death. After the publication of the 'French Revolution' he resumed his studies of the Puritan era. He bitterly complained of 'the shoreless lakes of bilge-water' through which he was compelled to wade. 'I get to see,' he wrote in his journal in 1840, 'that no history in that strict sense can be made of that unspeakable puddle of a time—a Golgotha of dead dogs. Yet I say to myself a great man does lie buried under this waste continent of cinders.' He visited the field of Naseby with Dr. Arnold, and stood in Ely cathedral on the spot where the historic order, 'Leave your fooling and come out, Sir,' was issued and obeyed. He finally determined to confine himself to a collection of Cromwell's letters and speeches,[1] and the scheme, thus narrowed, was rapidly carried out. The Protector had never found a friend. To royalists he was the man of blood, to republicans the great apostate, to sceptics like Hume 'a frantic enthusiast.' Macaulay admired without understanding him.

It was Carlyle's ambition to vindicate both the character and the policy of his hero. In the former his success was incontestable. Cromwell was disinterred from the load of misrepresentation and calumny which had weighed on him for nearly two centuries, and allowed to bear witness in his own defence. James Mozley and Church declared themselves wholly unconvinced, but they had stood almost alone.[2] Forster confessed himself a convert, and no rational being now believes the Protector to have been either a hypocrite or a fanatic. It was the proudest achievement of the historian's life to restore to England one of the greatest of her sons. His interpretation of policy, on the other hand, is far less convincing. He first realised how large a part in the struggle was played by the religious factor, but he failed to measure the strength of the demand for political self-government. Caring nothing himself for representative institutions, he never understood how they could be the object of passionate desire. Thus, instead of tracing the evolution of Cromwell's political ideas under the stress of events, he attributes to him his own belief in autocracy. The Clarke Papers were later

[1] See Firth's introduction to Lomas' edition, 1904. Wilbur Abbott's great edition, containing fresh material, appeared 1937–47, Harvard University Press, 4 vols.
[2] See J. B. Mozley, Essays, vol. i., 1878; and Church, Occasional Papers, vol. i., 1897.

to show how unwillingly the superman advanced towards supreme power, how earnestly he attempted to work with Parliament, how deep was his conviction of the frailty of a benevolent despotism. Carlyle never realised that even a good government maintained by the sword was not worth having. The time was out of joint and the hero was at hand to set it right. He pours scorn on Ludlow and Vane as Mommsen pours scorn on Cicero and Pompey. He believed that the history of the Commonwealth proved the incapacity of a popular assembly to govern. In reality it established the impossibility of Personal Government in modern England.

Carlyle was totally unfitted for the technical duties of an editor. He accepted the Squire Papers—forged after the publication of his book as a practical joke without asking to see the originals and without observing that they were filled with modern phraseology. He made little effort to seek the best text, allowed himself a wide licence in emendations, and modernised the speeches. Such proceedings would ruin the reputation of a professional scholar, but Carlyle cared little about technique so long as he could make his hero live. If, in the flattering words of Green, the work is characterised by the learning of an antiquary and the genius of a poet, it is no less remarkable for the resourcefulness of a showman. No one can dispute that he aids the reader to visualise the man, and that he occasionally makes sense of unintelligible passages. When the critic has done his worst, the 'Cromwelliad' remains a marvellous production. The battle of Dunbar and the death of the hero are masterpieces of literature. The 'Letters and Speeches' remains a classic, fearing no rivalry, a monument to two great and not wholly dissimilar souls.

The long association with Cromwell strengthened Carlyle's conviction that men of action formed the backbone of history. His view of British politics become more and more gloomy. The progress of which his contemporaries spoke was progress backwards. He believed neither in democracy nor science. The Reform Bill was a failure. Parliament was the weakness, not the strength of the state, an obstacle to work, not its instrument. As his belief in government by discussion waned, his admiration for benevolent autocrats waxed. The author of 'Latter Day Pamphlets' could not but look back with longing to the eighteenth century, which, though an era of religious scepticism, was also the age of flesh-and-blood rulers. A visit to the battle-fields of Frederick the Great in 1852 marks the definite inauguration of his last and most formidable historical task. Old Fritz had not figured in the lectures on Heroes, and after years of study he

remarked, 'I never cared very much about him.' Yet he pronounced him the last of the kings. If he lacked the faith of Abbot
Samson or Cromwell, he at any rate believed in facts and accepted
the gospel of work. If he deceived others, he never deceived
himself.

When Carlyle published his massive volumes, Frederick was
almost unknown in England: Macaulay's second essay was a
hindrance, not a help. Nor did he derive much help from his
German guides, whom he rudely dismissed as 'dark, chaotic
dullards.'[1] Preuss had collected a vast quantity of material, and
Ranke had sketched his policy and administration; no one had
reproduced his personality. It was this task which he set himself
to perform. The full-length portrait of Frederick William I is
perhaps the most successful part of the entire work. The silent
man of action, with his faith in God and his unresting labours for
his people, speaks straight to the heart of the historian. The
horseplay of the Tobacco Parliament attracted rather than
repelled the man who despised the tinsel of court life. The young
Frederick appeals to him less than his uncouth father. Carlyle
cared little more for verse-making and flute-playing than Frederick
William, but when the hero emerges as a man of action he offers
his homage. While the justice of the claim on Silesia interests
him little, he applauds the bold decision and the lightning stroke.
He had displayed in the 'Cromwell' his powers as a military
historian. A second visit to Germany in 1858 stamped every
detail of the battle-fields on his tenacious memory; so exact
were his descriptions of the campaigns that they served to
instruct German officers till the Prussian General Staff compiled
its own history. On the other hand, the ten fruitful years of reform
and reconstruction between the two great struggles are merely
outlined. When the Seven Years War ended in 1763 the reign
was only half over, but the last twenty-three years are dismissed in
half a volume mainly devoted to foreign policy. Of the unceasing
labour to reform the finances, develop the resources of the soil,
plan new industries, humanise the law, we hear little or nothing.
Henry Larkin,[2] who helped him with the work, testifies that
Carlyle contemplated a fairly complete account of Frederick's
reconstruction of his kingdom, which he regarded as the most
important and instructive lesson of his career; but the book was
already longer than he had anticipated, and his energies were

---

[1] For the early biographers see Hintze, *Historische u. Politische Aufsätze*,
vol. ii. For an authoritative German view see Krauske, 'Macaulay und
Carlyle,' *Hist. Zeitschrift*, vol. cii.

[2] *Carlyle*, 1886.

spent. Moreover, he believed that no living picture could be built up from official reports and statistics.

The 'Frederick' adds little to knowledge, but it is full of purple patches. It has been called the largest and most varied show-box in historical literature. Mrs. Carlyle, an exacting critic, pronounced it the best of her husband's works. It exhibits an undiminished power of *mise en scène*, humour, and characterisation. Emerson pronounced it the wittiest book ever written. Carlyle never composed anything more brilliant than the story of Voltaire's antics at Potsdam, and the portraits of the rulers of Europe are in his best style. Its immediate success was greater than that of the 'French Revolution' or 'Cromwell,' and it was at once translated into German. When he began his task few dreamed of the dramatic transformations to come; when he concluded, the first blows of Bismarck's hammer had fallen. The sensational rise of a new Power stimulated interest in the founder of Prussia's greatness, and Carlyle's services as an historian and a defender of the German cause in 1870 were rewarded by Frederick's own coveted Order 'Pour le Mérite.' Yet the book is too long for its readers, as it was too long for its author. The hero was less heroic than he had supposed. To Varnhagen he wrote that he had only labour and sorrow in the book, and added, 'What the devil had I to do with your Frederick?' Yet Old Fritz was in some ways an even greater king than he imagined, and Koser's masterpiece leaves an impression which the professional hero-worshipper fails to convey.

Carlyle at his best is the greatest of English historical portrait-painters. It was his habit, relates Gavan Duffy,[1] to paste on a screen engraved portraits of the people about whom he was writing. It kept the image of the man steadily in view, remarked the Sage, and one must have a clear image of him in the mind before it was possible to make the reader see him. But the writer who saw individuals with such incomparable clearness was blind to the very existence of the masses. His later years reveal something like contempt for the poor and ignorant. 'Shooting Niagara' gave almost brutal expression to his opinion of the working-classes in 1867. He told Wolseley, half in earnest, that he hoped he would lock the door of Parliament and turn the members out. He sided with the South in the slavery struggle, and with Governor Eyre against 'quashee nigger.' His whole philosophy was that the common herd must be drilled and punished by their superiors. As Englishmen became more optimistic and democratic he grew ever more reactionary and depressed.

[1] *Conversations with Carlyle*, 1892.

II

Carlyle's chief disciple and biographer, approaching history in the spirit of his master, accomplished work in which shining merits and glaring faults were inextricably mingled. An eminent Belgian critic who christened Froude[1] the national historian points out that he is almost unknown on the Continent, and that none of his books have been translated. 'He is passionately, fanatically, exclusively English.' His studies began under the auspices of the Oxford Movement. When Newman commenced a series of Lives of the Saints, he turned to the younger brother of Hurrell Froude to assist him, with the marching orders, 'Rationalise when the evidence is weak, and that will give credibility when you can show the evidence is strong.' Froude chose St. Neot, a contemporary of Alfred, and wound up his narrative with the words, 'This is all, and perhaps rather more than all, that is known of his life.' His tour through the cloudy region of hagiology made him half a sceptic, and though he was ordained in 1845 his faith gradually disappeared. The public burning of the 'Nemesis of Faith' in 1849 was the turning-point of his life. Deprived of his Fellowship, he left Oxford for London. It was at this dark moment that he met Carlyle, who helped him to a new faith. His historical and literary essays quickly became popular, and an article on Elizabethan Seamen inspired 'Westward Ho!'

No one could live through the Oxford Movement without thinking about the Reformation. Of all the disciples of Newman none had spoken with such fierce contempt of the Reformers as Hurrell Froude, but on beginning to study the sixteenth century for himself, the younger brother was struck by the popularity of Henry VIII during his lifetime. When the plan arose in his mind of a detailed narrative of the struggle of England against Rome he was warmly encouraged by Carlyle, who had recently scourged the Jesuits in a Latter Day Pamphlet and regarded the Roman Catholic Church as a gigantic imposture. The first four volumes of the 'History of England from 1529 to the death of Elizabeth' created a sensation only less than that of Macaulay. The High Church movement had made the Reformers widely unpopular, and Whigs like Hallam and Macaulay had attacked them for sycophancy. Froude's defence of Henry and

---

[1] See Herbert Paul's admirable *Life of Froude*, 1905; Sarolea, *Essais, Première Série*, 1905; Skelton, *The Table Talk of Shirley*, 1895; Frederic Harrison, *Tennyson, Ruskin, Mill*, etc., 1899; Algernon Cecil, *Six Oxford Thinkers*, 1909.

the Reformation rests on the broadest ground. Starting with the profound conviction that Rome was and always had been the enslaver of mind and soul, he entertained heartfelt gratitude to the men who broke its sway. He rejected Hume's contention that the people were like Eastern slaves, and refused to believe that an English Parliament could have supported the King for any other reason than that it agreed with his policy. Seen in this light there could be no question of despotism. Engaged in a life-and-death struggle the King was bound to use every weapon of offence and defence, and the people applauded his action. The Reformation was by far the greatest event in our history. It was not a conflict between rival dogmas but a struggle to decide whether England should govern herself or be ruled by priests. The breach with Rome was the beginning of the greatness of England, a blow struck for human freedom and intellectual honesty. That there were plenty of good men on the wrong side he readily admits, but those who believe that the right side won should be grateful to their deliverers.

Froude was not content with showing that Henry's victory was the salvation of our race. He convinced himself that the King was a much better man than was commonly believed—more conscientious, less cruel, less selfish, less sensual. He contends that the divorce was the result of genuine scruples, that Anne Boleyn and Catherine Howard were guilty of adultery, and that his subjects were no less anxious than he for legitimate male heirs. The marriage with Jane Seymour the day after the execution of Anne was 'an official act which his duty required at the moment.' He did not love her, but married her 'under the pressure of a sudden and tragic necessity.' The execution of More and Fisher is defended on the ground that they were prepared to bring over a foreign army and plunge the country into civil war. In these measures of swift decision the King was acting as the trustee of the national security. The dissolution of the monasteries was necessary, not only because they were the garrison of Rome, but because their morals were an offence; and the spoils went not only to the courtiers but to education and the national defences.

The volumes on Henry VIII were the most brilliant historical work produced in England in the middle of the century, with the single exception of Macaulay. The magnitude of the issues, the vivid portraiture of famous men, the figure of the masterful King, arrested attention. A born story-teller, Froude produces his effects by the simplest methods. The reader sails over sparkling waters. No English historian has possessed a style so easy, so flowing, so transparent. Yet, despite its enthusiastic welcome by militant Protestants of the school of Kingsley, it aroused sharp criticism. The *Edinburgh Review* delivered a sustained attack on the historian's conceptions of morality.[1] It was difficult to believe he had ever seen the face of English justice, and his reading of Henry VIII was a pervading paradox. He innocently assumed that the Parliament of 1529 was freely elected, whereas it was virtually nominated by the sheriffs. He found nothing suspicious in the fact that no judge or jury acquitted a victim in a Crown prosecution. He seized on the preambles to the Statutes as trustworthy evidence of public opinion. The whole work was vitiated by the worship of force. 'Carlyle,' concludes the critic, 'has a good deal to answer for by his splendid and dangerous example of spoiling what might have been so good a book.' Bergenroth declared the writer to be no historian. Pauli and Ranke rejected Froude's reading of the reign. In his superb lectures on Henry VIII Stubbs professed himself quite unable to accept Froude's view of the King, and Friedmann's studies of Anne Boleyn showed that Parliament was a shadow. The volumes on Edward and Mary are less striking, owing to the lack of a dominating figure, but they are of higher historical value. The notion that Cranmer was a mere sycophant is dead, and Froude did more than anyone to kill it. He was the first to show the stature of Somerset, his generous ideals, and his sympathy with the common people. Mary was conscientious enough, indeed too faithful an interpreter of a hateful religion. The fires of Smithfield reminded England what Catholicism really meant and completed its conversion. Thus her reign, despite its unspeakable horrors, was a blessing in disguise, and the lesson had never to be repeated.

The later and larger half of the work is devoted to Elizabeth. Artistically, despite many brilliant passages, it is inferior to the earlier volumes, for Froude presents too much of his material to his readers. He was not, however, without some excuse, for these volumes rest to a large extent on the archives of Simancas, which he was the first English historian to explore. As his early dislike of Henry had been turned to sympathy on closer investigation, so his youthful devotion to the Queen melted into something like contempt. He rejects the scandals relating to her personal character, but her career had never before been subjected to a microscopic examination and it could not sustain the scrutiny. 'The letters of Burleigh and Walsingham,' he wrote, 'have finally destroyed the prejudice that still clung to me that, despite her many faults, she was a woman of ability. The great results of

[1] July, 1858.

her reign were the fruits of a policy which did not belong to her and which she starved and thwarted.' To the pedestal from which Elizabeth is deposed her chief minister is exalted. 'Burleigh,' declares the historian in uncompromising terms, 'was the solitary author of Elizabeth's and England's greatness.' We owe to Froude our full knowledge of the tireless efforts of the great statesman. Less a brilliant than a cautious mind, he required ample time for his operations. He was allowed forty years, and he used them to establish Protestantism on an impregnable foundation. The Scottish scenes of the drama are at once the most brilliant and the least trustworthy. Mary Stuart is pursued with relentless hostility through thirty years, while her half-brother, the Regent Murray, stands out as a stainless knight in the crowd of selfish intriguers. The Casket Letters are accepted *en bloc*, and the stern Protestant moralist feels a righteous joy in unmasking the Catholic sinner. The hero of the story is Knox, the man after his own heart who saved the Reformation. The Irish chapters oppress the reader with their monotonous horror. The extracts from Simancas and the Burleigh papers were so considerable that the historian laid down his pen after the Armada. It was a wise decision. Twelve stout volumes had been occupied with the story of sixty years. Moreover, the book was a drama of conflict, and it was artistically desirable that it should end on a note of victory. For practical purposes the struggle for national freedom which began in 1529 ended in 1588. The chessplayer, in Froude's words, sweeps the pieces from the board when the end is in sight.

The strength and weakness of the work are now generally recognised. It was the first and it remains the only detailed survey by a single hand of one of the two most critical periods of our history. It restored the authors of the Reformation to life, and enriched English literature with innumerable pages of thrilling narrative. Freeman's attacks in the *Saturday Review* contained little substance. 'I fancy,' he wrote to a friend, 'that from endlessly belabouring Froude I get credit for knowing more of these times than I do. But one can belabour Froude on a very small amount of knowledge. I am profoundly ignorant of the sixteenth century.' He was right in his censure of Froude's indifference to the cruelty of his heroes. He was justified in complaining of his neglect to investigate the relations of the Crown with Parliament and the Courts. He was within his rights in calling attention to careless proof-reading and mistakes of detail. But his final verdict, delivered in 1870 on the conclusion of the work, exceeds the limits of fair criticism. 'Mr. Froude is not an historian. His work consists of four volumes of ingenious paradox and eight of ecclesiastical pamphlet. The blemishes which cut it off from any title to the name of history are utter carelessness as to facts and utter incapacity to distinguish right from wrong.' In vain the defendant challenged the *Saturday Review* to let two competent experts verify the references in any hundred pages. In a letter to Skelton he wrote, 'I acknowledge to five real mistakes in twelve volumes and about twenty trifling slips, equivalent to i's not dotted and t's not crossed, and that is all that the utmost malignity has discovered.' A few years later, when he published some articles on Becket, Freeman accused him of 'fanatical hatred towards the English Church, reformed or unreformed,' and charged him with 'an inborn and incurable twist which renders it impossible for him to make an accurate statement on any matter.' To this first signed attack Froude returned a dignified reply, pointing out that his critic had only discovered two or three trifling misprints and mistakes.

Freeman's vitriolic attacks have injured his own fame more than that of his victim. While the historian of the Norman Conquest eschewed manuscripts, most of Froude's materials were in the archives. In transcribing documents, often almost illegible and written in several languages, mistakes were inevitable. He was an exceptionally careless copyist and corrector of proofs, and did not always trouble to distinguish between quotation in full and his own abridgements. But deliberate alteration of his sources was impossible to him. In his imaginative sketch, 'A Siding at a Railway Station,' he defends himself against the charge of falsification. Skelton, the biographer of Maitland and Mary Stuart, declares that he had a passionate reverence for truth. Though he could not accept all his conclusions, he bears emphatic testimony to the inexhaustible industry and substantial accuracy of his friend. Andrew Lang, who worked over much of the same ground, pronounces that, though no historian was more honest, few or none of his merit had been so fallible. Brewer complained that in the narrative of Thomas Cromwell's early life scarcely a statement was correct. In editing a revised edition of Carlyle's 'Reminiscences' Charles Eliot Norton made 130 corrections in the first five pages of Froude's edition, and he declared that almost every letter in the 'Life' which he had collated was incorrectly printed. How treacherous was his memory was shown in his volumes of travel.

Though his carelessness in detail is a grave fault, it is lack of impartiality which excludes Froude from the first rank of historians. Pollard has argued that his conception of Henry VIII was less extravagant than his critics maintained, but his mind lacked serenity and insight into differing modes of thought. The main occupation of his life was to combat the Roman Church. On completing his defence of the Reformation he turned to a later chapter of the same struggle. Having boldly vindicated the cruelties of the Tudors, he undertook the even more unsavoury task of defending the English régime in Ireland. 'When Catholic and Protestant came into conflict,' confesses his sympathetic biographer, Herbert Paul, 'he took instinctively, almost involuntarily, the Protestant side.' His bias is far more offensive in the later than in the earlier work. In the eighteenth century the Government did not possess the excuse that a deadly struggle for the body and soul of England was in progress. 'The English in Ireland' breathes the very spirit of Carlyle. Though liking the Irish peasant and never happier than when fishing in Kerry, Froude shared his master's contempt for the race. 'I have grown to hate my Irish book,' he wrote to Skelton. 'It will make the poor Paddies hate me too, which I do not wish.' In his eyes the Irish were an inferior breed, Catholicism a degrading idolatry. On reaching the Grattan Parliament he takes his stand with the most fanatical Tories. While Grattan was led astray by the delirium of nationality, the true statesman was Clare. He condemns the concession of the franchise to Catholics in 1793, approves the recall of Fitzwilliam, exalts the Orange Lodges, and applauds the King's opposition to emancipation. There was some ground for the sneer that in Froude's eyes it was no crime to kill a Catholic. The book was an Orange manifesto, its purpose to show the folly of conciliation. He was one of those whom Gladstone had in his mind when he referred to the belief that the Irish had a double dose of original sin. Though containing a good deal of valuable material, the work was morally indefensible and politically mischievous. Undeterred by Burke's warning, he brought an indictment against a nation. Carlyle was delighted with a book which reflected his own prejudices, but its authority was quickly overthrown by Lecky.

After composing an eloquent rhapsody on Cæsar in the spirit of Mommsen and compiling the biography of Carlyle, Froude returned in old age to the sixteenth century with a volume on Catherine of Aragon which showed that he had learned nothing and forgotten nothing. He was disappointed that his reading of Henry VIII had not been accepted, and bitterly declared that it was no good trying to alter popular verdicts. Yet he found nothing to withdraw and little to alter. He did not pretend to impartiality, for he believed in the Reformation. 'The legislation of Henry and his Parliaments is the Magna Charta of the modern world. The stake played for was the liberty of mankind. Those who believe that the victory was of right over wrong have no need to blush for the actions of the brave men who in the pulpit or the Council Chamber, on the scaffold or at the stake, won for mankind the spiritual liberty which is now the law of the world.' The three courses of lectures delivered when he succeeded Freeman at Oxford, dealing with the Council of Trent, the seamen of the sixteenth century, and the Letters of Erasmus, breathe the same militant Protestantism. Froude closes the age of the amateurs. His great scenes are equal to Macaulay, and Frederick Harrison compared him to Livy and Froissart; but he was even less of a thinker than Carlyle, and his work has had to be done over again. He never realised that the duty of the historian is neither eulogy nor invective, but cool interpretation of complex processes and conflicting ideals.

CHAPTER XVII

THE OXFORD SCHOOL

I

WHILE the writings of Macaulay, Carlyle and Froude were selling by tens of thousands, more exact methods began to be applied. Stubbs[1] started to learn Anglo-Saxon while still at school, and employed his holidays in studying rolls in the old Court house of his native Knaresborough. By the time he went to Oxford he knew his way about mediæval documents. At the age of twenty-five he accepted a living in Essex, where during sixteen tranquil years he found leisure to become the greatest English mediævalist of his time. His first work was to trace the succession of bishops through the centuries. The 'Registrum Sacrum Anglicanum' was recognised by the few who could appreciate it as a valuable contribution to Church history, and at once became an indispensable work of reference.

His exact scholarship made him a severe critic of the publications of the Record Commission. Public money was wasted on printing documents of secondary importance, while contemporary authorities were rarely chosen. Moreover, the conception of the duties of editor was narrow. When the Lives of Edward the Confessor appeared he wrote, 'I am sorry to see the philological side of things is to be kept so exclusively in view in these publications.' The standard was soon to be raised by the critic himself. In 1857 Lord Romilly, Master of the Rolls, obtained permission from the Treasury for the publication of critical editions of the sources of English history till the end of the Middle Ages. The enterprise was mainly directed by Duffus Hardy, whose survey of the 'Sources and Documents of English History' was a work of enduring value. Stubbs at once offered his services, but it was not till 1863 that the greatest of editors received his commission. For twenty-five years he was to enrich the Rolls Series with masterpieces of technique and historical learning, which may be said to have inaugurated the critical

---

[1] See *Letters of William Stubbs*, ed. by W. H. Hutton, 1904; Maitland, *Eng. Hist. Review*, July, 1901; *Quarterly Review*, Jan. 1905. Helen Cam, 'Stubbs seventy years later,' *Cambridge Historical Journal*, 1948, 129–147, summarises subsequent criticism

study of mediæval sources in England. He possessed every qualification for his task—palæographic skill, abundant learning, and
a judicial mind. His first volume, the 'Itinerary of Richard I,'
appeared in 1864; his last, the concluding volume of 'William of
Malmesbury,' in 1889. That on Dunstan rescued the character of
one of the greatest of English ecclesiastics. Those on the early
Angevins were furnished with historical introductions which
presented the first adequate picture of the personality of the rulers.
The literary ability of these massive prefaces was as striking as
their erudition. He wrote under the immediate impression of his
sources. 'I am trying to do my Henry II by the light of nature,'
he remarked in 1866. 'I cannot write without feeling it is all
my own.'

While Stubbs was immersed in the Chronicles he was summoned to the Chair of Modern History at his own University in
1866. His appointment was greeted by Green in the *Saturday
Review* as an agreeable contrast to the nomination of a popular
novelist to Cambridge and the elevation of a leading metaphysician to the Chair of Ecclesiastical History at Oxford. He
was, in fact, the first trained historian to hold the post. His inaugural lecture explained very frankly the new Professor's conception of his task. 'The study of modern history is, next to theology
itself, the most thoroughly religious training the mind can receive.
It is Christianity that gives the modern world its unity and at the
same time cuts it off from the death of the past.' But his political
and religious beliefs were never obtruded in his work, and the
lecture ends with the expression of a hope that he might help to
found an historical school which should join with foreign workers
in a common task.

During his twenty years at Oxford Stubbs was occupied with
his lectures and the 'Constitutional History.' He groaned over
his statutory duty, to which, however, the world owes some of
his most brilliant pages. The discourses which he deemed worthy
of publication appeared on his resignation of the chair. The
'Lectures on Mediæval and Modern History' give a more complete impression of the historian than any of his other books.
The immense knowledge and variety of theme are not more
striking than the lightness of touch, the vivid characterisation,
the humour and the buoyancy. The superb discourses on Literature and Learning at the Court of Henry II, on Henry VII and
Henry VIII, stand out as masterpieces in a fascinating volume.
After his death other courses were published which added nothing
to his reputation. His main interest was the Constitution. It was
not creditable to an educated people, he declared, that while its

students were well acquainted with the machinery of Athens and Rome, they should be ignorant of the institutions of their own forefathers. In the year following his appointment he informed a friend that he was going to deliver eighteen lectures on constitutional history from Tacitus to Henry II, and that he had already written most of them. They were published after his death, and it is interesting to recover the first draft of his famous work. A second step was taken in 1870 by the publication of the 'Select Charters,' which has served as a model for similar volumes on other periods and other countries. A concise Introduction sketches constitutional history to Edward I in bold outline. Freeman hailed it as 'worthy of the unerring learning and critical power of the first of living scholars.' By selecting the most important sources laws and charters, treaties and chronicles— he gave reality to the study of early English history, and his concise elucidations threw light on many obscurities of law and practice. Repeatedly revised, the 'Charters' may be regarded as a volume of annotated authorities for the 'Constitutional History.'

Stubbs' masterpiece began to appear in 1874, and was immediately recognised as one of the half-dozen major historical works in the English language. Its scope is wider than the title indicates. It is virtually a history of England from Julius Cæsar to the accession of the Tudors, the first authoritative survey of our national life. There is little on diplomacy, economic conditions, or military detail, but it embraces Church and State, law and justice, administration and finance. Maitland has remarked that no work on constitutional development is so marvellously concrete. 'While the institutions grow and decay under our eyes, we are never allowed to forget that this process of evolution and dissolution consists of the acts of human beings.' By alternating analytical and narrative chapters he combines the study of structure with that of the national movement. Though he rightly felt that the reconstruction of the main lines of constitutional development was his greatest task, he never allows his readers to forget how many threads went to form the web of the nation's life.

Stubbs' work was the first attempt to grapple with the whole range of English constitutional problems of the Middle Ages. He was fond of law, and it was said of him that he might have been a great judge. Bryce, his Professorial colleague at Oxford, tells us that, unlike Freeman and Green, he had a great interest in legal points and unusual capacity for mastering them. The first volume, extending to the Norman Conquest, was the least original and the least enduring. The materials at that time were scanty and difficult of interpretation. 'Many an investigator,' wrote Maitland a generation later, 'will leave his bones to bleach in that desert before it is accurately mapped. It may be doubted if he was fully aware of the treachery of the ground that he traversed.' On the other hand his French critics Petit-Dutaillis and Bémont have complained that his conclusions were often timid, that he hesitated before badly documented periods, and shirked decisions on difficult problems. Yet caution was perhaps the path of wisdom. He was thoroughly acquainted with the works of Waitz and Gneist, the Maurers, Brunner and Sohm, and he sometimes followed his German guides with too great fidelity. Of his English predecessors he rated Kemble highest. In 1859 he called him 'my pattern scholar.' In 1866 he wrote, 'I am sorry to say that I do not believe in Palgrave. Kemble was just as much run away with by his own theories, but I think there is much more sense in his notions.' He was convinced that England rested on Teutonic foundations, and he accepted Maurer's theory of the Mark. It has been the work of a later generation to exhibit the complexity of Anglo-Saxon society, and he cannot be seriously blamed for failing to anticipate their researches. Nor can he be gravely censured for mistaking the nature of Folkland in company with every scholar before Vinogradoff. On reaching Norman times he is on much firmer ground. The sources were fuller, the problems less thorny. With Henry II and his sons he entered territory every by-path of which was known to him. So familiar was the period that he wrote his admirable little book on the Plantagenets for a popular series in six weeks. It is here that his touch is surest, that his characterisations are most vivid and convincing. Yet he skilfully maintains the interest of his story during the fourteenth and fifteenth centuries, 'a gloomy, worn-out, helpless age.' He exaggerated the anarchy of feudalism, shared the traditional error of regarding Magna Charta as the work of a self-conscious nation instead of an effort of the barons to retain their privileges, and praised Edward I beyond his deserts[1]; but the major blunders of the second and third volumes are few. The review of social and political influences at the close of the Middle Ages, with which the work concludes, exhibits his synthetic power at its highest.

Conspicuous among the merits of the 'Constitutional History' is its fairness. 'To read him is a training in justice,' declares Maitland, a man of widely different views in politics and religion.

[1] See Templeman, 'Edward I and the Historians,' in *The Cambridge Historical Journal*, vol. x., no. 1.

Outside his books Stubbs expressed opinions of a very pronounced character. He supported Austria in 1859, spoke of 'the wretched Italians,' denounced 'those horrid Poles' in 1863, and scoffed at Garibaldi's visit to England. Bryce records that he refused to meet a Unitarian minister, and the Professor himself proudly told an Oxford audience of his skill in piloting a volume of Renan from the hands of Green into the waste-paper basket. He solemnly burned a volume of Herbert Spencer while Canon of St. Paul's. He laughed at Freeman's zeal on behalf of the victims of Turkish misrule. Disliking Puritanism he disapproved Green's glowing narrative of the struggles of the seventeenth century. He defined himself as steeped in clerical and conservative principles. Yet this man of reactionary instincts and violent prejudices judged the conflicts of the distant past with remarkable impartiality, and could boast with truth that no one could tell his politics from his greatest work. Indeed he was criticised for his approval of the Lancastrians as the friends of Parliamentary government and for his severity towards the more authoritarian Yorkists. He said in one of his Oxford lectures that it was not his task to make men Whigs or Tories, but to make the Whigs good, sensible Whigs, and Tories good, sensible Tories. His pages are free from extravagant eulogy and depreciation. The highest justice, he declared, was only to be found in the deepest sympathy with erring and straying men. He resists the temptation to which Freeman succumbed of idealising Anglo-Saxon institutions, and holds the scales even between Henry II and Becket. Petit-Dutaillis, who showed his admiration by three volumes of corrective and supplementary studies,[1] goes so far as to describe the book as leaning rather to the liberal side. Stubbs, he declares, belonged to a generation which rejoiced in electoral reforms and the perfecting of political machinery, and shared the view of patriotic German scholars that primitive German institutions were the source of human dignity and independence.

'The history of institutions,' declared Stubbs in his pregnant Foreword, 'cannot be mastered, can scarcely be approached, without an effort. It has a point of view and a language of its own. It reads the exploits and characters of men by a different light from that shed by the false glare of arms. It holds out small temptation to the mind that requires to be tempted to the study of truth.' The severity of its subject-matter and the obscurity of many of its topics renders the 'Constitutional History' by no means easy reading, but the style is clear and vigorous, and in some passages it reaches a high level. In its two

[1] *Studies Supplementary to Stubbs*, 1908–29.

thousand pages there is not a superfluous word. The work was welcomed by scholars all over the world. The author declared that his first volume had met with more appreciative and intelligent reception in Germany than in England. If such were the case it was because there were more Germans capable of measuring its greatness. He visited Waitz at Göttingen, but the two scholars with whom he was most intimate belonged to a younger generation. Pauli, the historian of mediæval England, reviewed his writings as they appeared. Even closer was the friendship with Liebermann, who described him as the greatest historian of mediæval England, and whose monumental edition of the Anglo-Saxon laws was hailed by the Oxford Professor as 'a very splendid, invaluable work.' He was the recipient of many foreign distinctions, and was everywhere regarded as the head of the exact school of history in England. His most distinguished pupils were Tout and Round.

When Stubbs accepted the Bishopric of Chester in 1884, he announced in his farewell lecture that he had no intention of forsaking his old studies, and that he hoped to publish a fourth volume of the 'British Councils,' complete his edition of William of Malmesbury, and perhaps attempt a sketch of the constitutional history of the Reformation. Of these plans only the second was fulfilled. His new duties, by which he was frankly bored, left him scarcely any time for his library, and deprived the world of a revised 'Constitutional History.' He refused to abridge it, and the alterations he introduced in successive editions were trifling. He followed the activities of younger men with unflagging interest but made no real effort to incorporate their results. When Hubert Hall pointed out mistakes in his account of the customs, he corrected it. He accepted Vinogradoff's interpretation of folkland, but maintained that there was some public land, though giving no authority for his belief. He refers in a note to Round's discussion of knight-service, but does not modify his text. 'We feel we have had a king,' wrote Maitland on his death, 'and are now kingless.' No other Englishman, he added, had so completely displayed to the world the whole business of the historian from the winning of raw material to narrating and generalising. His teaching and example had made Oxford a centre of systematic study and research, but he was not a profound thinker. When Buckle's work appeared he remarked, 'I don't believe in the philosophy of history, so I don't believe in Buckle.' He rejected Freeman's notion of the unity of history and the more philosophic conception derived from Lessing which Bishop Temple explained in his famous essay on 'The Education of the Human Race.' He was the greatest British historian of his age, and he did more to introduce the methods of German scholarship than any other man.

II

Though Freeman[1] was slightly older than Stubbs he always regarded the latter as his master. With Green, who dedicated his most popular work to 'my masters in English History,' they form what is popularly known as the Oxford School. Yet the two historians differed widely in temperament and outlook. Stubbs was cool and reserved, Freeman a hero-worshipper and propagandist. Stubbs was concise, Freeman diffuse. The former was an extreme conservative, the latter a militant radical. The scope of their work was equally different. While Stubbs spent his life in mastering mediæval England, Freeman was equally at home in Athens and Rome, Aachen and Constantinople, Rouen and Winchester. Entering Oxford in 1841, while Newman's influence was at its height, he was attracted to ecclesiastical architecture, and wavered between the career of an architect and the ministry. But secular history gradually became his main interest, and he competed for a prize on the effects of the Norman Conquest, reading Thierry, Lingard, Palgrave and the chronicles. His first substantial work, 'A History of Architecture,' attacked the archæologists who neglected history. Soon after he published a work on Window Tracery, with his own illustrations, and a year or two later co-operated in a history of St. Davids. His love of architecture remained, but he came to value it less for its beauty than for its witness to the past.

Possessed of independent means, Freeman determined to dedicate his life to history. For twenty years after taking his degree he devoted most of his time to the classical world, especially to Greece. He described her enslavement as the most melancholy event in history, and dreamed of the recovery of Constantinople. He wrote letters and made speeches in modern Greek, sang the praises of Finlay, and formed an enduring friendship with Tricoupis. To the sneer that the Greeks were mongrels he replied that Greek blood was no more mixed than our own, while the national character had changed but little. His enthusiasm for the Christians of the Near East was equalled by his hatred of the Turks, and he vigorously opposed the

[1] See Stephens, *Life and Letters of Freeman*, 2 vols. 1895; Bryce, *Studies in Contemporary Biography*, 1903; Bémont in *Revue Historique*, vol. xlix.; York Powell, *Occasional Writings*, 1906.

Crimean War as an attempt to buttress up a savage tyranny. He planned a 'History of Federal Government,' starting with Greece and passing through Switzerland and the Netherlands to the United States. Only one volume was completed, but the massive fragment was a valuable contribution to the least known chapter of Greek history.[1] His exhaustive study of the federàtions in which Greece organised herself after the downfall of her liberty is still indispensable. After a visit to Switzerland, which was to form the subject of the second volume, he declared that he loved the Swiss from the bottom of his heart, and his enthusiasm for the simple democracy of the cantons was to find expression in the celebrated lectures on the English Constitution.

Whilst mainly engaged on the ancient world, Freeman never lost sight of later times. In 1865, at the age of forty-three, he determined to become the historian of the Norman Conquest. The most important event in our history before the Reformation had never been really studied. Thierry was uncritical and built on a false hypothesis. Palgrave died before he reached the Conqueror. Stubbs had not yet planned his 'Constitutional History.' The 'History of the Norman Conquest' opens with a sketch of Anglo-Saxon England and of the settlement of the Norsemen in France. The story of the Norman Dukes is related in an admirable chapter, and the study of the Danish Kings first revealed their interest and importance, but the author enters on his full stride with Edward the Confessor. The hero of the drama is Godwin, and in rescuing him from his enemies Freeman places him beside Simon de Montfort, names him 'the Great,' and pronounces a panegyric on his grave. The portrait of Harold is even more flattering than that of his father. In the struggle between Norman and Saxon his sympathies are with the latter. He is penetrated with a sense of William's greatness, but the picture, though accurate and conscientious, lacks life and colour. The Conquest was much less disturbing to the life of the nation than might have been expected. Above all the free constitution, the glory and pride of England, was not seriously disturbed. The popular elements were not submerged, and the great Witans met in 1085 and 1086 as the guardians of the sacred principle of self-government.

The book was a labour of love. Worshipping political liberty, he believed that he found it among the Teutonic nations and above all in his own country. 'One would say the old Saxon blood flowed unmixed in his veins,' declared a German critic. He declared that he would gladly have fought under Harold at Senlac.

[1] See Bury's preface to the edition of 1893.

Despite its vast length the book is alive. The spacious structure was built on solid foundations, and Green greeted it as a perfect miracle of research. His learning must be sought not only in the text but in the innumerable appendices attached to each volume, many of them dissertations of high value. A second source of his strength was a knowledge of the scene of the events which he described. He was the first English historian to realise the importance of exact knowledge of geographical sites and historical remains in the reconstruction of events. The 'Travels in Normandy and Maine' may be read as a companion to the 'Norman Conquest.' The birthplace and burial-place of the Conqueror and his wife, the towns where he lived, the battle-fields where he won his fame, the castles and churches he built—these tangible objects help bring the man back to life.

Freeman's view of the place of the Norman Conquest in history is subject to considerable reservations. In the reaction against Thierry's conception of a cataclysm he underestimates the area of disturbance and exaggerates the rapidity of racial amalgamation. In his eagerness to establish continuity he accepts evidence too readily, and interprets the Witans of the Conqueror's closing years too democratically. He exaggerated the popular element in the constitution both before the Conquest and after. 'The great changes in law and government,' he wrote, 'that we usually attribute to the Conqueror belong in most cases to Henry II.' But this is to attribute too much originality to the Angevin monarch, who developed the ideas of Henry I, which differed little from those of his father. His survey of the results of the Conquest lacks completeness owing to his neglect of important departments of national life, above all the relations of classes to one another and to the Crown. Here we touch the main weakness of the book. It is a political narrative, not a picture of the life of the people. In a series of outspoken criticisms in the *Saturday Review*, Green rightly complained of a certain narrowness of moral and intellectual sympathy.[1] 'He passes silently by religion, intellect, society. He admires the people gathered in its Witan, but he never takes us to the thegn's hall or the peasant's hut. Of the actual life, manners, tastes of our forefathers the book tells us nothing. It is essentially a work of historic reaction.' The criticism, though severe, was in the main justified.[2] Freeman believed action alone to be history, and in this sphere nothing was too insignificant to escape his notice. In the third volume, which deals with the Conquest itself, every detail is welcome,

[1] Republished in Green, *Historical Studies*, 1903.
[2] Cp. Pauli's criticism, *Hist. Zeitschrift*, vol. xxxvii.

but the narrative of petty wars and insurrections is not less detailed than that of the events which determined the fate of nations. He lacked the selective instinct which Stubbs and Green possessed.

Freeman's knowledge of the chronicles was exhaustive, but he had no taste for manuscripts and never learned palæography. Writing in his library at Somerleaze he depended on printed authorities, but not even of these did he make full use. Possessing little interest in law or the structure of society he never realised the importance of charters. His chapter on Domesday Book is superficial. Round[1] was largely justified when he declared that Freeman belonged to a bygone school. He made no discoveries, for discoveries were impossible without the study of manuscripts. That institutions and economic conditions were not less important than the vicissitudes of rulers and warriors was hidden from him. Among minor faults of the book are the aggressive Teutonism, the repetition of favourite phrases, the use of uncouth words such as unright, unlaw and mickle. In the heated controversy with Round on the battle of Hastings the verdict went against him, but the matter was of no great consequence.[2] Despite its sins of commission and omission, it is a work of enduring importance. The 'Norman Conquest' was supplemented by a work on William Rufus. Though the reign was short and relatively uneventful, two massive volumes are devoted to it. Every fact recorded in the chronicles is transferred to the historian's pages, accompanied in many cases by a prolix discussion. Pauli blamed him for accepting the scandalous charges brought against Rufus by his enemies the clergy, but it is impossible to prove they were wrong.

When Stubbs accepted a bishopric, Freeman was naturally appointed his successor. In addition to his massive treatises on Greece and Norman England he had published an important work on the 'Historical Geography of Modern Europe,' three volumes of essays, lectures on the Saracens and the Ottomans, 'The English Constitution' and 'Comparative Politics,' and innumerable studies of historic towns and districts. Like Stubbs, he found no pleasure in the delivery of his statutory lectures and lamented the paucity of advanced students, yet he spared no labour on his duties. Commencing with a course on the 'Methods of Historical Study,' he followed with surveys of Europe in the fifth and eighth centuries and with a sketch of the 'Chief

---

[1] Article on 'Historical Research,' *The Nineteenth Century*, Dec. 1898.
[2] See *Quarterly Review*, 1892–3, and Spatz, *Die Schlacht von Hastings*, 1896.

Periods of European History.' The Regius Professor of Modern History was curiously ignorant of the last four centuries, and wisely chose most of his themes from the Middle Ages.

His last years were mainly devoted to a subject which lay far from the province of his chair. His occupation with Norman England kindled his interest in the fair island which had also been ruled by Norman Kings. For a moment he considered the idea of a history of the Normans in Sicily, but he quickly convinced himself that he must go further back. The position of the island made it the theatre of strife between East and West. Should it be part of Africa or of Europe? 'No one has tried to treat the whole story as a contribution to Universal History. It is by this standard I would ask my work to be judged. Nowhere do we better learn the folly of those arbitrary divisions which have made the study of history vain and meaningless.' It was his intention to bring his narrative to the death of the Emperor Frederick II, but it was not to be. He had never learned how to condense, and when he died four large volumes only brought the story to the beginning of the third century B.C. He declared that whereas he had brought many facts to light in the 'Norman Conquest,' it was difficult to find an absolutely new fact in the early history of Sicily, so exhaustive had been the research of Holm. His own contribution lies rather in his knowledge of the island. His enthusiasm knew no bounds. 'The Greek tongue,' he declared, 'is the noblest part of the study of language, the history of Greece the most instructive part of the history of the world.' He returned with delight to Thucydides, 'the greatest of historical teachers,' and other judgments of his early manhood were confirmed. 'For the democracy of Syracuse, as of Athens, we have Grote to our master. And from renewed experience I can say once more that Thirlwall is not superseded even by him.'

The work opens with a chapter on Characteristics of Sicilian History. The panorama is wide and impressive, the comparison of Sicily with other islands suggestive; but there is much repetition, and many allusions confuse rather than enlighten. The description of the natural features of the island which follows is in his best style, and the foundation of Syracuse provides occasion for a fine rhetorical disquisition on the city's place in history. The wars with Carthage and Italy are related with wearisome detail, but no reader will quarrel with the minute narrative of the Athenian expedition. The fourth volume, left unfinished and prepared for publication by his son-in-law, Arthur Evans, brings the story down to the Tyranny of Agathocles. The work was translated into German and received with warm commendation by Holm. Adolf Bauer declared that no English work on antiquity since Grote showed such wide and profound erudition.[1] It is a noble fragment, marred indeed by prolixity, like the 'Norman Conquest,' but inspiring in the enthusiasm which animates all his writings.

Freeman's central doctrine was the Unity of History. From early Greece to the Roman Empire, from Imperial Rome to mediæval and modern Europe there was no break, and he rendered service to historical thinking and teaching by his emphasis on continuity. Yet Stubbs devoted part of one of his lectures to an attack on his friend's philosophy. Classical, mediæval and modern history, he declared, could be usefully studied apart. In the world of action there was continuity, but in the world of thought and feeling, about which Freeman knew little and cared less, there were deep gulfs. A graver criticism may now be made. Since he enunciated his doctrine the historian's horizon had widened. His vision was confined to Europe. But Greece can no longer be treated as the starting-point of civilisation, for the discovery of the Ancient East has altered our perspective. Moreover, though he insisted on the need of knowing alike the classical, the mediæval and the modern world, his conception of history was purely external. The 'Norman Conquest' contained a chapter on architecture, the 'History of Sicily' a few pages on early Greek literature and on Hieron's relation to Pindar and Æschylus. Yet nine-tenths of human history, complained Frederic Harrison, left him without living interest. 'The keynote of his character,' declared his old friend Bryce, 'was the extraordinary warmth of his interest in the persons, things and places he cared for and the scarcely less conspicuous indifference to matters which lay outside the well-defined boundary line of his sympathies. He regarded history as almost exclusively a record of political events. He was not interested in religion, philosophy, or social conditions, and he thought it strange that anyone should be.' He knew the churches and castles of England and Western Europe better than any historian of his time, but he is believed only once to have visited a picture-gallery, dragged thither by Green. While he cared nothing for Plato, the Greek tragedians and Shakespeare, he loved old English ballads, admired Scott, and rejoiced in Macaulay's Lays. The world of ideas had no existence for him. Regarding history solely as a record of happenings, he recognised continuity but not organic evolution. His partialities never led him into the extravagances of Carlyle and Froude, for he detested

[1] A. Bauer, *Die Forschungen zur Griechischen Geschichte*, 1899.

cruelty. He exaggerated the virtues of Godwin and Harold, but he never whitewashed a bad man. Green, who found so much to censure in the 'Norman Conquest,' recognised its lofty moral qualities. 'It glows with a passionate love of civil freedom and a passionate detestation of all that is cruel and unjust. If there is hero-worship it is not the mere craven worship of brute force.' His greatest admiration is reserved for men like Timoleon and Washington, who knew how to lay aside their power. Despite his prejudices and limitations he occupies a high place among the writers and teachers of history, and readers of every school may find instruction in his virile pages.

III

Though Green[1] learnt something from Stubbs and Freeman, he was far more original than either. As a boy he explored the churches near his Oxford home and took rubbings of brasses. At twenty-two he embarked on authorship by a series of articles on Oxford in the eighteenth century. The easy, graceful style is already virtually formed, and the picture of the ancient city with its Jacobite dons and rowdy undergraduates is skilfully drawn. Ordained at twenty-four he worked for nine years among the poor. He used to say in later life that his experience of the East End was of assistance to his literary work, for it was there that he gained his living interest in the masses. A paper on Dunstan, read at the Somerset Archæological Society in 1862, was a turning-point in his career, for there he met Freeman. The elder scholar was struck by the essay—'a noble defence of a noble and slandered man'—which showed that the writer could weigh evidence as well as narrate. Henceforth Freeman made it his duty, in his own words, 'to blow Johnny Green's trumpet.' Their friendship lasted unbroken till the latter's death twenty years later, despite their totally different conceptions of history. Freeman was annoyed at Green's imaginative methods, while the younger man regretted the elder's absorption in mere events. Yet they had many interests in common, and rejoiced in each other's society at home and abroad. Freeman generously recognised his debt to his brilliant companion. 'I owe the deepest obligations to Green's interest in municipal history. His gift of catching the leading features in the topography and history of a town was wonderful. Whatever I have tried to do in that way I have learned from

[1] See *Letters of J. R. Green*, ed. Leslie Stephen, 1901; Bryce, *Studies in Contemporary Biography*, 1903; York Powell, *Occasional Writings*, 1906; Monod, *Portraits et Souvenirs*, 1897; W. G. Addison, *J. R. Green*, 1946.

him.' A year later Green met Stubbs on a visit to their common friend. The Professor was a less expansive personality, and the relations of the older and the younger man were never very intimate. Yet Stubbs warmly appreciated his work and his services to English history, and never lost an opportunity of singing his praises.

The year 1869 witnessed the birth of the conception of the 'Short History of the English People.' There was no good modern summary even of the outward facts of English history, still less a survey of the development of civilisation. Its publication in 1874 forms an epoch in historiography, for the English-speaking world received the first coherent and satisfying account of its own past. The hero of the book was the people; only thus could English history be conceived as a whole. The deeds of kings fall into their proper place, and we hear little of drums and trumpets. Chaucer occupies more space than Crecy. Dynasties come and go, battles are won and lost, but the people remain. That this reading of history is now a commonplace is mainly the work of Green. Though not the first to enunciate it, he was the first to illustrate it in the history of a great nation. The pyramid which historians had tried to balance on its apex now rests on its base. His work possesses the living interest of a biography and the dramatic unity of an epic.

Not less admirable than the design was the execution. By skilful grouping of periods, the omission of burdensome detail, a vivid style, and sympathy with every aspect of life—social, religious, literary, artistic, no less than political—he succeeded in reconstructing the development of a nation within the compass of a single volume. The difficulty of such an achievement is suggested by the fact that no one had accomplished it in England or elsewhere. The first breach with tradition was in his division of periods not according to reigns or dynasties but according to their governing feature. His grouping was highly suggestive, though his commencement of the New Monarchy with Edward IV was sharply challenged. A second departure was the substitution of a brief sketch for a detailed narrative of war and diplomacy, thus transferring the emphasis from action and military glory to internal development, and concentrating attention on men, books, ideas and ideals which revealed or influenced national life. 'I dare say you would stare,' he wrote to Freeman, 'to see seven pages devoted to the Wars of the Roses and fifteen to Colet, Erasmus and More. The more I think over our story as a whole, the more its political history seems to spring out of and be moulded into form by the social and religious history you like to chaff me about.' His earlier studies had been mainly devoted to the Middle Ages, and this part of the 'Short History' is on the whole the best. The mere man of action such as Henry V excites little enthusiasm in comparison with Alfred or John Ball, Langland or Caxton. He emphasised the influence of towns, discussed the economic effects of the Black Death, and traced the Wars of the Roses to social and material changes. In surveying his task shortly before its completion he declared that the sections on the New Learning, the Peasant Revolt and the towns were by far the best things he had yet written. On entering modern history he was on less familiar ground, but the chapters on the Reformation are of high merit. The sections on the Stuarts are less satisfactory, and the eighteenth century provided less opportunities for his special gifts than any of its predecessors. The work ends with the conclusion of the Napoleonic War.

The success of the 'Short History' was instantaneous. No historical work since Macaulay had sold so rapidly. Though Freeman objected that much of it presupposed more than average knowledge, it became a manual for schools and a companion for the advanced student. Hundreds of thousands of all ages became for the first time intelligently interested in the history of their own country. The originality of conception and wide learning were generally recognised. The freshness of treatment and youthful buoyancy were the more remarkable in the work of a consumptive under sentence of death. The history of England was no longer an old almanack but the development of a living organism, the English people. The work indeed possesses a touch of genius to which neither of the author's masters could lay claim. Despite its immense success it did not escape criticism. 'All through the earlier part,' wrote Green himself, 'I see the indelible mark of the essayist, the tendency to little vignettes, the jerkiness, the slurring over the uninteresting parts. I learnt my trade as I wrote on.' In such a work mistakes were inevitable. The truth of the matter was stated by Stubbs. 'Like other people he made mistakes sometimes, but scarcely ever do they affect either the essence of the picture or the force of the argument.' It was also accused of offering a partisan presentation of national development. Brewer, the historian of Wolsey, denounced it in the *Quarterly*[1] as a democratic manifesto, which idealised the people and despised their rulers. James I was presented as an immoral buffoon, a coward and a drunkard; Charles I as a compound of avarice and baseness; George III as a vain, selfish and unscrupulous tyrant. He was equally possessed with

[1] Reprinted in Brewer, *English Studies*, 1881.

a singular hostility to the Church of England. He considered war to be mere butchery, and declared that it played a small part in the real story of European nations. He possessed unquestionable genius, but his sympathies appeared to be not with order but with disorder. 'Under the guise of a school history he has disseminated some very violent opinions in politics and religion. We protest emphatically against the whole tone and teaching of the book.'

Though Brewer's criticisms were absurdly exaggerated, he was correct in detecting a 'leftish' standpoint. Green became increasingly liberal year by year and was one of the earliest of English Home Rulers. He loved and honoured Gladstone, ardently sympathised with the sufferings and ideals of the people, and detested the men in Church and State who had oppressed them.[1] In any conflict between ruler and ruled he was sure to be found on the side of the latter. 'I shall go on loving freedom, and the men who won it for us to the end of the chapter,' he confessed to Freeman. Thus he relates with deep sympathy the Peasants' Revolt of 1381, and is an enthusiastic supporter of Parliament against the first two Stuarts. There is little attempt to understand the royalist position which Gardiner was beginning to interpret. Nor is there a trace of the large-mindedness which was to characterise Lecky's treatment of the revolt of the American colonies. Yet the work cannot fairly be described as partisan. In many instances it is conspicuously impartial. He is fair both to the Protestant and the Catholic martyrs and severe on their persecutors. He is just both to Pitt and Fox. The book is no rhapsody on the British race, no thick and thin defence of British policy. He tests politics by the principles of morality, and does not fear to condemn the treatment of Ireland and Scotland, India, America and France.

A further charge was advanced by Brewer. 'The demand for history, lively, attractive, sparkling, has produced the required supply. The temptation is great and Green has not always been able to resist it. He has a natural tendency to supply from his own fertile and fervid imagination the dramatic details lacking in his cold and colourless originals.' A milder variety of this indictment is occasionally met with in the ranks of his friends. 'The imaginative faculty,' declares Bryce, 'was the leading and distinctive quality of his mind and writing. The early editions occasionally purchased vividity at the price of exactitude. His judgment was sometimes dazzled by the brilliance of his ingenuity.' He saw everything in colour. 'The fault of his style,'

[1] Cp. Mrs. Green's speech at the unveiling of the tablet at Jesus College in *The Times*, June 7, 1909.

declared the *Edinburgh Review*, 'is a uniformity, sometimes almost a monotony, of picturesqueness. We sometimes feel a fatigue like that experienced in turning over the pages of a picture book.' Against such criticisms may be set Stubbs' admiration for 'the wonderful simplicity and beauty of the way he tells his tale.'

While the 'Short History' was selling by scores of thousands in many languages, Green resolved to narrate the fortunes of England in greater detail. He threw himself into his task with such vigour that four large volumes of the 'History of the English People' were completed by 1880. The scale of 'Big Book' was about double that of 'Little Book,' but the scheme and method are the same. As an introduction to English history it was superior to every work except its own predecessor, yet it may be questioned whether it was worth undertaking. It was written too soon to allow fresh study to modify his judgments on particular issues, and it exposed itself to the same criticisms. Gardiner censured his habitual negligence in regard to constitutional laws, specially marked in the seventeenth century in reference to ship-money, benevolences and other contested issues.

Though the deadly disease now held him tightly in its grip, Green plunged with heroic courage into fresh labours. He lamented that 'the age of national formation' should remain comparatively unknown, and that its struggles should still be to most Englishmen mere battles of kites and crows. 'The Making of England,' which he completed, and the 'Conquest of England,' which lacked his revision, contain some of his best work. Dean Stanley had once said to him, 'I see you are in danger of growing picturesque. Beware of it. I have suffered myself.' The warning was now taken. He possessed a rare power of seizing the features of scenery and their effect on historical development. He knew and loved England, and in 1880 he and his wife published a 'Geography of the British Isles.' This exact knowledge of the face of the country, its archæological remains, its forests, its marshes and its roads, stood him in good stead in the 'Making of England.' His numerous maps for the first time traced the boundaries of the Kingdoms at different epochs. In addition to a detailed study of the invasions and the civil wars, he devotes a striking chapter to the Settlement of the Conquerors, their culture and institutions. He rejected the continuance of Roman culture, and agreed with Freeman in making Anglo-Saxon institutions extremely democratic. In the 'Conquest of England,' which continues the story from Egbert, he paints Alfred and Canute in glowing colours and repeats his unfavourable estimate of Godwin. 'The difference between Green and Freeman,' wrote Creighton after reading the two works, 'is enormous. Freeman tries to make you understand each detail by isolating it and surrounding it with nineteenth-century settings. He iterates and reiterates, but you don't see it. In the 'Making' and the 'Conquest' the whole thing moves together.'[1]

Green's death in 1883 at the age of forty-six was a serious blow to historical studies. In discussing the choice of an epitaph he had said, 'Do you know what they will say of me? ''He died learning.''' Grant Duff declared that had he lived he would have been the greatest English historian since Gibbon. Bryce believed that many would place him near Macaulay, for, though less weighty, he was more subtle and not less fascinating. He also found in him something of Gibbon, 'the combination of a mastery of details with a large and luminous view of those far-reaching forces and relations which govern the fortunes of peoples and guide the course of empire.'

[1] Creighton's *Life*, i. 264, 1904.

CHAPTER XVIII

GARDINER, LECKY, SEELEY AND CREIGHTON

I

WHILE Froude was occupied with the Tudors a less brilliant but far more trustworthy historian began his lifelong study of the Stuarts. It is Gardiner's[1] glory to have narrated the most critical and controversial period of our history for the first time with complete knowledge and tranquil judgment. With the possible exception of Stubbs' 'Constitutional History' his volumes form the most solid and enduring achievement of British historiography in the latter half of the nineteenth century. No attempt had been made to discover how the events of the time appeared when investigated solely from contemporary records. Royalist and Whig historians had seen what they wished to see. Ranke's monumental work, was only beginning to appear. Gardiner used to censure Guizot for beginning his 'History of the English Revolution' with Charles I, on the ground that a thorough study of James I was essential to the understanding of the struggle. The first two volumes appeared in 1863, covering the first half of the reign. For nearly forty years the undertaking was pursued without haste and without rest. He set his heart on reaching the Restoration, but died while engaged on the year 1656.

His work was the first narrative based on an exhaustive study of the vast mass of authorities reposing in public and private archives. The evidence of newspapers and pamphlets was freely used. Memoirs, however illustrious their author, were treated as secondary, not as primary, authorities. To compare the footnotes of a chapter of Gardiner with those of any previous work is to realise the advance. The judge had at last all the facts before him, and he knew what use to make of them. He challenged the Whig version of the reign of the first two Stuarts which had prevailed since Hallam and the Reform Bill, but he never doubted

---

[1] See *Dict. Nat. Biog.* (by Firth); York Powell in *Eng. Hist. Review*, April 1902; 'Two Oxford Historians' (Green and Gardiner), in *Quarterly Review*, April 1902. R. G. Usher's attack on his impartiality in *Critical Study of the Historical Method of Samuel Rawson Gardiner* (1915) was answered by Firth in a series of contributions to the *Times Literary Supplement*, 1919.

that Parliament was on the side of the future and that it was well that the policy of James and Charles failed. His originality lay not in his judgment of the result of the great struggle, but in his delineation of the leading actors and in his estimate of the relation of the rival policies to the practice and tradition of the past. 'In this world of mingled motives,' he remarks quietly, 'the correctness of a political or religious creed does not form a test by which to distinguish the noble from the ignoble man.' If it be one of the chief duties of an historian to render the actors in his drama intelligible, Gardiner was one of the greatest. His complete knowledge and equable temper enabled him to understand men who could not understand one another. He saw the grandeur of the ideals of Bacon as clearly as Spedding, and respected the courage of Coke and Pym as much as Macaulay. His readers are never allowed to forget how much each side contributed to the making of England.

He departs from the Whig tradition in the first place in regard to James I. Previous writers had based their conception of James chiefly on the memoir-writers and anecdote-mongers, and the public took its notions from the 'Fortunes of Nigel.' While Macaulay described the face and emphasised the oddities, Gardiner has little to tell of the outer man. Rejecting the stories of drunkenness and immorality, he shows the monarch to have been very different from the buffoon of popular literature. 'He desired to act rightly, to see justice done to all, to direct his subjects in the ways of peace and concord, and to prevent religion from being used as a cloak for polemical bitterness. His own ideas were usually shrewd. But he had too little tact and too unbounded confidence in his own not inconsiderable powers to make a successful ruler.' His policy both at home and abroad was a failure, and he sowed the seeds of revolution and disaster. The portrait of his son is less opposed to the prevalent tradition, though the censure is gently conveyed. 'A want of imaginative power lay at the root of his faults. Conscious of the purity of his own motives, he never ceased to divide mankind into two simple classes—those who agreed with him and those who did not, into sheep to be cherished and goats to be rejected.' In dealing with the latter he persuaded himself that it was lawful to employ deception. Both sides could appeal to tradition. In the fifteenth century Parliamentary privilege stood high, in the sixteenth the prerogative. The spirit of the new world was with the Parliament, but all around strong monarchies were in existence. The conviction that enlightened autocracy was the best form of government was held not only by rulers themselves but by many of the noblest minds of the time. James had given powerful literary expression to his views before he ascended the English throne. Bacon sincerely believed that the philosophic King would rule more wisely than representatives of the people. To this ideal of enlightened and God-fearing autocracy Gardiner renders full justice, while recognising that James and Charles were too mediocre to carry it out and that it was only suitable to immature peoples.

England was advancing in wealth and culture, new ideas of political liberty had been sown by the Reformation, and the personal government which had seemed reasonable in the strong hands of Elizabeth appeared less natural in those of James. Moreover, the struggle for national existence ended with the defeat of the Armada. The controversy was sharpened by a circumstance which had no connection with politics. The purchasing power of money had fallen rapidly owing to the great increase of specie from the mines of Spanish America, and the old taxes no longer sufficed to meet the needs of the State. Thus the increased demand for money led to suspicion and to a claim for a closer supervision of its expenditure. A second factor of aggravation was that the Kings adopted the High Church Anglicanism which to many Puritans seemed hardly distinguishable from Rome. The suspicion was increased by their refusal to throw the whole weight of England into the Protestant scale in the Thirty Years War, and by their friendliness to the Catholic Powers. The marriage of Charles with a French princess suggested that the key of the fortress was being delivered to the enemy. Gardiner shows that the Kings were loyal Protestants, and that they were right in refusing to steer the ship direct into the tornado of the Continental war. European politics, he declares, formed for the Commons a labyrinth without a thread. No part of the work is of greater value than that which for the first time revealed the foreign policy of James, unskilful in execution but not unstatesmanlike in design. A third cause of friction was presented in a new light. Nothing exasperated opinion more than the favour shown by both monarchs to Buckingham, whom Whig historians had presented as a typical favourite, selfish, vain and incapable. Gardiner's portrait is less flattering than that of Ranke, but he credits him with patriotism. 'If, however, it is only just to class him among ministers rather than among favourites, he must rank among the most incapable ministers of this or any other country.' More striking is the interpretation of Strafford. Pointing out that he accepted the theory neither of a Parliamentary executive nor of Divine Right, Gardiner declares that his entry into the government was in no sense an apostasy, and pronounces him the heir of Bacon, a lesser Richelieu. His capital error was the failure to recognise that the Elizabethan system was out of date, and that no stable constitutional edifice could be raised with Charles for its foundation.

Though he dismisses the charges of autocratic innovations and treason to the national religion, Gardiner is none the less convinced that the system of personal rule was impossible and degrading, and that the King's lack of tact and scorn of compromise made it appear peculiarly odious. On the other hand, though his opinion of the character of the Parliamentary leaders is as high as that of any Whig historian, he finds their outlook in some respects narrower than that of the monarchs. 'We look in vain,' he remarks in discussing the quarrels of 1625, 'for any sign of openness to the reception of new ideas, or for any notion that the generation in which they lived was not to be as the generation which had preceded it.' His analysis of Coke's ideology reveals a mind at least as conservative as that of his sovereigns. Again, there is no ground for charging with sycophancy the judges who pronounced in favour of the prerogative. The precedents were conflicting, and men of honour might well differ in their verdict. While recognising the zeal and good intentions of Laud, he sums up strongly against his policy. The Archbishop was a loyal Protestant, but it was difficult for Puritans to believe it when they saw their friends imprisoned and mutilated. The vindictive punishment of ecclesiastical offences contributed more than anything else to the popular exasperation. The Star Chamber, which had hitherto been little concerned with political cases, now gained the reputation of a tool of despotism and the organ of the Romanising party. Laud, he declares with severity, sought to train up a generation in habits of thought which would have extinguished all desire for political liberty. In the early stages of the Long Parliament the historian is against the Court, and he places the main responsibility for the outbreak of war on the King. In claiming executive control for Parliament Pym broke with precedent and tradition; but the demand was only formulated after failing to obtain trusted ministers, and after convincing himself that nothing else would terminate the system of personal rule. When the war began the King's worst quality, duplicity, hurried him towards the abyss. Gardiner's minute research in foreign archives established the fact that he stuck at nothing to regain his power and that a compromise was impossible. So penetrated is he with the impossibility of Charles that he has no words of blame for his execution.

With Cromwell, from whom he was descended, we enter on

new problems. 'He was a brave, honourable man, striving, according to his lights, to lead his countrymen into the paths of peace and godliness.' He depicts him as opportunist, moderate, even conservative, frightened by the levelling doctrines around him, moving forward towards supreme power with unwilling steps, penetrated with the impermanence of any régime which did not rest on the assent of Parliament. The expulsion of the Rump was designed as a step to a return to representative government. When he had reached supreme power, his most earnest desire was to transform a military dictatorship into a civil state. While convinced of his lifelong sincerity, Gardiner pronounces it natural that other men should think him a hypocrite. His mature judgment of the man and his work was given in the Ford Lectures on 'Cromwell's Place in History' and in the illustrated monograph in the Goupil series. No historian has rendered more ample justice to his noble character and lofty ideals, but the estimate of his ability is a little grudging, and he is a sharp critic of his statesmanship. As a soldier he pronounces him inferior to Montrose. He condemns both his Irish record and his foreign policy. 'Puritanism still had a hold on his heart; but for all that it was the material, the mundane aspect of politics which had gained the upper hand, at least as far as foreign politics were concerned.' He is clear that the Protectorate was bound to end in failure owing to the inherent difficulties of his situation. Representing a minority, Oliver could only maintain himself by force. The army was expensive, and a representative Chamber would have refused supplies. We derive a melancholy impression of a good man struggling with adversity, his constructive work a failure. 'It is impossible to resist the conclusion that Cromwell effected nothing in the way of building up where he had pulled down, and that there was no single act of the Protectorate that was not swept away at the Restoration without hope of revival.'

Gardiner has been well described as a Puritan purged of all harshness and narrowness. It has been held that his connection with the Irvingites aided him to understand the exaltation of the sects, but no one could tell from his work to what Church or party he belonged. While it has been the task of many writers to rekindle and inflame the passions of the past, he was not only the judge but the peacemaker. His sovereign achievement is to have interpreted the Royalist and Parliamentary cause with equal insight to the modern world, but his work possesses many other merits. His account of foreign policy, based on researches in Spain and other lands, is one of the best we possess for any period of our history. His studies of finance broke new ground.

His competence as a military historian surprised the readers of the 'Civil War,' and the volumes on the Commonwealth and Protectorate showed him equally at home in naval warfare.

With one exception Gardiner possessed all the tools of his craft—an accurate mind, equanimity, insight into character, sympathy with ideas different from his own. The exception was style. Had he possessed that talisman, his noble work would have become a popular classic. His pages are lacking in grace and distinction, but from time to time we feel the pulse of life beating beneath the studied reserve. Perhaps the highest point is reached in the chapters on the trial and death of Strafford, impressive in their suggestion of inevitable doom. He employed a lifetime to narrate the events of two critical generations, and he performed his task so thoroughly that it need not be done again on the same ample scale. It is idle to blame him for devoting so little space to culture and economic conditions and social life. He discharged the duty that above all needed to be accomplished, and laid the foundation on which others could build. He lived the modest life of a scholar, happy in his work and the appreciation of historians all over the world, caring nothing for fame and fortune. In loyalty to his self-imposed task he refused the Regius Professorship at Oxford on the death of Froude. He contributed articles on his chosen period to the Dictionary of National Biography. For thirty years he was Director of the Camden Society, for which he edited a dozen volumes. He succeeded Creighton as Editor of the *English Historical Review*. When Father Gerard tried to prove that the Gunpowder Plot had been organised by Robert Cecil to ruin the Catholics and confirm his position, he vindicated the essentials of his narrative. No Englishman of his time did more to raise the standard of responsibility in historical work, and he left us the most satisfying account of any period in the history of our race. The highest tribute to his judgment is the fact that Firth, his only rival in the field, reached approximately the same conclusions.

II

While Gardiner devoted his life to a single century, Lecky[1] ranged at large over the past. Destined for a family living in the south of Ireland, he studied divinity at Trinity College, Dublin; but at twenty-one he published an anonymous work on the religious tendencies of the age which showed that the Church was no place for him. His earliest and strongest interest was in the

[1] See *Memoir of W. E. H. Lecky*, by his wife, 1909, and Auchmuty, *Lecky*, 1945.

history and literature of his country. 'He studied the speeches of the principal orators,' writes a college friend, 'and could repeat by heart many passages from them. He was saturated with the writings and poetry of the patriotic party, and he looked on the author of "Who fears to speak of '98?" with feelings of unbounded admiration. Patriotism seemed to be his one absorbing passion.' His youthful enthusiasm found vent in his 'Leaders of Public Opinion in Ireland.' Immaturity is stamped on its pages, and the epilogue breathes a fiery nationalism, but the essays are not without power. The author concealed his name, and only thirty copies were sold.

The failure of the book turned his energies into a widely different field. His multifarious readings, his travels, and his admiration for Buckle suggested a line of study of which the first fruits appeared in the 'History of Rationalism.' It was the work of a thinker and a scholar, though its author was only twenty-seven. George Eliot[1] pointed out its faults with rather excessive emphasis, but it remains one of the works which every student of the psychological evolution of humanity should read. The 'History of European Morals from Augustus to Charlemagne,' which appeared four years later, marks a further advance. Its learning is even more comprehensive, the arrangement more skilful, the style richer and stronger; it is not surprising that it remained its author's favourite work. Tennyson pronounced it 'a wonderful book for a young man to have written, a great book for any man to have written.' When the poet added that it proved the author to possess true genius he overshot the mark. Lecky's mind was critical, not creative. The picture of the steady and irresistible march of rationalism had caused widespread alarm. The survey of ethical theories in the introductory chapter of the later work announced the author's repudiation of utilitarian solutions, and declared his belief that the intellectual processes of the modern world would inflict no injury in the field of morals. The studies of Rationalism and Morals made their way all over the world, and they deserved their success, for they were among the earliest notable endeavours to broaden the conception of history by penetrating behind the screen of action. An interesting letter explains their author's purpose. 'The two books are closely connected. They are an attempt to examine the merits of certain theological opinions according to the historical method. The first is a history of the imposition of those opinions on the world, the second a history of their decay. They belong to a very small school of historical writings which began with Vico, was

[1] Her article is reprinted in her *Essays*.

continued by Condorcet, Herder, Hegel, Comte, and found its last great representative in Buckle. What characterises these writers is that they try to look at history, not as a series of biographies or accidents or pictures, but as a great organic whole.'

At the age of thirty Lecky had won a European reputation by his studies in the evolution of ideas, but the rest of his life was devoted to modern political history. Froude had claimed the sixteenth century, Gardiner was at work on the seventeenth; the eighteenth was still open. Stanhope's large scale narrative, conscientious and useful as it was, lacked breadth and colour. Lecky's ambition was to present a comprehensive survey of life and policy, of institutions and tendencies. Much of biographical, military and party interest was suppressed in order to find place for the Church and Dissent, the agricultural, manufacturing and commercial interests, the Press, social conditions, and the relations of the mother country to its dependencies. The 'History of England in the Eighteenth Century' appeared in eight volumes between 1878 and 1890, and immediately took rank as a classic. In a later edition the Irish chapters were disentangled from the English, and the work is most conveniently treated as consisting of two separate parts. The English volumes cannot be said to provide a history of the eighteenth century. The period preceding the accession of George III is a mere sketch, while the narrative stops in 1793 with the outbreak of the Great War. The survey of the development of the Whig party from the Revolution possesses considerable interest, but as a history in the grand style the work only covers the first thirty-three years of the reign of George III. Lecky possessed something of Gardiner's power to sympathise with both sides. The narrative of the American war is a triumph of impartiality. It is of these chapters that Acton wrote to the author that they were fuller of political instruction than anything which had appeared for a long time. If there is a hero it is neither Chatham nor Pitt, but Burke. There was more of the charlatan in Chatham, he declared, than in any other very great Englishman, and both he and his son delighted in a kind of ostentatious virtue. Burke and Fox, on the other hand, sacrificed incomparably more for their principles. Among the most successful portions of the work are two massive chapters which may almost be described as digressions, the first a survey of the work of Wesley and the state of religious thought, the second an analysis of the causes of the French Revolution.

The most original and important part of the whole work is that which concerns Ireland. Before commencing the history of the eighteenth century he had rewritten his 'Leaders of Public

Opinion,' omitting its rhetoric but retaining the nationalist stand-point. In approaching the composition of his principal work his determination to relate the critical period of Irish history in minute detail was mainly due to the appearance of Froude's volumes. 'His whole nature,' writes his wife, 'revolted against the spirit of intolerance of which Mr. Froude was the advocate and the use he made of his authorities.' After prolonged research in the archives of Dublin Castle he revealed the true history of the Grattan Parliament, the rebellion of 1798, and the Union. The work was so thoroughly done that it does not need to be repeated. These volumes rank with Gardiner's narrative of the struggles of the seventeenth century, and constitute his highest achievement.

The Irish volumes, like the English, but with more excuse, merely sketch the earlier half of the century. The stream broadens with the appearance of the Volunteers and the estab-lishment of an independent legislature in 1782. Though a Pro-testant Assembly elected by Protestant votes, the Parliament showed itself to be inspired by a healthy nationalism. Its attitude to the Catholic majority was not unfriendly, and its loyalty to the English connection beyond reproach. Its chief spokesman was perhaps the noblest political figure of his time, and the volumes form one long tribute to Grattan's character, policy and genius. A great step forward was taken with the concession of the franchise to Catholics in 1793, and the dispatch of Lord Fitz-william seemed to herald further concessions. In the controversy over his policy and recall Lecky takes his stand without hesita-tion on the side of the Viceroy, and in the terrible years which followed he is unstinting in his condemnation of blind repression. He contends that it was the harsh and blundering policy of the Government which drove masses of men into the rebel camp whom reasonable concessions would have kept loyal. He believes that the rebellion of 1798 made Union inevitable, but he does not yield to Grattan in indignation at the methods by which it was accomplished. His patient research enabled him to unravel every thread of that sordid story. He recognises the ability of Clare and the skill of Castlereagh, but he pronounces the whole unbribed intellect of Ireland to have been against the measure. His pages prove that the Union bore the same relation to ordinary legislation as martial law to civil jurisprudence.

While Lecky was at work on the Grattan Parliament the Home Rule controversy burst upon the country. His half-forgotten book on 'Irish Leaders' was pillaged for missiles, but he ranged himself without hesitation among Gladstone's opponents. The letters published in his biography dispel the charge of inconsistency.

He had welcomed the Land Act of 1870, and he entertained the greatest respect for such Home Rulers as his friends Gavan Duffy and O'Neill Daunt, but he detested Parnell and his associates. How intense was his distrust of the capacity of his countrymen appears in a curious letter of 1880. 'I think you will soon find the opinion growing up on all sides that Ireland is unfit for the amount of representative government she possesses, and that a government on the Indian model may become a necessity.' He disliked the Local Government Bill of 1898 passed by his own party, and 'hoped it would not do much harm.' The Home Rule conflict made him a politician and drove him into Parliament. He took a gloomy view of the future, and on the last day of 1893 he wrote in his commonplace book, 'the world seems to me to have grown very old and very sad.' It was under the influence of this pessimism that he wrote 'Democracy and Liberty,' a passionate attack on recent developments in the political and industrial world. The book is the work of an angry partisan, and no part of it is so bitter as that which deals with Ireland. Yet his reading of Irish history never altered. The closing months of his life were occupied with the further expansion of the work which he had published in 1861 and revised in 1871. Grattan is still the statesman working nobly for the progress of his country in cordial loyalty to England. The essay contained an exhaustive discussion of the recall of Fitzwilliam in the light of recent pronouncements by Lord Rosebery and Lord Ashbourne in their biographies of Pitt. He concedes that the Viceroy was guilty of technical mistakes, but maintains that Pitt committed an irreparable blunder in dismissing the man whom the great majority of Irishmen trusted and loved. The second volume was devoted to O'Connell. While gently recognising his faults, he is convinced of his sincerity and whole-hearted devotion to his country. Lecky had no objection to a nationalism which respected the rights of property, repudiated violence, and was loyal to the British Crown. It was fitting that the life of a scholar whose greatest achievement was the vindication of the Grattan Parliament should end with a mellow, almost tender, biography of the greatest of Irish nationalists.

III

Though no historian of his time took a more limited view of the province of history than Seeley,[1] it was not because his own

---

[1] See Prothero's memoir prefixed to his *Growth of British Policy*, 1895; Tanner, *Eng. Hist. Review*, July 1895; H. A. L. Fisher, *Fortnightly Review*, Aug. 1896; and Adolf Rein, *Seeley, Eine Studie über den Historiker*, 1912.

interests were few. Beginning with a critical edition of the first book of Livy, he scored his most brilliant success as the author of 'Ecce Homo,' and in his closing years wrote a charming sketch of Goethe. His first historical effort was the 'Lectures and Essays' published in 1870, a year after he succeeded Kingsley as Regius Professor of Modern History at Cambridge. The inaugural lecture was characteristically devoted to the teaching of politics. Why should history be studied? Because it is the school of statesmanship, came the answer. 'Our University is and must be a great seminary of politicians. Without at least a little knowledge of history no man can take a rational interest in politics, and no man can form a rational judgment about them without a good deal.' That this obvious truth was so little recognised was due to the common error that history dealt with the remote past. It was to modern history that he invited the attention of the young men 'from whom the legislators and statesmen of the next age must be taken,' and it was in modern history that he was to find the theme of his three chief historical works.

The earliest and largest was the 'Life and Times of Stein, or Germany and Prussia in the Napoleonic Age.' His plan was to approach the history of Napoleon from a new angle, and thus to illustrate the principles at issue between him and his enemies. The great work of constructive reform which followed the disaster of Jena was little understood, and Stein was merely a name in England. The book contained no revelations, for he consulted no manuscripts, but he knew all the printed authorities. His thesis was that a reform took place in Germany not less far-reaching than in France and without its attendant horrors. The problem of transforming Prussia into a modern State was accomplished in the main by Stein, whom Seeley, following Häusser, compares to Turgot. Though hero-worship was no temptation to his austere temperament and biographical details had no attraction for him, he does not conceal his admiration for the courage and sanity of the great statesman whose name stands at once for national independence and internal reform.

Seeley was possessed with a lifelong detestation of Napoleon and the conception of a universal state. He embodies the struggle of the good and evil principle—nationality *versus* universal dominion—in Stein and Napoleon. He censures Frederick William III for not drawing the sword a year before Jena, and again in 1809 and 1812. Had he joined Russia and Austria in the year of Austerlitz, the result might have been different, whereas in 1806 he stood alone. Had he joined Austria in 1809 he might have turned the scale. Had he attacked Napoleon in flank after the disasters of 1812 he might have saved the bloodshed of Leipzic and Waterloo. Seeley never doubts the patriotism of the colourless King, but the main burden was borne by other men. Next to Stein himself he places Fichte, of whose soul-stirring 'Addresses to the German People' he speaks with enthusiasm. His chapters provided English readers with the best summary of the epoch-making changes which abolished serfdom and established municipal self-government. The reform of the army by Scharnhorst and Gneisenau, the foundation of the University of Berlin, the noble personality of Niebuhr, the educational labours of the Humboldts, take their place among the factors of regeneration. The 'Life of Stein' never became a popular favourite, but its worth was recognised by those who took the trouble to read it. For England it was the revelation of a great statesman and an heroic epoch. The historian was justified in his claim that it was abundance of matter, not diffuseness of style, that had made the book so large. To Germany it was also welcome as the first adequate biography of the statesman whom the vast compilation of Pertz had hidden rather than revealed, and it retained its place till the appearance of Max Lehmann's exhaustive study a generation later. If the work has a fault it is its portrait of the Emperor. His 'Short Life of Napoleon,' written for the 'Encyclopædia Britannica' and republished in an expanded form, again revealed his inability to recognise the greatness of a man whose character and policy he abhorred.

If the 'Stein' met with less success than it deserved, Seeley's next work brought ample compensation. 'The Expansion of England' occupies a place in political history as well as in the annals of historiography, for it appeared at a moment when the nation was becoming interested in the colonies and the Empire. We had conquered and peopled half the world in a fit of absence of mind, he declared, and even now we had not ceased to think of ourselves as a race inhabiting an island off the northern coast of Europe. This insularity had affected historians, who made far too much of the parliamentary squabbles of the eighteenth century, and failed to perceive that our history was less in England than in America and Asia. The two courses of lectures dealt with the conquest of Canada and India, explaining with admirable clarity the relation between the foundation of the British Empire and the conflict with France. 'The main struggle of England from the time of Louis XIV to the time of Napoleon was for the possession of the New World.' Seeley produced his effects by focussing a brilliant light on the principal factors, exhibiting the connection between apparently isolated occurrences, and bringing the reader by a number of paths to the same conclusion. He loved panoramic surveys, comprehensive generalisations, international problems. 'He was much more at home,' wrote a pupil, 'dealing with a century than a decade. The whole drift of his mind was towards the suggestive treatment of large phenomena rather than the microscopic investigation of details. His method was astronomical. He swept the whole heaven with his telescope.' His thesis was less original than he suggested, but he was the first to work it out.

Though the 'Expansion of England' became the bible of British Imperialists, its spirit was by no means that of unrestrained enthusiasm for empire or for the methods by which it was built up. While emphasising the importance of the movement, he left it an open question whether it was a matter for exaltation or regret. 'Bigness is not necessarily greatness. If by remaining in the second rank of magnitude we can hold the first rank morally and intellectually, let us sacrifice mere material magnitude.' He draws a sharp distinction between the white colonies and India, the possession of which, he declared, increased our responsibilities but not our power. He rejects the notion that the vastness of the Empire proves either invincible heroism or supernatural genius for government in our nation. The book stimulates reflection rather than exultation, and emphasises rather the magnitude than the glory of our inheritance. Like Mahan's 'Sea Power in History' and Oliver's 'Alexander Hamilton,' it was as much a political dissertation as a scientific inquiry.

The last ten years of Seeley's life were mainly occupied with the study of British foreign policy. Like Ranke, to whom he owed most, he regarded history as concerned mainly with the life and relations of states. His books had been international studies, and he delighted to lecture on English diplomacy in the time of William and Marlborough. He collected a mass of original material, and he possessed the art of distilling its essence. His first plan was to begin with 1688, but as it became clear that some introduction was needed, he pushed his starting-point ever further back. Finally he commenced with the accession of Elizabeth, and when overtaken by death had only reached the reign of William III. The fragment filled two small volumes, which were published after his death. The 'Growth of British Policy' traced the making of a Great Power and the influence of the religious and dynastic struggles of the Continent on the statecraft of the island kingdom. 'English eyes,' he wrote, 'are always bent upon Parliament, English history always tends to shrink into mere Parliamentary history; and there is scarcely a great English historian who does not sink somewhat below himself in the treatment of foreign relations.' It was his ambition to produce an English counterpart to Droysen, but he describes the book as an essay, not a history. The foreground is occupied by the figures of Elizabeth, Cromwell and William III, who raised England to the lofty position she held among the nations when the eighteenth century dawned. The erudition is largely concealed. Scarcely a reference is given, and details are kept in the background, but few books leave such an impression of lucidity and grasp. His power of marshalling facts was unrivalled, and no one was more successful in making the reader feel the diplomatic unity of Europe. The work opens with a study of the growth of the House of Hapsburg, and there are chapters in which England is scarcely mentioned, but it is not long before the threads are interwoven. He believed that the destiny of a state depended less on its institutions than on its place in the world. Firth complained that, though the ideas of the book are bold and original, the facts are sometimes strained. Generalisation is a perilous art, and Seeley occasionally traced results too exclusively to diplomatic factors.

His output, though slender in quantity, is of high quality. His writings were completely elaborated before they were given to the world; he had a horror of lazy thinking, slovenly expression and careless scholarship. He felt a hearty contempt for the purveyors of the picturesque, and infuriated the youthful George Trevelyan by dismissing Carlyle and Macaulay as charlatans. It has been said that he handled facts like a lawyer, building up a case and making the lines of his argument converge on a single point. His conclusions are hammered into the mind and are impossible to misunderstand or forget. Though he deliberately excluded vast tracts of the life of the past from the purview of the historian, no one has more ardently proclaimed the capacity of history to guide and influence the present. History possessed a meaning and taught lessons which it was the main duty of the historian to discover. It was the direct reference to the problems of the day which helped to win for the 'Expansion of England' its phenomenal success. When the Historical Tripos was established, he claimed a leading place in it for political science. 'Historical details were worth nothing to him but as a basis for generalisation,' wrote his friend Prothero after his death. 'In dealing with history he always kept a definite end in view—the solution of some problem, the establishment of some principle, which would arrest the attention of the student and might be of use to the statesman. Narrative without generalisation had no interest for him.' Politics, he declared, were vulgar, when they were not liberalised by history, and history faded into mere literature when it lost sight of its relation to practical politics. The attempt to derive practical lessons from history and to build up a science of politics was pursued in stimulating Conversation Classes in his own house. It was a lofty ambition, but didactic history, however scientific in intention and stimulating, has its pitfalls. Moreover, his emphasis on the superior utility of the study of recent times ignores the truth that to-day is not only the child of yesterday but the heir of all the ages.

IV

Creighton,[1] like Seeley, was above all interested in the relations of states, the technique of diplomacy, the secrets of the council-chamber. Both approached their task in the cool, detached manner of Ranke; both were more interested in action than in ideas. His apprenticeship was served at Oxford, where he lectured on mediæval and modern history, and wrote popular sketches of Rome, Simon de Montfort and the Age of Elizabeth. The success of these elementary works encouraged him to more serious undertakings when he accepted a college living at Embleton in Northumberland. He was passionately attached to Italy, and had written on Æneas Sylvius and other Italian subjects. In 1877 he informed a friend that he was busy on what he intended to make the work of his life, a history of the Papacy from the beginning of the Great Schism to the Council of Trent. 'My book would be in no sense polemical or ecclesiastical. It aims at dealing with the larger political aspects of the time, and would embrace the history of Italy, its art and literature, as well as a survey of the whole of European history. It would fill a void between Milman, which becomes very scrappy towards its close, and Ranke's "Popes," and my object is to combine the picturesqueness of the one with the broad political views of the other.' He approached the Papacy with a good deal of sympathy. 'Popular Protestantism,' he wrote, 'has so grotesquely misrepresented facts concerning the Reformation that now one of the great means used by the Roman Catholics to make converts is to prove to anyone who will listen the falsity of their opinions regarding the facts of the past.' He had no theories, no philosophy of history, no wish to prove or disprove anything. His

[1] See *Life and Letters of Mandell Creighton*, by his wife, 2 vols., 1904; Richard Garnett in *Eng. Hist. Review*, April 1901; Gosse, *Portraits and Sketches*, 1912.

ambition was simply to collect materials for a picture of the pre-Reformation and Reformation era. Ecclesiastical history is but rarely approached in such a spirit, and the book realises its author's ideal of light without heat.

The first two volumes, bringing the story down to the middle of the fifteenth century, appeared in 1882. Their learning and impartiality, which were everywhere recognised, won him the Professorship of Ecclesiastical History at Cambridge. Hodgkin, his neighbour and fellow enthusiast for Italian history, looking back on his intercourse with Creighton during the composition of the work, testifies that the latter raised his standard of the way in which history ought to be written. 'I always like,' he said, 'to keep close to my authorities'; and the volumes showed how literally he interpreted his duty. The discussions of the sources are among the most valuable parts of the work. The volumes suffer, indeed, from an almost excessive severity of treatment. The intrigues of the period, the procession of Popes and anti-Popes, are narrated in minute detail. Were it not for the Hussite movement and the gallant attempts of the Councils to reform the Church, they might fairly be called dull, or even, as their author half seriously declared, very dull. It was not his fault that the Pontiffs, except Nicholas V and Pius II, were lacking in personality. 'When events are tedious,' he wrote, 'you must be tedious.' Yet the work built up a reputation among scholars at home and abroad, and it gave him special satisfaction that his fairness was recognised at Rome. Acton, whom he considered the only Englishman capable of judging the merits of the book, spoke of his sovereign impartiality, though he challenged the favourable verdict on the Conciliar movement and regretted that so little attention was devoted to the development of ideas. Creighton expected more opposition from his own camp, for his aim had been to 'clear away Protestant misconceptions about the steady growth of what they call an evangelical spirit.'

His most memorable achievement was the treatment of the early Renaissance Popes in the third and fourth volumes. His love of brilliant colour and striking personalities gave the age of the Italian princes a special fascination. The studies of scholarship and culture were unreservedly praised, but the handling of the Popes who made the Papacy a great Temporal Power found severe critics. It was not in his nature to moralise, to wring his hands, to hurl thunderbolts against crowned sinners. 'I am busy with the Borgias,' he wrote, 'and it is like spending one's day in a low police court. But I don't want to show how the Popes lived in Rome, but how they affected Europe.' He refused to exhibit

Rodrigo Borgia as a moral monster, and claimed for him not a few of the homelier virtues. 'Alexander's unparalleled wickedness,' he wrote before the book was published, 'is a result of the general desire to find a scapegoat for the decay of Italy in the sixteenth century. He was bad enough, but not exceptionally bad.' The exceptional infamy attaching to him was largely due to the fact that he did not add hypocrisy to his other vices. 'The good are not so good as they think themselves,' remarked Creighton; 'the bad are not so bad as the good think them.' Too much should not be expected from human nature.

The new volumes provoked Acton to something like indignation. 'He is not striving to prove a case or burrowing towards a conclusion, but wishes to pass through scenes of raging controversy and passion with serene curiosity, a suspended judgment, a divided jury and a pair of white gloves.' To the stern Catholic moralist the degradation of the Papacy was a shameful tragedy. 'It is the office of historical science to maintain morality as the sole impartial criterion of men and things, and the only one on which honest minds can be made to agree.' A second criticism from the same pen will carry more general conviction. Acton congratulated him on 'lightening his burden' by substituting life and action for thought and law. It was a delicate method of hinting that the treatment was external and therefore superficial. Creighton preferred pageantry to problems, narrative to reflection. The weighty criticism led to a memorable correspondence, in which Acton stated his views with increased emphasis. 'I cannot accept your canon that we are to judge Pope and King unlike other men, with a favourable presumption that they did no wrong. If there is any presumption it is the other way, against the holders of power, increasing as the power increases.' Creighton's rejoinder protested against making history a branch of moral science. Men who thought heresy a crime might be accused of an intellectual mistake, not necessarily of a moral crime. 'History supplies me with few heroes, and records few good actions; but the actors were men like myself, sorely tempted by the possession of power. Who am I that I should condemn them? Surely they knew not what they did.'

The features of which Acton complained reappear in an intensified degree in the concluding volume of the work, extending from the accession of Leo X to the sack of Rome. Creighton was well fitted by his calm temperament for dealing with controversial periods, but his mind was too secular to master the problems of the Reformation. In the admirable words of Richard Garnett:

'He prefers the learning of the fifteenth century to the theology of the sixteenth. Italians suit him better than Germans, statesmen better than warriors, scholars better than prophets.' The chapters on the German Humanists and the Reuchlin controversy, with which the volume opens, are written with his old ardour for culture. As men are born Platonists or Aristotelians, so are they born to love Luther or Erasmus. Creighton was on the side of Erasmus. Though there are brilliant passages in the volume, it did nothing to advance his fame. No real attempt is made to explain one of the greatest events in history. He has little to say of the grievances against Rome, the indignation at the worldliness of the Church, the protests of the moralist, the preacher and the satirist. That a great change was impending was obvious in the fifteenth century, but in his pages the Reformation arrives virtually unannounced. He opens his narrative by the curious words, 'The religious revolt, originated by Luther, fell like a thunderbolt from a clear sky.' He rejected the traditional Protestant notion that it was inevitable, and pronounced it a misfortune for Christendom that it took the form of a breach of the unity of the Church. Yet he declares that Luther made no demands which the Church could not have met. 'The Curia was responsible for driving Luther to revolt.'

Nowhere does the personality of the Reformer appear so unimpressive. To Catholics he is a bold bad man, to Protestants a bold good man, to Creighton a soul drifting rather than driving into rebellion. Luther was the first great man that Creighton met with in his history, and he failed to realise his stature. He was partly conscious of his failure. 'What I have written about Luther,' he wrote to Henry Charles Lea, 'does not satisfy me. Kolde admires it, but says that he must be understood from the religious side, whereas I treat him chiefly from the political side.' The criticism of the German scholar touches the heart of the matter. Creighton declared that he tried to take the view of a contemporary statesman, and his monograph on Wolsey portrays the secular world in which he felt himself most at home. He lacked insight into the life and thought of the masses and into the fiery convictions of religious reformers. Yet, despite its limitations, the 'History of the Papacy' is a notable book. Though there are no revelations—for Creighton never explored the twilight world of the archives—the printed sources are skilfully employed. His impartiality is conspicuous, his style clear and interesting. In dealing with men and movements with which he is in full sympathy he reaches a high level of portraiture and interpretation. The weakness of the book lies in its relative indifference to the more fundamental experiences of religious life. He had completed the greater part of the fifth volume before his appointment to a bishopric in 1891, which proved as fatal to historical production as with Stubbs. His latest work was a brief Introduction to the opening volume of the ' Cambridge Modern History,' in which he depicts the Renaissance as the beginning of the modern world.

CHAPTER XIX

ACTON AND MAITLAND

I

ACTON'S[1] descent from the Prime Minister of the Kingdom of Naples during the Napoleonic era and from the ancient German house of Dalberg secured him from his birth the entry into a cosmopolitan circle which was widened by the marriage of his mother to Lord Granville. His inability to enter Cambridge led him to Munich, where he lived for six years in the house of Döllinger, the greatest ornament of Catholic scholarship, who became the most potent influence in his life. He threw himself with extraordinary energy into the study of Church history and impressed all who met him with the strength and range of his intellect.[2] On leaving Munich he attended the lectures of Ranke and Böckh at Berlin, made a long tour through the United States, and accompanied his stepfather to the coronation of Alexander II.

The contrast between the stirring intellectual life of Germany and the stagnant Catholicism of his native land determined him to introduce the leaven of modern scholarship into England. With the aid of the brilliant convert Simpson, the biographer of Campion, he used the *Rambler* to survey the movement of European

[1] A collected edition of his writings, with hitherto unpublished correspondence, is in course of publication by Hollis and Carter. See Herbert Paul's memoir prefixed to *Acton's Letters to Mary Gladstone*, 1904; Introduction (by Figgis and Laurence) to *History of Freedom and other Essays*, 1907; *Edinburgh Review*, Ap. 1903; R. L. Poole, *Eng. Hist. Review*, Oct. 1902; Bryce, *Studies in Contemporary Biography*, 1903; Lady Blennerhassett in *Biographisches Jahrbuch*, 1905; Figgis in *Dict. Nat. Biog.*; Herbert Fisher, 'Acton's Historical Work,' *Quarterly Review*, July, 1911; Grant Duff, *Out of the Past*, vol. ii., 1903; Lally, *As Lord Acton Says*, 1942; Archbishop Matthew, *Acton: the Formative Years*, 1946; Gertrude Himmelfarb, Introduction to *Acton, Essays on Freedom and Power*, Boston, 1948; Butterfield, *Lord Acton* (Historical Association Pamphlet), 1948. The fullest analysis of his ideas are to be found in Ulrich Noack's three volumes, *Geschichtswissenschaft und Wahrheit, Katholizität und Geistesfreiheit*, and *Politische Sicherung der Freiheit*, 1935–47, and in Fasnacht, *Acton's Political Philosophy*.

[2] See Bernhard von Meyer, *Erlebnisse*, vol. i. ch. 12, 1875. 'With true joy I recall the time when I was privileged to enjoy the society of this young man, already possessed of extensive knowledge and consumed with zeal for German scholarship.'

thought and to discuss historical, political and philosophical problems.[1] From his boyhood he had read omnivorously in several languages, copying notable passages and arranging his extracts in boxes and drawers. At twenty-three he began to build up the magnificent library which was the delight of his life, and which was one day to find a home in Cambridge.[2] It was an uphill fight, for his message was not only the importance of learning but the sacredness of truth, the rights of conscience, the crime of civil and religious absolutism. He was eager to obtain the assistance of Newman, but the greatest of English Catholics was scarcely less repelled by the audacities of the *Rambler* than by the obscurantism of Manning and Ward. In reply to a letter criticising the treatment of Pius V Acton wrote a lugubrious reply. 'Public opinion does not admit the authority of science or the sanctity of truth for its own sake. Our aim is the encouragement of the true scientific spirit and the disinterested love of truth. I have nowhere seen this principle seriously adopted by any Catholic periodical.' When the monthly journal was suppressed the quarterly *Home and Foreign Review* was founded to carry on the campaign. 'There is only one thing you may not like,' wrote the editor to Newman on the appearance of the first number; 'Paul III had a son, not a nephew as he is usually called. I feel very strongly that this ought to be gibbeted, and I cannot avoid pointing out the wilful lie that it involves.' By 1864 the patience of his superiors was exhausted. He bowed to authority, and suppressed the *Review*.

The output of these six years was prodigious both in quantity and range.[3] The more important articles were republished after his death. Except for a study of James de la Cloche and an attack on Buckle, the essays are directly or indirectly concerned with Catholicism and its enemies. The earliest, 'Political Thoughts on the Church,' laments the supersession of religious motives by political opinions, which it traces to the usurpation by the Protestant states of the functions of the Church. Rome was attacked by Conservatives as a political danger and by Liberals as the foe of liberty. 'We must be prepared to do battle for our religious system in every other sphere as well as in that of doctrine.' The

[1] See Gasquet's Introduction to *Lord Acton and His Circle*, 1906; 'Gasquet and the Acton-Simpson Correspondence' in the *Cambridge Historical Journal*, 1950; and Wilfrid Ward's biographies of W. G. Ward and Newman.

[2] See Tedder, 'Lord Acton as a Book Collector,' *Proceedings of the British Academy*, vol. i.

[3] See the bibliographies compiled for the Royal Historical Society by W. A. Shaw, 1903, and in the volumes of Lally and Himmelfarb.

Middle Ages were a time 'in which were laid the foundations of all the happiness that has since been enjoyed and of all the greatness that has been achieved by men.' The Christian notion of conscience demanded a corresponding measure of personal liberty, and the Church could not tolerate any government in which this right was not recognised. She was the irreconcilable enemy of the despotism of the state, and thus the guardian of liberty as well as of conscience. Absolute monarchy had been her greatest enemy, but rationalist democracy was an equal danger. The Reformation was 'the great modern apostasy,' for which a day of reckoning would come as it had come for paganism. Yet England, 'in the midst of its apostasy and in spite of so much guilt towards religion,' had preserved the Catholic spirit in her political institutions more than any other country.

Acton followed the events of 1860 in Italy with indignation, and wrote a pungent essay on the death of Cavour, who sought the greatness of the State, not the liberty of the people. His attack on Austria in 1859 is pronounced unpardonable, and his hostility to the Church a calamity. 'The incompatibility of the Piedmontese laws and government with the freedom of the Church is the real danger in the loss of the Temporal Power.' The Temporal Power was the theme of a long article a few months later on Döllinger's new book, 'The Church and the Churches.' Like his master he pronounced Protestantism to be doomed— 'disorganised as a Church, its doctrines in a state of dissolution, despaired of by its divines, strong and compact only in its hostility to Rome.' The Primacy was essential to the Church of Christ, and without it the body broke up into warring atoms. The Reformation was a great movement against the freedom of conscience, for the rejection of the Pope led straight to the divine right of kings, which was invented by Luther. The government of the Papal States was in need of reform, but there was neither despotism nor spiritual decay. A remarkable article on the 'Protestant Theory of Persecution' carries the war boldly into the enemy's camp. Protestantism, he repeated, had swept away the only authority that could temper the omnipotence of the state. The Reformers preached and practised the punishment of error by death in an age when the disappearance of unity had deprived it of excuse. There is not a word in condemnation of Catholic persecution, and in an essay on Goldwin Smith's 'Irish History' he defended Rome against the charge of being a persecutor. Mediæval persecution was justified, for the sects were revolutionary parties, and Catholicism never persecuted those outside her fold. A long review of Hefele's life of Ximenes attacked the Spanish Inquisition for repressing religious thought and aiding absolutism, but pronounced it to have been useful in combating vice. Despite the militant Catholicism of the *Rambler*, Wiseman publicly attacked it for its 'absence of all reserve or reverence in its treatment of persons or of things deemed sacred, its grazing over the very edges of the most perilous abysses of error, and its habitual preference of uncatholic to Catholic instincts, tendencies and motives.' Acton issued a spirited reply in his new organ, vindicating his loyalty and his independence. 'Modern society has developed no security for freedom, no instrument of progress, no means of arriving at truth which we look upon with indifference or suspicion.' The defence failed to conciliate his critics, and the striking essay, 'Conflicts with Rome,' announces the termination of the *Home and Foreign Review* 'There is no lack of periodicals representing science apart from religion or religion apart from science. The *Review* has attempted to exhibit the two in union. The principles it has upheld will not die with it, but will find their destined advocates and triumph in their appointed time.'

Newman's letters show that it was rather Simpson than Acton who gave offence, but the position of a critical individualist in a Church claiming divine authority was bound to be difficult. Though Rome had not possessed such an advocate in England since the Reformation, the English leaders were becoming increasingly suspicious of the German scholarship which Döllinger and his pupil represented. Newman, Manning and Ward had left the Church of their baptism owing to its surrender to 'Liberalism,' and they had no mind to admit the evil spirit into the Church of their adoption. When Ambrose St. John visited Pius IX in 1869, the Pope spoke to him of those who were not Catholics *di cuore*, of whom Acton was the type.[1] The indefatigable propagandist contributed leading articles to a weekly journal called the *Chronicle*, which was founded in 1867 and only lived a year, and then helped to reorganise the *North British Review* on the lines of Liberal Catholicism. In the latter appeared the massive article on the Massacre of St. Bartholomew, which rebuked the attempts to dissociate the Church from responsibility. 'Such things will cease to be written when we perceive that truth is the only merit that gives dignity and worth to history.' The apologist was developing into the historian.

As the Vatican Council approached Acton joined his master in resisting a consummation which he felt would be equally disastrous to liberty and the Church. From Rome he sent to Döllinger full reports on which the 'Letters of Quirinus' were largely based.

[1] Ward's *Newman*, vol. ii. 167.

When defeated he published his 'Open Letter to a German Bishop' and an article in the *North British Review*. The former contrasted the bold words of the minority in the early stages with their silence at the critical moment, and declared that in duty to their reputation they must resist to the end. The latter surveyed in detail the origin, problems and course of the Council, which might have been used for reform had not the Pope been captured by the Jesuits. No appeal to revelation or tradition, to reason or conscience, had produced any effect. In recent years almost every writer who really served Catholicism had fallen sooner or later into disgrace or suspicion. Romanism was triumphing over Catholicism. The springing of Infallibility on the Council was a conspiracy. The final defeat of his ideal of a tolerant and scholarly Catholicism threw a lasting shadow over Acton's life. The Church of his dreams was as far from the Ultramontanism of Pius IX and Manning as was the Protestantism of Harnack from the fundamentalism of Spurgeon. Like Döllinger, he refused to join the Old Catholic Church, but he was regarded with suspicion by the victors, and Manning more than once invited explanations. He believed that he would be excommunicated, and told Gladstone that the only question was when the blow would fall.[1] He was not, however, molested, and he remained throughout life a devout Catholic. He was relieved to discover that the tremendous power claimed and recognised in 1870 was never employed during his lifetime, but his hatred of the spirit of Ultramontanism never varied. Herbert Paul compares him to Sarpi; but if he cared little more for the Curia, he had a far deeper interest in religion than the great Venetian. His last utterance on behalf of his Church was the series of letters to *The Times*[2] in 1874 in answer to Gladstone's attack on Vaticanism. In reply to the contention that Catholics could no longer be loyal owing to their allegiance to a foreign potentate, he maintained that, though the Pope had long claimed the power to depose princes, English Catholics had not acted and would not act seditiously. In his later writings confessionalism completely disappears.

The plan of a 'History of Liberty,' written throughout from the original sources, had been formed early in life; and in 1877 he delivered two lectures which indicate the direction of his thought. 'Liberty,' he begins, 'next to religion, has been the motive of good deeds and the common pretext of crime.' By liberty he meant the assurance that every man should be pro-

[1] Manning described him as the evil genius of Gladstone; see Purcell, *Manning*, vol. ii. 434-5 and 490-1, 1895.

[2] Reprinted in *Lord Acton's Correspondence*, i. 119-44, 1917.

tected in doing what he believed to be his duty against the influence of authority and majorities, custom and opinion. 'The most certain test by which we judge whether a country is really free is the amount of security enjoyed by minorities.' There was little liberty in Greece and Rome, for the individual was at the mercy of the state. The words of Christ, 'Render unto Cæsar the things that are Cæsar's, and unto God the things that are God's,' were the repudiation of absolutism and the inauguration of freedom. In the Middle Ages it was the resistance of the Church which prevented Europe from falling under a Byzantine despotism. From the conflict of the secular and ecclesiastical power arose civil liberty, for both were driven to acknowledge the sovereignty of the people. While the outcome of ancient politics was an absolute state planted on slavery, the Middle Ages witnessed the restriction of authority by representation and by the Church. This process was arrested by Machiavelli and the Reformers, who revived the theory of absolutism. Liberty was saved by England and America. The striking article of a year later on Erskine May's 'Democracy in Europe' covers much the same ground. 'Ancient democracy in its best days was never more than a partial and insincere solution of the problem of popular government.' Christianity introduced ideas which made for democracy, but they were not applied. Its revival was due neither to the Christian Church nor to the Teutonic State, but to the quarrel between them. After emphasising Luther's championship of passive obedience, he declares Lilburne among the first to understand the real conditions of democracy. To America is due its triumph and its influence in Europe. 'It was democracy in its highest perfection, armed and vigilant against its own weakness and excess.' He blames the French Revolution for imparting to modern democracy an implacable hatred of religion, and declares its theory of equality disastrous to liberty. He concludes by discussing federalism, proportional representation, and other guarantees of freedom. The lesson of history is that the only hope of liberty lies in the division of power.

The 'History of Liberty' was never written nor even commenced, and the task, as he conceived it, was beyond human power. 'Acton,' wrote Gregorovius in his diary in 1869, 'sets copyists to work all over the world to supply him with materials. I am afraid he may be swamped by their very copiousness.'[1] His words on Döllinger are only too applicable to himself. 'He would not write with imperfect materials, and to him the materials were always imperfect.' Döllinger had judged correctly when he

[1] *Roman Journals*, 340, 1910.

said that if Acton did not write a great book before he was forty, he would never do so. 'Twenty years ago,' records Bryce in a well-known passage, 'late at night, in his library at Cannes, he expounded to me his views of how such a history of liberty might be written, and how it might be made the central thread of all history. He spoke for six or seven minutes only; but he spoke like a man inspired, as if, from some mountain summit high in air, he saw beneath him the far-winding path of human progress from dim Cimmerian shores of pre-historic shadow into the fuller yet broken and fitful light of the modern time. The eloquence was splendid; but greater than the eloquence was the penetrating vision which discerned through all events and in all ages the play of those moral forces, now creating, now destroying, always transmuting, which had moulded and remoulded human institutions, and had given to the human spirit its ceaselessly changing forms of energy. It was as if the whole landscape of history had been suddenly lit up by a burst of sunlight. I have never heard from any other lips any discourse like this, nor from his did I ever hear the like again.'

The foundation of the *English Historical Review* in 1886 supplied a new stimulus to production.[1] Acton had long wished for something corresponding to the great reviews of Sybel and Monod, and promised his support. An article on 'German Schools of History,' the most impressive he ever wrote, opened the first number, and was hailed by Creighton, the first editor, as sufficient to establish the reputation of the journal throughout Europe. He presents the ideas which underlay the historical scholarship of the century, connecting historical studies with the movement of political, religious and economic thought throughout Europe. It is equally striking for its learning, its judgment and its pregnant style. Next in importance was the massive article on Döllinger, written on the death of his nonagenarian master, 'who formed his philosophy of history on the largest induction ever available to man.' The obituary of Giesebrecht, brief as it is, conveys a complete idea of the personality and achievement of the historian. His reviews were as striking as his articles. Those of Lea's 'History of the Inquisition' and Bryce's 'American Commonwealth' were worthy of the classics they discussed. The criticisms of less important books—Flint's 'Historical Philosophy in France,' Creighton's volumes on the Popes, de Broglie's study of Mabillon, Morse Stephens' 'History of the French Revolution,' Seeley's 'Napoleon,' and Bright's 'Victorian Era'—are crowded with judgments and reflections which give

[1] See Creighton's *Life*, vol. i. ch. 11, 1904.

them permanent interest. His style became increasingly epigrammatic and allusive, and he leaves the impression that he writes from a higher level of knowledge than other men. His contributions form the most striking feature in the first decade of the *Review*. In the *Nineteenth Century* he reviewed the biographies of George Eliot and Lord Houghton, and welcomed the memoirs of Talleyrand and Tocqueville. More remarkable was the massive Introduction to Burd's edition of the 'Prince,' in which he traces the conscious or unconscious adoption of the principles of Machiavelli through the centuries, and regretfully pronounces him not a vanishing type but a constant and contemporary influence.

Acton's appointment to the Chair of Modern History at Cambridge on the death of Seeley in 1895 aroused unusual interest.[1] Though his name was scarcely known to the public and he had never published a book, he had been a conspicuous figure for nearly forty years in the republic of learning, he had taken a leading part in the greatest ecclesiastical struggle of the century, he was familiar with the statesmen no less than the scholars of Europe, and he was one of the most erudite Englishmen of his time. Half German by birth and training, he brought an international atmosphere into the University. A Catholic Professor of History was a novelty, but the choice was abundantly justified. Cambridge has never had a teacher more capable of inspiring his students to research and reflection or more ready to enter into their life and interests. The Inaugural Lecture[2] struck a note which had never been heard at either University. In his opening paragraphs he shattered the fetters in which his predecessor had bound himself and attempted to bind his pupils. 'Politics and history are interwoven, but are not commensurate. Ours is a domain that reaches farther than affairs of state. It is our function to keep in view and to command the movement of ideas, which are not the effect but the cause of public events.' The first of human concerns was religion, the second liberty, and their fortunes were intertwined. Passing from the scope and content of history to the spirit which should govern its study he emphasised the sanctity of the moral code. 'I exhort you never to debase the moral currency, but to try others by the final maxim that governs your own lives, and to suffer no man and no cause to escape the undying penalty which history has

[1] See Pollock, 'Lord Acton at Cambridge,' *Independent Review*, Oct. 1904, and the Introduction (by Figgis and Laurence) to *Lectures on Modern History*, 1906.

[2] Its teaching was challenged by H. C. Lea, 'Ethical Values in History,' *American Historical Review*, vol. ix., and by Lamprecht in *Deutsche Zeitschrift für Geschichtswissenschaft*, 1898.

the power to inflict on wrong.' 'If in our uncertainty we must often err, it may be sometimes better to risk excess in rigour than in indulgence.' 'If we lower our standard in history, we cannot uphold it in Church and State.' The fear that he would shield his Church disappeared when it was realised that the severest sentences were pronounced where their religion should have taught men better. 'In judging men and things,' he had written to Creighton, 'ethics go before dogma, politics and nationality.'[1] He practised what he preached, and he never wrote or uttered a word as Regius Professor which revealed him as a member of one Church rather than another.

Acton delivered two courses of lectures which were published after his death. That on Modern History outlines developments from the Renaissance to the eve of the French Revolution. Designed primarily for undergraduates it naturally contains a great deal of familiar information, but we feel his personality in the pontifical judgments with which the book abounds, and many things appear in a new light. Though the book necessarily deals with events rather than with ideas, the dominant theme is the advance of mankind towards ordered liberty. 'We have no thread through the enormous intricacy of modern politics except the idea of progress towards more perfect and assured freedom and the divine right of free men.' He boldly declares the emancipation of conscience from authority to be the main content of modern history. His comments on the Augsburg settlement of 1555, the Edict of Nantes, the theorists of the English Revolution and the American War, to name a few passages, suggest the rich contribution of liberty to the life of mankind. Of the men of action William the Silent and Washington receive marks for good conduct, but for most of the outstanding rulers, from Charles V to Frederick the Great, he has little admiration. Religious and racial prepossessions fall into their proper place when the progress of humanity is taken as the test and measure of progress.

The course on the French Revolution is more interesting and characteristic. Acton was dealing with the greatest subject in modern history and with a movement in which ideas and action were intertwined. No brief summary can convey an adequate idea of the strength, the eloquence and the wealth of reflection in this fascinating book. The opening lecture on the Heralds of Revolution is remarkable for the prominent position assigned to Fénelon, 'the first man who saw through the majestic hypocrisy of the Court and knew that France was on the road to ruin.' He believed

[1] See the interesting correspondence in Creighton's *Life*, vol. i. ch. 13; and in Himmelfarb, 357–373.

that absolute power was poison, and that the only antidote was a Constitution. The *Philosophes* who succeeded him continued his work by undermining authority; but none of them, least of all Rousseau, desired or understood political liberty. 'The spark that turned thought into action was supplied by the Declaration of Independence.' The lecture on the Influence of America is one of the most valuable, not only for the extracts from American publicists and the discussion of the earlier philosophy of Burke, but also for his judgment of the great struggle. 'Their grievance was difficult to substantiate and trivial in extent. But if interest was on one side, there was a manifest principle on the other—a principle so sacred and so clear as imperatively to demand the sacrifice of men's lives, of their families and their fortune. They represented liberty as a thing so divine that the existence of society must be staked to prevent even the least infraction of its sovereign right.' When Acton speaks of liberty there is always a ring in his voice.

It was the combination of French theory and American practice that led to the events of 1789. The *Cahiers* gave a mandate for the abolition of feudalism and despotism, not for the establishment of a democratic republic. In contrast to Taine's lurid picture of the actors, Acton declares them to have been average men, with a large number above the common standard both in ability and character, while Mirabeau and Sieyès possessed genius. 'The Revolution will never be intelligently known to us till we discover its conformity to the common law, and recognise that it is not utterly singular and exceptional, that other scenes have been as horrible as these, and many men as bad.' The main responsibility for the degeneration of the reform movement is attributed to the Court. The King was ready to advance, but he was surrounded by evil advisers, the worst of them the Queen. Of the Declaration of Rights he speaks with enthusiasm. 'It is the triumphant proclamation of the doctrine that human obligations are not all assignable to contract or to interest or force. This single page of print outweighs libraries and is stronger than all the armies of Napoleon.' Yet it had one great fault. It sacrificed liberty to equality, and the absolutism of the King was succeeded by the absolutism of the Assembly.

Long before the Constituent Assembly had time to grapple with the most urgent problems, Europe began to threaten the Revolution. The Émigrés intrigued against the new order from the frontier, the King and Queen from the Tuileries. The flight to Varennes showed France in a flash that her King had been saying one thing and doing another. Differing in politics and religion, Acton and Aulard agreed that it was the intrigues of the Court with foreign Powers which drove the Revolution into fatal courses. On the other hand, the Civil Constitution, which the King abhorred, was a fatal blunder. The Constituent Assembly was better than the Legislative, and the Legislative superior to the Convention. He laments the fall of the Monarchy, and condemns the September massacres, the execution of the King and Queen, and the Terror, yet they all had their causes. The reign of violence began when the danger on the frontier became acute, and ended when it was removed. In face of the Brunswick manifesto, threatening death and destruction to the Revolution and all its works, a despotic executive was inevitable. Thus the Girondins went down before the Jacobins, who were worse men and cared even less for liberty, but knew how to defend the fatherland. Danton is judged with great severity, and all that can be said for him is that he was not so bad as Robespierre. In a characteristic thrust the lecturer pours scorn on the race of whitewashers. 'The strong man with the dagger is followed by the weaker man with the sponge.' Yet the Revolution, despite its horrors, was a great effort at human emancipation. 'The best things that are loved and sought by men are religion and liberty, not pleasure or prosperity, not knowledge or power. Yet the paths of both are stained with infinite blood.'

A few months after Acton's appointment the Cambridge University Press invited him to edit a comprehensive history of the modern world.[1] He accepted, 'because my office makes it a duty not to be declined, and because such an opportunity of promoting his own ideas for the treatment of history has seldom been given to any man.' In a detailed memorandum he explained his plan of campaign. 'We shall avoid the needless utterance of opinion or service of a cause. Contributors will understand that our Waterloo must satisfy French and English, Germans and Dutch alike; that nobody can tell, without examining the list of authors, where the Bishop of Oxford laid down the pen, and whether Fairbairn or Gasquet, Liebermann or Harrison took it up.' After reviewing the mass of publications of new matter in every country, he declares that the honest student finds himself continually deserted, retarded, misled by the classics of historical literature. 'Ultimate history we cannot have in this generation, but we can dispose of conventional history.' He looked forward with special pleasure to the later volumes, which would be enriched with secrets that could not be learned from books. 'Certain

[1] See The Cambridge Modern History, an Account of its Origin, Authorship and Production, 1907.

privately printed memoirs may not be absolutely inaccessible, and there are elderly men about town gorged with esoteric knowledge.' His essay on the 'Causes of the Franco-Prussian War,' written during his last years at Cambridge, suggests the wealth derived from men who had made history that was stored in a single brain. 'He was always hunting for the key to secret chambers,' remarks Bryce, 'believing that the grand staircase is only for show. One was sometimes disposed to wonder whether he did not think too much about the backstairs, but he had seen a great deal of history in the making.' The editor drew up a list of contributors and secured the acceptance of the greater number, but in the spring of 1901 he had a stroke and was compelled to resign his task. He died in 1902, shortly before the appearance of the first volume. Like Mark Pattison he carried an enormous cargo of unused knowledge to the grave.

Henry Sidgwick used to say that however much you knew about anything Acton was certain to know more. De Laveleye recorded his astonishment at finding on the table of his host 'all the new books on all subjects, read and annotated.' Tollemache tells us how Gladstone used to dismiss abstruse points that arose in conversation with the remark 'We must ask Lord Acton.' These tributes, of course, must not be taken too literally. He knew nothing of science, cared little for pure literature and the arts, and was only an oracle on the later Middle Ages and the modern world. To a wide knowledge of books he added an unrivalled knowledge of men. He had met many celebrities who had played a leading part in politics and scholarship in Europe and America for half a century. In early life he sat in the House of Commons, later in the House of Lords. Lord Morley records that Gladstone could never have enough of his company, and the 'Letters to Mary Gladstone' reveals the affectionate admiration of the scholar for the statesman.[1] A member of Grillion's and The Club, he knew the best of English society. Abroad his company was sought by men like Renan and Taine, Mommsen and Helmholtz no less than by Döllinger and Dupanloup. He would dine one evening with Thiers and the next with the Duc de Broglie. He counted the Empress Frederick among his friends. 'To be with Acton,' wrote a grateful pupil, 'was like being with the cultivated mind of Europe. In the deep tones of his voice there seemed to sound the accents of history.'

He believed that historical study was not merely the basis of insight into the present but a school of virtue and a guide to

[1] Cp. Mary Drew, 'Lord Acton's Legacy to Liberals,' *The Optimist*, Jan. 1908.

life. 'The great achievement of history is to develop and perfect and arm conscience.' It was above all a spiritual process, a record of the formation and operation of ideas and ideals. Liberty was the sign and the prize and the motive in the onward and upward advance of the race. 'We all know some twenty or thirty predominant currents of thought or attitudes of mind which jointly weave the web of human history. All these a serious man ought to understand, in whatever weakness and strength they possess, in their causes and effects and relations. The majority of them are either religious or substitutes for religion.' He drew up a list of a hundred books for a young man 'whose education is finished and who knows common things.'[1] Its object was set forth in noble words—'to perfect his mind and open windows in every direction, to raise him to the level of his age so that he may know the forces that have made our world what it is and still reign over it, to guard against surprises and the constant sources of error within, to supply him with the strongest stimulants and the surest guides, to give force and fullness and clearness and sincerity and independence and elevation and generosity and serenity to his mind, that he may know the method and law of the process by which error is conquered and truth is won, that he may learn to master what he rejects as fully as what he adopts, that he may understand the origin as well as the strength and the vitality of systems and the better motive of men who are wrong, to steel him against the charm of literary beauty and talent, so that each book may be a beginning of a new life.'

The historian, in his view, was not only the interpreter of events and ideologies but the guardian of morality. 'The inflexible integrity of the moral code,' he declared, 'is to me the secret of the authority, the dignity and the utility of history.' He believed that since the coming of Christianity men knew as well as they know to-day what was right and what was wrong; the Christian conscience was our compass and we needed nothing more to steer our course. 'Our judgment of men and parties,' he wrote in his review of Morse Stephens, 'is determined by the lowest point they touch. Murder, as the low-water mark, is invaluable as our basis of measurement. If we have no scientific zero to start from, it is idle to censure corruption, mendacity or treason, and morality and history go asunder.' He detested alike the superman and his votaries. 'Excepting Froude,' he wrote to Mary Gladstone on the death of Carlyle, 'I think him the most detestable of historians.' The series of aphorisms containing his

[1] See Clement Shorter, 'Lord Acton's Hundred Best Books,' *Pall Mall Magazine*, July, 1905.

advice to historians breathes an austerity which would have satisfied Sismondi and Schlosser. 'Judge not according to the orthodox standard of a system religious, philosophical, political, but according as things promote or fail to promote the delicacy, integrity and authority of conscience.' 'The greatest sin is homicide. The accomplice is no better than the assassin, and the theorist is worse.' 'Murder may be done by legal means, by plausible and profitable war, by calumny, as well as by dose or dagger.' History taught the student to seek and tell the whole truth, to insist on evidence, to suspect equivocation, to allow for bias. The historian was a judge, overawed neither by worldly greatness, success or flattery, a corrector of injustice, an avenger of innocence. He was dismayed at the cool detachment of his old master. 'Döllinger,' he wrote in 1879, 'looks for the root of differences in speculative systems, in defect of knowledge, in everything but moral causes; and in this I am divided from him by a gulf that is almost too deep for sympathy. He refuses to see all the evil there is in man.' This stubborn refusal to recognise that the moral atmosphere had changed like everything else was only modified on his death bed. 'During what was almost our last conversation,' writes his son,[1] 'he solemnly adjured me not to rash-judge others as he had done, but to take care to make allowance for human weakness.' It was a fitting close to a life devoted to the pursuit of truth that he should be learning to the end.

II

The most brilliant and original of English institutional historians prepared himself for his life work by the practice of law. An article on the reform of English Real Property Law, published in 1879 at the age of twenty-nine, revealing a knowledge of the work of Brunner and other foreign jurists, attracted the attention of Sir Frederick Pollock and led to the beginning of an historic friendship. 'I was a lawyer,' wrote Sir Frederick after the death of his friend, 'who had found it impossible to understand English law without much more historical criticism than was usual in text-books.' He found in Maitland[2] a kindred mind, equally

[1] Letter to *The Times*, Oct. 30, 1906. Acton's oracular judgments are challenged by Butterfield, *The Whig Interpretation of History*, ch. 6.

[2] See Fisher, *F. W. Maitland*, 1910; A. L. Smith, *Maitland, Two Lectures*, 1908; Sir F. Pollock, *Quarterly Review*, April 1907; Vinogradoff, *Eng. Hist. Review*, April 1907; *Selden Society*, vol. xxii., 1907; *Cambridge University Reporter*, July 22, 1907. For foreign appreciations see Bémont, *Revue Historique*, vol. xciii., and *Law Quarterly Review*, April 1907. There is a good centenary article in *The Cambridge Journal*, December, 1950.

interested in past and present. In 1884 a second notable friendship began when he met Vinogradoff at Oxford. 'That day determined the rest of my life.' Under the impulse of the conversation he found his way to the Record Office. The result was his book, 'Pleas of the Crown for the County of Gloster,' his native county, which he described as a photograph of English life early in the thirteenth century. In the same year he was appointed Reader in the History of English Law at Cambridge, and gave up his work as a conveyancer. His second venture owed its origin still more directly to the Russian scholar, who described in the *Athenæum* a manuscript in the British Museum containing hundreds of cases of Henry III, apparently compiled by or for Bracton, annotated by him, and used in the construction of his famous treatise. Maitland's studies confirmed the hypothesis of his friend, and in 1887 'Bracton's Note-book' appeared. Brilliantly edited, the cases threw light on many aspects of social life as well as on the legal conceptions and practices of the time. A year -later he was appointed Downing Professor of the Laws of England. He entitled his inaugural lecture 'Why the history of law is not written,' and answered his own question by pointing out its traditional isolation from every other study. Our records were unique both in mass and continuity, and they contained undreamed-of treasures. 'Legal documents are the best, often the only evidence we have for social and economic history, for the history of morality, for the history of practical religion. There are large and fertile tracts of history which the historian has to avoid because they are too legal for him.' Law must be regarded as part of the national life, and the ideas of which it was the expression must be recovered. 'The history of law must be the history of ideas.' The average historian possessed no detailed knowledge of law, while the average lawyer's mind was profoundly unhistorical. To bridge the gulf he undertook the largest task of his life.

The 'History of English Law,' published in 1895, though described as the work of Pollock and Maitland, was mainly written by the latter. The two hundred pages of the introductory sketch form a precious contribution to English history. Anglo-Saxon law was pronounced to be almost purely Germanic. If Celtic custom survived the Teutonic conquest it could not be traced. There was also no real evidence that Roman institutions outlived the invasions or contributed to the formation of our laws. 'Within the sphere of law everything that is Roman or Romanised can be accounted for by late importation. Whatever is Roman in the early Anglo-Saxon documents is ecclesiastical.

In the later reigns some Roman forms and phrases filtered in from France. It was not till the Norman Conquest that Roman elements, embedded in the Frankish system of government which was copied by the Norman Dukes, reached England in any quantity. It was not till the middle of the twelfth century that the tide began to flow in flood from the revived study of Justinian at Bologna; and a century later the tide began to ebb.' Since Edward I legal life has been continuous. Our law was never obliterated by a wholesale importation of Roman elements, as in Germany. The thirteenth century, the classic period of French and German law, had been thoroughly explored by Continental scholars, but European law could only be fully understood when every system had been carefully studied. 'We must know in isolation the things that are to be compared before we compare them. A small share in this preliminary labour we have tried to take.' While virtually confining themselves to the history of law the authors occasionally discuss a constitutional problem. 'We think that those who have endeavoured to explore the private law of the Middle Ages may occasionally see even in political events some clue which escapes eyes that are trained to look only or chiefly at public affairs.' In like manner incursions are made into the sphere of ecclesiastical law, while leaving on one side the constitution of the Church. The greater part of the two massive volumes is devoted to an analysis of Angevin law, the manifold varieties of tenure, the social classes, the different jurisdictions, contract and inheritance, marriage law, criminal law, procedure. Though parts of this encyclopædic survey are necessarily technical, it is enlivened by an alert style and constant glimpses at the wider national life. A second edition in 1898 added an illuminating chapter on pre-Saxon, that is Roman times.

It was the original intention of the authors to supplement their survey of Angevin law by a study of Domesday. 'Our one hope of coercing Domesday Book to deliver up its hoarded secrets, our one hope of making an Anglo-Saxon land-book mean something definite, lies in an effort to understand the law of the Angevin time.' The treatment of 'that enigmatical record' was held over, and 'Domesday Book and Beyond' appeared a year later, bearing the name of Maitland alone. The problem was far more difficult than the reconstruction of Angevin law, but his attempt was the most successful effort yet made to solve it. Seebohm's 'English Village Community,' with its vivid picture of mediæval husbandry, its massive scholarship and its skilful marshalling of the evidence for servile origins, had produced a

deep impression on its publication in 1883. Starting from the
familiar manorial system of the later Middle Ages, he traced its
main features back by slow stages through Domesday and the
Anglo-Saxon centuries to the Roman occupation. The Roman
villa, he concluded, was the ancestor of the manor, the village
community a Latin not a Teutonic creation. The theory of the
mark collapsed in a moment, and for a time it seemed as if his
charge had swept the Germanists from the field. Yet the new
theory was scarcely more watertight than the old. The chain of
evidence, which at first sight looked so complete, contained
yawning gaps. Facts of equal importance and of a different
orientation were overlooked. Closely resembling Fustel de
Coulanges in his habits of mind not less than in his conclusions,
Seebohm possessed a rare power of working in high relief. Vinogradoff's classical work on 'Villainage,' described by Maitland
as by far the greatest achievement in English legal history, soon
proved that the social structure was less simple than Seebohm
believed. Where the English scholar found a single system descend-
ing unbroken from Roman times, the Russian discovered a
number of types, a complex of legal and social relationships,
varying both with the century and the locality. While Vinogradoff's rejection of the hypothesis of servile origins was based
chiefly on post-Domesday evidence, Maitland's rested on his
study of Domesday itself. His conclusion is that the manor and
the seigneurial element were not the outcome of the Roman villa,
that free peasants become numerous as we go further back, that
free villages existed, that England was still only partially manori-
alised at the Norman Conquest, and that no real manorial system
existed till the twelfth century. The manors varied greatly in
character, freeholders were numerous, and there were many
grades of freedom. We begin with village communities, Germanic
in origin, of landowning ceorls and their slaves. This free class
was depressed by the growth of seigneurial justice and feudalism.
The free village community was agrarian, not political. It lacked
an assembly and court and was unrecognised by law. The treatise,
which discusses subjects of great difficulty with unusual lightness
of touch, overthrew the conception of a homogeneous servile
manorial England.

A second monograph followed a year later. The Ford Lectures
on 'Township and Borough,' though a less ambitious work,
grappled with the problem of the origins and privileges of towns
in the light of the records of Oxford and Cambridge. Here, again,
his task is to protest against over-simplification. He inclines to
Keutgen's theory that the borough originated in the county

fortress. The township, with market, court and rampart, became a borough or privileged town. After the Norman Conquest many towns asked for and obtained similar privileges, but no hypothesis explained every case. Cambridge, for instance, had no lord but the King. The book embraces a discussion of the corporate idea, a conception in which Maitland delighted as a blend of metaphysics, law and history. Gierke had shown the immense place held by corporations in the life of the Middle Ages: the Trust or Fellowship was a living organism, a real person, neither the creature of the State nor a fiction. This conception was explained and elaborated by Maitland in 1900 in the brilliant Introduction to his translation of Gierke's chapter on the theory of corporations.

A third monograph was of more general significance. The 'History of English Law' had briefly sketched the legal position of the clergy and discussed the ecclesiastical offences of heresy and sorcery, but no attempt was made to study Canon Law. When Maitland began to work in this field the greatest and indeed the only authority was Stubbs, who had lectured on it at Oxford and compiled a memorandum for the Royal Commission on Ecclesiastical Courts. From Stubbs' view that it had no binding force in the English Church till ratified by that Church, Maitland was converted by his study of the 'Provinciale' of Lyndwood, an official of the Archbishop of Canterbury, compiled in 1430. Other text-books pointed in the same direction, and his book proved that England was as much subject to the Canon Law as any other country. The tradition that England was largely independent of Rome and that the Reformation effected no great change disappeared. 'Canon Law in England' created excitement and even resentment in certain circles, but its conclusions have held their ground. Of scarcely less value was his description of the Elizabethan Settlement and the Scottish Reformation in the second volume of the 'Cambridge Modern History.' Though he had hitherto devoted little attention to the sixteenth century he rapidly grasped the nature of the problems he had to solve. In a single brief chapter he throws a flood of light on the Elizabethan Settlement, his mind, trained to seize and analyse conceptions half legal half political, piercing to the heart of the Reformation compromise. The Anglo-Catholicism of Henry VIII was dead and 'the long Elizabethan peace' had come. 'It appeared as part and parcel of a general amelioration. It was allied with honest money, cheap and capable government, national independence and a reviving of national pride.'

While thus busily engaged on narrative and investigation

Maitland devoted much time and thought to the Selden Society, which he had founded in 1887. Of the twenty-one volumes published during his life he edited no less than eight. The first set the standard for its successors. The Introduction to the 'Select Pleas of the Crown' explained the differentiation of the branches of the Royal Court during the first half of the thirteenth century. The 'Select Pleas of Manorial Courts' traced the decline of private jurisdiction. 'Bracton and Azo' measured Bracton's debt to Roman law and Italian learning, on which Maine had gone astray. While special topics were illuminated by the publications of the Selden Society, he aroused his countrymen to the importance of a vast and almost totally neglected department of materials for a knowledge of English law. 'Some day,' he declared, 'it will seem wonderful that men once thought they could write the history of mediæval England without using the Year-books.' It was because the Year-books had not been explored that the 'History of English Law' was not continued. He threw himself into the study with zest, and rejoiced to discover how much light they shed on every branch of law and administration. He began with the reign of Edward II, and completed three volumes. He had no difficulty in exhibiting the unique value of what he described as the earliest 'debates' in Europe. His translation of the French text is a remarkable achievement in philology, involving a reconstruction of the Anglo-French legal language. He was engaged on this abstruse task during the months of illness before he died.

Maitland's death at the age of fifty-six was an irreparable blow to scholarship. In twenty years he had laid the foundations of a history of English law and had mapped sections of it in considerable detail. He had inspired his pupils and fellow-workers, among them Mary Bateson, with a boundless devotion. His work and worth were fully recognised. Vinogradoff declared him a genius. Acton pronounced him the ablest historian in England while Stubbs and Gardiner were still alive. Dicey placed him beside Blackstone and Maine. In Germany his work was diligently studied. Liebermann declared that he had turned the dust of the archives into gold, Brunner that he had brought England out of isolation and plunged her into the mid-stream of European thought. Gierke found in him an inspiring interpreter of his own ideas and a fellow-worker in the study of corporations. Similar tributes came from the historians and jurists of France and America. The cause of this universal admiration must be sought in his possession of qualities rarely found in combination. 'No one since Gibbon,' writes A. L. Smith, 'so combined the scientific and the literary, the analyst and the artist, the Stubbs and the Froude.' He was both brilliant and exact, imaginative and industrious. His technique was faultless. He possessed a rare insight into the conceptions of which law and custom were the expression. While Stubbs was unrivalled in his analysis of institutions, Maitland was his superior in elucidating the ideas they embodied. By discovering the human interest behind procedure and parchments he related law to life. He interpreted history in the widest manner. 'What men have done and said, above all what they have thought—that is history.' The history of law was the history of ideas, not as abstractions but as forces acting through living men. The bright, graceful style reflects his alert and vivacious spirit. He was always ready with a modern parallel to visualise a conception or interpret a practice. The chapter on the Elizabethan Settlement shows that he might have been as successful in narrative as in the interpretation of institutions and ideas. His early lectures on the English Constitution sparkle with wit and gaiety. His Rede Lecture on 'English Law and the Renaissance' showed in a few broad strokes how England kept her own law while Roman law was effecting an entry in Germany and Scotland. The immense rapidity with which he worked left no rough edges, and he touched nothing which he did not adorn. In the considered opinion of Pollard he was not only the greatest historian of his time but the greatest that England has possessed.

It is impossible to do more than glance at the labours of many other British scholars. The most resolute attempt by a single scholar to narrate our mediæval history was made by Sir James Ramsay, whose painstaking volumes extend to the coming of the Tudors. Making no claim to originality and lacking literary charm, his work derives value from its careful study of the printed sources. Round threw light on the institutions of the Norman kings, Tait on the early boroughs. Kate Norgate followed up her volumes on the Angevins, undertaken at the suggestion of Green, by studies of John and the early years of Henry III. No chapter of later mediæval history was explored with greater thoroughness than the reign of Henry IV by Wylie. Brewer collected his incomparable prefaces to the State Papers of Henry VIII into two massive volumes which carried the story of the reign to the fall of Wolsey and revealed his greatness. Pollard covered the sixteenth century in a series of masterly monographs. British naval history was explored and popularised by Sir John Laughton, who launched the Navy Records Society, and by Sir Julian Corbett. Spedding dedicated his life to collecting the writings and defending the reputation of Bacon. David Masson used Milton as a peg on which to hang an encyclopædic survey of his times. By his editions of the Clarke Papers, Ludlow's Memoirs and many other sources, old and new, by his contributions to the 'Dictionary of National Biography,' by his monographs on Cromwell and Cromwell's Army, and by his continuation of Gardiner's narrative to the death of the Protector, Firth lit up every corner of the middle decades of the seventeenth century. The era of the Restoration inspired Christie's life of Shaftesbury and Miss Foxcroft's study of Halifax.

The leading statesmen of the eighteenth century are gradually finding biographers. Sichel composed a spirited apologia for Bolingbroke, Basil Williams provided the first adequate life of Chatham, Lord Fitzmaurice vindicated his ancestor Shelburne. After a sparkling sketch of the early life of Fox, Sir George Trevelyan returned to his hero at the close of his life, expanding the narrative into a history of the American War. John Morley's volumes on Burke won a place among the classics of English political literature. Holland Rose's lives of Napoleon and Pitt embody the researches of many years. Fortescue related the fortunes of the British Army with infinite detail and a sovereign contempt for political reputations. By his biographies of Perceval and Lord John Russell and his English History from 1815 to 1880 Spencer Walpole spanned the nineteenth century in a long array of volumes written in the spirit of a moderate Whig. The later decades of the Victorian era were sketched by Herbert Paul. The official political biographies in which England is so rich continued the process begun by the Greville Memoirs of unveiling the motives and projects of Victorian statesmen. The social and economic transition between the England of the eighteenth and the nineteenth century was lit up by the researches of Sidney and Beatrice Webb and Lawrence and Barbara Hammond. Narratives of Scottish history were compiled by Burton, Andrew Lang and Hume Brown. Irish history remains a battle-field. Mrs. J. R. Green sharply challenged the disparaging English conception of her country in the Middle Ages and was answered by Orpen. Bagwell told the story of the sixteenth and seventeenth centuries from the standpoint of the ruling race. The tragic death of Litton Falkiner removed the best equipped scholar in the field of modern Irish history since Lecky.

Among recent works produced by British scholars in the sphere of foreign history Bryce's 'Holy Roman Empire' occupies a high place. Repeatedly revised, it taught students all over the world to understand the theory and practice of mediæval Europe. Hodgkin's 'Italy and her Invaders' won a deserved popularity by its narrative power and the romantic interest of its theme. The English Dahn brought to life the centuries that lie between Alaric and Charles the Great, and few volumes in English historical literature are more fascinating than those which describe the Gothic Kingdom of Theodoric and its destruction by the armies of Justinian. Less popular but not less valuable are Howorth's 'History of the Mongols,' Armstrong's 'Life of Charles V,' Martin Hume's voluminous writings on Spain, and Ward's studies of the Thirty Years War and the Hanoverian Electorate. Sir William Hunter devoted his life to the history of India. Herbert Fisher studied Napoleonic administration in Germany, and Oman retold the story of the Peninsula War. Kinglake's voluminous 'History of the Crimean War,' once so eagerly read, is now almost forgotten. Fyffe wrote a luminous survey of European history from the French Revolution to the Congress of Berlin. Among recent works George Macaulay Trevelyan's volumes on Garibaldi won an enthusiastic welcome by their brilliant colouring. The fine English tradition of the learned amateur created by Gibbon and Grote has been well maintained, to the inestimable advantage both of scholarship and literature. The 'Victoria History of the Counties of England' pursues its leisurely course, and the publications of the English Place-Names Society fill gaps in our knowledge of early England. The 'Cambridge Modern History' contains some of the ripest work of British and foreign scholars.

CHAPTER XX

THE UNITED STATES

I

THE serious documentary study of American history begins with Jared Sparks, whose first task was to collect the writings of Washington.[1] The letters already published were scattered in many books, and the great mass of papers had never seen the light. At first the family, who were contemplating the publication of a selection of the private papers, refused him access to the treasures of Mount Vernon, but on the advice of Chief Justice Marshall they yielded. In 1828 Sparks visited the archives of London and Paris. The work, which appeared between 1834 and 1838 in twelve volumes, not only revealed the character and activity of the founder of the Republic, but offered the first detailed account of the critical period of American history. Its importance was at once recognised. Guizot sponsored an abridged French translation and prefixed an illuminating sketch of the hero, while Raumer prepared a German edition. While Sparks' industry was everywhere recognised, the performance of his editorial duties did not escape criticism. He was accused by Lord Mahon of suppressing passages reflecting on American officers, and by others of altering and polishing the letters. Sparks rejoined that if he omitted certain letters it was only because their contents were reproduced in those which he published. To his other critics he retorted that, as Washington left several drafts of many documents and in his old age had revised many of his earlier letters, he felt it his duty to print them in the form they finally assumed: his own share in the alteration of the text had been confined to the correction of obvious mistakes of the copyist. This was not quite correct, for a few passages were omitted for political reasons and some verbal changes were without excuse.

---

[1] See H. B. Adams, *Life of Jared Sparks*, 2 vols., 1893. For general surveys see J. F. Jameson, *History of Historical Writing in America*, 1891; Bassett, *The Middle Group of American Historians*, 1917; Michael Kraus, *A History of American History*, 1937; *The Marcus W. Jernegan Essays in American Historiography*, ed. by W. T. Hutchinson, 1937; H. E. Barnes, 'Historical Writing and Historical Science' in *Twentieth Century America*, ed. J. S. Roncek, 1950.

If Sparks was not an ideal editor and was ill-advised in preferring the later to the earlier draft, his bona fides is beyond cavil. At the instance of the Government he published twelve volumes of documents illustrating the diplomatic history of the Revolution, and collected the writings of Franklin and Gouverneur Morris. The 'Library of American Biography,' containing sixty lives, several of them from his own pen, covered the whole range of American history. Sparks was also a pioneer in another field. His appointment to a chair at Harvard in 1839 marks the first recognition of historical teaching in the Universities, and long before his death in 1861 he came to be regarded as the Nestor of American historians.

American history came of age with Bancroft,[1] who possesses the best claim to the title of the national historian. The young graduate of Harvard visited Europe in the quiet years following the Great War, heard Hegel and Schleiermacher, Savigny and Böckh in Berlin, Heeren in Göttingen, and visited Goethe. Though a native of Massachusetts he was a Jeffersonian Democrat. 'The popular voice,' he declared in a Fourth of July oration in 1826, 'is all powerful with us; this is our oracle; this, we acknowledge, is the voice of God.' His address on 'The Office of the People in Art, Government and Religion,' delivered in 1835, is another pæan to the crowd. 'True political science venerates the masses. Listen reverently to the voice of lowly humanity.' With this simple philosophy he entered on the composition of a history of America, the first volume of which appeared in 1834. 'The spirit of the colonies demanded freedom from the beginning. The United States have the precedence in the practice and defence of the equal rights of man.' There was no army and no debt. Religion was free. Intelligence was diffused with unparalleled universality. There is not a shadow in Bancroft's picture, and there is no mention of slavery. We breathe the buoyant atmosphere of the age of Andrew Jackson.

The centuries which led up to this state of perfection naturally claim their share of the credit. The first volume narrates the early voyages and settlements, and concludes with a Character of Puritanism. Its only fault was intolerance, and this was defensive and temporary. The Pilgrim Fathers made no attempt to convert others, and only defended their polity against attack. 'It was no more than a train of mists hanging over a fine river.' Their laws were mild except in regard to the lapses of married women. Americans could look back with pride to a golden age.

[1] See Mrs. Howe, *Life and Letters of George Bancroft*, 2 vols., 1908, and R. B. Nye, *George Bancroft*, 1945.

The volume was naturally hailed with delight. Bancroft uttered the thoughts of a new born nation, and shared the complacency and exuberance of a sanguine time. It is impossible not to be touched by his faith in popular government and the American constitution. The work also aroused interest in the Old World. 'It is one of my pleasantest thoughts,' wrote the aged Heeren from Göttingen, 'that I have helped somewhat in training the historian of the United States.' The second and third volumes, completing the colonisation of America, are written in the same strain of eulogy. Roger Williams is glorified as the foe of coercion in matters of conscience. George Fox and the Quakers are drawn with a loving hand, and the reputation of Penn is vigorously defended. Bancroft loathed every form of ecclesiastical domination, and proudly declares that priestcraft did not emigrate from the old world. The epidemic of witch-hunting is related with regret, but the reader is reminded that it did not last long. 'The selfishness of evil defeats itself, and God rules in the affairs of men.' In his 'Oration on the Progress of Mankind,' delivered in 1854, he declares that progress is inevitable, guaranteed by God's dwelling with humanity. 'Providence never disowns the race. No tramp of a despot's foot ever trod out one idea. The world cannot retrograde.' The early volumes, in the picturesque phrase of Franklin Jameson, voted for Jackson.

In thanking the author for a copy of his second volume in 1838 Carlyle wrote: 'Parts remind me of Johannes Müller's "Switzerland," one of our bravest books. But your theoretic matter gratifies me much less; you are too didactic.' Though Carlyle was hardly the man to complain of didactic history, the criticism was well founded. The philosophy of the book is childish, and the qualities which won applause two generations ago are those which are most offensive to modern taste. Yet it possessed solid worth, and its value increased as it advanced. Americans were proud to aid the national historian with their recollections and family papers. He explored the archives of the Prussian Foreign Office at Berlin. Pascual de Gayangos helped him with the Spanish archives, while friends and agents worked for him at the Hague, Paris and Vienna. After an interval of twelve years spent in political life and at the London Embassy, he issued the fourth volume in 1852. While three volumes carried the story down to 1748, seven were devoted to the quarrel with England and the establishment of independence. He speaks with extreme severity of British policy. 'The penal Acts of 1774,' he declares, 'dissolved the moral connection of the two countries. Great Britain made war on human freedom. Liberty in Europe and in

England itself was threatened. In taking up arms the colonies struck a blow for the progress of the whole of mankind.' England should have offered independence, for her lusty offspring had come of age. It was a cruel and unnatural war, yet it was followed by blessings for both countries. With the peace England abandoned for ever her evil ways. America, for her part, distinguished between the British Government and the British people. Respect and affection for the parent land remained. A nation was born without social upheaval. The Declaration of Independence, the immortal work of Jefferson, gave utterance to the eternal principles of justice and righteousness. The hand of God was evident throughout.

The narrative of the conflict with England suffers from the usual faults of patriotic history. The picture of the colonists as fired with a holy resolution to defend their liberties is a dream. It was left to younger writers to show how little enthusiasm there was for the struggle, how common were petty jealousies, how nearly the cause was wrecked. The Loyalists were representatives of a widely spread conviction. The help of France is insufficiently recognised, while the rôle of the German volunteers is exalted. Attention is too much confined to New England. The later volumes led to sharp controversy. Descendants of men who played a leading part in the war published pamphlets to expose the injustice to their ancestors. Though the author made vigorous replies, not a few of the criticisms were just. The work is discursive, rhetorical, sententious. As an introduction to the narrative of German assistance he goes back to the *Völkerwanderung*. Pages of trite reflection interrupt the narrative. Carlyle told him that he went too much into the origin of things generally known. The work, though not finished till 1874, never ceased to bear the marks of its origin. Jackson remained the statesman of his heart. 'Do you know what I say about you to my classes?' asked Ranke when Bancroft returned as Minister to Berlin. 'I tell them that your history is the best book ever written from the democratic point of view.' He winced a little at the criticism dressed up as a compliment, and remarked that if there was democracy in his pages it was due to the subject, not to the historian. Despite these faults of judgment and execution the book was a notable achievement. It was the first detailed and connected account of the history of the American colonies. It contained an immense mass of original material, drawn from the public and private archives of both hemispheres. He had known John Adams, Madison and many other makers of history. 'Every historian of the United States,' declared Von Holst, 'must stand on Bancroft's shoulders.' The later volumes displayed improvement in workmanship. The rate of production was slower, the research wider, the flag-waving less boisterous. Americans had learned by bitter experience that the New World was not exempt from the trials and imperfections of the Old.

In 1882, at the age of eighty-two, Bancroft added two volumes on the formation of the Constitution. It was the realisation of a very old ambition. To fulfil it he had visited the archives of most of the thirteen States and studied the reports of the ministers of Austria and Holland, France and England. The book is a sustained tribute to the greatness and goodness of Washington. Madison is hailed as the chief architect of the Constitution, and Hamilton receives something less than his due. He looks at the work and finds it good—good for order, good for liberty, good for the individuality of every citizen, a marvellous blend of strength and flexibility. The treatise closes with a glance at the contrasted circumstances of the Old and New World, the former groaning under tyranny and on the eve of revolution, the latter entering into the Promised Land. 'In America a new people had risen up without king, princes or nobles. They were more sincerely religious, better educated, of purer morals, of serener minds than the men of any former republic. In the happy morning of their existence they had chosen justice for their guide.'

Bancroft's idealisation of Puritan America was repeated by Palfrey, who wrote a 'History of New England' to the outbreak of the War of Independence. His admiration for the colonists is too great and his gratitude for their services to political liberty too deep to allow him to be critical. Without applauding religious intolerance, he finds excuses for it. He had delved deep in the English archives, and no previous historian had so closely studied the interaction of Old and New England during the critical decades of the Puritan era. Though inferior in popularity to Bancroft, he reached a higher level, and Jameson has pronounced his volumes the best single piece of work on any part of the colonial period. More critical methods were employed by Hildreth, who, though writing before Palfrey, belongs by spirit to a later generation. His 'History of the United States' was written with the express purpose of tempering the laudation which Bancroft had rendered fashionable. His aim, he informed his readers, was to give 'undress portraits of our progenitors.' The result of the experiment was described in the preface to the second edition. 'My presumption in bursting the bubble of a colonial golden age of fabulous purity and virtue has given very serious offence, especially in New England.' He audaciously declared that the period before 1789 was largely the domain of myth, and his sceptical volumes, like a cold north wind, blew away many a patriotic legend. Thus while Bancroft declares the Salem witchcraft to be merely a regrettable lapse, Hildreth, who relates it at pitiless length, finds in it the irrefragable evidence of an almost savage society. In the second part of his work, continuing the narrative to 1821, he broke new ground and supplied the first critical survey of the early Presidencies. American historians, like American politicians, were divided into Federalists and Democrats. Bancroft's hero was Jefferson, whom Hildreth dismissed as a demagogue; he preferred Hamilton, whose low opinion of the average man he shared. He had access to few official or private collections, and his style was poor, but his business-like narrative taught Americans that their history must be studied in the same critical spirit as that of other countries.

The scientific exploration of American history dates from the last two decades of the nineteenth century. The first authoritative account of the settlement of the American continent was provided in the co-operative work edited by Justin Winsor, the famous librarian of Harvard. The 'Narrative and Critical History of America' begins with a volume on the Aborigines, and traces the explorations and settlements of the European races, and concludes with the establishment of the United States. The critical essays on the sources of information, the elaborate notes, the illustrations and maps place the work in a position by itself. Among the most valuable chapters are those of the editor, himself a specialist in the history and cartography of early colonisation. Clements Markham narrated Pizarro's conquest of Peru and the emancipation of South America. The history of the English colonies, on the other hand, before and after the conflict with the Mother Country, is slight and disconnected. The work closes with a miscellaneous volume on the Hudson's Bay Company, Arctic exploration, Canada under the British Crown, and Spanish America. It is less a narrative history than a companion for the advanced student, summarising the labours of a century on the colonisation of the New World.

A less successful example of co-operation was given by the colossal compilation which owes its origin to the wealthy Californian amateur Hubert Howe Bancroft.[1] Retiring from a publishing business in middle age he spent enormous sums on the purchase of books and pamphlets, newspapers and manuscripts, and the copying of local records. A Russian was dispatched to

[1] He describes and defends his literary methods in his *Recollections*, 1912. Cp. J. W. Caughey, *H. H. Bancroft*, 1946.

Alaska and Spaniards to Mexico. Veteran pioneers were visited and their memories recorded. A superb library was formed as the foundation of an exhaustive survey of Central and Western America. With these materials the 'History of the Pacific States' was compiled in thirty-four stout volumes by a staff of assistants and revised by the editor. Useful from their freight of documents, they lack the higher qualities of historical writing. They may be compared to the guides of Baedeker or Murray, where the name and personality of the author are suppressed and in which the reader only looks for tabulated facts. Beginning with the States of Central America the work proceeds northwards through Mexico, Texas and California, to Oregon, Washington, British Columbia and Alaska. It is regrettable that the task of utilising the priceless collection of sources should have been entrusted to a literary bureau. The colonial period was described in a fairly objective spirit by Osgood and Beer. The admirable series of 'American Statesmen' covers the ground from the beginning of the conflict with England to the end of the Civil War. Nearly all are of high quality, while a few, notably Carl Schurz' 'Life of Clay,' are of enduring value. The most valuable work on the early Presidencies is the monumental study of Jefferson and Madison by Henry Adams, whose nine volumes rest on prolonged research in both hemispheres and present a lucid record of foreign and domestic policy during sixteen eventful years. MacMaster's colossal narrative, covering the period from the Revolution to the Civil War, is a useful compilation. After the appearance of Channing's large scale 'History of the United States' there was no further need to consult Bancroft or his contemporaries.

The most important study of recent events is the 'History of the United States from the Compromise of 1850,' by James Ford Rhodes, which narrates the critical years of the slavery struggle. He shares the repugnance of his contemporaries for slavery and rejoices at its disappearance, but he has no hard words for the men who appeared to be fighting for its maintenance. The first two volumes describe the gathering of the storm, the next three the conflict. He emphasises the vital fact that the combatants did not regard it as a struggle between slavery and freedom. Many northerners cared little about the slave; many Southerners, Lee among them, thought slavery wrong. The North fought for the maintenance of the Union, the South for the right of secession. No Southerner has paid a warmer tribute to the nobility of Lee or the courage of Stonewall Jackson. The statesmen are treated as generously as the soldiers, and Jefferson Davis himself is hailed as a worthy foeman. The portrait of Lincoln is a masterpiece of judgment and insight. The encyclopædic work of his secretaries, Nicolay and Hay, had appeared in 1890, but the unique personality was buried beneath ten massive volumes. Rhodes removes the halo, denies him military genius, and gently corrects the common exaggeration of his mental powers. But the President gains as much as he loses. He becomes more human, more lovable, when we watch him battling with his own temptations and groping his way through a forest of difficulties. More clearly than anyone he saw that the war must be proclaimed and conducted as a defence of the Union, not an attack on slavery. To have followed the lead of the extreme Abolitionists would have been to court disaster for the twin causes of which he was the guardian. Rhodes originally intended to bring his story down to 1884, when the election of the Democrat Cleveland showed that the old dividing lines had disappeared. As he came within sight of his goal he recognised that it was needless to travel so far, and decided to conclude with 1877, when the last Presidential election fought on the negro question was decided, the last troops were withdrawn, and the South was allowed to work out the negro problem in its own way. The two closing volumes which describe the period of Reconstruction display the same serenity. He is severe on Andrew Johnson and Blaine, emphasises Grant's political incapacity, and describes his rule as the high-water mark of corruption. The work marks the distance which American scholarship had travelled since Bancroft.[1] The crude elation and national arrogance are gone, and a younger generation has learned to respect the motives of men whose actions the world has agreed to condemn.

II

At the same time that Americans were beginning to study their national history, Washington Irving[2] turned his eyes to the Old World. He was essentially cosmopolitan, happy in every land and open to every influence. Though less an historian than an essayist and a humorist, he claims a place in the development of American historiography. His literary career began in 1809 with Knickerbocker's 'History of New York,' a picture of the Dutch occupation blending fact and fancy, humour and satire, which carried America by storm. A few years later he sailed for Europe, where he remained for seventeen years. The publication of his 'Sketch-book,' containing Rip van Winkle, made him a

[1] See M. A. de Wolfe Howe, *James Ford Rhodes*, 1929.
[2] See P. M. Irving, *Life and Letters of W. Irving*, 4 vols., 1862–4, and C. D. Warner's volume in *American Men of Letters*, 1884.

favourite in both worlds. His love of travel and romance led him to Spain in 1826, and two years later he issued a 'Life of Columbus' based on the collections of Navarette, supplemented by research in Madrid and Seville. The work was the first scholarly account of the great discoverer; written with his usual delicate grace, it appealed to lovers of literature as well as of history. Its popularity was so great that the author at once composed an abridgment to forestall American pirates. The narrative is perhaps a little over-coloured, but it is a poet's appreciation of a great dreamer.

In the following year Irving published the 'Chronicle of the Conquest of Granada,' which he regarded as the best of his works. As he fathered his comic history of Dutch America on an imaginary antiquarian, so he invented a Spanish friar to chronicle the fall of the Moorish Kingdom. Despite its fanciful setting, the book contained a good deal of substance and was enriched by the author's intimate knowledge of Granada. It was followed by a volume of sketches of the Alhambra, a medley of descriptive studies and tales which display his humour and sentiment at its best. Living within the ruins, he caught the spirit of the place which is for ever linked with his name. 'It is impossible to contemplate this delicious abode and not admire the genius and poetry of those who devised this earthly paradise. They deserved this beautiful country. They won it bravely, they enjoyed it generously and kindly. Everywhere I meet traces of their sagacity, courage, urbanity, high poetical feeling and elegant taste. I am almost tempted to say that they are the only people who ever deserved the country, and to pray that they may come over from Africa and conquer it again.' Irving returned to the United States in 1832 a famous man, and was appointed Minister to Madrid ten years later. His plan of a history of the conquest of Mexico was abandoned on learning that Prescott was engaged on the subject. The closing years were devoted to a 'Life of Washington.' He had little taste for research, and when confronted by the graver tasks of the historian he fails. In the lighter sphere of anecdote and romance he is supreme. His fame is secure as the father of American literature and the discoverer of the fascination of Spain.

Where Washington Irving had scratched the shining surface of Spanish history, Prescott[1] dug deep into its foundations. His residence at Harvard was rendered unhappily memorable by the

---

[1] See Ticknor's *Life of Prescott*, 1864, Ogden's volume in *American Men of Letters*, 1904, and Peck, *W. H. Prescott*, 1905. There is a good sketch in Seccombe's Introduction to *The Conquest of Peru*, Everyman's Library. Cp. *Ticknor's Life, Letters and Journals*, 2 vols., 1876.

accident which deprived him of the sight of one eye and inflicted irreparable damage in the other. Reading was always difficult and often impossible, but the love of learning was too strong to be quenched by physical disabilities. It is curious, in the light of his subsequent occupations, that his prolonged visit to Europe after leaving the University did not include a visit to Spain. His interest was at the time mainly attracted by French and Italian literature, and it was not till his friend Ticknor delivered his lectures on Spanish literature at Harvard in 1824 that he turned to the country with which his name is associated. After considering several historical themes, he determined to write a detailed narrative of the reign of Ferdinand and Isabella. His ample means allowed him to form a magnificent library, and he obtained books and manuscripts from the American Minister to Madrid. Since almost every line had to be read to him, ten years of study were required before the work appeared in 1837. Though the plums had been already picked out by Washington Irving, Prescott's volumes did not suffer by comparison with those of his brilliant countryman. His canvas was larger, his learning far more profound, his style not inferior. The clash of civilisations within the peninsula, the discovery of the New World, the union of Aragon and Castile into a strong kingdom, the personality of the two rulers, the beginnings of the Inquisition—here were themes to make the fortune of an historian. Ferdinand is portrayed as a wise and successful ruler despite his cold and selfish character. Isabella is the heroine of the book, equally eminent in mind and heart, a perfect woman with the brain of a man. Her only weakness, religious intolerance, was the fault of her time. Prescott writes of the Inquisition with a strength of feeling rare in his tranquil pages, but he is wholly free from prejudice against Catholicism. His Ximenes, though rigid and despotic, is a commanding figure; Columbus a hero without fear and without reproach; Gonsalvo, 'the Great Captain,' a man of many virtues, though capable of treachery. In addition to the full-length portraits, the historian devotes careful attention to administration, literature and manners.

During the long years of preparation Prescott often questioned his ability to do justice to so great a theme, and doubted the readiness of his countrymen to interest themselves in a detailed narrative. Such apprehensions were immediately dispelled. Daniel Webster declared that a comet had suddenly blazed out on the world in full splendour. Pascual da Gayangos, the friend of many Anglo-Saxon scholars, contributed a warm eulogy to the *Edinburgh Review*, while Ford, author of the famous 'Handbook,' praised it in the *Quarterly*. Lord Holland pronounced it the most important historical work since Gibbon. Guizot and Mignet were loud in its praise. Translated into several languages, it was the first historical work produced in America to enjoy an international reputation. 'The Reign of Ferdinand and Isabella' deserved its reputation. Though not the most brilliant, it is certainly the most solid achievement of its author, and it has never been superseded. Strengthened by new matter in successive editions, its value continually increased. In particular the third edition, appearing in 1841, was enriched through the good offices of Gayangos with the manuscript correspondence of 'the Catholic Kings,' found at the breaking up of the Saragossa convents. Not every part was watertight. The survey of Arab polity and culture before the fall of Granada was based largely on the brittle researches of Conde. The portrait of Isabella is too rose-coloured, though it is nearer life than Bergenroth's picture of a despotic hypocrite. Justin Winsor thought the picture of Columbus too flattering. The account of the Inquisition accepts Llorente too readily. But few works of the time require so little adaptation to satisfy students of to-day.

From Ferdinand and Isabella to the conquests in the New World was but a step. Prescott employed assistants to transcribe manuscripts in Spanish libraries relating to Mexico and Peru. Gayangos sent copies from the British Museum, and Calderon, the Spanish Minister to Mexico, himself a distinguished man of letters, collected documents *in situ*. The splendour of Montezuma's kingdom, degraded though it was by human sacrifices, provided a brilliant introduction to the story of the invasion. The march of Cortez from the coast constitutes the most arresting theme that he ever handled. The commanding figure of the leader dominates the stage. Ruthless as were the Conquistadores, the Empire they overthrew was still more cruel. The 'Conquest of Mexico' is the most popular of Prescott's books. It appealed and still appeals to all readers, young and old, who love adventure and romance. The descriptions of marches, of battles, of the siege of the capital took rank with the glowing pages of Macaulay, and found their way straight to the heart of every schoolboy. A few critics blamed his leniency to the invaders, but the historian, while condemning their acts, refused to castigate them for not being in advance of their time. 'Never call hard names,' he wrote in his diary; 'it is unhistorical, unphilosophical, ungentlemanlike.' He was at all times sparing of judgments. The book was praised by Catholics for its fairness to their Church, while Quincy Adams declared that it was difficult to tell whether the author was

Protestant or Catholic, monarchist or republican. The favourable judgment of the veteran Alexander von Humboldt, 'the most competent critic my work has to encounter,' gave him special pleasure. The verdict of Washington Irving was equally flattering. The gravest fault of the book passed unrecognised. When archæology revealed the secrets of Aztec Mexico, the civilisation of Montezuma turned out to be far less brilliant than Prescott, following the Spanish chroniclers, had believed. The 'Conquest of Peru' was a less arresting theme. Pizarro is of smaller calibre than Cortez, and there was less excuse for his fiendish cruelties. Moreover, the civil wars of the Conquistadores destroy the dramatic unity of the story. He complained of his subject as second-rate and spoke of the quarrels of banditti over their spoils. In Mexico his sympathies were on the whole with the Spaniard, in Peru against him. Once more the sketch of the indigenous civilisation is the weakest part of the work, for the researches of Clements Markham were to reveal a widely different world.

In 1842 Ford urged Prescott to write the life of Philip II, 'an almost virgin subject,' and the historian had made large collections before he was free to carry out his plan. Mignet procured copies of documents at Paris. Gayangos not only delved in the archives of London and Simancas, but secured the opening of the treasure-houses of the Alvas and other great families. The work was begun in 1849, and the first two volumes appeared in 1855. Abroad the struggle with England, the war in the Netherlands, the defeat of the Turks; at home the rebellion of the Moriscoes, the reign of the Inquisition, the tragedy of Don Carlos: here was a theme to tempt an historian who had already won world-wide fame. His death interrupted the narrative when it had reached 1580, but the three volumes form a noble torso. Judging Philip by the ideas of his time, he finds it possible to pardon and even to admire. 'You have by nature the judicial mind,' wrote the hot-blooded Motley, who confided to his wife that Prescott's Philip was 'altogether too mild and flattered a portraiture of that odious personage.' Among his achievements none is more notable than that of rendering the grim Catholic ruler intelligible.

While engaged on Philip, Prescott turned aside for a few months to record the closing days of his father. He had often been urged to write the history of Charles V, but he considered Robertson sufficiently trustworthy to render a comprehensive narrative unnecessary. He was willing, however, to supply an account of the Emperor's cloister life. He had sensed its character from documents copied for him at Simancas, and had utilised his materials in the first volume of 'Philip II,' written in 1851 but not published till 1854. During these intervening years the truth was revealed by no less than three historians. A Simancas archivist had compiled an account of the retreat and added large extracts from the archives. His manuscript had been bought by the French Government after his death and sent to the Foreign Office at Paris, where it lay neglected till Stirling-Maxwell, after a visit to Yuste in 1849, utilised it for his 'Cloister Life of Charles V,' which appeared in 1852. The success of the book led Mignet and Gachard to follow up the clue. All three were laid under contribution in the narrative written in 1855 by Prescott, who, however, added nothing to their researches. Enriched with this substantial supplement Robertson's old work entered on a new lease of life. Prescott was one of the most conspicuous of the brilliant amateurs whose works created a world-wide interest in history during the middle decades of the nineteenth century. He was more attracted by the concrete aspects of life than by ideas. He possessed a gift of stately narrative, and knew how to choose subjects which gave full scope to his talents. He was not always critical in the use of his authorities, nor was he a philosophic historian interested in social evolution. On the other hand, while Grote and Macaulay, Carlyle and Froude, Bancroft and Motley made their histories vehicles of political and religious propaganda, his pages are free from hero-worship and party bias. He stood aloof from public life, and had no ambition to play the prophet or the moralist. If this reserve renders his writings less vital, it saves them from the reaction which accompanies the discredit of popular slogans.

When Prescott had been at work for some years on the reign of Philip II, he learned that a young fellow-countryman was studying the revolt of the Netherlands. He encouraged him to continue, lent him materials, and heralded the publication of his work. The appearance of 'The Rise of the Dutch Republic' in 1856 satisfied him that his confidence had not been misplaced. A native of Massachusetts, like Bancroft and Prescott, Motley[1] was a precocious child, and his future eminence was clearly foreseen at Harvard by Oliver Wendell Holmes. Having learned German at a school where Bancroft was a master, he determined to follow his example. He entered Göttingen, where he formed a lifelong friendship with Bismarck, and when the two students migrated to Berlin they shared a lodging. After his return he. determined to narrate the rise of the Dutch Republic. 'I did not

[1] See O. W. Holmes, *Motley*, 1878, and *Correspondence of J. L. Motley* 2 vols., 1889, and *J. L. Motley and his Family: Further Letters*, 1910.

first make up my mind to write a history and then cast about for a subject. My subject had taken me up, drawn me in, and absorbed me into itself.' Leaving for Europe in 1851 he plunged into the archives of Belgium, Holland and Germany. He spoke of his digging in subterranean depths of black-letter folios in half a dozen languages, dark, grimy and cheerless as coalpits. But he added that he had not been working underground for so long without hoping that he would make some few people better and wiser. Above all, he had found one great, virtuous and heroic character, who was never inspired by any personal ambition and was worthy of a place beside Washington. He familiarised himself with the scenes of his drama. 'I haunt it,' he wrote of the Grande Place at Brussels, 'because it is my theatre. Here were enacted so many tragedies, so many stately dramas which have been familiar to me so long, that I have got to imagine myself invested with a kind of property in the place.' After ten years' incessant labour the book was published in London in 1856 at his own expense. Like Prescott, the unknown author won fame in a day. In the *Westminster Review* Froude declared that the book would take its place among historical classics, and that in dramatic description no modern historian, except perhaps Carlyle, surpassed him. Oliver Wendell Holmes compared him to Rubens. In his own country he was immediately placed at the side of Bancroft, Irving and Prescott. Guizot wrote an introduction to a French translation, and the Archivist-General of Holland superintended the Dutch edition.

The choice of the subject was a master-stroke. One of the greatest crises in history, one of the cardinal chapters in the development of modern liberty, had been left to men of letters. Motley's theme, indeed, surpassed those of Prescott himself in its tense passion and arresting fascination. The researches on which the work rested were wide and profound. Few productions of the age of amateurs are based so largely on contemporary documents. 'I go day after day to the archives,' he wrote to Holmes. 'Here I remain among my fellow-worms, feeding on these musty mulberry-leaves, out of which we are afterwards to spin our silk. It is something to read the real signs-manual of such fellows as William of Orange, Egmont, Alexander Farnese, Philip II, Cardinal Granvelle and the rest of them.' The work revealed one of the greatest stylists of the century. Free from the magniloquence of Bancroft and the stiffness of Prescott, it represents the high-water mark of achievement in American historical literature. The great scenes of the story, from the death of Egmont and Horn to the defence of Leyden and the assassination of William the Silent, rank among the noblest passages of English prose.

Motley, to whom liberty was a religion, entered keenly into the struggles which he set himself to record. He told his father of his satisfaction in 'pitching into Alva and Philip to my heart's content.' 'We may congratulate ourselves,' wrote Prescott when the book appeared, 'that it was reserved for one of our country-men to tell the story of this memorable revolution, which in so many of its features bears a striking resemblance to our own.' He regarded the revolt of the Dutch as every American of his generation regarded the revolt of the Thirteen Colonies, a struggle for freedom, a holy war. Philip is the villain of the piece, Alva his bloodthirsty agent, William the Silent the heroic champion of liberty who lives and dies for his people. For Motley as for Froude Catholicism, symbolised by the Inquisition, is the religion of slaves and bigots, Protestantism the faith of free men. Such passionate partisanship, natural enough half a century ago, is foreign to the cooler temper of to-day. Even at the moment of its appearance Guizot, staunch Protestant though he was, gently chided its partiality, adding that the bias was so obvious that it was not likely to do harm. Prescott complained that he had been rather hard on Philip. Kervyn de Lettenhove and other Catholic writers have removed more than one of Motley's heroes from the pedestal on which he set them. The Dutch historians themselves, led by Fruin and Blok, regard their ancestors with a more critical eye than their American champion. We enjoy the burning pages as much as our fathers, but the spell is broken.

Motley's plan embraced the War of Independence to the recognition of the Republic in 1648. The first part was hardly published when he set to work on the 'History of the United Netherlands.' 'My canvas is very broad, and I have not got a central heroic figure to give unity and flesh and blood to the scene. It will be, I fear, duller and less dramatic.' England entered the struggle, and the countries in combination succeeded in crippling the power of Spain, but the fate of the revolted pro-vinces long trembled in the balance. Farnese was a redoubtable foe, and the Protestants suffered from the loss of their beloved chief. Maurice was a better soldier than his father but had neither political instinct nor personal fascination. If the book is neces-sarily less popular than its predecessor, it is not the fault of the historian. He explored for the first time the foreign policy of the later years of Elizabeth, whose fame was not enhanced in the process. The first two volumes hardly yielded in interest to their predecessors, but the third and fourth were too full of diplomatic intrigues. 'I don't know whether my last two volumes are good or bad,' he wrote. 'I only know they are true—but that need not make them amusing.'

He had hoped to reach the Thirty Years War, and the 'Life of Barnevelt' was rather a digression than a continuation. It was no longer the strife of Holland against Spain, of Geneva against Rome, but a squalid story of domestic discord. He discovered at the Hague the autograph letters of Barnevelt during the last few years of his life, written in such a hand that no one had ever attempted to read them. This treasure-trove became the foundation of his work. He was delighted to do honour to a man too little known, whom he described as the Prime Minister of European Protestantism. His belief that he could handle the highly controversial subject more impartially than Barnevelt's countrymen was erroneous, for his proneness to hero-worship made him once again an eager partisan. As a Unitarian he naturally supported the Latitudinarians against the Calvinists. Each party claimed to represent the national religion. Of the seven Provinces only two were Arminian; Barnevelt therefore claimed for each Province the right to determine its official cult. When Maurice took possession of one of the churches he levied a body of mercenaries. The Statholder was supported by the States-General, and Barnevelt was executed after a sham trial. Convinced of his patriotism and sympathising with his dislike of an iron Calvinism, Motley hails him as a patriot and a martyr, while Maurice appears as the ruthless soldier who hurried his innocent rival to the scaffold.

While the earlier books had been received with rapture in Holland, the 'Barnevelt' provoked sharp criticism. Groen van Prinsterer, the editor of the Orange Correspondence, composed a voluminous reply.[1] The work which appeared to Guizot a great historical plea for religious and political liberty seemed to the Calvinist historian an insult to the memory of a national hero. He contrasts Motley's testimony to the political worth of Calvinism with his contempt for its faith and philosophy. The Unitarian, he added, did not care about evangelical religion. Barnevelt's death was not the work of Maurice but of the people, who arose to defend biblical religion against the sham Christianity of Arminius. Maurice merely defended the Reformed Church and the authority of the central government against attack. He had no desire for Barnevelt's death, though he might well have prevented it. That Motley did some injustice to the Statholder is evident, but Maurice was not quite so innocent as Groen

[1] *Maurice de Nassau et Barnevelt*, 1875

suggests. Barnevelt, declares Blok, sinned through obstinacy, wilfulness and intolerance, but his execution was a judicial murder. 'Both parties were culpable, but the dominant party committed the greater sin.' Three years after the publication of his last book Motley was dead. Though he had not accomplished his full purpose he had done enough to immortalise his name. He established the importance of the struggle of the Netherlands against Spain. No American historian approaches him in intensity of conviction and expression. Liberty was the passion of his life, and he makes his readers feel that the civilisation of to-day rests on the struggles and sacrifices of the past.

Unlike Prescott and Motley who woke up to find themselves famous, Parkman's[1] conquest of popularity was slow and difficult. Like other members of what Holmes called the Brahmin caste of New England, he was born in Boston and educated at Harvard. At school he devoured the novels of Fenimore Cooper. His interest in the struggle between France and England for North America began at college, and in his vacations he visited the battle-fields. In 1843, at the age of twenty, he dedicated his life to the task which was not completed till 1892. He visited the untamed Indian tribes in the North-West, living for weeks in a Sioux village. His experiences were recorded in his first book, 'The Oregon Trail,' which, despite its freshness and its picturesque descriptions, attracted little notice. 'The Conspiracy of Pontiac,' with which he made his début as an historian, fared scarcely better. The expulsion of France from Canada after the victory of Wolfe was followed by an Indian rising in 1763. Pontiac was the last great chief, and with his overthrow the Canadian Indians fade out of history. Parkman's knowledge of the theatre of war and of the surviving tribes enabled him to reconstruct the life and organisation of their ancestors. A few good judges were struck by the spirited style and the obvious mastery of the material, and the lack of encouragement did not deter him from the prosecution of his self-imposed task, though for ten years he was too ill to undertake exacting work. The hardships he had encountered during his sojourn among the Indians had shattered his health, and his eyes were of little more use to him than Prescott's.

'The Conspiracy of Pontiac' was rather an appendix than an introduction to the work of his life. While the final struggle of

---

[1] See Farnham, *Life of Parkman*, 1900; Sedgwick's volume in *American Men of Letters*, 1904; Wade, *Francis Parkman*, 1942; *Quarterly Review*, April 1897, and Seccombe, Introduction to *The Conspiracy of Pontiac*, Everyman's Library. His Journals were published in 2 vols., 1947.

Wolfe and Montcalm was familiar to everybody, the story of the colonisation of Canada by the French was almost unknown. 'The Pioneers of France in the New World' recorded the Huguenot settlement in Florida and its ruthless extinction by the Spaniards, followed by Cartier's exploration of the St. Lawrence and the foundation of Quebec by Champlain. Two years later a volume on the Jesuit missions revealed the devotion of the men who suffered unspeakable tortures and gave their lives in the effort to reclaim the Hurons and the Iroquois from savagery. No volume of the series is more thrilling than this tribute to Catholic missionaries by a Puritan freethinker. A third work was devoted to the bold attempt of La Salle to link Canada to the mouth of the Mississippi by a line of French forts and hem in the English colonies; a fourth to the Old Régime in Canada, a dark picture of French administration; a fifth to the work of Frontenac, the greatest and most masterful of the Governors, the central figure of the whole work and the hero of the historian.

The story had now reached 1701, but, instead of pursuing the narrative, Parkman, who was growing old, sprang over half a century to the dramatic struggle of Montcalm and Wolfe. The heroism of the two commanders and the greatness of the issue give an epic character to the conflict. Finally he bridged the gap by 'Half a Century of Conflict.' His reputation travelled slowly, and when Fiske, in a London lecture in 1880, pronounced him the first of American historians, his name was scarcely known to an English audience. He has, indeed, no superior among his countrymen. Theodore Roosevelt dedicated to him his 'Winning of the West.' 'Those of us who have spent much of our time on the frontier realise that your works must be the models for all historical treatment of the founding of new communities.' Hart called him the greatest of all writers who made America their theme. Goldwin Smith compared him to Tacitus. His theme, though of narrower appeal than the Spanish Monarchy or the Dutch Republic, was the prologue to the drama of the Revolution. The Colonies were powerless to expel the French, but the removal of France made the revolt against England possible.

Parkman's researches in American and European archives were profound. He knew every corner of the stage on which the drama was played, and was free from partisanship, though French Canadians declared that he had been unjust to them. His knowledge of the Indians was derived from life, not from books. His style, at first somewhat florid, gained in simplicity and power, and his descriptive passages are among the finest in American literature. He was fitted by his martial temper for describing

perils and adventures. Throughout life he retained a deep admiration for strong men and vigorous action. Nothing but an
iron will would have carried him through his troubles, and there
is no trace of the invalid in his books. He hated weakness, despised
the Abolitionists, and had no belief in democracy. 'Many of
his traits of mind and character,' records Farnham, his friend and
biographer, 'were those of a soldier. He liked a fight for its own
sake, and for the energy, courage and strength it called forth.'
He never forgave the Quakers for refusing to fight the Indians.
He longed to take part in the Civil War, but he had abundant
opportunity of showing his bravery in his own library.

When Parkman ceased to write, a new star was rising in the
historical firmament. When appointed Lecturer at the Naval War
College at Newport Mahan quickly realised that the influence of
sea power had never been seriously investigated.[1] The neglect of
the wider aspects of naval history was particularly noticeable
in England, the greatest of Maritime Powers. 'The Influence
of Sea Power upon History, 1660–1783,' published in 1889, opens
with a discussion of the conditions affecting maritime strength,
geographical position, physical conformation, extent of territory
and population, the characteristics of the people and the government of the State. The sea itself is a great highway, or, better,
a wide common. The history of Europe for more than two
centuries had been largely a struggle between the Western
Powers for the control of the sea. Beginning his survey with
the Dutch War of Charles II he emphasises the extent to which
the commercial interests of England were involved in the war
of the Spanish Succession, from which England emerged as a
Mediterranean Power with Gibraltar and Port Mahon. In the
Seven Years War Wolfe's success would have been impossible
without the fleet, which opened the St. Lawrence and prevented
the arrival of reinforcements from France. The importance of
sea power is enforced still more powerfully by the American War
of Independence. Choiseul had strengthened the French fleet
which, joined by the Spanish, nearly equalled that of England.
It was owing to them that George III failed to reduce the Atlantic
seaboard and was therefore unable to cope effectively with the
rebellion. Finally it was the presence of De Grasse in Chesapeake
Bay which led to the capitulation of York Town and virtually
to the collapse of the war. The resounding success of the book
encouraged the author to continue his survey. In 1892 appeared
a second work, tracing the history of the Great French War,

[1] See Taylor, *Life of Admiral Mahan*, 1920. For an expert appreciation
of his first two works see *Eng. Hist. Review*, Oct. 1893.

which he shows to have been a war of commerce for England. He defends Pitt against the attacks of Macaulay, for he realised that control of the sea was the key of the problem, and with Trafalgar the worst was over. 'Those far distant, storm-beaten ships, on which the Grand Army never looked, stood between it and the dominion of the world.' The Continental System, designed to ruin England, inflicted far greater damage on France; for the Orders in Council, together with the Berlin and Milan decrees to which they were a reply, went far to destroy the neutral carrier, thus injuring France most because she most needed his services.

Mahan next turned his attention to the grandest figure of those eventful years, 'the one man who summed up and embodied the greatness of the possibilities which sea power comprehends, the man for whom genius and opportunity worked together to make him the personification of the navy of Great Britain.' The novelty of the book, which contained little new material, lay in the discussion and explanation of Nelson's achievements. He shows that his strength lay in promptitude of action, which was not the fruit of brilliant improvisations but of profound deliberation before the fight. Mahan's main object was to measure the achievement of one 'the simple mention of whose name suggests not merely a personality or a career but a great force.' But he also desired to reveal the man himself and to disentangle him from his glory. In the embittered controversy relating to his treatment of the Neapolitan republicans he defends his conduct with great spirit. 'Sharer of our mortal weakness, he has bequeathed to us a type of single-minded self-devotion that can never perish.' The fourth work on the influence of sea power is devoted to the war of 1812, which arose from the measures taken by England during the fierce struggle with Napoleon. The value of the work is enhanced by the survey of the causes which led to the conflict. He points out that the British people was convinced of the right as well as of the need to seize their nationals for service wherever found, that Britain was engaged in a desperate contest, and that her neglect of conventional law was essential to her success. On the other hand America was right to resist practices which injured and wronged her.

Mahan's writings owe their importance to the new angle from which familiar events are regarded. Few new facts are brought to light, and the technical discussion sometimes becomes a little wearisome for the general reader. Occasionally the element of sea power in the determination of a particular result is over-emphasised at the expense of other factors. Yet, though not the earliest expert on naval history, he was the first to seize its wider bearings and to make it interesting to the non-professional reader. He may fairly be described as the founder of a school, for the study of sea power is being vigorously pursued both in the Old and the New World. His writings, moreover, possess a political as well as an historical importance. He strove to rouse the United States to the importance of developing their fleet. In his first book he showed how much American independence owed to the ships of France and Spain. His biography of Farragut recalled the importance of the fleet in the victory of the North. That his works made a profound impression on the German Emperor not less than on the directors of British policy is no secret. Once again an historian has helped to make history as well as to record it.

The present generation of American historians have confined themselves almost entirely to their own country. The age of brilliant amateurs is at an end. The serious transatlantic student now goes to Berlin and Leipsic to learn the technique of his profession. Historians gaze at the colonial period without being dazzled, while the high character of Governor Hutchinson and the conscientious convictions of the Loyalists are freely recognised. Charles Francis Adams has written with severity of the religious intolerance of 'the glacial period' of Massachusetts history, and with scant respect of the 'filiopietistic' school of Bancroft and Palfrey. From the vantage-point of Wisconsin Turner traced the moving frontier and the colonisation of the Middle West. If the contribution to the literature of the world is smaller than in the spacious days of Prescott, Motley, and Parkman, the gains of scholarship are more assured.

CHAPTER XXI

MINOR COUNTRIES

I

WHILE in most countries historical study accompanied the revival of national feeling, in Bohemia it created it.[1] The paralysis which began with the battle of the White Hill in 1620 lasted for two centuries. Czech ceased to be used for literary expression, its place being taken by German and Latin. Every book published in the Austrian dominions had to run the gauntlet of two censors, one representing the Government, the other the Church. Education was in the hands of the Jesuits. From this long slumber the country was roused by the efforts of five scholars. At the end of the eighteenth century Dobrowsky began to excite interest in Bohemian literature. Kollar published a collection of sonnets inspired by burning love for the Slavs, Jungmann wrote a history of Bohemian literature, and Safarik published his 'Slavic Antiquities.' But by far the most celebrated was Palacky, the greatest of Slav historians and the creator of the national consciousness of Bohemia. The child of Lutheran parents, he was brought up in the traditions of the Bohemian Brothers. Educated in Pressburg, he always declared that he was no child of German culture. Dobrowsky introduced him to the nobles who were interested in Bohemian history, and by whom the National Museum at Prague had recently been established. Little enthusiasm had hitherto been shown for the institution by the Czechs themselves and the Austrian officials looked on it with suspicion. When Palacky boldly maintained that the indifference was rather the fault of the directors than of the people, Count Sternberg, the leader of the enterprise, replied that it was too late to raise the Bohemian nation from the dead. The young scholar retorted that no attempt was being made. In 1828 he founded a Journal of the Museum,

[1] The best surveys of recent activities in the minor countries are in *Histoire et Historiens, 1876–1926*, 2 vols., 1927, and *Some Historians of Modern Europe*, ed. Bernadotte E. Schmitt, 1942. For Bohemia see Count Lützow, *Lectures on the Historians of Bohemia*, 1905, and *History of Bohemian Literature*, 1899; Seton-Watson, *History of the Czechs and Slovaks*, 1943; Leger, *Études Slaves*, vol. ii., 1875; Masaryk, *Palacky's Idee des Böhmischen Volkes*, 1899.

and the first-fruits of his studies were contained in a volume on early Bohemian historians.

When Palacky became aware of the wealth of material stored in the archives of the castles, he resolved to take the whole of Bohemian history for his province. He was appointed Historiographer with a salary, and though the appointment was vetoed at Vienna, the Diet was allowed to defray the expenses of publication. Thus encouraged he embarked on the composition of his work, of which the first volume, dealing with the settlement of the Slavs in Bohemia, appeared in 1836. Filled with patriotic fervour he idealised the culture and virtue of the early Czechs. The book only assumed national importance when the narrative reached the century of Hus; but the part which burst on his fellow-countrymen like a revelation was also the item which aroused the greatest resentment at Vienna. While Hus and his followers had been caricatured in German and Catholic publications as brutal fanatics, Palacky showed that Czech cruelties were surpassed by those of their enemies, and revealed the greatness of Ziska and Procopius. The censor challenged the statement that the courage of Hus at his trial forced even his adversaries to admiration. 'The Catholic Church,' he declared, 'does not see courage but insolence and obstinacy founded on utter blindness.' The historian addressed a manly protest to Vienna. 'I cannot believe it to be a necessity of Catholicism that every deed and thought of Hus should be unconditionally condemned and all circumstances favourable to him suppressed. This is what the censor seems to expect, but I would rather give up my work and abandon the study of history.' He was none the less compelled to suppress certain passages, and to insert interpolations from the censor's pen as his own work. Shortly after this unworthy coercion of a great scholar the Revolution of 1848 broke out. The police censorship of the press being abolished, the historian restored the omissions and expunged the interpolations. He was now a great national figure. He presided over the Slav Congress at Prague, and was elected to the Constituent Assembly at Vienna. When absolutism was restored he returned to his study, but with the beginning of a milder policy a decade later he was made a Life Peer. The promise of Francis Joseph to be crowned King at Prague delighted his closing years, for he could not foresee that it would never be fulfilled.

Palacky's first intention had been to bring his history to the fatal year 1620, but he finally determined to lay down his pen in 1526 with the accession of the Hapsburgs. The experience of the Catholic censor was sufficiently disagreeable. The guardian of Hapsburg prestige would have rendered an account of the Reformation century virtually impossible. Moreover his material was so extensive that ten volumes were needed even for his limited design. Written first in German it appeared after 1848 simultaneously in both languages, and on revision the early volumes were rendered into Czech. It was his achievement to recreate the history of a country, to discover and utilise a great mass of new material, to throw light on many dark places in the mediæval history of central Europe. The Hussite volumes formed the kernel of the book. Helfert wrote an opposition biography, but the most persistent of his critics was Höfler, who was brought from Munich to Prague to counteract him. Palacky had little difficulty in showing that Höfler's volumes, though printed by the Imperial press, were so uncritical as to be almost worthless, while his ignorance of Czech was a fatal handicap. Bachmann,[1] who covered the same ground at the turn of the century, declared that Palacky is now of no value, but this severe verdict is only true of the first volume. He was misled by the faked Königinhof manuscripts of songs of the ninth or tenth century, which revealed a lofty native culture independent of Teutonic influences. He confronted German contempt for Czech culture with an idealisation of the Slav, and maintained that Bohemia in the twelfth and thirteenth centuries was inferior to no country except France and Italy in civilisation. His work was not only an achievement in scholarship but a political event, a trumpet call to an oppressed nationality to raise its head and prove itself worthy of its past.

The lifelong labours of Palacky encouraged the writing as well as the reading of Bohemian history. The greatest of his pupils, Tomek,[2] devoted his life to the history of Prague. Though little known outside Bohemia his work, which is a great deal more than the story of a city, ranks next to that of his master in importance. Professor at Prague for forty years, first Rector of the Czech University founded in 1881, a politician and a deputy, he played a leading part in the intellectual life of his country. Twelve volumes, published between 1855 and 1901, brought the narrative down to 1609. The work is more critical and less rhetorical than that of Palacky, who belonged to the age of the romantics. Though a Catholic he draws a dark picture of the Church in the fifteenth century, and recognises the sincerity and noble ambitions of Hus. The third great Bohemian historian, Anton Gindely,[3] differed from his older contemporaries both in

---

[1] *Geschichte Böhmens*, vol. i., 1899.
[2] See Leger's article on Tomek in *La Renaissance Tchèque*, 1911.
[3] See Ward's article, *Eng. Hist. Review*, July 1893.

his mixed descent and in his freedom from racial bias. His German father spoke only his native tongue, his Czech mother both languages. His first important work was devoted to the Bohemian Brethren, and was designed to inaugurate an elaborate study of the Bohemian Reformation. He plunged into the archives at Brussels and the Hague, Paris and Simancas. In the latter he found unexpected treasures. 'Half of what I have collected,' he wrote, 'is wholly new, and the other half shows the already known in a wholly different light. I often feel intoxicated with joy.' On returning home he became Professor at Prague and Director of the Archives, supervising the publication of the proceedings of the Bohemian Diet at the beginning of the Thirty Years War. His history of the reign of Rudolf II, published after his return, threw a flood of light on a dark corner of history. It was succeeded by four volumes on the Thirty Years War, bringing the narrative to 1623. Breaking off at this point he composed a popular history of the war, based partly on lectures delivered to the Crown Prince Rudolf. He then issued monographs on the career of Wallenstein between 1625 and 1630 and on Bethlen Gábor. He was one of the most impartial of men. Though a Catholic, his religious views cannot be guessed from his writings. He exposed the political incapacity of the Protestant princes of the Empire, and rejected the dynastic and confessional glorification of Ferdinand II. But though he had no superstitious reverence for the House of Hapsburg, he treats Wallenstein as a traitor to the Emperor. He was more German than Czech, and when Prague University was divided he chose the German section.

It is hardly surprising that Hungarian history has been strongly patriotic.[1] The passionate sense of national self-consciousness sought in the story of the Magyars at once a vindication of Hungarian claims to autonomy and a source of strength in times of trouble. Thus general surveys have attracted historical scholars more than the patient investigation of problems and periods. Not till the emergence of Marczali did Hungarian historiography break the shackles of a narrow patriotism. His popular sketch of the development of the Hungarian people and his larger works on Hungary under Joseph II represent the highest achievement of Magyar scholarship.

Though the conception of Italian unity dates from the Napoleonic era, the fragmentation of the country encouraged the study of regional history, the Tuscan usually devoting himself

---

[1] See Flegler, 'Beiträge z. Würdigung d. ungarischen Geschichtschreibung,' *Historische Zeitschrift*, vol. xix; and *Revue de Synthèse historique*, vol. ii.

to Tuscany, the Venetian to Venice, the Neapolitan to Sicily and the South.[1] The two historians who attracted most attention during the years following the downfall of Napoleon gave their books a strong political flavour. In the early days of the French Revolution Botta[2] had been arrested as a republican, and later accompanied the French arms as a doctor. His chief work, the 'History of Italy during the Revolutionary and Napoleonic Wars,' was a manifesto of liberal and nationalist ideas. Italy is depicted as the victim of foreign barbarians, past and present, and her right to an independent life is loudly proclaimed. The vivid touches of a man who had witnessed many of the scenes he describes rendered the book a great favourite, and the glowing patriotism helped to keep alive the national idea in an era of reaction. Colletta's[3] 'History of the Kingdom of Naples,' before, during and after, the Great French War, is of higher importance. He fought against the French in 1798, but he knew the vices of the Bourbon régime and was not sorry when the army of the Revolution entered the city. He held important civil and military posts under King Joseph and Murat. Joining the revolution in 1820 he became Minister of War, and on the suppression of the constitutional movement he was imprisoned in Austria. Two years later he was permitted to live in Florence, where he wrote his masterpiece. The book is a prolonged and solemn denunciation of Bourbon rule. While detesting disorder and revolution he shows that they were rendered inevitable by misgovernment. The flattering picture of the reign of Murat makes the Bourbon Restoration loom all the darker. Colletta has been compared to Tacitus, whose lofty invective he strove to reproduce. Such a book could not be published in Italy, but the Geneva edition found its way back across the Alps.

In Italy, as in England and France, interest in the past was to a large extent created by the novel and the drama. 'I Promessi Sposi,' published in 1827, rested on a serious study of Lombardy in the seventeenth century; and though the pious Manzoni took care that the Church should appear to advantage, the picture of the life and thought of the time was sufficiently accurate. The greatest of Italian historical novels was the parent of a large progeny. Niccolini glorified the Sicilian Vespers in 'John of Procida,' and attacked the Papacy in 'Arnold of Brescia.' Of a

---

[1] See Croce, *Storia della Storiografia Italiana nel secolo Decimonono*, 2 vols. 1921.

[2] See Pavesio, *Carlo Botta*, 1874.

[3] See Luchaire, *Essai sur l'Évolution intellectuelle de l'Italie*, 1815–30, pp. 198–214, 1906.

similar type were the 'Fieramosca' and 'Niccolo de Lapi' of Cesare Balbo. The plays, novels and poems produced in rich profusion during the second quarter of the century did much to stimulate the pride in national development which in due time issued in the serious study of Italian history. The first of such works was the compilation of Troya[1] on the early Middle Ages. The Neapolitan scholar made prolonged researches in the archives of Monte Cassino and other monasteries. Though 'Italy in the Middle Ages' remained a vast torso, it is of considerable importance in the development of Italian studies. No one had examined the archives so thoroughly since Muratori, and his great collection of documents made a history of the Lombard Kingdom possible. 'My vocation,' he wrote to a friend, 'is to recount the facts—a humble sort of history, unworthy of Vico and Herder.' This modest ambition, which aimed neither at philosophy nor art, did not hinder the expression of his views. He exhibited the Lombards as barbarians and tyrants, and the Popes as the guardians of Roman law, the Latin language and Christian civilisation. The book pointed to the resurrection of Italy through the Vatican.

Troya's attitude towards history was shared by his fellow Neapolitan, the scholarly Abbot of Monte Cassino, who welcomed Pertz and Mommsen, Renan and Gregorovius to his library on the mountain top. Tosti[2] won reputation by his history of the monastery over which he presided, and his study of Boniface VIII defended the great Ultramontane as a champion of humanity and of Italy. He glorified the Church as representing mind against force, and behind the Papacy and the Guelfs he saw democracy and nationality. In 1848 appeared the 'Lombard League' written in the months preceding the revolution. The book, dedicated to Pius IX, displayed the Pope at the head of Italy in opposition to the invader. 'I lay these chapters at your feet as a sacred thing. Give us back the standard of Alexander III. The hour has struck, humanity awaits you.' Tosti was an uncompromising Guelf. The Italian republics reached a height of civilisation denied to the monarchies of other lands. Italy belonged to her citizens, other countries to their rulers. With these ideas he welcomed the year of revolutions, and the ensuing reaction was a bitter disappointment. Monte Cassino was occupied by the military, and its Abbot fled. The dream that the Papacy stood for liberty and independence was shattered when French bayonets destroyed the

---

[1] See Majocchi, *Troya*, 1876; Del Giudice, *Carlo Troya*, 1899; and Marc Monnier, *L'Italie, est-elle la terre des morts?* ch. xi., 1860.

[2] See Renan, *Essais de Morale et de Critique*, 1859.

short-lived Roman Republic of Mazzini and Garibaldi and restored Papal rule.

A conception of Italian history which agreed in some respects with that of Tosti was held by a far more gifted writer. Ferrari[1] left his country in 1840 and wrote his chief work in French. 'The Revolutions of Italy,' published in 1858, contained an eloquent survey from the fall of the Western Empire to the collapse of the Florentine Republic in 1530. Every writer, he declared, sought for some unifying principle, some in the Papacy, others in the cities. In truth the contending factions were Guelfs or Ghibellines under different names. Thus the 7,200 revolutions and the 700 massacres which took place between 1000 and 1500 were only the struggles of two parties. Pope and Emperor were mere symbols. His volumes suggest that the maze of bloodshed and confusion which makes up Italian history was really fruitful. Italians themselves, he affirms, never wished to exchange this feverish life for one of repose, for this perpetual effervescence was the condition of their creative achievements. While Sismondi lamented the disorders as the abuse of his adored liberty, Ferrari crowned them with roses. His book lacks accuracy and sobriety, and Croce dismisses him as an unhistorical mind, but it is the most daring reconstruction of the psychology of Italian city life ever attempted.

The greatest of South Italian scholars was the Sicilian Amari,[2] whose first success was mainly due to the political undertones of his work. His 'History of the Sicilian Vespers,' published in 1842, narrated the revolt in minute detail, but despite its thousand pages its author sprang into fame. The work passed through eight editions in his lifetime, and was translated into several languages. While recording the expulsion of the French, he and his readers were thinking of the Neapolitan Bourbons. The book was a serious study and the criticism of sources unusually thorough, but its subject and its success made it suspect. Amari was dismissed from his office and summoned to Naples, but he thought Paris would be safer. He returned to Palermo to take office in the Provisional Government of 1848, but on the collapse of the constitutional movement he once more sought refuge abroad. He occupied his exile by researches among the Arabic manuscripts in the Paris libraries. The six volumes of 'The Mussulmans in

---

[1] See Renan's essay, 'Les Révolutions d'Italie,' in *Essais de Morale et de Critique*, 1859.

[2] See Tommasini, *Scritti di Storia e Critica*, 1891; Derenbourg, *Opuscules d'un Arabisant*, 1905; Ancona, in *Carteggio di Amari*, vol. ii., 1896; and the sumptuous volumes, *Centenario della nascita di Amari*, 1910.

Sicily' are one of the few outstanding historical achievements of modern Italy. They lit up a dark corner of the Middle Ages and filled the gap between Roman and Norman times. Returning to his native island after the expedition of the Thousand, he served for some years as Minister of Education to the new Kingdom and died at the age of eighty-three.

While a few isolated scholars practised their trade in the South under discouraging circumstances, the northern States witnessed a more fruitful activity. Though not the most erudite of Piedmontese scholars the first and most popular·was Cesare Balbo,[1] who began his literary career with historical dramas and novels. His political activity being rewarded by banishment he settled in Paris, where he employed his leisure on a history of Italy, two volumes of which were published in 1820. Many years later he confessed that it had been a dream of his youth to write a history of his country, but his narrative, like that of Troya, only reached the end of the Lombards. Yet, though scarcely more than a chronicle of wars and invasions, it was welcomed as the first Italian summary of the early fortunes of Italy, and the vibrant national feeling was some compensation for the lack of higher qualities. His 'Summary of Italian History,' rapidly written for a Turin encyclopædia in 1845, obtained even greater popularity. Its moral was that happiness depended on independence, and that foreign rule was poison to a nation's soul. Like Troya and Tosti, Balbo pictured the Church as a bulwark of national independence, but at the same time emphasised the services of the House of Savoy. Among other Piedmontese scholars who won national fame were Count Sclopis, author of a history of Italian Legislation which is still indispensable, and Coppi,[2] who devoted his life to a continuation of the Annals of Muratori. Still more important was Count Litta's 'Famiglie Celebri,' the first part of which, devoted to the Sforza, appeared in 1819.[3] Before his death in 1852 he had completed over one hundred noble families, among them the Visconti, the Este, the Medici, the Gonzaga and the Bentivoglio. Before Litta Italian family history was a maze of forgeries. Charles Albert was angered by the exposure of the failings of his royal predecessors, and the historian was harassed by the Austrian and Piedmontese censorship.

Belonging to the same school of liberal Catholicism as Balbo which dominated Italian historiography during the first half of

---

[1] See Reumont, *Zeitgenossen*, vol. i., 1862.
[2] See Reumont, *Biographische Denkblätter*, 1878.
[3] See Reumont, *Zeitgenossen*, vol. ii.

the century, Cesare Cantu[1] played a similar part in Lombardy. His importance, however, extended beyond the frontiers of his province, for no one wrote so much or took such a large share in instructing Italians in their history. His 'Margherita Pusterla,' an historical novel of the fourteenth century, won immense popularity, and his study of Lombardy in the seventeenth century, designed as a commentary on the 'Promessi Sposi,' received help from Manzoni. The main task of his life was a complete history of Italy, which traced the fortunes of the peninsula in a dozen volumes from the foundation of Rome to the Crimean War. The survey of religion and literature, economic development and social life gave it a value of its own. Cantu was prolix and superficial, and there is little insight into the process of historic growth, but he possessed the art of popularisation.

During the decades that followed the fall of Napoleon Florence was the intellectual capital of Italy. The Government of Tuscany, like its fellows, was hostile to liberty of thought, but the police were less active and the censorship less galling. Among her citizens was the man who by knowledge, zeal and wealth contributed more to Italian historical studies in the middle decades of the century than any of his countrymen. Like Balbo and Cantu, Count Capponi belonged to the school of liberal Catholicism.[2] When in England he had been struck by the importance of the great reviews, and he dreamed of an Italian journal on the model of the *Edinburgh*. His plan was realised with the assistance of Vieusseux, a cultured Genevese who had settled in Florence. Though the censorship compelled the editor to confine himself in the main to literary topics, the *Antologia*, which began to appear in 1821, became a rallying-point for Italian scholarship. Twenty years later a still more important step was taken by the same two men in the foundation of the *Archivio Storico Italiano*. At first serving chiefly for the publication of documents it quickly became a true historical review, and survived to witness the birth of a number of regional journals. For half a century the Palazzo Capponi was a meeting-point for foreign as well as native scholars. Though a loyal subject of the Grand Duke and a champion of Italian federation under the Pope, he was too tolerant to quarrel with those who urged a bolder solution. There is no more attractive figure in modern Italian scholarship than the Tuscan Maecenas who, despite the blindness which overtook him in middle life, never lost his zest for study. His life-work was the early history of his native city and state. He accumulated a great body of

[1] See Tabarrini, *Studi di Critica storica*, 1876.
[2] See Reumont's admirable biography, *Gino Capponi*, 1880.

material and worked at intervals at his task, but he committed
the mistake of delaying publication. When it appeared in 1875
it failed to satisfy the expectations of a more critical age.
Like Balbo and Cantu, he displays throughout strong Guelf
sympathies.

For many years the history of Venice was studied in the pages
of Daru, but two scholars were at work in the city when his
volumes appeared who laid the foundations of a far deeper
insight. In 1824 was published the first volume of the Venetian
Inscriptions to which Cicogna[1] devoted a long and laborious life,
and it was owing to such researches that it became possible to
supersede Daru. Samuel Romanin, a Jew of Trieste, migrated to
Venice in 1821, and after years of research published his 'Storia
documentata di Venezia' in ten volumes, 1853–61.[2] The work
was valuable for its judgment no less than its new material, and
disproved many of Daru's charges. It is in the closing act of the
drama that the two historians differ most widely. While the
Frenchman traced the fall of the Republic to decadence, Romanin
contended that it only yielded to force.

Of the generation whose studies synchronised with or followed
the creation of the Italian Kingdom the most distinguished
was Villari.[3] Born in Naples in 1827 he migrated to Tuscany in
1849, and found his life-work in Florence. For ten years he
laboured at the biography of Savonarola and furnished the first
detailed study of the prophet based on the examination of his
writings and letters. He never wavered in his belief that the great
preacher was essentially Catholic, that he had no desire to subject
the world to the Church, and that he was one of the most glorious
of Italy's thinkers, heroes, and martyrs. The 'Life of Machiavelli'
was a larger and still more important work. 'When Machiavelli's
object is achieved,' wrote Macaulay in 1827, 'his tomb and name
will be reverenced.' The prophecy had come true. As a citizen of
united Italy, Villari looked back with gratitude to one of her
prophets. He discovered the unity of his writings in an overmastering desire to see his country united and free from foreign
domination. The work, though its standpoint was not altogether
new, came as a challenge. Capponi had recently denounced the
author of 'The Prince,' and foreign scholars pilloried him as
the type of Italian guile. Villari made a fair judgment possible
by reconstructing the historical background, and the scholarly
volumes of Tommasini were to confirm the favourable verdict.

[1] See Reumont, *Biographische Denkblätter*, 1878.
[2] See the 'Necrologia' by Polidori in the tenth volume.
[3] See Baldasseroni, *Pasquale Villari*, 1907.

His third important work, the 'Researches on the First Two Centuries of the History of Florence,' appeared in 1893, and was largely rewritten in 1904. The book is a series of essays, concluding with a picture of Florence in the time of Dante. The love of his adopted city occasionally breaks through the reserve of the scholar. 'In the darkness of the Middle Ages Florence appeared as a little point of electric light which illuminated the world.' Alone of Italian historians of the nineteenth century he gained not only a European reputation but a European public. Outside the political field Francesco de Sanctis' 'History of Italian Literature' holds the first place.

The first historical work produced in Spain in the nineteenth century owed its fame less to its merits than to its subject. Llorente's[1] 'History of the Inquisition' possesses the piquant interest of a revelation. The secretary to the Holy Office in Madrid took advantage of the expulsion of the Bourbons and the temporary suppression of the tribunal to compile its history with the aid of official documents. The book, which appeared in French in 1817 and shortly after in the original, was translated into several languages and increased the hatred with which the Inquisition was viewed in Protestant and liberal Europe; but the use of material is arbitrary, and it must be used with extreme caution. Of scarcely less celebrity was Conde's 'History of the Arabs in Spain.' In an age when a knowledge of Arabic was rare, Conde was believed to possess the key. Appointed librarian at Madrid by Joseph Bonaparte, the historian retired with the French to Paris, only returning in 1819 to die. His work appeared immediately after his death, was translated into several languages, and remained canonical for a generation. The first blow at his authority was struck by Pascual da Gayangos in his sumptuous edition of El Makkari's Mohammedan Dynasties, but it was not till the appearance of Dozy's 'Recherches sur l'histoire politique et littéraire de l'Espagne' in 1849 that it proved to be a house built upon sand. Conde knew little more of Arabic than the alphabet. 'With incomparable impudence he forges dates by hundreds and invents facts by thousands, while pretending to translate. It would be easier to cleanse the stables of Augeas than to correct all the faults and refute all the lies.' In his 'Recherches' and in the 'History of the Spanish Mussulmans' which followed it, the great Dutch Arabist dispersed the fog of monkish legends and rendered possible a critical history

[1] See the hostile analysis in Hefele, *Ximenes*, ch. xviii., 1844. H. C. Lea, the American historian of the Inquisition, has also exposed his reckless abuse of figures.

of mediæval Spain. His most resounding achievement was to recover the real character and chequered career of the Cid.

The early years of the Restoration also witnessed the first serious studies of the heroic age of the Spanish Monarchy. The Royal Academy of History began the great 'Collección de documentos inéditos' which has passed its hundredth volume: none of the minor countries could boast such a comprehensive work or one begun so early. With its publication scholars began to realise the importance of the national treasure-house at Simancas,[1] from which so many of its contents were drawn. In the eighteenth century Robertson had been refused permission to undertake researches for his 'Conquest of America,' and it was not till 1843 that Gachard entered the little village near Valladolid to copy the correspondence of Philip II. He was followed by a few other foreign scholars, all of whom complained of the physical hardships involved. Bergenroth and Maurenbrecher arrived from Germany, Gindely from Bohemia, De Leva from Italy, Froude and Gardiner from England. Bergenroth, who spent the best part of ten years in the archives, undermined his health and died of fever. Among the small number of Spanish pilgrims to the shrine was Lafuente,[2] author of the first detailed and complete history of Spain. His work, appearing in thirty volumes between 1850 and 1867, glorifies the Monarchy and the Church. While rejecting many absurdities of the old chronicles, he is not courageous enough to reject them all. The style is prolix, like that of most South European historians. Every part of the story has been modified by new discoveries, and the book was superseded by the 'Historia General,' written by members of the Academy of History under the guidance of Canovas, which began to appear in 1892. The famous Conservative statesman was a profound student, and his volumes on Philip IV revealed his capacity both for research and narrative. The most notable item of the collection is the documented work of Danvila y Collado on the reforming Ruler Charles III, the best of the Bourbon kings.

The Academy history is the most important effort of Spanish historiography, but other valuable works have been produced.[3] Altamira, known to English readers as a contributor to the Cambridge Histories, has written the best narrative in any

---

[1] There is a good account of the history of the archives in *Revue Historique*, vol. xcvi. Cp. Cartwright, *Gustave Bergenroth*, 1870. The archives have been transferred to Seville.

[2] See the detailed biography in vol. xxx. of his *Historia general de España*.

[3] See *Revue de Synthèse historique*, vols. vi. and ix.

language of the growth of Spanish civilisation.[1] Danvila y Collado has composed an exhaustive treatise on the Civil Power which, while emphasising legislation and administration, is scarcely less than a history of Spain from Ferdinand and Isabella to the Constitution of 1812. Fernandez Duro's work on the Armada revealed the Spanish side of the expedition. The greatest of modern Spanish scholars, Menendez y Pelayo, whose death at the age of fifty-six was a blow to European scholarship, threw more light on the development of the Spanish mind than any other writer, native or foreign. His massive monograph on the Spanish heretics, published when he was only twenty-six, told a painful story. His histories of Science and Æsthetic Ideas in Spain and his innumerable literary essays touch the national life at many points. No survey could ignore the historical novels of Perez Galdos, the Walter Scott of Spain. His 'National Episodes' relate the vicissitudes of the country from the battle of Trafalgar in two score volumes, and offer a wonderfully living picture of the revolt against Napoleon, the despotism of Ferdinand VII, and the atrocities of the Carlist wars.

Nowhere is the contrast between past and present more poignant than in Portugal, and in no country has the cult of the past been less discriminating. With the publication of the first work of Herculano de Carvalho[2] in 1846–9 serious historical studies began. Though the four volumes covered scarcely more than a century, three editions were quickly demanded, but the book created indignation as well as interest. Boldly declaring in his preface that patriotism was a bad counsellor for historians, he scraped off the legendary gilding and some venerable fables he did not even deign to mention. He showed that Portuguese history was less heroic, less glorious, less unique than had been believed, and wounded his compatriots in their tenderest spot by emphasising the large admixture of Moorish blood. The few scholars of whom Portugal could boast welcomed the book as an honest attempt to reach the truth, but the author was assailed by many critics as a traitor, a blasphemer and a Lutheran, who had been bought by foreign foes. He bitterly declared that he ought to have shown every Portuguese to be worth three Spaniards and two Frenchmen, and to have accepted the popular legends and pious falsehoods of old women. So disgusted was he by the ignorant bigotry of his countrymen that he left his work a fragment. On resolving to discontinue his history he turned to a

---

[1] See Some Historians of Modern Europe, ed. B. E. Schmitt, ch. 1.

[2] See Döllinger, Akademische Reden, vol. ii., 1889, and Baxmann in Historische Zeitschrift, vol. ix.

subject scarcely less inflammable. His massive monograph on the foundation of the Inquisition in Portugal was based throughout on unused acts and correspondence. Though more limited in scope and less famous than the work of Llorente, it is a far sounder performance. Southey had once said that the Portuguese Inquisition was an association to burn people whose property was coveted. This indictment was confirmed by the researches of Herculano, who called his story a drama of crimes. The reception of his second work was so hostile that the old admirer of Walter Scott turned to the historical novel. 'Eurich,' a tale of the destruction of the Visigothic Kingdom by the Moors, was translated into German by Heine and appeared in an abridged form in French. Herculano found some compensation for the complacent ignorance of the majority of his countrymen in the devotion and admiration of his pupils, though none of them reached the stature of their master.

In Switzerland,[1] as in Portugal, serious investigation was impossible till the haze of legend had been dispersed and the national traditions subjected to a critical inquiry. The work of iconoclasm was accomplished by Kopp,[2] an ardent patriot and a pious Catholic. A teacher of history at Lucerne, he edited a selection of passages from Johannes Müller[3] for schools, and his enthusiastic tribute to the 'immortal' work showed that he was troubled by no doubts. His conversion began when he undertook to write a memorial sketch for the fifth centenary of Lucerne's entrance into the Confederation. Turning to the archives he discovered that the stories of Tschudi, which Müller had naïvely copied into his pages, were mostly late inventions. The determination to accept no incident for which early testimony was not forthcoming revolutionised the study of Swiss history. His next task was to publish a volume of documents in 1835. The new version, from which Gessler and Tell disappeared, was received with consternation, but the critical insight brought fame beyond the frontier. Encouraged by friends he determined to narrate the beginnings of the confederation. The familiar anecdotes of Austrian tyranny and cruelty were dismissed as legends, and Austrians were delighted to read a vindication of Rudolf of Hapsburg. An historian who was so little of a 'patriot' naturally found most appreciation outside his country; but Waitz, the

---

[1] See G. von Wyss, *Geschichte der Historiographie in der Schweiz*, 1895, and Feller, *Die Schweizerische Geschichtschreibung im neunzehnten Jahrhundert*, 1938.

[2] See Lutolf, *J. E. Kopp*, 3 vols., 1868.

[3] See Henking, *Johannes Müller*, 2 vols., 1909–28.

greatest of mediævalists, and Böhmer, the most intimate of his friends, lamented that a work of such importance should be so badly written. Switzerland now reads her history not in his pages but in the manuals which incorporated his results. Most of the national effort, however, goes into the study of the various cantons, for pride in his canton is an instinct in every citizen. Among the influences which have helped to create interest in the past are the novels of Conrad Ferdinand Meyer.

The year 1830, which witnessed the birth of an independent Belgium, ushered in a period of eager historical research and production.[1] Belgian historians as a rule have distinguished themselves rather by the publication of materials than by brilliant narratives. Most attention has been paid to the critical sixteenth century, and it was to that epoch that Gachard devoted most of his long life. Born in France he came as a youth to Belgium, and in 1831 was appointed chief archivist of the new kingdom. His editions of the voluminous correspondence of William the Silent and of Philip II made a study of the great rivals possible. Though his main occupation was to discover and edit materials, he wrote a study of Don Carlos, a history of Belgium in the eighteenth century, and several volumes of essays. More popular but far less critical was Kervyn de Lettenhove, whose 'History of Flanders' is one of the most considerable narrative works that Belgium has produced. In his patriotic enthusiasm he plunges headlong into the strife between France and the Communes. His lack of judgment appears even more clearly in his most celebrated work, 'Les Huguenots et les Gueux.' Written from the standpoint of militant Catholicism, it turned Motley's picture upside down. He detests William the Silent and reviles his supporters. The successful revolt of 1830 was the chosen domain of Juste, whose numerous monographs on the 'Founders of the Belgian Monarchy' possess enduring value owing to his use of the private papers of King Leopold, Stockmar, Van de Weyer and other statesmen to whom the country owes its independence. During the last generation an historical school employing the expert methods of French and German Universities has arisen. It is owing to the devoted labours of two generations that Pirenne, the greatest of Belgian historians, was able to write a critical history of his country.

The country of Grotius and Hoofd has devoted close attention to its glorious history.[2] The place occupied in Belgium by Gachard

[1] See Potvin, *Histoire des Lettres en Belgique*, vol. iv., 1882, and *Biographie Nationale de Belgique*.

[2] See the brief sketch by Blok, *Die Geschichtschreibung in Holland*, 1924.

was filled in Holland by Groen van Prinsterer, whose life was largely devoted to the publication of the archives of the House of Orange down to 1688. A Calvinist and an ardent champion of the dynasty, his judgments are not always beyond cavil, but his introductions and elucidations are a real contribution to history.[1] A far greater name is Fruin,[2] a miniature Ranke, whose fame would have been wider had he written a work of large dimensions; but it may be doubted whether it would have been so useful as the stream of monographs in which he recorded his results. His most celebrated work, 'Ten Years of the Eighty Years War,' (1588–98), published in 1857, procured him the Chair of Dutch History at Leyden. Alike in scholarship, judgment and style this study of the critical period following the death of William the Silent is reckoned the most perfect historical work that Holland has produced. Ranging more particularly over the sixteenth and seventeenth centuries, the ten volumes of his collected essays and investigations constitute the most trustworthy guide to the glorious period of Dutch history. Fruin's successor at Leyden was his pupil Blok, whose 'History of the Dutch People' offered the first comprehensive and critical survey of national development. It at once took its place as the national history, and has received the honour of English and German translations. Every aspect of the national life—political and social, religious and literary, industrial and commercial—receives attention, and from time to time the author halts to survey the situation as a whole. The concluding volume, describing the eighteenth and nineteenth centuries, offers a welcome picture of a little known chapter in modern history. The example of Groen van Prinsterer in an earlier generation was followed by Japikse and Colenbrander in voluminous publications of material on the later history of the House of Orange.

The founder of Danish[3] historical scholarship was Allen, the author of the first modern history of Denmark, a work which, in a French translation, was for long the sole guide of foreign students. While his survey was merely a summary of known facts, his 'History of the Three Northern Kingdoms, 1497–1536,' was the fruit of prolonged research. The early history of Scandinavia was the chosen theme of Worsaae. Beginning with the primeval

[1] See Mackay, *Religious Thought in Holland*, Lecture 1, 1911.

[2] See the appreciations by Blok, *Verspreide Studien*, 1903, and Rackfahl, *Hist. Zeitschrift*, vol. xcviii.

[3] See Steenstrup, *Historieskrivninger i Danmark i det 19de Aarhundrede*, 1889, and Ellen Jörgensen, *Historiens Studium i Danmark i det 19 Aarhundrede*, 1943.

antiquities of Denmark, he traced the Norsemen to England, Scotland and Ireland, and followed with a survey of the Danish conquest of England and Normandy. His works, translated into English and German, were for a generation the chief source of knowledge for the Vikings, and his richly illustrated writings created a taste for Scandinavian antiquities. Building on his foundations but employing more critical methods, Steenstrup published his massive work on the Norsemen, the later volumes of which revealed the existence of more numerous traces of Scandinavian influence in England than had been generally realised. The story of the Danes may now be read in the co-operative work which began to appear in 1897, to which Steens-trup, Fridericia, Erslev, Edvard Holm and other tried scholars have contributed.

The father of historical study in Sweden was Geijer,[1] professor and poet, politician and economist, who published the first comprehensive history of his country in 1832. Passing lightly over the Middle Ages the narrative broadens with Gustavus Vasa, relates the career of Gustavus Adolphus in detail, and closes with the abdication of his daughter Christina. The book became a national possession and was translated into several languages. The story was continued by his pupil Carlson, who added a fifth and sixth volume, but died before he had completed the reign of Charles XII. Fryxell, the Swedish Freytag, did more to popularise the study than any other writer by his 'Stories from Swedish History' which began to appear in 1823, the forty-sixth volume being completed more than half a century later. Though it became more scholarly as it advanced, it never reached a high academic standard. Among living Swedish scholars no one compares in significance and influence with Harold Hjärne who occupies the chair of Geijer and Carlson at Upsala.

The first modern Norwegian historian was Rudolf Keyser, whose writings and lectures at Christiania created an interest in the early and mediæval history of Scandinavia. The greatest of his pupils, Munch, helped his master to publish the old Norwegian laws, and himself brought many sources to light. His principal work, the most important monument of Norwegian studies, was an eight volume 'History of the Norse People to the Union with Denmark in 1397,' in which society and culture receive not less attention than war and statecraft. His researches were not confined to his own country, and it was while studying manuscripts in Rome that he died. A master of Teutonic philology whose competence was recognised by Grimm, his lectures on

[1] See Nielsen, *Erik Geijer*, 1902.

language, mythology and history created a widespread interest in Norse civilisation. The Viking centuries were the chosen field of Alexander Bugge, and the humiliating period of Norwegian history under Danish rule was critically surveyed by Sars.

Russia's first national historian was Karamsin.[1] Under Catherine and Paul he had been a liberal and something of a cosmopolitan, but he came to regard Russia as a world apart, independent of and superior to the countries of the West. It was in this Slavophil spirit that he set to work, toning down the barbarism and throwing the warm colours of fancy around his narrative. The keynote of the coming work was struck by a Memoir on 'Ancient and Modern Russia,' glorifying the principles of autocracy and combating constitutional theories. The book was among the influences that weaned his patron Alexander I from his liberalism and led to the fall of Speranski. The 'History of the Russian State' appeared in twelve volumes between 1816 and 1829. He depicts the early princes as absolute rulers, and presents Ivan III, who freed Russian from the Tartars, as the ideal monarch. His book has been called the epic of despotism. The Church is the strength of the throne. 'Faith is one of the essential forces of the state.' Pushkin described the first official historiographer as the Columbus of ancient Russia, and Soloviev praised the book as a magnificent poem. It is true that he steered his course over an almost uncharted sea, but neither in scholarship nor judgment does he reach a high standard. He wrote well but had no critical instincts, accepted his authorities without challenge, and took little interest in the life of the people.

The second great name is that of Soloviev,[2] who relegated Karamsin to the upper shelf. The first volume appeared in 1851, and a further instalment followed every year. At his death in 1879 the twenty-ninth volume was almost ready for press. Karamsin reached 1611, Soloviev the reign of Catherine II. He made careful researches in the archives, and his volumes were an addition to as well as a summary of existing knowledge. Though filled with a deep reverence for the past, he regarded the craving for Western culture as natural and laudable. In reply to Katkov and the Moscow Slavophils he maintained that Russians were Europeans, and that nothing European could be alien to them.

---

[1] Karamsin is discussed in the histories of Russian literature by Reinholdt and Waliszewski, and in Pypin, *Die geistigen Bewegungen Russlands in der ersten Hälfte des 19ten Jahrhunderts*, ch. iv., 1894. The best general survey is by Mazour, *An Outline of Modern Russian Historiography*, 1939.

[2] See Guerrier's tribute, *Hist. Zeitschrift*, vol. xlv.

He emphasises the necessity of the work of Peter the Great, and shows how naturally it grew out of the past. He marks an immense advance in his ability to understand and sympathise with the ideals of the liberal as well as of the Slavophil, and he includes social, economic and cultural factors. His summary of Russian history, issued in 1859 in a single volume, enjoyed great popularity and in a French translation enables foreigners to form an estimate of its author's merits. The older historians were superseded by Kluchevsky, the greatest of Russian historical scholars, who after many years of fruitful activity at Moscow was persuaded to revise and publish his lectures.[1] Making no effort to rival his master Soloviev in detailed narrative of politics and war, and largely ignoring foreign affairs, he specialises in the social and economic life of the people. Masses of material have poured from the public archives and from those of the Worontzoff and other great families. De Martens spent forty years in editing the treaties concluded with foreign Powers, thereby rendering a history of Russian diplomacy possible. That synthetic works, utilising the material thus accumulated, are rare is partly due to the censorship. Waliszewski's brilliant biographies of the rulers from Ivan the Terrible to Paul found a European public. The greatest loss which the censure inflicted was the suppression of the larger part of Bilbassoff's work on Catherine II which was designed to fill twelve volumes. With the exception of a vast bibliography the work is still in manuscript. Hruschevski's large-scale history of the Ukraine, written in Ukrainian, is the equivalent of Palacky. Historical studies have suffered by the ejection or banishment of prominent teachers. Vinogradoff took refuge at Oxford, and Miliukov, the liberal historian of Russian culture, deprived of his chair, went into politics. The leaden obscurantism of the Tsarist régime weighed no less heavily on historical scholarship than on every other department of national life.

Polish historians, like those of Bohemia, laboured under the disability of writing subject to the censorship of an alien Power. Their trials are illustrated in the career of Lelewel.[2] As Professor of History at Wilna he aroused the enthusiasm of his pupils, and in the crusade against secret societies he lost his post. When the Revolution broke out in 1830 he was elected a member of the national government. On its failure he fled to Paris and thence to

[1] There is an English translation in 5 volumes. See *Some Historians of Modern Europe*, ed. B. E. Schmitt, ch. 9.
[2] See Nitzschmann's *Geschichte der Polnischen Literatur*; Morfill, *Poland*, ch. xiii.; and Dembinski, Halecki and Handelsman, *L'historiographie Polonaise*, 1933.

Brussels, where he spent the last thirty years of his life. His
'Poland in the Middle Ages' suffered from lack of access to the
archives, and the ardent democrat found more popular influences
in early Polish history than had ever existed. None the less he
remains a striking figure, and his learning and patriotism are
gratefully remembered in the land of his birth. No academic
historian has contributed so powerfully to the awakening of
national interest as the poetry of Mickiewicz and the patriotic
novels of Kraszewski and Sienkiewicz.

Nowhere except in Bohemia has the influence of historical
studies been greater than in Greece. The expulsion of the Turks
left the country poor and ignorant, and cultured Greeks found
comfort in the memory of classical civilisation. But at the very
moment of emancipation the Bavarian Fallmerayer startled
the learned world by his denial of the ethnic continuity of the
race: the modern 'Greeks', he declared, were virtually Slavs. The
attack was deeply resented, and Greeks witnessed with delight
the refutation of his paradox by Hopf, Finlay, Zinkeisen and
Hertzberg. The unbroken continuity of Greek life was the thesis
of the work of Paparrigopoulos. His reply to Fallmerayer and
other historical essays procured him the Chair of Greek History
when the University of Athens was founded in 1837. In 1865–76
he published the history which contained the result of his lifelong
researches. Like other 'national' histories it possesses the faults
of an apologia, emphasising the culture and heroism of the Greeks
and the vices of their oppressors. His message was repeated in
the short 'History of Greek Civilisation,' which appeared simultaneously in Greek and French in 1878. Foreign scholars, he
declared, hardly appreciated the intimate relation of the new to
the old Greeks. The West had sinned against Greece, and it must
now assist the little kingdom to embrace all lands where Greek
blood predominated. Students and teachers alike are filled with
enthusiasm for the epic traditions of their country. 'The exclusively Hellenic character of all the features, physical and intellectual, of the present Greeks,' declares Bikelas,[1] 'is a glorious
proof of the intensity of our national vitality.' No Greek writer
of a younger generation is so well known in the west as Andréadès,
the leading authority on the financial and economic history of
South-East Europe. In Roumania Jorga, historian of the Byzantine Empire, the Ottoman Empire and the Roumanians, has no
competitor. The wars and revolutions of the last hundred years
in the Balkan states provided unfavourable soil for tranquil
teaching and research.

---

[1] *Seven Essays on Christian Greece*, 1890.

CHAPTER XXII

THE ANCIENT EAST

AMONG the most sensational events of the nineteenth century is the resurrection of the Ancient East. We are now aware that Greece and Rome, far from standing near the beginning of recorded history, were the heirs of a series of mature civilisations. Our whole perspective has been changed. The ancient world ceases to be merely the vestibule to Christian Europe, and becomes in point of duration the larger part of recorded history.[1]

I

The discovery of early Egypt dates from Napoleon's expedition in 1798. The country was vaguely known by the obelisks and mummies scattered about the capitals of Europe and by references in books of travel, but interest in its life and art, religion and science, had been lost. The French army was accompanied by several scholars, whose observations were recorded in an array of magnificent volumes. but the inscriptions, being unintelligible, were transcribed with so little accuracy as to be useless to philologists. Of far greater importance was the discovery of a damaged slab of basalt, now in the British Museum, by a French officer while excavating for fortifications at the Rosetta mouth of the Nile. The Rosetta stone contained a priestly decree of 197 B.C. awarding honours to Ptolemy Epiphanes in Greek, hieroglyphics (the language of the priests), and demotic (the popular dialect). Here was a key to the history and civilisation of ancient Egypt, but who could fit it to the lock? The first attack was made by Sylvestre de Sacy and the Swede Akerblad, who guessed several letters in demotic and identified in both versions the groups of letters which appeared to correspond to the proper names. They maintained that the writing could not

---

[1] See Darmesteter, 'L'Orientalisme en France,' in his *Essais Orientaux*, 1883; Hogarth, *Authority and Archæology*, 1899; Hilprecht, *Explorations in Bible Lands*, 1903; *Cambridge Ancient History*, vol. i., chs. 3 and 4, 1923; Kenyon, *The Bible and Archæology*, 1940; Finegan, *Light from the Ancient East*, 1946; Ceram, *Götter, Gräber und Gelehrte*, 1949; Daniel, *A Hundred Years of Archæology*. 1950. Wallis Budge, *By Nile and Tigris*, 1920; Sayce, *Reminiscences*, 1923; and Petrie, *Seventy Years in Archæology*, 1931, are useful.

be wholly ideographic, as a foreign proper name could not be represented by an image, but they isolated the names without being able to determine their elements. A more successful attempt was that of Thomas Young, author of the undulatory theory of light, who identified the signs answering to the sounds n, f, p, t, i. In the words of Maspero, Young saw visions of the promised land but never entered it.

The riddle was guessed by Champollion,[1] who thereby became the High Priest of Egyptology. There is no more wonderful page in the annals of scholarship than the brief career of this man of genius. As Schliemann dreamed of Troy in his childhood, Champollion's thoughts turned to Egypt. Making the acquaintance of the physicist Fourier, who had taken part in the French expedition, the lad of eleven pored over his collections and listened enraptured to the traveller's tales. Chancing on a Coptic grammar at the age of fourteen, he threw himself into its study, believing that it might contain the key to the unknown. In Paris he worked under Sylvestre de Sacy, learning Arabic and other Oriental languages. Turning to the problem of the Rosetta stone, he noticed that certain papyri began with representations of religious scenes which he also found at the head of hieroglyphic inscriptions. Guessing that the text might also be the same, he detected the same signs in the hieroglyphics. Without having read a word, he had discovered that the writing on papyrus was simply cursive hieroglyphics. Turning from hieroglyphics he attacked the cursive script and identified the proper names, Berenice, Alexander and Cleopatra, which gave him nineteen letters, and with these he could partially read demotic. He then returned to hieroglyphics, and obtained the phonetic alphabet from some royal cartouches. These letters, tracked through the inscription, gave him a series of words very like the familiar Coptic. Thus the veil of Isis was raised. He had shown that hieroglyphics were about nine-tenths phonetic and one-tenth ideographic; that the three modes of writing, hieroglyphics, hieratic and demotic, formed a single system. The names of the rulers became legible, and the dynasties and monuments fell into their place. Darmesteter compares the rapidity and brilliance of his conquests to the career of the First Consul. Young belittled his rival's results, but Champollion had no difficulty in showing that his alphabet was false except for five signs. Sylvestre de Sacy hailed his pupil's triumph, but Klaproth bitterly accused him of falsifying texts. 'Not human criticism, but the intuition of the Divinity alone could work such a miracle, and we are asked to believe that a single scholar has

[1] See Hartleben's great biography, 2 vols., 1906.

done in a few years what reason and common sense prove to be impossible.' This sneering attack is the highest eulogy, for the discoveries announced in the *Lettre à Dacier*, 1822, and the *Précis du Système Hieroglyphique*, 1824, seemed beyond human power. Champollion was appointed Professor at Grenoble, but returned to Paris in 1826 as Keeper of the Egyptian Museum. Meanwhile he had studied the precious Turin papyrus which listed the kings down to Rameses II. In 1828 he visited Egypt with Rosellini under the auspices of the French and the Tuscan Governments. The tour shattered his health, but on his return to Paris in 1829 a Chair of Egyptian Archæology was founded for him. He only delivered his inaugural lecture, and died in 1831 at the age of forty-one. His was the greatest as well as the earliest of the achievements by which the ancient East was recovered for the modern world. His 'Monuments of Egypt,' the fruit of his journey, appeared after his death, and was followed by an 'Egyptian Grammar' and a 'Dictionary of Hieroglyphics.' His supreme service was the decipherment of hieroglyphics. He had not thoroughly mastered demotic, which finally yielded to the assault of Brugsch; but that could afford to wait, for the most important inscriptions were in hieroglyphics.

The second great step in Egyptology was taken by Lepsius.[1] After learning exact methods from Gottfried Hermann he entered Otfried Müller's *Seminar* at Göttingen, and decided to cultivate the archæological rather than the grammatical side of philology. Feeling the need of knowing antiquity as a whole, he heard Heeren as well as Ewald, Böckh as well as Bopp. For his doctor's degree he chose the Eugubian Tablets, seven copper plates found in the fifteenth century in a vault at Gubbio. The inscriptions, which formed the oldest monuments of an Italian tongue, made it possible to reconstruct the Umbrian language, and threw light on ritual and religion. The tablets had been analysed by Otfried Müller in his book on the Etruscans, and the attention of Lepsius had been drawn to them by his beloved master. By carrying the discussion of the problem far beyond where Müller had left it, he proved his capacity for deciphering unknown tongues. He completed his student's career by a year in Paris, where he attended the lectures of Letronne, who questioned many of Champollion's results. He now received an invitation to Italy from Bunsen, who desired him to study the Egyptian language. Before accepting he decided to inquire whether Champollion's work rested on a firm foundation. The result of his investigations was satisfactory, and the splendid possibilities

[1] See Ebers, *Richard Lepsius*, Eng. trans., 1887.

of Egyptology burst upon him. He learned Coptic, and then
attacked demotic and hieroglyphics. Bunsen and Humboldt
watched over him with fatherly care, and procured a grant from
the Berlin Academy. Rosellini sent him his results, and he was
allowed access to the manuscripts of Champollion. After exhaust-
ing the resources of Paris, he examined the treasures of Turin,
above all the papyrus list of the kings. Bunsen believed that
he had found the man to continue the work of Champollion.
He was then planning his work on 'Egypt's Place in History,'
and was anxious that the young scholar should collaborate. The
plan was not to be realised, but the two men formed a lifelong
friendship.

In 1837 Lepsius published his 'Letter to Rosellini,' confirming
the main discoveries of Champollion and rejecting the methods of
his critics. The unlocking of the treasure-house was the signal
for a number of amateurs to rush in. It was his merit to insist on
the application of strict critical principles, and to sweep away
fancies and speculations. In 1842 he sketched out the 'Book of
Kings,' to which he made additions after his visit to Egypt. He
also occupied himself with mythology, marshalling the motley
throng of deities into ordered ranks. On his first visit to Turin
he had realised that most of the religious texts on monuments,
mummies and papyri belonged to a work which he christened the
'Book of the Dead,' a thorough study of which was obviously
necessary to the comprehension of mythology. In 1842 he published the Turin papyrus in facsimile, and, though it was a late
and faulty copy, the book held its place till Naville published the
best texts forty years later. When Lepsius asked Bunsen to procure help for a visit to Egypt, the minister promised to do his
best. Humboldt supported the application, and the accession of
Frederick William IV in 1840 made the project practicable. A
Chair of Egyptology was created for him at Berlin, and the plan
of a private journey ripened into that of a scientific expedition.

Lepsius landed in Egypt at the end of 1842, having learned
all that Europe could teach him. Mehemet Ali gave him a free
hand in excavation, and presented to the King of Prussia whatever he cared to select. The expedition sent home about 15,000
antiquities and plaster casts. Three tombs were dispatched
from Memphis, columns from Thebes and Philæ, obelisks, statues,
sarcophagi, papyri and innumerable other objects. The story of
the expedition, which lasted three years, was told by its leader
in his 'Letters from Egypt, Ethiopia and the Sinai Peninsula.'
Making a long stay at Memphis, he explored the Old Empire,
excavated over one hundred tombs, separated the twelfth from

the eighteenth dynasty, dated the invasion of the Hyksos, and
investigated the methods of construction employed in the Pyramids. Inscriptions at Philæ enabled him to determine the sequence
of the Ptolemies, and he studied the Nile valley beyond the First
Cataract for the first time, visiting Meroe and opening up the
civilisation of Ethiopia. He passed six months at Thebes, rejoicing
in the mighty rulers of the eighteenth and nineteenth dynasties.
After a visit to the Sinai peninsula he returned home laden with
precious spoil. His highest expectations had been exceeded. He
was appointed Director of the Egyptian Museum, Berlin, of which
he was virtually the creator, and the King supplied funds for the
publication of his results, which appeared in twelve large volumes
containing nearly a thousand plates. The 'Monuments of Egypt
and Ethiopia' contains an inexhaustible treasure of inscriptions,
maps, sketches and pictures, many of them in colour. Marginal
notes indicate the locality and the reign, but there is no
explanatory text. The 'Book of Kings,' begun before the Egyptian
journey and published in 1852, is therefore an almost indispensable companion. In the words of Ebers, the 'Monuments'
must ever remain the most fundamental work for the student of
Egyptology.

An intelligible view of Egyptian history was impossible without a secure chronological basis. The treatise of Lepsius on the
'Chronology of the Egyptians,' published in 1849, rested not
only on a study of the monuments but on an attempt to reconstruct the lost work of Manetho, the Ptolemaic historian, from
fragmentary extracts in later writers. Though it made no claim
to be a narrative, he firmly outlined the history of Egypt. His
later life was occupied by incessant work and travel. On revisiting
Egypt in 1866 he discovered the Tablet of Canopus, a long inscription in hieroglyphics, demotic and Greek, which proved that the
decipherment of the Rosetta stone and of other texts on the same
principles was correct. At the age of seventy he published a
Nubian Grammar, at which he had worked since his visit to
Ethiopia, and the introduction to which surveys in broad perspective the nations and languages of Africa. Busy to the end,
and loaded with honours from the learned societies of the world,
Lepsius died in 1884 at the age of seventy-four, having accomplished more for Egyptology than anyone except its founder.
His cautious methods and exact scholarship render his work
peculiarly solid. With the exception of Brugsch all the great
German scholars who carried on his work, Ebers and Dümichen,
Erman and Wiedemann, were his pupils. 'Lepsius was one of the
last survivors of our heroic age,' wrote Maspero on his death.

'For long he had been the master of us all. I only hope that when I die I may be held to have done for our science one half as much as he.'

Shortly after Lepsius returned from his first expedition, Mariette[1] was sent by the Louvre to the country with which his name is imperishably associated. A few weeks later he discovered an avenue of 141 sphinxes which led up to the Serapeum or Temple of Osiris near Memphis. The temple had disappeared but the huge vaults remained where the sacred Apis bulls were buried. He also found sixty-four tombs ranging from the eighteenth dynasty to the Ptolemies, with innumerable inscriptions and works of art. He then unearthed the temple of the Sphinx at Gizeh. He returned to Paris in 1853, intending to publish a full account of his discoveries; but though he had rapidly classified them he was too little of a scholar for exact interpretation, and only a brief description appeared. In 1857 he was named by the Khedive Director of Antiquities and founded the Museum at Bulak. He found hundreds of tombs at Memphis and Sakkara, excavated the city of Abydos, explored the Ptolemaic temples at Dendera and Edfu, and cleared out the palaces of Medinet Habu and Der el Behari in the hills near Thebes. Though his technique was crude, he was the first and greatest of the excavators. He regarded the Museum as his greatest achievement. Knowing where his best work could be done, he refused the offer of the Chair of Egyptology at the Collège de France. 'Mariette,' said Brugsch, his devoted friend and colleague, 'was more a poet than a scholar. He was weak in deciphering hieroglyphics, and was fully conscious of the uncertainty of his renderings. He confessed that he had absolutely no gift for the philological side of the science, and deeply lamented it.'

Mariette stands besides Champollion and Lepsius as the third great figure in Egyptology. His supreme achievement was to reveal the Old Empire, of which he has been truly described as the Columbus. His discovery of royal tombs of the sixth dynasty at Sakkara brought to light the first long religious texts of the Old Empire, the 'Book of the Dead' belonging to the Middle and the New. He showed that its art and civilisation, far from being primitive, were highly developed, and that it was itself the culmination of ages of development. 'Mariette,' writes Darmesteter, 'had to struggle not only with the unknown but with nature and man. His thirty years of triumph are years of incessant and

<hr>

[1] See Maspero's ' Notice biographique ' in Mariette, Œuvres Diverses, vol. i., 1904, and G. Charmes, L'Égypte, 1891. Both were personal friends.

devouring conflict with fever, stupidity, apathy and prejudice. He had to perform prodigies of diplomacy to force the foolish possessors of these treasures to understand their value. The monopoly of discoveries saved Egypt from the utter ruin which another century of tourists and speculators in antiquities would have consummated.' When he died, the Khedive sent a granite sarcophagus for his remains. 'He sleeps, guarded by four sphinxes from the Serapeum, at the entrance to his museum, on the threshold of the forty centuries restored by his genius.'

Champollion's death had been followed by a good deal of fanciful speculation, and it was not till de Rougé[1] that Egyptology in France again began to advance on sound lines. The worth of his scholarly monographs was recognised by his appointment as Conservator of Egyptian Monuments at the Louvre, and in 1860 he succeeded to the Chair of Egyptology. When he paid a long visit to Egypt, Mariette acted as his cicerone. Though his name is connected neither with sensational discoveries nor with comprehensive treatises, his services to scientific Egyptology are rated highest by those most qualified to judge them. A still more brilliant philologist was Brugsch,[2] the second great German Egyptologist. The publication of his 'Demotic Grammar' in 1848 brought him at a bound into the front rank of scholars, and, acting on the advice of Humboldt, Frederick William IV sent him to Egypt to decipher demotic inscriptions. He was with Mariette when the Serapeum area was brought to light, and formed a lifelong friendship with the prince of excavators. His relations with Lepsius were strained and sometimes openly hostile. When Humboldt, the friend and patron of both, attempted to secure the appointment of the younger scholar as Director of the Berlin Museum, Lepsius announced that he would resign his professorship and leave the capital unless the post was awarded to himself. Yet he expressed his admiration of Brugsch's greatest work, the 'Dictionary of Hieroglyphics and Demotic,' and declared that there was nothing like it in Egyptology. Ebers, the friend and pupil of both, declares Brugsch far superior as a decipherer and investigator of the evolution of Egyptian languages. Eduard Meyer has pronounced him the equal of Champollion in genius, many-sidedness and divinatory instinct. While Lepsius confined himself to inscriptions, Brugsch boldly grappled with manuscripts. Though above all a philologist, Brugsch made the first detailed

[1] See Maspero's sketch in Rougé, *Œuvres Diverses*, vol. i., 1907, and Wallon, *Éloges*, vol. i., 1882.

[2] See his autobiography, *Mein Leben u. Wandern*, 1894, and Naville's article in *Allg. Deutsche Biog.*

attempt to narrate the history of Egypt from contemporary records. Lepsius, he declared, had done all that was possible to one starting from Manetho, but the monuments had largely discredited the Ptolemaic priest. The book is liberally supplied with translations from inscriptions and papyri. The Early and Middle Empires are sketched without great detail, but half the first volume is devoted to the tale of the majestic eighteenth dynasty, which became fully known to students through his pen. The work enjoyed wide popularity, but it was not wholly satisfactory, being too largely composed of texts and too liberal in hypothesis. A third scholar associated with Mariette was Dümichen.[1] When the great excavator uncovered the temple of Seti at Abydos, he did not pause to examine in detail the treasures which it contained. Shortly afterwards Dümichen, on his first visit to Egypt, discovered on the walls a table of the Kings—Seti and his son Rameses II making offering to a long line of ancestors. This perfectly preserved list became the main foundation of Egyptian chronology.

The closest friend of Mariette's later years was Maspero, who succeeded him as the Director of the Museum and of Egyptian Antiquities. Like Champollion, he showed a taste for hieroglyphics while still at school. In 1867 he met Mariette, who was then in Paris in connection with the exhibition. The famous Egyptologist gave him two new and difficult texts to study, and the self-taught scholar translated them. In 1869, at the age of twenty-three, he was appointed to teach Egyptian at the newly founded École des Hautes Études, and on the death of de Rougé Mariette procured for him the coveted chair at the Collège de France. Visiting Egypt in 1880 as head of a mission which later developed into the French Institute of Oriental Archæology, he remained till after the death of Mariette. His first task was to open a Sakkara pyramid, which provided thousands of religious texts. His most sensational find was that of royal tombs of the eighteenth to the twenty-first dynasties, and the mummies, heaped together in a pit, of Seti, Rameses II and III, and Thothmes, in the Valley of the Kings near Thebes in 1881. He superintended the removal of the Museum to Cairo and the publication of its catalogue. He first popularised Egyptology in France. The works of Champollion and de Rougé had been too abstruse, Mariette's reports too sketchy, to secure a wide circle of readers. Explorer, philologist and historian, his larger and smaller histories of the Peoples of the East first set the picture in its frame.

[1] See Ebers, *Aegyptische Studien*, 1900.

Till the death of Mariette the main work of Egyptology had been carried on by French and Germans, and it was now the turn of England to take a hand. The foundation of the Egyptian Exploration Fund in 1883 marks the beginning of organised effort. The chief agent in its early years was Flinders Petrie,[1] who first visited Egypt in 1880. Beginning with the Delta, he excavated Tanis, the Zoan of the Bible, and identified Naukratis by its early Greek inscriptions, which revealed three centuries of Greek settlement hitherto unsuspected. Shortly after a second Greek city, Daphne, was discovered. He then turned to the Fayum, working at Hawara, where he entered the pyramids and discovered a cemetery with treasures ranging from precious gems to children's dolls. In his eyes no find was too small to be of importance. He located Lake Moeris and the Labyrinth and explored Tel-el-Amarna, the short-lived city of the religious reformer Aknaton, father-in-law of Tutankamun, who deserted Thebes about 1380 to free himself from the power of the priests. In 1887 a peasant woman stumbled on some crumbling wooden chests with hundreds of clay tablets of the fourteenth century in Babylonian cuneiform containing correspondence of Egyptian rulers and vassals in Syria and Palestine, which, when edited by Winckler, opened a new world to historians of the early East. Some of the letters were bought by the British Museum. A great Hyksos camp was found in 1905 twenty miles north of Cairo. A lengthening row of illustrated monographs, including sites in every part of Egypt and extending to the Sinai peninsula, bears witness to his fruitful labours. As an excavator Petrie ranks with Mariette and Maspero, and his co-operative 'History of Egypt,' of which he wrote the first four volumes, was the first authoritative narrative in English.

America came late to Egyptology, but Breasted[2] is a host in himself. The lofty traditions of French scholarship were continued by Revillout and Amélineau, the former devoting himself to law, the latter to moral and religious ideas. Lumbroso based a detailed review of the political and economic life of the Ptolemaic era on the papyri and inscriptions. Ebers[3] edited the great medical treatise of the sixteenth century B.C. known as the Ebers papyrus which he found at Thebes, compiled popular illustrated

[1] His early discoveries were summarised in *Ten Years' Digging in Egypt*, 1892, and the whole story was told in his *Seventy Years in Archæology*, 1931.

[2] See C. Breasted, *Pioneer of the Past: the Story of J. H. Breasted*, 1947.

[3] See Ebers, *The Story of My Life*, 1893, and Eduard Meyer, *Kleine Schriften*, 1910.

descriptive works, and presented a series of scenes from Egyptian history in the 'Egyptian Princess' and other novels which made their way all over the world. Erman, the successor of Lepsius at Berlin, in addition to his great Egyptian Dictionary, painted scholarly and comprehensive pictures of Egyptian life and thought.

The main event of the last two decades has been the revelation of Egyptian origins.[1] When Maspero published his narrative in 1895 the story began with the pyramid-builders of the fourth dynasty. We have now recovered not only the early dynasties but neolithic and palæolithic Egypt. Strange pottery and flints had long been known, but it was not till the systematic examination of the primitive cemeteries between Abydos and Edfu by de Morgan that the existence of a stone age was recognised. Petrie, who had suggested their connection with Libyan invaders between the Old and Middle Empires, was converted, and has classified the phases of the prehistoric epochs by the pottery. The discovery of this primitive civilisation sets the history of Egypt in a new perspective. Equally recent is our knowledge of the first three dynasties. The invaders, probably of Semitic origin, were grouped round two centres in Upper and Lower Egypt, and the Kings of Hierakonpolis ultimately conquered the north and formed the first dynasty. Here again light shines from the tombs. To the labours of de Morgan and Amélineau, Petrie and Quibell at Abydos and Hierakonpolis we owe this new chapter of ancient history. The change of capital to Memphis, which was founded under the first dynasty, was made by the third, and the systematic exploration of the vast site was commenced by Petrie. The excavations of Nubian Meroe belong to the other end of Egyptian history. Though marvellous progress has been made, two great gaps remain. Darkness descends after the sixth dynasty, and the curtain only rises on the widely different world of the eleventh. In like manner the collapse of the Middle Empire leaves the stage in gloom, and though we know a little of the Hyksos our information is still of the scantiest. That their culture was low is clear; that they left behind them a memory of loathing we learn from Manetho. Yet no traces of destruction wrought by them have been discovered, and they employed hieroglyphics and worshipped Egyptian gods. That they came from Asia is agreed, but were they Bedouin Arabs or a race from Asia Minor related to the Hittites? The chronology of the Early and Middle Kingdoms remains uncertain, owing to these two

[1] Admirably summarised by King and Hall, *Egypt and Western Asia in the Light of Recent Discoveries*, 1907.

dark periods. Petrie, following the traditional computation, places the first dynasty about 4300, while Erman, Eduard Meyer and Breasted date it at about 3400. Maspero rejects both extremes.

II

The discovery of Mesopotamian civilisation was even more sensational.[1] While numerous remains of vanished greatness had always been visible in the valley of the Nile, Mesopotamia was remote and inaccessible, and adventurous visitors found nothing but a few mounds on the plain. Once again a vanished world has been recovered by the joint exertions of the philologist and the excavator. The first step was to decipher the inscriptions collected by travellers. The key of cuneiform lay in inscriptions of the Persian Kings at Persepolis and Susa which were available in the transcripts of Carsten Niebuhr. In 1802 Grotefend identified the three languages of the Persepolis inscriptions as Persian, Median and Babylonian, recovered the names of Darius Hystaspes and his son Xerxes, and identified some letters. A few more letters were identified by Burnouf and Lassen in 1836, but the decisive victory was won by Henry Rawlinson,[2] the Champollion of cuneiform. Travelling in Persia in 1835 he noticed two cuneiform inscriptions in Hamadan, and identified the names of Persian Kings. He now made acquaintance with the efforts of Grotefend, and declared that twenty-two of the thirty letters of his alphabet were wrong. In 1838 he published a translation of the first two paragraphs of the Persian inscription at Behistun. Burnouf then sent him his memoir on the Hamadan inscriptions, containing several differences in interpretation, and his researches on Zend, an early form of Persian though later than the inscriptions, which aided him in seizing the grammatical structure of the language. With Lassen Rawlinson began to correspond in 1838, and the two men found that they agreed in regard to almost every letter.

Appointed to Bagdad as Political Agent in 1844, Rawlinson at once set off for Behistun. The Rosetta stone contained a Greek key, but the inscription of Darius was in three scripts all equally unknown. Moreover while the Rosetta stone could be studied in comfort, the proclamation was cut on the side of a precipitous

[1] See Hilprecht, *Explorations in Bible Lands*, 1903; Budge, *The Rise and Progress of Assyriology*, 1925; Kenyon, *The Bible and Archæology*, 1940; and G. E. Daniel, *A Hundred Years of Archæology*, 1950. Brief summaries are given in Darmesteter, *Essais Orientaux*, and the histories of Hommel, Rogers and Eduard Meyer.

[2] See Canon Rawlinson, *Sir H. Rawlinson*, 1898.

rock 300 feet above the plain. The Persian cuneiform was current
in Persia, the Babylonian in Babylonia, while the Median was
found in more than one locality. With immense difficulty he
copied the Persian and the Median, but the Babylonian version
he was at first unable to reach. The Persian which his predecessors
had endeavoured to decipher was the easiest, and to this he
devoted his chief attention. Using as his key the letters of the
three names deciphered in the Hamadan inscriptions, Hystaspes,
Darius and Xeres, he essayed a translation of the whole inscription, which, with his dissertations, appeared in the *Journal of the
Royal Asiatic Society*. Oppert, the most authoritative of judges,
declared in 1895 that after Rawlinson it was only possible to
glean in the field of Persian cuneiform interpretation. He next
turned to the Babylonian script, which was far more difficult, for
there were several signs for the same letter and about 300 characters were in use. Moreover, while in the Persian script he had
predecessors, in Babylonian he had none. As Layard's treasures
floated down the Tigris to Bagdad he took copies of the inscriptions, and noticed that the script of the Assyrian tablets was
almost exactly the same as the Babylonian version at Behistun.
He therefore made a second journey in 1847, and, being himself
unable to reach the face of the rock, employed a Kurdish boy to
take a squeeze. Nearly half the inscription was decayed and
therefore conjectural, but he managed to extract its main secrets.
Returning to England in 1849, he published papers in the *Journal
of the Royal Asiatic Society* on the Babylonian and Assyrian
records. Ten years later a cylinder containing the annals of the
first Tiglath-Pileser in 800 lines was found and submitted to
Rawlinson, Oppert, Talbot and Hincks, whose translations were
virtually the same. The problem was now practically solved,
though even to-day there is uncertainty about certain characters.
Rawlinson never worked seriously at the Median version, but the
Persian and Babylonian capitulated at his summons. His later
life was largely spent at the British Museum, piecing together
and translating broken fragments of clay and stone; and with
the aid of George Smith and Pinches he edited the great collection
of 'Cuneiform Inscriptions of Western Asia' for the Trustees. In
1904 the Trustees of the British Museum sent two members of
their staff to make fresh squeezes of the Behistun inscription,
and a definitive edition appeared in 1907.

The placing of Assyriology on a scientific basis was above all
the achievement of Schrader and Friedrich Delitzsch. The former,
a pupil of Ewald, published in 1872 his 'Cuneiform Inscriptions
and the Old Testament,' the first careful discussion of the new

light thrown on the history of the Jews.[1] At the same time he began to lecture on Assyriology at Jena, whence he was shortly summoned to Berlin. Till now German scholars had been inclined to scoff at the new science, and Gutschmid[2] had expressed his scepticism before Schrader commenced to write. The Assyriologist aided Duncker with a new edition of his 'History of Antiquity,' and when the latter was challenged by Gutschmid hurried to his rescue. Gutschmid turned from Duncker and launched a violent attack on Schrader in his 'Assyriology in Germany.' Schrader, he declared, was an enthusiast who lacked rigorous philological schooling and was destitute of critical instinct. The critic was more learned and possessed a more powerful brain than the Berlin Professor, and his brilliant invective was like a cavalry charge. He succeeded in exposing some vulnerable conclusions, and the result of his onslaught was to teach greater caution; but the indictment was grossly exaggerated, and he shut his eyes to the growing volume of established fact. Schrader replied in his greatest work, 'Cuneiform Inscriptions and Historical Research.' Though a poor controversialist, his book carried conviction by its solid learning, and the world of scholarship no longer doubted that the foundations of Assyriology were well and truly laid. Long before his death the exact philological methods of Delitzsch, his greatest pupil, placed the study beyond the reach of further attack.

During the years in which Burnouf, Lassen and Rawlinson were deciphering cuneiform, the excavation of the remains of Mesopotamian civilisation was inaugurated. When Botta arrived at Mosul in 1842 as French Consul, he was instructed by the French Government to excavate Khorsabad, and was rewarded by the discovery of the Palace of Sargon, the conqueror of Samaria. Many of the remains were dispatched to Paris, where they formed the first Assyrian Museum. The revelation of a rich and powerful civilisation excited world-wide interest, and the gigantic winged bulls aroused popular enthusiasm. Where Botta led the way, Layard[3] followed. While travelling in Mesopotamia in 1840 he cast longing glances at the mounds, and in 1845 he led an expedition to Nimrud, near Mosul, where he unearthed the palaces of great Assyrian rulers and the magnificent monuments now in the British Museum. He then turned to Koujunik, the ancient Nineveh, where he unearthed the Palace of Sennacherib,

---

[1] See Eduard Meyer's masterly sketch, *Kleine Schriften*, 1910.

[2] See Rühl's sketch in Gutschmid, *Kleine Schriften*, vol. v., 1894.

[3] In addition to his descriptive writings, see his *Autobiography and Letters*, 2 vols., 1903.

the wall sculptures of which revealed the civilisation of Western
Asia—dress and customs, hunting scenes and boats, the career
and government of the King. The royal library contained tablets
on astronomy and astrology, records and chronological lists,
hymns and incantations, reports on administration and State
affairs. Among these treasures none equalled in interest that
which narrated the Assyrian story of the Deluge, deciphered by
George Smith in 1872.

The startling discoveries in Assyria were quickly followed by
an attack on the older and more southerly civilisation of Babylon.
Layard scratched the mound at Nippur near Bagdad. Rawlinson
explored Birs Nimrud, long regarded as the Tower of Babel.
Loftus laboured at Warka, Taylor at Ur, and Oppert led a
French mission to Babil. But marble and stone were rare, and
the lack of imposing remains damped the ardour of the West.
Moreover the country was inhabited by lawless and ignorant
tribes and was often under water. On the other hand it gradually
became clear from the Nineveh tablets that most of the literary
treasures of Assyria were merely copies of Babylonian originals,
and when the world again turned its attention to Babylonia,
sensational discoveries awaited it. Methodical excavation was
begun by de Sarzec, French Consul at Basra, in 1877.[1] Resolving
to explore South Babylonia, or Chaldæa, he selected Tello, the
ancient Lagash, and worked at it till his death more than twenty
years later. The finds were examined and described by Heuzey,
Curator of Oriental Antiquities at the Louvre. Since Botta and
Layard had revealed the wonders of Assyria, no Asiatic discoveries approached in importance those at Tello. Texts had been
found in the Nineveh library which Rawlinson pronounced to be
pre-Semitic, and Loftus and Taylor had stumbled on similar
inscriptions further south; but for the purpose of history the
Sumerians were discovered at Tello, where thousands of tablets
were found, mostly accounts. The excavations of the American
Pumpelly expedition at Anau in Russian Turkestan suggests
a possible origin of the race which possessed a complicated
language, a system of irrigation, and a highly developed art.
A magnificent collection of diorite statues suggests the glories
of the reign of Gudea, King of Lagash, about 2600 B.C. The
inscriptions told of trade with Arabia, the Sinai peninsula and
the Mediterranean. When de Sarzec died in 1901 he had written
a new chapter of history. The palaces of the Assyrian rulers

---

[1] The explorations at Tello are described by Hilprecht. Later excavations are summarised in King and Hall, *Egypt and Western Asia in the
Light of Recent Discoveries*, 1907.

Sargon and Sennacherib, at which Europe had marvelled in the middle of the century, appeared relatively modern beside the vast antiquity of Tello. The chain of human experience lengthened when it was realised that a large part of Babylonian culture, including the art of writing, was inherited by the Semites from the Sumerians.

While de Sarzec was busy at Tello, an American expedition was sent to Nippur fifty miles south of Babylon in 1886 under the lead of Peters and Hilprecht. Nowhere had so many inscriptions been recovered, thousands of tablets having formed part of the temple library. The long array of magnificent volumes in which the results are recorded constitutes the most important addition to our knowledge of Northern Babylonia. The most interesting find was a Sumerian version of the Flood, centuries older than the Assyrian and the Jewish narratives. Still more recently the Deutsche Orientgesellschaft, founded in 1898, excavated the disappointing site of Babylon, the ancient glories of which have been tentatively reconstructed in Koldewey's plans. Though no monuments have been brought to light in stoneless Babylonia so impressive as those discovered by Botta and Layard in Assyria, the evidences of culture are far more numerous and important. Since the cylinder of the Flood no find aroused such world-wide interest as that of the code of Hammurabi, discovered by Jacques de Morgan[1] at Susa in 1901 and translated by Scheil. The block of diorite, eight feet high, containing 282 paragraphs of laws as elaborate as those of Moses, revealed in a flash a complex and refined civilisation. After expelling the Elamites, Hammurabi, the greatest ruler of the First Dynasty of Babylon, united the North and the South into a single State and, desiring to enforce uniform laws, issued the code which bears his name. Beneath the relics of Persian, Parthian and Arab rule de Morgan also found a mass of inscriptions which reveal the early history of Elam, hitherto vaguely known from Babylonian and Assyrian records. The spoils of Susa fill two halls of the Louvre. During the last decade the exploration of Assyria has been resumed. The unexhausted site of Nineveh has been once more attacked, and Andrae's examination of Shergat on the Tigris, between Mosul and Bagdad, revealed the city of Assur, the first Assyrian capital, which has been systematically investigated by the German

---

[1] In addition to his great series of reports, see his brief summary, *Histoire et Travaux de la Délégation en Perse*, 1905. Visiting Susa in Southern Persia in 1891, where he found four large mounds, de Morgan persuaded the French Government to purchase from the Shah the monopoly of excavation in Persia. The work began in 1897 in Susa and elsewhere.

Oriental Society. We thus learn of Assyria before the days of its greatness, when it was still a province under Babylonian viceroys. Preliminary attempts have been made to uncover the secrets of Ur.

While Duncker provided the first comprehensive account of the ancient East in his 'History of Antiquity,' the English equivalent was supplied by George Rawlinson, who received help from his famous brother and George Smith. 'The Five Great Monarchies of the Ancient Eastern World' dealt with the geography and history, religion and customs, arts and sciences of Chaldæa, Assyria, Babylonia, Media and Persia, and was followed by volumes on Parthia, the Sassanid or New Persian Empire, and Phœnicia. Like Duncker he was ignorant of Oriental languages, but his survey was a scholarly performance. He devoted more attention to culture, and the illustrations formed a novel and welcome feature. Maspero's short 'History of the Ancient Peoples of the East' first appeared in 1875, and twenty years later he covered the ground in far more detail in three sumptuous volumes. While he only writes with first-hand authority on Egypt, the work is a careful survey of the fortunes of the early empires. Finally Eduard Meyer, in his great 'History of Antiquity,' described with the hand of a master the earliest civilisations of Babylonia. First published in 1884, the second edition, appearing in 1909, was less a revision than a new work—so great was the mass of material that had come to light in the interval. The discoveries of the last two decades have been utilised in Winckler's contribution to Helmolt's 'History of Mankind' and in King's admirable history of Babylonian civilisation.

We are now able to reconstruct tentatively and in outline the features of the lands watered by the Tigris and the Euphrates. Eduard Meyer's conviction that the Semites occupied the country before the Sumerians is not generally shared, but it is not yet possible to determine when the rival races entered the region which bears the stamp of both. The country appears to have been long divided among city-states—Kish, Lagash, Ur and others—whose fortunes and relations to one another were constantly changing. In the third millennium Sargon bulks largely not only as the ruler of Accad and Sumer but as the founder of an empire stretching to the Mediterranean. His edifice was overthrown by the Elamites, but when the wave receded, the city of Babylon became the centre of a brilliant and powerful Empire. Of the dynasties which succeeded one another we know most of the first, about 2000, of which Hammurabi was the greatest figure. The great mass of official correspondence, judicial decisions

and legal documents, in addition to his elaborate Code, reveal
a startingly modern civilisation. Of the history of Assyria, which
gradually rose from vassalage to independence, the early chapters
are as meagre as the later are detailed. If Winckler's verdict,
'a military robber-state,' be too severe, it was at any rate far less
cultured than the venerable empire which it ultimately overthrew.
It has been maintained that Babylonia was to the ancient East
what Rome has been to Europe. In law and science, religion and
art, its influence was incalculable. The revelation of the debt of
the Jews aroused not only interest but in some camps consternation. The legend of the Flood was only the first of the many
borrowings which the inscriptions have revealed, and though the
measure of obligation is differently assessed no scholar denies
the immense influence of the older on the younger religion.

III

Among the most recent sensational episodes in the revelation
of the Ancient East is the discovery of an advanced civilisation
in Crete in the second and third millennia before Christ. In Egypt
and Babylonia the frontiers of knowledge were pushed further
back; in Crete, as in Mycenæ, an unknown world was brought to
light. Its romantic interest was enhanced by the establishment
of an ancient foundation for one of the most famous legends
of the ancient world. How the Minotaur, half man half bull,
devoured the septennial tribute of youths and maidens from
Athens in the labyrinth, how Theseus joined the victims, how
Ariadne, daughter of Minos, falling in love with him, gave him
a sword to slay the Minotaur and a thread to retrace his steps,
was known to every Greek child and has thrilled the imaginations
of the centuries. The exploration of the city called by Homer
'Great Knossos' was among the ambitions of Schliemann, but
the task had to wait for the expulsion of the Turks and the
appearance of a wealthy Englishman.[1] Noting seals at Athens
with an unknown script, Arthur Evans purchased part of the site
of Knossos in 1895 and the rest in 1900. He was equipped for his
task by encyclopædic knowledge of the history and geography
of the Mediterranean lands. In his first season he unearthed a
pre-Mycenæan palace, vastly larger than those of Tiryns and

[1] The biography of Sir Arthur Evans has been admirably written by
his half-sister Joan Evans. The full story is told in *The Palace of Minos*,
1921–35, by the discoverer himself. R. M. Burrows, *The Discoveries in
Crete*, 1907; George Glasgow, *The Minoans*, 1923; and Pendlebury, *The
Archæology of Crete*, 1939, are useful summaries.

Mycenæ, adorned with frescoes denoting a high stage of civilisation. The elaborate low-necked garments of the ladies were scarcely distinguishable from evening dress, and provoked a French savant to exclaim, '*Mais ce sont Parisiennes.*' A gaming board of superb design confirmed the impression that the culture was far richer than that of Mycenæ. The frescoes of bull-grappling —catching the horns of the charging animal and vaulting over it—and other evidences showed the prominent place in the life and thought of the people occupied by the bull. The ramifications of the lower parts of the palace were so extensive as to suggest that the labyrinth was within, not without the building. The nine weeks' work in 1900 opened up new vistas of incalculable importance for the early history of the eastern Mediterranean, and the explorations of the following years fulfilled the promise of the dawn. Though the palace was pillaged and burned about the year 1400 B.C., enough is left both of the structure and its contents to reconstruct the life of the Minoan capital. The lack of defensive preparations and of warlike themes and frescoes shows that it felt secure from attack, in eloquent contrast to the massive walls of Tiryns and Mycenæ and the military emblems of Egypt and Assyria.

The pioneering work at Knossos inspired research in other parts of the island. Italian scholars explored Phæstos, which boasts a fine palace, and Hagia Triada, a country edifice close by. Harriet Boyd discovered a town at Gournia, and the British School at Athens brought to light another at Palaiokastro. Though the inscriptions remain unintelligible it is now possible to outline the early history of Crete, with pottery as our chief guide. Archaic fragments suggest the existence of settlements earlier than the Minoan civilisation, which may be divided into the Early, Middle and Late epochs, each containing three divisions. The palace at Knossos was begun in the third period of Middle Minoan and finished during the first two divisions of Late Minoan. Its destruction followed swiftly on its completion. The simultaneous annihilation of Phæstos and Hagia Triada shows that the whole of Minoan culture was overwhelmed in a common ruin about 1200 B.C., perhaps by the Mycenæans, themselves driven forth by the Achæans. For a time artistic production continued, but darkness descends with the coming of the Dorians. That intercourse with Egypt was common during the Old and Middle Kingdoms is proved by an ever-increasing mass of evidence in both countries; but as Egyptian chronology only becomes certain with the eighteenth dynasty, the exact limits of the earlier stages of Minoan civilisation cannot be established. Sir Arthur Evans sides with the scholars who shorten Egyptian history, and dates Early Minoan about 3400. In any case the Cretan excavations reveal the history of at least two thousand years. Minoan civilisation was one of the sources of Greek culture, and among its contributions was the alphabet, the signs of which were merely simplified by the Phœnicians. If we are to seek for the pioneers of European civilisation, they may well be found in the first lords of the sea, the rulers of Minoan Crete.

The latest civilisation to be revealed is that of the Hittites.[1] Eighteenth and early nineteenth century travellers reported monuments in Asia Minor which they could not identify and inscriptions they could not read. The references in the Old Testament suggest a good deal of intercourse in the earliest days of Israel, but more illumination has come from Egypt. We possess the Egyptian copy of a treaty between Rameses II and the King of the Kheta, the first recorded treaty in history, and they are mentioned in the Tell-el-Amarna letters. Assyrian records speak of the Khatti as a powerful people in Northern Syria about 1100 B.C. and at intervals till 717 when Sargon II relates that he put an end to their independence. A little additional evidence comes from the Van inscriptions in Armenia, which have been partially deciphered. From these sources it became clear that the Hittites were an important power in Northern Syria and Eastern Asia Minor for over a thousand years before they were swallowed up by Assyria, that they were at first military and aggressive, later commercial and wealthy, and that they had close political and commercial relations with neighbouring peoples. This evidence has been largely supplemented during recent years by a study of the sites. The sculptures seen by George Smith at Jerablus on the Euphrates, supposed to be Carchemish, led to excavations by the British Museum, and the inscriptions were pronounced to be Hittite. A study of the rock monuments at Boghaz Keui and other rock sculptures in different parts of Asia Minor led Sayce to declare in 1880 that a great Hittite Empire, worthy to rank with Egypt and Assyria, had extended from the Taurus to the Ægean. In 1884 Wright, a British missionary, published his 'Empire of the Hittites,' the earliest work on the subject, which discussed the evidence of the Old Testament, Egypt and Assyria. Sayce made the first attempt to decipher the inscriptions, but Messerschmidt, the editor of the Hittite

---

[1] Eduard Meyer, *Reich u. Kultur der Chetiter*, 1914, gives an excellent brief survey. Cowley, *The Hittites*, 1920, and Hogarth, *Kings of the Hittites*, 1926, are useful Schweich Lectures. All previous treatises were superseded by Garstang, *The Land of the Hittites*, 1929.

Corpus, declared at the turn of the century that only one sign of the two hundred hieroglyphics which were known could be interpreted with certainty. The boldest attempt was made by the Hungarian Hrozny.

Though the language remains unread, exploration and excavation have made rapid progress. The most important work has been done at Boghaz Keui in North Cappadocia, the systematic exploration of which was begun in 1906 by a joint expedition of the Berlin Archæological and the Nearer Asia Societies under the guidance of Winckler. The 20,000 clay tablets of the fourteenth century—the most sensational discovery of ' written records since the Tell-el-Amarna letters—in Hittite and Babylonian cuneiform found in the ruins of the palace should ultimately supply the key to many problems. Of considerable importance is Sakje-Geuzi, in North Syria, recently excavated by Garstang. In 1911 the British Museum began the excavation of Carchemish, the capital of the North Syrian section of the Empire. Sinjerli and Tell-Halaf have been examined by a German expedition. All these North Syrian sites exhibit a powerful Assyrian influence. The pictures of Kheta warriors in Egypt closely resemble those of the Hittite sculptures. The history has been tentatively sketched by Garstang, whose theory of two periods of Hittite power, the former with its centre at Boghaz Keui, the latter at Carchemish, has been generally accepted.

Till recently excavations in Asia Minor were mainly confined to Hellenistic and Greco-Roman sites, and Troy was too remote to throw much light on the general history of the peninsula. In these circumstances it was natural to suppose that Greece owed to the Phœnicians the major part of what they learned from the East. But the fame of the men of Tyre and Sidon has been sadly dimmed since the days of Movers. Arthur Evans showed that the Cretan script was independent of and indeed earlier than Phœnician, and every addition to the remains of Phœnician art has confirmed the impression of its mediocrity. Nobody now shares Perrot's belief that Cyprus was a mere artistic dependency of Phœnicia. We possess no Phœnician monument or coin before the ninth century and no writing till later, though the Old Testament and Homer show that they possessed civilisation earlier. Their commercial activity is not in doubt, but they were not the only nor the principal purveyors of the culture of the East. The discovery of a Hittite Empire brings meaning and order into the history of Asia Minor, and explains the permeation of Oriental influences.[1] Out of its ruins arose the power of Phrygia and

[1] See Hogarth's admirable lectures, *Ionia and the East*, 1909.

Lydia. The former vividly impressed the Greek imagination and has left imposing remains; the latter was the last link between Greece and the East. The excavation of Sardes was commenced by Americans in 1910. Hogarth's exploration of the deeper strata of the shrine of Artemis at Ephesus, which Wood left untouched, has revealed a wealth of Oriental influence. While the culture of the East reached Greece to some extent through the Minoans and the Phœnicians, there can be little doubt that the main pathway was by land, not by sea, and that the route ran through the wide dominions of the Hittite empire.

Few parts of the world have guarded their secrets so jealously as Arabia, perhaps the cradle of the Semitic race. The interior is still unvisited, nature and man combining to warn off intruders at peril of their lives, but Carsten Niebuhr and Burckhardt, Burton and Palgrave, Doughty and Bent, lifted corners of the veil. It was not till the last three decades of the nineteenth century that Halévy and Glaser revealed the outlines of early Arabian civilisation in the south.[1] In the course of several journeys they explored the country round Sana, and collected hundreds of inscriptions which have been published in the Corpus of Semitic Inscriptions. Glaser's 'History and Geography of Arabia before Mohammed,' laid the foundation on which subsequent scholars have built. The fragmentary knowledge derived from the references of Jewish and classical writers was slightly enlarged from Assyrian sources, but it was the Arabian inscriptions which revealed a great civilisation for a thousand years before Christ. Most of them are votive, and the few that are historical are undated, yet it is possible to register a few results. Four civilised kingdoms can be traced, two of which, the Sabæan and the Minæan, are known in some detail. In the former, the Sheba of the Old Testament, the inscriptions go back to about 800, indicate the periods, rulers and capitals, and reveal their mythology and religion. The Minæan Kingdom is less known.

The rise of Islam was not seriously investigated till the middle of the nineteenth century. The first step was taken by Weil, a German Jew who learned Arabic under de Sacy. On the basis of the earliest sources available in Europe he compiled a life of the prophet, and his more important 'History of the Khalifs' was a conscientious paraphrase of the Arab historians, printed and unprinted. The second step was taken by Sprenger, whose massive volumes are still of use. The sketch of religious movements in Arabia before Mohammed and the exhaustive analysis

[1] See Otto Weber, *Glaser's Forschungsreisen in Südarabien*, 1909, and Hogarth, *The Penetration of Arabia*, 1904.

of the Koran, to the comprehension of which he boasted that he had supplied the key, were among the striking features of the book. For the founder himself he had little admiration, castigating his sensuality, pronouncing him weak and hysterical, and denying him genius. His low opinion was shared by Muir, whose larger and smaller biographies gave the English-speaking world the first trustworthy account of the rise of Islam based on first-hand acquaintance with the sources. Precious contributions to the history and background of early Muhammedanism have been made by De Goeje's monumental edition of Tabari, Prince Caetani's 'Annali dell' Islam,' Wellhausen's studies of pre-Islamic Arabia, and the researches on the Koran by Nöldeke and Goldziher. The 'Encyclopædia of Islam,' with contributions by Sir Thomas Arnold and other leading Arabists, began to appear at Leiden in 1908.

The first important step in the recovery of ancient Persia[1] was taken in 1754 when Anquetil Du Perron, at the age of twenty, set forth for India to obtain the sacred books of Zoroastrianism. Enlisting as a private under the French East India Company he reached Surat, the goal of his journey, after four years of war and illness. He spent three years among the Parsis, learning Zend and Pehlvi, and studying their religious practices. In 1762 he returned to Paris with his manuscripts, and in 1771 appeared his translation of the Zend Avesta with an account of the customs and rites of the Parsis. The work was denounced in some quarters as a modern forgery, in others as a fantastic absurdity, and the significance of one of the most heroic feats in the history of scholarship was rarely recognised. The discovery appeared to remain sterile till the second founder of Zend studies appeared. Burnouf was above all a Sanskritist, but his researches into the languages and civilisation of India led him to study Zend, which he took to be the language of ancient Persia. He quickly found that Anquetil's translation was of little assistance, since he had learned from men who fully understood neither Zend nor Pehlvi, into which the sacred books had been translated in the Middle Ages. It was Burnouf's achievement to render himself independent of the degenerate scholarship of the modern Parsis by means of a Sanskrit translation of one of the sacred books. His 'Commentary on the Yasna' established the real character both of the language and religion of ancient Persia. Believing that the language of the Persian Kings could not differ materially from that of the sacred books, he turned his attention to the

[1] See Darmesteter, ' L'Orientalisme en France, ' ch. i. *Essais Orientaux*, 1883.

cuneiform inscriptions of Persepolis and carried their interpretation far beyond the point at which Grotefend had left it. After
his death Persian studies were pursued rather by German than
French scholars, but it was on Burnouf's foundations that
Gutschmid and Nöldeke built their reconstruction of Persian
history.

The study of ancient India[1] was rendered possible by the
linguistic researches of Sir William Jones, Colebrooke and Bopp.
In studying Sanskrit Jones was quickly struck by its resemblance
to Latin and Greek. During his residence in India as a judge
he founded the Bengal Asiatic Society, translated specimens of
Sanskrit literature, and wrote on many aspects of ancient India.
Though his scholarship was not profound, his enthusiasm aroused
widespread interest. His work was continued by Colebrooke,
the first great Sanskrit scholar of Europe, who spent most of his
life as an Indian judge. Learning Sanskrit in order to read the
Hindu lawbooks, he published an essay on the Vedas in 1805
which gave the first authentic account of them, and compiled a
Sanskrit grammar. His exact translations and analyses came as a
wholesome corrective to the fantastic speculations of amateurs.
If the first step towards the revelation of ancient India was taken
by English scholars, the second was due to Germans. In his
brilliant essay on the 'Language and Wisdom of the Indians'
Friedrich Schlegel showed the close connection of Sanskrit with
other tongues, and it was the work of Bopp to prove it in detail.
In reading the Mahabharata and Ulfilas he was amazed at the
close resemblance of Sanskrit to Gothic. He planned a comparative grammar of 'Sanskrit and its daughters,' and in 1816 published his 'System of Conjugation' which established the relations
of Sanskrit with Latin, Greek and Persian. He followed up his
success by a Sanskrit grammar and devoted his later years to his
greatest work, the 'Comparative Grammar.' His unwearying
labours brought the Indo-European languages into relation with
one another, and a searchlight was thrown upon vast spaces of
unrecorded experience.

Sanskrit once thoroughly understood, it was not long before
attempts were made to reconstruct the civilisation of ancient
India. The first comprehensive survey was undertaken by
Lassen,[2] a Norwegian trained at Bonn, who published his

---

[1] See Benfey, *Geschichte der orientalischen Philologie*, 1869; Darmesteter,
'L'Orientalisme en France,' ch. ii.; Max Müller's essay on Colebrooke, in
Chips from a German Workshop, vol. ii.; Lefmann, *Franz Bopp*, 2 vols.,
1891–7.

[2] See *Allg. Deutsche Biog.*

encyclopædic survey between 1847 and 1862. His work deals with geography and natural conditions, history to the foundation of the European settlements, literature and art, religion and customs. Though the field was too vast for every part to be authoritative, Lassen's massive volumes gave an immense impetus to study. In the reconstruction of ancient India no chapter is more important than that of the discovery of Buddhist scriptures by Brian Hodgson, who, on arriving as Assistant Resident in Nepal in 1821, persuaded a pundit to procure copies of the chief manuscripts in the monasteries.[1] His conclusions were not always correct, but his fame as the founder of the study of Buddhism is secure. He divided his treasures among six libraries, giving each enough for a comprehensive study of Buddhism. One of the largest shares fell to Paris, where they attracted the attention of Burnouf, and it was on them that he based his epoch-making 'Introduction to the Study of Indian Buddhism.' The investigation of the most attractive of Asiatic religions has been eagerly pursued. The attempt of Sénart and a few other scholars to challenge the existence of Buddha has failed, and the assured results of half a century of research were summarised by Oldenberg. Max Müller's collection of Sacred Books of the East enabled English students to judge for themselves how much Asia could teach us in the religious sphere. The superbly illustrated 'Histoire de l'Art dans l'Antiquité,' by Perrot and Chipiez, though partly out of date owing to the rapid advance of archæology, retains its value for the whole expanse of the Ancient East. The first encyclopædic survey of the Far East was undertaken in the twelve volumes of Captain Brinkley's 'Japan and China,' published 1903–4.

[1] See Sir William Hunter, *Life of Brian Hodgson*, 1896.

CHAPTER XXIII

GREECE AND BYZANTIUM

I

OWING to the early death of Otfried Müller the task of gathering up the sheaves fell to two younger men. Duncker's[1] 'History of Antiquity' played a useful part in popularising a knowledge of the ancient world. The third and fourth volumes were devoted to Greece, but the narrative only reached the Persian wars. At the end of his life he returned to the classical world, rewrote the work, which had not been revised since 1860, and added two volumes continuing the story to the death of Pericles. It was rather his political insight than his scholarship that gave the Greek volumes their importance. For Duncker the paramount necessity for a State is the power to defend itself against attack. His hero is Themistocles, 'the founder of Attic power, the most far-seeing and powerful of all Greeks.' While recognising the personal eminence of Pericles, he denies his military capacity and censures his policy. He made Athens free and brilliant, but did not give her the power to defend her treasures.

The political approach was widely different from that of Ernst Curtius,[2] who was won for classical studies by the lectures and friendship of Otfried Müller. 'To hear him,' wrote the young Göttingen student to his father, 'is an invaluable privilege; he is an incomparable teacher. The clearness of his thought, the lively grace of his lectures, the fullness of his knowledge fascinate me afresh every day and evoke new enthusiasm for the science which he has revivified.' Accompanying Brandis and his family to Athens as tutor in 1836 he acted as guide when his beloved master paid his fatal visit in 1840. Curtius was with him to the last, and dedicated his life to the enterprise which had been the main object of the journey. On Müller's death he returned to Germany, and in 1844 sprung into notice by a lecture on the Acropolis delivered before a distinguished audience in Berlin. The brilliant young scholar became the tutor of the Crown Prince Frederick

---

[1] See Haym, *Das Leben Max Dunckers*, 1891.
[2] See *Ernst Curtius, Ein Lebensbild in Briefen*, 1903; H. Gelzer, 'Wanderungen u. Gespräche mit Ernst Curtius,' in *Ausgewählte Kleine Schriften*, 1907; Freeman, *Historical Essays*, Second Series, 1873.

and a lecturer at Berlin. His first important work was an historical geography of the Peloponnesus, resting on an intimate acquaintance with the country and a thorough study of the literary and monumental sources. In receiving Curtius into the Prussian Academy in 1853 the veteran Böckh gave warm expression to his admiration. 'I have spent my life testing and sifting details, the necessary foundation of further research. But you have seen the land itself, the frame of the picture.' The address reads like a *Nunc Dimittis*, and the younger scholar may well have felt it a summons to exhibit Greek civilisation as the unity which floated before the master's vision.

In 1856 Curtius was appointed to the Chair of Otfried Müller at Göttingen, and in the following year began the publication of his 'History of Greece.' Written for the same series as Mommsen's 'Rome,' the work was designed as a summary of existing knowledge for the cultured public. 'It is a book,' he wrote to his pupil the Crown Prince, 'not for scholars but for all who care for history, a book to be read, without notes or fragments of Greek or Latin.' For such an undertaking he possessed rare qualifications. He was an enthusiastic admirer of Greek civilisation, which he saw through the eyes of Winckelmann, Goethe and Hölderlin. He combined the idealism of the romantics with the exact scholarship of the critical school. Above all he was thoroughly acquainted with the land itself and the remains of its ancient glories. On the other hand he had shown little interest in the political side of Greek history. These qualities were to assert themselves in the History, to earn its fame and to limit its authority. He begins with a comprehensive survey of the country, and his recognition of the part played by nature set an example to future historians. 'I have read your first volume line by line,' wrote the aged Alexander von Humboldt; 'your survey of the country is a masterpiece of nature painting.' Curtius points out that the position of the peninsula on the frontier between Europe and Asia facilitated the intercourse which proved so fruitful for its development. Like Duncker he rejects Grote's hostile view of the Tyrants, and equally refuses to share his admiration for Cleisthenes. It is in the description of culture and civilisation at different epochs that he excels. The chapter on 'The Unity of Greece' passes in review the bonds which held together the scattered members of the Greek world—the games and the oracles, literature and art. The pictures of sacred places, such as Delphi and Olympia, reveal the intimate touch of personal knowledge. Himself deeply religious, he took Greek religion more seriously than most historians. The account of the Persian wars is mediocre, but the chapter on 'The Years of Peace' is one of the gems of the book. In no other history is the glamour of the age of Pericles more vividly realised. To Grote Greece meant democracy, to Curtius she stood for culture. Athenian civilisation was an imperishable possession of humanity, the spring-time of the spirit. He rejects the view that the Macedonians were barbarians, maintaining that Philip had learnt to value Hellenic culture; yet he places Demosthenes beside Pericles, though his task was beyond human power. The uprising under his inspired leadership was the last great deed of free Greece, and the narrative ends with Chæronea.

The weakness of the work lies in the treatment of action. Bernays remarked that he was more successful with *res* than with *res gestae*. It was a temperamental disqualification for whioh no perfection of scholarship could atone. His poetical nature never cared much for institutions, war and party faction. In his pictures of culture he surpasses Thirlwall, Grote and Duncker as much as he falls behind them in his handling of political problems. Though it was mainly the representation of culture that won fame for the book, even this part of the work has not escaped criticism. He himself had been among the first to visit the enchanted land, and the brightness of the vision never faded. Greece stands out in his pages rather as an exquisite jewel than as a link in the chain of history. Wilamowitz has spoken of its soft, elegiac tone, of the gentle mourning for lost beauty, of the mood which ruined cities awake. His style is fluent and polished, and the entire work sugggests grace, not strength. Bunsen aptly described it as a civilising book. It was of real service in providing Germany with the first detailed survey of Greek history based on a complete knowledge of recent research, but it was not a work which, like that of Mommsen, warned competitors off the course.

The later years of his life were in part devoted to archæological research. His friendship with the Crown Prince enabled him to secure substantial help for the complete excavation of Olympia, which had been demanded by Winckelmann and begun by the French expedition of 1829. The work was commenced in 1875 and yielded a rich harvest, including the Hermes of Praxiteles. His last important composition was an historical survey of Athens, tracing the fortunes of the city throughout the ages. He was not only a scholar but a missionary. His gospel was the glory and beauty of Greece, and his popular essays and addresses, collected into volumes, carried the message into the widest circles. The immense sale of his History was a compensation for the cold

looks of the specialists. 'The good German savant,' he wrote
sarcastically in 1881, 'shrugs his shoulders when a book is readable and when there are no beads of perspiration on the author's
brow.' He was profoundly convinced that a knowledge of Greek
civilisation was not only an indispensable part of culture but an
aid to the development of character. Greece alone taught the
lesson of harmonious self-realisation. He never quite forgave
Gelzer for plunging into the Byzantine Empire. No historian
brought more single-minded devotion to his task than this
scholar, the High Priest of Hellenism in its most spiritual form.

After Thirlwall and Grote, Duncker and Curtius, it might
seem as if there was only room for monographs, but during the
last quarter of the century the discoveries of Schliemann[1] revolutionised the treatment of early Greek history. At seven he saw
a picture of the burning of Troy and longed to visit the site,
declaring that the fortifications could not have wholly vanished.
At ten he wrote a Latin essay on the Trojan war. His father's
poverty compelled him to earn at fourteen, and it was not till
the age of thirty-four that he began to learn Greek. At forty-one
he was a rich man and retired from business. In 1870 he began
the excavations of Hissarlik, the site of Troy, and in 1874 published his 'Trojan Antiquities.' The learned world laughed at his
naïve identifications of the objects and buildings described in the
Iliad, which he treated as a factual record, and he confused the
different strata superimposed upon one another. His discoveries
aroused world-wide interest, while his shortcomings were only
known to scholars. Hindered in his work at Troy by the Turkish
Government he transferred his attention to Mycenæ, where he
discovered the graves of the kings filled with gold and other
ornaments. In a telegram to the King of the Hellenes he announced
that he had found Agamemnon and his household, but more
careful study revealed the fact that the treasures did not belong
to a single period and that the number and sex of the persons did
not agree with the legend. It was, however, of minor importance
whether the body of Agamemnon or of other kings had been
found, for he had revealed a vanished civilisation. He next discovered at Orchomenos the so-called Treasury of Minyas, and
laid bare the fortress-city of Tiryns, the neighbour of Mycenæ.

When Schliemann died in 1890 he had filled the world with
his fame. In twenty years he had unearthed three cities, revealed
Mycenæan civilisation, and given an incalculable impetus to
archæological research. He was filled with a romantic attachment

---

[1] See Schuchhardt, *Schliemann's Excavations*, 1891, and Emil Ludwig,
Schliemann of Troy, 1931.

to Greece. Marrying a Greek lady, he called his son Agamemnon and his daughter Andromache. But he possessed neither the training nor the patience required for the task of scientific excavation. He held the Mycenæans to be Homer's Achæans. It was left to others to point out that the civilisation of Mycenæ was pre-Homeric, and to Dörpfeld, the colleague of his later years, to prove that the city of Hector and Achilles was the sixth, not the second. Schliemann was a pioneer, a *conquistador*,[1] a dilettante of genius. If he revealed the romantic possibilities of excavation, his errors emphasised the need of *expertise*.

The discoveries of Schliemann provided the most precious new material for Greek history, but only second in importance was the Aristotelian treatise on the Constitution of Athens, published in Kenyon in 1891. The growing mass of inscriptions and papyri, the exploration of sites, the recovery of innumerable objects of art, and the reconstruction of the civilisations of the ancient East encouraged fresh attempts at a history of Greece.[2] The massive work of Busolt, which began to appear in 1885, aimed less at a detailed narrative than at an exhaustive review of the sources and of modern scholarship. The second edition was described by the author as a new work, for the discovery of the *Politeia* rendered mere revision inadequate. His volumes present a minute survey of the materials for a knowledge of Mycenæan civilisation, and show the world of Homer to be later and simpler. The foundation of the historical states, the rise and decline of the Athenian Empire are discussed with cautious scholarship. 'My history,' he frankly declares, 'is written rather for learning than for reading, and it makes no pretence to compare in attractiveness with Curtius or Duncker.' More than half the book consists of notes.

Very different is the well-known history of Holm,[3] who, like Curtius, wrote for the cultured public. His wish, he declared, was to summarise results and to separate fact from hypothesis. 'The Greeks did not always hit on the best or nearly the best course of action, but they were an exceptionally high type of humanity, the great seekers after perfection.' He holds the balance evenly between Sparta and Athens. He brushes aside Curtius' exaggeration of the influence of Delphi, contending that the Oracle manifested little originality or foresight, and merely sanctioned what

[1] Salomon Reinach's phrase.
[2] Recent studies are summarised in Bauer, *Die Forschungen zur Griechischen Geschichte*, 1899, and Kroll, *Die Altertumswissenschaft im letzten Vierteljahrhundert*, 1905.
[3] See *Biographisches Jahrbuch für die Altertumswissenschaft* for 1901.

had been already decided. He pays homage to the genius of Themistocles, and denies that he was a traitor. His keen admiration of Pericles as a great statesman, the equal and successor of Solon, does not blind him to his lack of military talent. On reaching the fourth century he contests the decay of the Athenians, but he pronounces the Macedonians to be Greeks in the wider sense of the word. 'Chæronea was not less glorious for the conquered than for the conquerors.' The success of Demosthenes, he declares, would have continued the old exploitation of Greece by Persia and the civil wars of the States. Alexander was a genuine Greek in whose achievement the good vastly outweighs the evil. The fourth and concluding volume, bringing the story to Augustus, first attempted a comprehensive survey of the age of political decline. Holm's work is sound and scholarly, without any attempt at paradox or propaganda. He had no instinct for politics, like Droysen and Duncker, and the chapters on literature and culture are rather commonplace. Economic phenomena are inadequately handled. Yet the book possesses merits of its own. It has drawn more from coins than any of its rivals. 'There is great charm,' he writes, 'in making use of numismatics. There is more history in these studies than in many a laborious criticism of authorities.' The Sicilian chapters possess an authority which no other history of Greece approaches. The illustrative and critical notes are admirable throughout. In its English dress it took the place of Grote and Curtius as a handbook for learners and teachers.

A few years later Beloch, the distinguished scholar who long held the chair of ancient history at Rome, produced a history differing widely from that of Holm. Though less suitable for beginners, it is far more stimulating for advanced students and scholars—audacious, unconventional, a ringing challenge to tradition. Writing in the spirit of the *Aufklärung* he sees in Greece not the inventor of democracy nor the mirror of beauty, but rather the mother of science and the champion of reason. 'Our whole modern civilisation rests on a Hellenic foundation. Thence come the goods which make our life worth living—our science, our art, our ideals of intellectual and political freedom.' In words that seem like a voice from the grave of Buckle he declares that all progress in civilisation is in the last resort progress in knowledge. The first volume extends to the Peloponnesian war, and presents a less detailed summary than that of his predecessors. He is thoroughly sceptical about early times, and dismisses the Dorian invasion as an invention of scholars. But, though much is omitted, one important aspect of Greek history receives special attention. He had long studied the economic aspects of history, and his work on population in Greece and Rome had opened up a new and fruitful field. He complains that the economic history of Greece has been neglected since Böckh, and his chapters on social changes, trade, industry, the growth of towns, population, the rise of prices and other vital questions form the most original part of the book. His highly critical estimate of Athenian democracy had been already announced in a striking monograph. He calls Pericles a great Parliamentarian, which in his mouth is no eulogy. He failed to maintain the empire at the height to which it had been raised by Themistocles and Cimon, and his legacy was the Peloponnesian war. Like Grote, with whom he differs in almost everything else, he has a good word for Cleon. He rejects the idea that the Greeks were demoralised by the war with Sparta, for the moral level of the fifth century was low. On the contrary they were rendered more humane by the growth of the scientific movement. Sophocles and Herodotus were still naïvely superstitious, whereas Thucydides and Euripides reveal the beginning of scientific thinking.

Since Beloch had no great admiration for the Athenian empire, he sheds no tears over its fall. Particularism prevented the Greek communities, separately or in combination, from fulfilling the first duty of a State, namely self-defence. Such a condition could not continue, and the battle of Chæronea brought the unity which the best Greeks had long vainly tried to attain. Local self-government was left, and Philip was an indulgent master. He maintains that Greeks and Macedonians felt themselves one, and that the opposition was in no sense a national movement. They spoke Greek with only a dialect difference, and were closely connected by race. The Greeks only regarded them as barbarians owing to their lack of culture, a fault that was quickly cured. While the historian hurries over the familiar story of independent Greece, he allows himself ample space for the ever widening empire of Greek culture which began with the conquests of Alexander. He has no exalted opinion of Alexander as a general or statesman. His claim to divinity was the first reaction of the East on the conquerors, the first step along the road which led the freest of peoples to Byzantinism. He died when he was beginning his full work, but the forces he set in motion continued to operate and changed the face of the world. A masterly survey of the new regions unlocked by his sword fills half a large volume, and embraces trade, coinage, banking, population, finance, society, education, religion and science, literature and art. 'The world belonged to the Greeks,' he writes, 'but could they hold it?' The fourth and concluding volume answers the question in the negative. The break up of Alexander's empire ushers in a dreary period, which even Beloch fails to make interesting.

Eduard Meyer's volumes on Greece form the larger part of the vast survey of antiquity to which he devoted his life. 'For the great tasks of history salvation is only to be found when it becomes conscious of its universal character, in ancient as well as in modern times.' Only by treating Greece in connection with the Mediterranean peoples could its real nature be seized and the baseless hypotheses of generations of scholars be swept away. European history, he declares, begins on the Ægean, and his knowledge of the early Mediterranean empires gives special authority to his judgments on Mycenæan civilisation. Though it did not exist in western Greece, its wares and graves have been found in Italy, Sicily and Sardinia. The only great Mycenæan city in Asia Minor was Troy. Mycenæan art was strongly oriental, but the culture as a whole was essentially Greek. He accepts the Dorian invasion, but adds that it is uncertain whether the Dorians came together or by infiltration. In any case their numbers were large enough to swamp the population they found. Mycenæan culture gradually died out everywhere, for it had outlived itself. Dorian civilisation is but little known, and has to be reconstructed from Homer and such survivals as Sparta. The glory of the period was the epic. 'Homer' was the outcome of centuries of composition, ending in repeated editing and unification. The most important achievement of the Greek Middle Ages was the colonisation of the Mediterranean and the gradual ousting of the Phœnicians, a process in regard to which we possess no sources, but of which the sites themselves are sufficient testimony.

Solon is the first Greek statesman whose personality we know, and his importance is greater than that of Cleisthenes. Meyer describes the rise of the Persian Empire with a fullness of knowledge which no historian of Greece had approached. His picture of fifth-century Athens in many ways resembles that of Beloch. Themistocles, he declares, was the greatest of Athenians: after him there were great deeds but no lasting successes. Demos was a cruel master, as merciless as the most capricious despot, and was responsible for disgraceful condemnations from Miltiades and Themistocles downwards. Athens possessed no real government and suffered from permanent anarchy. Pericles was less of a statesman than Themistocles, because he was more of an idealist. 'The vices of radical democracy were unveiled when the balance caused by his greatness was removed.' The abyss was already opening under his feet, and he only postponed the crash. Neither he nor any man could provide the stable foreign policy which every state needs. The fate of Athens was also the fate of Greece. Before Philip drew his sword the strength of the nation was consumed by conflict. 'When Greek culture had reached its highest point and was ripe to become world-culture, the nation had lost all political importance. It was broken to pieces, and the ruins lay there for anyone to pick up.' The narrative breaks off with Epaminondas, but there is no doubt what the verdict on the Macedonian conquest would have been. Meyer's critical notes contain a complete account of the sources and of modern scholarship. Though politics are in the foreground, he is equally at home in literature and art, philosophy and religion. That his work rests throughout on independent study was further revealed by the 'Forschungen,' the first volume of which discusses the problems of early history, the second those of the fifth century. The studies of Herodotus and Thucydides are of peculiar interest. He declares that the political bias of the former has never been fully realised, and maintains that his object was to champion Athenian hegemony as the Prussian School championed the hegemony of Prussia. For Thucydides, on the other hand, his admiration is without limit, and he brushes aside all reflections on his impartiality. 'The speeches are the real nerve-centre of the work and also the highest point of his and all historical art.'

While the task of rewriting Greek history in the light of new discoveries has been mainly undertaken by German scholars, two other attempts deserve notice. When Duruy had finished his volume on Rome, he compiled a history of Greece in which inscriptions and archæology were utilised. The work makes no pretence to profound or original research, but it was a scholarly summary presented in an attractive form. He is more sparing of political judgments than in his volumes on Rome, but he has a kindlier feeling for the Greek democracies than is common in Germany. The first important history produced by an English scholar since Grote and the only attempt to utilise the vast mass of new material is that of Bury. At once scientific and popular, this relatively brief summary forms an admirable introduction. Making no attempt at detailed description of literature and art, philosophy and religion, the author confines himself in the main to a political narrative to the death of Alexander.

Greece is no exception to the rule that much of the most valuable work is contained in monographs. Among living men no one has contributed so much to a knowledge of Greek civilisation as Wilamowitz.[1] His studies of Homer and Euripides have

[1] See his delightful autobiography, English translation, 1930.

illuminated the history of literature and religion. His massive treatise, 'Aristotle and Athens,' has reconstructed the Athenian state in the light of the *Politeia*. His innumerable dissertations and lectures have lit up every aspect of Greek life. With Meyer and Wilamowitz to guide him the student will not go far astray. The discovery of Mycenæan civilisation has naturally been followed by lively discussion. We know that it was pre-Homeric and pre-Dorian, but no certain conclusions have been reached as to who the Mycenæans were. No work equals in audacious suggestiveness Ridgeway's volumes on 'The Early Age of Greece.' Unlike Hall, who pronounces the Mycenæans to have been Achæans, he contends that the Pelasgi were the original inhabitants of Greece and authors of the Mycenæan civilisation, and were afterwards conquered successively by the Achæans and the Dorians. The Homeric problem continues to exert an irresistible attraction, but no positive results have been established. 'We shall never know,' declares Holm categorically, 'whether Homer existed, who he was, or what he wrote.' Wolf placed the introduction of writing centuries too late, and Lachmann's theory of an aggregate of ballads is equally untenable. Andrew Lang restated the case for the unity of Homer, and Gilbert Murray, has given a fascinating sketch of the rise of the Greek epic from the opposite standpoint. Bérard has written a suggestive sketch of the Odyssey in the light of geographical knowledge and the explorations of the Phœnicians. The period between Homer and Solon is still dark, as there are few inscriptions before the Persian wars, but the excavation of Sparta has shown the Dorian capital to be more artistic than we thought. We have travelled far from the æstheticism of Curtius, and the Athenian Empire is now discussed in the light of the problem of food supply. A brilliant picture of the political and economic life of the Athenian Commonwealth in the fifth century has been painted by Zimmern.

If we now look at Greece less through Athenian spectacles, and increasing attention is paid to the period which followed the fall of the Athenian empire, it is largely due to the commanding personality of Droysen,[1] whose 'Alexander the Great' appeared in 1833. Droysen emphasised not what he destroyed but what he had created. The interaction of East and West was pronounced to have inaugurated a richer historic life. The Macedonians were a kindred race, and Demosthenes was the worst friend of his country. The young historian, only twenty-four years old, was almost intoxicated by the glory of his hero, and he first revealed his world-historic influence. In later editions the exuberance was

[1] See G. Droysen, *J. G. Droysen*, vol. i., 1910.

toned down and the sources more critically handled, and the book, which possesses something of the power and passion of Mommsen, still retains its place. After launching the 'Alexander' he proceeded to trace the fortunes of his successors. 'In my opinion,' he wrote to Welcker, 'no period of such importance has been so much neglected as that which I have ventured to christen Hellenism.' It was his intention to survey the era as a whole, its culture and religion no less than its wars and its rulers, but he began with political history and never went further. The 'History of Hellenism' is an imposing fragment, not the panoramic survey of his dreams. Even Droysen could not make the struggles and the rivalries of the Diadochi attractive, but he keeps steadily before the reader the significance of an age pregnant with great issues. Carefully revised in later life in the intervals of other studies, his volumes continue to occupy an honourable place in historical literature. Schäfer's fine monograph on Demosthenes saluted the genius and wisdom of the great orator. Niese's 'History of Greece from the battle of Chæronea,' a convenient political narrative, warmly eulogises the character and states-manship of Alexander. Kärst, on the other hand, in his 'History of the Hellenistic Age,' while praising the moderation of Philip, depicts his son as consumed with a mad ambition for divinity and the conquest of the world. While opinions of the conquerors continue to differ, it is now realised that Chæronea was not the end of Greek history but the beginning of the world-mission of Hellenism. For the story of the leagues Freeman's volume on Federal Government is still unsurpassed. No human being can make interesting the broken fragments of Alexander's empire, but Bevan's volumes on the House of Seleucus and Bouché-Leclercq's detailed picture of the Ptolemies are important con-tributions to an eventful period. Though Greek institutions have been the theme of numerous monographs, no work corresponding to Mommsen's 'Staatsrecht,' which Wilamowitz has declared the most urgent of needs, has been attempted, for the multi-plicity and variety of states render a synthetic view peculiarly difficult.

The volume of effort directed to the study of Greek culture is enormously greater than that devoted to Rome. Mahaffy's studies of Greek Life and Thought form a useful introduction, but for an adequate handling of the different provinces we must turn to the labours of specialists. Brandis published a penetrating analysis of pre-Socratic thinkers, and Heinrich Ritter compiled a survey of ancient philosophy marked by irreproachable scholar-ship and lucid presentation; but both failed to establish a logical connection between thinker and thinker.[1] It was this task which Hegel first attempted to fulfil in his Lectures, which applied the dialectic process to the succession of schools; but the work made no claim to expert scholarship, and his construction, though always suggestive, was often arbitrary. A far greater advance was made in 1851 with Zeller's 'Philosophy of the Greeks,' which was frequently revised and forms one of the glories of German scholarship. More recently Gomperz' 'Greek Thinkers' has won almost equal popularity.

The study of religion is a more formidable affair. The contention of Adalbert Kuhn and Max Müller that Greek mythology was part of the common stock of the Indo-Germanic races and was mainly solar theory no longer finds supporters. In the difficult task of recovering the evolution of belief no scholars have shown more flair than Usener and Dietrich. The inscriptions have led to a more correct valuation of some of the cults, certain of which, like that of Zeus of Dodona, prove to have been occupied only with trivialities. Apollo has ceased to be a Dorian or even a Greek deity and has been annexed by Lycia. An encyclopædic survey of the cults of the Greek States has been undertaken by Farnell. The study of the Mysteries has been vigorously pursued. Though Creuzer's naïve idea that they embodied a mass of esoteric truth was destroyed by Lobeck, it is clear that they supplied the emotional nourishment which the cults were unable to provide, resembling the Christian Sacraments and miracle plays, offering scenes and rites, not doctrines or theology. In the dim world, where Orpheus and Dionysus hold sway, Foucart and Reitzenstein, Cornford and Jane Harrison have trodden with undaunted footsteps. Rohde's masterpiece, 'Psyche,' the most satisfying monograph on any aspect of Greek religion, traces the conception of immortality through the ages. Many themes are treated with brilliant originality in the voluminous writings of Salomon Reinach. Frazer has analysed the testimony of Pausanias, and the detailed results of modern scholarship must be sought in Roscher's 'Dictionary of Mythology.' The study of art has made rapid progress with the advance of excavation. Perrot and Chipiez treated Greece against a broad background in their encyclopædic survey of antiquity. Furtwängler's fascinating 'Masterpieces of Greek Sculpture,' with its audacious attributions, stimulated research. The course of literature has been mapped by the Croiset brothers, Christ and Mahaffy. New territory has been brought into cultivation by Susemihl's massive study of Alexandrian literature and Rohde's monograph on the Greek novel.

[1] See Zeller's *Kleine Schriften*, vol. i., 1910.

The sources of Greek history increase every year. Böckh's Corpus contained 8,000 inscriptions, a smaller number than the Attic Corpus alone, itself only a part of the great collection which the Berlin Academy has undertaken with the assistance of Paris and Vienna. Their decipherment owes much to Kirchhoff's brilliant studies of the alphabet, distinguishing localities and dates by the formation of letters, and to the scholarship of Ulrich Köhler.[1] The Papyri[2] and the Ostraka have fructified every department of the Hellenistic world, though rather in the fields of administration and culture than of politics. The technique of excavation has been perfected, and the foundation of archæological schools at Athens has ensured a supply of zealous and competent workers.[3] The French, under the direction of Homolle, removed the village under which lay Delphi and explored the island of Delos, which has been described as a Greek Pompeii. The Americans, after excavating the Heræum at Argos, have begun to reveal Corinth, and the British School has explored Sparta. In recovering the history of their own land Greek scholars have taken an active part.[4] The Archæological Society has discovered pre-Mycenæan remains on the Acropolis, excavated Epidaurus and Dodona, and completed the labours of the French at Eleusis. Across the sea the remains of civilisation in Cyprus have been recovered by Cesnola, an American Consul, Ohnefalsch-Richter and Myres. Gems and jewellery have been brought to light in the tombs of South Russia, and the early history of the Scythian cultures and Greek colonisation from the mouths of the Danube to the Caucasus has been summarised in the magnificent quarto 'Scythians and Greeks' by Ellis Minns. Dörpfeld completed the exploration of Troy and showed the bottom city to be pre-Mycenæan. Humann has explored Pergamum. The Temple of Artemis at Ephesus, one of the Seven Wonders of the ancient world, discovered by Wood in 1873, has been further unearthed by Hogarth. To the *Politeia* have been added in recent years the poems of Bacchylides and Herondas, fragments of Sappho and Pindar, speeches of Hypereides, 800 lines of Theopompus, and considerable sections of Menander and Euripides. No site

[1] For a good popular sketch see Newton, 'On Greek Inscriptions,' in *Essays on Art and Archæology*, 1880.

[2] Wilcken, *Die Griechischen Papyrusurkunden*, 1897, gives an excellent sketch of papyrology.

[3] See Michaelis, *Archæological Discoveries in the Nineteenth Century*, 1908; Percy Gardner, *New Chapters in Greek History*, 1892; and Radet, *L'Histoire de l'École française d'Athènes*, 1901.

[4] See Théodore Reinach's chapter in *Greece in Evolution*, ed. Abbott, 1909.

has yielded so rich a harvest of papyri as Oxyrhynchus, in the Fayum, where Grenfell and Hunt, working for the Egypt Exploration Fund, have kept the academic world in a state of joyful expectation. Though the finds are often of no great moment, they represent collectively a real addition to our knowledge of a civilisation in regard to which every grain of information is gold.

II

The nineteenth century witnessed few more important developments in the field of scholarship than the revival of interest in the Eastern Empire. Byzantine studies[1] were founded in the seventeenth century by Ducange, but the seed did not germinate for two hundred years. The eighteenth century, unjust to the Middle Ages as a whole, showed itself particularly unfriendly to the Greek Empire. For Voltaire Byzantine history was a series of horrible and disgusting incidents, for Montesquieu a tissue of sedition and perfidy. The vast compilation of their countryman Lebeau confirmed the popular impression of its repulsive dullness, and his unhappy title, the 'Lower Empire,' stuck. Worse than all Gibbon failed to realise its true character and importance. The chapters on Constantine and Julian, Theodosius and Justinian are incomparable, but after Heraclius his interest wanes, and he marches a procession of colourless figures wearily across the stage. It is a 'tedious and uniform tale of weakness and misery,' a corrupt and effeminate State with a thin veneer of civilisation. Of its services to civilisation, of the greatness of many of its figures, he had no conception.

Interest revived with the Greek War of Independence and the controversy as to the racial derivation of modern Greeks. Owing in part to his friendship with a Greek fellow-student at Göttingen, George Finlay resolved to visit Greece and judge for himself the condition of the people and the chances of the war.[2] In 1823 he was with Byron in Missolonghi. 'You are young and enthusiastic,' said the poet, 'and you are sure to be disappointed when you know the Greeks as well as I do.' The prophecy was to come true. When independence was achieved he bought an estate in Attica.

---

[1] See Diehl, *Études Byzantines*, 1905; Krumbacher, *Geleitwort zur Byzant. Zeitschrift*, reprinted in his *Populäre Aufsätze*, 1909; and Gerland, *Das Studium der Byzantinischen Geschichte*, 1934. Russia's contributions are summarised in Vasiliev, *History of the Byzantine Empire*, vol. i., ch. 1, 1928.

[2] See the brief autobiography in Tozer's edition, vol. i., 1877. There are eulogies of his work in Freeman, *Historical Essays*, Third Series, 1879, and Fallmerayer, *Ges. Werke*, vol. iii., 1861.

'I lost my money and my labour, but I learned how the system of tenths has produced a state of society and habits of cultivation against which one man can do nothing. When I had wasted as much as I possessed, I turned my attention to study.' His life-work appeared as a series of monographs between 1844 and 1861. His closing years were devoted to a thorough revision, and to the continuation of the narrative to 1864. After his death his volumes were issued as a single work under the title 'A History of Greece from its Conquest by the Romans.' Freeman described it in 1855 as the greatest work of English historical literature since Gibbon, and the most original history in the language. Krumbacher, prince of critics, warmly praised the knowledge of Greek character and the narrative talent.

Finlay courageously chose an unpopular subject and claimed attention for it. Beginning where historians of classical Greece left off, he surveyed the Byzantine Empire from beginning to end, and continued his story for four centuries after its fall. Though Greece is always in the foreground, he offers a fairly complete summary of the history of the Eastern Empire. He showed that the government reached a far higher standard than any other state during the Middle Ages, and maintained that the moral condition of the people under the Iconoclasts was superior to that of any equal number of human beings, at the time or earlier, in any part of the world. Law was highly developed, order was fairly maintained, justice was tolerably administered. On the other hand he admits the fiscal oppression and the unprogressive centralisation which sterilised the Empire. The most novel feature of the work was the emphasis on social and economic conditions. He was, indeed, rather a student of law and economics than a professed historical scholar, and his personal knowledge of the evils of independent Greece led him to trace their influence back through the centuries. He wrote without any exaggerated sympathy for the Greek people. He relates the capture of Constantinople in 1453 without emotion, praises Mohammed II, and proclaims the moral superiority of the Turks at the time of the conquest. But he draws a sinister picture of Turkish rule, of which the tribute of Christian children to form the Janissaries was the keystone. In the account of the War of Independence he castigates the leaders while admiring the patriotism and endurance of the people. Though his picture of contemporary Greece is highly critical, he admits that her progress was as great as could reasonably be hoped. While Finlay pointed out the speculative character of much of Fallmerayer's evidence, it was above all the work of Hopf, who begins with Alaric's invasion, to refute the contention of wholesale displacement. His researches were buried in Ersch and Gruber's Encyclopædia, and are in consequence unknown to the general reader, yet no one did so much to place the study of the Greek Middle Ages on a secure foundation. His results have filtered into the text-books through the medium of Hertzberg, whose history of Greece from the close of the classical age presents the researches of other men in a well-ordered narrative.

The epoch of lengthy narratives gave way to the epoch of monographs about 1870. The lead in Byzantine studies, which had hitherto been taken by Germany and England, reverted to France with the publication of Rambaud's 'Constantine Porphyrogenitus.' Though a study of a single ruler, the book embodied a definite conception of Byzantine history. Autocracy and administrative centralisation, he declared, were essential, as the Empire was always on a war footing; the union of Church and State was necessary, because the Empire could only disarm the barbarians by Christianity; its rulers were often compelled to bribery and deceit, as they had to deal with barbarous and faithless tribes. 'We have been pitiless for its vices without noticing the virtues which it must have possessed to survive the Western Empire for a thousand years.' No European State, he adds, had to meet such assaults. Rambaud possessed every qualification for an historian of the Byzantine Empire, including a knowledge of Russian, but he seldom revisited the field where he won his fame. His lead was followed by Schlumberger, who, after earning applause by a treatise on the 'Coins of the Latin Orient,' published his sumptuous work on 'Byzantine Sigillography' in 1884. The volume, enriched by over a thousand illustrations, proved of immense value for iconography, the dignitaries and ceremonies of the Court, the geography and administrative divisions of the Empire. It was largely with the aid of monumental sources that he carried out the series of richly illustrated monographs on Byzantine rulers by which he is best known. The first was devoted to Nicephorus Phocas, whom he rescued from the spiteful imputations of Liutprand; a second to the towering personality of Basil, the 'Slayer of the Bulgarians'; the final volume to Basil's successors. Though these biographies only cover a century, they reveal every aspect of the life of the Empire and refute the tradition of a decadent State. The third French scholar to dedicate himself to the Eastern Empire was Diehl, who was trained in the French Schools at Athens and Rome. Beginning with studies of administration in the Exarchate of Ravenna and in Africa, he wrote a richly illustrated survey of Justinian and the civilisation of the sixth century. A separate monograph on Theodora pictures a woman of strong will and rare intelligence, outliving her stormy youth and leaving a memory deeply cherished by the Emperor. His study of Byzantine art is the best survey of a fascinating territory. No scholar has done more to popularise Byzantine history, and his work was rewarded by his appointment as first holder of the Chair of Byzantine History created at the Sorbonne in 1899. Chalandon's volumes on the Comneni, though of less popular appeal, are of not inferior merit.

In England Bury's erudite narrative of the Eastern Empire till the ninth century and his edition of Gibbon won him a place in the front ranks of scholars. William Miller and Rennell Rodd illumined the darkness of mediæval Greece, and Edwin Pears reconstructed the tragedies of 1204 and 1453. The greatest of German Byzantinists was Krumbacher, for whom a chair was founded in Munich in 1892, and whose encyclopædic survey of Byzantine Literature is the most important single work in the whole field of Byzantine studies. Far from being a mere analytical catalogue of writers, it throws light on every aspect of the Empire. Of no less service was his creation of the 'Byzantinische Zeitschrift.' Zacharia von Lingenthal explored the territory, unknown to Savigny, of Byzantine law. Pichler traced the separation of the Eastern and Western Churches, and Hergenröther's majestic monograph on Photius, Patriarch of Constantinople, threw light on the early history of the Empire, and the relations between the Eastern and Western churches. Gregorovius related the fortunes of mediæval Athens, and Röhricht devoted a laborious life to the Crusades. Heyd's exhaustive investigation of Levantine trade, a classic of economic history, illustrated the commercial history of the Empire and the fortunes of the foreign settlements. In Slavonic Europe interest grew apace when it was realised that the history of the Slavs is unintelligible without a knowledge of Byzantine influences. A Byzantine Review was founded by Russian scholars in 1894, and an Institute of Archæology was created at Constantinople under Uspenski in 1895. The most original treatises on Byzantine art are the work of Strzygowski, an Austrian Pole.

Byzantine studies have made immense progress in the last half-century, but the territory is so vast that there is even now no more promising field of historical research. The Byzantine Corpus, which began to appear at Bonn under the auspices of Niebuhr, was so imperfectly edited as to be of slender value, and it is only in the last three decades of the century that scholarly editions of the sources became available. No work has aroused so much controversy as the 'Historia Secreta'; but the view of Dahn, the historian of the *Völkerwanderung* and author of the superb historical novel 'Ein Kampf um Rom,' that it was indeed the work of Procopius is now generally accepted. In 1904 the International Association of Academies determined on a Corpus of Greek mediæval charters. There are now Byzantine Chairs at Paris and Munich, Leyden and Leipsic, St. Petersburg, Odessa and Buda-Pesth. From the scholarship of two generations a new Byzantium[1] has emerged, not anæmic and inert but the mother of great statesmen and soldiers, the home of Greek culture while central and western Europe was plunged in darkness, the rampart of Christian Europe for a thousand years, the civiliser of the Slavonic races, no longer a degenerate descendant of Greece or a parody of Rome, but a Christian state with its own individuality. The virile Isaurians hold their own beside any dynasty of the West. Freeman truly remarked that it was for ages the only regular and systematic government in the world. Nothing but a centralised bureaucracy could have held together so many countries and races. Its administrative machine was the most elaborate that the world had seen, and the Byzantine Court was to mediæval Europe like Versailles to the rulers of the seventeenth and eighteenth centuries. Travellers and ambassadors marvelled at the splendour of the capital, and felt themselves in the presence of a more complex and highly organised civilisation than they knew at home. Yet there is no disposition to pass from the extreme of depreciation to exaggerated eulogy. The Eastern Empire was a bureaucracy in which political liberty was unknown. In literature it produced no masterpiece; in science, theology and philosophy it took little interest. In the region of the arts alone was it creative. 'The mission of Christian Constantinople,' declares Bikelas with truth, 'was not to create but to save.' Yet to preserve Greek culture during the barbarism of the early Middle Ages and to defend it against the assaults of Islam was to deserve well of civilisation.

[1] Popularly sketched by Frederic Harrison in the Rede Lecture, 1900, reprinted in *Among My Books*, 1912.

CHAPTER XXIV

MOMMSEN AND ROMAN STUDIES

I

THE history of Roman studies since the death of Niebuhr is largely the record of the amazing activities of a single man. The son of a Schleswig pastor, Theodor Mommsen[1] was the eldest of three brothers, all of whom gained distinction in classical research. The study of law at Kiel turned his attention to Rome, and his interest in the classical world was increased by the lectures of Otto Jahn. His first works, a Latin dissertation on Roman Associations and a study of Roman Tribes, won the notice of scholars, and at the age of twenty-six he was already a master of his craft. A travelling scholarship from the Danish Government, supplemented by a small grant from the Berlin Academy, was employed to visit Italy, and the Italian tour played as great a part in his life as in that of Ranke. His headquarters in the Eternal City was the Archæological Institute,[2] founded by Bunsen and Gerhard in 1829; and with its secretary Henzen, who had already begun to collect inscriptions, he formed a close friendship.

In his dissertation on Roman Associations the young scholar had expressed a wish for a Corpus of Latin Inscriptions. There had been a dozen collections before 1800, all of which contained forgeries.[3] The foundation of Latin epigraphy had been laid by Marini, whose work on the Fratres Arvales (1795) contained a thousand unknown inscriptions. His example was followed by his pupil Borghesi,[4] who reconstructed the Fasti of the Roman magistrates. After some correspondence Mommsen visited him in his home at San Marino, and discussed the prospects of a

---

[1] The fullest account is by Hartmann, *Mommsen*, 1908. The best appreciations are by Neumann, *Hist. Zeitschrift*, vol. cxii.; Kärst, *Hist. Vierteljahrschrift*, 1904; Haverfield, *Eng. Hist. Review*, Jan. 1904; Camille Jullian, *Revue historique*, vol. lxxxiv; Otto Hirschfeld, *Kleine Schriften*, 1913. Guilland's essay, in *L'Allemagne Nouvelle et ses Historiens*, 1899, over-emphasises his political ideas.

[2] See Michaelis, *Gesch. des deutschen Archäologischen Instituts*, 1879.

[3] See Hübner, *Römische Epigraphik*, in Iwan Müller's *Handbuch*.

[4] See the notice in Borghesi, *Œuvres*, vol. x., 1897.

Latin Corpus. The Berlin Academy invited Otto Jahn to undertake the work, and Jahn asked his old pupil to help. But the
French Academy had not at this time given up the idea of a
Corpus, and Borghesi had promised his aid. In view of the competition Mommsen resolved to carry out an independent work
with the Samnite inscriptions, and then, on the advice of Borghesi,
passed to the Neapolitan Kingdom. After prolonged wanderings
in the South he revisited San Marino before crossing the Alps.
When the 'Inscriptions of the Neapolitan Kingdom' appeared
in 1852 they were dedicated to Borghesi, 'Magistro, Patrono,
Amico.' While searching for inscriptions he had kept his eyes
open for other aspects of antiquity. The chief result of his Italian
journey, after the Inscriptions, was the mastery of ancient
dialects. His 'Oscan Studies,' followed by his 'Lower Italian
Dialects,' were an epoch-making contribution to the history and
ethnography not less than to the languages of pre-Roman
Italy.

Mommsen returned to Kiel in time to take part in the stirring
events of 1848. A slight injury sustained in a street riot in Hamburg prevented him from joining his brothers as volunteers
against Denmark, but he found compensation in helping to
edit the *Schleswig-Holstein Zeitung*, the organ of the Provisional
Government. The close contact with war and revolution gave him
an insight into the forces and passions which build up history,
while his brief experience of journalism developed the incisive
style to which the 'Roman History' was to owe part of its fame.
The failure of the national movement made Holstein too hot for
him, and he accepted a call to the Chair of Roman Law at Leipsic,
where he lived in close companionship with Otto Jahn and
Moritz Haupt. But the arm of reaction was long, and in 1851
Beust, the Saxon Prime Minister, dismissed the three scholars
from their posts. Mommsen accepted an invitation to Zurich,
where he collected Swiss inscriptions, but the sphere was too
small, and he soon moved to Breslau.

The almost accidental origin of the 'Roman History' was
related in a letter to Gustav Freytag. 'In my youth I thought of
all sorts of things, of Roman criminal law, an edition of legal
documents, a compendium of the Pandects, but never of historical writing. Invited to give a public lecture while at Leipsic, I
delivered an address on the Gracchi. Reimer and Hirzel, the publishers, were present, and two days later they asked me to write
a Roman History for their series.' 'It is high time for such a
work,' he wrote to Henzen; 'it is more than ever necessary to
present to a wider circle the results of our researches.' A year

later, in 1851, he declared that he was weighed down by the end-less difficulty of the undertaking. His first plan was to devote two volumes to the Republic and a third to the Empire, but he quickly realised that the latter could only be treated when the Inscriptions had been collected. The three volumes were therefore devoted to the Republic. He obeyed the order to fill his book with results instead of processes. In Niebuhr the thread of narrative is lost in the labyrinth of dissertation. Mommsen only asked tradition to confirm or illustrate inferences drawn from the survival of institutions and usages. While he glides rapidly past the problems which occupy other historians, he reconstructs in broad strokes the ethnology, institutions and social life of early Italy. The fully historical period begins with Pyrrhus. The account of Hannibal is less striking than that by Arnold, and the picture of the Gracchi is lacking in sympathy. He reaches his full stride with Marius and Sulla, and portrays the dying struggles of the Republic with incomparable power and brilliancy.

The 'Roman History' was quickly translated into several languages.[1] For the first time the modern world was provided with a complete survey of the Republic. Its sureness of touch, its throbbing vitality, and the Venetian colouring of its portraits left an ineffaceable impression on every reader. Almost at the same moment Grote and Mommsen brought Athens and Rome into the consciousness and culture of the modern world. While the public welcomed the book with delight and scholars testified to its impeccable erudition, some specialists were annoyed at finding old hypotheses rejected and new ones advanced as if they were incontrovertible facts. Others complained of the lack of tranquillity and dignity. It is indeed the work of a publicist as well as of a scholar. Labienus was a Napoleonic marshal; Sulla, Don Juan; Cato, Sancho Panza. We read of Junkers and *haute finance*. 'Much might be said about the modern tone,' he wrote to Henzen. 'I wanted to bring down the ancients from their fan-tastic pedestal into the real world. That is why the consul had to become the burgomaster. Perhaps I have overdone it, but my intention was sound enough.'

A more serious charge was directed against the closing volume. No part of the 'Roman History' possesses such vitality as the tale of the struggle of Cæsar with his enemies, for the his-torian steps down from his conning-tower and leaps into the fray. Pompey, Cicero and Cato are scourged as if they were the living chiefs of a hated political faction, while his idol dominates the

[1] For an English judgment see Freeman, *Historical Essays*, Second Series, 1873. Cp. Carl Peter, *Studien zur Römischen Geschichte*, 1863.

stage, radiant, peerless, irresistible, the saviour of society. Mommsen has no love for ineffectual angels. He censures Pompey for his lack of passion in good or evil. 'He had met Ciceros in 1848,' remarks Haverfield, 'who talked admirably and acted feebly.' He spoke contemptuously of the honest mediocrities of the Senate. Cæsar was the man of destiny, seeing and doing what was needed, desiring neither to conquer the world nor to call himself King. His aim was the political, military, moral and intellectual renaissance of his degraded nation. Surveying his reforms, he declares each stone in the fabric enough to make a man immortal. 'What senseless idealisation of Cæsar!' commented Strauss. 'An historian may blame, but not scold; praise, but not lose his balance.' Freeman lamented that he had no notion of right and wrong. Even his friend Gustav Freytag regretted the intensity of his dislikes.

The charge that he took sides left Mommsen unmoved. 'Those who have lived through historical events, as I have,' he wrote, 'begin to see that history is neither written nor made without love or hate.' He rejected every absolute standard in politics and scoffed at legitimism. 'When a Government cannot govern,' he declared, 'it ceases to be legitimate, and he who has the power to overthrow it has also the right.' These utterances were music to Napoleon III, who invited the historian to dinner when in Paris and sent him his own life of Cæsar in return. But Mommsen was anxious that the world should not confound his defence of Cæsar with a defence of Cæsarism, and in a second edition he explained his standpoint. The Republic was rotten. Cæsar's work was necessary and wholesome, not because it brought or could bring blessing, but because it was the lesser evil. Under other circumstances it would have been an usurpation. 'By the same natural law that the least organism is far more than the most skilful machine, so is every imperfect constitution which gives room for the free self-determination of a majority of citizens infinitely more than the most humane and wonderful absolutism; for one is living, the other is dead.' The Emperors held the State together and enlarged it mechanically, while within it lost its sap and died. It was well that he left the book virtually in its original form, for only thus could it retain the character which won it world-wide fame. It was a work of genius and passion, the creation of a young man, and is as fresh and vital to-day as when it was written. In sheer brilliance and sustained power no historical work in the German language, save Treitschke's 'Deutsche Geschichte,' approaches it.

The excellence of the editions of the Samnite and Neapolitan inscriptions had impressed every scholar. In 1853 the Berlin Academy gave Mommsen a salary for six years to work at the Corpus,[1] and in 1858 he was called as a member of the Academy to Berlin, where he received a Chair. It was the end of his wanderings. The immense scope of the work, far larger than the twin enterprise of Böckh, demanded a man possessing the power of rapid as well as accurate work, and capable of inspiring and controlling his colleagues. The first of the massive folios appeared in 1863, containing the Republican inscriptions, edited by Mommsen himself, and the Consular Fasti, edited by Henzen. The duty of each scholar was to see the originals where possible, to examine printed volumes, to interpret the local and personal references, to establish the date, to suggest the reconstruction of mutilated passages. Of the twenty volumes which appeared during his lifetime he edited nearly half, including Cisalpine Gaul, South Italy, the Danube and the East, while every section underwent his revision and bears his mark. A school of skilled epigraphists grew up under the eye of the master, ready to continue the work as Henzen, De Rossi and other veterans dropped out of the ranks. In the year before his death he finished revising the inscriptions of the East, and in his last weeks he planned a new edition of the first volume. He had estimated the inscriptions at 80,000; but that number has already been doubled, and new material is continually accumulating. New editions and supplements keep the work up to date, and the *Ephemeris Epigraphica*, established in 1872, facilitates the communication of discoveries and the discussion of plans. No work has ever approached the Corpus in fruitfulness for Roman studies. Every department of private and public life was irradiated—the administration, the towns, the army, taxation, religion, art, social conditions, communications. Haverfield has well compared it to a cardinal discovery in science, and Camille Jullian has pronounced it the greatest service ever rendered by any scholar to the knowledge of the past.

While thus engaged on a task that would have consumed the entire energy of ordinary men, Mommsen produced a series of treatises each of which marked an epoch in its department. The first was the 'Chronology' of the Republic, in which he grappled with a thorny problem hitherto scarcely touched. The work, which was in the nature of pioneering, is the least enduring of his productions; but the controversies which it provoked were

[1] See Hirschfeld's memorial address, in *Abhandlungen der Berliner Akademie*, 1904; Harnack, *Geschichte der Akademie der Wissenschaften*, 1901; and Waltzing, *Le Recueil Général des Inscriptions latines*, 1892.

fruitful, and it was on the results of the discussions of a quarter of a century that Soltau built the edifice that largely superseded that of his master. The 'History of the Coinage,' published in 1860, was more important. Mommsen had begun his numismatic studies during the Italian tour, and now essayed an encyclopædic survey of a vast and largely untravelled country. He bore eloquent testimony to his great predecessors, Eckhel[1] and Borghesi, but pointed out the incompleteness of their work. Moreover, while they wrote solely as numismatists, Mommsen never forgot that he was an historian. Beginning with the Greco-Asiatic coinage from which the Roman grew, he traces the development from Rome to Italy, from Italy to the world, discussing the circulation and duration of types, the rights of minting, the problems of trade and finance. He reviewed the new material for the French translation issued by De Blacas; but he never found time to issue a revised edition, and the work is now out of date. None the less, he followed the progress of numismatics with unflagging interest. He was instrumental in founding the *Zeitschrift für Numismatik*, and he supported the Corpus Nummorum, presenting to it the money given to him on his doctor's jubilee.

The most important of the books written during his occupation with the Corpus was the treatise on 'Roman Public Law.'[2] Double the length of the 'Roman History,' the 'Staatsrecht' was regarded by the author as the greatest of his achievements. A work so vast and detailed could never win popularity, but its consummate scholarship renders it the admiration and despair of historians. It is perhaps the greatest historical treatise on political institutions ever written. 'As long as jurisprudence ignored the State and the people,' he declared, 'and history and philology ignored law, both knocked vainly at the door of the Roman world.' It is one of the secrets of his greatness that he was a lawyer no less than an historian. He had already published the first critical edition of the 'Digest,' thenceforward the companion of every jurist.

The 'Staatsrecht' fills over three thousand pages, and surveys the whole course and system of Roman government and administration. Every statement is buttressed by arguments and authorities, and scarcely less than one-third of the space is occupied by notes. It is a series of monographs, not a constitutional history. The institutions are studied separately, yet as limbs of

---

[1] See Kenner, *Joseph von Eckhel*, 1871.

[2] See Bernays, 'Die Behandlung des Römischen Staatsrechts,' *Ges. Abhandlungen*, vol. ii., 1885.

an organic system of public law. The most original part of the work in the treatment of the Principate. Historians had seen in the régime of Augustus a violent rupture with the old order and the creation of a system which lasted virtually unchanged for three centuries. Mommsen pointed out that he wished to found a dyarchy, and deliberately gave the Senate a large share of power. The office of Princeps was not hereditary. The ruler was only the first citizen, raised above other officers of state by enjoying his power for life and having no colleague. To the command of army and navy and the control of selected provinces were gradually added new powers till a real Empire was reached. He showed that the system was neither empire nor monarchy; that it was a new magistracy set in an old framework; that it rested on a balance of power between the Princeps and the Senate; that it was a compromise between the old oligarchy and the absolutism of Cæsar; and that it was not till Diocletian that unqualified autocracy made its appearance. Thus Rome underwent a gradual evolution from the Principate to the Empire. The same story is told from the other side in the volume on the Senate. Complaints were heard that as a jurist he exaggerated the significance of legal forms and that the whole picture was too tidy and systematic. In particular his theory of the dyarchy has not escaped criticism. Gardthausen maintained that he exaggerated the power of the Senate and underestimated the tendency of the Principate to develop into a world-monarchy: the belief of Romans that they were living under personal rule was stronger evidence than certain republican survivals. A pendant appeared ten years later in the volume of a thousand pages on 'Criminal Law.'[1] No part of the vast territory of Roman law was so closely contiguous to history. The work surveys the officials, the procedure, the classes of crime and the punishments from the beginning of Roman history till Justinian, and in the course of his long journey the historian throws light on many aspects of Roman civilisation— on morals, marriage and religion.

When Mommsen terminated his history with the death of Cæsar it was his intention to continue it after a foundation had been laid by a collection of the whole mass of extant inscriptions. As the decades passed the world ceased to hope for the work which he alone was able to write, though it was long before he surrendered the idea. A fragment written in 1877 was published after his death, and in 1885 there appeared what was described as the fifth volume of the 'Roman History.' The 'History of the

[1] See the masterly analysis by Strachan-Davidson, *Eng. Hist. Review*, April 1901.

Roman Provinces from Augustus to Diocletian' was based on the Corpus.[1] A vanished world was reconstructed by the genius of a single man, and it became possible to estimate the real character and influence of the Empire. Earlier writers had perforce regarded it through the eyes of the Roman historians and satirists, who placed the personality of the ruler in the forefront of the picture. It was Mommsen's achievement to establish that Rome was not the Empire, and that the cruelties and eccentricities of the monarch had but little effect throughout the boundless expanse of the Roman world.

His researches proved that the lurid horrors of the capital were in no way typical. The authority of Tacitus before Mommsen was that of Livy before Niebuhr. The legend, consecrated by Gibbon, of the contrast between the first and second centuries, between the age of Tiberius and the age of the Antonines, was swept away. The provinces, declares the historian, enjoyed a tolerable evening after a sultry day, for the greatest achievement of the Empire was to provide three centuries of peace. For the tradition of an age of despotism and decay he substituted the picture of a stable order from which Western civilisation was to arise. In the next place he revealed the exact nature of the administrative machine. We learn of the Forward policy and the Buffer policy, the border-lands and vassal states, the military system, the garrisons, the towns, taxation and trade. It is, indeed, a gazetteer of the Empire with Italy left out. The British chapter, for which the inscriptions were scanty, is necessarily thin and unsatisfying. Scarcely more adequate is the treatment of Spain. But these constitute only a minute fraction of the work, in which every chapter represents a substantial addition to knowledge. He was at his best in the countries whose inscriptions he had himself edited, such as the Danubian lands and Asia Minor. The section on Greece is notable for its discussions of the causes of decay, though Nöldeke declared the picture of Hellenistic culture too dark. The treatment of the Jews received universal praise. The infectious buoyancy of the 'Roman History' is gone; the author rarely allows himself to be picturesque, and the human element is absent. It is a disinterested study of a system of government, not a record of passion and struggle. It would have gained by a general view of provincial policy and administration, a discussion of the relations of the central to the local government, and a review of social and economic forces; but his main ideas may be gleaned without difficulty. The incomparable

[1] See W. T. Arnold, *Eng. Hist. Review*, April 1886, and Pöhlmann, *Aus Altertum u. Gegenwart*, 1895.

value of the 'Staatsrecht' and the 'Roman Provinces' increases the regret that the great historian never set the crown on his labours. We should have had a wonderful portrait gallery of the Emperors, a masterly exposition of the place of Roman law in the Imperial system, a brilliant picture of the growth and persecutions of Christianity.

The later years of the historian's life were largely devoted to the study of texts. The most celebrated of his editions was that of the testament of Augustus. The original at Rome was lost but an almost perfect copy had been discovered at Ancyra, in Asia Minor, by Busbecq in the sixteenth century. It was not till the French expedition of Perrot in 1861 that a critical edition became possible and it was from this version that Mommsen printed the inscription in the Corpus, reissued as a separate volume in 1865. But part of the Greek translation was still lacking. In 1882 Humann was chosen to uncover the hidden parts and take a plaster cast of the whole. On the strength of the new material Mommsen issued a new edition with a revised commentary. A brisk controversy arose as to the origin of the most famous of all Roman inscriptions. The editor contended that it was set up in the lifetime of Augustus, while others maintained that it was drawn up by him and engraved by his successor with the necessary additions. He joined the executive of the *Monumenta*, becoming responsible for the Auctores Antiquissimi which covered the centuries of the *Völkerwanderung*. The history of the Goths was illustrated by editions of Jordanes and Cassiodorus, while the Liber Pontificalis, Nennius and other minor chronicles of the fourth to the seventh centuries threw light on an obscure period. 'The dark transition between antiquity and modern history,' he wrote, 'must be illustrated from both sides, and science stands before it as engineers before a mountain tunnel.' His last task was an edition of the Theodosian Code, with elaborate Prolegomena. Thus the sphere of his studies was extended till Rome was swallowed up in the Middle Ages.

Mommsen took a prominent part in organising or encouraging all enterprises directed to the elucidation of Roman history. Among them was the project of exploring the *Limes* or Roman wall from the Rhine to the Danube. An organisation was founded in 1890, a journal was instituted to record the progress of the work, and a museum established to exhibit the objects discovered. The exploration threw light not only on the frontier but on methods of fortification and defence. A second work in which he took a lively interest was the 'Prosopographia' or biographical dictionary, based almost wholly on the Corpus, compiled by his friend and colleague Dessau under the auspices of the Berlin Academy. He hailed with delight the work of pioneers. Though he was an old man when the importance of papyri began to be realised, his pupil Wilcken testifies that he was among the first to seize the significance of these brown rags. The new science touched his own work above all in connection with the Roman province of Egypt. He helped to found a special journal, while the scheme of a Corpus Papyrorum flitted before his mind. He desired that the scholars of every country should combine in enterprises too vast for the resources of a single state. One of these was a 'Thesaurus Linguæ Latinæ,' a history of every Latin word till the sixth century. In 1892 he endeavoured to unite the Academies of Germany and Austria for such undertakings, and sketched the statutes for a federation. But the Berlin Academy, while approving co-operation in the Thesaurus, rejected the plan for a closer union. The decision was a disappointment, but his efforts prepared the way for the International Association of Academies, which held its first meeting in Paris in 1901. The range of vision of the aged historian grew wider and wider. His eyes were not dim nor his natural force abated. He eagerly followed the sensational discoveries which revealed the ancient civilisations of the East and placed Greece and Rome in a new perspective. His thoughts were much occupied with the bearing of the new knowledge on the old, and among his last activities was the framing of a set of questions relating to the oldest criminal law of civilised communities, which he sent to specialists in Greek, Teutonic, Indian, Moslem and Jewish law with a view to co-ordinating the broad results of their researches. The questions relating to Rome he answered himself.

One of the elements of his greatness as an historian was his vivid interest in every aspect of life.[1] The prince of scholars was at the same time an active politician and a leader of thought. His brilliant eyes and mobile face expressed every emotion of a vibrant temperament. He had fought with his pen in 1848, and had sacrificed his position at Kiel and Leipsic to his convictions. In 1861 he entered the Prussian Parliament as a member of the Fortschrittspartei. In 1881 he became a member of the Reichstag, joining the Radical party, led by his friend Bamberger, which seceded from the National Liberals when Bismarck introduced Protection. He was one of those who felt that the unification of Germany imposed the duty of a higher culture, and in his Rectorial Address of 1874 he declared that Germans could not rest

[1] For an intimate appreciation see Harnack, *Aus Wissenschaft u. Leben*, vol. ii., 1911.

on their laurels. Yet, like Ranke, he was dismayed at what he described as the dehumanising tendencies of the time. He fought the outbreak of anti-Semitism led by Stöcker and Treitschke. He denounced the Agrarians as corn speculators and brandy-burners. When he defined Protection as a policy of swindling, Bismarck prosecuted him, but he was acquitted. He opposed the colonial movement as jingoism and the Zedlitz school bill as obscurantism. A child of the *Aufklärung*, he resisted every infringement of liberty in science, literature and art. His last political pronouncement was a resounding attack on the Agrarian tariff of 1902. He died in his sleep in 1903 at the age of eighty-six, learning and teaching to the end.

Mommsen and Ranke stand together and alone in the first class of nineteenth-century historians. Ranke's works were almost entirely of a narrative character, while Mommsen earned fame not only as a master of narration but as an interpreter of institutions and an editor of inscriptions and texts. They resembled each other in their productiveness and their combination of critical technique with synthetic vision. Both were the honoured masters of generations of eager students, and both lived to see their fame established beyond all rivalry. Mommsen's publications extended over sixty years. There is no immaturity in his early works and no decline in the later. He alone achieved the complete assimilation and reproduction of a classic civilisation for which scholars have struggled since Scaliger. Rome before Mommsen was like modern Europe before Ranke. *Latericiam accepit, marmoream reliquit.*[1]

II

Two of Mommsen's German contemporaries wrote histories which enjoyed considerable popularity. The first edition of Peter's narrative appeared in 1853, the second after the 'Roman History' had taken the world by storm. As a Niebuhrian he was among the critics of the great historian, but he repudiated the charge that he was more conservative. He briefly sketched the legends of the Kings, warning his readers that they are unhistorical, but he accepts tradition as a guide to the form and growth of the constitution. His narrative only grows detailed when Polybius comes to the rescue. He admires the patriotic, moral, orderly life of the Republic, but agrees that decay set in after the Gracchi. His

[1] For a general survey see Kroll, *Die Altertumswissenschaft im letzen Vierteljahrhundert*, 1905. *The Year's Work in Classical Studies* began to appear in 1906.

estimate of the protagonists in the final struggles is sane and moderate. 'We cannot blame Cicero,' he remarks, 'for not seeing, as we see, that the Republic was doomed.' He admits that Cæsar governed wisely and well, but he denies his power to rejuvenate the State. 'We cannot look at the picture of the Roman State at its highest point—that is, during the Punic wars—without admiration.' But their conquests led to their own destruction, and the century of civil war destroyed the respect for law. The ruins of the old Roman character were further broken up by Augustus and Tiberius, and trampled under foot by Caligula, Claudius and Nero.

A more popular narrative was that of Ihne, who confined himself to the Republic and treated it in greater detail. Appearing at intervals between 1868 and 1890, the work was written in some respects as a counterblast to Mommsen, for whom he entertained no friendly feelings. His ambition was to tread in the footsteps of Arnold. 'If Arnold had finished his work,' he wrote, 'and it had been kept up to date, I should probably not have written my book.' His wish was to summarise existing knowledge rather than to advance solutions. His account of early Rome bears unmistakable traces of Niebuhr and Schwegler. He has no heroes, and he deplores the cruelty of the Roman character. 'I am accused of unfairness to Rome,' he declared. 'That is not the case; but I am fair to Greece and Carthage, remembering that the Roman historians, who are not always very veracious, have had the ear of the world and have silenced all opposing voices.' In reaching the closing days of the Republic he accepts the foundation of personal rule as inevitable. Cæsar and Pompey strove and struggled, but did not really deflect the course of history. 'The Republic fell not by Cæsar's decision or ambition. If he had died early the Republic would none the less have found a master. He solved the problem without passion, with grandeur and elevation of spirit.' Though the book lacked power and originality, its balanced tone made it a favourite with those who were repelled by the strident partisanship of Mommsen.

Outside Germany the most ambitious history was written by Duruy,[1] the enlightened Minister of Napoleon III. The first two volumes were published in 1843-4; but though the third and fourth were ready by 1850 they were held back till 1872, as they eulogised Cæsar and the Empire. He leans on Niebuhr and Schwegler in the early centuries, and anticipates Mommsen in his view of the transition to the Empire. Writing in 1880 he remarked that the Republicans were but a narrow oligarchy who,

[1] See Lavisse, *Victor Duruy*, 1895.

when they had conquered the world, did not know how to govern it. On its fall a hundred families suffered loss, but eighty millions profited. In the volumes written in later life Duruy made full use of the Inscriptions, and shared Mommsen's view of the services of the Empire to civilisation. In an elaborate survey of society in the first two centuries he contends that the life of the provinces was as wholesome as that of the capital was corrupt. He continued his work to the death of Theodosius, thus achieving the only detailed narrative of Roman history from beginning to end. The popularity of the book was enhanced by the illustrations which the author added to a later edition, and it was translated into German, Italian and English. Though it was impossible for Duruy, who was also the author of histories of France and Greece, to be a profound student, his powerful mind and immense energy made him a serviceable guide. The most important recent attempt at a detailed narrative is that of Gaetano de Sanctis, whose 'Storia dei Romani' was the first large scale attempt to gather up the results of research since Mommsen. He steers a middle course between scepticism and credulity, dealing fully with the early races and with the Greeks in Italy. Reviving a favourite idea of Niebuhr, he believes that a large quantity of popular poetry once existed and that the legends were derived from it, and even that some of the old ballads could be tentatively reconstructed from tradition. Heitland's survey of the Republic aims at a judicial narrative, discarding the paradoxes of fellow-students and advancing none of his own. He shows his independence of Mommsen in his portraits of Caius Gracchus and Sulla, Cicero and Cæsar. His recognition of the necessity of Cæsar's work does not involve approval of his character or condemnation of the champions of a hopeless cause.

Valuable contributions to Roman history have been made by men who have chosen special problems or periods. Our knowledge of pre-Roman Italy is being slowly increased by the combined labours of archæology, ethnology and philology. The influence of physical conditions was for the first time thoroughly explored by Nissen.[1] As historians of Greece before Curtius had known nothing of the physical characteristics of the peninsula, so Niebuhr, Schwegler and even Mommsen had paid little attention to the stage on which their drama was enacted. Nissen's study of the mountains, the rivers, the coasts, the natural resources and the climate supplied a new background for historic events. The works of Ettore Pais on Sicily and Italy to the Punic Wars reveal utter scepticism in regard to the traditions of early Rome, and

[1] *Italische Landeskunde*, 2 vols., 1883-1902.

maintain that the Consular Fasti were falsified. He has more confidence in the evidence of archæology, language and place names. The 'Ancient Legends of Roman History' form a pendant to his larger work and discuss recent discoveries in the Forum. He believes that many Roman traditions were merely mythical personifications of the seven hills of Rome. Since Otfried Müller wrote his brilliant survey of the Etruscans excavations have steadily continued, and their religion, art and social conditions are now known in considerable detail. Yet their origin and racial affinities are still in doubt, and their language still defies interpretation.

It was a common complaint against Mommsen that he did not discuss the value of his sources, the critical analysis of which was inaugurated by Nissen, whose studies of the fourth and fifth decades of Livy examined the writings and personality of the historian with a thoroughness never before approached. His results, which were less negative than those commonly accepted, were attacked by Peter, who maintained that Livy's work was intended rather as an exhortation to patriotism and virtue than as a serious narrative. His conclusions, however, were supported by Nitzsch, whose 'Römische Annalistik' declared that we can reach contemporary evidence through works of second and third hand. He has been called the last of the Niebuhrians, and he certainly belongs rather to the school of Niebuhr than of Mommsen. Nitzsch also worked at a history of the Republic, fragments of which, supplemented by his lectures, appeared after his death. The power and freshness of the treatment evoked lively regrets that he had not written a complete survey. While Mommsen's main interest was in the life of the State, Nitzsch devoted his attention rather to social and economic factors, emphasising the struggle of the peasantry with the new capitalism of commerce and transport.

The closing scenes of the Republic have continued to attract historians more than all the earlier or later centuries. A detailed narrative was written by George Long, which, though lacking colour, rested on profound acquaintance with the literary sources and displayed a balanced judgment. Forty years later Greenidge planned a work embracing the last century of the Republic and the early Empire to A.D. 70. The book opens with a valuable review of social and economic conditions, and is mainly devoted to the Gracchi. While Tiberius was contented with social reform, Caius demanded also political and judical changes. Both legislated without the Senate, which was already an obstruction, and the first bloodshed was the beginning of the civil wars. The death of

Greenidge after the completion of the first volume was a serious blow to Roman studies. Other English scholars have made valuable contributions to a knowledge of the period of transition. Warde Fowler's popular life of Cæsar virtually adopts Mommsen's view of the hero. Cæsar, he declares, possessed high aims and true humanity. Rome needed and wished for absolutism: the city-state was played out, the Senate selfish and incapable. Though technically guilty of treason, he was justified by the need of introducing a rational government, and no statesman has accomplished work of such lasting value. Though far from perfect and guilty of occasional cruelties, he was affectionate and lovable. He and Cicero were the noblest characters of the age. Vindication of Cicero has been carried further by Strachan-Davidson's biography and Tyrrell's edition of the Letters. Cæsar's campaigns in Gaul and Britain have been studied with incomparable thoroughness by Rice Holmes. In his admirable handbook of Roman history and in the Oxford lectures which his hearers will never forget, Pelham devoted special attention to the relation between the Republic and the Principate.

No work since Mommsen aroused such world-wide interest as Ferrero's 'Greatness and Decline of Rome.'[1] Though coldly received by scholars, its ability and suggestiveness are unquestionable. Beginning life as a pupil of Lombroso he became an active politician, and it was from the point of view of a sociologist that he approached the study of the ancient world. He traces the fall of the Republic to the advent of the mercantile era in an old agricultural and aristocratic society. The fall of Carthage was followed by an influx of riches which led to an increase of luxury and a higher standard of needs. The conflict of rich and poor became acute. Foreign policy and internal evolution were determined by changes in the distribution of wealth, and individual actors in the drama are borne helplessly along on the current of economic change. Thus the critical period of Roman history is primarily an economic problem, a struggle rather of economic forces than of political groups. The Republic was slain not by Sulla or Cæsar but by Imperialism. 'Great men are unaware of the historic work of which they are the instruments and victims, for they, like their fellows, are the sport of what we may call the destiny of history.' For the old vision of soldiers struggling with one another for power was substituted that of the conflict of men

---

[1] Among the best criticisms are those by Besnier, *Revue Historique*, vol. xcv., and Haverfield, 'Roman History since Mommsen,' *Quarterly Review*, Oct. 1912. Croce dismisses the book as a discredit to Italian scholarship. *Storia della Storiografia Italiana*, ii., 245–7.

with a fate that was too strong for them. Ferrero is still more audacious than Mommsen in his efforts to visualise the past. He compares the Romans of the early Republic to the Boers, Lucullus to Napoleon, Cæsar to a Tammany boss, the power of Augustus to the President of the United States. But these and other comparisons, though irritating to the scholar, attracted readers who shrink from academic works.

The narrative becomes detailed when Sulla dies. One of the novelties of the book is the importance attached to Lucullus, 'the strongest man in the history of Rome,' who turned Italy from civil war to the conquest of the East. But it was only a temporary diversion, and quarrels quickly arose about the spoils. He blames Mommsen's fanatical admiration for Cæsar, whom he regards as an accomplished opportunist. He was 'the unconscious instrument of Destiny for an immense work,' but he never saw the goal or fathomed the meaning of his own enterprises. He fought in Gaul because there was nowhere else to fight, ignorant of the fact that its conquest would be the beginning of European history. He was above all a destroyer, and he founded nothing durable. As Cæsar dominates the first half of the book, his nephew pervades the second. While most critics deem Mommsen to have underestimated the power of the Princeps, Ferrero believes he exaggerated it. Augustus emerges from his pages a man of small calibre and limited vision, cowardly and nervous at first, though growing in mind and will in later years. He was not the successor but the antithesis of Cæsar. The régime of Augustus was not a monarchy, not even a dyarchy. His desire was to replace the State under the control of the Senate and to give the Senate the assistance of a Moderator. Thus he was but the President of a constitutional republic, and Ferrero calls his volume 'The Republic of Augustus.' Augustus presided over the transition wisely. The Empire was neither phenomenally wicked nor particularly happy. The historian is at his best in illustrating the connection between economic phenomena and political evolution. His studies of character and his estimate of statesmanship are weak. His mechanical philosophy reduces history to little more than a struggle of blind forces. Yet he denies that he is a materialist. He declared that the political, economic and social crises of Rome depended on the change of customs caused by the augmentation of wealth, expenditure and needs, which was in essence a psychological change.[1] 'The fundamental force in history is psychological, not economic.' It is the

---

[1] See *Characters and Events of Roman History from Caesar to Nero*, Lowell Lectures for 1908.

language as well as the spirit of Lamprecht. The key to Roman history is 'the automatic increase of ambitions and desires.' The mixture of East and West was at once the glory and weakness of Rome. The corruption of Rome has been greatly exaggerated. There was in reality only the same increase in wealth and wants which we are witnessing to-day. The appetite for pleasure and luxury grew, changing mentality and morality, policy and institutions. The rich parvenus succeeded the aristocracy, and the rich, then as now, were restless, neurotic and pessimistic. Such changes are at once the condition and the penalty of progress.

No adequate history of the Empire has been written. A provisional attempt was made by Hermann Schiller, a pupil of Mommsen, but his conscientious volumes lack distinction. Bury compiled a brief but useful summary of the first two centuries of the Empire. Seeck's six volumes, 'Geschichte des Untergangs der antiken Welt,' survey the politics and culture of Rome from Diocletian to 476. Among monographs on the Cæsars Gardthausen's monumental survey of the life and work of Augustus holds pride of place. Henderson's monograph on Nero typifies the reaction against Tacitean conceptions of the Empire. Gregorovius devoted a pleasant volume to Hadrian. The detailed study of the Provinces in the light of inscriptions, coins and archæology has made considerable advance. Otto Hirschfield's analysis of the Imperial administration added new details to his master's picture. Camille Jullian's vast survey of Roman Gaul is a classic. Haverfield dedicated his life to Roman Britain. The Austrian jurist Mitteis devoted a monograph of monumental learning, based on papyri and inscriptions, to the transition from Hellenic to Roman law in the Eastern Provinces.

Though the constitutional history of Rome owes most to Mommsen, valuable contributions have been made by scholars working on independent lines. The first thorough exploration of the institutions of the Republic was undertaken in Ludwig Lange's 'Roman Antiquities.'[1] His caution is in striking contrast to the dash and certitude of Mommsen. In a review of the 'Staatsrecht,' which attempted to present Roman government as an organism, Lange defended his antiquarian method on the ground that by following Mommsen's lead concrete facts might be sacrificed to juristic symmetry.[2] The 'Staatsrecht' found another and more hostile critic in Madvig.[3] The great Danish scholar had studied law in his youth, but quickly deserted it for

---

[1] See Neumann, *Ludwig Lange,* 1886.
[2] Lange, *Kleine Schriften,* vol. ii., 1887.
[3] See Nettleship, *Lectures and Essays,* Second Series, 1895.

Latin texts. In his old age, when blindness put a stop to his favourite studies, he dictated his volumes on the Constitution. To begin with the Magistracy, he declared, passing over the Senate and people, was to build the roof before the foundation. Mommsen explained political forms by modern theories, and some of his hypotheses were strained and fanciful. Madvig rejected the attempt to recover the conceptions which alone could afford deep insight into the institutions and their connection with one another. He treats the Empire in the old way of lacking all constitutional character. Neglecting the inscriptions, it was dismissed by Otto Hirschfeld as out of date before its publication. A middle course is steered between the descriptive and juristic schools by Herzog's 'History and System of the Roman Constitution,' which emphasised the necessity of seizing the spirit of Roman public law, while contesting the success of Mommsen's endeavour. Unlike Mommsen, Herzog relates the growth of the constitution as a whole in its chronological development.

Life and culture have been diligently explored, but the extreme paucity of materials makes the recovery of the civilisation of the early Republic almost impossible. The most daring attempt was made by Fustel de Coulanges, who offered a complete interpretation of Roman civilisation in the terms of religion. The cult of the family, he declared in 'La Cité Antique,' was the keystone of the fabric. Early Roman society, which was founded on a religious basis, was simple and pure. With the break up of the family came the decline of the Republic. Though Fustel oversimplified a complex problem and attempted to unlock the life of centuries by a single master-key, he presented an extraordinarily suggestive reconstruction of society. Less harmonious but more convincing pictures of religious life and thought have been painted by Wissowa and Warde Fowler. The civilisation of the Empire has been the theme of three works of outstanding importance. Friedländer's 'Sittengeschichte,' published in 1860, immediately became a European classic. Revised by a group of specialists after the author's death, it still offers the most complete picture of Roman civilisation from Augustus to the end of the Antonines. Next in time come the fascinating studies of Gaston Boissier, whose 'Roman Religion' discussed the entry of Oriental faiths, the rise of the worship of the Emperor, and the philosophy of Seneca. His later work, 'The End of Paganism,' continues the narrative. Dill's delightful volumes on Roman Society in the second and fourth centuries are distinguished for their insight and learning. The Empire has profited by the works of scholars working in other fields, such as Renan and Harnack, Neumann and Ramsay, de Rossi's explorations in the catacombs and Cumont's studies of Mithraism.

No province has been more sedulously cultivated than the archæology of Rome. The partial excavation of the Forum by Fea during the French occupation gave the needed impetus to research, and during the years of the Restoration Nibby and Canina worked at the reconstruction of the city. Systematic treatment began with Bunsen's 'Description of the City of Rome' and Becker's masterly sketches in his 'Roman Antiquities.' The 'Roman Topography' of Jordan, a pupil of Moritz Haupt, marked the first decisive advance since Bunsen. Boni's excavations in the Forum and on the Palatine have produced sensational results. A journal of the excavations was established in 1876, and the results were popularised by Lanciani and Hülsen. The exploration of Ostia has begun. The excavation of Pompeii moves slowly forward, and the rich harvest of results was garnered by Mau. The resurrection of Herculaneum was delayed by the expense involved in the necessity of removing a village and cutting through the solid rock. Excavation has largely increased the known remains of classical art, and the traditional conception of Roman sculpture as purely derivative has been overthrown. Italy still hides many secrets in her bosom, and the Schools of Archæology in the Eternal City look forward to a future of fruitful rivalry. Outside the peninsula the richest harvest has been gathered at Timgad, the pearl of Roman Africa.

CHAPTER XXV

THE JEWS AND THE CHRISTIAN CHURCH

I

THE recovery of the civilisations of the early East has run parallel with and fostered the application of critical methods to the Jewish Scriptures.[1] As Niebuhr's main conclusions were anticipated in the seventeenth and eighteenth centuries, several results of Old Testament scholarship were foreseen by isolated thinkers of an earlier time. Hobbes denied the Mosaic origin of the Pentateuch, and Spinoza noted its composite character. Père Simon provoked the wrath of Bossuet by suggesting that the Old Testament should be criticised like other books. A long step forward was taken when in 1753 the French Jew Astruc separated the Elohim and Jehovah strains of the Pentateuch. But the era of systematic criticism opens with Eichhorn, who caught the spirit of historical research prevailing at Göttingen. He regarded the books of the Old Testament as possessing an oriental character, and requiring interpretation in the light of Semitic ideas. The attempt to substitute a less mechanical conception of the sacred writings was simultaneously made by Herder, who described the Old Testament as a mirror of the folk-soul of Israel. Bound by close friendship, Eichhorn and Herder independently reached broadly similar results. Many years later Goethe looked back with gratitude to the two men who had opened up a new source of delight in the literature of the Jews. Eichhorn's 'Introduction to the Old Testament,' published in 1783, was the first comprehensive attempt to apply critical methods to the sacred books. He had worked, he declared, in an unknown field. He only knew of Astruc's discovery at second hand, and testified that he had reached the same goal independently. He classified the component parts of the Pentateuch according as they belonged to the Jehovistic or Elohistic version, and pointed out that many of the books of the Old Testament had passed through several hands.

If Eichhorn was the founder of Old Testament criticism, his

---

[1] See Cheyne's *Founders of Old Testament Criticism*, 1893; Duff, *History of Old Testament Criticism*, 1910.

pupil Ewald[1] was the first critical historian of the Jews. 'What Wolf and Niebuhr have done for Greece and Rome,' wrote Arnold to Bunsen in 1835, 'seems sadly wanted for Judæa.' Milman's 'History of the Jews,' written in 1829, was useful in insisting that the Bible should be studied like any other historical book and the Jews as a member of the Semitic family; but, though described by Stanley as the first decisive inroad of German theology into England, the treatment was too brief and the author's knowledge too slight to meet the need of students. Born at Göttingen, where he was to pass most of his life, Ewald embarked on the study of Oriental languages while still at school and sat at the feet of Eichhorn. Equally interested in philology, theology and history, he succeeded to his master's chair in 1827. He lectured on Sanskrit, Persian and Turkish, as well as on Semitic languages, and won his first triumph by a Hebrew Grammar. His commentaries on the Psalms, Job, Proverbs and Ecclesiastes, which he described collectively as the Poetical Books, showed that his religious insight was worthy of his philological equipment, and he penetrated deeper into the meaning of the prophets than any of his predecessors.

As a young man Ewald formed the design of a 'History of the People of Israel,' and after the completion of the Prophets he set himself to gather up the results that had been obtained by half a century of scholarship. The work began to appear in 1843, and the author lived to issue a third edition in 1864–8. In a long Introduction he declared that the gaps in the historical books could be filled by the poetic and prophetic writings, which best conveyed the feelings of the age. The first volume reaches the death of Moses, and treats the early history as mythical, not fictitious. He describes Abraham as a representative man, and explains the quarrel of Jacob and Esau as the conflict between Hebrew and Arabian tribes. Moses is clearly historical and is the greatest founder of a religion after Christ. The passage of the Red Sea is historical, though not miraculous. Of the Israelites themselves the historian gives an eloquent but over-coloured picture. They discerned God and dared the uttermost under His guidance. The Law of Moses first proclaimed a God who delivers those who seek Him in spirit, obedience and faith. In this 'glorious primeval age' the belief in Jehovah gave strength in battle and stimulated every aspect of life. Before Moses religion was individual; with him it became national as well. Ewald's treatment

---

[1] The most authoritative study is by Wellhausen, in *Festschrift zur Feier d. 150jährigen Bestehens der Akademie der Wissenschaften zu Göttingen,* 1901.

of early history was stimulating but arbitrary. Like Niebuhr, he was often praised for his faculty of divination when he was merely giving rein to his imagination. On reaching the Kings he is on firmer ground. His portraits of Saul, David and Solomon are painted with vigour. He makes a hero of David and idealises his people, whom he affirms to be as yet uncorrupted. His picture of Elijah glows with colour. The narrative of the later centuries is less impressive than that of the heroic age.

To read Ewald is to measure the gulf that separates the middle from the end of the nineteenth century. In the first place, his story is drawn almost exclusively from the Old Testament itself. In narrating the conquest of Samaria in his revision of 1865 he declares Assyrian too little understood to be available for the purposes of an historian. Neither the revelation of ancient civilisations nor the nascent science of comparative religion is mirrored in his work. Secondly, the Jews are throughout the Chosen People, who, though not free from grave faults, are in the early centuries at any rate worthy of their privileged position. Their leading figures are too much idealised. Finally, he has no suspicion of the late origin of the law, and Wellhausen places the 'History' below the philological works. 'I cannot admit that he opened the gate or pointed the way, like De Wette or Vatke. He was rather the great holder-up, who by his authority prevented the true interpretation of Jewish history being accepted.' Pfleiderer pronounced the book a didactic romance, and convicted the author of retarding biblical criticism by a generation. Despite these faults of commission and omission his volumes occupy a prominent place in historiography. His Semitic scholarship was beyond cavil, and no one could read him without feeling that the history of the Jews was equal in dramatic interest to that of Greece and Rome. The book found a warm welcome in England. Stanley pronounced it a noble work, building on it his own 'Lectures on the History of the Jewish Church,' which utilised the author's knowledge of the Holy Land.

The revolution in our conception of the Old Testament which is associated with the name of Wellhausen, and which put Ewald on the shelf, was prepared by the independent labours of several scholars. De Wette, in Wellhausen's words, 'the epoch-making pioneer of historical criticism in this field,' was the first to notice that the Mosaic law was unknown to Judges, Kings and Prophets alike, and to contend that Deuteronomy was little, if at all, older than King Josiah; but the bold hypotheses of his earlier works were toned down in his later years, and the solution of the problem was reserved for a younger scholar. Vatke's 'Biblical

Theology,' published in 1835, contended that the religion of Israel was subject to the law of development; but it was less the Hegelian philosophy of the work than his discovery of the real sequence of the sacred books which gives it its outstanding importance.[1] Yet the assertion of the late origin of the priestly code was buried in a large and difficult volume. His greatest achievement is to have led Wellhausen to write, 'I have learned most and best from Vatke.' While Vatke was propounding new ideas at Berlin, similar conclusions had been reached by Reuss[2] at Strassburg. It flashed upon him that the Prophets were earlier than the Law, and the Psalms later than both. In seeking a clue to the religious development of the Jews he was confronted by the alleged existence of the complete Levitical system in the earliest stage of Jewish history, coupled with the absence of any knowledge of it in the Prophets. His conclusions were formulated in 1833 in twelve theses, which were so novel that he dared not publish them, and which were worked up half a century later in his 'History of the Old Testament Scriptures.' He found Vatke's book so forbidding in appearance that he did not read it, and it was not till his ideas were developed by his own pupils that he returned to the problems of his youth. Among his hearers was Graf, whose 'Historical Books of the Old Testament,' published in 1866, grew out of the germ planted in his mind a generation earlier. The Grafian hypothesis, as it came to be called, was adopted in Duhm's classical work on the Prophets, which placed them at the centre of the religious development of the Jews; but other powerful voices had to be raised before traditional errors could be overthrown.

Kuenen's studies of the Old Testament won him the reputation of a consummate scholar, and his 'Religion of Israel,' published in 1869, adopted the Grafian hypothesis.[3] Though lacking the eloquence of Ewald, the Leyden Professor inspires far more confidence. He denied the exceptional origin and the unique character of the Jewish religion, rejected the miracles of the Old Testament, and pronounced the early history in the Pentateuch and Joshua mainly legendary. No firm ground could be reached till about 800, when contemporary materials began. A history of the religious ideas of the Jews, he declared, had been rendered possible by the new chronological arrangement of the books of the Old Testament. Beginning with a sketch of religion in the

[1] See Benecke's full length biography, *Wilhelm Vatke*, 1883.

[2] *Reuss' Briefwechsel mit Graf*, 1904, is of interest for the development of Old Testament studies.

[3] See Réville, *Abraham Kuenen*, 1890.

eighth century, he glances back at the origins. Abraham, Isaac and Jacob may have existed. Moses certainly did exist. The Exodus probably took place about 1300. Polytheism was not an innovation but the creed of the majority till the Exile. The priestly legislation, drawn up and written down after the Exile, had arisen at various times and been more than once worked up before reaching its final form. The third volume is devoted to a survey of Judaism, and the narrative ends with the fall of Jerusalem. Kuenen's work, with its lengthy appendices and notes, is rather a string of dissertations than a narrative, but his abiding merit is to have interpreted the successive stages of the religion of Israel which Ewald had failed to grasp.

With the publication of Wellhausen's 'Composition of the Hexateuch' in 1876 and his 'History of Israel' in 1878 the hypothesis which Vatke, Graf and Kuenen had expounded in their books, and Reuss and Lagarde in their lectures, ceased to be the possession of isolated scholars and became public property.[1] Though starting as a pupil of Ewald he sensed that the Law and the Prophets were different worlds, and he welcomed the Grafian hypothesis on its appearance. In Judges, Kings and·Prophets there was no sign of the Law, whereas after the Exile it at once became prominent. These facts told their own tale. The Mosaic law was not the starting-point of the history of ancient Israel but of Judaism. Deuteronomy was found in the Temple under Josiah. The Levitical law was not written till after the fall of the Kingdom of Judah, and the Pentateuch was not accepted as authoritative till Ezra. It thus became possible to estimate the originality and significance of the Prophets. The book aroused the greatest excitement among historians and theologians all over the world. The work was never continued, and reappeared in later editions under the more suitable title of 'Prolegomena to the History of Israel'; but he contributed a brief 'History of Israel and Judah' to the ninth edition of the 'Encyclopædia Britannica,' and in 1894 published a fuller narrative.

Wellhausen's book divided Old Testament scholars into two camps, but most of the experts enlisted under his banner. It was generally recognised that his reconstruction alone rendered the religious development of the Jews intelligible, and three years later Stade began to publish a history of Israel based on its conclusions. The tone of the work is highly critical, indeed almost polemical. 'Our science lags behind other historical sciences

[1] Wellhausen's results are well summarised in Pfleiderer, *Development of Theology since Kant*, 1890. Cp. Robertson Smith's review in *Lectures and Essays*, 1912.

because it has been almost monopolised by theologians.' To advance it needed the aid of philologists, historians and students of comparative religion. In his pages there is little left of the traditional story of early Israel. He finds no evidence for the sojourn in Egypt, and declares the narratives of the conquest of Canaan mere sagas. With David we reach solid ground, but we must be on our guard against the colossal exaggerations of the chroniclers. The realm of David and Solomon was small, its culture primitive, the splendours of court and temple a myth. David was a typical ruler of one of the many little principalities into which Syria was then divided. The discovery of King Mesa's inscription reveals Moab with its tribal god and its identical order of ideas. There was no monotheism before the Prophets, and ancestor-worship and belief in spirits were general. The practical difference between Elohim and Yahweh was small. Adopting Wellhausen's results, Stade finds no trace of the Mosaic law before King Josiah. The exile in Babylon he believes to have been in no way painful except in the diminished opportunity for religious devotion. No reader can fail to be impressed by the power and erudition of the first large critical history of the Jews, but the undertone of controversy and the constant emphasis on the falsity of tradition interfere with its enjoyment.

The chief exponent of Wellhausen's views in England was his friend Robertson Smith.[1] Having learned the secrets of Semitic philology from Lagarde at Göttingen, he was appointed at the age of twenty-four 'to a professorship of Oriental languages and the Old Testament at the Free Church College at Aberdeen in 1870. In 1875 he contributed an article on the Bible to the ninth edition of the 'Encyclopædia Britannica' which led to a charge of heresy. The prolonged trial aroused as much interest as that of Colenso. The Professor was finally acquitted of heresy but deprived of his chair. Confident in his critical principles he delivered lectures to large audiences in Edinburgh and Glasgow, which were published under the title of 'The Old Testament in the Jewish Church,' and 'The Prophets of Israel.' Though popular in treatment they combined exhaustive knowledge of Continental scholarship with original views. His appointment to the Arabic chair at Cambridge was followed by his 'Kinship and Marriage in Early Arabia' and his 'Lectures on the Religion of the Semites,' a systematic comparison of Hebrew religion with the beliefs and practices of other branches of the Semitic family. He pointed out that beliefs varied and were difficult to date, and that only

[1] See the biography by Black and Chrystal, 1912. Cp. Burkitt, *Eng. Hist. Review*, Oct. 1894.

religious observances were primitive and fixed. His investigations led him to reject the notion of fundamental differences between Semites and Aryans. These volumes are full of profound research and brilliant analysis. Though less popular than his early lectures, they revealed the existence in England of a Semitic scholar equal in learning and insight to the greatest names in Holland and Germany. His early death was an irreparable loss to the study of the Old Testament and to the nascent science of comparative religion.

The critical treatment of Jewish history on the lines of Well-hausen was inaugurated in France by Renan.[1] His work on the 'Origins of Christianity' completed, he returned to the field in which he had won his spurs. He had written a learned history of Semitic languages, had visited the scenes of Jewish history, and had persuaded the Academy of Inscriptions to undertake a Corpus of Semitic Inscriptions. 'To have been consistent,' he declared, 'I should have commenced my "Origins of Christianity" with the volume I publish to-day, for they go back to the great prophets who introduced morality into religion.' He adds that he chose the most urgent part of his task first owing to the un-certainty of life. But at sixty he found himself still in good health, plunged boldly into his task, and lived to complete in five volumes the most readable though not the most convincing history of the Jewish people ever written.

The first volume extends to David, and embraces the legend-ary history of the Israelites. Renan is convinced that tradition contains precious elements, if not of fact, at least of atmosphere. In traversing this twilight world the historian needs imagination. 'Even if I have guessed wrongly on some points, I am certain that I have grasped the unique work which the breath of God, that is the soul of the world, has realised through Israel.' He warns his readers that he is providing less a history than a half imaginative reconstruction of society and religion before the historical period. The outlines can be traced—the life in Baby-lonia, the sojourn in Egypt, the exodus under Moses or some other leader; but before David there are no certain facts. It is useless to ask what happened; we can only picture various ways in which things may have happened. Every sentence should include a 'perhaps.' The book pleased the public far more than the experts. Kuenen declared that in omitting an analysis of the sources he was setting sail without a chart, and complained that he accepted

---

[1] The best books on Renan are by Grant Duff, 1893; Séailles, 1895; Mme. Darmesteter, 1897. Darmesteter, *Notice sur la Vie et l'Œuvre de Renan*, 1893, gives an expert's verdict on the Semitic scholar.

and rejected material with equal caprice. Wellhausen condemned the volume as unworthy of his reputation. Robertson Smith pronounced his reconstruction of the patriarchal age altogether wrong. The patriarchs, declared Smith, were quite different from nomads, and resembled the great householders of the time of the Kings. Equally baseless was his conviction of the monotheistic tendency of the Semites, for it was only in Israel, and then owing only to the Prophets, that monotheism developed. He exaggerated the difference between Yahweh and Elohim, and the latter was a creature of his fancy. He idealised the early Israelities and believed that they degenerated, whereas their religious ideas were clarified and purified by time. Thus the first volume, despite its literary charm, is the weakest of the five.[1]

With David, the founder of Jerusalem and the dynasty, the historical period is declared to begin, but the portrait is as darkly shadowed as that of Ewald erred by excess of colour. The king makes no appeal to Renan, who believes his power to have been magnified by tradition and points out that he can no longer claim credit for the Psalms. He is compared to one of the kinglets of Abyssinia or to Abd-el-Kader, the warrior chief of Algeria, a ruthless potentate surrounded by his harem and supported by mercenaries, lacking religious and moral ideas. Solomon was a miniature Louis XIV, more intelligent than his father, but a thorough epicurean. Of the divided Kingdom Renan paints a sombre picture. The times were rude, the Kings were cruel, and Yahweh encouraged every abomination. Of Elijah, whom he pronounces in large measure a legendary figure, he writes with detestation for his savage intolerance. Ahab appears as a tolerant and enlightened ruler. The most important event of the time was the reduction to writing of the legends of the patriarchs and the wars, followed by the independent Yahwist and Elohistic compositions which were long after worked up into the Pentateuch.

The picture of the Prophets was universally criticised. Renan often declares that the Jews stood for religion as the Greeks for intellect; but though admitting that Israel owes them its historic importance, he finds as much to blame as to praise. Amos is sombre and narrow, passionately threatening the day of wrath, urging men to rend their hearts, not their garments. Hosea is like a preacher of the *Ligue* or a Puritan pamphleteer. Isaiah's reputation is largely due to his supposed authorship of the writings

[1] For specialist criticisms see Robertson Smith, *Lectures and Essays*, 1912, and Kuenen, 'Drei Wege, Ein Ziel,' in *Gesammelte Abhandlungen*, 1894.

of the far greater genius who lived during the Exile. The prophet was the conscience of his people; but he was a publicist not less than a preacher, a politician not less than a theologian, a forerunner of Calvin, Knox and Cromwell. Renan cannot conceal his contempt for the shrill intolerance of Jeremiah, whom he pillories as one of the founders of religious persecution and an enemy of the Monarchy and the State. Ezekiel suggested the 'Châtiments' of Victor Hugo and the social visions of Fourier. Exclusive preoccupation with moral standards does not tend either to culture or to national strength, and the Prophets hastened the doom of a people who had in any case no talent for politics. Yet they possess undying importance. They transmuted a tribal God into the righteous Lord of the universe. They pleaded the cause of the poor and humble. They were the founders of the religion of humanity, the forerunners of Jesus. Early Israel possessed no real religion. The Elohim were the spirits of the air, Yahweh the capricious despot of a tiny world who exacted sacrifice but not a pure and contrite heart. It was the Prophets who turned dross into gold and evolved the idea of ethical monotheism. No one has written with greater enthusiasm of the Second Isaiah, the last and greatest of the Prophets. 'With him we are on a mountain top whence we discern Jesus on the summit of another mountain, with a deep depression between.'

The transformation of a secular state into a theocracy, which had begun before the Captivity, is traced in detail, but without sympathy. Renan sharply castigates the futility of the Priestly Code and the sterile scholasticism of its commentators. Nehemiah is described as the first Jesuit, who turned Jerusalem into a tomb. The Law was the most terrible instrument of torture ever invented, an unpardonable departure from the tradition of the Prophets whose work was only resumed by Christ. The spirit was slain by the letter. The chapters on Judaism, though containing a good deal of sound criticism, are far too polemical. He admires the heroism of Judas Maccabæus, but dwells with most pleasure on the emancipating influence of Hellenism, the cultured scepticism of the Sadducees and Ecclesiastes, the large-hearted charity of Hillel and Philo. The richly-coloured studies of culture and literature, of society and thought, of the ideals and superstitions which made up the atmosphere of the Hellenistic era, show that the hand of the historian, though old and weary, had not lost its cunning. He had fulfilled the ambition of his life, for his two great works form an organic whole. 'All that the Frenchman of ordinary culture knows of the ancient East,' testified Brunetière, 'of comparative religion, of exegesis, comes directly or indirectly from Renan.' His achievement is to have aroused interest. It is the task of more prosaic scholars to continue and correct his work.

The acceptance of Wellhausen's reconstruction was by no means unanimous or unconditional. The elder Delitzsch lamented that, if he was right, it would no longer be possible to speak of 'the Law and the Prophets.' Hommel accepted him for a time and subsequently reverted to the traditional view. Immediately after the appearance of Stade's iconoclastic volumes, Kittel came forward with a rival interpretation of Jewish history till the Captivity. Though dismissed by Robertson Smith as a dilution of Wellhausen, and though certain concessions are made to the critical school, the book belongs to the conservative camp of Dillmann. He believes in Abraham and Joseph, regards the Decalogue as Mosaic, and finds fragments of genuine tradition in the historical books which other scholars dismiss as accretions. The work is a compromise between the traditional and the critical schools, and the attribution of the main part of the Priestly Code to the reign of Hezekiah tangles the threads of development. Its chief merit is the detailed analysis of the sources. Other critics of Wellhausen, while accepting his view as to the late redaction of the Law, believe that parts of it are far older, in substance if not in form, than he allows. A Jewish view of Jewish history in the light of modern research has been presented with admirable skill in the Hibbert Lectures of Montefiore.

In addition to general histories, innumerable monographs add stone after stone to the edifice. Useful surveys of the literature of the Old Testament have been provided by Reuss, Cornill and Driver. George Adam Smith's 'Historical Geography of the Holy Land' is a classic. Gunkel studied the sources and character of Hebrew cosmology. Eduard Meyer analysed the legends of the Patriarchs and reviewed the neighbours of early Israel. The post-exilic era has attracted increasing attention. A sensation was caused when Kosters, a Dutch theologian, asserted that the return from captivity under Cyrus was a myth, and that the Temple was built by those who had remained behind. The contention was rebutted by Eduard Meyer, whose 'Origin of Judaism' established the authenticity of the Persian documents in Ezra. Cheyne painted one of the best pictures of religious life after the Exile. Schürer's monumental 'History of the Jewish People in the Time of Christ' is a panorama of the politics, religion and philosophy, the literature and society of three centuries, utilising the new evidence of inscriptions, papyri and coins.

The history of the Jews has benefited far less by archæological research than that of Egypt or Assyria.[1] No splendid buildings or sculpture have been brought to light at Jerusalem, the inscriptions are few, and discoveries in other lands throw little light on the Bible narrative. The first systematic explorations of the country were made by Edward Robinson, an American teacher of Hebrew, who published the record of his first journey in 1838, and by Tobler, whose seven volumes of historical topography correspond to Leake's survey of Greece. The foundation of the Palestine Exploration Fund in 1865 and of the German Palestine Society in 1878 provided the machinery for co-operative effort. American and German schools of Archæology were established in Jerusalem. Lachish was explored by Flinders Petrie and Bliss, who discovered the remains of eleven cities dating from about 1700 to 400 B.C. Some of the secrets of Megiddo were unveiled by Schumacher, to whom we also owe our scanty knowledge of Samaria. Sellin can point to fruitful labours at Taanach and Jericho. The historic life of Gezer has been minutely revealed by Macalister, the strata of seven cities reaching to the neolithic age. The most piquant result of his excavations has been to rehabilitate the Philistines, the authors of the most artistic objects found in the accumulations of two thousand years. We can now trace Palestine back far into the third millennium, and watch the cave-dwellers being gradually dispossessed by Semite invaders. A partial excavation of Jerusalem has revealed a network of pre-historic tunnels and aqueducts. The most sensational finds come from beyond the borders of Israel and Judah. The stele of Mesha, commonly known as the Moabite stone, the earliest inscription in a Semitic alphabet, dating from the time of Ahaziah and Jehosophat, was discovered in 1868. Assyrian inscriptions, among them those of Sargon and Sennacherib describing the capture of Samaria and the siege of Jerusalem under Hezekiah, supplement the Old Testament narrative. The Tell-el-Amarna letters, which light up the politics and culture of Palestine in the fourteenth century, speak of the Chabiri, whom some scholars believe to be the Hebrews. The much-discussed inscription of Merenptah found by Petrie in 1896 containing the name Isirar is believed by some experts to denote the existence of Israelites under his rule in Palestine, but no decisive evidence of a sojourn of Israel in Egypt has come to light. The discovery in 1904 of papyri records of a Jewish military colony at Elephantine, an island near the

---

[1] See Père Vincent, Canaan d'après l'Exploration récente, 1907; Driver, Schweich Lectures, 1909; Bliss, The Development of Palestine Exploration, 1906; Hilbrecht, Explorations in Bible Lands, 1903; Macalister, A Century of Excavation in Palestine, 1925; Kenyon, The Bible and Archæology, 1940.

first cataract, throws welcome light on the fifth century. Aramaic had already supplanted Hebrew, and though worshippers of Yahweh the settlers were not monotheists.

The most notable feature of recent Old Testament study has been the discussion of the debt of the Jews to Babylonian religion and culture, but it was not until Delitzsch delivered a lecture in Berlin in 1902 that the relationship became a topic of universal discussion. 'Babel and Bible' sold by tens of thousands and was followed at intervals by a series of discourses confirming and developing its contentions. Till recently, he declared, Israel had been held to be one of the oldest of civilisations and to have formed a world by itself, while the Old Testament was regarded as the main authority for the Ancient East. But an older and vaster civilisation had been discovered from which Israel derived not only her science but her religion. The Tell-el-Amarna tablets revealed the supremacy of Babylonian culture from the Euphrates to the Nile, and the Israelites drew in its influence with their earliest breath. The saga of the Flood arose naturally in a land subject to constant inundations. The Creation legends were Babylonian, the creator being the God Marduk. The story of the forbidden fruit, the serpent and the fall appears on a Babylonian cylinder. Though polytheism prevailed, the idea of a supreme God was general. The moral level of Babylonian civilisation was not conspicuously lower than that of Israel, and the position of women, a legacy from the Sumerians, was higher. Astronomy was invented in the plains of Mesopotamia, with the division of the hour into sixty minutes and the minute into sixty seconds. The Jews were no more original in religion and ethics than in science and law.

The denial of the originality of the Jews brought the champions of tradition into the field. The fiercest rejoinder came from Hommel, who roundly declared that what was new in the lectures was not true. The Israelites, he asserted, made their own religion. Delitzsch was wrong in his conception of Babylonian monotheism, and Biblical origins were Chaldaic, not Babylonian. The Pentateuch, though not the work of Moses, was composed not very long after his time, and Canaanite-Babylonian influences only appeared in additions. Less rigidly conservative scholars were also far from satisfied. The science was so young, declared Kittel, that some sensation-mongering was inevitable. The differences between the cosmology of Babylon and the Bible were fundamental. Babylonia was heathen, the Bible monotheist. The elements taken from Babylon were transmuted, and the later form was more truly original than the first conception. Israel turned dross into gold; Babylonia was a quarry, not a model. Delitzsch held his ground, offering fresh illustrations of his central thesis for which the excavations at Babylon supplied him with new material.

The indebtedness of the Jews to Babylonia is equally the message of Winckler, who elaborated the astral theory of Babylonian religion, and of Jeremias and Zimmern, who followed in his footsteps. In his 'History of Israel' the former contends that the legends from Abraham to Solomon belong to a system resting on Babylonian astrology. In his ingenious book, 'The Old Testament in the Light of the Ancient East,' Jeremias works out the influence in detail. He claims that Babylonia was the source of the highest conceptions found among the Jews, and that, while the popular religion of the Israelites was pagan, the pure cult of Yahweh, which came from Babylonia, was the faith of the leaders. So enduring was the Babylonian influence that it is to be found even in the Book of Revelation. The speculations of Winckler and his school, however fanciful, served to focus attention on the derivation of Jewish religion. The precise nature of the debt to Babylonia it is still too early to decide, but its recognition has sufficed to revolutionise the study of early Israel and to provide a new background for the religious history of the world. The chequered post-biblical fortunes of the Jews were first fully described in the voluminous work of Graetz.

II

The winning of ecclesiastical history[1] for science by Protestant scholarship has been one of the triumphs of the nineteenth century. The conflict of the Churches never slackens, the battle of belief and unbelief continues, yet some order and fixity are being introduced even into such controversial territory as the origins of Christianity and the Reformation.

The first detailed narrative was compiled by the Magdeburg centuriators; but their ardent Protestantism found nothing but a steady deterioration from the primitive Church, and in the Bishop of Rome they detected the features of Antichrist. The official answer was composed by Baronius with the help of the Vatican archives, and his mighty tomes are still of use. The

[1] See Baur, *Die Epochen der Kirchlichen Geschichtschreilbung*, 1852; Headlam, 'Methods of Early Church History,' in his *History, Authority and Theology*, 1909; Bratke, *Wegweiser zur Quellenkunde der Kirchengeschichte*, 1890; Conybeare, *History of New Testament Criticism*, 1910; Nigg, *Die Kirchengeschichtschreibung*, 1934; and the biographies in *Realencyklopädie für Protestantische Theologie u. Kirche.*

reaction against the hard-shelled formalism in which the Lutheran Church was imprisoned gave birth to pietism, and it was in the conviction that the Christian life was of infinitely higher value than a mechanical orthodoxy that Gottfried Arnold wrote his 'Impartial History of Churches and Heretics' in 1699.[1] The Reformation had begun in a revolt against the secularisation of the Church, but quickly imitated its faults. Recognising, like Flacius, an ever-increasing degeneration, he does not attribute it to the Papacy alone but to all the influences which turned the Church into a hierarchy and petrified Christianity into dogma. The message of Christ is to be found chiefly in the heretics, the heroes of the book, who arise in succession to protest against clericalism. In Mosheim[2] we miss the propagandist zeal of Flacius and the mystical piety of Arnold. He approached his subject without passion or unction, and wrote the first ecclesiastical history which belongs to the modern world. For him the Church is an institution like the State; his treatment is predominantly external, political, secular. The Göttingen Professors related the history of the Church to secular events and rejected a mass of legendary detail, but they lacked insight into distant times and other modes of thought. Spittler, the ablest of them, dismissed Athanasius as a clerical and Bernard as a despot. No one learned at Göttingen to love Church history or to reverence the saints.

The romantic movement restored sentiment and imagination to their thrones. The Ages of Faith rose into favour, and historians cared more to trace the operation of Christian principles than to castigate Rome. The embodiment of the new spirit was a Jew, David Mendel, who embraced Christianity at the age of seventeen, and took the name of August Neander.[3] Initiated into the philosophy of religion by Schleiermacher and nourished on Böhme and Plato, he found the teaching of Planck at Göttingen too rationalist for his taste. 'A new life of faith,' he declared many years later, 'had awakened which began to inspire study. A superficial, heartless enlightenment, which despised the greatness and the glory of the ages, was condemned both by life and by science.' He quickly learned to love the Fathers, but was satisfied with a simple pietistic Christianity. After a thesis on Clement of Alexandria, he wrote his first important work on Julian in 1812. In the following year, at the age of twenty-four,

---

[1] There is an interesting chapter on Arnold in Ritschl, *Geschichte des Pietismus*, vol. ii., 1884.

[2] See Heussi, *Die Kirchengeschichtschreibung Mosheims*, 1904.

[3] See Schaff, *August Neander*, 1886; Harnack, *Reden u. Aufsätze*, vol. i., 1904; Lichtenberger, *History of German Theology in the 19th Century*, 1889.

he was appointed to the Chair of Church History in the newly founded University of Berlin, which he occupied till his death in 1850. Monographs on St. Bernard, Gnosticism, Chrysostom and Tertullian followed in rapid succession. In 1822 he published 'Memorials of Christian Life,' a gallery of portraits illustrating the spirit and effects of Christianity, and in 1825 appeared the first volume of his 'History of the Christian Church.'

Church history meant for Neander less the development of dogma or institutions than a picture of saintly lives. As a disciple of Schleiermacher he regarded religion as above all an expression of feeling, its different manifestations carrying with them their own justification. Even Julian is treated sympathetically in view of his sincere convictions. He was not much interested in the Church as a Great Power, regarding its complex machinery and its secular activities as a derogation from the simple purity of primitive Christianity. His task was to emphasise the beauty and fragrance of the dedicated life, to make the study of Christian men and women an instrument of personal edification. Interrupted by death before reaching the Reformation, his pages breathe a spirit of gratitude for the heritage that is common to Rome and Wittenberg. Though convinced of the truth of Christian dogma, he never indulges in heresy-hunting or maintains the importance of doctrine apart from moral results. Believing Christianity to be a divine leaven, he seeks and finds it in an infinite variety of forms. Harnack salutes him as a Protestant Benedictine. The spirit of the whole work is profoundly irenic. The sympathetic handling of the great figures of the Church was a refreshing change from the chilly *Aufklärung*, but it was accompanied by serious weaknesses. Though he emphasises the sacredness of individuality and protests against whatever cramps it, his portraits tend to be a trifle monotonous. Thus, while he succeeds with congenial types of character, he sometimes fails in his portraiture of the more rugged personalities. He prefers the saint to the statesman, the scholar and the mystic to the man of action. His dislike of the worldliness of the hierarchy blinds him to the necessity of a powerful and permanent organisation. Further, he shared with other members of the Romantic school a weakness in critical technique. He took his sources as he found them and never realised the duty of establishing their value.

Neander exercised not less influence as a teacher than as a writer.[1] His lecture-room was crowded with eager students, and from his *Seminar* issued the scholars who were to continue and surpass his work. His lectures not only breathed enthusiasm for

[1] See Lenz, *Geschichte der Universität zu Berlin*, i. 614–16, 1910.

his subject but inculcated an attitude towards life. He uttered grave warnings against excessive intellectualism, whether in the form of rationalism or dogmatism. Though he disliked the critical spirit which was springing up around him, he opposed the expulsion of De Wette from Berlin, and, when asked his opinion as to the prohibition of Strauss' 'Life of Jesus,' advised against it. Indeed Hengstenberg, the leader of militant orthodoxy, denounced him as only half a believer. No figure among ecclesiastical historians is more attractive than that of this learned and loving Christian. Though Church history needed more critical methods, it would be unjust to overlook his services. He made his appeal to all Christians. Möhler, who attended his lectures, pronounced him the first German Protestant with a real knowledge of the Fathers, and paid a tribute to his wonderful comprehension of Catholic dogmas and the early sects. Like Chateaubriand in France, he rescued the Christian Church from the hostility or half-contemptuous patronage of the *Aufklärung*.

In 1826, the year after the first volume of Neander's principal work appeared, Ferdinand Christian Baur[1] was appointed to the Chair of Historical Theology at Tübingen. Standing at the opposite pole and differing in temperament, method and results, he exerted a far more permanent influence, and laid the foundations of the critical treatment of ecclesiastical history. Though few of the contentions of the Tübingen School are now accepted, it gave an incalculable impetus to research. The son of a Württemberg pastor, Baur studied theology at Tübingen, and a work on the 'Symbolism and Mythology of Antiquity' won him the chair which he occupied till his death in 1860. His lectures were written out and formed the basis of the publications which followed one another with bewildering rapidity for over thirty years. These writings fall roughly into three classes, dealing respectively with the development of dogma, the books of the New Testament, and Church History. Though the dominating influence of his early life was Schleiermacher, Hegel gradually displaced him. Beginning with monographs on Manichæism and Gnosticism, he discussed the theory of the Atonement and the doctrine of the Trinity in works remarkable for their skill in connecting the links in a chain of ideas. It was his achievement to introduce the conception of law and growth into the realm of dogma. 'Baur's

[1] See Zeller's masterly essays, 'F. C. Baur' and 'Die Tübinger historische Schule,' *Vorträge und Abhandlungen*, vol. i., 1875; Weizsäcker, *F. C. Baur*, 1892; Mark Pattison, 'The Present State of Theology in Germany,' *Essays*, vol. ii.; Pfleiderer, *Development of Theology since Kant*, 1890; and Dilthey, *Gesammelte Schriften*, iv., 403-32.

mastery in tracing the march of ideas through the ages, over the heads of men, was a thing new to literature.'[1] He interprets the dialectical development of Christian dogma as Hegel had interpreted Greek philosophy. His business was less with facts than with ideas. The idea, not the fact, of the Resurrection was the basis of the Christian faith: whether it occurred, he declares, was beyond the scope of history. It was no necessary part of the historian's duty to pronounce whether Christianity is a natural or supernatural phenomenon.

In a second group of writings Baur grappled with the date and authorship of the books of the New Testament. He approached his task in the conviction that they must be studied like other documents, and that the personality and standpoint of the writer must be taken into account. While earlier scholars devoted their chief attention to the Gospels, he started with the writings of Paul, and his conception of the great Apostle of the Gentiles dominates his view of early Christianity: the key to the whole period seemed to him to lie in the opposition between Peter and Paul. Christianity, he declared, was not a complete revelation, but a complex of ideas and tendencies which developed gradually. It was at first wholly Jewish, the early Christians recognising Jesus as the fulfilment of the Messianic prophecies. It was Paul who made Christianity a universal religion, and in so doing he broke with the Twelve. This struggle of Pauline universalism and Petrine Judaism enables us to date the Canonical books. Romans, Galatians and Corinthians, which clearly reflect the controversy, are the only authentic epistles. The writings in which the conflict is toned down date from the era of compromise in the second century, when the dangers from Gnosticism on the one hand and persecution on the other compelled the leaders to put aside their quarrels. Among these late works are the Gospels, which were compiled from narratives now lost. Matthew is the nearest to these primitive writings, as it most faithfully reproduces the Judæo-Christian atmosphere. Luke comes from the other camp, but has been modified for the purposes of conciliation. Mark is later still, as all traces of the antagonism have disappeared. John is a philosophical, not an historical work. Acts are an ingenious attempt at conciliation. This bold reconstruction gave an impetus to study, but the edifice was built on sand. He enormously exaggerated the antagonism in the primitive Church, and neglected other forces and movements. Above all he takes little account of the personality of Christ. It has often been said that in Baur's eyes Paul was the founder of Christianity. He thinks of Christ as

[1] Acton, in 'German Schools of History.'

the author of a system of ideas which the disciples discussed rather than as a person whom they followed. His dating of books according to their attitude towards the strife of Petrinism and Paulinism falls to the ground with the contention on which it is based. It is sufficient condemnation of the hypothesis that it compels him to place Matthew first and Mark last of the synoptics.

A third group of writings, relating to the general history of the Church, was the main occupation of his closing years. They were preceded by his monograph on ecclesiastical historians, in one and all of whom he detects the lack of insight into the processes of evolution. The first volume, devoted to the first three centuries, was published in 1853, and possesses importance as a summary of the views he had long been enunciating. A second appeared in 1859, and three more, completing the survey, were issued after his death, the last two being merely a reproduction of his lectures. His strength lay in the early centuries, and his studies of mediæval and modern times possess no special authority. His devoted pupil and colleague, Zeller, declares the 'Church History' the most perfect in form and method, though not the most important, of his works. He is at his best in tracing the development of ideas, at his weakest in dealing with individuals. While Neander's approach is from the emotions, that of Baur is from the intellect. Both views are radically incomplete. Yet Baur, like Neander, rendered immense services, and even his mistakes are often suggestive. His erudition, his capacity for abstract thought, his unceasing output, the long tenure of his chair, made the Tübingen Professor by far the most influential Protestant theologian of his time. There was nothing of the iconoclast about him. Weizsäcker testifies that no orthodox student need have been deterred from entering the Ministry by attending his lectures. He treated the rise of Christianity as an historical phenomenon, leaving his hearers to decide for themselves whether it was human or divine.

Baur's influence was increased by the fact that he was surrounded by disciples who co-operated with him in the endeavour to rescue the early Church for science. The most famous of them, however, cannot be reckoned a member of his school. While Baur devoted his main attention to the Apostolic age, Strauss[1] attempted to separate the legendary from the historical elements in the Gospels and denied the divinity of Christ. The challenge led to a more critical examination of the sources; without the leaven of Strauss and Baur the study of Christian origins would

[1] See Hausrath, *D. F. Strauss*, 2 vols., 1876–8, and Eck, *D. F. Strauss*, 1899.

have made far less rapid progress. The most brilliant member of the Tübingen school, properly so called, was Schwegler,[1] whose work on the Post-Apostolic age summarised the master's results and exaggerated the antagonism of Peter and Paul. More cautious was Zeller, who, after attempting a critical examination of the Acts, deserted theology for Greek philosophy. Hilgenfeld displayed greater independence, placing the synoptics earlier than his master, and extending the list of authentic Pauline writings. If he can only be described with reserve as a member of the Tübingen school, Ritschl,[2] the most influential theologian who ever attended Baur's lectures, stands clearly outside it. His 'Origin of the Early Church,' written in 1850 and recast in 1857, reduced the antagonism of Petrinism and Paulinism to its proper dimensions. His analysis of Paul's teaching revealed elements more closely allied to Judaic Christianity than Baur allowed, and he successfully challenged the notion of a long duration of Petrinism. Critical opinion now accepts more of the Pauline Epistles than Baur, and places the Synoptic Gospels and the Acts in the later decades of the first century.

Immense progress has been made in every department of Church history since the death of Baur. The necessity of a careful study of the soil out of which Christianity grew has been recognised, and the works of Schürer and Bousset, Hausrath and Pfleiderer, have recreated the world into which Christ was born. The debt of the early Church to Greece has been brilliantly assessed by Hatch. Holtzmann and Jülicher summarised the scholarship of a century in their Introductions to the New Testament. Zahn devoted a laborious life to the history of the Canon. In his classical 'Apostolic Times' Weizsäcker, the successor of Baur at Tübingen, described the early Christian communities, their distribution and institutions, their customs and beliefs, and drew an impressive portrait of Paul. The constitution of the primitive Church has given rise to prolonged controversy. The first important step was taken by Rothe,[3] who was rather a thinker than an historian; and the first part of his only historical work is devoted to a discussion of the idea of the Church, which he defined as a means not an end. He contends that Christ did not found a Church, and that the first disciples thought more of the message than of organisation. Before the fall of Jerusalem there were only isolated congregations: it was only when the Apostles

---

[1] See Zeller's tribute, *Vorträge u. Abhandlungen*, vol. 2.

[2] See O. Ritschl, *Albrecht Ritschl*, 2 vols., 1894-6.

[3] See Nippold, *Richard Rothe*, 2 vols., 1873, and Hausrath, *Rothe u. Seine Freunde*, 2 vols., 1902.

died and doctrinal differences began to threaten that episcopacy was born.

The most impressive picture of democratic origins was drawn by Sohm in 1892 as an introduction to his study of Canon Law.[1] The Church, declared the famous Leipsic jurist, is spiritual, while law is secular; therefore Canon Law is in opposition to the essence of the Church. The Catholic asserts that the constitution of Pope, bishop and priest is divine, the Anglican builds on the bishop, the Presbyterian on the presbyter. The earliest officers were, however, not teachers but administrators. Whether they were copied from the Synagogue or heathen associations or from neither is unimportant. The organisation was purely local, for the early Christians were simply the people of Christ, a community, not a Church. 'Where two or three are gathered together in My name, there am I in the midst of them.' Not till the middle of the second century did the danger of Gnosticism lead to the creation of a Church, the demand for organisation proving stronger than the confidence in God's guidance. 'The history of Canon Law is the history of the progressive disfigurement of Christian truth.' Thus Christianity was lost in Catholicism. From bishop to Pope was but a step, and the Vatican decrees of 1870 followed logically from the great apostasy the identification of the invisible with the visible Church. This conception of early Christianity was set forth with extraordinary power and ample learning; but its exaggerations were gently corrected by Harnack,[2] who pointed out that organisation was natural as well as necessary, that a soul needed a body, and that law aimed at embodying Christian ideals.

The evolution of dogma has been studied with zeal and profit. Among the many apologetic works provoked by Strauss' 'Life of Jesus' Dorner's 'History of the Doctrine of the Person of Christ' holds pride of place. Breathing the spirit of Schleiermacher and Neander, and tracing the Person of Christ through the ages as the dominant fact in Christian life and thought, this monumental treatise remains an indispensable companion to the student. Not less important was Ritschl's study of the theory of Justification.

The history of the early Church was related for the first time in popular form in Renan's sparkling volumes. In his youthful work, the 'Future of Science,' written in 1849, he declared that a history of the origins of Christianity, if scientifically written, would revolutionise thought and would be the most important

[1] *Kirchenrecht*, vol. i., 1892.
[2] *Constitution and Law of the Church*, Appendix, 1910.

book of the nineteenth century. His mission to Phœnicia in 1860 gave him the opportunity of visiting the Holy Land, where the plan of a life of Jesus and a study of Christian origins was formed. The *Vie de Jésus*, though the most celebrated part of the work, possesses the least value, and the conception of Christ satisfied neither believers nor unbelievers. 'The Apostles' sketched Jewish, Roman and Christian society, and illustrated the enthusiasm of a nascent religion by the rise and persecutions of Babism. The volume on Paul is scarcely more adequate than the *Vie de Jésus*. His influence on Christianity is pronounced to be wholly unfavourable: he was the father of theology who transformed Christianity from ethics into dogma. He was a great man of action, but neither saint, savant nor poet. He did little for religion, and his place in the Christian hierarchy is below St. Francis and Thomas à Kempis. 'Antichrist' describes the Neronian persecution. The fifth and sixth volumes cover the reigns of Trajan and Hadrian and sketch the rise of Gnosticism. The seventh, which bears the name of Marcus Aurelius, pictures the pagan world when the triumph of Christianity is within sight. The transcendent importance of the whole drama, the wide learning, the sympathy with different forms of thought, the vivid description of historic localities and the exquisite style won it instant popularity. While Baur records the rise and fall of doctrines, Renan exhibits a pageant of living men.

Our knowledge of the early Church has been enormously increased during recent decades by the aid of archæology and inscriptions. The discovery at Oxyrhynchus of a papyrus leaf of the third century containing sayings attributed to Jesus aroused worldwide interest. Ramsay's explorations in Asia Minor, above all in Phrygia, recovered some almost unknown chapters, and enabled him to throw new light on the journeys of St. Paul and to present a vivid picture of 'The Church of the Roman Empire.' Cumont described Mithraism and other rivals of Christianity. Lightfoot's superb editions of Clement, Ignatius and Polycarp lit up the life and organisation of the second century, and Gwatkin's treatise on Arianism is a classic. The 'Dictionary of Christian Biography' is a noble monument of British scholarship. No man, alive or dead, has done so much for the study of the early Church as Harnack.[1] The *Texte und Untersuchungen*, which he edited since 1882 and to which he contributed innumerable monographs, illuminated every corner of the first three centuries. He initiated and directed the Prussian Academy's

[1] See the full-length biography by his daughter, Agnes von Zahn-Harnack, 1936.

edition of the Ante-Nicene Fathers. As editor of the *Theologische Literaturzeitung* he recorded every advance of scholarship. His New Testament studies, though the least of his achievements, are full of acute analysis. His 'History of Dogma' is an indispensable guide through the maze of speculation. His survey of 'Christian Literature till Eusebius' is a monument of exact learning and critical acumen. His study of the 'Constitution of the Early Church' summarises the results of two generations of research. The 'Mission and Expansion of Christianity' attempted the first detailed survey of the actual growth of Christian communities in many lands before the conversion of Constantine. Christianity, he declares, possessed every quality inviting acceptance—the Person of the Saviour and the healer, the gospel of charity and the pure life, a marvellous power of assimilating foreign elements. It covered every aspect of the life of man, and provided the form for the monotheism towards which the world was feeling its way.

The ecclesiastical history of the Middle Ages was known to English readers for half a century chiefly through Milman's 'History of Latin Christianity.'[1] He won fame by a singularly independent 'History of the Jews.' 'It is splendid,' wrote Lockhart, 'but some wise folks shake their heads at some passages about miracles. You would disarm them by writing a history of Christianity.' The Dean of St. Paul's acted on the advice and produced a survey of the early Church of no great importance. The work, however, to which it served as an introduction ranks with the outstanding historical achievements of the early Victorian era. The 'History of Latin Christianity' from Theodosius to the eve of the Reformation relieved England from Newman's reproach that she possessed no ecclesiastical history but Gibbon. His friend Dean Stanley declared it 'indispensable and inestimable, a complete epic and philosophy of mediæval Christendom.' The testimony of Froude was no less handsome. 'You have written the finest historical work in the English language. Calmness and impartiality, a belief that in a divinely governed world no systems of faith or policy have taken enduring hold on mankind unless the truth in them has been greater than the falsehood—these are essentials of a great writer, and these you possess more than anyone who has taken such subjects in hand.' Milman had no desire to edify his readers: he portrayed the Church rather as an institution than as an influence. He was more interested in action than in thought or feeling, for his mind

[1] See A. Milman, *Memoir of H. H. Milman*, 1900, and Lecky, *Historical Essays*, 1908.

was essentially secular. Like Stanley he cared little for doctrinal controversy. Dean Church, while recognising his power and impartiality, complained that he lacked a due appreciation of the reality and depth of those eternal problems of thought and feeling which have made theology. Yet this detachment saved him from the hostility to Catholicism then common among Protestant historians; he detested credulity, intolerance and sacerdotalism wherever they appeared. He recognised the greatness of certain Popes and the immense contribution of monasticism and the mediæval church to European civilisation. Macaulay declared that, though the substance of the book was excellent, the style was bad. It certainly lacks grace and colour, but it possesses something of the solidity of Grote. To those who knew him, testifies Lecky, the man seemed even greater than his work. 'Very few historians,' he adds, 'have combined in larger measure the three great requisites of knowledge, soundness of judgment, and inexorable love of truth.'

The best work on the mediæval Church is to be found in monographs. Reuter drew a full-length portrait of Alexander III, Luchaire of Innocent III. Sabatier produced the entrancing biography of St. Francis for which the world had been waiting. Hauck devoted his life to a vast narrative of the Church in Germany to the close of the Middle Ages. Hook compiled the lives of the Archbishops of Canterbury. The evolution of Canon Law was traced by Richter and his greatest pupil Hinschius. Renan measured the impact of Averroes, and Lechler the challenge of Wyclif. No one accomplished so much as Henry Charles Lea,[1] whose 'History of the Mediæval Inquisition' was rightly described by Acton as the most important contribution of the New World to the religious history of the Old, and whose works on Sacerdotal Celibacy, the Spanish Inquisition, Confession and Indulgences, and the Ordeal repay diligent study. His erudition excites the more astonishment that it was acquired during the leisure of a publisher's life, and that his materials for the most part had to be copied and sent across the Atlantic. Though lacking distinction of style, these massive monographs light up many curious tracts of human experience. The opening of the Vatican archives in 1881 supplied mediævalists with an overwhelming mass of fresh material, and the French School at Rome has published many a precious volume of the Papal letters. Paul Kehr inaugurated the 'Regesta Pontificum Romanorum' with volumes on Italy and was followed by Brackmann's collection

[1] See E. S. Bradley, *H. C. Lea*, 1931, and Baumgarten's attack, *H. C. Lea's Historical Writings*, 1909.

on Germany. Finke dedicated his life to collecting materials for a history of the Council of Constance.

It is natural that Protestants not less than Catholics should devote special attention to the Reformation.[1] No Protestant historian of the struggle enjoyed such popularity as Merle d'Aubigné, who portrayed Luther and Calvin with an aureole round their heads. The pious Swiss pastor had studied the writings of the Reformers with loving care, but his volumes belong to the literature of edification and are now forgotten. A more critical generation derives its knowledge of Luther from Köstlin, Kolde and Kawerau. Köstlin's biography, in its latest edition, the second volume of which was revised by Kawerau, represents the last word in Luther scholarship. Fully alive both to the weaknesses of the Reformers and to the merits of their opponents, the latter approaches more closely than any Protestant historian to a dispassionate view of the conflict. Erasmus and Melanchthon await definitive biographies, but Strauss' eulogy of Hutten and Barge's life of Carlstadt are of outstanding importance. The complete Weimar edition of Luther's writings began to appear in 1883, and the Association for the History of the Reformation, also dating from the quatercentenary of his birth, has issued a long series of monographs. Doumergue's sumptuous volumes on Calvin have erected the memorial to which the Genevese reformer is entitled. Canon Dixon and Gairdner described the transition in England from the standpoint of advanced Anglicanism. The historical, doctrinal and moral controversies between the Churches were analysed in Karl Hase's 'Handbook of Protestant Polemics.' Among the outstanding works on the Church history of the last three centuries are Dorner's survey of Protestant theology, Schweitzer's monumental treatise on the 'Central Dogmas of Protestantism,' Pfleiderer's 'History of the Philosophy of Religion,' Tulloch's sketch of Cambridge Platonists, and Ritschl's volumes on Pietism. Nippold surveyed the whole field from the middle of the eighteenth century from the angle of a vibrant Protestantism. Abbey and Overton explored the religious history of England from the Non-Jurors to the Reform Bill. Dean Church wrote a sketch of the Oxford Movement which combines personal memories with sureness of judgment. The greatest monument of Protestant scholarship is Herzog's 'Encyclopædia of Protestant Theology,' the third edition of which appeared under the direction of Hauck.

[1] Catholic writers on the Reformation are described in the following chapter.

CHAPTER XXVI

CATHOLIC HISTORIOGRAPHY

I

WHILE most of the valuable work on Church history has been accomplished by Protestant scholars, contributions of importance have come from the rival camp. The revival of the Roman Church during the generation following the downfall of Napoleon was felt in the domain of historical study not less than in social life. Its earliest centre was South Germany, its first and most brilliant figure Möhler,[1] who began to teach Church history at Tübingen shortly before Baur. The publication in 1825 of 'The Unity of the Church as exemplified in the Fathers' was an event in the life of Catholic Germany. 'He who truly lives in the Church will also live in the first age of the Church and understand it; and he who does not live in the present Church will not live in the old and will not understand it, for they are the same.' The first part discussed the unity of the spirit, the second the unity of the body of the Church. The power and eloquence of the book made a deep impression. 'It fascinated us young men,' remarked Döllinger to Friedrich fifty years later. 'We felt that Möhler had discovered a fresh, living Christianity. The ideal of a Church purified from its abuses became our goal, and the revival of theological science would bring with it the reform of the Church.' Two years later a more ambitious work, 'Athanasius and the Church of his Time,' revealed the historian's ability both to portray character and to analyse philosophic conceptions. His most celebrated production, the 'Symbolik,' a study of the dogmatic differences of Protestantism and Catholicism, was the most formidable attack on the Reformation since Bossuet. Its aim was to prove from patristic literature that Protestantism was unfaithful to the teaching of the primitive Church. His colleague Baur wrote a pointed criticism, to which he replied in a supplementary volume, contending that his opponent argued his case from the standpoint of Schleiermacher and Hegel, not of the

---

[1] See Friedrich, *J. A. Möhler*, 1894; Knöpfler, *J. A. Möhler*, 1896; and Vigener, *Drei Gestalten aus dem modernen Katholizismus*, 1927. The revival of German Catholicism may be studied in Werner, *Geschichte der Katholischen Theologie*, 1866; Friedrich, *Geschichte des Vatikanischen Conzils*, vol. i., 1877; and Goyau, *L'Allemagne Religieuse*, vols. i.–ii., 1905.

Reformers, and that he only defended Protestantism by mis-stating its teaching. Falling in the same decade as Strauss' 'Life of Jesus,' the duel of Möhler and Baur gave a further impetus to the study of ecclesiastical history and doctrine.

Deeply wounded by the stinging attack of his Tübingen col-league, Möhler accepted a call to Munich. Among his staunchest‧ admirers was Döllinger, who surrendered the Chair of Church History, taking for himself that of Canon Law and Doctrine. But the brilliant scholar's career in his new sphere was short, for he was carried off by consumption at the age of forty-one. The grief in Catholic Germany resembled the consternation in the world of classical studies on the death of Otfried Müller. Both men entered the dusty world of research like a breath of spring, inspiring young and old alike with fresh enthusiasm. The publi-cation of his remains enabled the world to realise even more fully its irreparable loss. A large work on Patrology surveyed the Christian literature of the first three centuries, and a genera-tion later his lectures on Church history were published from the notes of pupils. Though his main strength lies in the early Church, he possessed a considerable knowledge of the Reformation. He writes with severity of Luther, the colossal egoist whom he com-pares to the world-conquerors bringing destruction‧in their train. His authority remained so great that when the ranks of Catholic scholarship were split by the Vatican decrees both parties claimed his support. His attitude towards the Papacy was certainly not Ultramontane; for he had declared General Councils the supreme tribunal and the sole legitimate authority for the Church, and his hostility to the Jesuits was unconcealed. When the question of the recall of the Society to Lucerne arose, a pupil published notes of lectures delivered in 1831 in which he had bracketed the Jesuits with the Protestants and declared the dissolution of‧the Order a just punishment. But when Strauss[1] declares that he shut his eyes to the defects of his Church and was never quite happy in it, he goes too far. His position was equi-distant from the Ultramontane and Old Catholic camps into which his friends and pupils were to be divided.

. When Möhler's meteoric career was over, his place as the leader of German Catholic theology was taken by Döllinger.[2] The

[1] *Vermischte Schriften*, vol. ii.

[2] See Friedrich's great biography, 3 vols., 1899–1901; Acton, 'Döllinger's Historical Work,' in *History of Freedom and Other Essays*, 1907; Stieve, *Abhandlungen*, 1900; Cornelius, *Historische Arbeiten*, 1899; Luise von Kobell, *Conversations of Dr. Döllinger*, 1892; Vigener, *Drei Gestalten*, 1927. For Ultramontane attacks see Michael, *Döllinger*, 1892, and Jörg, *His-torisch-Politische Blätter* for 1890, 237–62.

son of a Professor at Wurzburg, his earliest friend was Platen, the sceptical poet, who described him as 'very enlightened and tolerant, but a Christian.' A more important influence was Baader, from whom he learned to love the mystics. At eighteen he buried himself in Sarpi and set sail on the vast ocean of Baronius. He saw that the battle of the Churches must be fought out with the weapons of the historian, not of the metaphysician. When De Maistre's treatise on the Papacy appeared, he coldly remarked that it lacked historical proofs. On the publication of his first book in 1826 he was appointed to the Chair at Munich which he was to make the most influential in the Catholic world. He already appears in the rôle his fidelity to which was to lead his bark into stormy seas. The first and holiest law of the Catholic Church, he declared, was to accept no dogma which was not based on the tradition of all the centuries. His lectures covered the whole field of ecclesiastical history, and it was an easy task to write a handbook. The work grew under his hands, and became so large that on reaching the Reformation he decided not to continue it. Translated into English, French and Italian it carried the fame of its author throughout the Catholic world.

Shortly after the publication of the 'Church History,' a far more important work on the Reformation began to appear. The growth of rationalism and the quarrels of the sects seemed to him to announce the speedy downfall of Protestantism. The bond of a common Christianity between Rome and Wittenberg was loosening. The Catholic student of Protestant theology, he remarked, was like a man standing on the shore watching a little boat driven by the waves he knows not whither. He determined to show how misleading was Ranke's picture of the national life, how weak the theology, how baneful the moral and intellectual results of the Lutheran revolt. He collects all the evidence he can find of evil and confusion and attributes it to the Reformation, above all to Luther's favourite doctrine of Justification by Faith and his attack on 'good works.' Such a partial diagnosis, however, can never explain a great historic movement. Greeted with enthusiasm in Catholic Germany, it aroused angry hostility among Protestants, but its vast length and unskilful arrangement rendered popularity impossible. When the third volume sold badly, the author discontinued his work. It remains a quarry in which historians of all creeds have delved, a treasure-house of rare and curious learning. Döllinger was now the uncontested chief of Catholic scholarship, and he voiced the demands of the Church in the Frankfurt Parliament. In 1851 the discovery of the 'Philosophumena' led to a sharp controversy as to its authorship. Döllinger accepted the attribution to Hippolytus, but defended the reputation of the Church. Soon after he published his 'Vestibule of Christianity,' a survey of the civilisation of antiquity which drew commendation from Protestants no less than Catholics. Being ignorant of German, Newman had the work translated at the Oratory and read it with pleasure. It was quickly followed by a study of the 'First Age of Christianity,' which was also approved in conservative circles. It was the last book written by the great scholar before entering on the path which was to lead the veteran academic champion of Catholicism to excommunication.

Next to Möhler and Döllinger the name of Hefele[1] counted for most in the world of scholarship. After winning a solid reputation by twenty years of patristic, liturgical and historical studies and a biography of Ximenes, he published the first volume of his 'History of the Councils' in 1855. In the preface to a later instalment he declares that it was his wish to produce an objective work, and his volumes were the most authoritative produced by any Catholic of his time in the domain of Church history. His first plan had been to concentrate on the dogmatic aspect, but he finally decided to include canon law, liturgy and morals and thus make his book of use to the canonist and the historian of culture. 'Till now the councils have been treated separately. I try to regard each as a link in the chain of development.' Thus the work grew into something like a history of the Church. Its value is still universally recognised. With the fifth volume, covering the centuries from Hildebrand to the end of the Hohenstaufen, 'the grandest period of the Middle Ages,' the work broadens into a history of the struggle of Pope and Emperor. After completing the Council of Constance he was appointed Bishop of Rottenburg; and as his official duties and lack of access to a great library made research difficult he brought the work to an end with the Councils of Florence and Basel. Looking back on his seven massive volumes he repeats that he is not conscious of any bias. 'Have I always succeeded? Has any historian always succeeded? *In magnis voluisse sat est.*' Revision was begun in 1873 and completed by Knöpfler.

A fourth member of the Munich circle was the veteran controversialist Görres'.[2] As a child of the Rhineland he had welcomed the French Revolution, but he took a leading part in the opposition to Napoleon. With equal energy he combated the Holy Alliance, and declared that, as the princes were arrayed against

---

[1] See articles in *Allg. Deutsche Biog.* and Herzog's *Realencyklopädie.*
[2] See Sepp, *Görres,* 1877.

liberty, the people must look to Rome. As an ardent champion of Catholicism he received the Chair of History at Munich, but his mind was unfitted for systematic study. His chief historical effort was his vast survey of Christian Mysticism. He passes the early saints and Fathers in review, accepting the miracles of St. Antony and tracing visions and ecstasy through the ages. The second half of the work is devoted to evil spirits—to possession, witchcraft and magic. The name and fame of Görres helped to make Munich the capital of Catholic Germany, but brought no reinforcement to its academic prestige.

The circle was further reinforced by the arrival of a zealous convert from the north. George Phillips,[1] the child of English parents living at Königsberg, studied under Savigny and Eichhorn, and began to teach law at Berlin in 1827. In the following year he joined the Roman Church and soon accepted a call to Munich. In 1845 he began to publish the vast work on Canon Law to which he devoted the rest of his life. Tracing everything to the Papacy, which he believed to have been infallible from the beginning and supreme over the world, his work was an Ultramontane manifesto. Its influence in Germany and Austria, whither he migrated in 1848, was immense, and it was one of the principal sources of the movement which culminated in 1870. By 1838 the Munich circle felt strong enough to found a journal. While the *Tübingen Quarterly*, to which Möhler and Hefele had been frequent contributors, stood for scholarship, the *Historisch-Politische Blätter* was designed for the defence of the Church in every field. Among minor members of the school may be mentioned Jarcke, Höfler and Lasaulx. The former, a bosom friend and fellow convert of Phillips at Berlin, accompanied him south. Höfler, a much more serious historical scholar and a pupil of Döllinger, won fame by a history of the German Popes and was called to Prague in 1851 to combat Palacky and the champions of Hus. Lasaulx[2] had little more aptitude for history than Görres. When he read his 'Fall of Hellenism' to Döllinger, the great scholar shuddered at the confusion of dates and authorities, and his lectures were equally incoherent. Yet all these men helped to make Munich the centre of Catholic studies, and future champions of the Church, among them Ketteler and Moufang, came to seek their training within its walls.

Though the Catholic revival reached its greatest development in South Germany, there was a corresponding movement in France. When Chateaubriand rendered Christianity fashionable,

---

[1] See Schulte's article in *Allg. Deutsche Biog.*
[2] See Stölzle, *Ernst von Lasaulx*, 1904.

other voices were quickly raised in its support. Bonald demanded the restoration of the Jesuits, De Maistre pleaded for the recognition of the Pope as the anchor of Europe, Lamennais attacked Gallicanism and indifference. The latter broke with Rome and dropped out of the fighting line, but younger men, among them some of his own disciples, came forward. The struggle for the freedom of Catholic schools and the condemnation of the journal *L'Avenir* by the Pope had made the name of Montalembert[1] familiar throughout France before he was thirty. His disappointments turned his eyes towards the Middle Ages. Travelling in Germany he reached Marburg on St. Elizabeth's Day, but found her forgotten and her shrine neglected by a Lutheran people. He followed her footsteps wherever she had trod, and wrote her biography. 'I do not regret the institutions which have perished, but I do bitterly regret the divine breath which animated them. Everyone knew what he was to believe, what he could know, what he ought to think of all those problems of life and destiny which to-day are sources of torment. There was an immense moral healthfulness which neutralised all the maladies of the social body. I believe the day will come when humanity will demand its release from the dreary waste in which it has been enthralled. It will ask to hear again the songs of its infancy, to present its thirsty lips at the breast of its mother. And that mother will come forth more beautiful, powerful and merciful than ever.' The biography is a work of edification, not of science, but it gave an impetus to the Catholic revival. Perhaps its most important result was its share in the conversion of the incomparable gladiator, Louis Veuillot.

A far more ambitious work was the 'History of the Monks of the West.' Montalembert's first intention was to paint a full-length portrait of St. Bernard, but the introduction was ultimately transformed into a comprehensive history of monasticism. The author of the famous battle-cry, 'We are the sons of the Crusades and we will never yield to the sons of Voltaire,' was not the man for objective study, and he frankly described the work as 'a Catholic book.' The Middle Ages, he declares, have been ridiculously calumniated. 'A devouring desire to learn and to work animated every mind.' The narrative opens with a sombre picture of the dying Roman Empire. Civilisation, he declares, was rescued by the joint efforts of the barbarians and the monks. After a rapid sketch of the hermits of the desert we reach Benedict, the first commanding figure in the portrait gallery. The narrative

[1] See the biographies by Mrs. Oliphant, 1872, Foisset, 1877, and Lecanuet, 3 vols., 1900-2.

attains its highest flight in the volumes on the Irish missionaries. While rejoicing in their prowess he makes no attempt to exhibit them as immaculate. Both Columbanus and Columba were thoroughly human, the latter far more a fighter than a dove. He is equally alive to the failings of Wilfrid, whose career he follows with loving interest. He accompanies Hildebrand from the cloister to the throne, and warmly supports him in the mortal struggle with the Emperor. The task was interrupted by death when the majestic figure of St. Bernard was almost in sight. The famous orator was more at home in the tribune than the study, and his use of the sources is thoroughly uncritical. A more serious student was Ozanam,[1] whose doctor's thesis was a study of 'Dante and Catholic Philosophy.' In 1844 he succeeded Fauriel as Professor of Foreign Literature at Paris, and the remaining years of his short life witnessed a remarkable output. His 'Germanic Studies' and his survey of civilisation in the fifth century sketched the beginnings of the Middle Ages. The 'Franciscan Poets' was a contribution both to ecclesiastical and literary history. Dying of consumption in 1853 at the age of forty, he left the memory of an exquisite personality and a scholar of rare attainments. His devotion to the Middle Ages equalled that of Montalembert, but he is free from the gush that sometimes disfigures the pages of his friend. His main task was to emphasise the services of Christianity to the barbarian nations. Where Gibbon had seen in the Church one of the destroyers of ancient culture, Ozanam pronounced it the bridge from the civilisation of Rome to the modern world.

Of larger calibre was the elaborate study of 'The Church and the Empire in the Fourth Century' by Albert De Broglie,[2] who was later to win European fame by his record of the diplomacy of Louis XV and his political activities during the Third Republic. No more eloquent apologia had ever been written. Admitting his 'profound devotion to the cause of the Church,' he depicts her as the wise and tender mother of the human race. After her ruthless persecution by the Pagan Empire she might have retaliated, but she preferred persuasion to force. Placing the sign of the cross on Roman civilisation, she transformed a whole society by the moral effect of a doctrine, saving whatever was worth preservation in the ancient world. Convinced that human weakness has never been able to endanger the purity of her doctrine, he judges the actors in the drama with considerable freedom. The three great rulers Constantine, Julian and Theodosius, the three mighty

---

[1] See O'Meara, *Frederic Ozanam*, 1878.
[2] See Fagniez, *Le Duc de Broglie*, 1902.

Churchmen Athanasius, Basil and Ambrose, fill the stage. He admits the crimes of Constantine, the servility of Eusebius, and the virtues of Julian, but we are never allowed to forget that the Church saved the world. The book was suggested by the thought that France needed conversion like the Roman Empire. Though neither decadent nor pagan, she had become estranged from the Church, and it was the act of a good patriot as well as a good Catholic to urge her to submit once more.

Crétineau-Joly[1] belonged to a different school and chose more modern themes for his text. His admiring biographer confesses that for him history was not an object of curiosity but a weapon. Himself a Vendéan, his 'La Vendée militaire' was as much a polemic as a history. His friend and patron Gregory XVI was delighted with the book, and suggested that he should become the chronicler of the Jesuits. Were they not the Vendéans of the Church ? He responded to the appeal and quickly produced a voluminous history. The Jesuits assisted the work, believing that the public would be impressed by the testimony of a man who was not a member of the Order. On finishing his task he accepted their invitation to write a history of their suppression. As the book hotly attacked Clement XIV its sale was forbidden in the Papal States, and Theiner, the archivist of the Vatican, issued a reply. His later years were devoted to a survey of the struggle between the Church and the Revolution. He was rather a journalist than an historian, more akin to Louis Veuillot than to Montalembert or Ozanam, but his access to documents gives his books a certain importance.

While these writers were appealing to the great world of controversy and culture, tasks of a less popular character were being performed by scholars of whom the public knew little. Determined to restore the French Benedictines to the position they had occupied before the Revolution, Dom Guéranger purchased the Benedictine Abbey of Solesmes, which had been deserted since 1802. He set the example of research by works on the early Church and the history of ritual; but the greatest ornament of the abbey was his pupil and colleague Pitra,[2] whose researches in many archives were rewarded by a Cardinal's hat. In his heroic enterprise the 'Patrologia Græca et Latina' Migne received precious assistance from the scholars of Solesmes. Le Blant's edition of the Inscriptions of Christian Gaul unlocked a new world. Studied separately, he declared, they meant little;

---

[1] See Abbé Maynard, *Crétineau-Joly*, and Druffel, *Hist. Zeitschrift*, vol. lii.

[2] See Cabrol, *Cardinal Pitra*, 1893.

studied together they revealed the beliefs, the hopes, the secrets of their ancestors. It was his aim to do for the flock what the Benedictine 'Gallia Christiana' had done for the shepherds. In 1893 the aged scholar published a work on the Persecutions, sifting the wheat from the chaff and building a foundation for a critical knowledge of the early martyrs.

In Italy a priceless contribution to ecclesiastical history was made by De Rossi,[1] by whom the treasures of the catacombs were first methodically explored. The marvellous underworld of the Eternal City had been rediscovered in the sixteenth century and described in the seventeenth by Bosio, whom his great successor hailed as the Columbus of Christian archæology. He aroused the interest of Pius IX, who supplied him with money for excavation. The discovery of the graves of several popes of the third century in the catacomb of St. Callistus in 1852 attracted the attention of the world, and for the remaining forty years of his life one triumph succeeded another. He began the publication of the Christian inscriptions of Rome in 1861, and left the work almost complete at his death. But his greatest achievement was the sumptuously illustrated 'Roma Sotteranea,' which appeared in three quarto volumes between 1864 and 1877, and described the history, topography, architecture and frescœs of the catacombs. Among his other services were the foundation of a quarterly 'Bulletin of Christian Archæology,' the creation of the Lateran museum, and an exhaustive study of the mosaics of the Roman churches. Mommsen, with whom he collaborated in the Corpus, has emphasised the combination of qualifications which made the founder of Christian archæology and epigraphy one of the great figures of his time—his knowledge of Christian and classical literature, his mastery of palæography and inscriptions, his intimate acquaintance with the Roman Empire and with the classical and mediæval city.

II

It was but for a short time that Catholics could congratulate themselves on the revival of historical scholarship. In the fifties there were a few rumblings of the coming storm, in the sixties an internecine struggle. In 1870 the Vatican decrees embodied the triumph of Ultramontanism and drove the Old Catholics into the wilderness. These great events exerted an incalculable influence on the study of history.

[1] See Baumgarten, *G. B. de Rossi*, 1892; Guiraud, in *Revue Historique* vol. lviii.; Mommsen, in *Reden und Aufsätze*, 1905.

After Döllinger had split with the Vatican it became fashionable in Ultramontane circles to declare that he had been a heretic while he was still regarded as the champion of Catholic claims. There was, however, no public indication of divergence before the celebrated lectures in 1861, in which he declared that the fall of the Temporal Power was not improbable and would not be fatal. 'The Church and the Churches,' written in the same year, an expansion and explanation of the lectures, was intended as an apologia for Catholicism; and Pius IX declared that, though he could not agree with everything in it, it could do nothing but good. But the treatment of the Reformation showed that a different spirit had come over him, and the suspicions aroused by the lectures were confirmed by the striking volume on the 'Papal Fables of the Middle Ages.' He sharply attacked the Syllabus of 1864, and in 1867 he challenged the œcumenical character of the Council of Trent on the ground that it was dominated by Rome and packed with Italian bishops. 'What would my old friends Möhler and Görres have said,' he wrote in 1868, 'if they had lived to see such times? They would have said to the Ultramontanes, "Away with you, we have no dealings with you."'

When the Vatican Council was summoned and its object announced, Döllinger, under the pseudonym of Janus, wrote the most famous of all his books, 'The Pope and the Council,' the most vigorous historical indictment ever brought against Ultramontanism. Though promptly placed on the Index, it was read all over the world and mobilised opinion against Infallibility before the Council met. While it was sitting he kept up a running fire in his 'Letters of Quirinus' in the *Allgemeine Zeitung*, based on information sent from Rome by Acton, Friedrich and Strossmayer. The victory of the Ultramontanes was followed by the excommunication of the historian and the foundation of the Old Catholic Church, of which he never became a member. Precious sparks flew from his forge in his 'Lectures on Reunion' and his addresses to the Munich Academy; but though he laboured with undiminished energy till his death at the age of ninety, he would have communicated to the world little of his vast stores of knowledge but for the help of Reusch, who aided him to prepare for publication his early researches into mediæval sects, his edition of Bellarmine's Autobiography, and his elaborate survey of the moral controversies in the Roman Church during the seventeenth and eighteenth centuries.

Döllinger was revered as their leader by a number of younger scholars who shared his hostility to the Vatican decrees. Among them was Reusch,[1] a native of Westphalia, who when the crisis arrived unhesitatingly followed his old master. 'I cannot act against my conviction,' he told his bishop. 'You speak too much of conviction,' was the reply. 'I have always respected you; your only fault was that you thought too much of science and too little of authority.' After taking an active part in the foundation of the Old Catholic Church, he withdrew on the abolition of clerical celibacy. A monograph on Luis de Leon, one of the *causes célèbres* of the Spanish Inquisition, was followed by a searching analysis of the trial of Galileo. But it is by his monumental work on the 'Index of Forbidden Books' that his name will endure. Its two thousand pages cast a broad ray of light on the last three centuries, and leave an overwhelming impression of the obscurantism of Rome. Though Reusch excelled rather as a collector of material than as a literary artist, the work is perhaps the greatest achievement of Old Catholic scholarship.

Even more intimately associated with Döllinger was Friedrich, his pupil, colleague and biographer, who accompanied Cardinal Hohenlohe as his theologian to the Vatican Council. He published his diary of the eventful months in Rome, edited the official documents, and then proceeded to compile the history of the Council. The massive introductory volume, which contains a panoramic survey of the growth of Ultramontanism, is, despite its obvious bias, a work of enduring value. On his master's death he composed the monumental biography which is at once a testimony to their friendship and a contribution of rare interest to the ecclesiastical history of the century. Among other members of the circle none was more valued than Johannes Huber. Though he never wrote a large work, his knowledge of Church history was profound, and he aided his master in 'The Pope and the Council.' When Infallibility was proclaimed, he continued the struggle in his work on the Jesuits, dedicated to Döllinger, who, with Reusch, Friedrich and Acton had aided him in the task. It was, he explained, just a century since Clement XIV had dissolved the Order, but it had risen from its ashes and now freedom and culture were threatened by its deadly embrace.

Equally bound to Döllinger by friendship and community of principles was Cornelius,[2] who won fame in 1855 by his study of the Anabaptists at Munster. In the following year he and Sybel were called to Munich where he worked quietly among his pupils till his death in 1903, producing little but fragments. Among younger members of the circle were Lossen and Druffel, whose

---

[1] See Goetz, *F. H. Reusch*, 1901.
[2] See Friedrich, *Rede auf Cornelius*, 1904.

early death was a blow to the cause of liberal Catholic scholarship. The former's monograph on the 'War of Cologne' explored an important episode in the Counter-Reformation, and as Secretary of the Munich Academy he aided Döllinger in the publication of his Academic Addresses. Druffel collected materials for the history of the Counter-Reformation and the Council of Trent. To complete the survey of Old Catholic scholarship three more names must be mentioned. Maassen, Professor of Law at Graz, issued the first volume of a work on the sources and literature of Canon Law, which, though a fragment, is a monument of erudition. Langen's massive 'Church History' till Innocent III is of interest as the only detailed survey of the early Middle Ages from the pen of an Old Catholic. Finally Schulte issued an exhaustive history of the sources of Canon Law, and compiled the most authoritative account of the Old Catholic movement.

While Döllinger, Reusch, Schulte and most of their friends rejected the Vatican Decrees, they were accepted by other scholars of scarcely less distinction. To the surprise of his friends Hefele submitted, though with obvious reluctance. Their most active champion was Hergenröther, who, when 'Janus' was carrying public opinion by storm, came forward with a reply which claimed that Ultramontanism possessed a longer pedigree than Döllinger was disposed to admit. His later years were devoted to the continuation of Hefele's masterpiece on the Councils. His volumes, which conclude the fifteenth and commence the sixteenth century, derive value from the documents in the Vatican library, of which he was appointed Prefect. His services were recognised by a Cardinal's hat.

Of the historians who welcomed the new Ultramontanism the most influential was Janssen.[1] A son of the Rhineland he was brought up in a strongly Catholic atmosphere, and his mother took him with her on pilgrimages. He refused to believe that the Middle Ages, which created Gothic cathedrals, were a time of darkness. In 1854, at the age of twenty-five, he was appointed Professor of History for Catholic students at the gymnasium of Frankfurt, and passed the rest of his life in the Imperial city. The dominant influence in his life was Böhmer, a Catholic in everything but name. Stopping before a statue of Charles the Great he remarked, 'This shows us what we lack—a history of the German people from the pen of a Catholic historian; for what we know as German history is only a farce.' These words determined the young priest's vocation, and the 'History of the German People' took shape in his mind. Before

[1] See Pastor, *Johannes Janssen*, 1894.

settling down to the main task of his career he wrote the life and collected the correspondence of Böhmer, and edited the reports of the Frankfurt representatives in the Diet. Böhmer had suggested a complete history of the German people, but Janssen decided to begin with the end of the Middle Ages. In 1874 he read the first chapter to Pastor, who remarked, 'That opens up a new world'; the author rejoined that he had the same feeling. In 1875 the first half of the first volume appeared, and was hailed with enthusiasm by the Catholic world. When he died in 1891 he had reached the eve of the Thirty Years War. The eight massive volumes were read with avidity. No large Catholic historical work of the nineteenth century obtained such resounding success or led to so much controversy.

Döllinger had stressed the chaos produced by the Lutheran movement, but Protestant historians ignored his results. Janssen went further back, and prefaced his study of the Reformation by a detailed investigation of the fifteenth century. His object was to establish that it was not a time of moral or intellectual decrepitude, with a few 'Reformers before the Reformation' like voices crying in the wilderness, but of healthy activity and prosperity. He describes the flourishing state of religious and secular education, and announces that there were not less than fifteen complete translations of the Bible before Luther. Art was vigorous and creative. The value of his work as a corrective of Protestant tradition was generally recognised. In the second half of the first volume he dealt with agriculture, industry and trade, showing the comfort of the peasants and the prosperity of the towns. For the first time shadows appear in the picture— riches leading to luxury and immorality, the despotism of capital, the horrors of usury. The evil was increased by Roman law, the economic teaching of which was contrary to Christian principles. Curiously enough the condition of religion is not described, Janssen excusing himself on the ground that he was not writing Church history and that the Lutheran revolution was rather economic, social and legal than ecclesiastical or intellectual.

While the first volume found admirers in both Churches, the second, which embraced the early years of the Reformation, was naturally less welcomed in Protestant circles. Unlike Döllinger, who traced doctrinal development, and Ranke, who related political history, Janssen devoted his attention chiefly to culture and social life. He brings a severe, almost savage, indictment against the Humanists. Erasmus, he declares, was sceptical, frivolous, selfish; the younger Humanists were rather heathen than Christian, and some of them were of bad character. The worst was Hutten. Of Luther himself he has little to say, and he avoids invective, but he paints a terrible picture of the material and moral chaos when the religious conflict arose. Though he does not attribute the Peasants' Revolt exclusively to the Reformation, he traces its ferocity mainly to that cause. The third volume, extending to the abdication of Charles V, though severe on the Protestant actors in the drama, is not sparing in criticism of Catholics. He admits the existence of evils in the Church and sharply censures the German bishops as secular princes with ecclesiastical titles. The later volumes are devoted to the Counter-Reformation and to the generation preceding the Thirty Years War. Here the picture is one of unrelieved gloom—immorality and drunkenness, ignorance, tyranny and superstition. Hundreds of pages are devoted to popular literature, hundreds to the hideous crimes which disgraced the country, half a volume to the belief in witchcraft which infected the whole population. Thus the story which opened with the bright colours of the fifteenth century closes in deep shadow. Its message is that Germany was ruined not by the Thirty Years War but by the Reformation.

Janssen's erudition established a claim to attention, and the novelty both of his method and results aroused universal interest. At last Catholics were able to boast of an historian who could meet Protestant scholars on equal terms. The importance of his work was emphasised by the attacks it provoked. Baumgarten, the biographer of Charles V, Kawerau and Köstlin, Kolde and Lenz, biographers of Luther, fell upon the audacious iconoclast. Delbrück declared him a false coiner, and denounced the work as a vast lie. Janssen replied to his critics in two successive volumes, in which, while accepting some minor corrections, he pointed out errors into which they had fallen. Now that the dust of controversy has cleared away, it is not difficult to estimate the character of the book. It is, in the first place, a substantial addition to our knowledge of the life of the German people. Secondly, it has modified the traditional Protestant view of the fifteenth century as an age of degeneracy and chaos. Thirdly, it has confirmed the contention of Döllinger that the Lutheran movement was accompanied by great confusion and by a temporary decline of culture and prosperity. Taine truly remarked that no one could in future write of the Reformation without knowing and weighing the Catholic side. On the other hand, Janssen cannot be numbered among historians of the first rank. He prided himself on 'letting the sources speak'; but his accumulation of all the passages that are damaging to Protestantism and his suppression of many facts that are damaging to Catholicism

produces a misleading result. He tells the truth, but it is not
the whole truth. His use of materials is often uncritical. Good
and bad authorities are lumped together, isolated particulars are
often made the basis of far-reaching generalisations. In a word
even in Pastor's revised version it is a dexterous polemic, not a
work of disinterested research.

Second in popularity among the Ultramontane historians of
the generation following the Vatican Council was Pastor, the
biographer of Janssen and historian of the Renaissance Popes.[1]
His aim was to describe the great religious struggle of the sixteenth century as reflected in the history of the Papacy, as
Janssen depicted it mirrored in the life of the German people.
Neither Ranke nor Creighton had been able to use the Vatican
archives. Drawing most of his material from this inexhaustible
reservoir, he supplemented it by researches in the archives of
the Lateran, the Inquisition, the Propaganda, in the libraries of
princely houses, in the chief cities of Italy, France and Germany,
Austria and Switzerland. While Janssen used little but printed
sources, Pastor prefers the testimony of manuscripts. Though
he declares that the best apologia for the Popes is to show what
they have done, he is no unreserved admirer of certain princes of
the Church. The early volumes describe the period of the New
Learning, the influence of which was deeply felt in the Vatican.
Keenly interested in art and culture, he deals at length with the
Humanism of Pius II, the artistic activities of his successors, and
the world-famous painters, sculptors and architects of the Papal
Court. He distinguishes between the heathen and the Christian
Renaissance, between Valla and Poggio on the one hand and
Nicholas V and Vittorino da Feltre on the other. The Popes, he
confesses, welcomed all humanists without troubling about their
paganism; for they were themselves temporal princes, and the
only vigorous assault on the pagan Renaissance came from
Savonarola. He shelters himself behind the dictum of Leo I,
Petri dignitas etiam in indigno hærede non deficit. He deplores the
corruption and intrigue at papal elections. In the third volume,
devoted to Alexander VI and Julius II, he is less indulgent than
Creighton. Employing the Borgia Regesta for the first time, he
declares that they render it impossible to defend the Pope. Yet
he pronounces him the best temporal sovereign of his time,
attributes his crimes to his affection for his family, and praises
his watch over the purity of Church teaching. He admits that the
character of Julius was not papal, but suggests that it was per-

[1] See the massive volume, *Pastor, Tagebücher, Briefe, Erinnerungen,*
1950.

haps necessary in a time of force to possess a militant champion of the Papacy. He blames the company kept by Leo X and the policy of Clement VII in Germany and England. He laments the absence of reforming popes at the crisis of the Church's fate, and makes no attempt to hide the faults of Paul III.

Pastor's volumes are the result of immense industry and contain a mass of new material, but he too is not in the front rank of historians. His conception of the dual nature of the Renaissance is untenable, for the Christian and pagan elements were so mingled that the era must be considered and judged as a whole. He is by standpoint and belief out of sympathy with a movement which was above all a revolt against the Ages of Faith. He never really faces the fact that both the conciliar movement and the German revolt were the expression of deep-seated and vital convictions. He explains the shortcomings of the Popes by the worldliness and demoralisation of society, but it does not occur to him that the corruption of the Church itself was one of its causes. He is severe on Savonarola, whose work he compares to the Salvation Army, and whom he condemns for disobeying Rome and mixing in politics. Instead of judging the Church more severely than the world for its moral lapses, he hints excuses and tempers blame. Despite its moderate tone the work is vitiated by fundamental bias. Like other Catholic historians, he fails to render the Reformation intelligible.

A far more powerful personality was the Austrian Dominican Denifle,[1] whose first important writings were devoted to the German mystics. In opposition to Protestant tradition he maintained that mysticism grew out of scholasticism, and that the mystics were in no sense anti-clericals or forerunners of the Reformation. Summoned to Rome by his Order he was invited by Leo XIII to assist in the official edition of Aquinas, after the Bull 'Aeterni Patris' in 1879 recommending special study of the greatest of the Schoolmen. In pursuance of this task he visited the archives of Europe, collecting material not only for the enterprise but for plans of his own. Appointed archivist at the Vatican he found such rich stores relating to mediæval Universities that he undertook to write their history. The first volume, which appeared in 1885, was an apologia for the Universities and incidentally for the Church and the Middle Ages, but it was also a vast compendium of knowledge. His scheme embraced five volumes, but it was largely owing to the success of the first that it had no successor. The most eloquent praise came from Paris in the form of an invitation by the French Government to edit a documentary

[1] See Grabmann, *Heinrich Denifle*, 1905.

history of the University. He accepted the task, and in ten years six volumes of documents saw the light. The discovery of the originals swept away a mass of forgeries and interpolations. The work was also a contribution to French history, throwing light on the relations of the French Court and Church to the Papacy, on the Orders, on the reception of Aristotle, and on mediæval theology. While thus employed the indefatigable scholar found relaxation in a documented work on the 'Dissolution of the Church in France, in the fourteenth and fifteenth centuries,' a mine of information on art and liturgies, saints and relics, Church property and organisation. Like all his other writings, it was unfinished; for the study of the fifteenth century directed his thoughts to Luther.

Denifle's 'Luther and Lutheranism,' published in 1904, gave evidence of profound study in the Vatican and in German archives. He had been compelled to write the book, he remarked, by the virulent attacks of Protestant historians on his Church and their unreasoning idolatry of Luther. Protestant theologians, he declared bitterly, were allowed to doubt the divinity of Christ but not to lay an impious hand on the reformer. Luther and his friends lost their belief for moral reasons. To know Luther as he was is to understand his revolt. 'This book is not intended for the young. Such is the real Luther!' He concludes a passionate preface with the words, 'May God open the eyes of Protestants to his character, and bring them back to the Catholic Church.' The massive volume of 800 pages hurled at the memory of the Reformer is one of the most repulsive works in historical literature. The Reformers, he declares, were apostles of the flesh; their philosophy was summarised in the precept, Follow Nature, and among the most fleshly was Luther himself. Far from being too good for the Church, the Church was too good for him, for he was dominated by a coarse, sensual nature. A large part of the volume is devoted to an analysis of his work on Monastic Vows, in which the impossibility of struggling against natural instincts is proclaimed, and the marriage of priests, in Denifle's scornful words, is preached as a cure for the breach of vows. We are also informed that Luther drank, and a chapter on his physiognomy emphasises the verdict of the written evidence.

The work fell like a bomb in the Lutheran camp. The attack was more concentrated than that of Janssen, and Denifle expressed his contempt for the Lutheran specialists. 'Their original sin,' he declared, 'is that they are unscientific. If only they had treated Luther as they treat the God-man!' He reads them a lesson in editorial technique by pointing out errors in the Weimar edition of his works. This bitter attack brought numerous replies, notably from Harnack, Seeberg and Kolde. They pointed to mistakes in detail, to the omission of evidence which told in Luther's favour, to neglect of comparison with Catholic standards. Hausrath, who published a life of the reformer in 1904, declared that Denifle twisted phrases and took jokes and lamentations too literally. Luther was much fiercer in words than in deeds, and his violence was the only way to arouse his countrymen. He was cast in a heroic mould, 'God's Wundermann,' as Myconius called him, a genius and a child. Denifle replied in a pamphlet directed against Harnack and Seeberg,[1] and then rapidly wrote a volume on pre-Lutheran discussions of Justification, after journeying through Germany, France and England in search of manuscript commentaries on St. Paul. Among his discoveries was an early commentary on Romans by Luther himself.

Following the lead of Janssen and Denifle, Catholic historians have devoted special attention to the German Reformation.[2] Pastor sponsored a series of useful monographs, described as 'Illustrations to Janssen's History.' The life of Luther was explored in great detail by Elvers, a convert, and Grisar devoted a large scale work to his personality and the development of his ideas. Majunke, a gladiator of the *Kulturkampf*, maintained that he had committed suicide, a legend finally exploded by Nicholas Paulus. Gasquet related the dissolution of the English Monasteries, and Ehses threw new light on the divorce of Catherine of Aragon from the Vatican archives. The defence of the Jesuits was vigorously undertaken by Duhr. Choosing a few from 'the thousands of fables,' he deals with the poisoning of Clement XIV, 'the end justifies the means,' the assassination of tyrants, obscurantism, lack of patriotism, avarice and wealth, responsibility for the Thirty Years War. Though not free from human weakness and mistakes, he concludes they have nothing to fear. Hilgers defended the Index of Forbidden Books. Brück, Bishop of Mainz, traced the fortunes of the Church in Germany in the nineteenth century, and Wilfrid Ward described its revival in England in biographies of Wiseman, Newman, and his father W. G. Ward.

The Görres Society, founded in 1876, established an historical review, created an Institute in Rome with an organ of its own, and published the materials relating to the Council of Trent. Only second in importance has been the activity radiating from the Jesuits of Maria-Laach. Beginning with occasional pamphlets

---

[1] *Luther in rationalistischer und christlicher Belenchtung*, 1904.
[2] See Köhler, *Katholizismus und Reformation*, 1905.

after the publication of the Syllabus in 1864, the *Stimmen aus Maria-Laach* grew into a regular journal after the Vatican Council. The revised edition of the encyclopædia of Wetzer and Welte measures the advance made since its appearance in the middle of the century. The Belgian Jesuits, led by De Smedt and Delehaye, have continued the *Vitae Sanctorum*, which has now reached the month of November. The Benedictines possess a review of their own, the pages of which are enriched by the erudition of Dom Morin. Dom Cabrol, Abbot of Farnborough, has launched a vast 'Dictionary of Christian Archæology.' Grisar and Mgr Mann have begun large scale narratives of the mediæval Popes.

Midway between Ultramontanes and Old Catholics have stood a few historical scholars who, without openly revolting, were out of sympathy with the newer tendencies. Of these the most important are Kraus and Duchesne. The former studied philology at Bonn, where he began a lifelong friendship with Reusch.[1] When a little over thirty he produced a 'Handbook of Church History,' which superseded the compendium of Alzog whom he followed at Freiburg. A second edition, published in 1882, was so critical that he was invited by the Vatican to suppress it. He had written sharply of papal claims, the Jesuits and scholasticism, and complained that Ultramontanism had brought the Church to the edge of the precipice. Yielding to necessity he withdrew it and published an emasculated edition, saying that an officer must obey his general, but he afterwards regretted his concessions and spoke of it as an *édition de demoiselles*. It was in large measure the desire to escape from his fetters which induced him to devote his later life to the less dangerous topic of Christian art. His survey of the monuments of Alsace-Lorraine formed a model for other provinces. He had met De Rossi in Rome, and he issued a German edition of Northcote and Brownlow's abridgment of the 'Roma Sotteranea,' with substantial contributions of his own. He edited a 'Dictionary of Christian Antiquities,' which embraced not only archæology, but the constitution, ritual and private life of the first six centuries. For his 'Christian Inscriptions of the Rhineland' he was appointed Conservator of the ecclesiastical monuments of Baden. His greatest work, the 'History of Christian Art,' began to appear in 1896. Written with loving insight and superbly illustrated, it is not only the best survey of Christian art but a substantial contribution to ecclesiastical history. In his monograph on Dante he announces himself a Ghibelline, for he

---

[1] See Hauviller, *F. X. Kraus*, 1904, and Braig, *Zur Erinnerung an F. X. Kraus*, 1902.

loved papal domination in the Middle Ages as little as in his own day. He was above all a humanist, an historian of culture rather than of the Church. He had nothing in common with Ultramontanism. His hero was Rosmini, to whom he devoted the longest of his essays. In his life of Cavour he sharply attacks the political Church and welcomes its downfall. He regarded the Jesuits as hopelessly obscurantist, and was the friend of Cardinal Hohenlohe and other priests on whom the Vatican frowned. He admired Harnack, and made Duchesne and Loisy known in Germany. His passionate desire was to reconcile Christianity and culture, Church and nationality, the Vatican and the Quirinal. But he was not a reformer of the type which goes to the stake for his convictions.

Duchesne's critical study of the sources and editions of the 'Liber Pontificalis' was rewarded by his appointment as Professor of Church History at the Institut Catholique at Paris. His lectures aroused the enthusiasm of his pupils, among whom was Loisy; but his methods were too independent to be tolerated by an Ultramontane Church,[1] and he migrated to the more temperate climate of the École des Hautes Études. His edition of the 'Liber Pontificalis' elicited a warm tribute from Mommsen. Of not less importance was his 'Episcopal Fasti of ancient Gaul,' arranged under provinces, which deflated some of the legends of the saints. More popular was his study of early Christian worship, which reviews the origin of the Mass, the development of liturgies, the rites of ordination, the use of vestments, the celebration of festivals, and other aspects of organised Christian life. In a volume of lectures on the beginnings of the temporal sovereignty of the Popes, 754–1073, he declared that even when the grosser scandals had been rejected the character of almost all the Popes of those times was far removed from the apostolic ideal. A volume on the 'Separated Churches' added to the suspicion in which he was held by the stricter circles of his communion. In 1905 he began to publish his 'History of the Early Church,' based on lectures which had already circulated in manuscript. He had mastered Protestant scholarship, and the names of Harnack and Schürer, Zahn and Lipsius, Loofs and Krüger appear at the foot of his pages. Harnack remarked that any Protestant scholar might be proud to have written the book. Duchesne recognises that at first there was neither canon nor creed, and that the episcopate arose as a defence against heresy. His pages lack unction, and he skates lightly over thin ice. In discussing the vision of Constantine he

[1] See Houtin, *La Question biblique chez les Catholiques au Dix-neuvième Siècle*, 1902.

cautiously remarks that it is difficult to measure the value of such testimony and to scrutinise such intimate events. Constantine himself is no hero for the historian, who finds too much blood in his story. The fifth century is an age of sadness, ruin and decrepitude. The book was written for scholars, and no large scale Catholic work of our time reaches such a lofty standard of objective treatment.

The first two volumes were published shortly before the condemnation of Modernism, and received the imprimatur of the Master of the Sacred Palace, the theologian of the Pope. They were hailed by the Catholic press as a proof that learning and orthodoxy could be combined, and the University of Louvain made him a Doctor. When an Italian translation was undertaken Duchesne made a few corrections and again obtained an imprimatur. He presented a copy to Pius X, who declared himself satisfied with its orthodoxy, but no sooner had the translation appeared than a storm of criticism burst over his head. The Consistorial Congregation of nine Cardinals denounced it as 'dangerous and sometimes even deadly,' and forbade its use in Italian Seminaries. The translation was imperfect and was at once withdrawn. A Jesuit, Bottagisio, launched a series of critical articles in a Florentine paper and republished them in a volume, dedicated to the Pope. The historian replied with a 'Confidential Letter to the Bishops of the Catholic Church,' declaring the book a travesty of his views. But the hunt for modernists was now in full swing, and old supporters, like Cardinal Mercier, fell away. No specific charge of heresy was made, but the author was accused of flippancy and lack of reverence. The ambition of his enemies was fulfilled in 1912, when the chief work of the greatest modern French Catholic scholar was placed on the Index. The fourth volume only appeared after his death in 1922.

CHAPTER XXVII

THE HISTORY OF CIVILISATION

I

THE scope of history has gradually widened till it has come to include every aspect of the life of humanity. No one would now dare to maintain with Seeley that history was the biography of states, and with Freeman that it was past politics. The growth of nations and empires, the achievements of men of action, the rise and fall of parties remain among the most engrossing themes of the historian. But the influence of nature, the pressure of economic factors, the origin and transformation of ideas and ideals, the contribution of science and art, religion and philosophy, literature and law, the material conditions of life, the fortunes of the masses now claim his attention in no less degree. He must see life steadily and see it whole.

The literary genre which embraces the non-political aspects of civilisation is most conveniently termed *Kulturgeschichte*.[1] Its founder was Voltaire, whose 'Siècle de Louis XIV' was the first work in which the whole life of a nation is portrayed. His 'Essai sur les Mœurs' is the first real history of civilisation, the first work in which an attempt is made to weave numberless threads into a single design. Where Voltaire opened the way, other historians followed. Winckelmann treated the history of ancient art as a revelation of the Greek mind. Heeren explored the development of commerce. Justus Möser discovered the peasant, and exhibited the connection between economic and political organisation. Herder and the Romantics listened to the whisperings of the Folk-soul. Though the histories of Schlosser and Guizot march on a broad front, the full importance of *Kulturgeschichte* was rarely recognised during the first half of the nineteenth century.

The revolution of 1848 directed the attention of statesmen and historians to the Fourth Estate. This event in the main determined the life-work of Riehl,[2] a member of the Triumvirate

---

[1] See Jodl, *Die Culturgeschichtschreibung*, 1897, and Schaumkell, *Geschichte der deutschen Kulturgeschichtschreibung*, 1905.

[2] See Simonsfeld, *W. H. Riehl*, 1898; Gothein, in *Preussische Jahrbücher*, April 1898; Lorenz, *Die Geschichtswissenschaft*, 1886.

to whom historians of culture look back as the pioneers of their craft. Lorenz selects him as the chief representative of the genre, while Steinhausen claims primacy for Burckhardt and Gustav Freytag. It is true that Riehl never produced a classic and was little read outside Germany; but he devoted a long life as Professor, author and itinerant lecturer to proclaiming the importance of historical sociology. His father was Superintendent of the Castles of the Duke of Nassau, and took the lad on his journeys of inspection. The romantic movement, with its enthusiasm for the creative capacity of the people, and the development of Germanistic studies under the inspiration of the brothers Grimm moulded the thought of the young Rhinelander. A residence in Augsburg strengthened his interest in the town life of old Germany. In 1854, at the age of thirty-one, he was summoned to Munich by Maximilian II, and became an honoured guest at his Round Table. Acton attended his classes and recorded his impressions long after. 'One man living has an equal grasp of the moving and abiding forces of society. Over thirty years ago, before Burckhardt or Friedländer, Buckle or Symonds, Riehl began to lecture on the history of civilisation, revealing to his fortunate audience new views of history, deeper than any existing in literature.'

Folk-study, he declared, was the creation of the last century, but the materials were as old as history. Homer and the Old Testament were rich in ore, and Herodotus, who had a clear conception of ethnography, was the father of folk-study as well as of history. Tacitus first systematically related the people to the country in his 'Germania.' Not till Justus Möser, the true founder of social history, was a further step taken.[1] The 'History of Osnabrück' was the first work in which the mass of the people came by their rights. The next half-century witnessed contributions to an historical sociology from various sources—the creation of a science of statistics by Achenwall, Adam Smith's studies of economic life, Karl Ritter's emphasis on geography, Savigny's natural history of law, above all the mythological and philological researches of the Grimms. It was now recognised that man could only develop within the limits imposed by nature. It was on these foundations that Riehl's chief work, the 'Natural History of the German People,' rested. In the preface to the first volume, 'Land and People,' he explains that he has learned from his wanderings over the country that types and characters have a definite historical and natural origin. The people, once merely a decorative background, are now the chief figure in the picture, and the main task alike of the historian and the

[1] See P. Klassen, *Justus Möser*, 1936.

politician is to understand the laws of their growth. Of these the most fundamental is nature. He divides Germany into three districts, the differences of climate, soil, mountain or plain leading to different customs, use of the land, food, clothing, houses and even beliefs. While towns quickly become cosmopolitan the life of the countryside flows on, determined less by the action of governments or the infiltration of ideas than by the influence of natural factors. The analysis of the action of nature on social and economic life is richly suggestive, and there is a sense of the open air in his pages.

Riehl proceeds in a second volume to formulate the laws of society. There are two great forces in social life, each incorporated in two classes. The first, that of inertia or social conservatism, is most powerfully represented by the peasant, but it is a demo cratic conservatism. During the French Revolution, when the towns seethed with excitement over the rights of man, the peasants asked for privileges in wood and meadow. The second element representing persistence or inertia is the aristocracy. Stein wisely recognised that to remove its oppressive privileges was to strengthen and perpetuate its social and political influence. The second of the fundamental forces, that of movement, operates primarily in the towns. On the maintenance of equilibrium between the forces of persistence and movement depend the health and well-being of the state. Pursuing his way from the general to the particular, Riehl deals in a third volume with 'The Family,' the sheet-anchor of society. 'The more we change in the state and society,' he declares, 'the more we cling to the family.' The family rests on nature's division of labour between the sexes; the growth of culture differentiates them still further, since in primitive communities the women work like the men. He directs attention to the factors, traditional and otherwise, which give a character to each separate household. This family individuality, which speaks from the pictures of Ludwig Richter, he adjures his countrymen to retain. He calls his volume 'The Idyll of the German Home.'

The study of the Palatinate, a detailed application of the methods recommended in the 'Natural History,' was intended as a contribution to group psychology. The natural features of the country, the history of the people, the monuments of the Roman Empire and the Middle Ages, the villages and towns, clothes and food, political and social characteristics, religion and dialect, are passed in review. Riehl essayed a similar task in his exploration of Augsburg, which has been sometimes described as his masterpiece. 'In folk study, as in natural science,' he declared, 'there are no small matters.' Everywhere he finds an organic relation between nature and man. His methods were applied in a great co-operative work on the 'Land and People of Bavaria,' edited by himself at the command of the King, and in the foundation of a National Museum at Munich, of which he was the first director. An essential part of his work for *Kulturgeschichte* was his emphasis on art. Himself a musician and a musical critic, he contended that music was as great a factor in culture as poetry or science, and that the evolution of musical forms solved many a problem in the history of German sentiment. Again, the cathedrals and other monuments of the past formed an illustrated history of the land and the people. In addition to his historical works he wrote a large number of stories, designed to illustrate a thousand years of German life. 'Each is only a little genre picture, but together they make a great historical panorama.'

Riehl's keen insight into the connection of nature and man was not accompanied by the recognition of other factors. His relative indifference to the state led Treitschke to dismiss him as a publicist of the salon. Like Jakob Grimm, he preferred the type to the individual. He looked first to the living people, only then to the printed word. He was the most unprofessional of historians. His achievement was to emphasise the inexhaustible interest of the life of the people, to inquire by what influences it was determined and through what channels it expressed itself. Gothein testifies to the delight with which his contemporaries welcomed the pictures of Riehl, and how they set out on walking tours of observation and discovery. He found interest and meaning in the dullest districts and people, and turned dust to gold. He was sometimes described by liberal critics as the theorist of the reaction after 1848, but it was the gentle, poetic conservatism which loved the 'good old times.' He advanced the highest claims for *Kulturgeschichte*, describing it as the true philosophy of history. He refused to recognise an antagonism between Politics and Culture. 'The dualism will vanish, and *Kulturgeschichte* will become the stem, with the State, the Church, Art and other departments as branches.'

As intensely German as Riehl, Gustav Freytag[1] won a far wider popularity in his attempt to reconstruct the historic life of his people. A native of Silesia, where the shadow of the Slavonic world intensified racial self-consciousness, he early developed an absorbing interest in German literature and history. Initiated into

---

[1] See Freytag, *Erinnerungen*, 1887; Alberti, *Gustav Freytag*, 1885; Hanstein, *G. F.*, 1895; Lindau, *G. F.*, 1907; Dove, *Ausgewählte Schriftchen*; *Freytag u. Treitschke im Briefwechsel*, 1900.

mediæval philology by Lachmann, he took his Doctor's degree
with a thesis on the origin of German dramatic poetry, following
it up with a study of Roswitha. These early explorations of the
old festival-plays, the mysteries, the comedies, half pagan and
half Christian, revealed to him the life and voice of the people.
The events of 1848 drove him into the forum. He bought the
Grenzboten, moved to Leipsic, and made it the organ of German
unification under Prussian hegemony. Henceforth he combined
politics with history. It was in the columns of his own paper that
his 'Scenes from German History' began to appear in 1852. 'The
life of the people,' he wrote long after in his autobiography,
'which flows in a dark current beneath political events, had
always greatly attracted me—the circumstances, sorrows and joys
of millions of humble men and women.' He collected innumerable
pamphlets, fly-sheets, woodcuts and other treasures. 'To these
little books I owe all sorts of knowledge of customs and modes
of life of which the longer works say nothing.' Beginning with
sketches of the sixteenth and seventeenth centuries, it was only
later, and owing to their warm welcome, that he determined to
cover the whole of German history.

Freytag's 'Bilder,' surveying the life of the German people
from beginning to end in five volumes, was praised by scholars
as highly as by the great public. They are a work at once of
patriotism, science and art. 'It is the best German history we
have,' pronounced Scherer, 'or, if that is too much to say, we find
in it more that we demand from a good German history than
anywhere else.' Erich Schmidt places him in the first flight of
Germanists and historians. Even to-day the book is without a
rival. His hope that it might become 'a friend of the home' was
realised. By setting the people in the foreground of the picture
he gives unity to a span of two thousand years, and by his extracts
from contemporary witnesses he brings the past within sight.
'You put a piece of your heart into everything that your pen
touches,' remarked Treitschke. 'After Jakob Grimm,' wrote
Scherer, 'no one has filled me with such love for our people as
you.' Yet he resists the temptation to idealise the past. It is in
vain, he declares, that the German seeks for the good old times.
In every period of the past life was harder and poorer than it is
to-day. There was little safety, few rights, no public opinion; the
individual soul was less free. He avoids the danger of forgetting
the individual in the mass. He once spoke of *Kulturgeschichte* as
being too often like an old clo' shop—garments with no one to
wear them. He fully realises the importance of dominant personalities. He reaches the first impressive figure in Charles the

Great, and Barbarossa, 'the last real German Emperor,' is portrayed with loving care. The centre of the whole work is Luther, and the sketch of the Reformer became the cherished possession of Protestant Germany, as Michelet's picture of Joan of Arc carried a breath of patriotic idealism into the schools of France. Only second in importance is the detailed study of the work and character of Frederick the Great. If these portraits are the most popular part of the book, its most valuable feature is the picture of the Thirty Years War. He portrays the army, camp life, the villages, the towns, the superstitions and vices, the robbers and the police. No historian has more realistically revealed the moral and material disasters of a struggle that threw back Germany for a century.

The book was completed in 1866, when Germany came within sight of unification. 'This year,' wrote Freytag, 'Germans have regained what to many had become as unfamiliar as the *Völkerwanderung* or the Crusades—their state. It has become a joy to be German, and it will soon be reckoned a great honour among the nations of the earth.' A life of his friend Mathy, the Baden Minister and one of the champions of German unity, may be regarded as a continuation of the story in another form. But his work as the interpreter of the life of the German people was not completed. In his autobiography he relates how the campaign of 1870, in which he accompanied the Crown Prince to the front, gave rise to visions which were to take shape in 'The Ancestors.' The whole history of the race seemed to unroll like a map before his eyes. 'I was always deeply interested in the connection of man with his ancestors,' he writes, 'in their mysterious influence on body and soul. What science cannot fathom the poet may attempt.' He formed a plan by which a single family should take part in the decisive events of German history. While the novels of Willibald Alexis had dealt with Brandenburg and presented little interest to the members of other states, Freytag determined to appeal to every citizen of united Germany. The first instalment, appearing in 1872, related the fortunes of Ingo at the time of the Roman peril; the second dealt with the Slav invasion in the East and the coming of Boniface, the third and fourth with the rise and fall of chivalry. The fifth, 'Marcus König,' brings us to the Reformation, mirrored in the career of a merchant of Thorn living under Polish rule but German in feeling. The sixth portrays the Thirty Years War, the seventh the reign of Frederick William I. The eighth embraces the Wars of Liberation and incorporates matter relating to his own family, for the latest member of the family, Victor König, becomes a journalist in 1848.

Freytag described his work as a symphony in eight parts. But while the individual is presented as the heir of the ages, he is never limited or fettered by the lengthening chain of tradition. The ancestors are an inspiration, not a burden. Though the pearls are strung on an almost invisible thread, the series possesses an emotional unity. Read with avidity during the years succeeding the crowning mercy of 1870, 'Die Ahnen' brought vividly before united Germany the crowding memories of the past. The book took its place as a poetical rendering of the 'Bilder,' as Schiller's Wallenstein dramas grew out of his 'Thirty Years' War.' Together they did more to interest German men and women all over the world in their own history than the writings of any other man.

While Riehl and Freytag devoted their strength to the fortunes of the German people and the common man, their greater Swiss contemporary, Burckhardt,[1] called attention to thought and conduct, religion and art, scholarship and speculation—the reconstruction of the mental and moral atmosphere of the past. As Riehl loved the peasant and Freytag the burgher, Burckhardt preferred the *élite*. All three contributed to widen the scope of history; but while the two Germans wrote only of their own country the Swiss scholar embraced the whole field of civilisation and his fame is in every land. At Berlin he heard Böckh, Jakob Grimm and Ranke, but he was most attracted by Franz Kugler, whose 'History of Art' was then beginning to appear. He had already, as a young man of twenty, written on Swiss Cathedrals, and on entering at Bonn he wrote on the Churches of the Rhine. In 1844 he was appointed lecturer on history and art at Basel, and began to attract the eager listeners who were to throng his lecture-room for half a century. In 1847, at the request of the author, he edited Kugler's 'Handbook of Painting,' adding material of his own.

Though his labours had been hitherto chiefly in the world of art, Burckhardt's first considerable work showed that he was keenly alive to other aspects of civilisation. 'For me,' he wrote in 1842, 'the background is the chief consideration, and that is provided by *Kulturgeschichte*, to which I intend to dedicate myself.' His 'Times of Constantine the Great,' published in

---

[1] See Trog, *Jakob Burckhardt*, 1898; Neumann in *Allg. Deutsche Biog.*; Gelzer, *Ausgewählte Kleine Schriften*, 1907; Gothein in *Preussische Jahrbücher*, vol. xc.; Meinecke, *Ranke und Burckhardt*, 1948; Krittermeyer, *Jakob Burckhardt*, 1949; Werner Kaegi, *Jakob Burckhardt*, vol. i., 1947; vol. ii., 1951. A sumptuous edition of his works in 14 volumes appeared 1929–34. The first volume of his *Briefe*, ed. by Max Burckhardt, appeared in 1949.

1852, aimed at seizing the features of a period of rapid transition. In studying the fourth century for his lectures, he had been struck by the prevailing ignorance of the atmosphere. He desired to depict the psychology of an age in which the leading characteristic was insecurity and the dominant tendency a longing for novelty. The old and the new were concentrated in Diocletian and Constantine. He reviews the elements which fermented in the old world and prepared the way for Christianity, but he regards Constantine himself as a calculating realist. To those who contended that the ruler's religious convictions were a mystery he rejoins that he had none. Moreover Christianity itself rapidly degenerated when it became the official religion, and the better elements took refuge in asceticism and monasticism. The book is a panorama of the life of the Empire and its government, the provinces and the capitals, heathenism, neo-platonism and the mysteries, the persecution of the Christians, the relation of Church and State. The old world, he concludes, was destroyed neither by the barbarians nor by Christianity, but by itself. The work was welcomed by scholars, but though it brought him at a bound into the front rank of historians it never became a popular favourite.[1]

Burckhardt's first and strongest passion was art. He had already paid a flying visit to Italy, and after finishing 'Constantine' he spent over a year in the peninsula. The result was his 'Cicerone,' or guide to the art treasures of Italy, a book in small format of a thousand pages, divided into sections on architecture, sculpture and painting. The work won warm praise from Kugler and other historians of art, and in later editions, revised by other hands, it was to become the guide, philosopher and friend to innumerable travellers. Though his earlier architectural works had been devoted to Gothic, he warmly appreciates Renaissance, emphasising its originality in the treatment of space. He is less at home in sculpture but is stimulating in his judgments on painting. Throughout the book he offers his own impressions, regardless of tradition or expert opinion. After studying the art of the Renaissance he turned to the exploration of other aspects of its life. He determined to submit Italy to the same searching analysis as he had devoted to the age of Constantine, and the new subject suited him better than the old. He had too little sympathy with Christianity to understand certain aspects of the fourth century; but in the fifteenth, with its intellectual audacity, its art and scholarship, he was thoroughly at home. His 'Culture of the Renaissance,' published in 1860, immediately took its place

[1] An English translation appeared in 1949.

among historical classics, revealing to the world the potentialities of *Kulturgeschichte*, and raising it to a position of authority among historical genres. No historian has seized and interpreted the psychology of an epoch with greater power and insight. In the Middle Ages, he declares, one was a member of a class, a corporation, a family; society was a hierarchy, tradition was supreme. With the Renaissance man discovered himself and became a spiritual individual. The fetters of a thousand years were burst, self-realisation became the goal, and new valuations of the world and of man became current. Dazzling personalities of the type of the Emperor Frederick II had been witnessed once or twice in the Middle Ages: the complete man, *l'uomo universale*, now became common in the world of action, of thought and art. 'The fifteenth century is, above all, that of the many sided man.' The soil from which these wonderful human plants grew was composed of many elements—the intense life of the City State, the revival of the art and philosophy of antiquity, the weakening of authority, the disintegration of belief. The Tyrant and the Condottiere, despite their ruthlessness, were political artists, men cast in a gigantic mould. The great ladies developed a brilliancy never attained by women before or since.

Burckhardt was too great an historian to be blinded by the brilliance which flashes out between the Middle Ages and the Reformation. The detailed analysis of morality and religion with which the book closes makes no attempt to hide the savagery and bestiality, the gross superstition existing side by side with limitless scepticism. He is appalled by 'the disinterested love of evil' in Cæsar Borgia and Sigismondo Malatesta; yet he realises that the fundamental vice of the upper class, unbridled individualism, was a condition of its greatness. 'The Italian of the Renaissance had to bear the first mighty surging of a new age. Through his gifts and his passions he has become the most characteristic representative of all the heights and all the depths of his time.' Despite its faults the Renaissance was the springtime of the modern world. Burckhardt's masterpiece is one of the most original works in historical literature. Many readers have complained of the omission of art; and though Taine has replied that we do not miss it, because we are more interested in the man as a man than as an artist, it renders the survey incomplete. Others maintain that he greatly exaggerates the rapidity of the transition from mediæval twilight to the fierce light of the Renaissance. His knowledge of the literary sources of the Renaissance was immense, but he had made no profound study of the Middle Ages. Some critics assert that the view of the Renaissance is too flattering, others that the political chapters are inadequate. As a citizen of the country where the state counted for less than anywhere in Europe, he took little interest in the problems of government and had no use for empires, old or new. Some readers complain that he overestimated the influence of the rediscovery of the classical world,[1] others that he omits the material foundation of Italian culture and that his survey mixes up different generations. Such criticisms, few of which are wholly without substance, leave the reputation of the book intact as, in Acton's words, 'the most penetrating and subtle treatise on the history of civilisation that exists in literature.'

Though he lived nearly forty years longer, Burckhardt never published another book. He devoted infinite pains to his lectures, to the wealth and originality of which Nietzsche and other hearers have borne witness. He refused the flattering offer of Ranke's Chair at Berlin when the veteran historian retired. The chief occupation of his later life was an encyclopædic survey of Greek civilisation, based on his lectures. Two volumes had been ready for many years at the time of his death in 1897, and two further volumes were prepared for the press by a pupil. He had sketched a course in 1868 on the Spirit of Antiquity, and had often lectured on Greece during the following years. Under pressure from his hearers he reduced them to writing, but he could never conquer the conviction that they were too imperfect for publication, and he only gave permission on his death-bed. When urged he replied ironically, 'No—such a poor outsider dare not. I am a heretic and an ignoramus, and I should be torn in pieces by the *viri eruditissimi.*' These facts must be remembered if we are to understand the imperfections of the book and the sharp criticisms by specialists. While the manuscript was lying in his desk Greek studies were making rapid strides. He knew he was being left behind, but he believed that a thorough knowledge of the literary sources was a guarantee against serious error. He never grasped the importance of the inscriptions and other new evidence.

The 'History of Greek Civilisation' is a detailed and comprehensive survey.[2] 'The highest culture,' he declared, 'can only arise on ground made safe by might.' Yet he does not tie culture to politics, and he recognises the sovereignty of genius.

---

[1] Sellery, *The Renaissance: its Nature and Origins*, 1950, is the latest attack on Burckhardt's presentation of the period as a sudden illumination.

[2] The best discussion of the book is by Carl Neumann, 'Griechische Kulturgeschichte in der Auffassung Burckhardts,' *Hist. Zeitschrift*, vol. xxxv.

In particular, art may flourish when the state is weak. To religion he devotes an entire volume. The third volume deals with art and literature, science and philosophy, while the fourth portrays the individual Greek in the successive stages of his development from Homer to Pausanias. He rejects the idealisation of the Greek world which Curtius had inherited from Otfried Müller, Goethe and Winckelmann. The very fact that he was not a specialist, that he came to Greece late in life with an eye trained in other fields, gives his book unusual freshness. Its most striking feature is the depth of the shadows. He had been accused of being dazzled by the Renaissance: he was certainly not dazzled by Greece. He emphasises the cruelties, the intolerance, the dark stain of slavery. Though he was sometimes called 'the pagan,' he yielded to none in his acceptance of Christian ethics Wilamowitz declared categorically that it did not exist for science, but such good judges as Holm and Kärst praised the work. For Burckhardt the inner life was much more interesting than the outer world of forms and institutions which he valued chiefly as supplying favourable conditions for its expression. It was his power of penetrating to the soul of an epoch that aroused the enthusiasm of Taine. He was too individual to form a school, but where is the historian who has set out to interpret the psychology of an age or a people who has not drunk deeply at his spring?

II

When Riehl, Freytag and Burckhardt had rendered *Kulturgeschichte* fashionable, an army of workers appeared to carry their methods into new territory. Friedländer's incomparable picture of the civilisation of the Roman Empire was followed by Lecky's fascinating histories of Rationalism and Morals. Such works as Gregorovius' monumental 'History of the City of Rome in the Middle Ages,' Vossler's studies of Dante and his age, Rashdall's panorama of mediæval universities, Lynn Thorndike's detailed record of mediæval science and magic, Henry Adams' 'Mont St. Michael and Chartres,' a sympathetic interpretation of thirteenth century Christendom, Comparetti's astonishing story of the influence of 'Virgil in the Middle Ages,' enriched and enlarged the conception of history. Among notable contributions to the understanding of the modern European mind may be mentioned Symonds' 'Renaissance in Italy,' Ruffini's 'History of Religious Liberty,' Paulsen's 'History of Higher Education in Germany,' Leslie Stephen's 'English Thought in the Eighteenth Century,' and 'The English Utilitarians,' Kuno Fischer's 'History of

Modern Philosophy,' based on his lectures at Heidelberg, Merz' 'European Thought in the Nineteenth Century,' Haym's biographies of Herder and Humboldt, Justi's glowing portrait of Winckelman and his age, and Dilthey's illuminating studies of German thinkers from the Reformation to Schleiermacher. The introduction of the historic method into the study of economics by Roscher directed attention to social history. Half a century after Hallam lamented that we could never know the life of an English mediæval village, Thorold Rogers laid the foundation of a history of rural England by the seven volumes of his 'History of Agriculture and Prices.' Cunningham and Ashley attempted the first comprehensive surveys of our economic development. Levasseur devoted a long life to tracing the fortunes of the French working-classes. Nitzsch lectured at Berlin on the social history of the German people, and Inama-Sternegg wrote the first scholarly economic history of Germany. Kovalevsky traced the economic development of Europe from the fall of the Roman Empire, Sombart and Max Weber the evolution of capitalism since the sixteenth century. The school of Schmoller, whose early treatise on the cloth industry at Strassburg served as a model, illuminated every country with monographs of the highest standard. No one so powerfully emphasised the intimate connection of economic phenomena with the life of the state and society as the venerable Berlin professor, whose Seminar attracted students from many lands.

The history of civilisation was eagerly studied by a group of men who wrote under the impact of the scientific discoveries and generalisations of the middle of the nineteenth century. Comte's limited knowledge of history discounts the value of his survey of development, and his law of the three states was oversimplified. Marx imprisoned himself in his system of economic determinism. Buckle's[1] torso was of greater service in stimulating reflection on the causes and connections of events and in emphasising the enduring influence of natural conditions, while his brilliant sketches of intellectual development in England and Scotland, France and Spain, are among the most fascinating pages in historical literature. It was his ambition to transform the history of civilisation from a compilation into something like a science, resting on a solid basis of comparison and induction from the whole boundless field of politics and culture. His thesis that progress was the result of growing knowledge was sharply challenged; but though he shares the facile dogmatism of the mid-Victorian era, his book marked an epoch in the life of many

[1] See J. M. Robertson's challenging work, *Buckle and his Critics*, 1895.

readers and gave an immense impetus to the sociological investigation of the past. It was as a champion of similar naturalistic ideas that Hellwald,[1] the well-known traveller and geographer compiled his 'History of Civilisation in its Natural Development' in 1874. 'I try,' he wrote, 'to examine if supernatural forces are necessary to explain the phenomena of civilisation.' He concluded that they were not, and pronounced cultural development a natural process, conditioned by race, geography and climate. Civilisation means the mastering of nature and the taming of man, not the growth of morality. The struggle for existence dominates the whole course of historic life. The best part of the book is that which deals with prehistoric society, where nature rules as an autocrat, not as a constitutional monarch. Though Hellwald's knowledge of world history was limited, his tone polemical, his philosophy shallow, the book won wide popularity. The fourth edition, published after his death, was revised by specialists and superbly illustrated. Helmolt edited a large co-operative 'History of Mankind' which similarly emphasises the sovereign influences of nature and geography. Primitive civilisation has been brought within the circle of historical study. The discoveries of Boucher des Perthes in the Somme basin and of Pitt Rivers in England threw back the opening of the human drama thousands of years, and created the science of prehistoric archæology. In the hands of Tylor and McLennan, Mannhardt and Ratzel, Frazer and Westermarck, anthropology has become a science, and the habits and beliefs of our ancestors have been rendered intelligible. Maine devoted his massive intellect to the interpretation of early law.

The increasing popularity of *Kulturgeschichte* gave rise to prolonged controversy as to its character and importance. The discussions which aroused the widest interest were those between Gothein and Schäfer and those which arose out of Lamprecht's 'German History.' In his inaugural lecture at Tübingen in 1888 Dietrich Schäfer,[2] known for his studies of the Hanseatic League, declared that if history was to have unity and scientific character it must concentrate on the state. In our democratic age many writers found the key to the story in the masses, and studied habits and circumstances rather than the expressions of the highest faculties of man. Large volumes were devoted to such trifles as the mediæval house. It was time to reassert that the

[1] See *Allg. Deutsche Biog.* The naturalistic school is discussed by Barth, *Die Philosophie der Geschichte als Soziologie*, 1897. Carlo Antoni, *Dallo Storicismo alla Sociologia*, 1940, is useful.

[2] *Das eigentliche Arbeitsgebiet der Geschichte.*

vitalising breath, without which history was a mass of dead knowledge, must always come from the state. Even the Renaissance was largely political, and its typical figure was Machiavelli. The Reformation gave man a national consciousness, and Luther proclaimed the divine origin of the state. 'The historian's task is to make the state understand its origin, its task, the conditions of its life.' If he enters the region of religion or law, literature or art, he must remember that he is walking along side-paths.

This uncompromising assertion of the traditional political standpoint called forth a reply from the ablest of the younger German practitioners of *Kulturgeschichte*.[1] Gothein had attracted attention by a study of the civilisation of Southern Italy, and increased his fame by a massive study of Loyola and the Counter-Reformation. Growing sciences, he declared, needed no anxious limitation of their scope. The state was only one form of human association. It might be the greatest, but all were indispensable. The separate aspects of historic life—the state, religion, art, law, economics—involve and presuppose a higher unity in which they combine, an organism of which they are limbs. Schäfer had spoken as if *Kulturgeschichte* dealt only with the material conditions of life. He rebuts the assertion that it neglects the individual by declaring that Freytag comes nearest the great secret of the connection of the single life with the folk-life, and that his Luther and Frederick tower like oaks in the underwood. To the criticism that it dwarfs the state he replies that in many of the critical moments of human development the key is to be found beyond the frontier of politics. In the era of Constantine the cardinal event was the transition from paganism to Christianity. In the Renaissance, the Reformation and the Counter-Reformation, ideas shattered the ancient moulds and transformed the face of the world. In such periods only the historian of culture is in a position to bring order out of the chaos of politics. The growth of Prussia was essentially a political problem, but such exceptions are rare. Events are the products of forces, and forces are the children of ideas. A reply from Schäfer[2] brought the controversy to a close. He admits that history includes all aspects of life, but he pleads that no human mind can embrace the whole, and maintains that Ranke and all other great historians focussed their glance on the state. He challenges the contention that certain periods are almost wholly cultural. Luther, he declares, would never have succeeded without national feeling behind him. The

---

[1] *Die Aufgaben der Kulturgeschichte*, 1889.
[2] *Geschichte und Kulturgeschichte*, 1891.

Counter-Reformation would never have won its sensational successes without the treasure of Mexico and Peru. Neither controversialist convinced the other, and each continued to work at the subjects which interested him most. Gothein's plea for a wider conception of the historian's task proved useful not only in broadening the political school but in recalling champions of *Kulturgeschichte* to their graver obligations.

The controversy arising out of the publication of Lamprecht's 'German History'[1] was more bitter and prolonged. Lamprecht won reputation by a massive monograph on mediæval economic life on the Mosel and the middle Rhine. The industry in bringing together the greatest collection of original material ever made for a German district was generally recognised, but the use of his treasures was sharply criticised. Below pronounced his methods arbitrary and his constructions capricious. Gierke complained that his juristic conceptions lacked clarity. Schmoller declared that the book was published too soon, and was cloudy in thought and difficult to read. In 1891 the 'German History' began to appear. No preface explained the purpose of the author, but a few introductory sentences were added to the second edition of the first volume published three years later. The purely political historian, he declares, inquires with Ranke 'how it actually was'—*wie ist es eigentlich gewesen?* He himself desired to know 'how it became'—*wie ist es eigentlich geworden?* The genetic method must be substituted for the narrative, and this involves a survey of the whole mass of circumstances, material and intellectual, out of which events emerge. Living in a scientific age the historian must investigate causation. In the political parts of the work he made no claim to research, but in the surveys of social organisation and culture he was on his own ground. The main object of the book was to trace the development of the German consciousness. He believed in a national folk-soul, which developed according to immanent laws, though affected by outside influences.

Beginning with Pytheas, Lamprecht sketches the natural differences between his time and our own. Anthropology and philology are laid under contribution, but his picture of primitive German life compares unfavourably with the lucidity of such a master as Wilhelm Arnold. The political narrative, which begins

[1] The literature on Lamprecht is extensive. There are useful sketches of the controversy in Goldfriedrich, *Die historische Ideenlehre in Deutschland*, 431–65, 1902; Bernheim, *Lehrbuch der historischen Methode*, 710–18, 1908; Kötzschke u. Tille, *Karl Lamprecht*, 1915; *Some Historians of Modern Europe*, ed. B. E. Schmitt, ch. x.

with Cæsar and Varus, is weak and colourless, while every form of art is lovingly reviewed. Charles the Great is the first living being we meet, but he does not enjoy a very vigorous vitality. The history of conditions supersedes that of persons, and culture takes precedence of politics. Two rulers of the tenth century interest the author—Henry the Fowler, 'the real founder of the Empire' and the patron of the towns, and the short-lived Otto III, the child of a Greek mother. In the conflict between Henry IV and Hildebrand he scarcely seems conscious of the greatness of the greatest of the Popes. The third volume opens with a valuable survey of the towns in the eleventh century and their political influence. The personality of Barbarossa, the greatest figure since Charles the Great, is dismissed in a few lines as the type of a romantic hero of Wolfram or Hartmann von Aue. Frederick II, the most striking personality of the Middle Ages, called by his contemporaries *Stupor Mundi*, flits past like a shadow. After the fall of the Hohenstaufen the absence of great political figures makes us less conscious of the historian's limitations, but even in his own field of *Kulturgeschichte* he is not always satisfactory. He has little to say of the great mystics, the glory of the fourteenth century. We reach the close of the Middle Ages with a feeling that our guide lacks the key to their deeper secrets. With Luther we meet the first personality whose importance seems to be fully grasped. He offers a fair account of his writings, and so far departs from his common practice as to quote passages from the Table Talk. In pointing out the Reformer's failure to understand the Revolt of 1525 he carefully studies its social and economic causes.

At this stage, having produced five volumes in rapid succession, Lamprecht halted to reply to his critics who came at him like a swarm of bees. When he was praised by amateurs, declared Lenz,[1] scholars must protest. The distinction between *gewesen* and *geworden* was ridiculous, for Ranke had excelled in the genetic treatment of historical problems. Lamprecht explained far less than Ranke, for he made no attempt to relate German history to the main current of European affairs, and he was blind to the importance of great national figures. Examining the volume on the Reformation, his own special period, Lenz declares that every page, almost every line, aroused protest. Rackfahl made a list of errors in a few pages on the sixteenth century, and showed in parallel columns how he plagiarised the work of other scholars. Johannes Haller, the editor of the Acts of the Council of Basel, declared that there were almost as many mistakes in the account

[1] *Hist. Zeitschrift*, vol. lxxvii.

of the Council as sentences. Finke wrote a small volume to correct
the picture of ecclesiastical conditions at the end of the Middle
Ages.[1]

Lamprecht's first comprehensive reply appeared in his essays
entitled 'Old and New Tendencies.'[2] In writing his 'German
History,' he declared, he knew he would come into conflict with
the dominant school, yet no serious history was possible without
some intellectual standpoint. Earlier schools had explained
historic happenings by individual actions, that is by individual
psychology: a new path had been opened by the study of social
and economic development. He who recognised the operation
of economic influences was often regarded as a materialist,
because economic phenomena were 'material' in opposition to
art, literature or philosophy, yet every economic act and change
was psychologically conditioned as much as any intellectual
effort. The causal method was most easily applied in social and
economic phenomena, and it was well to begin there. While the
history of persons must always contain an element of romance
and speculation, because we can only guess at their motives, the
history of conditions will one day reach approximately scientific
truth. The key to history is to be found in collective psychology.
In the long essay on Ranke which follows he carries the war into
the enemy's camp. The great historian, he declares, sprinkled his
pages with philosophic reflections; he was a mystic who believed
that the development of humanity took place in obedience to
unknown laws. The first task was to analyse the factors of historic
life. It was this which he had attempted in the 'German History,'
which was less a narrative than an essay in genetic interpretation.

The controversy was waged for several years in pamphlet
and periodical, the Leipsic Professor defending himself with
extraordinary determination against a host of assailants. His
most comprehensive utterance is to be found in the lectures on
Modern Historical Science, delivered in the United States in
1904.[3] The fight, he declared, had been between the champions of
individual and social psychology, between those who found the
motive power in heroes and those who found it in conditions.
Herder had discovered the psyche of the masses, and the Romantics continued his work. Ranke, and still more the Prussian
School, had revived the individualist method. 'It was a time
of almost purely political activity. The nation yearned in the

[1] *Die kirchlichen Verhältnisse zu Ende des Mittelalters nach der Darstellung Lamprechts,* 1896.
[2] *Alte und neue Richtungen in der Geschichtswissenschaft,* 1896.
[3] *What is History?* 1905.

very fibre of its soul for the long-coveted unity. With its attainment a new psychic no less than a new political world came into existence. Description was no longer the watchword, but comprehension.' Lamprecht pronounces primitive Germany symbolic, when imagination was strong and the individual was lost in the family and the clan. The early Middle Ages witnessed the development of types. The later Middle Ages, a time of territorial rule and city life, was an era of conventions. The towns and the tenants, for instance, were not wholly free, and the period forms a transition to the era of individuals, which begins with the Renaissance and Reformation, and culminates in the *Aufklärung*. The fifth or subjective stage begins with the romantic movement, the reaction of feeling against the cult of reason. We were now living in a period of nervous tension, marked by the spirit of enterprise, speculation, haste and anxiety, but inspired by no ruling ideal. These psychic stages occur in all countries. A vast work remains to be done in assessing the action of economic changes on social and psychic life; and though they are not the only factor, material and hence social progress is the dominant stimulus to general advance.

On resuming his History, Lamprecht showed that the criticisms of the first five volumes had left no trace. The treatment of the centuries since the Reformation exhibits the same faults as their predecessors. Those aspects which interest him are treated at length, while others of equal or greater importance receive little notice. Thus in the sixth volume we find a long chapter on early music and the development of instruments, in the seventh a detailed study of art. On reaching the Napoleonic era we approach as near to political narrative as he allows; but though he writes with ardent patriotism of the Wars of Liberation he has little to say of Stein and his colleagues. The sections dealing with philosophy, literature and art, with Kant and Beethoven, are vigorous and thoughtful, and the volumes on the nineteenth century bear ample witness to his many-sided interest in the modern world. The work is completed by three supplementary volumes on German history since 1870. 'I know it is bold to write on my own time, as many know the parts and some know the whole better than I. For these I have not written.' What was needed was insight into the driving spiritual forces. The first volume surveys art, literature and speculation, and discusses Wagner, Nietzsche, Stefan George, and other pioneers. Wundt is hailed as the greatest philosopher since Kant, the founder of experimental psychology on which the further progress of philosophy depends. The second volume groups the phenomena of economic life round the twin principles of need and enjoyment, and describes the extension of communications, the development of international credit, advances in production, invention and technical education, the application of chemistry to industry and agriculture, the development of the Fourth Estate, emigration, rings, the Polish labourer and many other questions. The third discusses the growth of parties, foreign relations, the colonies and the development of *Welt-Politik*. The work ends on a note of challenge to the political historians with whom Lamprecht's life was a ceaseless feud. 'Human development is in no slavish dependence on political fortunes. Political self-preservation depends on the development of the ideal values of art and science, religion, law and morality; for only in their cultivation do national and cosmopolitan tendencies combine.'

The 'German History' is a work of rare intellectual vigour and originality. Its insistence on economic factors, its theory of rhythmic psychological transformations, and its emphasis on art and culture contributed to broaden the conception of history, but it is excluded from the front rank by serious faults. A detailed survey of the whole course of civilisation in Germany can only be successfully attempted by the co-operative method. Lamprecht is well versed in economics and art, but the student of political and ecclesiastical history will derive little aid from his pages. The book is of little value to scholars, and its daring generalisations are a snare to the beginner. In his reaction against the political school he presents Germania without her political backbone. His neglect of the element of personality is a grave flaw. Finally his abstract terminology and barbarous compounds give the work a somewhat forbidding air. Yet whatever be thought of his theories and writings, the growing popularity of *Kulturgeschichte* is partly due to his strenuous activities. Among the most capable workers in the field is his pupil Steinhausen, who founded the *Archiv für Kulturgeschichte* in 1903. The most important of his monographs, the 'History of German Letterwriting,' is an excursion into a little-known world. The value of the book was at once recognised, and the author received assistance from the Berlin Academy in the publication of German letters of the Middle Ages.

If political history and *Kulturgeschichte* have sometimes appeared to be antagonistic, it is because both have been too narrowly defined. They are equally needed to attain the goal, which is nothing less than the record and interpretation of the life of humanity. Time has smoothed the jealousies of the rival schools: the one is no more bound to neglect conditions than the other to ignore individuals. The method varies with the theme, for civilisation is the fruit of effort and achievement daily working along many lines. While historical science is thus extending its conquests in every direction, the philosophy of history lags behind. We continue to analyse, to generalise and to speculate, but guesswork it remains. Yet though it is not yet possible to formulate laws satisfactorily explaining the pattern of human evolution, every true historian contributes to our knowledge of the ascent of man.

INDEX